Textbooks in Language Sciences

Editors: Stefan Müller, Martin Haspelmath
Editorial Board: Claude Hagège, Marianne Mithun, Anatol Stefanowitsch, Foong Ha Yap

In this series:

1. Müller, Stefan. Grammatical theory: From transformational grammar to constraint-based approaches.

2. Schäfer, Roland. Einführung in die grammatische Beschreibung des Deutschen.

ISSN: 2364-6209

Grammatical theory

From transformational grammar to constraint-based approaches

Stefan Müller

language science press

Stefan Müller. 2016. *Grammatical theory: From transformational grammar to constraint-based approaches* (Textbooks in Language Sciences 1). Berlin: Language Science Press.

This title can be downloaded at:
http://langsci-press.org/catalog/book/25

© 2016, Stefan Müller

ISBN: Digital, complete work: 978-3-944675-21-3 ;
        Hardcover: vol1:   978-3-946234-29-6; vol. 2 978-3-946234-40-1
        Softcover: vol1:   978-3-946234-30-2; vol. 2 978-3-946234-41-8
        Softcover US: vol1:   978-1-530465-62-0 ; vol. 2 978-1-523743-82-7
ISSN: 2364-6209

Cover and concept of design: Ulrike Harbort
Translators: Andrew Murphy, Stefan Müller
Typesetting: Stefan Müller
Proofreading: Viola Auermann, Armin Buch, Andreea Calude, Rong Chen, Matthew Czuba, Leonel de Alencar, Christian Döhler, Joseph T. Farquharson, Andreas Hölzl, Gianina Iordăchioaia, Paul Kay, Anne Kilgus, Sandra Kübler, Timm Lichte, Antonio Machicao y Priemer, Michelle Natolo, Stephanie Natolo, Sebastian Nordhoff, Parviz Parsafar, Conor Pyle, Daniela Schröder, Eva Schultze-Berndt, Alec Shaw, Benedikt Singpiel, Anelia Stefanova, Neal Whitman, Viola Wiegand
Open reviewing: Armin Buch, Leonel de Alencar, Andreas Hölzl, Gianina Iordăchioaia, Paul Kay, Dick Hudson, Paul Kay, Timm Lichte, Antonio Machicao y Priemer, Andrew McIntyre, Arne Nymos, Sebastian Nordhoff, Neal Whitman
Fonts: Linux Libertine, Arimo, DejaVu Sans Mono
Typesetting software: XƎLᴬTEX

Language Science Press
Habelschwerdter Allee 45
14195 Berlin, Germany
langsci-press.org
Storage and cataloguing done by FU Berlin

Freie Universität Berlin

For Max

Contents

Contents

Contents

Contents

Contents

Preface

This book is an extended and revised version of my German book *Grammatiktheorie* (Müller 2013b). It introduces various grammatical theories that play a role in current theorizing or have made contributions in the past which are still relevant today. I explain some foundational assumptions and then apply the respective theories to what can be called the "core grammar" of German. I have decided to stick to the object language that I used in the German version of this book since many of the phenomena that will be dealt with cannot be explained with English as the object language. Furthermore, many theories have been developed by researchers with English as their native language and it is illuminative to see these theories applied to another language. I show how the theories under consideration deal with arguments and adjuncts, active/passive alternations, local reorderings (so-called scrambling), verb position, and fronting of phrases over larger distances (the verb second property of the Germanic languages without English).

The second part deals with foundational questions that are important for developing theories. This includes a discussion of the question of whether we have innate domain specific knowledge of language (UG), the discussion of psycholinguistic evidence concerning the processing of language by humans, a discussion of the status of empty elements and of the question whether we construct and perceive utterances holistically or rather compositionally, that is, whether we use phrasal or lexical constructions.

Unfortunately, linguistics is a scientific field with a considerable amount of terminological chaos. I therefore wrote an introductory chapter that introduces terminology in the way it is used later on in the book. The second chapter introduces phrase structure grammars, which plays a role for many of the theories that are covered in this book. I use these two chapters (excluding the Section 2.3 on interleaving phrase structure grammars and semantics) in introductory courses of our BA curriculum for German studies. Advanced readers may skip these introductory chapters. The following chapters are structured in a way that should make it possible to understand the introduction of the theories without any prior knowledge. The sections regarding new developments and classification are more ambitious: they refer to chapters still to come and also point to other publications that are relevant in the current theoretical discussion but cannot be repeated or summarized in this book. These parts of the book address advanced students and researchers. I use this book for teaching the syntactic aspects of the theories in a seminar for advanced students in our BA. The slides are available on my web page. The second part of the book, the general discussion, is more ambitious and contains the discussion of advanced topics and current research literature.

This book only deals with relatively recent developments. For a historical overview, see for instance Robins (1997); Jungen & Lohnstein (2006). I am aware of the fact that chapters on Integrational Linguistics (Lieb 1983; Eisenberg 2004; Nolda 2007), Optimality Theory (Prince & Smolensky 1993; Grimshaw 1997; G. Müller 2000), Role and Reference Grammar (Van Valin 1993) and Relational Grammar (Perlmutter 1983, 1984) are missing. I will leave these theories for later editions.

The original German book was planned to have 400 pages, but it finally was much bigger: the first German edition has 525 pages and the second German edition has 564 pages. I added a chapter on Dependency Grammar and one on Minimalism to the English version and now the book has 808 pages. I tried to represent the chosen theories appropriately and to cite all important work. Although the list of references is over 85 pages long, I was probably not successful. I apologize for this and any other shortcomings.

Available versions of this book

The canonical version of this book is the PDF document available from the Language Science Press webpage of this book[1]. This page also links to a Print on Demand version. Since the book is very long, we decided to split the book into two volumes. The first volume contains the description of all theories and the second volume contains the general discussion. Both volumes contain the complete list of references and the indices. The second volume starts with page 431. The printed volumes are therefore identical to the parts of the PDF document.

Acknowledgments

I would like to thank David Adger, Jason Baldridge, Felix Bildhauer, Emily M. Bender, Stefan Evert, Gisbert Fanselow, Sandiway Fong, Hans-Martin Gärtner, Kim Gerdes, Adele Goldberg, Bob Levine, Paul Kay, Jakob Maché, Guido Mensching, Laura Michaelis, Geoffrey Pullum, Uli Sauerland, Roland Schäfer, Jan Strunk, Remi van Trijp, Shravan Vasishth, Tom Wasow, and Stephen Wechsler for discussion and Monika Budde, Philippa Cook, Laura Kallmeyer, Tibor Kiss, Gisela Klann-Delius, Jonas Kuhn, Timm Lichte, Anke Lüdeling, Jens Michaelis, Bjarne Ørsnes, Andreas Pankau, Christian Pietsch, Frank Richter, Ivan Sag, and Eva Wittenberg for comments on earlier versions of the German edition of this book and Thomas Groß, Dick Hudson, Sylvain Kahane, Paul Kay, Haitao Liu (刘海涛), Andrew McIntyre, Sebastian Nordhoff, Tim Osborne, Andreas Pankau, and Christoph Schwarze for comments on earlier versions of this book. Thanks to Leonardo Boiko and Sven Verdoolaege for pointing out typos. Special thanks go to Martin Haspelmath for very detailed comments on an earlier version of the English book.

This book was the first Language Science Press book that had an open review phase (see below). I thank Dick Hudson, Paul Kay, Antonio Machicao y Priemer, Andrew McIntyre, Sebastian Nordhoff, and one anonymous open reviewer for their comments. Theses comments are documented at the download page of this book. In addition the book went through a stage of community proofreading (see also below). Some of the proofreaders

---

[1] http://langsci-press.org/catalog/book/25

did much more than proofreading, their comments are highly appreciated and I decided to publish these comments as additional open reviews. Armin Buch, Leonel de Alencar, Andreas Hölzl, Gianina Iordăchioaia, Timm Lichte, Antonio Machicao y Priemer, and Neal Whitman deserve special mention here.

I thank Wolfgang Sternefeld and Frank Richter, who wrote a detailed review of the German version of this book (Sternefeld & Richter 2012). They pointed out some mistakes and omissions that were corrected in the second edition of the German book and which are of course not present in the English version.

Thanks to all the students who commented on the book and whose questions lead to improvements. Lisa Deringer, Aleksandra Gabryszak, Simon Lohmiller, Theresa Kallenbach, Steffen Neuschulz, Reka Meszaros-Segner, Lena Terhart and Elodie Winckel deserve special mention.

Since this book is built upon all my experience in the area of grammatical theory, I want to thank all those with whom I ever discussed linguistics during and after talks at conferences, workshops, summer schools or via email. Werner Abraham, John Bateman, Dorothee Beermann, Rens Bod, Miriam Butt, Manfred Bierwisch, Ann Copestake, Holger Diessel, Kerstin Fischer, Dan Flickinger, Peter Gallmann, Petter Haugereid, Lars Hellan, Tibor Kiss, Wolfgang Klein, Hans-Ulrich Krieger, Andrew McIntyre, Detmar Meurers, Gereon Müller, Martin Neef, Manfred Sailer, Anatol Stefanowitsch, Peter Svenonius, Michael Tomasello, Hans Uszkoreit, Gert Webelhuth, Daniel Wiechmann and Arne Zeschel deserve special mention.

I thank Sebastian Nordhoff for a comment regarding the completion of the subject index entry for *recursion*.

Andrew Murphy translated part of Chapter 1 and the Chapters 2–3, 5–10, and 12–23. Many thanks for this!

I also want to thank the 27 community proofreaders (Viola Auermann, Armin Buch, Andreea Calude, Rong Chen, Matthew Czuba, Leonel de Alencar, Christian Döhler, Joseph T. Farquharson, Andreas Hölzl, Gianina Iordăchioaia, Paul Kay, Anne Kilgus, Sandra Kübler, Timm Lichte, Antonio Machicao y Priemer, Michelle Natolo, Stephanie Natolo, Sebastian Nordhoff, Parviz Parsafar, Conor Pyle, Daniela Schröder, Eva Schultze-Berndt, Alec Shaw, Benedikt Singpiel, Anelia Stefanova, Neal Whitman, Viola Wiegand) that each worked on one or more chapters and really improved this book. I got more comments from every one of them than I ever got for a book done with a commercial publisher. Some comments were on content rather than on typos and layout issues. No proofreader employed by a commercial publisher would have spotted these mistakes and inconsistencies since commercial publishers do not have staff that knows all the grammatical theories that are covered in this book.

During the past years, a number of workshops on theory comparison have taken place. I was invited to three of them. I thank Helge Dyvik and Torbjørn Nordgård for inviting me to the fall school for Norwegian PhD students *Languages and Theories in Contrast*, which took place 2005 in Bergen. Guido Mensching and Elisabeth Stark invited me to the workshop *Comparing Languages and Comparing Theories: Generative Grammar and Construction Grammar*, which took place in 2007 at the Freie Universität Berlin and Andreas Pankau invited me to the workshop *Comparing Frameworks* in 2009 in Utrecht. I really enjoyed the discussion with all participants of these events and this book benefited enormously from the interchange.

I thank Peter Gallmann for the discussion of his lecture notes on GB during my time in Jena. The Sections 3.1.3–3.4 have a structure that is similar to the one of his script and take over a lot. Thanks to David Reitter for the LATEX macros for Combinatorial Categorial Grammar, to Mary Dalrymple and Jonas Kuhn for the LFG macros and example structures, and to Laura Kallmeyer for the LATEX sources of most of the TAG analyses. Most of the trees have been adapted to the forest package because of compatibility issues with XƎLATEX, but the original trees and texts were a great source of inspiration and without them the figures in the respective chapters would not be half as pretty as they are now.

I thank Sašo Živanović for implementing the LATEX package forest. It really simplifies typesetting of trees, dependency graphs, and type hierarchies. I also thank him for individual help via email and on stackexchange. In general, those active on stackexchange could not be thanked enough: most of my questions regarding specific details of the typesetting of this book or the implementation of the LATEX classes that are used by Language Science Press now have been answered within several minutes. Thank you! Since this book is a true open access book under the CC-BY license, it can also be an open source book. The interested reader finds a copy of the source code at https://github.com/langsci/25. By making the book open source I pass on the knowledge provided by the LATEX gurus and hope that others benefit from this and learn to typeset their linguistics papers in nicer and/or more efficient ways.

Viola Auermann and Antje Bahlke, Sarah Dietzfelbinger, Lea Helmers, and Chiara Jancke cannot be thanked enough for their work at the copy machines. Viola also helped a lot with proof reading prefinal stages of the translation. I also want to thank my (former) lab members Felix Bildhauer, Philippa Cook, Janna Lipenkova, Jakob Maché, Bjarne Ørsnes and Roland Schäfer, which were mentioned above already for other reasons, for their help with teaching. During the years from 2007 until the publication of the first German edition of this book two of the three tenured positions in German Linguistics were unfilled and I would have not been able to maintain the teaching requirements without their help and would have never finished the *Grammatiktheorie* book.

I thank Tibor Kiss for advice in questions of style. His diplomatic way always was a shining example for me and I hope that this is also reflected in this book.

On the way this book is published

I started to work on my dissertation in 1994 and defended it in 1997. During the whole time the manuscript was available on my web page. After the defense, I had to look for a publisher. I was quite happy to be accepted to the series *Linguistische Arbeiten* by Niemeyer, but at the same time I was shocked about the price, which was 186.00 DM for a paperback book that was written and typeset by me without any help by the publisher (twenty times the price of a paperback novel).[2] This basically meant that my book was depublished: until 1998 it was available from my web page and after this it was available in libraries only. My Habilitationsschrift was published by CSLI Publications for a much more reasonable price. When I started writing textbooks, I was looking for alternative distribution channels and started to negotiate with no-name print on demand publishers. Brigitte Narr, who runs the Stauffenburg publishing house, convinced me to publish my HPSG textbook with her. The copyrights for the German version of the book remained with me so that I could publish it on my web page. The collaboration was successful so that I also published my second textbook about grammatical theory with Stauffenburg. I think that this book has a broader relevance and should be accessible for non-German-speaking readers as well. I therefore decided to have it translated into English. Since Stauffenburg is focused on books in German, I had to look for another publisher. Fortunately the situation in the publishing sector changed quite dramatically in comparison to 1997: we now have high profile publishers with strict peer review that are entirely open access. I am very glad about the fact that Brigitte Narr sold the rights of my book back to me and that I can now publish the English version with Language Science Press under a CC-BY license.

Language Science Press: scholar-owned high quality linguistic books

In 2012 a group of people found the situation in the publishing business so unbearable that they agreed that it would be worthwhile to start a bigger initiative for publishing linguistics books in platinum open access, that is, free for both readers and authors. I set up a web page and collected supporters, very prominent linguists from all over the world and all subdisciplines and Martin Haspelmath and I then founded Language Science Press. At about the same time the DFG had announced a program for open access monographs and we applied (Müller & Haspelmath 2013) and got funded (two out of 18 applications got funding). The money is used for a coordinator (Dr. Sebastian Nordhoff) and an economist (Debora Siller), two programmers (Carola Fanselow and Dr. Mathias Schenner), who work on the publishing plattform Open Monograph Press (OMP) and on conversion software that produces various formats (ePub, XML, HTML) from our LaTeX code. Svantje Lilienthal works on the documentation of OMP, produces screencasts and does user support for authors, readers and series editors.

OMP is extended by open review facilities and community-building gamification tools (Müller 2012b; Müller & Haspelmath 2013). All Language Science Press books are reviewed by at least two external reviewers. Reviewers and authors may agree to publish these reviews and thereby make the whole process more transparent (see also Pullum (1984) for the suggestion of open reviewing of journal articles). In addition there is an optional second review phase: the open review. This review is completely open to ev-

---

[2] As a side remark: in the meantime Niemeyer was bought by de Gruyter and closed down. The price of the book is now 139.95 €/ $ 196.00. The price in Euro corresponds to 273.72 DM.

erybody. The whole community may comment on the document that is published by Language Science Press. After this second review phase, which usually lasts for two months, authors may revise their publication and an improved version will be published. This book was the first book to go through this open review phase. The annotated open review version of this book is still available via the web page of this book.

Currently, Language Science Press has 17 series on various subfields of linguistics with high profile series editors from all continents. We have 18 published and 17 forthcoming books and 146 expressions of interest. Series editors and authors are responsible for delivering manuscripts that are typeset in LaTeX, but they are supported by a web-based typesetting infrastructure that was set up by Language Science Press and by volunteer typesetters from the community. Proofreading is also community-based. Until now 53 people helped improving our books. Their work is documented in the Hall of Fame: http://langsci-press.org/about/hallOfFame.

If you think that textbooks like this one should be freely available to whoever wants to read them and that publishing scientific results should not be left to profit-oriented publishers, then you can join the Language Science Press community and support us in various ways: you can register with Language Science Press and have your name listed on our supporter page with almost 600 other enthusiasts, you may devote your time and help with proofreading and/or typesetting, or you may donate money for specific books or for Language Science Press in general. We are also looking for institutional supporters like foundations, societies, linguistics departments or university libraries. Detailed information on how to support us is provided at the following webpage: http://langsci-press.org/about/support. In case of questions, please contact me or the Language Science Press coordinator at contact@langsci-press.org.

Berlin, March 11, 2016   Stefan Müller

Part I

Background and specific theories

1 Introduction and basic terms

The aim of this chapter is to explain why we actually study syntax (Section 1.1) and why it is important to formalize our findings (Section 1.2). Some basic terminology will be introduced in Sections 1.3–1.8: Section 1.3 deals with criteria for dividing up utterances into smaller units. Section 1.4 shows how words can be grouped into classes; that is I will introduce criteria for assigning words to categories such as verb or adjective. Section 1.5 introduces the notion of heads, in Section 1.6 the distinction between arguments and adjuncts is explained, Section 1.7 defines grammatical functions and Section 1.8 introduces the notion of topological fields, which can be used to characterize certain areas of the clause in languages such as German.

Unfortunately, linguistics is a scientific field with a considerable amount of terminological chaos. This is partly due to the fact that terminology originally defined for certain languages (e.g., Latin, English) was later simply adopted for the description of other languages as well. However, this is not always appropriate since languages differ from one another considerably and are constantly changing. Due to the problems caused by this, the terminology started to be used differently or new terms were invented. When new terms are introduced in this book, I will always mention related terminology or differing uses of each term so that readers can relate this to other literature.

1.1 Why do syntax?

Every linguistic expression we utter has a meaning. We are therefore dealing with what has been referred to as form-meaning pairs (de Saussure 1916b). A word such as *tree* in its specific orthographical form or in its corresponding phonetic form is assigned the meaning *tree'*. Larger linguistic units can be built up out of smaller ones: words can be joined together to form phrases and these in turn can form sentences.

The question which now arises is the following: do we need a formal system which can assign a structure to these sentences? Would it not be sufficient to formulate a pairing of form and meaning for complete sentences just as we did for the word *tree* above?

That would, in principle, be possible if a language were just a finite list of word sequences. If we were to assume that there is a maximum length for sentences and a maximum length for words and thus that there can only be a finite number of words, then the number of possible sentences would indeed be finite. However, even if we were to restrict the possible length of a sentence, the number of possible sentences would still be enormous. The question we would then really need to answer is: what is the maximum length of a sentence? For instance, it is possible to extend all the sentences in (1):

(1)   a. This sentence goes on and on and on and on …

        b. [A sentence is a sentence] is a sentence.

        c. that Max thinks that Julius knows that Otto claims that Karl suspects that Richard confirms that Friederike is laughing

In (1b), something is being said about the group of words *a sentence is a sentence*, namely that it is a sentence. One can, of course, claim the same for the whole sentence in (1b) and extend the sentence once again with *is a sentence*. The sentence in (1c) has been formed by combining *that Friederike is laughing* with *that*, *Richard* and *confirms*. The result of this combination is a new sentence *that Richard confirms that Friederike is laughing*. In the same way, this has then been extended with *that*, *Karl* and *suspects*. Thus, one obtains a very complex sentence which embeds a less complex sentence. This partial sentence in turn contains a further partial sentence and so on. (1c) is similar to those sets of Russian nesting dolls, also called *matryoshka*: each doll contains a smaller doll which can be painted differently from the one that contains it. In just the same way, the sentence in (1c) contains parts which are similar to it but which are shorter and involve different nouns and verbs. This can be made clearer by using brackets in the following way:

(2)   that Max thinks [that Julius knows [that Otto claims [that Karl suspects [that Richard confirms [that Friederike is laughing]]]]]

We can build incredibly long and complex sentences in the ways that were demonstrated in (1).[1]

It would be arbitrary to establish some cut-off point up to which such combinations can be considered to belong to our language (Harris 1957: 208; Chomsky 1957: 23). It is also implausible to claim that such complex sentences are stored in our brains as a single complex unit. While evidence from psycholinguistic experiments shows that highly frequent or idiomatic combinations are stored as complex units, this could not be the case for sentences such as those in (1). Furthermore, we are capable of producing utterances that we have never heard before and which have also never been uttered or written down previously. Therefore, these utterances must have some kind of structure, there must be patterns which occur again and again. As humans, we are able to build such complex structures out of simpler ones and, vice-versa, to break down complex utterances into their component parts. Evidence for humans' ability to make use of rules for combining words into larger units has now also been provided by research in neuroscience (Pulvermüller 2010: 170).

It becomes particularly evident that we combine linguistic material in a rule-governed way when these rules are violated. Children acquire linguistic rules by generalizing from

---

[1] It is sometimes claimed that we are capable of constructing infinitely long sentences (Nowak, Komarova & Niyogi 2001: 117; Kim & Sells 2008: 3; Dan Everett in O'Neill & Wood (2012) at 25:19) or that Chomsky made such claims (Leiss 2003: 341). This is, however, not correct since every sentence has to come to an end at some point. Even in the theory of formal languages developed in the Chomskyan tradition, there are no infinitely long sentences. Rather, certain formal grammars can describe a set containing infinitely many finite sentences (Chomsky 1957: 13). See also Pullum & Scholz (2010) and Section 13.1.8 on the issue of recursion in grammar and for claims about the infinite nature of language.

the input available to them. In doing so, they produce some utterances which they could not have ever heard previously:

(3)   Ich festhalte   die.   (Friederike, 2;6)
      I   PART.hold them

      Intended: 'I hold them tight.'

Friederike, who was learning German, was at the stage of acquiring the rule for the position of the finite verb (namely, second position). What she did here, however, was to place the whole verb, including a separable particle *fest* 'tight', in the second position although the particle should be realized at the end of the clause (*Ich halte die fest.*).

If we do not wish to assume that language is merely a list of pairings of form and meaning, then there must be some process whereby the meaning of complex utterances can be obtained from the meanings of the smaller components of those utterances. Syntax reveals something about the way in which the words involved can be combined, something about the structure of an utterance. For instance, knowledge about subject-verb agreement helps with the interpretation of the following sentences in German:

(4)   a. Die Frau   schläft.
         the woman sleep.3SG

         'The woman sleeps.'

      b. Die Mädchen schlafen.
         the girls   sleep.3PL

         'The girls sleep.'

      c. Die Frau   kennt   die Mädchen.
         the woman know.3SG the girls

         'The woman knows the girls.'

      d. Die Frau   kennen   die Mädchen.
         the woman know.3PL the girls

         'The girls know the woman.'

The sentences in (4a,b) show that a singular or a plural subject requires a verb with the corresponding inflection. In (4a,b), the verb only requires one argument so the function of *die Frau* 'the woman' and *die Mädchen* 'the girls' is clear. In (4c,d) the verb requires two arguments and *die Frau* 'the woman' and *die Mädchen* 'the girls' could appear in either argument position in German. The sentences could mean that the woman knows somebody or that somebody knows the woman. However, due to the inflection on the verb and knowledge of the syntactic rules of German, the hearer knows that there is only one available reading for (4c) and (4d), respectively.

It is the role of syntax to discover, describe and explain such rules, patterns and structures.

1.2 Why do it formally?

The two following quotations give a motivation for the necessity of describing language formally:

> Precisely constructed models for linguistic structure can play an important role, both negative and positive, in the process of discovery itself. By pushing a precise but inadequate formulation to an unacceptable conclusion, we can often expose the exact source of this inadequacy and, consequently, gain a deeper understanding of the linguistic data. More positively, a formalized theory may automatically provide solutions for many problems other than those for which it was explicitly designed. Obscure and intuition-bound notions can neither lead to absurd conclusions nor provide new and correct ones, and hence they fail to be useful in two important respects. I think that some of those linguists who have questioned the value of precise and technical development of linguistic theory have failed to recognize the productive potential in the method of rigorously stating a proposed theory and applying it strictly to linguistic material with no attempt to avoid unacceptable conclusions by ad hoc adjustments or loose formulation. (Chomsky 1957: 5)

> As is frequently pointed out but cannot be overemphasized, an important goal of formalization in linguistics is to enable subsequent researchers to see the defects of an analysis as clearly as its merits; only then can progress be made efficiently. (Dowty 1979: 322)

If we formalize linguistic descriptions, it is easier to recognize what exactly a particular analysis means. We can establish what predictions it makes and we can rule out alternative analyses. A further advantage of precisely formulated theories is that they can be written down in such a way that computer programs can process them. When a theoretical analysis is implemented as a computationally processable grammar fragment, any inconsistency will become immediately evident. Such implemented grammars can then be used to process large collections of text, so-called corpora, and they can thus establish which sentences a particular grammar cannot yet analyze or which sentences are assigned the wrong structure. For more on using computer implementation in linguistics see Bierwisch (1963: 163), Müller (1999a: Chapter 22) and Bender (2008b) as well as Section 3.6.2.

1.3 Constituents

If we consider the sentence in (5), we have the intuition that certain words form a unit.

(5) Alle Studenten lesen während dieser Zeit Bücher.
     all   students   read during   this   time books
     'All the students are reading books at this time.'

For example, the words *alle* 'all' and *Studenten* 'students' form a unit which says something about who is reading. *während* 'during', *dieser* 'this' and *Zeit* 'time' also form a unit which refers to a period of time during which the reading takes place, and *Bücher* 'books' says something about what is being read. The first unit is itself made up of two parts, namely *alle* 'all' and *Studenten* 'students'. The unit *während dieser Zeit* 'during this time' can also be divided into two subcomponents: *während* 'during' and *dieser Zeit* 'this time'. *dieser Zeit* 'this time' is also composed of two parts, just like *alle Studenten* 'all students' is.

Recall that in connection with (1c) above we talked about the sets of Russian nesting dolls (*matryoshkas*). Here, too, when we break down (5) we have smaller units which are components of bigger units. However, in contrast to the Russian dolls, we do not just have one smaller unit contained in a bigger one but rather, we can have several units which are grouped together in a bigger one. The best way to envisage this is to imagine a system of boxes: one big box contains the whole sentence. Inside this box, there are four other boxes, which each contain *alle Studenten* 'all students', *lesen* 'reads', *während dieser Zeit* 'during this time' and *Bücher* 'books', respectively. Figure 1.1 illustrates this.

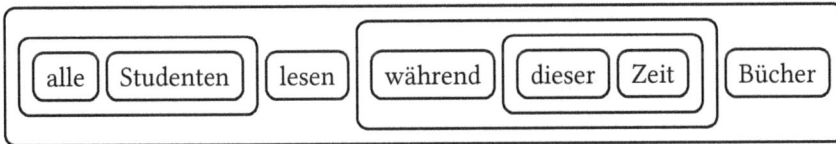

Figure 1.1: Words and phrases in boxes

In the following section, I will introduce various tests which can be used to show how certain words seem to "belong together" more than others. When I speak of a *word sequence*, I generally mean an arbitrary linear sequence of words which do not necessarily need to have any syntactic or semantic relationship, e.g., *Studenten lesen während* 'students read during' in (5). A sequence of words which form a structural entity, on the other hand, is referred to as a *phrase*. Phrases can consist of words as in *this time* or of combinations of words with other phrases as in *during this time*. The parts of a phrase and the phrase itself are called *constituents*. So all elements that are in a box in Figure 1.1 are constituents of the sentence.

Following these preliminary remarks, I will now introduce some tests which will help us to identify whether a particular string of words is a constituent or not.

1.3.1 Constituency tests

There are a number of ways to test the constituent status of a sequence of words. In the following subsections, I will present some of these. In Section 1.3.2, we will see that there are cases when simply applying a test "blindly" leads to unwanted results.

1.3.1.1 Substitution

If it is possible to replace a sequence of words in a sentence with a different sequence of words and the acceptability of the sentence remains unaffected, then this constitutes evidence for the fact that each sequence of words forms a constituent.

In (6), *den Mann* 'the man' can be replaced by the string *eine Frau* 'a woman'. This is an indication that both of these word sequences are constituents.

(6) a. Er kennt [den Mann].
he knows the man
'He knows the man.'

b. Er kennt [eine Frau].
he knows a woman
'He knows a woman.'

Similarly, in (7a), the string *das Buch zu lesen* 'the book to read' can be replaced by *der Frau das Buch zu geben* 'the woman the book to give'.

(7) a. Er versucht, [das Buch zu lesen].
he tries the book to read
'He is trying to read the book.'

b. Er versucht, [der Frau das Buch zu geben].
he tries the woman the book to give
'He is trying to give the woman the book.'

This test is referred to as the *substitution test*.

1.3.1.2 Pronominalization

Everything that can be replaced by a pronoun forms a constituent. In (8), one can for example refer to *der Mann* 'the man' with the pronoun *er* 'he':

(8) a. [Der Mann] schläft.
the man sleeps
'The man is sleeping.'

b. Er schläft.
he sleeps
'He is sleeping.'

It is also possible to use a pronoun to refer to constituents such as *das Buch zu lesen* 'the book to read' in (7a), as is shown in (9):

(9) a. Peter versucht, [das Buch zu lesen].
Peter tries the book to read
'Peter is trying to read the book.'

b. Klaus versucht das auch.
Klaus tries that also
'Klaus is trying to do that as well.'

The pronominalization test is another form of the substitution test.

1.3.1.3 Question formation

A sequence of words that can be elicited by a question forms a constituent:

(10)   a. [Der Mann] arbeitet.
        the man   works

        'The man is working.'

      b. Wer arbeitet?
        who works

        'Who is working?'

Question formation is a specific case of pronominalization. One uses a particular type of pronoun (an interrogative pronoun) to refer to the word sequence.

Constituents such as *das Buch zu lesen* in (7a) can also be elicited by questions, as (11) shows:

(11)   Was versucht er?
      what tries   he

      'What does he try?'

1.3.1.4 Permutation test

If a sequence of words can be moved without adversely affecting the acceptability of the sentence in which it occurs, then this is an indication that this word sequence forms a constituent.

In (12), *keiner* 'nobody' and *diese Frau* 'this woman' exhibit different orderings, which suggests that *diese* 'this' and *Frau* 'woman' belong together.

(12)   a. dass keiner [diese Frau] kennt
        that nobody this   woman knows

      b. dass [diese Frau] keiner kennt
        that this   woman nobody knows

      'that nobody knows this woman'

On the other hand, it is not plausible to assume that *keiner diese* 'nobody this' forms a constituent in (12a). If we try to form other possible orderings by trying to move *keiner diese* 'nobody this' as a whole, we see that this leads to unacceptable results:[2]

(13)   a. * dass Frau keiner diese kennt

      b. * dass Frau kennt keiner diese

---

[2] I use the following notational conventions for all examples: '*' indicates that a sentence is ungrammatical, '#' denotes that the sentence has a reading which differs from the intended one and finally '§' should be understood as a sentence which is deviant for semantic or information-structural reasons, for example, because the subject must be animate, but is in fact inanimate in the example in question, or because there is a conflict between constituent order and the marking of given information through the use of pronouns.

Furthermore, constituents such as *das Buch zu lesen* 'to read the book' in (7a) can be moved:

(14) a. Er hat noch nicht [das Buch zu lesen] versucht.
          he has PART not   the book to read   tried

          'He has not yet tried to read the book.'

      b. Er hat [das Buch zu lesen] noch nicht versucht.
          he has the book to read   PART not   tried

      c. Er hat noch nicht versucht, [das Buch zu lesen].
          he has PART not   tried   the book to read

1.3.1.5 Fronting

Fronting is a further variant of the movement test. In German declarative sentences, only a single constituent may normally precede the finite verb:

(15) a. [Alle Studenten] lesen   während der vorlesungsfreien Zeit Bücher.
          all   students   read.3PL during the lecture.free   time books

          'All students read books during the semester break.'

      b. [Bücher] lesen alle Studenten während der vorlesungsfreien Zeit.
          books   read all students   during the lecture.free   time

      c. * [Alle Studenten] [Bücher] lesen während der vorlesungsfreien Zeit.
          all   students   books   read during the lecture.free   time

      d. * [Bücher] [alle Studenten] lesen während der vorlesungsfreien Zeit.
          books   all students   read during the lecture.free   time

The possibility for a sequence of words to be fronted (that is to occur in front of the finite verb) is a strong indicator of constituent status.

1.3.1.6 Coordination

If two sequences of words can be conjoined then this suggests that each sequence forms a constituent.

In (16), *der Mann* 'the man' and *die Frau* 'the woman' are conjoined and the entire coordination is the subject of the verb *arbeiten* 'to work'. This is a good indication of the fact that *der Mann* and *die Frau* each form a constituent.

(16) [Der Mann] und [die Frau]   arbeiten.
      the man   and the woman work.3PL

      'The man and the woman work.'

The example in (17) shows that phrases with *to*-infinitives can be conjoined:

(17)   Er hat versucht, [das Buch zu lesen] und [es dann unauffällig verschwinden zu
       he had tried   the book to read   and it then secretly   disappear   to

       lassen].
       let

       'He tried to read the book and then make it quietly disappear.'

1.3.2 Some comments on the status of constituent tests

It would be ideal if the tests presented here delivered clear-cut results in every case, as
the empirical basis on which syntactic theories are built would thereby become much
clearer. Unfortunately, this is not the case. There are in fact a number of problems with
constituent tests, which I will discuss in what follows.

1.3.2.1 Expletives

There is a particular class of pronouns – so-called *expletives* – which do not denote people, things, or events and are therefore non-referential. An example of this is *es* 'it' in
(18).

(18)   a.   Es regnet.
            it rains

            'It is raining.'

       b.   Regnet es?
            rains   it

            'Is it raining?'

       c.   dass es jetzt regnet
            that it now rains

            'that it is raining now'

As the examples in (18) show, *es* can either precede the verb, or follow it. It can also be
separated from the verb by an adverb, which suggests that *es* should be viewed as an
independent unit.

   Nevertheless, we observe certain problems with the aforementioned tests. Firstly, *es*
'it' is restricted with regard to its movement possibilities, as (19a) and (20b) show.

(19)   a.   * dass jetzt es regnet
              that now it rains

            Intended: 'that it is raining now'

       b.   dass jetzt keiner   klatscht
            that now nobody claps

            'that nobody is clapping now'

(20) a. Er sah es   regnen.
          he saw it.ACC rain

          'He saw that it was raining.'

      b. * Es   sah er regnen.
          it.ACC saw he rain

          Intended: 'he saw that it was raining.'

      c. Er sah einen Mann klatschen.
          he saw a.ACC man   clap

          'He saw a man clapping.'

      d. Einen Mann sah er klatschen.
          a.ACC man   saw he clap

          'A man, he saw clapping.'

Unlike the accusative object *einen Mann* 'a man' in (20c,d), the expletive in (20b) cannot be fronted.

Secondly, substitution and question tests also fail:

(21) a. * Der Mann / er regnet.
           the man   he rains

      b. * Wer / was regnet?
           who   what rains

Similarly, the coordination test cannot be applied either:

(22) * Es und der Mann regnet / regnen.
        it and the man   rains   rain

The failure of these tests can be easily explained: weakly stressed pronouns such as *es* are preferably placed before other arguments, directly after the conjunction (*dass* in (18c)) and directly after the finite verb in (20a) (see Abraham 1995: 570). If an element is placed in front of the expletive, as in (19a), then the sentence is rendered ungrammatical. The reason for the ungrammaticality of (20b) is the general ban on accusative *es* appearing in clause-initial position. Although such cases exist, they are only possible if *es* 'it' is referential (Lenerz 1994: 162; Gärtner & Steinbach 1997: 4).

The fact that we could not apply the substitution and question tests is also no longer mysterious as *es* is not referential in these cases. We can only replace *es* 'it' with another expletive such as *das* 'that'. If we replace the expletive with a referential expression, we derive a different semantic interpretation. It does not make sense to ask about something semantically empty or to refer to it with a pronoun.

It follows from this that not all of the tests must deliver a positive result for a sequence of words to count as a constituent. That is, the tests are therefore not a necessary requirement for constituent status.

1.3.2.2 Movement

The movement test is problematic for languages with relatively free constituent order, since it is not always possible to tell what exactly has been moved. For example, the string *gestern dem Mann* 'yesterday the man' occupies different positions in the following examples:

(23)   a. weil   keiner gestern   dem Mann geholfen hat
             because nobody yesterday the man   helped   has

            'because nobody helped the man yesterday'

       b. weil   gestern   dem Mann keiner geholfen hat
             because yesterday the man   nobody helped   has

            'because nobody helped the man yesterday'

One could therefore assume that *gestern* 'yesterday' and *dem Mann* 'the man', which of course do not form a constituent, have been moved together. An alternative explanation for the ordering variants in (23) is that adverbs can occur in various positions in the clause and that only *dem Mann* 'the man' has been moved in front of *keiner* 'nobody' in (23b). In any case, it is clear that *gestern* and *dem Mann* have no semantic relation and that it is impossible to refer to both of them with a pronoun. Although it may seem at first glance as if this material had been moved as a unit, we have seen that it is in fact not tenable to assume that *gestern dem Mann* 'yesterday the man' forms a constituent.

1.3.2.3 Fronting

As mentioned in the discussion of (15), the position in front of the finite verb is normally occupied by a single constituent. The possibility for a given word sequence to be placed in front of the finite verb is sometimes even used as a clear indicator of constituent status, and even used in the definition of *Satzglied*[3]. An example of this is taken from Bußmann (1983), but is no longer present in Bußmann (1990):[4]

> **Satzglied test** A procedure based on → topicalization used to analyze complex constituents. Since topicalization only allows a single constituent to be moved to the beginning of the sentence, complex sequences of constituents, for example adverb phrases, can be shown to actually consist of one or more constituents. In the example *Ein Taxi quält sich im Schrittempo durch den Verkehr* 'A taxi was struggling at walking speed through the traffic', *im Schrittempo* 'at walking speed' and *durch den Verkehr* 'through the traffic' are each constituents as both can be fronted independently of each other. (Bußmann 1983: 446)

---

[3] *Satzglied* is a special term used in grammars of German, referring to a constituent on the clause level (Eisenberg et al. 2005: 783).

[4] The original formulation is: **Satzgliedtest** [Auch: Konstituententest]. Auf der → Topikalisierung beruhendes Verfahren zur Analyse komplexer Konstituenten. Da bei Topikalisierung jeweils nur eine Konstituente bzw. ein → Satzglied an den Anfang gerückt werden kann, lassen sich komplexe Abfolgen von Konstituenten (z. B. Adverbialphrasen) als ein oder mehrere Satzglieder ausweisen; in *Ein Taxi quält sich im Schrittempo durch den Verkehr* sind *im Schrittempo* und *durch den Verkehr* zwei Satzglieder, da sie beide unabhängig voneinander in Anfangsposition gerückt werden können.

The preceding quote has the following implications:

- Some part of a piece of linguistic material can be fronted independently →
  This material does not form a constituent.

- Linguistic material can be fronted together →
  This material forms a constituent.

It will be shown that both of these prove to be problematic.
   The first implication is cast into doubt by the data in (24):

(24)　a.　Keine Einigung　erreichten Schröder und Chirac über　den Abbau　　der
　　　　　　no　　agreement reached　　Schröder and Chirac about the　reduction of.the
　　　　　　Agrarsubventionen.[5]
　　　　　　agricultural.subsidies

　　　　　　'Schröder and Chirac could not reach an agreement on the reduction of agri-
　　　　　　cultural subsidies.'

　　　　b.　[Über　den Abbau　　der　　Agrarsubventionen] erreichten Schröder und
　　　　　　　about the　reduction of.the agricultural.subsidies reached　　Schröder and
　　　　　　Chirac keine Einigung.
　　　　　　Chirac no　　agreement

Although parts of the noun phrase *keine Einigung über den Abbau der Agrarsubventionen*
'no agreement on the reduction of agricultural subsidies' can be fronted individually, we
still want to analyze the entire string as a noun phrase when it is not fronted as in (25):

(25)　Schröder und Chirac erreichten [keine Einigung　über　den Abbau　　der
　　　　Schröder and Chirac reached　　no　　agreement about the　reduction of.the
　　　　Agrarsubventionen].
　　　　agricultural.subsidies

The prepositional phrase *über den Abbau der Agrarsubventionen* 'on the reduction of
agricultural subsidies' is semantically dependent on *Einigung* 'agreement' cf. (26):

(26)　Sie　einigen sich über　die Agrarsubventionen.
　　　　they agree　REFL about the agricultural.subsidies

　　　　'They agree on the agricultural subsidies.'

   This word sequence can also be fronted together:

(27)　[Keine Einigung　über　den Abbau　　der　　Agrarsubventionen] erreichten
　　　　no　　agreement about the　reduction of.the agricultural.subsidies reached
　　　　Schröder und Chirac.
　　　　Schröder and Chirac

In the theoretical literature, it is assumed that *keine Einigung über den Abbau der Agrarsubventionen* forms a constituent which can be "split up" under certain circumstances.

---

[5] tagesschau, 15.10.2002, 20:00.

In such cases, the individual subconstituents can be moved independently of each other (De Kuthy 2002) as we have seen in (25).

The second implication is problematic because of examples such as (28):

(28)   a.   [Trocken] [durch   die Stadt] kommt man am   Wochenende auch mit   der
            dry   through the city   comes one at.the weekend   also with the
            BVG.[6]
            BVG

            'With the BVG, you can be sure to get around town dry at the weekend.'

       b.   [Wenig] [mit Sprachgeschichte] hat der dritte Beitrag   in dieser Rubrik
            little   with language.history has the third contribution in this   section
            zu tun, [...][7]
            to do

            'The third contribution in this section has little to do with language history.'

In (28), there are multiple constituents preceding the finite verb, which bear no obvious syntactic or semantic relation to each other. Exactly what is meant by a "syntactic or semantic relation" will be fully explained in the following chapters. At this point, I will just point out that in (28a) the adjective *trocken* 'dry' has *man* 'one' as its subject and furthermore says something about the action of 'travelling through the city'. That is, it refers to the action denoted by the verb. As (29b) shows, *durch die Stadt* 'through the city' cannot be combined with the adjective *trocken* 'dry'.

(29)   a.   Man ist / bleibt trocken.
            one is   stays dry

            'One is/stays dry.'

       b.   * Man ist / bleibt trocken durch   die Stadt.
            one is   stays dry   through the city

Therefore, the adjective *trocken* 'dry' does not have a syntactic or semantic relationship with the prepositional phrase *durch die Stadt* 'through the city'. Both phrases have in common that they refer to the verb and are dependent on it.

One may simply wish to treat the examples in (28) as exceptions. This approach would, however, not be justified, as I have shown in an extensive empirical study (Müller 2003a).

If one were to classify *trocken durch die Stadt* as a constituent due to it passing the fronting test, then one would have to assume that *trocken durch die Stadt* in (30) is also a constituent. In doing so, we would devalue the term *constituent* as the whole point of constituent tests is to find out which word strings have some semantic or syntactic relationship.[8]

---

[6] taz berlin, 10.07.1998, p. 22.

[7] Zeitschrift für Dialektologie und Linguistik, LXIX, 3/2002, p. 339.

[8] These data can be explained by assuming a silent verbal head preceding the finite verb and thereby ensuring that there is in fact just one constituent in initial position in front of the finite verb (Müller 2005c, 2015b). Nevertheless, this kind of data are problematic for constituent tests since these tests have been specifically designed to tease apart whether strings such as *trocken* and *durch die Stadt* or *wenig* and *mit Sprachgeschichte* in (30) form a constituent.

(30) a. Man kommt am   Wochenende auch mit der BVG trocken durch die
  one comes at.the weekend   also with the BVG dry   through the
  Stadt.
  city

  'With the BVG, you can be sure to get around town dry at the weekend.'

  b. Der dritte Beitrag   in dieser Rubrik hat wenig mit Sprachgeschichte zu
  the third contribution in this   section has little with language.history to
  tun.
  do

  'The third contribution in this section has little to do with language history.'

The possibility for a given sequence of words to be fronted is therefore not a sufficient diagnostic for constituent status.

We have also seen that it makes sense to treat expletives as constituents despite the fact that the accusative expletive cannot be fronted (cf. (20a)):

(31) a. Er bringt es bis   zum Professor.
  he brings EXPL until to.the professor

  'He makes it to professor.'

  b. # Es bringt er bis   zum Professor.
  it brings he until to.the professor

There are other elements that can also not be fronted. Inherent reflexives are a good example of this:

(32) a. Karl hat sich nicht erholt.
  Karl has REFL not   recovered

  'Karl hasn't recovered.'

  b. * Sich hat Karl nicht erholt.
  REFL has Karl not   recovered

It follows from this that fronting is not a necessary criterion for constituent status. Therefore, the possibility for a given word string to be fronted is neither a necessary nor sufficient condition for constituent status.

1.3.2.4 Coordination

Coordinated structures such as those in (33) also prove to be problematic:

(33) Deshalb   kaufte der Mann einen Esel   und die Frau   ein Pferd.
  therefore bought the man a   donkey and the woman a   horse

  'Therefore, the man bought a donkey and the woman a horse.'

At first glance, *der Mann einen Esel* 'the man a donkey' and *die Frau ein Pferd* 'the woman a horse' in (33) seem to be coordinated. Does this mean that *der Mann einen Esel* and *die Frau ein Pferd* each form a constituent?

As other constituent tests show, this assumption is not plausible. This sequence of words cannot be moved together as a unit:[9]

(34) * Der Mann einen Esel   kaufte deshalb.
         the man   a   donkey bought therefore

Replacing the supposed constituent is also not possible without ellipsis:

(35)   a. # Deshalb kaufte er.
             therefore bought he

       b. * Deshalb kaufte ihn.
             therefore bought him

The pronouns do not stand in for the two logical arguments of *kaufen* 'to buy', which are realized by *der Mann* 'the man' and *einen Esel* 'a donkey' in (33), but rather for one in each. There are analyses that have been proposed for examples such as (33) in which two verbs *kauft* 'buys' occur, where only one is overt, however (Crysmann 2008). The example in (33) would therefore correspond to:

(36) Deshalb kaufte der Mann einen Esel   und kaufte die Frau   ein Pferd.
       therefore bought the man   a   donkey and bought the woman a   horse

This means that although it seems as though *der Mann einen Esel* 'the man a donkey' and *die Frau ein Pferd* 'the woman a horse' are coordinated, it is actually *kauft der Mann einen Esel* 'buys the man a donkey' and *(kauft) die Frau ein Pferd* 'buys the woman a horse' which are conjoined.

We should take the following from the previous discussion: even when a given word sequence passes certain constituent tests, this does not mean that one can automatically infer from this that we are dealing with a constituent. That is, the tests we have seen are not sufficient conditions for constituent status.

Summing up, it has been shown that these tests are neither sufficient nor necessary for attributing constituent status to a given sequence of words. However, as long as one keeps the problematic cases in mind, the previous discussion should be enough to get an initial idea about what should be treated as a constituent.

1.4 Parts of speech

The words in (37) differ not only in their meaning but also in other respects.

(37) Der dicke Mann lacht   jetzt.
       the fat   man laughs now
       'The fat man is laughing now.'

---

[9] The area in front of the finite verb is also referred to as the *Vorfeld* 'prefield' (see Section 1.8). Apparent multiple fronting is possible under certain circumstances in German. See the previous section, especially the discussion of the examples in (28) on page 15. The example in (34) is created in such a way that the subject is present in the prefield, which is not normally possible with verbs such as *kaufen* 'to buy' for reasons which have to do with the information-structural properties of these kinds of fronting constructions. Compare also De Kuthy & Meurers 2003b on subjects in fronted verb phrases and Bildhauer & Cook 2010: 72 on frontings of subjects in apparent multiple frontings.

Each of the words is subject to certain restrictions when forming sentences. It is common practice to group words into classes with other words which share certain salient properties. For example, *der* 'the' is an article, *Mann* 'man' is a noun, *lacht* 'laugh' is a verb and *jetzt* 'now' is an adverb. As can be seen in (38), it is possible to replace all the words in (37) with words from the same word class.

(38) Die dünne Frau   lächelt immer.
      the thin   woman smiles always

      'The thin woman is always smiling.'

This is not always the case, however. For example, it is not possible to use a reflexive verb such as *erholt* 'recovers' or the second-person form *lächelst* in (38). This means that the categorization of words into parts of speech is rather coarse and that we will have to say a lot more about the properties of a given word. In this section, I will discuss various word classes/parts of speech and in the following sections I will go into further detail about the various properties which characterize a given word class.

The most important parts of speech are *verbs, nouns, adjectives, prepositions* and *adverbs*. In earlier decades, it was common among researchers working on German (see also Section 11.6.1 on Tesnière's category system) to speak of *action words, describing words*, and *naming words*. These descriptions prove problematic, however, as illustrated by the following examples:

(39) a. die *Idee*
          the idea

      b. die *Stunde*
          the hour

      c. das laute *Sprechen*
          the loud speaking

          '(the act of) speaking loudly'

      d. Die *Erörterung* der   Lage   dauerte mehrere Stunden.
          the discussion of.the situation lasted   several   hours

          'The discussion of the situation lasted several hours.'

(39a) does not describe a concrete entity, (39b) describes a time interval and (39c) and (39d) describe actions. It is clear that *Idee* 'idea', *Stunde* 'hour', *Sprechen* 'speaking' and *Erörterung* 'discussion' differ greatly in terms of their meaning. Nevertheless, these words still behave like *Mann* 'man' and *Frau* 'woman' in many respects and are therefore classed as nouns.

The term *action word* is not used in scientific linguistic work as verbs do not always need to denote actions:

(40) a. Ihm gefällt das Buch.
          him pleases the book

          'He likes the book.'

  b. Das Eis schmilzt.
     the ice melts

     'The ice is melting.'

  c. Es regnet.
     it rains

     'It is raining.'

One would also have to class the noun *Erörterung* 'discussion' as an action word.

Adjectives do not always describe properties of objects. In the following examples, the opposite is in fact true: the characteristic of being a murderer is expressed as being possible or probable, but not as being true properties of the modified noun.

(41) a. der mutmaßliche Mörder
      the suspected   murderer

    b. Soldaten sind potenzielle Mörder.
      soldiers are potential murderers

The adjectives themselves in (41) do not actually provide any information about the characteristics of the entities described. One may also wish to classify *lachende* 'laughing' in (42) as an adjective.

(42) der lachende Mann
    the laughing man

If, however, we are using properties and actions as our criteria for classification, *lachend* 'laughing' should technically be an action word.

Rather than semantic criteria, it is usually formal criteria which are used to determine word classes. The various forms a word can take are also taken into account. So *lacht* 'laughs', for example, has the forms given in (43).

(43) a. Ich lache.
      I laugh

    b. Du lachst.
      you.SG laugh

    c. Er lacht.
      he laughs

    d. Wir lachen.
      we laugh

    e. Ihr lacht.
      you.PL laugh

    f. Sie lachen.
      they laugh

In German, there are also forms for the preterite, imperative, present subjunctive, past subjunctive and infinitive forms (participles and infinitives with or without *zu* 'to'). All of these forms constitute the inflectional paradigm of a verb. Tense (present, preterite, future), mood (indicative, subjunctive, imperative), person (1st, 2nd, 3rd) and number (singular, plural) all play a role in the inflectional paradigm. Certain forms can coincide in a paradigm, as (43c) and (43e) and (43d) and (43f) show.

Parallel to verbs, nouns also have an inflectional paradigm:

(44) a. der   Mann
          the.NOM man

      b. des   Mannes
          the.GEN man.GEN

      c. dem   Mann
          the.DAT man

      d. den   Mann
          the.ACC man

      e. die   Männer
          the.NOM men

      f. der   Männer
          the.GEN men

      g. den   Männern
          the.DAT men.DAT

      h. die   Männer
          the.ACC men

We can differentiate between nouns on the basis of gender (feminine, masculine, neuter). The choice of gender is often purely formal in nature and is only partially influenced by biological sex or the fact that we are describing a particular object:

(45) a. die   Tüte
          the.F bag(F)
          'the bag'

      b. der   Krampf
          the.M cramp(M)
          'cramp'

      c. das   Kind
          the.N child(N)
          'the child'

As well as gender, case (nominative, genitive, dative, accusative) and number are also important for nominal paradigms.

Like nouns, adjectives inflect for gender, case and number. They differ from nouns, however, in that gender marking is variable. Adjectives can be used with all three genders:

(46) a. eine kluge   Frau
          a.F clever.F woman

    b. ein kluger   Mann
        a   clever.M man

    c. ein kluges   Kind
        a   clever.N child

In addition to gender, case and number, we can identify several inflectional classes. Traditionally, we distinguish between strong, mixed and weak inflection of adjectives. The inflectional class that we have to choose is dependent on the form or presence of the article:

(47) a. ein alter Wein
          an old   wine

    b. der alte Wein
        the old wine

    c. alter Wein
        old   wine

Furthermore, adjectives have comparative and superlative wordforms:

(48) a. klug
          clever

    b. klüg-er
        clever-er

    c. am   klüg-sten
        at.the clever-est

This is not always the case. Especially for adjectives which make reference to some end point, a degree of comparison does not make sense. If a particular solution is optimal, for example, then no better one exists. Therefore, it does not make sense to speak of a "more optimal" solution. In a similar vein, it is not possible to be "deader" than dead.

There are some special cases such as color adjectives ending in -*a* in German *lila* 'purple' and *rosa* 'pink'. These inflect optionally (49a), and the uninflected form is also possible:

(49) a. eine lilan-e   Blume
          a   purple-F flower

    b. eine lila   Blume
        a   purple flower

In both cases, *lila* is classed an adjective. We can motivate this classification by appealing to the fact that both words occur at the same positions as other adjectives that clearly behave like adjectives with regard to inflection.

The parts of speech discussed thus far can all be differentiated in terms of their inflectional properties. For words which do not inflect, we have to use additional criteria. For example, we can classify words by the syntactic context in which they occur (as we did for the non-inflecting adjectives above). We can identify prepositions, adverbs, conjunctions, interjections and sometimes also particles. Prepositions are words which occur with a noun phrase whose case they determine:

(50) a. in diesen Raum
          in this.ACC room

      b. in diesem Raum
          in this.DAT room

wegen 'because' is often classed as a preposition although it can also occur after the noun and in these cases would technically be a postposition:

(51) des Geldes   wegen
      the money.GEN because

      'because of the money'

It is also possible to speak of *adpositions* if one wishes to remain neutral about the exact position of the word.

Unlike prepositions, adverbs do not require a noun phrase.

(52) a. Er schläft in diesem Raum.
          he sleeps in this   room

      b. Er schläft dort.
          he sleeps there

Sometimes adverbs are simply treated as a special variant of prepositions (see page 92). The explanation for this is that a prepositional phrase such as *in diesem Raum* 'in this room' shows the same syntactic distribution as the corresponding adverbs. *in* differs from *dort* 'there' in that it needs an additional noun phrase. These differences are parallel to what we have seen with other parts of speech. For instance, the verb *schlafen* 'sleep' requires only a noun phrase, whereas *erkennen* 'recognize' requires two.

(53) a. Er schläft.
          he sleeps

      b. Peter erkennt   ihn.
          Peter recognizes him

Conjunctions can be subdivided into subordinating and coordinating conjunctions. Coordinating conjunctions include *und* 'and' and *oder* 'or'. In coordinate structures, two units with the same syntactic properties are combined. They occur adjacent to one another. *dass* 'that' and *weil* 'because' are subordinating conjunctions because the clauses

that they introduce can be part of a larger clause and depend on another element of this
larger clause.

(54)   a. Klaus glaubt, dass er lügt.
            Klaus believes that he lies

            'Klaus believes that he is lying.'

        b. Klaus glaubt   ihm nicht, weil   er lügt.
            Klaus believes him not   because he lies

            'Klaus doesn't believe him because he is lying.'

Interjections are clause-like expressions such as *Ja!* 'Yes!', *Bitte!* 'Please!' *Hallo!* 'Hel-
lo!', *Hurra!* 'Hooray!', *Bravo!* 'Bravo!', *Pst!* 'Psst!', *Plumps!* 'Clonk!'.

If adverbs and prepositions are not assigned to the same class, then adverbs are normally used as a kind of "left over" category in the sense that all non-inflecting words
which are neither prepositions, conjunctions nor interjections are classed as adverbs.
Sometimes this category for "left overs" is subdivided: only words which can appear
in front of the finite verb when used as a constituent are referred to as adverbs. Those
words which cannot be fronted are dubbed *particles*. Particles themselves can be subdivided into various classes based on their function, e.g., degree particles and illocutionary
particles. Since these functionally defined classes also contain adjectives, I will not make
this distinction and simply speak of *adverbs*.

We have already sorted a considerable number of inflectional words into word classes.
When one is faced with the task of classifying a particular word, one can use the decision
diagram in Figure 1.2 on the next page, which is taken from the Duden grammar of
German (Eisenberg et al. 2005: 133).[10]

If a word inflects for tense, then it is a verb. If it displays different case forms, then
one has to check if it has a fixed gender. If this is indeed the case, then we know that
we are dealing with a noun. Words with variable gender have to be checked to see if
they have comparative forms. A positive result will be a clear indication of an adjective. All other words are placed into a residual category, which the Duden refers to as
pronouns/article words. Like in the class of non-inflectional elements, the elements in
this remnant category are subdivided according to their syntactic behavior. The Duden
grammar makes a distinction between pronouns and article words. According to this
classification, pronouns are words which can replace a noun phrase such as *der Mann*
'the man', whereas article words normally combine with a noun. In Latin grammars,
the notion of 'pronoun' includes both pronouns in the above sense and articles, since
the forms with and without the noun are identical. Over the past centuries, the forms
have undergone split development to the point where it is now common in contemporary Romance languages to distinguish between words which replace a noun phrase and
those which must occur with a noun. Elements which belong to the latter class are also
referred to as *determiners*.

---

[10] The Duden is the official document for the German orthography. The Duden grammar does not have an
official status but is very influential and is used for educational purposes as well. I will refer to it several
times in this introductory chapter.

```
                              part of speech
              _____|_____
             |                                                 |
          inflects                                    does not inflect
      _____|_____                                         |
     |                |                                        |
 for tense        for case                                     |
     |         _____|_____                                |
     |        |                |                               |
     |   fixed gender    flexible gender                       |
     |        |           _____|_____                        |
     |        |          |             |                       |
     |        |    no comparative   comparative                |
     |        |          |             |                       |
     |        |          |             |                       |
   verb     noun    article word    adjective              adverb
                      pronoun                            conjunction
                                                         preposition
                                                         interjection
```

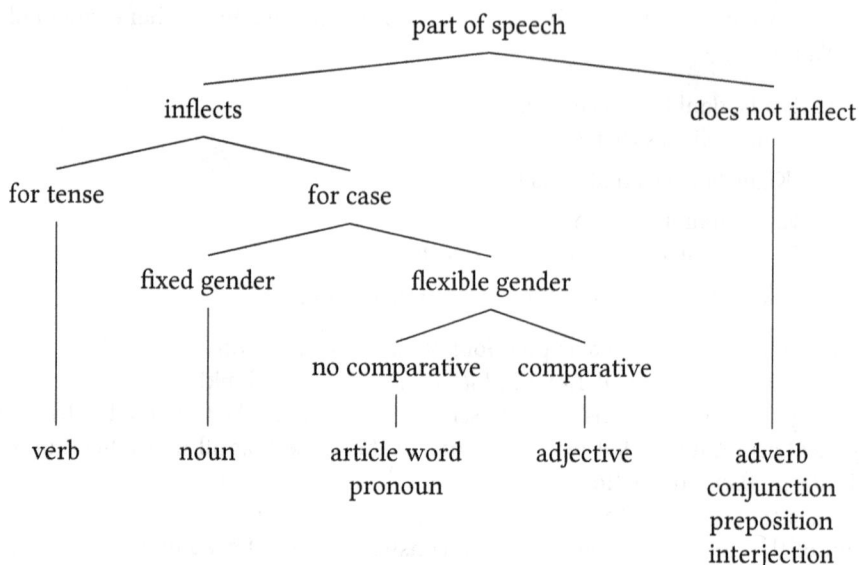

Figure 1.2: Decision tree for determining parts of speech following Eisenberg et al. (2005: 133)

If we follow the decision tree in Figure 1.2, the personal pronouns *ich* 'I', *du* 'you', *er* 'he', *sie* 'her', *es* 'it', *wir* 'we', *ihr* 'you', and *sie* 'they', for example, would be grouped together with the possessive pronouns *mein* 'mine', *dein* 'your', *sein* 'his'/'its', *ihr* 'her'/ 'their', *unser* 'our', and *euer* 'your'. The corresponding reflexive pronouns, *mich* 'myself', *dich* 'yourself', *sich* 'himself'/'herself'/'itself', 'themselves', *uns* 'ourselves', *euch* 'yourself', and the reciprocal pronoun *einander* 'each other' have to be viewed as a special case in German as there are no differing gender forms of *sich* 'himself'/'herself'/'itself' and *einander* 'each other'. Case is not expressed morphologically by reciprocal pronouns. By replacing genitive, dative and accusative pronouns with *einander*, it is possible to see that there must be variants of *einander* 'each other' in these cases, but these variants all share the same form:

(55) a. Sie gedenken   seiner   / einander.
         they commemorate him.GEN each.other

      b. Sie helfen ihm   / einander.
         they help   him.DAT each.other

      c. Sie lieben ihn   / einander.
         they love   him.ACC each.other

So-called pronominal adverbs such as *darauf* 'on there', *darin* 'in there', *worauf* 'on where', *worin* 'in where' also prove problematic. These forms consist of a preposition (e.g., *auf* 'on') and the elements *da* 'there' and *wo* 'where'. As the name suggests, *pronominal adverbs* contain something pronominal and this can only be *da* 'there' and *wo* 'where'. However, *da* 'there' and *wo* 'where' do not inflect and would therefore, following the decision tree, not be classed as pronouns.

The same is true of relative pronouns such as *wo* 'where' in (56):

(56) a. Ich komme eben aus der Stadt, *wo*   ich Zeuge eines Unglücks gewesen
          I   come PART from the city   where I   witness of.an accident been
          bin.[11]
          am

          'I come from the city where I was witness to an accident.'

      b. Studien haben gezeigt, daß mehr Unfälle   in Städten passieren, *wo*   die
          studies have shown that more accidents in cities   happen   where the
          Zebrastreifen   abgebaut werden, weil   die Autofahrer unaufmerksam
          zebra.crossings removed become because the drivers   unattentive
          werden.[12]
          become

          'Studies have shown that there are more accidents in cities where they do
          away with zebra crossings, because drivers become unattentive.'

      c. Zufällig   war ich in dem Augenblick zugegen, *wo*   der Steppenwolf
          coincidentally was I   in the moment   present where the Steppenwolf
          zum erstenmal unser Haus betrat und bei meiner Tante sich einmietete.[13]
          to.the first.time our   house entered and by my   aunt REFL took.lodgings

          'Coincidentally, I was present at the exact moment in which Steppenwolf en-
          tered our house for the first time and took lodgings with my aunt.'

If they are uninflected, then they cannot belong to the class of pronouns according to the decision tree above. Eisenberg (2004: 277) notes that *wo* 'where' is a kind of *uninflected relative pronoun* (he uses quotation marks) and remarks that this term runs contrary to the exclusive use of the term pronoun for nominal, that is, inflected, elements. He therefore uses the term *relative adverb* for them (see also Eisenberg et al. (2005: §856, §857)).

There are also usages of the relatives *dessen* 'whose' and *wessen* 'whose' in combination with a noun:

(57) a. der Mann, dessen Schwester ich kenne
          the man   whose sister   I   know

      b. Ich möchte   wissen, wessen Schwester du   kennst.
          I   would.like know   whose sister   you know

          'I would like to know whose sister you know.'

According to the classification in the Duden, these should be covered by the terms *Relativartikelwort* 'relative article word' and *Interrogativartikelwort* 'interrogative article

---

[11] Drosdowski (1984: 672).

[12] taz berlin, 03.11.1997, p. 23.

[13] Herman Hesse, *Der Steppenwolf.* Berlin und Weimar: Aufbau-Verlag. 1986, p. 6.

word'. They are mostly counted as part of the relative pronouns and question pronouns (see for instance Eisenberg (2004: 229)). Using Eisenberg's terminology, this is unproblematic as he does not make a distinction between articles, pronouns and nouns, but rather assigns them all to the class of nouns. But authors who do make a distinction between articles and pronouns sometimes also speak of interrogative pronouns when discussing words which can function as articles or indeed replace an entire noun phrase.

One should be prepared for the fact that the term *pronoun* is often simply used for words which refer to other entities and, this is important, not in the way that nouns such as *book* and *John* do, but rather dependent on context. The personal pronoun *er* 'he' can, for example, refer to either a table or a man. This usage of the term *pronoun* runs contrary to the decision tree in Figure 1.2 and includes uninflected elements such as *da* 'there' and *wo* 'where'.

Expletive pronouns such as *es* 'it' and *das* 'that', as well as the *sich* 'him'/'her'/'itself' belonging to inherently reflexive verbs, do not make reference to actual objects. They are considered pronouns because of the similarity in form. Even if we were to assume a narrow definition of pronouns, we would still get the wrong results as expletive forms do not vary with regard to case, gender and number. If one does everything by the book, expletives would belong to the class of uninflected elements. If we assume that *es* 'it' as well as the personal pronouns have a nominative and accusative variant with the same form, then they would be placed in with the nominals. We would then have to admit that the assumption that *es* has gender would not make sense. That is we would have to count *es* as a noun by assuming neuter gender, analogous to personal pronouns.

We have not yet discussed how we would deal with the italicized words in (58):

(58)   a. das *geliebte* Spielzeug
          the beloved toy

   b. das *schlafende* Kind
          the sleeping   child

   c. die Frage   des   *Sprechens* und *Schreibens* über Gefühle
          the question of.the talking   and writing   about feelings
          'the question of talking and writing about feelings'

   d. Auf dem Europa-Parteitag   fordern die *Grünen* einen ökosozialen
          on   the Europe-party.conference demand the Greens a   eco-social
          Politikwechsel.
          political.change
          'At the European party conference, the Greens demanded eco-social political change.'

   e. Max lacht   *laut*.
          Max laughs loudly

   f. Max würde *wahrscheinlich* lachen.
          Max would probably   laugh

geliebte 'beloved' and *schlafende* 'sleeping' are participle forms of *lieben* 'to love' and *schlafen* 'to sleep'. These forms are traditionally treated as part of the verbal paradigm. In this sense, *geliebte* and *schlafende* are verbs. This is referred to as lexical word class. The term *lexeme* is relevant in this case. All forms in a given inflectional paradigm belong to the relevant lexeme. In the classic sense, this term also includes the regularly derived forms. That is participle forms and nominalized infinitives also belong to a verbal lexeme. Not all linguists share this view, however. Particularly problematic is the fact that we are mixing verbal with nominal and adjectival paradigms. For example, *Sprechens* 'speaking.GEN' is in the genitive case and adjectival participles also inflect for case, number and gender. Furthermore, it is unclear as to why *schlafende* 'sleeping' should be classed as a verbal lexeme and a noun such as *Störung* 'disturbance' is its own lexeme and does not belong to the lexeme *stören* 'to disturb'. I subscribe to the more modern view of grammar and assume that processes in which a word class is changed result in a new lexeme being created. Consequently, *schlafende* 'sleeping' does not belong to the lexeme *schlafen* 'to sleep', but is a form of the lexeme *schlafend*. This lexeme belongs to the word class 'adjective' and inflects accordingly.

As we have seen, it is still controversial as to where to draw the line between inflection and derivation (creation of a new lexeme). Sag, Wasow & Bender (2003: 263–264) view the formation of the present participle (*standing*) and the past participle (*eaten*) in English as derivation as these forms inflect for gender and number in French.

Adjectives such as *Grünen* 'the Greens' in (58d) are nominalized adjectives and are written with a capital like other nouns in German when there is no other noun that can be inferred from the immediate context:

(59) A: Willst du   den roten Ball haben?
        want you the red   ball have

      'Do you want the red ball?'

      B: Nein, gib mir bitte   den grünen.
        no   give me please the green

      'No, give me the green one, please.'

In the answer to (59), the noun *Ball* has been omitted. This kind of omission is not present in (58d). One could also assume here that a word class change has taken place. If a word changes its class without combination with a visible affix, we refer to this as *conversion*. Conversion has been treated as a sub-case of derivation by some linguists. The problem is, however, that *Grüne* 'greens' inflects just like an adjective and the gender varies depending on the object it is referring to:

(60) a. Ein Grüner hat vorgeschlagen, ...
         a   green.M has suggested

       'A (male) member of the Green Party suggested ...'

      b. Eine Grüne hat vorgeschlagen, ...
         a   green.F has suggested

       'A (female) member of the Green Party suggested ...'

We also have the situation where a word has two properties. We can make life easier for ourselves by talking about *nominalized adjectives*. The lexical category of *Grüne* is adjective and its syntactic category is noun.

The word in (58e) can inflect like an adjective and should therefore be classed as an adjective following our tests. Sometimes, these kinds of adjectives are also classed as adverbs. The reason for this is that the uninflected forms of these adjectives behave like adverbs:

(61) Max lacht   immer / oft   / laut.
      Max laughs always often   loud

      'Max (always/often) laughs (loudly).'

To capture this dual nature of words some researchers distinguish between lexical and syntactic category of words. The lexical category of *laut* 'loud(ly)' is that of an adjective and the syntactic category to which it belongs is 'adverb'. The classification of adjectives such as *laut* 'loud(ly)' in (61) as adverbs is not assumed by all authors. Instead, some speak of adverbial usage of an adjective, that is, one assumes that the syntactic category is still adjective but it can be used in a different way so that it behaves like an adverb (see Eisenberg 2004: Section 7.3, for example). This is parallel to prepositions, which can occur in a variety of syntactic contexts:

(62) a. Peter schläft im   Büro.
          Peter sleeps in.the office

          'Peter sleeps in the office.'
      b. der Tisch im   Büro
          the table in.the office

          'the table in the office'

We have prepositional phrases in both examples in (62); however, in (62a) *im Büro* 'in the office' acts like an adverb in that it modifies the verb *schläft* 'sleeps' and in (62b) *im Büro* modifies the noun *Tisch* 'table'. In the same way, *laut* 'loud' can modify a noun (63) or a verb (61).

(63) die laute Musik
      the loud music

1.5 Heads

The head of a constituent/phrase is the element which determines the most important properties of the constituent/phrase. At the same time, the head also determines the composition of the phrase. That is, the head requires certain other elements to be present in the phrase. The heads in the following examples have been marked in *italics*:

(64) a. *Träumt* dieser   Mann?
          dreams this.NOM man

          'Does this man dream?'

b. *Erwartet* er   diesen Mann?
expects   he.NOM this.ACC man

'Is he expecting this man?'

c. *Hilft* er   diesem Mann?
helps he.NOM this.DAT man

'Is he helping this man?'

d. *in* diesem Haus
in this.DAT house

e. ein   *Mann*
a.NOM man

Verbs determine the case of their arguments (subjects and objects). In (64d), the preposition determines which case the noun phrase *diesem Haus* 'this house' bears (dative) and also determines the semantic contribution of the phrase (it describes a location). (64e) is controversial: there are linguists who believe that the determiner is the head (Vennemann & Harlow 1977; Hellan 1986; Abney 1987; Netter 1994, 1998) while others assume that the noun is the head of the phrase (Van Langendonck 1994; Pollard & Sag 1994: 49; Demske 2001; Müller 2007b: Section 6.6.1; Hudson 2004; Bruening 2009).

The combination of a head with another constituent is called a *projection of the head*. A projection which contains all the necessary parts to create a well-formed phrase of that type is a *maximal projection*. A sentence is the maximal projection of a finite verb.

Figure 1.3 shows the structure of (65) in box representation.

(65)   Der Mann liest einen Aufsatz.
the man   reads an   essay

'The man is reading an essay.'

Unlike Figure 1.1, the boxes have been labelled here.

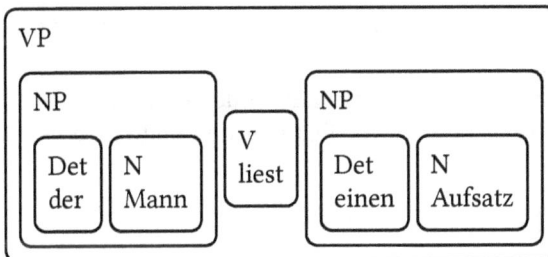

Figure 1.3: Words and phrases in annotated boxes

The annotation includes the category of the most important element in the box. VP stands for *verb phrase* and NP for *noun phrase*. VP and NP are maximal projections of their respective heads.

Anyone who has ever faced the hopeless task of trying to find particular photos of their sister's wedding in a jumbled, unsorted cupboard can vouch for the fact that it is most definitely a good idea to mark the boxes based on their content and also mark the albums based on the kinds of photos they contain.

An interesting point is that the exact content of the box with linguistic material does not play a role when the box is put into a larger box. It is possible, for example, to replace the noun phrase *der Mann* 'the man' with *er* 'he', or indeed the more complex *der Mann aus Stuttgart, der das Seminar zur Entwicklung der Zebrafinken besucht* 'the man from Stuttgart who takes part in the seminar on the development of zebra finches'. However, it is not possible to use *die Männer* 'the men' or *des Mannes* 'of the man' in this position:

(66) a. * Die Männer liest einen Aufsatz.
            the men   reads an   essay

  b. * Des   Mannes liest einen Aufsatz.
          of.the man.GEN reads an   essay

The reason for this is that *die Männer* 'the men' is in plural and the verb *liest* 'reads' is in singular. The noun phrase bearing genitive case *des Mannes* can also not occur, only nouns in the nominative case. It is therefore important to mark all boxes with the information that is important for placing these boxes into larger boxes. Figure 1.4 shows our example with more detailed annotation.

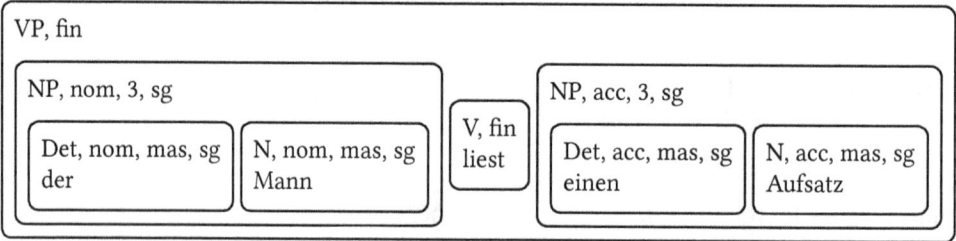

Figure 1.4: Words and word strings in annotated boxes

The features of a head which are relevant for determining in which contexts a phrase can occur are called *head features*. The features are said to be *projected* by the head.

1.6 Arguments and adjuncts

The constituents of a given clause have different relations to their head. It is typical to distinguish between arguments and adjuncts. The syntactic arguments of a head correspond for the most part to their logical arguments. We can represent the meaning of (67a) as (67b) using predicate logic.

(67) a. Peter helps Maria.

  b. *help'(peter', maria')*

The logical representation of (67b) resembles what is expressed in (67a); however, it abstracts away from constituent order and inflection. *Peter* and *Maria* are syntactic arguments of the verb *help* and their respective meanings (*Peter′* and *Maria′*) are arguments of the logical relation expressed by *help′*. One could also say that *help* assigns semantic roles to its arguments. Semantic roles include agent (the person carrying out an action), patient (the affected person or thing), beneficiary (the person who receives something) and experiencer (the person experiencing a psychological state). The subject of *help* is an agent and the direct object is a beneficiary. Arguments which fulfil a semantic role are also called *actants*. This term is also used for inanimate objects.

This kind of relation between a head and its arguments is covered by the terms *selection* and *valence*. Valence is a term borrowed from chemistry. Atoms can combine with other atoms to form molecules with varying levels of stability. The way in which the electron shells are occupied plays an important role for this stability. If an atom combines with others atoms so that its electron shell is fully occupied, then this will lead to a stable connection. Valence tells us something about the number of hydrogen atoms which an atom of a certain element can be combined with. In forming H_2O, oxygen has a valence of 2. We can divide elements into valence classes. Following Mendeleev, elements with a particular valence are listed in the same column in the periodic table.

The concept of valence was applied to linguistics by Tesnière (1959): a head needs certain arguments in order to form a stable compound. Words with the same valence – that is which require the same number and type of arguments – are divided into valence classes. Figure 1.5 shows examples from chemistry as well as linguistics.

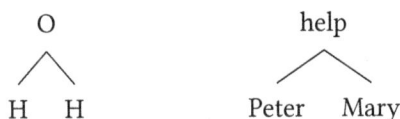

O   help

H   H   Peter   Mary

Figure 1.5: Combination of hydrogen and oxygen and the combination of a verb with its arguments

We used (67) to explain logical valence. Logical valence can, however, sometimes differ from syntactic valence. This is the case with verbs like *rain*, which require an expletive pronoun as an argument. Inherently reflexive verbs such as *sich erholen* 'to recover' in German are another example.

(68) a. Es regnet.
         it rains

         'It is raining.'

      b. Klaus erholt   sich.
         Klaus recovers REFL

         'Klaus is recovering.'

The expletive *es* 'it' with weather verbs and the *sich* of so-called inherent reflexives such as *erholen* 'to recover' have to be present in the sentence. Germanic languages have expletive elements that are used to fill the position preceding the finite verb. These positional expletives are not realized in embedded clauses in German, since embedded clauses have a structure that differs from canonical unembedded declarative clauses, which have the finite verb in second position. (69a) shows that *es* cannot be omitted in *dass*-clauses.

(69)   a. * Ich glaube, dass regnet.
          I   think   that rains

             Intended: 'I think that it is raining.'

    b. * Ich glaube, dass Klaus erholt.
          I   believe that Klaus recovers

             Intended: 'I believe that Klaus is recovering.'

Neither the expletive nor the reflexive pronoun contributes anything semantically to the sentence. They must, however, be present to derive a complete, well-formed sentence. They therefore form part of the valence of the verb.

Constituents which do not contribute to the central meaning of their head, but rather provide additional information are called *adjuncts*. An example is the adverb *deeply* in (70):

(70)   John loves Mary deeply.

This says something about the intensity of the relation described by the verb. Further examples of adjuncts are attributive adjectives (71a) and relative clauses (71b):

(71)   a. a *beautiful* woman
    b. the man *who Mary loves*

Adjuncts have the following syntactic/semantic properties:

(72)   a. Adjuncts do not fulfil a semantic role.
    b. Adjuncts are optional.
    c. Adjuncts can be iterated.

The phrase in (71a) can be extended by adding another adjunct:

(73)   a beautiful clever woman

If one puts processing problems aside for a moment, this kind of extension by adding adjectives could proceed infinitely (see the discussion of (38) on page 65). Arguments, on the other hand, cannot be realized more than once:

(74)   * The man the boy sleeps.

If the entity carrying out the sleeping action has already been mentioned, then it is not possible to have another noun phrase which refers to a sleeping individual. If one wants to express the fact that more than one individual is sleeping, this must be done by means of coordination as in (75):

(75)   The man and the boy are sleeping.

One should note that the criteria for identifying adjuncts proposed in (72) is not sufficient, since there are also syntactic arguments that do not fill semantic roles (e.g., *es* 'it' in (68a) and *sich* (REFL) in (68b)) or are optional as *pizza* in (76).

(76)   Tony is eating (pizza).

Heads normally determine the syntactic properties of their arguments in a relatively fixed way. A verb is responsible for the case which its arguments bear.

(77)   a.   Er gedenkt   des   Opfers.
             he remembers the.GEN victim.GEN

             'He remembers the victim.'

       b. * Er gedenkt   dem   Opfer.
             he remembers the.DAT victim

       c.   Er hilft dem   Opfer.
             he helps the.DAT victim

             'He helps the victim.'

       d. * Er hilft des   Opfers.
             he helps the.GEN victim.GEN

The verb *governs* the case of its arguments.

   The preposition and the case of the noun phrase in the prepositional phrase are both determined by the verb:[14]

(78)   a.   Er denkt an seine   Modelleisenbahn.
             he thinks on his.ACC model.railway

             'He is thinking of his model railway.'

       b. # Er denkt an seiner   Modelleisenbahn.
             He thinks on his.DAT model.railway

       c.   Er hängt an seiner   Modelleisenbahn.
             He hangs on his.DAT model.railway

             'He clings to his model railway.'

       d. * Er hängt an seine   Modelleisenbahn.
             he hangs on his.ACC model.railway

The case of noun phrases in modifying prepositional phrases, on the other hand, depends on their meaning. In German, directional prepositional phrases normally require a noun phrase bearing accusative case (79a), whereas local PPs (denoting a fixed location) appear in the dative case (79b):

---

[14] For similar examples, see Eisenberg (1994b: 78).

(79)   a.   Er geht in die   Schule / auf den   Weihnachtsmarkt / unter die
          he goes in the.ACC school   on the.ACC Christmas.market   under the.ACC
          Brücke.
          bridge

          'He is going to school/to the Christmas market/under the bridge.'

     b.   Er schläft in der   Schule / auf dem   Weihnachtsmarkt / unter der
          he sleeps in the.DAT school   on the.DAT Christmas.market   under the.DAT
          Brücke.
          bridge

          'He is sleeping at school/at the Christmas market/under the bridge.'

An interesting case is the verb *sich befinden* 'to be located', which expresses the location of something. This cannot occur without some information about the location pertaining to the verb:

(80)   * Wir befinden   uns.
       we   are.located REFL

The exact form of this information is not fixed – neither the syntactic category nor the preposition inside of prepositional phrases is restricted:

(81)   Wir befinden uns hier / unter der Brücke / neben dem Eingang / im Bett.
     we   are   REFL here under the bridge   next.to the   entrance in bed

     'We are here/under the bridge/next to the entrance/in bed.'

Local modifiers such as *hier* 'here' or *unter der Brücke* 'under the bridge' are analyzed with regard to other verbs (e.g., *schlafen* 'sleep') as adjuncts. For verbs such as *sich befinden* 'to be (located)', we will most likely have to assume that information about location forms an obligatory syntactic argument of the verb.

The verb selects a phrase with information about location, but does not place any syntactic restrictions on its type. This specification of location behaves semantically like the other adjuncts we have seen previously. If I just consider the semantic aspects of the combination of a head and adjunct, then I also refer to the adjunct as a *modifier*.[15] Arguments specifying location with verbs such as *sich befinden* 'to be located' are also subsumed under the term *modifier*. Modifiers are normally adjuncts, and therefore optional, whereas in the case of *sich befinden* they seem to be (obligatory) arguments.

In conclusion, we can say that constituents that are required to occur with a certain head are arguments of that head. Furthermore, constituents which fulfil a semantic role with regard to the head are also arguments. These kinds of arguments can, however, sometimes be optional.

---

[15] See Section 1.7.2 for more on the grammatical function of adverbials. The term adverbial is normally used in conjunction with verbs. *modifier* is a more general term, which normally includes attributive adjectives.

Arguments are normally divided into subjects and complements.[16] Not all heads require a subject (see Müller 2007b: Section 3.2). The number of arguments of a head can therefore also correspond to the number of complements of a head.

1.7 Grammatical functions

In some theories, grammatical functions such as subject and object form part of the formal description of language (see Chapter 7 on Lexical Functional Grammar, for example). This is not the case for the majority of the theories discussed here, but these terms are used for the informal description of certain phenomena. For this reason, I will briefly discuss them in what follows.

1.7.1 Subjects

Although I assume that the reader has a clear intuition about what a subject is, it is by no means a trivial matter to arrive at a definition of the word *subject* which can be used cross-linguistically. For German, Reis (1982) suggested the following syntactic properties as definitional for subjects:

- agreement of the finite verb with it

- nominative case in non-copular clauses

- omitted in infinitival clauses (control)

- optional in imperatives

I have already discussed agreement in conjunction with the examples in (4). Reis (1982) argues that the second bullet point is a suitable criterion for German. She formulates a restriction to non-copular clause because there can be more than one nominative argument in sentences with predicate nominals such as (82):

(82)   a. Er   ist ein Lügner.
       he.NOM ist a   liar.NOM

       'He is a liar.'

   b. Er   wurde ein Lügner genannt.
       he.NOM was   a   liar.NOM called

       'He was called a liar.'

Following this criterion, arguments in the dative case such as *den Männern* 'the men' cannot be classed as subjects in German:

---

[16] In some schools the term complement is understood to include the subject, that is, the term complement is equivalent to the term argument (see for instance Groß 2003: 342). Some researchers treat some subjects, e.g., those of finite verbs, as complements (Pollard 1996b; Eisenberg 1994a: 376).

(83)   a. Er hilft den   Männern.
           he helps the.DAT men.DAT

           'He is helping the men.'

       b. Den   Männern wurde   geholfen.
           the.DAT men.DAT were.3SG helped

           'The men were helped.'

Following the other criteria, datives should also not be classed as subjects – as Reis (1982) has shown. In (83b), *wurde*, which is the 3rd person singular form, does not agree with *den Männern*. The third of the aforementioned criteria deals with infinitive constructions such as those in (84):

(84)   a.   Klaus behauptet, den   Männern zu helfen.
            Klaus claims   the.DAT men.DAT to help

            'Klaus claims to be helping the men.'

       b.   Klaus behauptet, dass er den   Männern hilft.
            Klaus claims   that he the.DAT men.DAT helps

            'Klaus claims that he is helping the men.'

       c.   * Die Männer behaupten, geholfen zu werden.
            the men   claim   helped   to become

            Intended: 'The men are claiming to be helped.'

       d.   * Die Männer behaupten, elegant   getanzt zu werden.
            the men   claim   elegantly danced to become

            Intended: 'The men claim that there is elegant dancing.'

In the first sentence, an argument of the verb *helfen* 'to help' has been omitted. If one wishes to express it, then one would have to use the subordinate clause beginning with *dass* 'that' as in (84b). Examples (84c,d) show that infinitives which do not require a nominative argument cannot be embedded under verbs such as *behaupten* 'to claim'. If the dative noun phrase *den Männern* 'the men' were the subject in (83b), we would expect the control construction (84c) to be well-formed. This is, however, not the case. Instead of (84c), it is necessary to use (85):

(85)   Die Männer behaupten, dass ihnen   geholfen wird.
        the men.NOM claim   that them.DAT helped   becomes

        'The men claim that they are being helped.'

In the same way, imperatives are not possible with verbs that do not require a nominative. (86) shows some examples from Reis (1982: 186).

(86)   a.   Fürchte dich nicht!
            be.scared REFL not

            'Don't be scared!'

   b. * Graue nicht!
      dread not

      'Don't dread it!'

   c. Werd einmal unterstützt und …
      be   once   supported and

      'Let someone support you for once and …'

   d. * Werd einmal geholfen und …
      be   once   helped   and

      'Let someone help you and …'

The verb *sich fürchten* 'to be scared' in (86a) obligatorily requires a nominative argument as its subject (87a). The similar verb *grauen* 'to dread' in (86b) takes a dative argument (87b).

(87) a. Ich   fürchte   mich vor   Spinnen.
         I.NOM be.scared REFL   before spiders

         'I am scared of spiders.'

      b. Mir   graut vor   Spinnen.
         me.DAT scares before spiders

         'I am dreading spiders.'

Interestingly, dative arguments in Icelandic behave differently. Zaenen et al. (1985) discuss various characteristics of subjects in Icelandic and show that it makes sense to describe dative arguments as subjects in passive sentences even if the finite verb does not agree with them (Section 3.1) or they do not bear nominative case. An example of this is infinitive constructions with an omitted dative argument (p. 457):

(88) a. Ég vonast til   að verða hjálpað.
         I   hope   for to be   helped

         'I hope that I will be helped.'

      b. Að vera hjálpað í   prófinu   er óleyfilegt.
         to be   helped   on the.exam is not.allowed

         'It is not allowed for one to be helped during the exam.'

In a number of grammars, clausal arguments such as those in (89) are classed as subjects as they can be replaced by a noun phrase in the nominative (90) (see e.g., Eisenberg 2004: 63, 289).

(89) a. Dass er schon   um sieben kommen wollte, stimmt nicht.
         that he already at   seven   come   wanted is.true not

         'It's not true that he wanted to come as soon as seven.'

      b. Dass er Maria geheiratet hat, gefällt   mir.
         that he Maria married   has pleases me

         'I'm glad that he married Maria.'

(90) a. Das stimmt nicht.
        that is.true not

        'That isn't true.'

    b. Das gefällt mir.
        that pleases me

        'I like that.'

It should be noted that there are different opinions on the question of whether clausal arguments should be treated as subjects or not. As recent publications show, there is still some discussion in Lexical Function Grammar (see Chapter 7) (Dalrymple & Lødrup 2000; Berman 2003b, 2007; Alsina, Mohanan & Mohanan 2005; Forst 2006).

If we can be clear about what we want to view as a subject, then the definition of object is no longer difficult: objects are all other arguments whose form is directly determined by a given head. As well as clausal objects, German has genitive, dative, accusative and prepositional objects:

(91) a. Sie gedenken des   Mannes.
        they remember the.GEN man.GEN

        'They remember the man.'

    b. Sie helfen dem   Mann.
        they help   the.DAT man.DAT

        'They are helping the man.'

    c. Sie kennen den   Mann.
        they know   the.ACC man.ACC

        'They know the man.'

    d. Sie denken an den Mann.
        they think   on the man

        'They are thinking of the man.'

As well as defining objects by their case, it is commonplace to talk of *direct objects* and *indirect objects*. The direct object gets its name from the fact that – unlike the indirect object – the referent of a direct object is directly affected by the action denoted by the verb. With ditransitives such as the German *geben* 'to give', the accusative object is the direct object and the dative is the indirect object.

(92) dass er   dem   Mann   den   Aufsatz gibt
    that he.NOM the.DAT man.DAT the.ACC essay.ACC gives

    'that he gives the man the essay'

For trivalent verbs (verbs taking three arguments), we see that the verb can take either an object in the genitive case (93a) or, for verbs with a direct object in the accusative, a second accusative object (93b):

(93) a. dass er den   Mann   des   Mordes   bezichtigte
          that he the.ACC man.ACC the.GEN murder.GEN accused
          'that he accused the man of murder'

     b. dass er den   Mann   den   Vers   lehrte
          that he the.ACC man.ACC the.ACC verse.ACC taught
          'that he taught the man the verse'

These kinds of objects are sometimes also referred to as indirect objects.

Normally, only those objects which are promoted to subject in passives with *werden* 'to be' are classed as direct objects. This is important for theories such as LFG (see Chapter 7) since passivization is defined with reference to grammatical function. With two-place verbal predicates, the dative is not normally classed as a direct object (Cook 2006).

(94) dass er dem   Mann   hilft
      that he the.DAT man.DAT helps
      'that he helps the man'

In many theories, grammatical function does not form a primitive component of the theory, but rather corresponds to positions in a tree structure. The direct object in German is therefore the object which is first combined with the verb in a configuration assumed to be the underlying structure of German sentences. The indirect object is the second object to be combined with the verb. On this view, the dative object of *helfen* 'to help' would have to be viewed as a direct object.

In the following, I will simply refer to the case of objects and avoid using the terms direct object and indirect object.

In the same way as with subjects, we consider whether there are object clauses which are equivalent to a certain case and can fill the respective grammatical function of a direct or indirect object. If we assume that *dass du sprichst* 'that you are speaking' in (95a) is a subject, then the subordinate clause must be a direct object in (95b):

(95) a. Daß du   sprichst, wird erwähnt.
          that you speak   is   mentioned
          'The fact that you're speaking is being mentioned.'

     b. Er erwähnt, dass du   sprichst.
          he mentions that you speak
          'He mentions that you are speaking.'

In this case, we cannot really view the subordinate clause as the accusative object since it does not bear case. However, we can replace the sentence with an accusative-marked noun phrase:

(96) Er erwähnt diesen   Sachverhalt.
      he mentions this.ACC matter
      'He mentions this matter.'

If we want to avoid this discussion, we can simply call these arguments clausal objects.

1.7.2 The adverbial

Adverbials differ semantically from subjects and objects. They tell us something about the conditions under which an action or process takes place, or the way in which a certain state persists. In the majority of cases, adverbials are adjuncts, but there are – as we have already seen – a number of heads which also require adverbials. Examples of these are verbs such as *to be located* or *to make one's way*. For *to be located*, it is necessary to specify a location and for *to proceed to* a direction is needed. These kinds of adverbials are therefore regarded as arguments of the verb.

The term *adverbial* comes from the fact that adverbials are often adverbs. This is not the only possibility, however. Adjectives, participles, prepositional phrases, noun phrases and even sentences can be adverbials:

(97) a. Er arbeitet sorgfältig.
          he works   carefully

      b. Er arbeitet vergleichend.
          he works   comparatively

          'He does comparative work.'

      c. Er arbeitet in der Universität.
          he works   in the university

          'He works at the university.'

      d. Er arbeitet den ganzen Tag.
          he works   the whole day.ACC

          'He works all day.'

      e. Er arbeitet, weil   es ihm   Spaß macht.
          he works   because it him.DAT fun makes

          'He works because he enjoys it.'

Although the noun phrase in (97d) bears accusative case, it is not an accusative object. *den ganzen Tag* 'the whole day' is a so-called temporal accusative. The occurrence of accusative in this case has to do with the syntactic and semantic function of the noun phrase, it is not determined by the verb. These kinds of accusatives can occur with a variety of verbs, even with verbs that do not normally require an accusative object:

(98) a. Er schläft den ganzen Tag.
          he sleeps the whole day

          'He sleeps the whole day.'

      b. Er liest den   ganzen   Tag diesen   schwierigen Aufsatz.
          he reads the.ACC whole.ACC day this.ACC difficult.ACC essay

          'He spends the whole day reading this difficult essay.'

      c. Er gibt den   Armen   den   ganzen   Tag Suppe.
          he gives the.DAT poor.DAT the.ACC whole.ACC day soup

          'He spends the whole day giving soup to the poor.'

The case of adverbials does not change under passivization:

(99) a. weil   den   ganzen   Tag gearbeitet wurde
         because the.ACC whole.ACC day worked   was

         'because someone worked all day'

    b. * weil   der   ganze   Tag gearbeitet wurde
         because the.NOM whole.NOM day worked   was

1.7.3 Predicatives

Adjectives like those in (100a,b) as well as noun phrases such as *ein Lügner* 'a liar' in (100c) are counted as predicatives.

(100) a. Klaus ist *klug.*
          Klaus is clever

     b. Er isst den Fisch *roh.*
        he eats the fish   raw

     c. Er ist *ein Lügner.*
        he is a   liar

In the copula construction in (100a,c), the adjective *klug* 'clever' and the noun phrase *ein Lügner* 'a liar' is an argument of the copula *sein* 'to be' and the depictive adjective in (100b) is an adjunct to *isst* 'eats'.

For predicative noun phrases, case is not determined by the head but rather by some other element.[17] For example, the accusative in (101a) becomes nominative under passivization (101b):

---

[17] There is some dialectal variation with regard to copula constructions: in Standard German, the case of the noun phrase with *sein* 'to be' is always nominative and does not change when embedded under *lassen* 'to let'. According to Drosdowski (1995: § 1259), in Switzerland the accusative form is common which one finds in examples such as (ii.a).

(i) a. Ich bin dein   Tanzpartner.
        I   am your.NOM dancing.partner

    b. Der wüste Kerl ist ihr   Komplize.
       the wild guy is her.NOM accomplice

    c. Laß den   wüsten Kerl [...] meinetwegen ihr   Komplize sein.
       let the.ACC wild.ACC guy   for.all.I.care her.NOM accomplice be

       'Let's assume that the wild guy is her accomplice, for all I care.' (Grebe & Gipper 1966: § 6925)

    d. Baby, laß mich   dein   Tanzpartner   sein.
       baby let me.ACC your.NOM dancing.partner be

       'Baby, let me be your dancing partner!' (Funny van Dannen, Benno-Ohnesorg-Theater, Berlin, Volksbühne, 11.10.1995)

(ii) a. Er lässt den   lieben   Gott 'n frommen Mann sein.
          he lets the.ACC dear.ACC god a pious.ACC man be

          'He is completely lighthearted/unconcerned.'

     b. * Er lässt den   lieben   Gott 'n frommer   Mann sein.
          he lets the.ACC dear.ACC god a pious.NOM man be

(101) a. Sie nannte ihn   einen Lügner.
           she called   him.ACC a.ACC liar

           'She called him a liar.'

       b. Er   wurde ein   Lügner genannt.
           he.NOM was   a.NOM liar   called

           'He was called a liar.'

Only *ihn* 'him' can be described as an object in (101a). In (101b), *ihn* becomes the subject and therefore bears nominative case. *einen Lügner* 'a liar' refers to *ihn* 'him' in (101a) and to *er* 'he' in (101b) and agrees in case with the noun over which it predicates. This is also referred to as *agreement case*.

For other predicative constructions see Eisenberg et al. (2005: § 1206) and Müller (2002a: Chapter 4, Chapter 5) and Müller (2008).

1.7.4 Valence classes

It is possible to divide verbs into subclasses depending on how many arguments they require and on the properties these arguments are required to have. The classic division describes all verbs which have an object which becomes the subject under passivization as *transitive*. Examples of this are verbs such as *love* or *beat*. Intransitive verbs, on the other hand, are verbs which have either no object, or one that does not become the subject in passive sentences. Examples of this type of verb are *schlafen* 'to sleep', *helfen* 'to help', *gedenken* 'to remember'. A subclass of transitive verbs are ditransitive verbs such as *geben* 'to give' and *zeigen* 'to show'.

Unfortunately, this terminology is not always used consistently. Sometimes, two-place verbs with dative and genitive objects are also classed as transitive verbs. In this naming tradition, the terms intransitive, transitive and ditransitive are synonymous with one-place, two-place and three-place verbs.

The fact that this terminological confusion can lead to misunderstandings between even established linguistics is shown by Culicover and Jackendoff's (2005: 59) criticism of Chomsky. Chomsky states that the combination of the English auxiliary *be* + verb with passive morphology can only be used for transitive verbs. Culicover and Jackendoff claim that this cannot be true because there are transitive verbs such as *weigh* and *cost*, which cannot undergo passivization:

(102) a. This book weighs ten pounds / costs ten dollars.

       b. * Ten pounds are weighed / ten dollar are cost by this book.

Culicover and Jackendoff use *transitive* in the sense of a verb requiring two arguments. If we only view those verbs whose object becomes the subject of a passive clause as transitive, then *weigh* and *cost* no longer count as transitive verbs and Culicover and Jackendoff's criticism no longer holds.[18] That noun phrases such as those in (102) are no

---

[18] Their cricitism also turns out to be unjust even if one views transitives as being two-place predicates. If one claims that a verb must take at least two arguments to be able to undergo passivization, one is not necessarily claiming that all verbs taking two or more arguments have to allow passivization. The property of taking multiple arguments is a condition which must be fulfilled, but it is by no means the only one.

ordinary objects can also be seen by the fact they cannot be replaced by pronouns. It is therefore not possible to ascertain which case they bear since case distinctions are only realized on pronouns in English. If we translate the English examples into German, we find accusative objects:

(103)   a. Das Buch kostete einen   Dollar.
              the book costs   one.ACC dollar

             'The book costs one dollar.'

         b. Das Buch wiegt   einen   Zentner.
              the book weighs one.ACC centner

             'The book weighs one centner.'

In the following, I will use *transitive* in the former sense, that is for verbs with an object that becomes the subject when passivized (e.g., with *werden* in German). When I talk about the class of verbs that includes *helfen* 'to help', which takes a nominative and dative argument, and *schlagen* 'to hit', which takes a nominative and accusative argument, I will use the term *two-place* or *bivalent verb*.

1.8 A topological model of the German clause

In this section, I introduce the concept of so-called *topological fields* (*topologische Felder*). These will be used frequently in later chapters to discuss different parts of the German clause. One can find further, more detailed introductions to topology in Reis (1980), Höhle (1986) and Askedal (1986). Wöllstein (2010) is a textbook about the topological field model.

1.8.1 The position of the verb

It is common practice to divide German sentences into three types pertaining to the position of the finite verb:

- verb-final clauses

- verb-first (initial) clauses

- verb-second (V2) clauses

The following examples illustrate these possibilities:

(104)   a. (Peter hat erzählt,) dass er das Eis   gegessen *hat.*
              Peter has told   that he the ice.cream eaten   has

             'Peter said that he has eaten the ice cream.'

         b. *Hat* Peter das Eis   gegessen?
              has Peter the ice.cream eaten

             'Has Peter eaten the ice cream?'

c. Peter *hat* das Eis   gegessen.
Peter has the ice.cream eaten
'Peter has eaten the ice cream.'

1.8.2 The sentence bracket, prefield, middle field and postfield

We observe that the finite verb *hat* 'has' is only adjacent to its complement *gegessen* 'eaten' in (104a). In (104b) and (104c), the verb and its complement are separated, that is, discontinuous. We can then divide the German clause into various sub-parts on the basis of these distinctions. In (104b) and (104c), the verb and the auxiliary form a "bracket" around the clause. For this reason, we call this the *sentence bracket (Satzklammer)*. The finite verbs in (104b) and (104c) form the left bracket and the non-finite verbs form the right bracket. Clauses with verb-final order are usually introduced by conjunctions such as *weil* 'because', *dass* 'that' and *ob* 'whether'. These conjunctions occupy the same position as the finite verb in verb-initial or verb-final clauses. We therefore also assume that these conjunctions form the left bracket in these cases. Using the notion of the sentence bracket, it is possible to divide the structure of the German clause into the prefield (*Vorfeld*), middle field (*Mittelfeld*) and postfield (*Nachfeld*). The prefield describes everything preceding the left sentence bracket, the middle field is the section between the left and right bracket and the postfield describes the position after the right bracket. Table 1.1 on the following page gives some examples of this. The right bracket can contain multiple verbs and is often referred to as a *verbal complex* or *verb cluster*. The assignment of question words and relative pronouns to the prefield will be discussed in the following section.

1.8.3 Assigning elements to fields

As the examples in Table 1.1 show, it is not required that all fields are always occupied. Even the left bracket can be empty if one opts to leave out the copula *sein* 'to be' such as in the examples in (105):

(105)   a. [...] egal,   was noch passiert, der Norddeutsche Rundfunk
         regardless what still happens the north.German broadcasting.company
     steht schon jetzt als Gewinner fest.[19]
     stands already now as winner PART
     'Regardless of what still may happen, the North German broadcasting company is already the winner.'

  b. Interessant, zu erwähnen, daß ihre Seele völlig   in Ordnung war.[20]
     interesting to mention that her soul completely in order was
     'It is interesting to note that her soul was entirely fine.'

---

[19] Spiegel, 12/1999, p. 258.

[20] Michail Bulgakow, *Der Meister und Margarita*. München: Deutscher Taschenbuch Verlag. 1997, p. 422.

Table 1.1: Examples of how topological fields can be occupied

Prefield	Left bracket	Middle field	Right bracket	Postfield
Karl	schläft.			
Karl	hat		geschlafen.	
Karl	erkennt	Maria.		
Karl	färbt	den Mantel	um	den Maria kennt.
Karl	hat	Maria	erkannt.	
Karl	hat	Maria als sie aus dem Zug stieg sofort	erkannt.	
Karl	hat	Maria sofort	erkannt	als sie aus dem Zug stieg.
Karl	hat	Maria zu erkennen	behauptet.	
Karl	hat		behauptet	Maria zu erkennen.
	Schläft	Karl?		
	Schlaf!			
	Iss	jetzt dein Eis	auf!	
	Hat	er doch das ganze Eis alleine	gegessen.	
	weil	er das ganze Eis alleine	gegessen hat	ohne mit der Wimper zu zucken.
	weil	er das ganze Eis alleine	essen können will	ohne gestört zu werden.
wer		das ganze Eis alleine	gegessen hat	
der		das ganze Eis alleine	gegessen hat	
mit wem		du	geredet hast	
mit dem		du	geredet hast	

    c. Ein Treppenwitz der   Musikgeschichte, daß die Kollegen von Rammstein
       an afterwit   of.the history.of.music that the colleagues of Rammstein
       vor   fünf Jahren noch im   Vorprogramm von Sandow spielten.[21]
       before five years still in.the pre.programme of Sandow played

       'One of the little ironies of music history is that five years ago their colleagues
       of Rammstein were still an opening act for Sandow.'

The examples in (105) correspond to those with the copula in (106):

(106)   a. Egal   ist, was noch passiert, ...
         regardless is what still happens

         'It is not important what still may happen ...'

    b. Interessant ist zu erwähnen, dass ihre Seele völlig   in Ordnung war.
       interesting is to mention   that her soul completely in order   was

       'It is interesting to note that her soul was completely fine.'

    c. Ein Treppenwitz der   Musikgeschichte ist, dass die Kollegen von
       an afterwit   of.the music.history   is that the colleagues of
       Rammstein vor   fünf Jahren noch im Vorprogramm von Sandow spielten.
       Rammstein before five years still in pre.programme of Sandow played

       'It is one of the little ironies of music history that five years ago their col-
       leagues of Rammstein were still an opening act for Sandow.'

When fields are empty, it is sometimes not clear which fields are occupied by certain constituents. For the examples in (105), one would have to insert the copula to be able to ascertain that a single constituent is in the prefield and, furthermore, which fields are occupied by the other constituents.

    In the following example taken from Paul (1919: 13), inserting the copula obtains a different result:

(107)   a. Niemand da?
         nobody there

    b. Ist niemand da?
       is nobody there

       'Is nobody there?'

Here we are dealing with a question and *niemand* 'nobody' in (107a) should therefore not be analyzed as in the prefield but rather the middle field.

    In (108), there are elements in the prefield, the left bracket and the middle field. The right bracket is empty.[22]

---

[21] Flüstern & Schweigen, taz, 12.07.1999, p. 14.

[22] The sentence requires emphasis on *der* 'the'. *der Frau, die er kennt* 'the woman' is contrasted with another woman or other women.

(108) Er   gibt der Frau   das Buch,   die   er kennt.
       he.M gives the woman(F) the book.(N) that.F he knows

       'He gives the book to the woman that he knows.'

How should we analyze relative clauses such as *die er kennt* 'that he knows'? Do they form part of the middle field or the postfield? This can be tested using a test developed by Bech (1955: 72) (*Rangprobe*): first, we modify the example in (108) so that it is in the perfect. Since non-finite verb forms occupy the right bracket, we can clearly see the border between the middle field and postfield. The examples in (109) show that the relative clause cannot occur in the middle field unless it is part of a complex constituent with the head noun *Frau* 'woman'.

(109) a. Er hat [der Frau]   das Buch gegeben, [die er kennt].
           he has the woman the book given   that he knows

           'He has given the book to the woman that he knows.'

       b. * Er hat [der Frau]   das Buch, [die er kennt,] gegeben.
            he has the woman the book that he knows given

       c. Er hat [der Frau,   die er kennt,] das Buch gegeben.
           he has the woman that he knows the book given

This test does not help if the relative clause is realized together with its head noun at the end of the sentence as in (110):

(110) Er gibt das Buch der Frau,   die er kennt.
       he gives the book the woman that he knows

       'He gives the book to the woman that he knows.'

If we put the example in (110) in the perfect, then we observe that the lexical verb can occur before or after the relative clause:

(111) a. Er hat das Buch [der Frau]   gegeben, [die er kennt].
           he has the book the woman given   that he knows

           'He has given the book to the woman he knows.'

       b. Er hat das Buch [der Frau,   die er kennt,] gegeben.
           he has the book the woman that he knows given

In (111a), the relative clause has been extraposed. In (111b) it forms part of the noun phrase *der Frau, die er kennt* 'the woman that he knows' and therefore occurs inside the NP in the middle field. It is therefore not possible to rely on this test for (110). We assume that the relative clause in (110) also belongs to the NP since this is the most simple structure. If the relative clause were in the postfield, we would have to assume that it has undergone extraposition from its position inside the NP. That is, we would have to assume the NP-structure anyway and then extraposition in addition.

    We have a similar problem with interrogative and relative pronouns. Depending on the author, these are assumed to be in the left bracket (Kathol 2001; Eisenberg 2004: 403) or the prefield (Eisenberg et al. 2005: §1345; Wöllstein 2010: 29–30, Section 3.1) or even in the middle field (Altmann & Hofman 2004: 75). In Standard German interrogative or relative clauses, both fields are never simultaneously occupied. For this reason, it is not immediately clear to which field an element belongs. Nevertheless, we can draw parallels to main clauses: the pronouns in interrogative and relative clauses can be contained inside complex phrases:

(112) a. der Mann, [mit dem] du gesprochen hast
          the man   with whom you spoken   have

       'the man you spoke to'

       b. Ich möchte wissen, [mit wem] du gesprochen hast.
          I   want.to know   with whom you spoken   have

       'I want to know who you spoke to.'

Normally, only individual words (conjunctions or verbs) can occupy the left bracket,[23] whereas words and phrases can appear in the prefield. It therefore makes sense to assume that interrogative and relative pronouns (and phrases containing them) also occur in this position.

   Furthermore, it can be observed that the dependency between the elements in the *Vorfeld* of declarative clauses and the remaining sentence is of the same kind as the dependency between the phrase that contains the relative pronoun and the remaining sentence. For instance, *über dieses Thema* 'about this topic' in (113a) depends on *Vortrag* 'talk', which is deeply embedded in the sentence: *einen Vortrag* 'a talk' is an argument of *zu halten* 'to hold', which in turn is an argument of *gebeten* 'asked'.

(113) a. Über dieses Thema habe ich ihn gebeten, einen Vortrag zu halten.
          about this   topic have I   him asked   a   talk   to hold

       'I asked him to give a talk about this topic.'

       b. das Thema, über das   ich ihn gebeten habe, einen Vortrag zu halten
          the topic   about which I   him asked   have a   talk   to hold

       'the topic about which I asked him to give a talk'

The situation is similar in (113b): the relative phrase *über das* 'about which' is a dependent of *Vortrag* 'talk' which is realized far away from it. Thus, if the relative phrase is assigned to the *Vorfeld*, it is possible to say that such nonlocal frontings always target the *Vorfeld*.

   Finally, the Duden grammar (Eisenberg et al. 2005: §1347) provides the following examples from non-standard German (mainly southern dialects):

---

[23] Coordination is an exception to this:

   (i) Er [kennt und liebt] diese Schallplatte.
        he knows and loves this record

   'He knows and loves this record.'

(114)   a. Kommt drauf   an, mit wem dass sie zu tun haben.
            comes there.upon PART with whom that you to do have

            'It depends on whom you are dealing with.'

(115)   a. Lotti, die wo   eine tolle Sekretärin ist, hat ein paar merkwürdige
            Lotti who where a   great secretary is has a   few   strange
            Herren   empfangen.
            gentlemen welcomed

            'Lotti, who is a great secretary, welcomed a few strange gentlemen.'

      b. Du bist der beste Sänger, den wo   ich kenn.
            you are the best singer who where I   know

            'You are the best singer whom I know.'

These examples of interrogative and relative clauses show that the left sentence bracket is filled with a conjunction (*dass* 'that' or *wo* 'where' in the respective dialects). So if one wants to have a model that treats Standard German and the dialectal forms uniformly, it is reasonable to assume that the relative phrases and interrogative phrases are located in the *Vorfeld*.

1.8.4 Recursion

As already noted by Reis (1980: 82), when occupied by a complex constituent, the prefield can be subdivided into further fields including a postfield, for example. The constituents *für lange lange Zeit* 'for a long, long time' in (116b) and *daß du kommst* 'that you are coming' in (116d) are inside the prefield but occur to the right of the right bracket *verschüttet* 'buried' / *gewußt* 'knew', that is they are in the postfield of the prefield.

(116)   a. Die Möglichkeit, etwas   zu verändern, ist damit   verschüttet für lange
            the possibility something to change   is there.with buried   for long
            lange Zeit.
            long time

            'The possibility to change something will now be gone for a long, long time.'

      b. [Verschüttet für lange lange Zeit] ist damit   die Möglichkeit, etwas
            buried   for long long time ist there.with the possibility   something
            zu verändern.
            to change

      c. Wir haben schon seit   langem gewußt, daß du kommst.
            we have PART since long   known that you come

            'We have known for a while that you are coming.'

      d. [Gewußt, daß du kommst,] haben wir schon seit   langem.
            known   that you come   have we PART since long

Like constituents in the prefield, elements in the middle field and postfield can also have an internal structure and be divided into subfields accordingly. For example, *daß* 'that' is the left bracket of the subordinate clause *daß du kommst* in (116c), whereas *du* 'you' occupies the middle field and *kommst* 'come' the right bracket.

Comprehension questions

1. How does the head of a phrase differ from non-heads?

2. What is the head in the examples in (117)?

   (117)   a. he
           b. Go!
           c. quick

3. How do arguments differ from adjuncts?

4. Identify the heads, arguments and adjuncts in the following sentence (118) and in the subparts of the sentence:

   (118)   Er hilft   den kleinen Kindern in der Schule.
           he helps the small   children in the school

           'He helps small children at school.'

5. How can we define the terms prefield (*Vorfeld*), middle field (*Mittelfeld*), postfield (*Nachfeld*) and the left and right sentence brackets (*Satzklammer*)?

Exercises

1. Identify the sentence brackets, prefield, middle field and postfield in the following sentences. Do the same for the embedded clauses!

   (119)   a. Karl isst.
              Karl eats

              'Karl is eating.'
           b. Der Mann liebt eine Frau,   den Peter kennt.
              the man loves a   woman who Peter knows

              'The man who Peter knows loves a woman.'
           c. Der Mann liebt eine Frau,   die Peter kennt.
              the man loves a   woman that Peter knows

              'The man loves a woman who Peter knows.'

  d. Die Studenten haben behauptet, nur wegen   der Hitze
     the students   have   claimed   only because.of the heat
     einzuschlafen.
     to.fall.asleep
     'The students claimed that they were only falling asleep because of the
     heat.'

  e. Dass Peter nicht kommt, ärgert Klaus.
     that Peter not   comes   annoys Klaus
     '(The fact) that Peter isn't coming annoys Klaus.'

  f. Einen Mann küssen, der ihr nicht gefällt, würde sie nie.
     a   man kiss   that her not   pleases would she never
     'She would never kiss a man she doesn't like.'

Further reading

Reis (1980) gives reasons for why field theory is important for the description of the position of constituents in German.

Höhle (1986) discusses fields to the left of the prefield, which are needed for left-dislocation structures such as with *der Mittwoch* in (120), *aber* in (121a) and *denn* in (121b):

(120)   Der Mittwoch,   der passt mir gut.
        the Wednesday that fits   me good
        'Wednesday, that suits me fine.'

(121)   a. Aber würde denn jemand   den Hund füttern morgen   Abend?
           but would PART anybody the dog feed   tomorrow evening
           'But would anyone feed the dog tomorrow evening?'

        b. Denn   dass es regnet, damit   rechnet keiner.
           because that it rains   there.with reckons nobody
           'Because no-one expects that it will rain.'

Höhle also discusses the historical development of field theory.

2 Phrase structure grammar

This chapter deals with phase structure grammars (PSGs), which play an important role in several of the theories we will encounter in later chapters.

2.1 Symbols and rewrite rules

Words can be assigned to a particular part of speech on the basis of their inflectional properties and syntactic distribution. Thus, *weil* 'because' in (1) is a conjunction, whereas *das* 'the' and *dem* 'the' are articles and therefore classed as determiners. Furthermore, *Buch* 'book' and *Mann* 'man' are nouns and *gibt* 'gives' is a verb.

(1) weil   er das Buch dem Mann gibt
      because he the book the man   gives

      'because he gives the man the book'

Using the constituency tests we introduced in Section 1.3, we can show that individual words as well as the strings *das Buch* 'the book' and *dem Mann* 'the man', form constituents. These get then assigned certain symbols. Since nouns form an important part of the phrases *das Buch* and *dem Mann*, these are referred to as *noun phrases* or NPs, for short. The pronoun *er* 'he' can occur in the same positions as full NPs and can therefore also be assigned to the category NP.

    Phrase structure grammars come with rules specifying which symbols are assigned to certain kinds of words and how these are combined to create more complex units. A simple phrase structure grammar which can be used to analyze (1) is given in (2):[1,2]

(2) NP → Det N   NP → er   N → Buch
     S → NP NP NP V   Det → das   N → Mann
                             Det → dem   V → gibt

We can therefore interpret a rule such as NP → Det N as meaning that a noun phrase, that is, something which is assigned the symbol NP, can consist of a determiner (Det) and a noun (N).

---

[1] I ignore the conjunction *weil* 'because' for now. Since the exact analysis of German verb-first and verb-second clauses requires a number of additional assumptions, we will restrict ourselves to verb-final clauses in this chapter.

[2] The rule NP → er may seem odd. We could assume the rule PersPron → er instead but then would have to posit a further rule which would specify that personal pronouns can replace full NPs: NP → PersPron. The rule in (2) combines the two aforementioned rules and states that *er* 'he' can occur in positions where noun phrases can.

We can analyze the sentence in (1) using the grammar in (2) in the following way: first, we take the first word in the sentence and check if there is a rule in which this word occurs on the right-hand side of the rule. If this is the case, then we replace the word with the symbol on the left-hand side of the rule. This happens in lines 2–4, 6–7 and 9 of the derivation in (3). For instance, in line 2 *er* is replaced by NP. If there are two or more symbols which occur together on the right-hand side of a rule, then all these words are replaced with the symbol on the left. This happens in lines 5, 8 and 10. For instance, in line 5 and 8, Det and N are rewritten as NP.

(3)

	words and symbols						rules that are applied
1	er	das	Buch	dem	Mann	gibt	
2	NP	das	Buch	dem	Mann	gibt	NP → er
3	NP	Det	Buch	dem	Mann	gibt	Det → das
4	NP	Det	N	dem	Mann	gibt	N → Buch
5	NP		NP	dem	Mann	gibt	NP → Det N
6	NP		NP	Det	Mann	gibt	Det → dem
7	NP		NP	Det	N	gibt	N → Mann
8	NP		NP		NP	gibt	NP → Det N
9	NP		NP		NP	V	V → gibt
10						S	S → NP NP NP V

In (3), we began with a string of words and it was shown that we can derive the structure of a sentence by applying the rules of a given phrase structure grammar. We could have applied the same steps in reverse order: starting with the sentence symbol S, we would have applied the steps 9–1 and arrived at the string of words. Selecting different rules from the grammar for rewriting symbols, we could use the grammar in (2) to get from S to the string *er dem Mann das Buch gibt* 'he the man the book gives'. We can say that this grammar licenses (or generates) a set of sentences.

The derivation in (3) can also be represented as a tree. This is shown by Figure 2.1. The

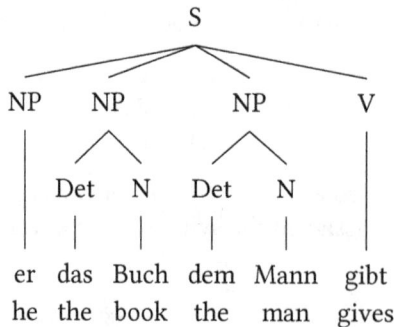

```
                        S
          ┌──────────┬─────────┬──────────┐
         NP         NP        NP          V
          │        ╱  ╲      ╱  ╲          │
          │      Det   N   Det   N         │
          │       │    │    │    │         │
         er      das  Buch dem  Mann      gibt
         he      the  book the  man      gives
```

Figure 2.1: Analysis of *er das Buch dem Mann gibt* 'he the book the woman gives'

symbols in the tree are called *nodes*. We say that S immediately dominates the NP nodes and the V node. The other nodes in the tree are also dominated, but not immediately dominated, by S. If we want to talk about the relationship between nodes, it is common to use kinship terms. In Figure 2.1, S is the *mother node* of the three NP nodes and the V node. The NP node and V are *sisters* since they have the same mother node. If a node has two daughters, then we have a binary branching structure. If there is exactly one daughter, then we have a unary branching structure. Two constituents are said to be *adjacent* if they are directly next to each other.

Phrase structure rules are often omitted in linguistic publications. Instead, authors opt for tree diagrams or the compact equivalent bracket notation such as (4).

(4) [s [NP er] [NP [Det das] [N Buch]] [NP [Det dem] [N Mann]] [v gibt]]
         he   the   book   the   man   gives

Nevertheless, it is the grammatical rules which are actually important since these represent grammatical knowledge which is independent of specific structures. In this way, we can use the grammar in (2) to parse or generate the sentence in (5), which differs from (1) in the order of objects:

(5) [weil]   er   dem   Mann das   Buch gibt
       because he.NOM the.DAT man   the.ACC book gives

     'because he gives the man the book'

The rules for replacing determiners and nouns are simply applied in a different order than in (1). Rather than replacing the first Det with *das* 'the' and the first noun with *Buch* 'book', the first Det is replaced with *dem* 'the' and the first noun with *Mann*.

At this juncture, I should point out that the grammar in (2) is not the only possible grammar for the example sentence in (1). There is an infinite number of possible grammars which could be used to analyze these kinds of sentences (see exercise 1). Another possible grammar is given in (6):

(6)   NP → Det N   NP → er   N → Buch
      V → NP V   Det → das   N → Mann
                          Det → dem   V → gibt

This grammar licenses binary branching structures as shown in Figure 2.2 on the following page.

Both the grammar in (6) and (2) are too imprecise. If we adopt additional lexical entries for *ich* 'I' and *den* 'the' (accusative) in our grammar, then we would incorrectly license the ungrammatical sentences in (7b–d):[3]

---

[3] With the grammar in (6), we also have the additional problem that we cannot determine when an utterance is complete since the symbol V is used for all combinations of V and NP. Therefore, we can also analyze the sentence in (i) with this grammar:

(i) a. * der Mann erwartet
          the man expects

     b. * des   Mannes er   das   Buch dem   Mann gibt
          the.GEN man.GEN he.NOM the.ACC book the.DAT man   gives

```
                          V
                      ┌───────┴───────┐
                    NP                  V
                     │           ┌──────┴──────┐
                     │         NP                V
                     │       ┌──┴──┐       ┌──────┴──────┐
                   Det   N          NP           V
                     │     │       ┌──┴──┐        │
                     │     │     Det    N         │
                     │     │      │      │         │
                    er   das   Buch  dem  Mann  gibt
                    he   the   book  the  man   gives
```

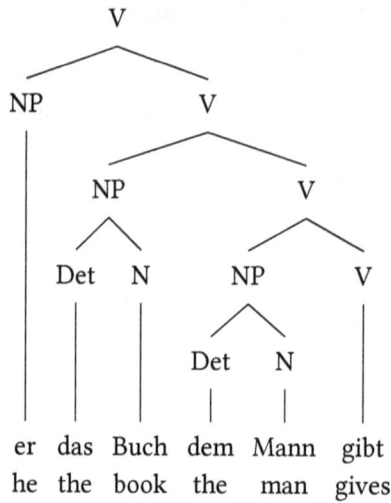

Figure 2.2: Analysis of *er das Buch dem Mann gibt* with a binary branching structure

(7) a.   er   das   Buch dem   Mann gibt
          he.NOM the.ACC book the.DAT man   gives
          'He gives the book to the man.'

  b. * ich   das   Buch dem   Mann gibt
        I.NOM   the.ACC book the.DAT man   gives

  c. * er   das   Buch den   Mann gibt
        he.NOM the.ACC book the.ACC man   gives

  d. * er   den   Buch   dem Mann gibt
        he.NOM the.M   book(N) the man   gives

In (7b), subject-verb agreement has been violated, in other words: *ich* 'I' and *gibt* 'gives' do not fit together. (7c) is ungrammatical because the case requirements of the verb have not been satisfied: *gibt* 'gives' requires a dative object. Finally, (7d) is ungrammatical because there is a lack of agreement between the determiner and the noun. It is not possible to combine *den* 'the', which is masculine and bears accusative case, and *Buch* 'book' because *Buch* is neuter gender. For this reason, the gender properties of these two elements are not the same and the elements can therefore not be combined.

In the following, we will consider how we would have to change our grammar to stop it from licensing the sentences in (7b–d). If we want to capture subject-verb agreement, then we have to cover the following six cases in German, as the verb has to agree with the subject in both person (1, 2, 3) and number (sg, pl):

The number of arguments required by a verb must be somehow represented in the grammar. In the following chapters, we will see exactly how the selection of arguments by a verb (valence) can be captured in various grammatical theories.

(8) a. Ich schlafe.   (1, sg)
          I   sleep

     b. Du schläfst.   (2, sg)
          you sleep

     c. Er schläft.   (3, sg)
          he sleeps

     d. Wir schlafen.   (1, pl)
          we   sleep

     e. Ihr schlaft.   (2, pl)
          you sleep

     f. Sie schlafen.   (3, pl)
          they sleep

It is possible to capture these relations with grammatical rules by increasing the number of symbols we use. Instead of the rule S → NP NP NP V, we can use the following:

(9) S → NP_1_sg NP NP V_1_sg
     S → NP_2_sg NP NP V_2_sg
     S → NP_3_sg NP NP V_3_sg
     S → NP_1_pl NP NP V_1_pl
     S → NP_2_pl NP NP V_2_pl
     S → NP_3_pl NP NP V_3_pl

This would mean that we need six different symbols for noun phrases and verbs respectively, as well as six rules rather than one.

In order to account for case assignment by the verb, we can incorporate case information into the symbols in an analogous way. We would then get rules such as the following:

(10) S → NP_1_sg_nom NP_dat NP_acc V_1_sg_nom_dat_acc
      S → NP_2_sg_nom NP_dat NP_acc V_2_sg_nom_dat_acc
      S → NP_3_sg_nom NP_dat NP_acc V_3_sg_nom_dat_acc
      S → NP_1_pl_nom NP_dat NP_acc V_1_pl_nom_dat_acc
      S → NP_2_pl_nom NP_dat NP_acc V_2_pl_nom_dat_acc
      S → NP_3_pl_nom NP_dat NP_acc V_3_pl_nom_dat_acc

Since it is necessary to differentiate between noun phrases in four cases, we have a total of six symbols for NPs in the nominative and three symbols for NPs with other cases. Since verbs have to match the NPs, that is, we have to differentiate between verbs which select three arguments and those selecting only one or two (11), we have to increase the number of symbols we assume for verbs.

(11) a.   Er schläft.
           he sleeps
           'He is sleeping.'

b. * Er schläft das Buch.
    he sleeps the book

c. Er kennt das Buch.
    he knows the book

    'He knows the book.'

d. * Er kennt.
    he knows

In the rules above, the information about the number of arguments required by a verb is included in the marking 'nom_dat_acc'.

In order to capture the determiner-noun agreement in (12), we have to incorporate information about gender (fem, mas, neu), number (sg, pl), case (nom, gen, dat, acc) and the inflectional classes (strong, weak)[4].

(12) a. der   Mann, die   Frau,   das   Buch   (gender)
          the.M man(M) the.F woman(F) the.N book(N)

      b. das Buch,   die Bücher   (number)
          the book.SG the books.PL

      c. des   Buches, dem   Buch   (case)
          the.GEN book.GEN the.DAT book

      d. ein Beamter,   der Beamte   (inflectional class)
          a   civil.servant the civil.servant

Instead of the rule NP → Det N, we will have to use rules such as those in (13):[5]

(13) NP_3_sg_nom → Det_fem_sg_nom N_fem_sg_nom
      NP_3_sg_nom → Det_mas_sg_nom N_mas_sg_nom
      NP_3_sg_nom → Det_neu_sg_nom N_neu_sg_nom
      NP_3_pl_nom → Det_fem_pl_nom N_fem_pl_nom
      NP_3_pl_nom → Det_mas_pl_nom N_mas_pl_nom
      NP_3_pl_nom → Det_neu_pl_nom N_neu_pl_nom

      NP_3_sg_nom → Det_fem_sg_nom N_fem_sg_nom
      NP_3_sg_nom → Det_mas_sg_nom N_mas_sg_nom
      NP_3_sg_nom → Det_neu_sg_nom N_neu_sg_nom
      NP_3_pl_nom → Det_fem_pl_nom N_fem_pl_nom
      NP_3_pl_nom → Det_mas_pl_nom N_mas_pl_nom
      NP_3_pl_nom → Det_neu_pl_nom N_neu_pl_nom

(13) shows the rules for nominative noun phrases. We would need analogous rules for genitive, dative, and accusative. We would then require 24 symbols for determiners (3 ∗ 2 ∗ 4), 24 symbols for nouns and 24 rules rather than one. If inflection class is taken into account, the number of symbols and the number of rules doubles.

---

[4] These are inflectional classes for adjectives which are also relevant for some nouns such as *Beamter* 'civil servant', *Verwandter* 'relative', *Gesandter* 'envoy'. For more on adjective classes see page 21.

[5] To keep things simple, these rules do not incorporate information regarding the inflection class.

2.2 Expanding PSG with features

Phrase structure grammars which only use atomic symbols are problematic as they cannot capture certain generalizations. We as linguists can recognize that NP_3_sg_nom stands for a noun phrase because it contains the letters NP. However, in formal terms this symbol is just like any other symbol in the grammar and we cannot capture the commonalities of all the symbols used for NPs. Furthermore, unstructured symbols do not capture the fact that the rules in (13) all have something in common. In formal terms, the only thing that the rules have in common is that there is one symbol on the left-hand side of the rule and two on the right.

We can solve this problem by introducing features which are assigned to category symbols and therefore allow for the values of such features to be included in our rules. For example, we can assume the features person, number and case for the category symbol NP. For determiners and nouns, we would adopt an additional feature for gender and one for inflectional class. (14) shows two rules augmented by the respective values in brackets:[6]

(14) NP(3,sg,nom) → Det(fem,sg,nom) N(fem,sg,nom)
       NP(3,sg,nom) → Det(mas,sg,nom) N(mas,sg,nom)

If we were to use variables rather than the values in (14), we would get rule schemata as the one in (15):

(15) NP(3,Num,Case) → Det(Gen,Num,Case) N(Gen,Num,Case)

The values of the variables here are not important. What is important is that they match. For this to work, it is important that the values are ordered; that is, in the category of a determiner, the gender is always first, number second and so on. The value of the person feature (the first position in the NP(3,Num,Case)) is fixed at '3' by the rule. These kind of restrictions on the values can, of course, be determined in the lexicon:

(16) NP(3,sg,nom)   → es
       Det(mas,sg,nom) → des

The rules in (10) can be collapsed into a single schema as in (17):

(17) S → NP(Per1,Num1,nom)
          NP(Per2,Num2,dat)
          NP(Per3,Num3,acc)
          V(Per1,Num1,ditransitive)

The identification of Per1 and Num1 on the verb and on the subject ensures that there is subject-verb agreement. For the other NPs, the values of these features are irrelevant. The case of these NPs is explicitly determined.

---

[6] Chapter 6 introduces attribute value structures. In these structure we always have pairs of a feature name and a feature value. In such a setting, the order of values is not important, since every value is uniquely identified by the corresponding feature name. Since we do not have a feature name in schemata like (13), the order of the values is important.

2.3 Semantics

In the introductory chapter and the previous sections, we have been dealing with syntactic aspects of language and the focus will remain very much on syntax for the remainder of this book. It is, however, important to remember that we use language to communicate, that is, to transfer information about certain situations, topics or opinions. If we want to accurately explain our capacity for language, then we also have to explain the meanings that our utterances have. To this end, it is necessary to understand their syntactic structure, but this alone is not enough. Furthermore, theories of language acquisition that only concern themselves with the acquisition of syntactic constructions are also inadequate. The syntax-semantics interface is therefore important and every grammatical theory has to say something about how syntax and semantics interact. In the following, I will show how we can combine phrase structure rules with semantic information. To represent meanings, I will use first-order predicate logic and λ-calculus. Unfortunately, it is not possible to provide a detailed discussion of the basics of logic so that even readers without prior knowledge can follow all the details, but the simple examples discussed here should be enough to provide some initial insights into how syntax and semantics interact and furthermore, how we can develop a linguistic theory to account for this.

To show how the meaning of a sentence is derived from the meaning of its parts, we will consider (18a). We assign the meaning in (18b) to the sentence in (18a).

(18) a. Max schläft.
      Max sleeps

      'Max is sleeping.'

      b. *schlafen'(max')*

Here, we are assuming *schlafen'* to be the meaning of *schläft* 'sleeps'. We use prime symbols to indicate that we are dealing with word meanings and not actual words. At first glance, it may not seem that we have really gained anything by using *schlafen'* to represent the meaning of (18a), since it is just another form of the verb *schläft* 'sleeps'. It is, however, important to concentrate on a single verb form as inflection is irrelevant when it comes to meaning. We can see this by comparing the examples in (19a) and (19b):

(19) a. Jeder Junge schläft.
      every boy   sleeps

      'Every boy sleeps.'

      b. Alle Jungen schlafen.
      all boys   sleep

      'All boys sleep.'

To enhance readability I use English translations of the predicates in semantic representations from now on.[7] So the meaning of (18a) is represented as (20) rather then (18b):

(20) *sleep'(max')*

---

[7] Note that I do not claim that English is suited as representation language for semantic relations and concepts that can be expressed in other languages.

When looking at the meaning in (20), we can consider which part of the meaning comes from each word. It seems relatively intuitive that *max'* comes from *Max*, but the trickier question is what exactly *schläft* 'sleeps' contributes in terms of meaning. If we think about what characterizes a 'sleeping' event, we know that there is typically an individual who is sleeping. This information is part of the meaning of the verb *schlafen* 'to sleep'. The verb meaning does not contain information about the sleeping individual, however, as this verb can be used with various subjects:

(21)   a. Paul schläft.
           Paul sleeps
           'Paul is sleeping.'

       b. Mio schläft.
           Mio sleeps
           'Mio is sleeping.'

       c. Xaver schläft.
           Xaver sleeps
           'Xaver is sleeping.'

We can therefore abstract away from any specific use of *sleep'* and instead of, for example, *max'* in (19b), we use a variable (e.g., x). This x can then be replaced by *paul'*, *mio'* or *xaver'* in a given sentence. To allow us to access these variables in a given meaning, we can write them with a λ in front. Accordingly, *schläft* 'sleeps' will have the following meaning:

(22) $\lambda x\ sleep'(x)$

The step from (20) to (22) is referred to as *lambda abstraction*. The combination of the expression (22) with the meaning of its arguments happens in the following way: we remove the λ and the corresponding variable and then replace all instances of the variable with the meaning of the argument. If we combine (22) and *max'* as in (23), we arrive at the meaning in (18b).

(23) $\lambda x\ sleep'(x)\ max'$

The process is called β-reduction or λ-conversion. To show this further, let us consider an example with a transitive verb. The sentence in (24a) has the meaning given in (24b):

(24)   a. Max mag Lotte.
           Max likes Lotte
           'Max likes Lotte.'

       b. *like'(max', lotte')*

The λ-abstraction of *mag* 'likes' is shown in (25):

(25) $\lambda y \lambda x\ like'(x,y)$

Note that it is always the first λ that has to be used first. The variable y corresponds to the object of *mögen*. For languages like English it is assumed that the object forms a verb phrase (VP) together with the verb and this VP is combined with the subject. German differs from English in allowing more freedom in constituent order. The problems that result for form meaning mappings are solved in different ways by different theories. The respective solutions will be addressed in the following chapters.

If we combine the representation in (25) with that of the object *Lotte*, we arrive at (26a), and following β-reduction, (26b):

(26)   a. $\lambda y \lambda x \; like'(x, y) \, lotte'$
       b. $\lambda x \; like'(x, lotte')$

This meaning can in turn be combined with the subject and we then get (27a) and (27b) after β-reduction:

(27)   a. $\lambda x \; like'(x, lotte') \, max'$
       b. $like'(max', lotte')$

After introducing lambda calculus, integrating the composition of meaning into our phrase structure rules is simple. A rule for the combination of a verb with its subject has to be expanded to include positions for the semantic contribution of the verb, the semantic contribution of the subject and then the meaning of the combination of these two (the entire sentence). The complete meaning is the combination of the individual meanings in the correct order. We can therefore take the simple rule in (28a) and turn it into (28b):

(28)   a. $S \rightarrow NP(nom) \; V$
       b. $S(V' \; NP') \rightarrow NP(nom, NP') \; V(V')$

V' stands for the meaning of V and NP' for the meaning of the NP(nom). V' NP' stands for the combination of V' and NP'. When analyzing (18a), the meaning of V' is $\lambda x \; sleep'(x)$ and the meaning of NP' is *max'*. The combination of V' NP' corresponds to (29a) or after β-reduction to (18b) – repeated here as (29b):

(29)   a. $\lambda x \; sleep'(x) \, max'$
       b. $sleep'(max')$

For the example with a transitive verb in (24a), the rule in (30) can be proposed:

(30) $S(V' \; NP2' \; NP1') \rightarrow NP(nom, NP1') \; V(V') \; NP(acc, NP2')$

The meaning of the verb (V') is first combined with the meaning of the object (NP2') and then with the meaning of the subject (NP1').

At this point, we can see that there are several distinct semantic rules for the phrase structure rules above. The hypothesis that we should analyze language in this way is called the *rule-to-rule hypothesis* (Bach 1976: 184). A more general process for deriving the meaning of linguistic expression will be presented in Section 5.1.4.

2.4 Phrase structure rules for some aspects of German syntax

Whereas determining the direct constituents of a sentence is relative easy, since we can very much rely on the movement test due to the somewhat flexible order of constituents in German, it is more difficult to identify the parts of the noun phrase. This is the problem we will focus on in this section. To help motivate assumptions about $\overline{\text{X}}$ syntax to be discussed in Section 2.5, we will also discuss prepositional phrases.

2.4.1 Noun phrases

Up to now, we have assumed a relatively simple structure for noun phrases: our rules state that a noun phrase consists of a determiner and a noun. Noun phrases can have a distinctly more complex structure than (31a). This is shown by the following examples in (31):

(31)   a. eine Frau
         a   woman

        b. eine Frau,   die wir kennen
         a   woman who we know

        c. eine Frau   aus Stuttgart
         a   woman from Stuttgart

        d. eine kluge Frau
         a   smart woman

        e. eine Frau   aus Stuttgart, die wir kennen
         a   woman from Stuttgart who we know

        f. eine kluge Frau   aus Stuttgart
         a   smart woman from Stuttgart

        g. eine kluge Frau,   die wir kennen
         a   smart woman who we know

        h. eine kluge Frau   aus Stuttgart, die wir kennen
         a   smart woman from Stuttgart who we know

As well as determiners and nouns, noun phrases can also contain adjectives, prepositional phrases and relative clauses. The additional elements in (31) are adjuncts. They restrict the set of objects which the noun phrase refers to. Whereas (31a) refers to a being which has the property of being a woman, the referent of (31b) must also have the property of being known to us.

Our previous rules for noun phrases simply combined a noun and a determiner and can therefore only be used to analyze (31a). The question we are facing now is how we can modify this rule or which additional rules we would have to assume in order to analyze the other noun phrases in (31). In addition to rule (32a), one could propose a rule such as the one in (32b).[8, 9]

(32) a. NP → Det N
      b. NP → Det A N

However, this rule would still not allow us to analyze noun phrases such as (33):

(33) alle weiteren schlagkräftigen Argumente
      all further   strong   arguments
      'all other strong arguments'

In order to be able to analyze (33), we require a rule such as (34):

(34) NP → Det A A N

It is always possible to increase the number of adjectives in a noun phrase and setting an upper limit for adjectives would be entirely arbitrary. Even if we opt for the following abbreviation, there are still problems:

(35) NP → Det A* N

The asterisk in (35) stands for any number of iterations. Therefore, (35) encompasses rules with no adjectives as well as those with one, two or more.

The problem is that according to the rule in (35) adjectives and nouns do not form a constituent and we can therefore not explain why coordination is still possible in (36):

(36) alle [[geschickten Kinder] und [klugen Frauen]]
      all   skillful   children and smart   women
      'all the skillful children and smart women'

If we assume that coordination involves the combination of two or more word strings with the same syntactic properties, then we would have to assume that the adjective and noun form a unit.

The following rules capture the noun phrases with adjectives discussed thus far:

(37) a. NP → Det $\overline{\text{N}}$
      b. $\overline{\text{N}}$ → A $\overline{\text{N}}$
      c. $\overline{\text{N}}$ → N

These rules state the following: a noun phrase consists of a determiner and a nominal element ($\overline{\text{N}}$). This nominal element can consist of an adjective and a nominal element (37b), or just a noun (37c). Since $\overline{\text{N}}$ is also on the right-hand side of the rule in (37b), we can apply this rule multiple times and therefore account for noun phrases with multiple adjectives such as (33). Figure 2.3 on the following page shows the structure of a noun phrase without an adjective and that of a noun phrase with one or two adjectives. The

---

[8] See Eisenberg (2004: 238) for the assumption of flat structures in noun phrases.

[9] There are, of course, other features such as gender and number, which should be part of all the rules discussed in this section. I have omitted these in the following for ease of exposition.

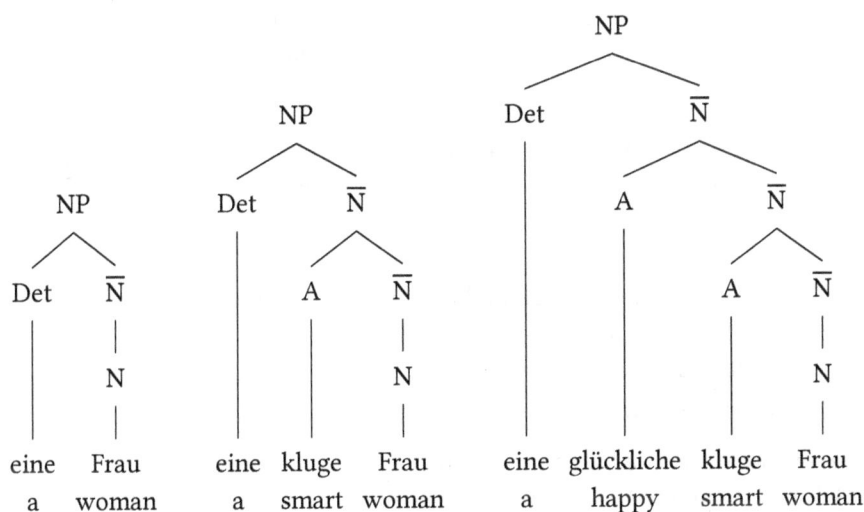

Figure 2.3: Noun phrases with differing numbers of adjectives

adjective *klug* 'smart' restricts the set of referents for the noun phrase. If we assume an additional adjective such as *glücklich* 'happy', then it only refers to those women who are happy as well as smart. These kinds of noun phrases can be used in contexts such as the following:

(38) A: Alle klugen Frauen sind unglücklich.
       all   smart women are   unhappy
    B: Nein, ich kenne eine glückliche kluge Frau.
       no   I   know   a   happy   smart woman

We observe that this discourse can be continued with *Aber alle glücklichen klugen Frauen sind schön* 'but all happy, smart women are beautiful' and a corresponding answer. The possibility to have even more adjectives in noun phrases such as *eine glückliche kluge Frau* 'a happy, smart woman' is accounted for in our rule system in (37). In the rule (37b), $\overline{\text{N}}$ occurs on the left as well as the right-hand side of the rule. This kind of rule is referred to as *recursive*.

We have now developed a nifty little grammar that can be used to analyze noun phrases containing adjectival modifiers. As a result, the combination of an adjective and noun is given constituent status. One may wonder at this point if it would not make sense to also assume that determiners and adjectives form a constituent, as we also have the following kind of noun phrases:

(39) diese schlauen und diese neugierigen Frauen
     these smart   and these curious   women

Here, we are dealing with a different structure, however. Two full NPs have been conjoined and part of the first conjunct has been deleted.

(40) diese schlauen ~~Frauen~~ und diese neugierigen Frauen
       these smart   women and these curious   women

One can find similar phenomena at the sentence and even word level:

(41)   a. dass Peter dem Mann das Buch ~~gibt~~ und Maria der Frau   die Schallplatte
           that Peter the man   the book gives and Maria the woman the record
           gibt
           gives

           'that Peters gives the book to the man and Maria the record to the woman'
       b. be- und ent-laden
           PRT and PRT-load

           'load and unload'

Thus far, we have discussed how we can ideally integrate adjectives into our rules for
the structure of noun phrases. Other adjuncts such as prepositional phrases or relative
clauses can be combined with $\overline{\text{N}}$ in an analogous way to adjectives:

(42)   a. $\overline{\text{N}} \rightarrow \overline{\text{N}}$ PP
       b. $\overline{\text{N}} \rightarrow \overline{\text{N}}$ relative clause

With these rules and those in (37), it is possible – assuming the corresponding rules for
PPs and relative clauses – to analyze all the examples in (31).

  (37c) states that it is possible for $\overline{\text{N}}$ to consist of a single noun. A further important
rule has not yet been discussed: we need another rule to combine nouns such as *Vater*
'father', *Sohn* 'son' or *Bild* 'picture', so-called *relational nouns*, with their arguments.
Examples of these can be found in (43a–b). (43c) is an example of a nominalization of a
verb with its argument:

(43)   a. der Vater von Peter
           the father of Peter

           'Peter's father'
       b. das Bild   vom Gleimtunnel
           the picture of.the Gleimtunnel

           'the picture of the Gleimtunnel'
       c. das Kommen des   Installateurs
           the coming of.the plumber

           'the plumber's visit'

The rule that we need to analyze (43a,b) is given in (44):

(44) $\overline{\text{N}} \rightarrow$ N PP

Figure 2.4 shows two structures with PP-arguments. The tree on the right also contains
an additional PP-adjunct, which is licensed by the rule in (42a).

  In addition to the previously discussed NP structures, there are other structures where
the determiner or noun is missing. Nouns can be omitted via ellipsis. (45) gives an

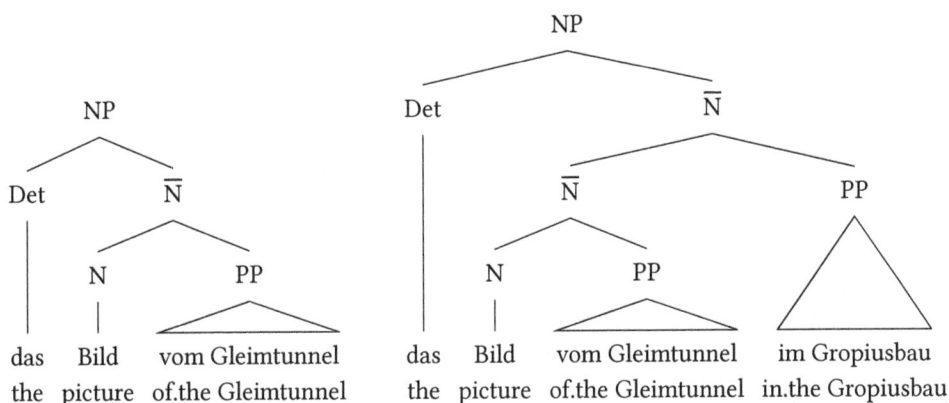

Figure 2.4: Combination of a noun with PP complement *vom Gleimtunnel* to the right with an adjunct PP

example of noun phrases, where a noun that does not require a complement has been omitted. The examples in (46) show NPs in which only one determiner and complement of the noun has been realized, but not the noun itself. The underscore marks the position where the noun would normally occur.

(45) a. eine kluge _
          a   smart
          'a smart one'

      b. eine kluge große _
          a   smart tall
          'a smart tall one'

      c. eine kluge _ aus Hamburg
          a   smart   from Hamburg
          'a smart one from Hamburg'

      d. eine kluge _, die alle   kennen
          a   smart   who everyone knows
          'a smart one who everyone knows'

(46) a. (Nein, nicht der Vater von Klaus), der _ von Peter war gemeint.
          no   not   the father of Klaus   the of Peter was meant
          'No, it wasn't the father of Klaus, but rather the one of Peter that was meant.'

      b. (Nein, nicht das Bild   von der Stadtautobahn), das _ vom Gleimtunnel war
          no   not   the picture of the motorway   the of.the Gleimtunnel was
          beeindruckend.
          impressive
          'No, it wasn't the picture of the motorway, but rather the one of the Gleimtun-nel that was impressive.'

   c. (Nein, nicht das Kommen des   Tischlers), das _ des   Installateurs ist
      no   not   the coming of.the carpenter the   of.the plumber   is
      wichtig.
      important

      'No, it isn't the visit of the carpenter, but rather the visit of the plumber that
      is important.'

In English, the pronoun *one* must often be used in the corresponding position,[10] but in
German the noun is simply omitted. In phrase structure grammars, this can be described
by a so-called *epsilon production*. These rules replace a symbol with nothing (47a). The
rule in (47b) is an equivalent variant which is responsible for the term *epsilon production*:

(47)   a. N →

      b. N → ϵ

The corresponding trees are shown in Figure 2.5. Going back to boxes, the rules in (47)

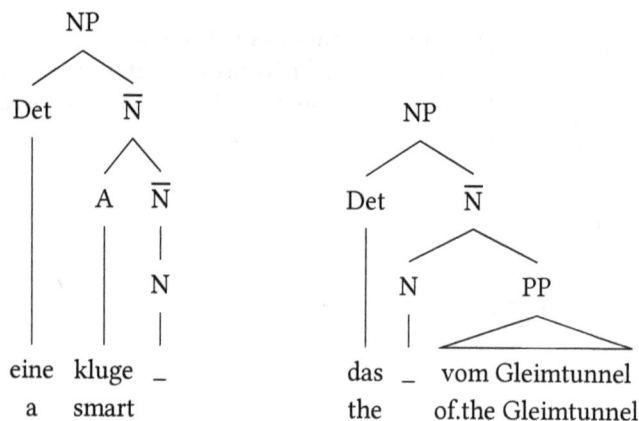

Figure 2.5: Noun phrases without an overt head

correspond to empty boxes with the same labels as the boxes of ordinary nouns. As we
have considered previously, the actual content of the boxes is unimportant when con-
sidering the question of where we can incorporate them. In this way, the noun phrases
in (31) can occur in the same sentences. The empty noun box also behaves like one with
a genuine noun. If we do not open the empty box, we will not be able to ascertain the
difference to a filled box.

    It is not only possible to omit the noun from noun phrases, but the determiner can
also remain unrealized in certain contexts. (48) shows noun phrases in plural:

(48)   a. Frauen
        women

      b. Frauen, die wir kennen
        women who we know

---

[10] See Fillmore et al. (2012: Section 4.12) for English examples without the pronoun *one*.

    c. kluge Frauen
       smart women

    d. kluge Frauen, die wir kennen
       smart women who we know

The determiner can also be omitted in singular if the noun denotes a mass noun:

(49) a. Getreide
       grain

    b. Getreide, das gerade gemahlen wurde
       grain   that just   ground   was

       'grain that has just been ground'

    c. frisches Getreide
       fresh   grain

    d. frisches Getreide, das gerade gemahlen wurde
       fresh   grain   that just   ground   was

       'fresh grain that has just been ground'

Finally, both the determiner and the noun can be omitted:

(50) a. Ich helfe klugen.
       I   help smart

       'I help smart ones.'

    b. Dort drüben steht frisches, das gerade gemahlen wurde.
       there over   stands fresh   that just   ground   was

       'Over there is some fresh (grain) that has just been ground.'

Figure 2.6 shows the corresponding trees.

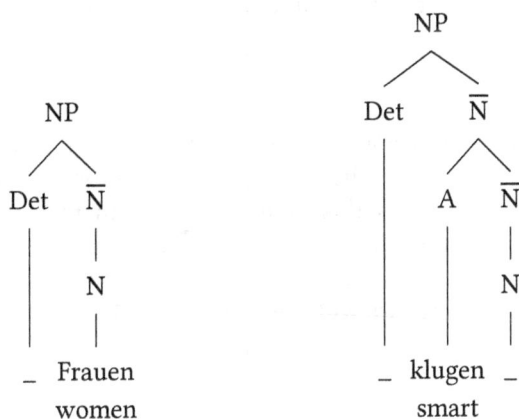

Figure 2.6: Noun phrases without overt determiner

    It is necessary to add two further comments to the rules we have developed up to this point: up to now, I have always spoken of adjectives. However, it is possible to have very complex adjective phrases in pre-nominal position. These can be adjectives with complements (51a,b) or adjectival participles (51c,d):

(51) a. der seiner Frau treue   Mann
          the his.DAT wife faithful man

          'the man faithful to his wife'

      b. der auf seinen Sohn stolze Mann
          the on his.ACC son   proud man

          'the man proud of his son'

      c. der seine   Frau   liebende Mann
          the his.ACC woman loving   man

          'the man who loves his wife'

      d. der von seiner   Frau geliebte Mann
          the by his.DAT wife loved   man

          'the man loved by his wife'

Taking this into account, the rule (37b) has to be modified in the following way:

(52) $\overline{N} \rightarrow AP \, \overline{N}$

An adjective phrase (AP) can consist of an NP and an adjective, a PP and an adjective or just an adjective:

(53) a. AP → NP A
      b. AP → PP A
      c. AP → A

There are two imperfections resulting from the rules we have developed thus far. These are the rules for adjectives or nouns without complements in (53c) as well as (37c) – repeated here as (54):

(54) $\overline{N} \rightarrow N$

If we apply these rules, then we will generate unary branching subtrees, that is trees with a mother that only has one daughter. See Figure 2.6 for an example of this. If we maintain the parallel to the boxes, this would mean that there is a box which contains another box which is the one with the relevant content.

In principle, nothing stops us from placing this information directly into the larger box. Instead of the rules in (55), we will simply use the rules in (56):

(55) a. A → kluge
      b. N → Mann

(56) a. AP → kluge
      b. $\overline{N} \rightarrow$ Mann

(56a) states that *kluge* 'smart' has the same properties as a full adjective phrase, in particular that it cannot be combined with a complement. This is parallel to the categorization of the pronoun *er* 'he' as an NP in the grammars (2) and (6).

Assigning $\overline{N}$ to nouns which do not require a complement has the advantage that we do not have to explain why the analysis in (57b) is possible as well as (57a) despite there not being any difference in meaning.

(57) a. [$_{NP}$ einige [$_{\overline{N}}$ kluge [$_{\overline{N}}$ [$_{\overline{N}}$ [$_{N}$ Frauen] und [$_{\overline{N}}$ [$_{N}$ Männer]]]]]]
           some   smart   women and   men

    b. [$_{NP}$ einige [$_{\overline{N}}$ kluge [$_{\overline{N}}$ [$_{N}$ [$_{N}$ Frauen] und [$_{N}$ Männer]]]]]
           some   smart   women and   men

In (57a), two nouns have projected to $\overline{N}$ and have then been joined by coordination. The result of coordination of two constituents of the same category is always a new constituent with that category. In the case of (57a), this is also $\overline{N}$. This constituent is then combined with the adjective and the determiner. In (57b), the nouns themselves have been coordinated. The result of this is always another constituent which has the same category as its parts. In this case, this would be N. This N becomes $\overline{N}$ and is then combined with the adjective. If nouns which do not require complements were categorized as $\overline{N}$ rather than N, we would not have the problem of spurious ambiguities. The structure in (58) shows the only possible analysis.

(58) [$_{NP}$ einige [$_{\overline{N}}$ kluge [$_{\overline{N}}$ [$_{\overline{N}}$ Frauen] und [$_{\overline{N}}$ Männer]]]]
        some   smart   women and   men

2.4.2 Prepositional phrases

Compared to the syntax of noun phrases, the syntax of prepositional phrases (PPs) is relatively straightforward. PPs normally consist of a preposition and a noun phrase whose case is determined by that preposition. We can capture this with the following rule:

(59) PP → P NP

This rule must, of course, also contain information about the case of the NP. I have omitted this for ease of exposition as I did with the NP-rules and AP-rules above.

The Duden grammar (Eisenberg et al. 2005: §1300) offers examples such as those in (60), which show that certain prepositional phrases serve to further define the semantic contribution of the preposition by indicating some measurement, for example:

(60) a. [[Einen Schritt] vor   dem Abgrund] blieb   er stehen.
           one   step   before the abyss   remained he stand

    'He stopped one step in front of the abyss.'

    b. [[Kurz]   nach dem Start] fiel die Klimaanlage   aus.
           shortly after the   take.off fell the air.conditioning out

    'Shortly after take off, the air conditioning stopped working.'

c. [[Schräg] hinter der Scheune] ist ein Weiher.
   diagonally behind the barn   is a   pond

   'There is a pond diagonally across from the barn.'

d. [[Mitten] im   Urwald] stießen   die Forscher   auf einen alten Tempel.
   middle in.the jungle   stumbled the researchers on an   old   temple

   'In the middle of the jungle, the researches came across an old temple.'

To analyze the sentences in (60a,b), one could propose the following rules in (61):

(61)   a. PP → NP PP

      b. PP → AP PP

These rules combine a PP with an indication of measurement. The resulting constituent is another PP. It is possible to use these rules to analyze prepositional phrases in (60a,b), but it unfortunately also allows us to analyze those in (62):

(62)   a. * [$_{PP}$ einen Schritt [$_{PP}$ kurz   [$_{PP}$ vor   dem Abgrund]]]
           one   step   shortly   before the abyss

      b. * [$_{PP}$ kurz   [$_{PP}$ einen Schritt [$_{PP}$ vor   dem Abgrund]]]
           shortly   one   step   before the abyss

Both rules in (61) were used to analyze the examples in (62). Since the symbol PP occurs on both the left and right-hand side of the rules, we can apply the rules in any order and as many times as we like.

We can avoid this undesired side-effect by reformulating the previously assumed rules:

(63)   a. PP → NP $\overline{\text{P}}$

      b. PP → AP $\overline{\text{P}}$

      c. PP → $\overline{\text{P}}$

      d. $\overline{\text{P}}$ → P NP

Rule (59) becomes (63d). The rule in (63c) states that a PP can consist of $\overline{\text{P}}$. Figure 2.7 on the following page shows the analysis of (64) using (63c) and (63d) as well as the analysis of an example with an adjective in the first position following the rules in (63b) and (63d):

(64)   vor   dem Abgrund
      before the   abyss

      'in front of the abyss'

At this point, the attentive reader is probably wondering why there is no empty measurement phrase in the left figure of Figure 2.7, which one might expect in analogy to the empty determiner in Figure 2.6. The reason for the empty determiner in Figure 2.6 is that the entire noun phrase without the determiner has a meaning similar to those with a determiner. The meaning normally contributed by the visible determiner has to somehow

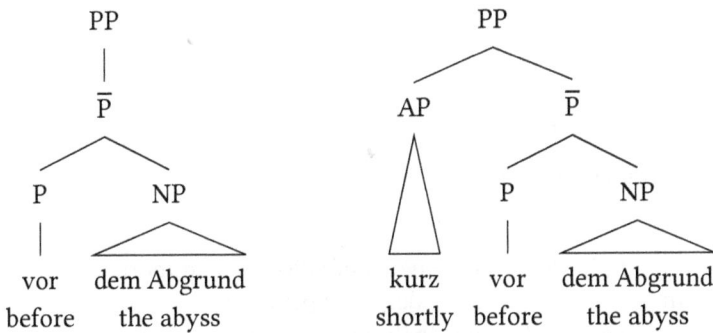

Figure 2.7: Prepositional phrases with and without measurement

be incorporated in the structure of the noun phrase. If we did not place this meaning in the empty determiner, this would lead to more complicated assumptions about semantic combination: we only really require the mechanisms presented in Section 2.3 and these are very general in nature. The meaning is contributed by the words themselves and not by any rules. If we were to assume a unary branching rule such as that in the left tree in Figure 2.7 instead of the empty determiner, then this unary branching rule would have to provide the semantics of the determiner. This kind of analysis has also been proposed by some researchers. See Chapter 19 for more on empty elements.

Unlike determiner-less NPs, prepositional phrases without an indication of degree or measurement do not lack any meaning component for composition. It is therefore not necessary to assume an empty indication of measurement, which somehow contributes to the meaning of the entire PP. Hence, the rule in (63c) states that a prepositional phrase consists of $\overline{\text{P}}$, that is, a combination of P and NP.

2.5 $\overline{\text{X}}$ theory

If we look again at the rules that we have formulated in the previous section, we see that heads are always combined with their complements to form a new constituent (65a,b), which can then be combined with further constituents (65c,d):

(65)   a. $\overline{\text{N}} \rightarrow \text{N PP}$
       b. $\overline{\text{P}} \rightarrow \text{P NP}$
       c. $\text{NP} \rightarrow \text{Det } \overline{\text{N}}$
       d. $\text{PP} \rightarrow \text{NP } \overline{\text{P}}$

Grammarians working on English noticed that parallel structures can be used for phrases which have adjectives or verbs as their head. I discuss adjective phrases at this point and postpone the discussion of verb phrases to Chapter 3. As in German, certain adjectives in English can take complements with the important restriction that adjective phrases with complements cannot realize these pre-nominally in English. (66) gives some examples of adjective phrases:

(66) a. He is proud.
      b. He is very proud.
      c. He is proud of his son.
      d. He is very proud of his son.

Unlike prepositional phrases, complements of adjectives are normally optional. *proud* can be used with or without a PP. The degree expression *very* is also optional.

The rules which we need for this analysis are given in (67), with the corresponding structures in Figure 2.8.

(67) a. AP → $\overline{A}$
      b. AP → AdvP $\overline{A}$
      c. $\overline{A}$ → A PP
      d. $\overline{A}$ → A

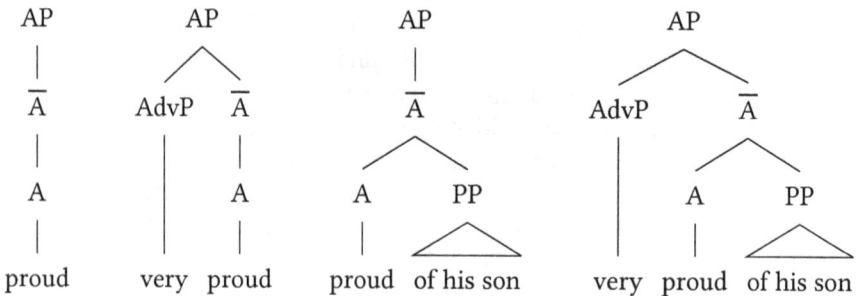

Figure 2.8: English adjective phrases

As was shown in Section 2.2, it is possible to generalize over very specific phrase structure rules and thereby arrive at more general rules. In this way, properties such as person, number and gender are no longer encoded in the category symbols, but rather only simple symbols such as NP, Det and N are used. It is only necessary to specify something about the values of a feature if it is relevant in the context of a given rule. We can take this abstraction a step further: instead of using explicit category symbols such as N, V, P and A for lexical categories and NP, VP, PP and AP for phrasal categories, one can simply use a variable for the word class in question and speak of X and XP.

This form of abstraction can be found in so-called $\overline{X}$ theory (or X-bar theory, the term *bar* refers to the line above the symbol), which was developed by Chomsky (1970) and refined by Jackendoff (1977). This form of abstract rules plays an important role in many different theories. For example: Government & Binding (Chapter 3), Generalized Phrase Structure Grammar (Chapter 5) and Lexical Functional Grammar (Chapter 7). In HPSG

(Chapter 9), $\overline{X}$ theory also plays a role, but not all restrictions of the $\overline{X}$ schema have been adopted.

(68) shows a possible instantiation of $\overline{X}$ rules, where the category X has been used in place of N, as well as examples of word strings which can be derived by these rules:

(68)

$\overline{X}$ rule	with specific categories	example strings
$\overline{\overline{X}} \rightarrow$ specifier $\overline{\overline{X}}$	$\overline{\overline{N}} \rightarrow \overline{\overline{\text{DET}}}\ \overline{\overline{N}}$	the [picture of Paris]
$\overline{X} \rightarrow \overline{X}$ adjunct	$\overline{N} \rightarrow \overline{N}$ REL_CLAUSE	[picture of Paris] [that everybody knows]
$\overline{X} \rightarrow$ adjunct $\overline{X}$	$\overline{N} \rightarrow \overline{\overline{A}}\ \overline{N}$	beautiful [picture of Paris]
$\overline{X} \rightarrow X$ complement*	$\overline{N} \rightarrow N\ \overline{\overline{P}}$	picture [of Paris]

Any word class can replace X (e.g., V, A or P). The X without the bar stands for a lexical item in the above rules. If one wants to make the bar level explicit, then it is possible to write X^0. Just as with the rule in (15), where we did not specify the case value of the determiner or the noun but rather simply required that the values on the right-hand side of the rule match, the rules in (68) require that the word class of an element on the right-hand side of the rule (X or $\overline{X}$) matches that of the element on the left-hand side of the rule ($\overline{X}$ or $\overline{\overline{X}}$).

A lexical element can be combined with all its complements. The '*' in the last rule stands for an unlimited amount of repetitions of the symbol it follows. A special case is zerofold occurrence of complements. There is no PP complement of *Bild* 'picture' present in *das Bild* 'the picture' and thus N becomes $\overline{N}$. The result of the combination of a lexical element with its complements is a new projection level of X: the projection level 1, which is marked by a bar. $\overline{X}$ can then be combined with adjuncts. These can occur to the left or right of $\overline{X}$. The result of this combination is still $\overline{X}$, that is the projection level is not changed by combining it with an adjunct. Maximal projections are marked by two bars. One can also write XP for a projection of X with two bars. An XP consists of a specifier and $\overline{X}$. Depending on one's theoretical assumptions, subjects of sentences (Haider 1995, 1997a; Berman 2003a: Section 3.2.2) and determiners in NPs (Chomsky 1970: 210) are specifiers. Furthermore, degree modifiers (Chomsky 1970: 210) in adjective phrases and measurement indicators in prepositional phrases are also counted as specifiers.

Non-head positions can only host maximal projections and therefore complements, adjuncts and specifiers always have two bars. Figure 2.9 on the following page gives an overview of the minimal and maximal structure of phrases.

Some categories do not have a specifier or have the option of having one. Adjuncts are optional and therefore not all structures have to contain an $\overline{X}$ with an adjunct daughter. In addition to the branching shown in the right-hand figure, adjuncts to XP and head-adjuncts are sometimes possible. There is only a single rule in (68) for cases in which a head precedes the complements, however an order in which the complement precedes the head is of course also possible. This is shown in Figure 2.9.

Figure 2.10 on page 77 shows the analysis of the NP structures *das Bild* 'the picture' and *das schöne Bild von Paris* 'the beautiful picture of Paris'. The NP structures in Figure 2.10

$$
\begin{array}{c}
\text{XP}
\end{array}
$$

XP   XP

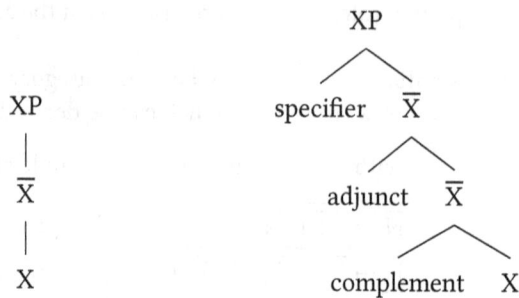

Figure 2.9: Minimal and maximal structure of phrases

and the tree for *proud* in Figure 2.8 show examples of minimally populated structures. The left tree in Figure 2.10 is also an example of a structure without an adjunct. The right-hand structure in Figure 2.10 is an example for the maximally populated structure: specifier, adjunct, and complement are present.

The analysis given in Figure 2.10 assumes that all non-heads in a rule are phrases. One therefore has to assume that there is a determiner phrase even if the determiner is not combined with other elements. The unary branching of determiners is not elegant but it is consistent.[11] The unary branchings for the NP *Paris* in Figure 2.10 may also seem somewhat odd, but they actually become more plausible when one considers more complex noun phrases:

(69)   a.   das Paris der   dreißiger Jahre
            the Paris of.the thirty   years

            '30's Paris'

     b.   die Maria aus   Hamburg
            the Maria from Hamburg

            'Maria from Hamburg'

Unary projections are somewhat inelegant but this should not concern us too much here, as we have already seen in the discussion of the lexical entries in (56) that unary branching nodes can be avoided for the most part and that it is indeed desirable to avoid such structures. Otherwise, one gets spurious ambiguities. In the following chapters, we will discuss approaches such as Categorial Grammar and HPSG, which do not assume unary rules for determiners, adjectives and nouns.

Furthermore, other $\overline{\text{X}}$ theoretical assumptions will not be shared by several theories discussed in this book. In particular, the assumption that non-heads always have to be maximal projections will be disregarded. Pullum (1985) and Kornai & Pullum (1990) have shown that the respective theories are not necessarily less restrictive than theories which adopt a strict version of the $\overline{\text{X}}$ theory. See also the discussion in Section 13.1.2.

---

[11] For an alternative version of $\overline{\text{X}}$ theory which does not assume elaborate structure for determiners see Muysken (1982).

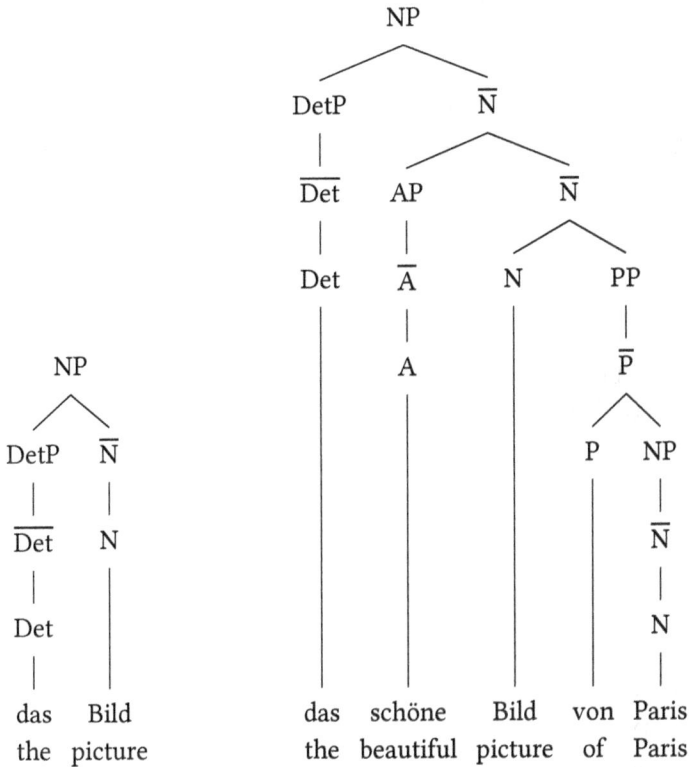

Figure 2.10: $\overline{X}$ analysis of *das Bild* 'the picture' and *das schöne Bild von Paris* 'the beautiful picture of Paris'

Comprehension questions

1. Why are phrase structure grammars that use only atomic categories inadequate for the description of natural languages?

2. Assuming the grammar in (6), state which steps (replacing symbols) one has to take to get to the symbol V in the sentence (70).

   (70) er das Buch dem Mann gibt
         he the book the man   gives
         'He gives the book to the man.'

   Your answer should resemble the analysis in (3).

3. Give a representation of the meaning of (71) using predicate logic:

(71)   a. Ulrike kennt Hans.
          Ulrike knows Hans

       b. Joshi freut   sich.
          Joshi is.happy REFL
          'Joshi is happy.'

Exercises

1. On page 55, I claimed that there is an infinite number of grammars we could use to analyze (1). Why is this claim correct?

2. Try to come up with some ways in which we can tell which of these possible grammars is or are the best?

3. A fragment for noun phrase syntax was presented in Section 2.4.1. Why is the interaction of the rules in (72) problematic?

(72)   a. NP → Det $\overline{\text{N}}$
       b. $\overline{\text{N}}$ → N
       c. Det → ϵ
       d. N → ϵ

4. Why is it not a good idea to mark *books* as NP in the lexicon?

5. Can you think of some reasons why it is not desirable to assume the following rule for nouns such as *books*:

(73)   NP → Modifier* books Modifier*

The rule in (73) combines an unlimited number of modifiers with the noun *books* followed by an unlimited number of modifiers. We can use this rule to derive phrases such as those in (74):

(74)   a. books
       b. interesting books
       c. interesting books from Stuttgart

Make reference to coordination data in your answer. Assume that symmetric coordination requires that both coordinated phrases or words have the same syntactic category.

6. Fillmore et al. (2012) suggested treating nounless structures like those in (75) as involving a phrasal construction combining the determiner *the* with an adjective.

   (75)   a. Examine the plight of the very poor.
          b. Their outfits range from the flamboyant to the functional.
          c. The unimaginable happened.

   (76) shows a phrase structure rule that corresponds to their construction:

   (76)   NP → the Adj

   Adj stands for something that can be a single word like *poor* or complex like *very poor*.

   Revisit the German data in (45) and (46) and explain why such an analysis and even a more general one as in (77) would not extend to German.

   (77)   NP → Det Adj

7. Why can $\overline{\text{X}}$ theory not account for German adjective phrases without additional assumptions? (This task is for (native) speakers of German only.)

8. Come up with a phrase structure grammar that can be used to analyze the sentence in (78), but also rules out the sentences in (79).

   (78)   a. Der   Mann hilft der   Frau.
              the.NOM man   helps the.DAT woman

              'The man helps the woman.'
          b. Er   gibt ihr   das Buch.
              he.NOM gives her.DAT the book

              'He gives her the book.'
          c. Er   wartet auf ein Wunder.
              he.NOM waits on a   miracle

              'He is waiting for a miracle.'

   (79)   a. * Der   Mann hilft er.
                the.NOM man   helps he.NOM
          b. * Er   gibt ihr   den Buch.
                he.NOM gives her.DAT the.M book.N

9. Consider which additional rules would have to be added to the grammar you developed in the previous exercise in order to be able to analyze the following sentences:

(80)   a.   Der   Mann hilft der   Frau   jetzt.
            the.NOM man   helps the.DAT woman now

      'The man helps the woman now.'

      b.   Der   Mann hilft der   Frau   neben dem Bushäuschen.
            the.NOM man   helps the.DAT woman next.to the bus.shelter

      'The man helps the woman next to the bus shelter.'

      c.   Er   gibt ihr   das   Buch jetzt.
            he.NOM gives her.DAT the.ACC book now

      'He gives her the book now.'

      d.   Er   gibt ihr   das   Buch neben dem Bushäuschen.
            he.NOM gives her.DAT the.ACC book next.to the   bus.shelter

      'He gives her the book next to the bus shelter.'

      e.   Er   wartet jetzt auf ein Wunder.
            he.NOM waits now on a   miracle

      'He is waiting for a miracle now.'

      f.   Er   wartet neben dem   Bushäuschen auf ein Wunder.
            he.NOM waits next.to the.DAT bus.shelter   on a   miracle

      'He is waiting for a miracle next to the bus shelter.'

10. Install a Prolog system (e.g., SWI-Prolog[12]) and try out your grammar. Details for the notation can be found in the corresponding handbook under the key word Definite Clause Grammar (DCG).

Further reading

The expansion of phrase structure grammars to include features was proposed as early as 1963 by Harman (1963).

The phrase structure grammar for noun phrases discussed in this chapter covers a large part of the syntax of noun phrases but cannot explain certain NP structures. Furthermore, it has the problem, which exercise 3 is designed to show. A discussion of these phenomena and a solution in the framework of HPSG can be found in Netter (1998) and Kiss (2005).

The discussion of the integration of semantic information into phrase structure grammars was very short. A detailed discussion of predicate logic and its integration into phrase structure grammars – as well as a discussion of quantifier scope – can be found in Blackburn & Bos (2005).

---

[12] http://www.swi-prolog.org

3 Transformational Grammar – Government & Binding

Transformational Grammar and its subsequent incarnations (such as Government and Binding Theory and Minimalism) were developed by Noam Chomsky at MIT in Boston (Chomsky 1957, 1965, 1975, 1981a, 1986a, 1995b). Manfred Bierwisch (1963) was the first to implement Chomsky's ideas for German. In the 60s, the decisive impulse came from the *Arbeitsstelle Strukturelle Grammatik* 'Workgroup for Structural Grammar', which was part of the Academy of Science of the GDR. See Bierwisch 1992 and Vater 2010 for a historic overview. As well as Bierwisch's work, the following books focusing on German or the Chomskyan research program in general should also be mentioned: Fanselow (1987), Fanselow & Felix (1987), von Stechow & Sternefeld (1988), Grewendorf (1988), Haider (1993), Sternefeld (2006).

The different implementations of Chomskyan theories are often grouped under the heading *Generative Grammar*. This term comes from the fact that phrase structure grammars and the augmented frameworks that were suggested by Chomsky can generate sets of well-formed expressions (see p. 54). It is such a set of sentences that constitutes a language (in the formal sense) and one can test if a sentence forms part of a language by checking if a particular sentence is in the set of sentences generated by a given grammar. In this sense, simple phrase structure grammars and, with corresponding formal assumptions, GPSG, LFG, HPSG and Construction Grammar (CxG) are generative theories. In recent years, a different view of the formal basis of theories such as LFG, HPSG and CxG has emerged such that the aforementioned theories are now *model theoretic* theories rather than generative-enumerative ones[1] (See Chapter 14 for discussion). In 1965, Chomsky defined the term *Generative Grammar* in the following way (see also Chomsky 1995b: 162):

> A grammar of a language purports to be a description of the ideal speaker-hearer's intrinsic competence. If the grammar is, furthermore, perfectly explicit – in other words, if it does not rely on the intelligence of the understanding reader but rather provides an explicit analysis of his contribution – we may call it (somewhat redundantly) a *generative grammar*. (Chomsky 1965: 4)

In this sense, all grammatical theories discussed in this book would be viewed as generative grammars. To differentiate further, sometimes the term *Mainstream Generative Grammar* (MGG) is used (Culicover & Jackendoff 2005: 3) for Chomskyan models. In this

---

[1] Model theoretic approaches are always constraint-based and the terms *model theoretic* and *constraint-based* are sometimes used synonymously.

chapter, I will discuss a well-developed and very influential version of Chomskyan grammar, GB theory. More recent developments following Chomsky's Minimalist Program
are dealt with in Chapter 4.

3.1 General remarks on the representational format

This section provides an overview of general assumptions. I introduce the concept of
transformations in Section 3.1.1. Section 3.1.2 provides background information about
assumptions regarding language acquisition, which shaped the theory considerably, Section 3.1.3 introduces the so-called T model, the basic architecture of GB theory. Section 3.1.4 introduces the $\overline{\text{X}}$ theory in the specific form used in GB and Section 3.1.5 shows
how this version of the $\overline{\text{X}}$ theory can be applied to English. The discussion of the analysis
of English sentences is an important prerequisite for the understanding of the analysis
of German, since many analyses in the GB framework are modeled in parallel to the
analyses of English. Section 3.1.6 introduces the analysis of German clauses in a parallel
way to what has been done for English in Section 3.1.5.

3.1.1 Transformations

In the previous chapter, I introduced simple phrase structure grammars. Chomsky (1957:
Chapter 5) criticized this kind of rewrite grammars since – in his opinion – it is not clear
how one can capture the relationship between active and passive sentences or the various ordering possibilities of constituents in a sentence. While it is of course possible to
formulate different rules for active and passive sentences in a phrase structure grammar
(e.g., one pair of rules for intransitive (1), one for transitive (2) and one for ditransitive
verbs (3)), it would not adequately capture the fact that the same phenomenon occurs in
the example pairs in (1)–(3):

(1)   a. weil   dort noch jemand   arbeitet
             because there still   somebody works

             'because somebody is still working there'

        b. weil   dort noch gearbeitet wurde
             because there still   worked   was

             'because work was still being done there'

(2)   a. weil   er den Weltmeister   schlägt
             because he the world.champion beats

             'because he beats the world champion'

        b. weil   der Weltmeister   geschlagen wurde
             because the world.champion beaten   was

             'because the world champion was beaten'

(3) a. weil   der Mann der Frau   den Schlüssel stiehlt
         because the man the woman the key   steals

      'because the man is stealing the key from the woman'

     b. weil   der Frau   der Schlüssel gestohlen wurde
         because the woman the key   stolen   was

      'because the key was stolen from the woman'

Chomsky (1957: 43) suggests a transformation that creates a connection between active and passive sentences. The passive transformation for English that he suggested has the form in (4):

(4) NP V NP → 3 [$_{AUX}$ be] 2en [$_{PP}$ [$_P$ by] 1]
     1 2 3

This transformational rule maps a tree with the symbols on the left-hand side of the rule onto a tree with the symbols on the right-hand side of the rule. Accordingly, 1, 2 and 3 on the right of the rule correspond to symbols, which are under the numbers on the left-hand side. *en* stands for the morpheme which forms the participle (*seen, been, …*, but also *loved*). Both trees for (5a,b) are shown in Figure 3.1.

(5) a. John loves Mary.
     b. Mary is loved by John.

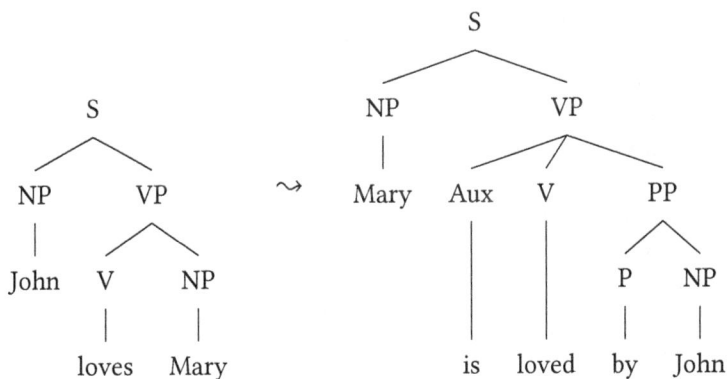

Figure 3.1: Application of passive transformation

The symbols on the left of transformational rules do not necessarily have to be in a local tree, that is, they can be daughters of different mothers as in Figure 3.1.

Rewrite grammars were divided into four complexity classes based on the properties they have. The simplest grammars are assigned to the class 3, whereas the most complex are of Type-0. The so-called context-free grammars we have dealt with thus far are of Type-2. Transformational grammars which allow symbols to be replaced by arbitrary other symbols are of Type-0 (Peters & Ritchie 1973). Research on the complexity of natural languages shows that the highest complexity level (Type-0) is too complex for natural language. It follows from this – assuming that one wants to have a restrictive formal apparatus for the description of grammatical knowledge (Chomsky 1965: 62) – that the form and potential power of transformations has to be restricted.[2] Another criticism of early versions of transformational grammar was that, due to a lack of restrictions, the way in which transformations interact was not clear. Furthermore, there were problems associated with transformations which delete material (see Klenk 2003: Section 3.1.4). For this reason, new theoretical approaches such as Government & Binding (Chomsky 1981a) were developed. In this model, the form that grammatical rules can take is restricted (see Section 3.1.4). Elements moved by transformations are still represented in their original position, which makes them recoverable at the original position and hence the necessary information is available for semantic interpretation. There are also more general principles, which serve to restrict transformations.

After some initial remarks on the model assumed for language acquisition in GB theory, we will take a closer look at phrase structure rules, transformations and constraints.

3.1.2 The hypothesis regarding language acquisition: Principles & Parameters

Chomsky (1965: Section I.8) assumes that linguistic knowledge must be innate since the language system is, in his opinion, so complex that it would be impossible to learn a language from the given input using more general cognitive principles alone (see also Section 13.8). If it is not possible to learn language solely through interaction with our environment, then at least part of our language ability must be innate. The question of exactly what is innate and if humans actually have an innate capacity for language remains controversial and the various positions on the question have changed over the course of the last decades. Some notable works on this topic are Pinker (1994), Tomasello (1995), Wunderlich (2004), Hauser, Chomsky & Fitch (2002) and Chomsky (2007). For more on this discussion, see Chapter 13.

Chomsky (1981a) also assumes that there are general, innate principles which linguistic structure cannot violate. These principles are parametrized, that is, there are options. Parameter settings can differ between languages. An example for a parametrized principle is shown in (6):

(6)   Principle: A head occurs before or after its complement(s) depending on the value of the parameter POSITION.

The Principles & Parameters model (P&P model) assumes that a significant part of language acquisition consists of extracting enough information from the linguistic input in order to be able to set parameters. Chomsky (2000: 8) compares the setting of parameters to flipping a switch. For a detailed discussion of the various assumptions about language acquisition in the P&P-model, see Chapter 21.6. Speakers of English have to learn that

---

[2] For more on the power of formal languages, see Chapter 17.

heads occur before their complements in their language, whereas a speaker of Japanese has to learn that heads follow their complements. (7) gives the respective examples:

(7) a. be showing pictures of himself

    b. zibun -no   syasin-o mise-te   iru
        REFL from picture   showing be

As one can see, the Japanese verb, noun and prepositional phrases are a mirror image of the corresponding phrases in English. (8) provides a summary and shows the parametric value for the position parameter:

(8)

Language	Observation	Parameter: head initial
English	Heads occur before complements	+
Japanese	Heads occur after complements	−

Investigating languages based on their differences with regard to certain assumed parameters has proven to be a very fruitful line of research in the last few decades and has resulted in an abundance of comparative cross-linguistic studies.

After these introductory comments on language acquisition, the following sections will discuss the basic assumptions of GB theory.

3.1.3 The T model

Chomsky criticized simple PSGs for not being able to adequately capture certain correlations. An example of this is the relationship between active and passive sentences. In phrase structure grammars, one would have to formulate active and passive rules for intransitive, transitive and ditransitive verbs (see the discussion of (1)–(3) above). The fact that the passive can otherwise be consistently described as the suppression of the most prominent argument is not captured by phrase structure rules. Chomsky therefore assumes that there is an underlying structure, the so-called *Deep Structure*, and that other structures are derived from this. The general architecture of the so-called T model is discussed in the following subsections.

3.1.3.1 D-structure and S-structure

During the derivation of new structures, parts of the Deep Structure can be deleted or moved. In this way, one can explain the relationship between active and passive sentences. As the result of this kind of manipulation of structures, also called transformations, one derives a new structure, the *Surface Structure*, from the original Deep Structure. Since the Surface Structure does not actually mirror the actual use of words in a sentence in some versions of the theory, the term *S-structure* is sometimes used instead as to avoid misunderstandings.

(9) *Surface Structure* = S-structure
    Deep Structure   = D-structure

Figure 3.2 gives an overview of the GB architecture: phrase structure rules and the lexicon license the D-structure from which the S-structure is derived by means of transformations. S-structure feeds into Phonetic Form (PF) and Logical Form (LF). The model is

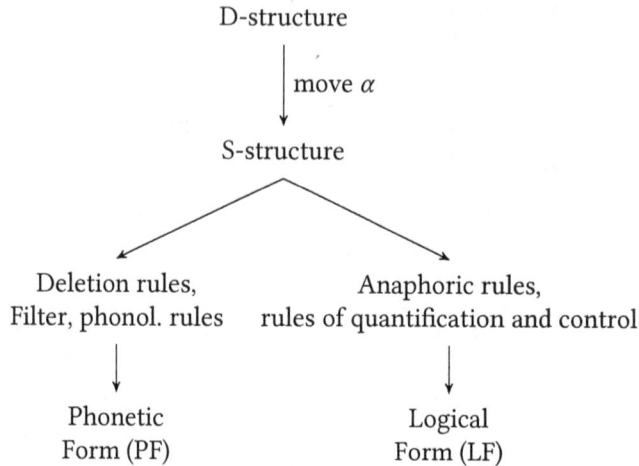

D-structure

$\downarrow$ move α

S-structure

Deletion rules,   Anaphoric rules,
Filter, phonol. rules   rules of quantification and control

$\downarrow$ $\downarrow$

Phonetic   Logical
Form (PF)   Form (LF)

Figure 3.2: The T model

referred to as the *T-model* (or Y-model) because D-structure, S-structure, PF and LF form an upside-down T (or Y). We will look at each of these individual components in more detail.

Using phrase structure rules, one can describe the relationships between individual elements (for instance words and phrases, sometimes also parts of words). The format for these rules is $\overline{\text{X}}$ syntax (see Section 2.5). The lexicon, together with the structure licensed by $\overline{\text{X}}$ syntax, forms the basis for D-structure. D-structure is then a syntactic representation of the selectional grid (= valence classes) of individual word forms in the lexicon.

The lexicon contains a lexical entry for every word which comprises information about morphophonological structure, syntactic features and selectional properties. This will be explained in more detail in Section 3.1.3.4. Depending on one's exact theoretical assumptions, morphology is viewed as part of the lexicon. Inflectional morphology is, however, mostly consigned to the realm of syntax. The lexicon is an interface for semantic interpretation of individual word forms.

The surface position in which constituents are realized is not necessarily the position they have in D-structure. For example, a sentence with a ditransitive verb has the following ordering variants:

(10)   a. [dass] der   Mann der   Frau   das   Buch gibt
            that the.NOM man   the.DAT woman the.ACC book gives
            'that the man gives the woman the book'

b. Gibt der   Mann der   Frau   das   Buch?
   gives the.NOM man   the.DAT woman the.ACC book

   'Does the man give the woman the book?'

c. Der   Mann gibt der   Frau   das   Buch.
   the.NOM man   gives the.DAT woman the.ACC book

   'The man gives the woman the book.'

The following transformational rules for the movements above are assumed: (10b) is derived from (10a) by fronting the verb, and (10c) is derived from (10b) by fronting the nominative noun phrase. In GB theory, there is only one very general transformation: Move α = "Move anything anywhere!". The nature of what exactly can be moved where and for which reason is determined by principles. Examples of such principles are the Theta-Criterion and the Case Filter, which will be dealt with below.

The relations between a predicate and its arguments that are determined by the lexical entries have to be accessible for semantic interpretation at all representational levels. For this reason, the base position of a moved element is marked with a trace. This means, for instance, that the position in which the fronted *gibt* 'gives' originated is indicated in (11b). The respective marking is referred to as a *trace* or a *gap*. Such empty elements may be frightening when one encounters them first, but I already motivated the assumption of empty elements in nominal structures in Section 2.4.1 (page 68).

(11) a. [dass] der Mann der Frau   das Buch gibt
         that   the man   the woman the book gives

         'that the man gives the woman the book'

      b. Gibt$_i$ der Mann der Frau   das Buch _$_i$?
         gives the man   the woman the book

         'Does the man give the woman the book?'

      c. [Der Mann]$_j$ gibt$_i$ _$_j$ der Frau   das Buch _$_i$.
         the man   gives   the woman the book

         'The man gives the woman the book.'

(11c) is derived from (11a) by means of two movements, which is why there are two traces in (11c). The traces are marked with indices so it is possible to distinguish the moved constituents. The corresponding indices are then present on the moved constituents. Sometimes, *e* (for *empty*) or *t* (for *trace*) is used to represent traces.

The S-structure derived from the D-structure is a surface-like structure but should not be equated with the structure of actual utterances.

3.1.3.2 Phonetic Form

Phonological operations are represented at the level of Phonetic Form (PF). PF is responsible for creating the form which is actually pronounced. For example, so-called *wanna*-contraction takes place at PF (Chomsky 1981a: 20–21).

(12) a. The students want to visit Paris.

     b. The students wanna visit Paris.

The contraction in (12) is licensed by the optional rule in (13):

(13) want + to → wanna

3.1.3.3 Logical Form

Logical Form is the syntactic level which mediates between S-structure and the semantic interpretation of a sentence. Some of the phenomena which are dealt with by LF are anaphoric reference of pronouns, quantification and control.

    Syntactic factors play a role in resolving anaphoric dependencies. An important component of GB theory is Binding Theory, which seeks to explain what a pronoun can or must refer to and when a reflexive pronoun can or must be used. (14) gives some examples of both personal and reflexive pronouns:

(14) a. Peter kauft einen Tisch. Er gefällt ihm.
       Peter buys a   table.M he likes   him

       'Peter is buying a table. He likes it/him.'

    b. Peter kauft eine Tasche. Er gefällt ihm.
       Peter buys a   bag.F   he likes him

       'Peter is buying a bag. He likes it/him.'

    c. Peter kauft eine Tasche. Er gefällt sich.
       Peter buys a   bag.F   he likes himself

       'Peter is buying a bag. He likes himself.'

In the first example, *er* 'he' can refer to either Peter, the table or something/someone else that was previously mentioned in the context. *ihm* 'him' can refer to Peter or someone in the context. Reference to the table is restricted by world knowledge. In the second example, *er* 'he' cannot refer to *Tasche* 'bag' since *Tasche* is feminine and *er* is masculine. *er* 'he' can refer to Peter only if *ihm* 'him' does not refer to Peter. *ihm* would otherwise have to refer to a person in the wider context. This is different in (14c). In (14c), *er* 'he' and *sich* 'himself' must refer to the same object. This is due to the fact that the reference of reflexives such as *sich* is restricted to a particular local domain. Binding Theory attempts to capture these restrictions.

    LF is also important for quantifier scope. Sentences such as (15a) have two readings. These are given in (15b) and (15c).

(15) a. Every man loves a woman.

    b. $\forall x \exists y (man(x) \rightarrow (woman(y) \land love(x, y)))$

    c. $\exists y \forall x (man(x) \rightarrow (woman(y) \land love(x, y)))$

The symbol ∀ stands for a *universal quantifier* and ∃ stands for an *existential quantifier*. The first formula corresponds to the reading that for every man, there is a woman who he loves and in fact, these can be different women. Under the second reading, there is exactly one woman such that all men love her. The question of when such an ambiguity arises and which reading is possible when depends on the syntactic properties of the given utterance. LF is the level which is important for the meaning of determiners such as *a* and *every*.

Control Theory is also specified with reference to LF. Control Theory deals with the question of how the semantic role of the infinitive subject in sentences such as (16) is filled.

(16)   a.   Der Professor schlägt   dem Studenten vor, die Klausur noch mal   zu
          the professor suggests the   student   PRT the test   once again to
          schreiben.
          write

          'The professor advises the student to take the test again.'

     b.   Der Professor schlägt   dem Studenten vor, die Klausur nicht zu bewerten.
          the professor suggests the   student   PRT the test   not   to grade

          'The professor suggests to the student not to grade the test.'

     c.   Der Professor schlägt   dem Studenten vor, gemeinsam ins   Kino   zu gehen.
          the professor suggests the   student   PRT together   into cinema to go

          'The professor suggests to the student to go to the cinema together.'

3.1.3.4 The lexicon

The meaning of words tells us that they have to be combined with certain roles like "acting person" or "affected thing" when creating more complex phrases. For example, the fact that the verb *beat* needs two arguments belongs to its semantic contribution. The semantic representation of the contribution of the verb *beat* in (17a) is given in (17b):

(17)   a.   Judit beats the grandmaster.
     b.   *beat'*(x,y)

Dividing heads into valence classes is also referred to as *subcategorization*: *beat* is subcategorized for a subject and an object. This term comes from the fact that a head is already categorized with regard to its part of speech (verb, noun, adjective, ...) and then further subclasses (e.g., intransitive or transitive verb) are formed with regard to valence information. Sometimes the phrase *X subcategorizes for Y* is used, which means *X selects Y*. *beat* is referred to as the predicate since *beat'* is the logical predicate. The subject and object are the arguments of the predicate. There are several terms used to describe the set of selectional requirements such as *argument structure, valence frames, subcategorization frame, thematic grid* and *theta-grid* or *θ-grid*.

Adjuncts modify semantic predicates and when the semantic aspect is emphasized they are also called *modifiers*. Adjuncts are not present in the argument structure of predicates.

Following GB assumptions, arguments occur in specific positions in the clause – in so-called argument positions (e.g., the sister of an X^0 element, see Section 2.5). The Theta-Criterion states that elements in argument positions have to be assigned a semantic role – a so-called theta-role – and each role can be assigned only once (Chomsky 1981a: 36):

Principle 1 (Theta-Criterion)
- *Each theta-role is assigned to exactly one argument position.*

- *Every phrase in an argument position receives exactly one theta-role.*

The arguments of a head are ordered, that is, one can differentiate between higher- and lower-ranked arguments. The highest-ranked argument of verbs and adjectives has a special status. Since GB assumes that it is often (and always in some languages) realized in a position outside of the verb or adjective phrase, it is often referred to as the *external argument*. The remaining arguments occur in positions inside of the verb or adjective phrase. These kind of arguments are dubbed *internal arguments* or *complements*. For simple sentences, this often means that the subject is the external argument.

When discussing types of arguments, one can identify three classes of theta-roles:

- Class 1: agent (acting individual), the cause of an action or feeling (stimulus), holder of a certain property

- Class 2: experiencer (perceiving individual), the person profiting from something (beneficiary) (or the opposite: the person affected by some kind of damage), possessor (owner or soon-to-be owner of something, or the opposite: someone who has lost or is lacking something)

- Class 3: patient (affected person or thing), theme

If a verb has several theta-roles of this kind to assign, Class 1 normally has the highest rank, whereas Class 3 has the lowest. Unfortunately, the assignment of semantic roles to actual arguments of verbs has received a rather inconsistent treatment in the literature. This problem has been discussed by Dowty (1991), who suggests using proto-roles. An argument is assigned the proto-agent role if it has sufficiently many of the properties that were identified by Dowty as prototypical properties of agents (e.g., animacy, volitionality).

The mental lexicon contains *lexical entries* with the specific properties of syntactic words needed to use that word grammatically. Some of these properties are the following:

- form

- meaning (semantics)

- grammatical features: syntactic word class + morphosyntactic features

- theta-grid

(18) shows an example of a lexical entry:

(18)

form	*hilft* 'helps'
semantics	*helfen'*
grammatical features	verb,
	3rd person singular indicative present active

theta-grid		
theta-roles	<u>agent</u>	beneficiary
grammatical particularities		dative

Assigning semantic roles to specific syntactic requirements (beneficiary = dative) is also called *linking*.

Arguments are ordered according to their ranking: the highest argument is furthest left. In the case of *helfen*, the highest argument is the external argument, which is why the agent is underlined. With so-called unaccusative verbs,[3] the highest argument is not treated as the external argument. It would therefore not be underlined in the corresponding lexical entry.

3.1.4 $\overline{\mathrm{X}}$ theory

In GB, it is assumed that all syntactic structures licensed by the core grammar[4] correspond to the $\overline{\mathrm{X}}$ schema (see Section 2.5).[5] In the following sections, I will comment on the syntactic categories assumed and the basic assumptions with regard to the interpretation of grammatical rules.

3.1.4.1 Syntactic categories

The categories which can be used for the variable X in the $\overline{\mathrm{X}}$ schema are divided into lexical and functional categories. This correlates roughly with the difference between open and closed word classes. The following are lexical categories:

- V = verb

- N = noun

---

[3] See Perlmutter (1978) for a discussion of unaccusative verbs. The term *ergative verb* is also common, albeit a misnomer. See Burzio (1981, 1986) for the earliest work on unaccusatives in the Chomskyan framework and Grewendorf (1989) for German. Also, see Pullum (1988) on the usage of these terms and for a historical evaluation.

[4] Chomsky (1981a: 7–8) distinguishes between a regular area of language that is determined by a grammar that can be acquired using genetically determined language-specific knowledge and a periphery, to which irregular parts of language such as idioms (e.g., *to pull the wool over sb.'s eyes*) belong. See Section 16.3.

[5] Chomsky (1970: 210) allows for grammatical rules that deviate from the $\overline{\mathrm{X}}$ schema. It is, however, common practice to assume that languages exclusively use $\overline{\mathrm{X}}$ structures.

- A = adjective

- P = preposition/postposition

- Adv = adverb

Lexical categories can be represented using binary features and a cross-classification:[6]

Table 3.1: Representation of four lexical categories using two binary features

	−V	+V
−N	P = [−N, −V]	V = [−N, +V]
+N	N = [+N, −V]	A = [+N, +V]

Adverbs are viewed as intransitive prepositions and are therefore captured by the decomposition in the table above.

Using this cross-classification, it is possible to formulate generalizations. One can, for example, simply refer to adjectives and verbs: all lexical categories which are [+V] are either adjectives or verbs. Furthermore, one can say of [+N] categories (nouns and adjectives) that they can bear case.

Apart from this, some authors have tried to associate the head position with the feature values in Table 3.1 (see e.g., Grewendorf 1988: 52; Haftka 1996: 124; G. Müller 2011: 238). With prepositions and nouns, the head precedes the complement in German:

(19) a. *für* Marie
         for Marie

      b. *Bild*   von Maria
         picture of   Maria

With adjectives and verbs, the head is final:

(20) a. dem König *treu*
         the king loyal
         'Loyal to the king'

      b. der [dem Kind *helfende*] Mann
         the the   child helping   man
         'the man helping the child'

      c. dem Mann *helfen*
         the man help
         'help the man'

---

[6] See Chomsky (1970: 199) for a cross-classification of N, A and V, and Jackendoff (1977: Section 3.2) for a cross-classification that additionally includes P but has a different feature assignment.

This data seems to suggest that the head is final with [+V] categories and initial with [−V] categories. Unfortunately, this generalization runs into the problem that there are also postpositions in German. These are, like prepositions, not verbal, but do occur after the NP they require:

(21)   a. des Geldes *wegen*
           the money because

           'because of the money'

       b. die Nacht *über*
           the night during

           'during the night'

Therefore, one must either invent a new category, or abandon the attempt to use binary category features to describe ordering restrictions. If one were to place postpositions in a new category, it would be necessary to assume another binary feature.[7] Since this feature can have either a negative or a positive value, one would then have four additional categories. There are then eight possible feature combinations, some of which would not correspond to any plausible category.

For functional categories, GB does not propose a cross-classification. Usually, the following categories are assumed:

C   Complementizer (subordinating conjunctions such as *dass* 'that')
I   Finiteness (as well as Tense and Mood);
    also Infl in earlier work (inflection),
    T in more recent work (Tense)
D   Determiner (article, demonstrative)

3.1.4.2 Assumptions and rules

In GB, it is assumed that all rules must follow the $\overline{\text{X}}$ format discussed in Section 2.5. In other theories, rules which correspond to the $\overline{\text{X}}$ format are used along other rules which do not. If the strict version of $\overline{\text{X}}$ theory is assumed, this comes with the assumption of

---

[7] Martin Haspelmath has pointed out that one could assume a rule that moves a post-head argument into a pre-head position (see Riemsdijk 1978: 89 for the discussion of a transformational solution). This would be parallel to the realization of prepositional arguments of adjectives in German:

(i)   a. auf seinen Sohn stolz
          on his   son proud

          'proud of his son'

      b. stolz   auf seinen Sohn
          proud of his   son

But note that the situation is different with postpositions here, while all adjectives that take prepositional objects allow for both orders, this is not the case for prepositions. Most prepositions do not allow their object to occur before them. It is an idiosyncratic feature of some postpositions that they want to have their argument to the left.

endocentricity: every phrase has a head and every head is part of a phrase (put more technically: every head projects to a phrase).

Furthermore, as with phrase structure grammars, it is assumed that the branches of tree structures cannot cross (*Non-Tangling Condition*). This assumption is made by the majority of theories discussed in this book. There are, however, some variants of TAG, HPSG, Construction Grammar, and Dependency Grammar which allow crossing branches and therefore discontinuous constituents (Becker, Joshi & Rambow 1991; Reape 1994; Bergen & Chang 2005; Heringer 1996: 261; Eroms 2000: Section 9.6.2).

In $\overline{\text{X}}$ theory, one normally assumes that there are at most two projection levels (X′ and X″). However, there are some versions of Mainstream Generative Grammar and other theories which allow three or more levels (Jackendoff 1977; Uszkoreit 1987). In this chapter, I follow the standard assumption that there are two projection levels, that is, phrases have at least three levels:

- X^0 = head

- X′ = intermediate projection ($\overline{\text{X}}$, read: X bar)

- XP = highest projection (= X″ = $\overline{\overline{\text{X}}}$), also called *maximal projection*

3.1.5 CP and IP in English

Most work in Mainstream Generative Grammar is heavily influenced by previous publications dealing with English. If one wants to understand GB analyses of German and other languages, it is important to first understand the analyses of English and, for this reason, this will be the focus of this section. The CP/IP system is also assumed in LFG grammars of English and thus the following section also provides a foundation for understanding some of the fundamentals of LFG presented in Chapter 7.

In earlier work, the rules in (22a) and (22b) were proposed for English sentences (Chomsky 1981a: 19).

(22) a. S → NP VP
      b. S → NP Infl VP

Infl stands for *Inflection* as inflectional affixes are inserted at this position in the structure. The symbol AUX was also used instead of Infl in earlier work, since auxiliary verbs are treated in the same way as inflectional affixes. Figure 3.3 on the following page shows a sample analysis of a sentence with an auxiliary, which uses the rule in (22b).

Together with its complements, the verb forms a structural unit: the VP. The constituent status of the VP is supported by several constituent tests and further differences between subjects and objects regarding their positional restrictions.

The rules in (22) do not follow the $\overline{\text{X}}$ template since there is no symbol on the right-hand side of the rule with the same category as one on the left-hand side, that is, there is no head. In order to integrate rules like (22) into the general theory, Chomsky (1986a: 3)

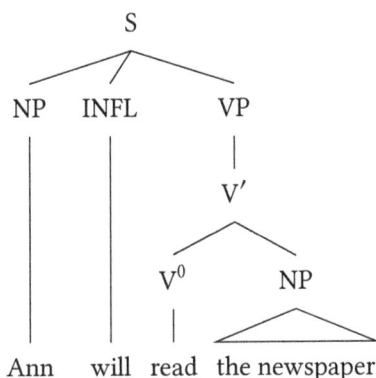

Figure 3.3: Sentence with an auxiliary verb following Chomsky (1981a: 19)

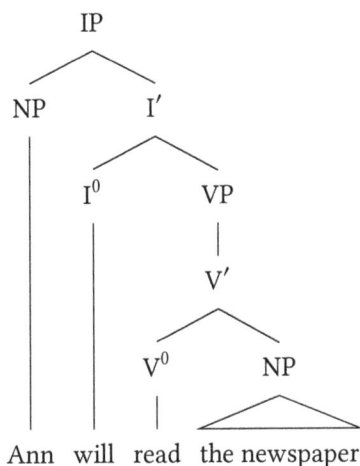

Figure 3.4: Sentence with auxiliary verb in the CP/IP system

developed a rule system with two layers above the verb phrase (VP), namely the CP/IP system. CP stands for *Complementizer Phrase*. The head of a CP can be a complementizer. Before we look at CPs in more detail, I will discuss an example of an IP in this new system. Figure 3.4 shows an IP with an auxiliary in the I^0 position. As we can see, this corresponds to the structure of the $\overline{X}$ template: I^0 is a head, which takes the VP as its complement and thereby forms I'. The subject is the specifier of the IP.

The sentences in (23) are analyzed as complementizer phrases (CPs), the complementizer is the head:

(23)   a. that Ann will read the newspaper
       b. that Ann reads the newspaper

In sentences such as (23), the CPs do not have a specifier. Figure 3.5 on the next page shows the analysis of (23a).

Yes/no-questions in English such as those in (24) are formed by moving the auxiliary verb in front of the subject.

(24)   Will Ann read the newspaper?

Let us assume that the structure of questions corresponds to the structure of sentences with complementizers. This means that questions are also CPs. Unlike the sentences in (23), however, there is no subordinating conjunction. In the D-structure of questions, the C^0 position is empty and the auxiliary verb is later moved to this position. Figure 3.6 on the following page shows an analysis of (24). The original position of the auxiliary is marked by the trace $_k$, which is coindexed with the moved auxiliary.

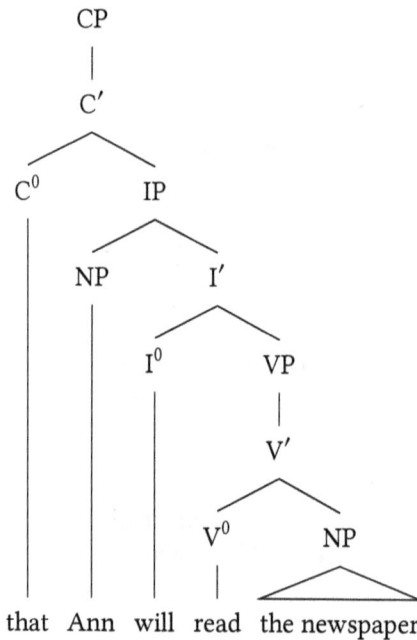

Figure 3.5: Complementizer phrase

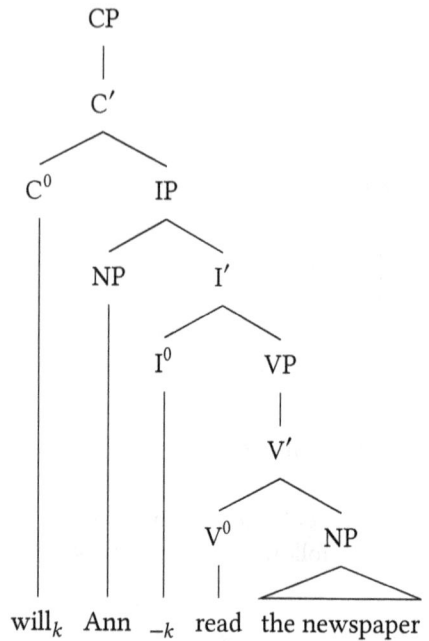

Figure 3.6: Polar question

wh-questions are formed by the additional movement of a constituent in front of the auxiliary; that is into the specifier position of the CP. Figure 3.7 on the following page shows the analysis of (25):

(25)   What will Ann read?

As before, the movement of the object of *read* is indicated by a trace. This is important when constructing the meaning of the sentence. The verb assigns some semantic role to the element in its object position. Therefore, one has to be able to "reconstruct" the fact that *what* actually originates in this position. This is ensured by coindexation of the trace with *what*.

Until now, I have not yet discussed sentences without auxiliaries such as (23b). In order to analyze this kind of sentences, one has to assume that the inflectional affix is present in the I^0 position. An example analysis is given in Figure 3.8 on the following page. Since the inflectional affix precedes the verb, some kind of movement operation still needs to take place. For theory-internal reasons, one does not wish to assume movement operations to positions lower in the tree, hence the verb has to move to the affix and not the other way around.

Following this excursus on the analysis of English sentences, we can now turn to German.

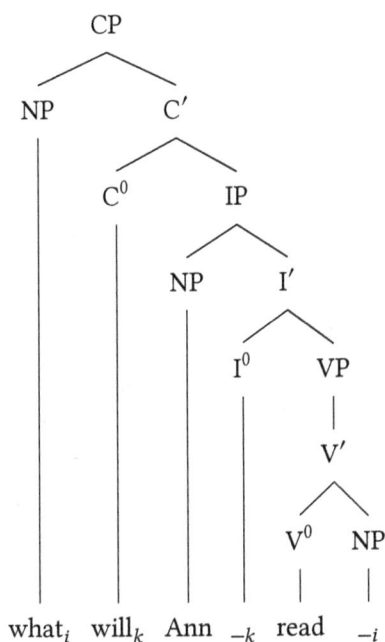

Figure 3.7: *wh*-question

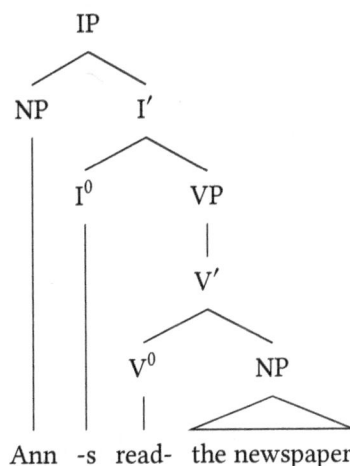

Figure 3.8: Sentence without auxiliary

3.1.6 The structure of the German clause

The CP/IP model has been adopted by many scholars for the analysis of German.[8] The categories C, I and V, together with their specifier positions, can be linked to the topological fields as shown in Figure 3.9 on the next page.

Note that SpecCP and SpecIP are not category symbols. They do not occur in grammars with rewrite rules. Instead, they simply describe positions in the tree.

As shown in Figure 3.9, it is assumed that the highest argument of the verb (the subject in simple sentences) has a special status. It is taken for granted that the subject always occurs outside of the VP, which is why it is referred to as the external argument. The VP itself does not have a specifier. In more recent work, however, the subject is generated in the specifier of the VP (Fukui & Speas 1986; Koopman & Sportiche 1991). In some languages, it is assumed that it moves to a position outside of the VP. In other languages such as German, this is the case at least under certain conditions (e.g., definiteness, see Diesing 1992). I am presenting the classical GB analysis here, where the subject is outside the VP. All arguments other than the subject are complements of the V, that are realized within the VP, that is, they are internal arguments. If the verb requires just one

---

[8] For GB analyses without IP, see Bayer & Kornfilt (1989), Höhle (1991a: 157), Haider (1993, 1997a) and Sternefeld (2006: Section IV.3). Haider assumes that the function of I is integrated into the verb. In LFG, an IP is assumed for English (Bresnan 2001: Section 6.2; Dalrymple 2001: Section 3.2.1), but not for German (Berman 2003a: Section 3.2.3.2). In HPSG, no IP is assumed.

CP

C′

IP

I′

VP

XP   C⁰   XP   V⁰   I⁰

SpecCP prefield	C⁰ left SB	IP (without I⁰, V⁰) middle field		V⁰, I⁰ right SB
		SpecIP subject position	phrases inside the VP	

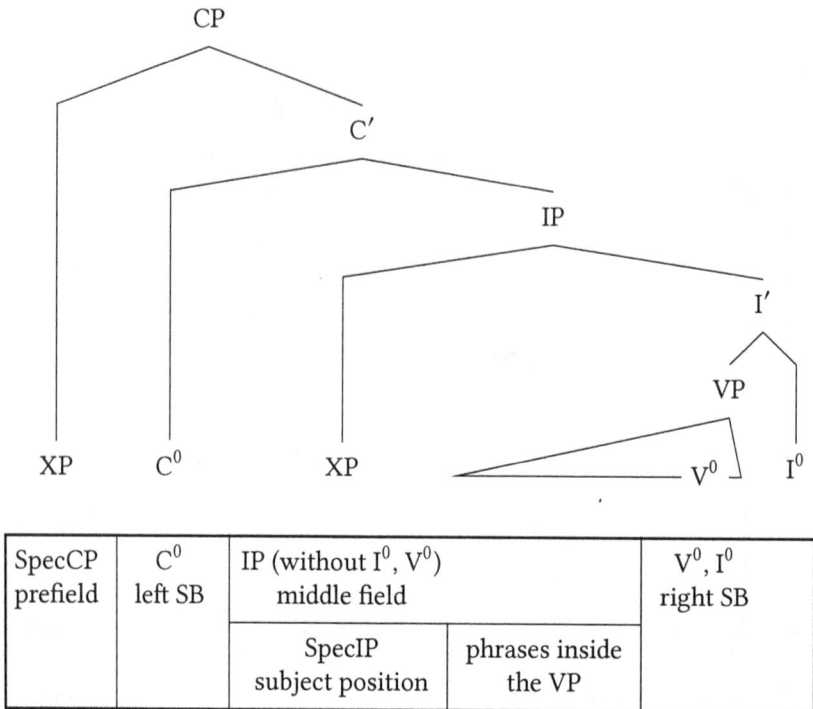

Figure 3.9: CP, IP and VP and the topological model of German

complement, then this is the sister of the head V^0 and the daughter of V′ according to the $\overline{\overline{X}}$ schema. The accusative object is the prototypical complement.

Following the $\overline{X}$ template, adjuncts branch off above the complements of V′. The analysis of a VP with an adjunct is shown in Figure 3.10 on the following page.

(26) weil   der Mann morgen   den Jungen trifft
      because the man tomorrow the boy   meets
      'because the man is meeting the boy tomorrow'

3.2 Verb position

In German, the position of the heads of VP and IP (V^0 and I^0) are to the right of their complements and V^0 and I^0 form part of the right sentence bracket. The subject and all other constituents (complements and adjuncts) all occur to the left of V^0 and I^0 and form the middle field. It is assumed that German – at least in terms of D-structure – is an SOV language (= a language with the base order Subject–Object–Verb). The analysis of German as an SOV language is almost as old as Transformational Grammar itself. It

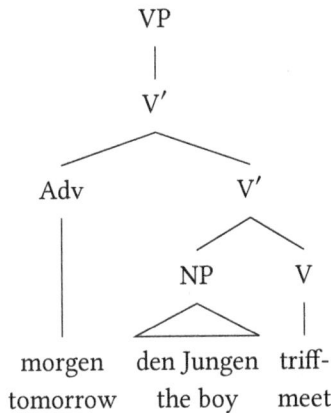

Figure 3.10: Analysis of adjuncts in GB theory

was originally proposed by Bierwisch (1963: 34).[9] Unlike German, Germanic languages like Danish, English and Romance languages like French are SVO languages, whereas Welsh and Arabic are VSO languages. Around 40 % of all languages belong to the SOV languages, around 35 % are SVO (Dryer 2013c).

The assumption of verb-final order as the base order is motivated by the following observations:[10]

1. Verb particles form a close unit with the verb.

(27) a. weil   er morgen an-fängt
          because he tomorrow PRT-starts

          'because he is starting tomorrow'

    b. Er fängt morgen   an.
        he starts tomorrow PRT

        'He is starting tomorrow.'

This unit can only be seen in verb-final structures, which speaks for the fact that this structure reflects the base order.

---

[9] Bierwisch attributes the assumption of an underlying verb-final order to Fourquet (1957). A German translation of the French manuscript cited by Bierwisch can be found in Fourquet (1970: 117–135). For other proposals, see Bach (1962), Reis (1974), Koster (1975) and Thiersch (1978: Chapter 1). Analyses which assume that German has an underlying SOV pattern were also suggested in GPSG (Jacobs 1986: 110), LFG (Berman 1996: Section 2.1.4) and HPSG (Kiss & Wesche 1991; Oliva 1992; Netter 1992; Kiss 1993; Frank 1994; Kiss 1995; Feldhaus 1997; Meurers 2000; Müller 2005b, 2015b).

[10] For points 1 and 2, see Bierwisch (1963: 34–36). For point 4 see Netter (1992: Section 2.3).

Verbs which are derived from a noun by back-formation (e.g., *uraufführen* 'to perform something for the first time'), can often not be divided into their component parts and V2 clauses are therefore ruled out (This was first mentioned by Höhle (1991b) in unpublished work. The first published source is Haider (1993: 62)):

(28) a. weil   sie   das Stück heute ur-auf-führen
          because they the play today PREF-PART-lead

      'because they are performing the play for the first time today'

  b. * Sie ur-auf-führen heute das Stück.
       they PREF-PART-lead today the play

  c. * Sie   führen heute das Stück ur-auf.
       they lead   today the play PREF-PART

The examples show that there is only one possible position for this kind of verb. This order is the one that is assumed to be the base order.

2. Verbs in non-finite clauses and in finite subordinate clauses with a conjunction are always in final position (I am ignoring the possibility of extraposing constituents):

(29) a. Der Clown versucht, Kurt-Martin die Ware zu geben.
          the clown tries   Kurt-Martin the goods to give

      'The clown is trying to give Kurt-Martin the goods.'

  b. dass der Clown Kurt-Martin die Ware gibt
      that the clown Kurt-Martin the goods gives

      'that the clown gives Kurt-Martin the goods'

3. If one compares the position of the verb in German with Danish (Danish is an SVO language like English), then one can clearly see that the verbs in German form a cluster at the end of the sentence, whereas they occur before any objects in Danish (Ørsnes 2009a: 146):

(30) a. dass er ihn gesehen$_3$ haben$_2$ muss$_1$
          that he him seen   have   must

  b. at han må$_1$ have$_2$ set$_3$ ham
      that he must have   seen him

      'that he must have seen him'

4. The scope relations of the adverbs in (31) depend on their order: the left-most adverb has scope over the two following elements.[11] This was explained by assuming the following structure:

(31)   a. weil   er [absichtlich   [nicht lacht]]
          because he intentionally   not   laughs

       'because he is intentionally not laughing'

       b. weil   er [nicht [absichtlich   lacht]]
          because he not   intentionally laughs

       'because he is not laughing intentionally'

It is interesting to note that scope relations are not affected by verb position. If one assumes that sentences with verb-second order have the underlying structure

---

[11] At this point, it should be mentioned that there seem to be exceptions from the rule that modifiers to the left take scope over those to their right. Kasper (1994: 47) discusses examples such as (i), which go back to Bartsch & Vennemann (1972: 137).

(i)   a. Peter liest gut wegen   der Nachhilfestunden.
         Peter reads well because.of the tutoring

      b. Peter liest wegen   der Nachhilfestunden gut.
         Peter reads because.of the tutoring   well

      'Peter can read well thanks to the tutoring.'

As Koster (1975: Section 6) and Reis (1980: 67) have shown, these are not particularly convincing counterexamples as the right sentence bracket is not filled in these examples and therefore the examples are not necessarily instances of normal reordering inside of the middle field, but could instead involve extraposition of the PP. As noted by Koster and Reis, these examples become ungrammatical if one fills the right bracket and does not extrapose the causal adjunct:

(ii) a. * Hans hat gut wegen   der Nachhilfestunden gelesen.
            Hans has well because.of the tutoring   read

      b. Hans hat gut gelesen wegen   der Nachhilfestunden.
         Hans has well read   because.of the tutoring

      'Hans has been reading well because of the tutoring.'

However, the following example from Crysmann (2004: 383) shows that, even with the right bracket occupied, one can still have an order where an adjunct to the right has scope over one to the left:

(iii) Da   muß es schon   erhebliche Probleme mit der Ausrüstung gegeben haben, da   wegen
       there must it already serious   problems with the equipment given   have since because.of
       schlechten Wetters ein Reinhold Messmer niemals aufgäbe.
       bad   weather a   Reinhold Messmer never   would.give.up

       'There really must have been some serious problems with the equipment because someone like Reinhold Messmer would never give up just because of some bad weather.'

Nevertheless, this does not change anything regarding the fact that the corresponding cases in (31) and (32) have the same meaning regardless of the position of the verb. The general means of semantic composition may well have to be implemented in the same way as in Crysmann's analysis.

in (31), then this fact requires no further explanation. (32) shows the derived S-structure for (31):

(32)   a.   Er lacht$_i$ [absichtlich   [nicht $_{-i}$]].
           he laughs intentionally   not

           'He is intentionally not laughing.'

     b.   Er lacht$_i$ [nicht [absichtlich $_{-i}$]].
           he laughs not   intentionally

           'He is not laughing intentionally.'

After motivating and briefly sketching the analysis of verb-final order, I will now look at the CP/IP analysis of German in more detail. C^0 corresponds to the left sentence bracket and can be filled in two different ways: in subordinate clauses introduced by a conjunction, the subordinating conjunction (the complementizer) occupies C^0 as in English. The verb remains in the right sentence bracket, as illustrated by (33).

(33)   dass jeder   diesen Mann kennt
      that everybody this   man   knows

      'that everybody knows this man'

Figure 3.11 on the following page gives an analysis of (33). In verb-first and verb-second clauses, the finite verb is moved to C^0 via the I^0 position: $V^0 \rightarrow I^0 \rightarrow C^0$. Figure 3.12 on page 104 shows the analysis of (34):

(34)   Kennt jeder   diesen Mann?
      knows everybody this   man

      'Does everybody know this man?'

The C^0 position is empty in the D-structure of (34). Since it is not occupied by a complementizer, the verb can move there.

3.3 Long-distance dependencies

The SpecCP position corresponds to the prefield and can be filled by any XP in declarative clauses in German. In this way, one can derive the sentences in (36) from (35) by moving a constituent in front of the verb:

(35)   Gibt der   Mann dem   Kind jetzt den   Mantel?
      gives the.NOM man   the.DAT child now the.ACC coat

      'Is the man going to give the child the coat now?'

(36)   a.   Der   Mann gibt dem   Kind jetzt den   Mantel.
           the.NOM man   gives the.DAT child now the.ACC coat

           'The man is giving the child the coat now.'

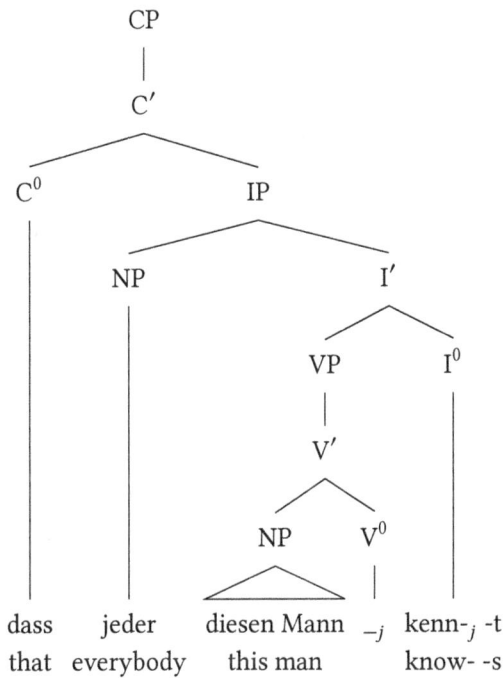

Figure 3.11: Sentence with a complementizer in C^0

b. Dem   Kind gibt der   Mann jetzt den   Mantel.
   the.DAT child gives the.NOM man   now the.ACC coat

c. Den   Mantel gibt der   Mann dem   Kind jetzt.
   the.ACC coat   gives the.NOM man   the.DAT child now

d. Jetzt gibt der   Mann dem   Kind den   Mantel.
   now gives the.NOM man   the.DAT child the.ACC coat

Since any constituent can be placed in front of the finite verb, German is treated typologically as one of the verb-second languages (V2). Thus, it is a verb-second language with SOV base order. English, on the other hand, is an SVO language without the V2 property, whereas Danish is a V2 language with SVO as its base order (see Ørsnes 2009a for Danish).

Figure 3.13 on page 105 shows the structure derived from Figure 3.12. The crucial factor for deciding which phrase to move is the *information structure* of the sentence. That is, material connected to previously mentioned or otherwise-known information is placed further left (preferably in the prefield) and new information tends to occur to the right. Fronting to the prefield in declarative clauses is often referred to as *topicalization*. But this is rather a misnomer, since the focus (informally: the constituent being asked for) can also occur in the prefield. Furthermore, expletive pronouns can occur there and these

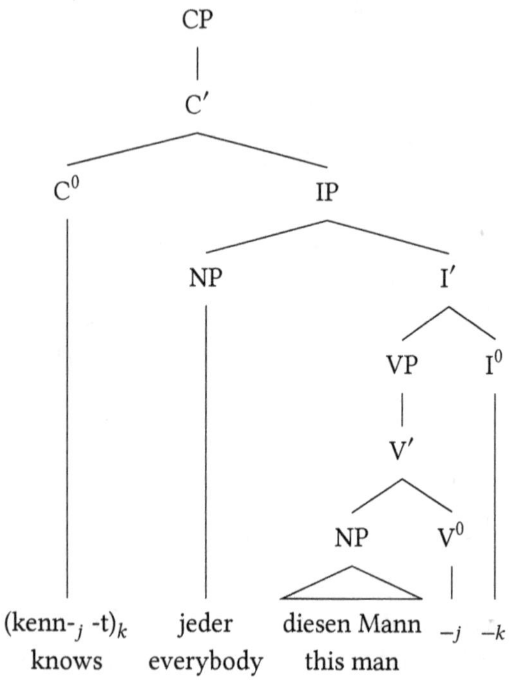

Figure 3.12: Verb position in GB

are non-referential and as such cannot be linked to preceding or known information, hence expletives can never be topics.

Transformation-based analyses also work for so-called *long-distance dependencies*, that is, dependencies crossing several phrase boundaries:

(37) a. [Um   zwei Millionen Mark]$_i$ soll   er versucht haben, [eine
         around two   million   Deutsche.Marks should he tried   have   an
         Versicherung $_i$ zu betrügen].[12]
         insurance.company   to deceive

      'He apparently tried to cheat an insurance company out of two million Deutsche Marks.'

   b. „Wer$_i$, glaubt   er, daß er $_i$ ist?" erregte sich ein Politiker vom   Nil.[13]
         who believes he that he   is   retort REFL a politician from.the Nile

      ' "Who does he think he is?", a politician from the Nile exclaimed.'

---

[12] taz, 04.05.2001, p. 20.
[13] Spiegel, 8/1999, p. 18.

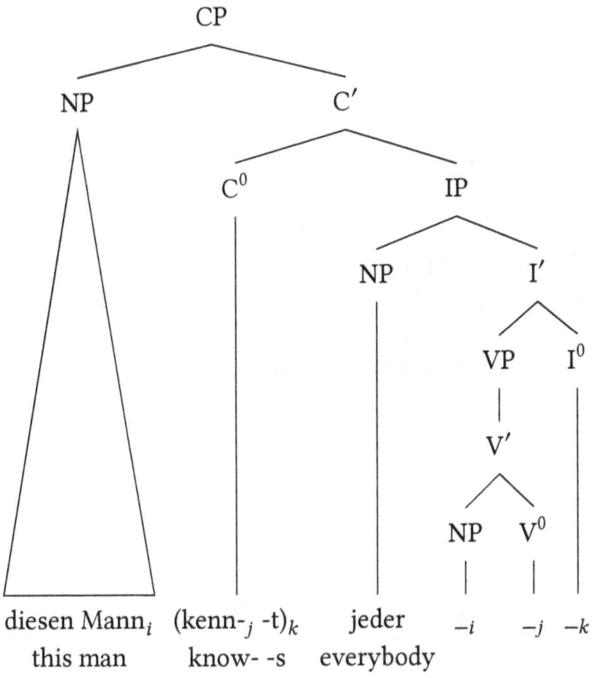

CP

NP   C′

C⁰   IP

NP   I′

VP   I⁰

V′

NP   V⁰

diesen Mann$_i$ (kenn-$_j$ -t)$_k$ jeder   –i –j –k
this man   know- -s   everybody

Figure 3.13: Fronting in GB theory

c. Wen$_i$ glaubst du, daß ich _$_i$ gesehen habe?[14]
   who believe you that I   seen   have

   'Who do you think I saw?'

d. [Gegen ihn]$_i$ falle es den Republikanern hingegen schwerer,
   against him fall it the Republicans   however more.difficult
   [[Angriffe _$_i$] zu lancieren].[15]
     attacks   to launch

   'It is, however, more difficult for the Republicans to launch attacks against
   him.'

The elements in the prefield in the examples in (37) all originate from more deeply embedded phrases. In GB, it is assumed that long-distance dependencies across sentence
boundaries are derived in steps (Grewendorf 1988: 75–79), that is, in the analysis of
(37c), the interrogative pronoun is moved to the specifier position of the *dass*-clause and
is moved from there to the specifier of the matrix clause. The reason for this is that there
are certain restrictions on movement which must be checked locally.

---

[14] Scherpenisse (1986: 84).
[15] taz, 08.02.2008, p. 9.

3.4 Passive

Before I turn to the analysis of the passive in Section 3.4.2, the first subsection will elaborate on the differences between structural and lexical case.

3.4.1 Structural and lexical case

The case of many case-marked arguments is dependent on the syntactic environment in which the head of the argument is realized. These arguments are referred to as arguments with *structural case*. Case-marked arguments, which do not bear structural case, are said to have *lexical case*.[16]

The following are examples of structural case:[17]

(38) a. Der   Installateur kommt.
         the.NOM plumber   comes

         'The plumber is coming.'

      b. Der Mann lässt den   Installateur kommen.
         the man   lets the.ACC plumber   come

         'The man is getting the plumber to come.'

      c. das Kommen des   Installateurs
         the coming   of.the plumber

         'the plumber's visit'

In the first example, the subject is in the nominative case, whereas *Installateur* 'plumber' is in accusative in the second example and even in the genitive in the third following nominalization. The accusative case of objects is normally structural case. This case becomes nominative under passivization:

(39) a. Karl schlägt den   Weltmeister.
         Karl beats   the.ACC world.champion

         'Karl beats the world champion.'

      b. Der   Weltmeister   wird geschlagen.
         the.NOM world.champion is   beaten

         'The world champion is being beaten.'

---

[16] Furthermore, there is a so-called *agreeing case* (see page 41) and *semantic case*. Agreeing case is found in predicatives. This case also changes depending on the structure involved, but the change is due to the antecedent element changing its case. Semantic case depends on the function of certain phrases (e.g., temporal accusative adverbials). Furthermore, as with lexical case of objects, semantic case does not change depending on the syntactic environment. For the analysis of the passive, which will be discussed in this section, only structural and lexical case will be relevant.

[17] Compare Heinz & Matiasek (1994: 200).

    (38b) is a so-called AcI construction. AcI stands for *Accusativus cum infinitivo*, which means "accusative with infinitive". The logical subject of the embedded verb (*kommen* 'to come' in this case) becomes the accusative object of the matrix verb *lassen* 'to let'. Examples for AcI-verbs are perception verbs such as *hören* 'to hear' and *sehen* 'to see' as well as *lassen* 'to let'.

Unlike the accusative, the genitive governed by a verb is a lexical case. The case of a genitive object does not change when the verb is passivized.

(40) a. Wir gedenken der   Opfer.
        we remember the.GEN victims

    b. Der   Opfer wird gedacht.
        the.GEN victims are remembered

        'The victims are being remembered.'

(40b) is an example of the so-called *impersonal passive*. Unlike example (39b), where the accusative object became the subject, there is no subject in (40b). See Section 1.7.1.

Similarly, there is no change in case with dative objects:

(41) a. Der Mann hat ihm   geholfen.
        the man   has him.DAT helped

        'The man has helped him.'

    b. Ihm   wird geholfen.
        him.DAT is   helped

        'He is being helped.'

It still remains controversial as to whether all datives should be treated as lexical or whether some or all of the datives in verbal environments should be treated as instances of structural case. For reasons of space, I will not recount this discussion but instead refer the interested reader to Chapter 14 of Müller (2007b). In what follows, I assume – like Haider (1986a: 20) – that the dative is in fact a lexical case.

3.4.2 Case assignment and the Case Filter

In GB, it is assumed that the subject receives case from (finite) I and that the case of the remaining arguments comes from V (Chomsky 1981a: 50; Haider 1984: 26; Fanselow & Felix 1987: 71–73).

Principle 2 (Case Principle)
- *V assigns objective case (accusative) to its complement if it bears structural case.*

- *When finite, INFL assigns case to the subject.*

The Case Filter rules out structures where case has not been assigned to an NP.

Figure 3.14 on the following page shows the Case Principle in action with the example in (42a).[18]

---

[18] The figure does not correspond to $\overline{\text{X}}$ theory in its classic form, since *der Frau* 'the woman' is a complement which is combined with V′. In classical $\overline{\text{X}}$ theory, all complements have to be combined with V^0. This leads to a problem in ditransitive structures since the structures have to be binary (see Larson (1988) for a treatment of double object constructions). Furthermore, in the following figures the verb has been left in V^0 for reasons of clarity. In order to create a well-formed S-structure, the verb would have to move to its affix in I^0.

(42)   a. [dass] der Mann der   Frau   den   Jungen zeigt
           that the man   the.DAT woman the.ACC boy   shows

       'that the man shows the boy to the woman'

       b. [dass] der Junge   der   Frau   gezeigt wird
           that   the boy.NOM the.DAT woman shown   is

       'that the boy is shown to the woman'

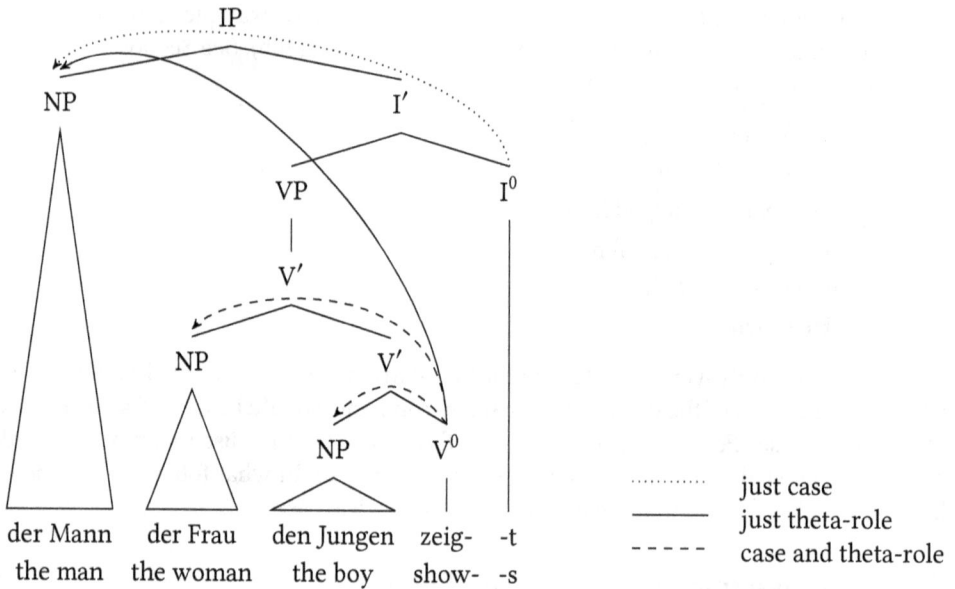

Figure 3.14: Case and theta-role assignment in active clauses

The passive morphology blocks the subject and absorbs the structural accusative. The object that would get accusative in the active receives only a semantic role in its base position in the passive, but it does not get case the absorbed case. Therefore, it has to move to a position where case can be assigned to it (Chomsky 1981a: 124). Figure 3.15 on the following page shows how this works for example (42b).

This movement-based analysis works well for English since the underlying object always has to move:

(43)   a. The mother gave [the girl] [a cookie].

       b. [The girl] was given [a cookie] (by the mother).

       c. * It was given [the girl] [a cookie].

(43c) shows that filling the subject position with an expletive is not possible, so the object really has to move. However, Lenerz (1977: Section 4.4.3) showed that such a movement is not obligatory in German:

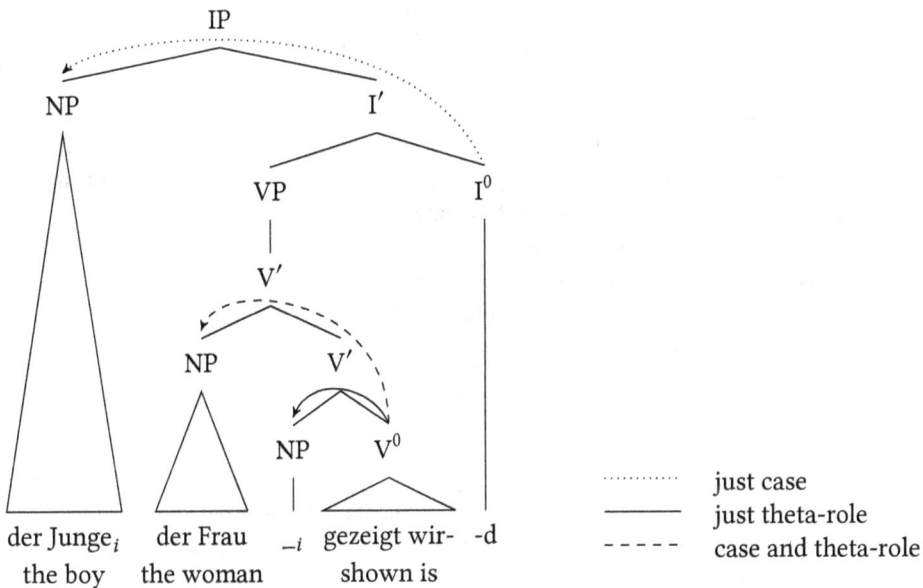

Figure 3.15: Case and theta-role assignment in passive clauses

					· · · · · · · · ·	just case	

(just case / just theta-role / case and theta-role — legend)

(44) a. weil   das   Mädchen dem   Jungen den   Ball schenkte
         because the.NOM girl   the.DAT boy   the.ACC ball gave
         'because the girl gave the ball to the boy'

   b. weil   dem   Jungen der   Ball geschenkt wurde
      because the.DAT boy   the.NOM ball given   was
      'because the ball was given to the boy'

   c. weil   der   Ball dem   Jungen geschenkt wurde
      because the.NOM ball the.DAT boy   given   was

In comparison to (44c), (44b) is the unmarked order. *der Ball* 'the ball' in (44b) occurs in the same position as *den Ball* in (44a), that is, no movement is necessary. Only the case differs. (44c) is, however, somewhat marked in comparison to (44b). The analysis which has been proposed for cases such as (44b) involves abstract movement: the elements stay in their positions, but are connected to the subject position and receive their case information from there. Grewendorf (1993: 1311) assumes that there is an empty expletive pronoun in the subject position of sentences such as (44b) as well as in the subject position of sentences with an impersonal passive such as (45):[19]

(45)   weil   heute nicht gearbeitet wird
        because today not   worked   is
        'because there will be no work done today'

---

[19] See Koster (1986: 11–12) for a parallel analysis for Dutch as well as Lohnstein (2014) for a movement-based account of the passive that also involves an empty expletive for the analysis of the impersonal passive.

A silent expletive pronoun is something that one cannot see or hear and that does not carry any meaning. For discussion of this kind of empty elements, see Section 13.1.3 and Chapter 19.

In the following chapters, I describe alternative treatments of the passive that do without mechanisms such as empty elements that are connected to argument positions and seek to describe the passive in a more general, cross-linguistically consistent manner as the suppression of the most prominent argument.

A further question which needs to be answered is why the accusative object does not receive case from the verb. This is captured by a constraint, which goes back to Burzio (1986: 178–185) and is therefore referred to as *Burzio's Generalization.*[20]

(46) Burzio's Generalization (modified):
If V does not have an external argument, then it does not assign (structural) accusative case.

Koster (1986: 12) has pointed out that the passive in English cannot be derived by Case Theory since if one allowed empty expletive subjects for English as well as German and Dutch, then it would be possible to have analyses such as the following in (47) where np is an empty expletive:

(47) np was read the book.

Koster rather assumes that subjects in English are either bound by other elements (that is, non-expletive) or lexically filled, that is, filled by visible material. Therefore, the structure in (47) would be ruled out and it would be ensured that *the book* would have to be placed in front of the finite verb so that the subject position is filled.

3.5 Local reordering

Arguments in the middle field can, in principle, occur in an almost arbitrary order. (48) exemplifies this:

---

[20] Burzio's original formulation was equivalent to the following: a verb assigns accusative if and only if it assigns a semantic role to its subject. This claim is problematic from both sides. In (i), the verb does not assign a semantic role to the subject, however there is nevertheless accusative case:

(i) Mich friert.
me.ACC freezes
'I am freezing.'

One therefore has to differentiate between structural and lexical accusative and modify Burzio's Generalization accordingly. The existence of verbs like *begegnen* 'to bump into' is problematic for the other side of the implication. *begegnen* has a subject but still does not assign accusative but rather dative:

(ii) Peter begegnete einem Mann.
Peter met a.DAT man
'Peter met a man.'

See Haider (1999) and Webelhuth (1995: 89) as well as the references cited there for further problems with Burzio's Generalization.

(48) a. [weil]   der Mann der Frau   das Buch gibt
         because the man   the woman the book gives

       'because the man gives the book to the woman'

      b. [weil]   der Mann das Buch der Frau   gibt
         because the man   the book the woman gives

      c. [weil]   das Buch der Mann der Frau   gibt
         because the book the man   the woman gives

      d. [weil]   das Buch der Frau   der Mann gibt
         because the book the woman the man   gives

      e. [weil]   der Frau   der Mann das Buch gibt
         because the woman the man   the book gives

      f. [weil]   der Frau   das Buch der Mann gibt
         because the woman the book the man   gives

In (48b–f), the constituents receive different stress and the number of contexts in which each sentence can be uttered is more restricted than in (48a) (Höhle 1982). The order in (48a) is therefore referred to as the *neutral order* or *unmarked order*.

Two proposals have been made for analyzing these orders: the first suggestion assumes that the five orderings in (48b–f) are derived from a single underlying order by means of Move-α (Frey 1993). As an example, the analysis of (48c) is given in Figure 3.16 on the following page. The object *das Buch* 'the book' is moved to the left and adjoined to the topmost IP.

An argument that has often been used to support this analysis is the fact that scope ambiguities exist in sentences with reorderings which are not present in sentences in the base order. The explanation of such ambiguities comes from the assumption that the scope of quantifiers can be derived from their position in the surface structure as well as their position in the deep structure. If the position in both the surface and deep structure are the same, that is, when there has not been any movement, then there is only one reading possible. If movement has taken place, however, then there are two possible readings (Frey 1993):

(49) a. Es ist nicht der Fall, daß er mindestens einem Verleger fast   jedes Gedicht
         it is not   the case that he at.least   one   publisher almost every poem
         anbot.
         offered

       'It is not the case that he offered at least one publisher almost every poem.'

      b. Es ist nicht der Fall, daß er fast   jedes Gedicht$_i$ mindestens einem Verleger
         it is not   the case that he almost every poem   at.least   one   publisher
         _$_i$ anbot.
            offered

       'It is not the case that he offered almost every poem to at least one publisher.'

```
                              IP
             ┌────────────────┴────────┐
         NP[acc]ᵢ                      IP
            ╱│╲            ┌────────────┴────────┐
           ╱ │ ╲       NP[nom]                   I′
          ╱  │  ╲        ╱│╲            ┌─────────┴───────┐
         ╱   │   ╲      ╱ │ ╲          VP                 I⁰
        ╱    │    ╲    ╱  │  ╲          │                 │
       ╱     │     ╲  ╱   │   ╲         V′                │
      ╱      │      ╲╱    │    ╲  ┌──────┴──────┐         │
     ╱       │       ╲    │   NP[dat]          V′         │
    ╱        │        ╲   │     ╱╲        ┌─────┴───┐     │
   ╱         │         ╲  │    ╱  ╲      NP    V⁰         │
  ╱          │          ╲ │   ╱    ╲      │     │         │
 das Buch   der Mann   der Frau    _ᵢ   gib-   -t
 the book   the man    the woman        give-  -s
```

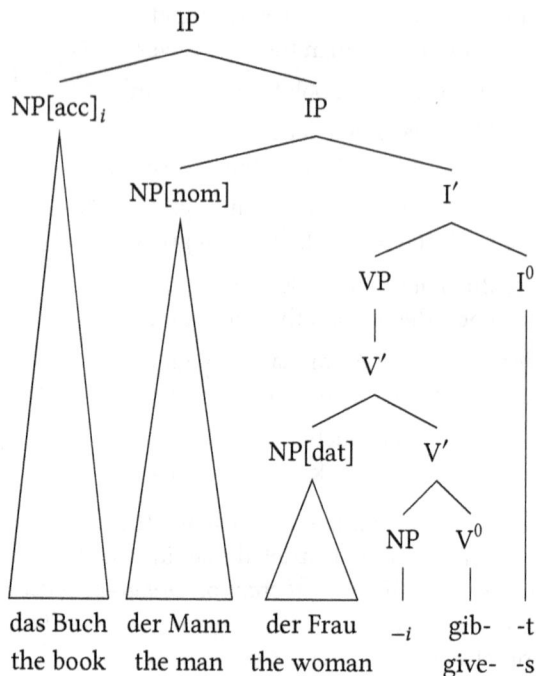

Figure 3.16: Analysis of local reordering as adjunction to IP

It turns out that approaches assuming traces run into problems as they predict certain readings for sentences with multiple traces which do not exist (see Kiss 2001: 146 and Fanselow 2001: Section 2.6). For instance in an example such as (50), it should be possible to interpret *mindestens einem Verleger* 'at least one publisher' at the position of $_{-i}$, which would lead to a reading where *fast jedes Gedicht* 'almost every poem' has scope over *mindestens einem Verleger* 'at least one publisher'. However, this reading does not exist.

(50) Ich glaube, dass mindestens einem Verlegerᵢ fast   jedes Gedichtⱼ nur dieser
      I   believe that at.least   one publisher almost every poem   only this
      Dichter $_{-i}$ $_{-j}$ angeboten hat.
      poet   offered   has
      'I think that only this poet offered almost every poem to at least one publisher.'

Sauerland & Elbourne (2002: 308) discuss analogous examples from Japanese, which they credit to Kazuko Yatsushiro. They develop an analysis where the first step is to move the accusative object in front of the subject. Then, the dative object is placed in front of that and then, in a third movement, the accusative is moved once more. The last movement can take place to construct either the S-structure[21] or as a movement to

---

[21] The authors are working in the Minimalist framework. This means there is no longer S-structure strictly speaking. I have simply translated the analysis into the terms used here.

construct the phonological form. In the latter case, this movement will not have any semantic effects. While this analysis can predict the correct available readings, it does require a number of additional movement operations with intermediate steps.

The alternative to a movement analysis is so-called *base generation*: the starting structure generated by phrase structure rules is referred to as the *base*. One variant of base generation assumes that the verb is combined with one argument at a time and each θ-role is assigned in the respective head-argument configuration. The order in which arguments are combined with the verb is not specified, which means that all of the orders in (48) can be generated directly without any transformations.[22] This kind of analysis has been proposed for GB by Fanselow (2001).[23] For the discussion of different approaches to describing constituent position, see Fanselow (1993).

3.6 Summary and classification

Works in GB and some contributions to the Minimalist Program (see Chapter 4) have led to a number of new discoveries in both language-specific and cross-linguistic research. In the following, I will focus on some aspects of German syntax.

The analysis of verb movement developed in Transformational Grammar by Bierwisch (1963: 34), Reis (1974), Koster (1975), Thiersch (1978: Chapter 1) and den Besten (1983) has become the standard analysis in almost all grammar models (possibly with the exception of Construction Grammar and Dependency Grammar).

The work by Lenerz (1977) on constituent order has influenced analyses in other frameworks (the linearization rules in GPSG and HPSG go back to Lenerz' descriptions). Haider's work on constituent order, case and passive (1984; 1985b; 1985a; 1986a; 1990b; 1993) has had a significant influence on LFG and HPSG analyses of German.

The entire configurationality discussion, that is, whether it is better to assume that the subject of finite verbs in German is inside or outside the VP, was important (for instance Haider 1982; Grewendorf 1983; Kratzer 1984, 1996; Webelhuth 1985; Sternefeld 1985b; Scherpenisse 1986; Fanselow 1987; Grewendorf 1988; Dürscheid 1989; Webelhuth 1990; Oppenrieder 1991; Wilder 1991; Haider 1993; Grewendorf 1993; Frey 1993; Lenerz 1994; Meinunger 2000) and German unaccusative verbs received their first detailed discussion in GB circles (Grewendorf 1989; Fanselow 1992a). The works by Fanselow and Frey on constituent order, in particular with regard to information structure, have advanced German syntax quite considerably (Fanselow 1988, 1990, 1993, 2000a, 2001, 2003b,c, 2004a; Frey 2000, 2001, 2004a, 2005). Infinitive constructions, complex predicates and partial

---

[22] Compare this to the grammar in (6) on page 55. This grammar combines a V and an NP to form a new V. Since nothing is said about the case of the argument in the phrase structure rule, the NPs can be combined with the verb in any order.

[23] The base generation analysis is the natural analysis in the HPSG framework. It has already been developed by Gunji in 1986 for Japanese and will be discussed in more detail in Section 9.4. Sauerland & Elbourne (2002: 313–314) claim that they show that syntax has to be derivational, that is, a sequence of syntactic trees has to be derived. I am of the opinion that this cannot generally be shown to be the case. There is, for example, an analysis by Kiss (2001) which shows that scope phenomena can be explained well by constraint-based approaches.

fronting have also received detailed and successful treatments in the GB/MP frameworks (Bierwisch 1963; Evers 1975; Haider 1982, 1986b, 1990a, 1991, 1993; Grewendorf 1983, 1987, 1988; den Besten 1985; Sternefeld 1985b; Fanselow 1987, 2002; von Stechow & Sternefeld 1988; Bayer & Kornfilt 1989; G. Müller 1996a, 1998; Vogel & Steinbach 1998). In the area of secondary predication, the work by Winkler (1997) is particularly noteworthy.

This list of works from subdisciplines of grammar is somewhat arbitrary (it corresponds more or less to my own research interests) and is very much focused on German. There are, of course, a wealth of other articles on other languages and phenomena, which should be recognized without having to be individually listed here.

In the remainder of this section, I will critically discuss two points: the model of language acquisition of the Principles & Parameters framework and the degree of formalization inside Chomskyan linguistics (in particular the last few decades and the consequences this has). Some of these points will be mentioned again in Part II.

3.6.1 Explaining language acquisition

One of the aims of Chomskyan research on grammar is to explain language acquisition. In GB, one assumed a very simple set of rules, which was the same for all languages ($\overline{X}$ theory), as well as general principles that hold for all languages, but which could be parametrized for individual languages or language classes. It was assumed that a parameter was relevant for multiple phenomena. The Principles & Parameters model was particularly fruitful and led to a number of interesting studies in which commonalities and differences between languages were uncovered. From the point of view of language acquisition, the idea of a parameter which is set according to the input has often been cricitized as it cannot be reconciled with observable facts: after setting a parameter, a learner should have immediately mastered certain aspects of that language. Chomsky (1986b: 146) uses the metaphor of switches which can be flipped one way or the other. As it is assumed that various areas of grammar are affected by parameters, setting one parameter should have a significant effect on the rest of the grammar of a given learner. However, the linguistic behavior of children does not change in an abrupt fashion as would be expected (Bloom 1993: 731; Haider 1993: 6; Abney 1996: 3; Ackerman & Webelhuth 1998: Section 9.1; Tomasello 2000, 2003; Newmeyer 2005). Furthermore, it has not been possible to prove that there is a correlation between a certain parameter and various grammatical phenomena. For more on this, see Chapter 16.

The Principles & Parameters model nevertheless remains interesting for cross-linguistic research. Every theory has to explain why the verb precedes its objects in English and follows them in Japanese. One can name this difference a parameter and then classify languages accordingly, but whether this is actually relevant for language acquisition is being increasingly called in question.

3.6.2 Formalization

In his 1963 work on Transformational Grammar, Bierwisch writes the following:[24]

> It is very possible that the rules that we formulated generate sentences which are outside of the set of grammatical sentences in an unpredictable way, that is, they violate grammaticality due to properties that we did not deliberately exclude in our examination. This is meant by the statement that a grammar is a hypothesis about the structure of a language. A systematic check of the implications of a grammar that is appropriate for natural languages is surely a task that cannot be done by hand any more. This task could be solved by implementing the grammar as a calculating task on a computer so that it becomes possible to verify to which degree the result deviates from the language to be described. (Bierwisch 1963: 163)

Bierwisch's claim is even more valid in light of the empirical progress made in the last decades. For example, Ross (1967) identified restrictions for movement and long-distance dependencies and Perlmutter (1978) discovered unaccusative verbs in the 70s. For German, see Grewendorf (1989) and Fanselow (1992a). Apart from analyses of these phenomena, restrictions on possible constituent positions have been developed (Lenerz 1977), as well as analyses of case assignment (Yip, Maling & Jackendoff 1987; Meurers 1999c; Przepiórkowski 1999b) and theories of verbal complexes and the fronting of parts of phrases (Evers 1975; Grewendorf 1988; Hinrichs & Nakazawa 1994; Kiss 1995; G. Müller 1998; Meurers 1999b; Müller 1999a, 2002a; De Kuthy 2002). All these phenomena interact!

Consider another quote:

> A goal of earlier linguistic work, and one that is still a central goal of the linguistic work that goes on in computational linguistics, is to develop grammars that assign a reasonable syntactic structure to every sentence of English, or as nearly every sentence as possible. This is not a goal that is currently much in fashion in theoretical linguistics. Especially in Government-Binding theory (GB), the development of large fragments has long since been abandoned in favor of the pursuit of deep principles of grammar. The scope of the problem of identifying the correct parse cannot be appreciated by examining behavior on small fragments, however deeply analyzed. Large fragments are not just small fragments several times over – there is a qualitative change when one begins studying large fragments. As the range of constructions that the grammar accommodates increases, the number of undesired parses for sentences increases dramatically. (Abney 1996: 20)

---

[24] Es ist also sehr wohl möglich, daß mit den formulierten Regeln Sätze erzeugt werden können, die auch in einer nicht vorausgesehenen Weise aus der Menge der grammatisch richtigen Sätze herausfallen, die also durch Eigenschaften gegen die Grammatikalität verstoßen, die wir nicht wissentlich aus der Untersuchung ausgeschlossen haben. Das ist der Sinn der Feststellung, daß eine Grammatik eine Hypothese über die Struktur einer Sprache ist. Eine systematische Überprüfung der Implikationen einer für natürliche Sprachen angemessenen Grammatik ist sicherlich eine mit Hand nicht mehr zu bewältigende Aufgabe. Sie könnte vorgenommen werden, indem die Grammatik als Rechenprogramm in einem Elektronenrechner realisiert wird, so daß überprüft werden kann, in welchem Maße das Resultat von der zu beschreibenden Sprache abweicht.

So, as Bierwisch and Abney point out, developing a sound theory of a large fragment of a human language is a really demanding task. But what we aim for as theoretical linguists is much more: the aim is to formulate restrictions which ideally hold for all languages or at least for certain language classes. It follows from this, that one has to have an overview of the interaction of various phenomena in not just one but several languages. This task is so complex that individual researchers cannot manage it. This is the point at which computer implementations become helpful as they immediately flag inconsistencies in a theory. After removing these inconsistencies, computer implementations can be used to systematically analyze test data or corpora and thereby check the empirical adequacy of the theory (Müller, 1999a: Chapter 22; 2015a; 2014d; Oepen & Flickinger 1998; Bender 2008b, see Section 1.2).

More than 50 years after the first important published work by Chomsky, it is apparent that there has not been one large-scale implemented grammatical fragment on the basis of Transformational Grammar analyses. Chomsky has certainly contributed to the formalization of linguistics and developed important formal foundations which are still relevant in the theory of formal languages in computer science and in theoretical computational linguistics (Chomsky 1959). However, in 1981, he had already turned his back on rigid formalization:

> I think that we are, in fact, beginning to approach a grasp of certain basic principles of grammar at what may be the appropriate level of abstraction. At the same time, it is necessary to investigate them and determine their empirical adequacy by developing quite specific mechanisms. We should, then, try to distinguish as clearly as we can between discussion that bears on leading ideas and discussion that bears on the choice of specific realizations of them. (Chomsky 1981a: 2–3)

This is made explicit in a letter to *Natural Language and Linguistic Theory*:

> Even in mathematics, the concept of formalization in our sense was not developed until a century ago, when it became important for advancing research and understanding. I know of no reason to suppose that linguistics is so much more advanced than 19th century mathematics or contemporary molecular biology that pursuit of Pullum's injunction would be helpful, but if that can be shown, fine. For the present, there is lively interchange and exciting progress without any sign, to my knowledge, of problems related to the level of formality of ongoing work. (Chomsky 1990: 146)

This departure from rigid formalization has led to there being a large number of publications inside Mainstream Generative Grammar with sometimes incompatible assumptions to the point where it is no longer clear how one can combine the insights of the various publications. An example of this is the fact that the central notion of government has several different definitions (see Aoun & Sporticche 1983 for an overview[25]).

---

[25] A further definition can be found in Aoun & Lightfoot (1984). This is, however, equivalent to an earlier version as shown by Postal & Pullum (1986: 104–106).

This situation has been cricitized repeatedly since the 80s and sometimes very harshly by proponents of GPSG (Gazdar, Klein, Pullum & Sag 1985: 6; Pullum 1985, 1989a; Pullum 1991: 48; Kornai & Pullum 1990).

The lack of precision and working out of the details[26] and the frequent modification of basic assumptions[27] has led to insights gained by Mainstream Generative Grammar rarely being translated into computer implementations. There are some implementations that are based on Transformational Grammar/GB/MP models or borrow ideas from Mainstream Generative Grammar (Petrick 1965; Zwicky, Friedman, Hall & Walker 1965; Kay 1967; Friedman 1969; Friedman, Bredt, Doran, Pollack & Martner 1971; Morin 1973; Marcus 1980; Abney & Cole 1986; Kuhns 1986; Correa 1987; Stabler 1987, 1992, 2001; Kolb & Thiersch 1991; Fong 1991; Crocker & Lewin 1992; Lohnstein 1993; Fordham & Crocker 1994; Nordgård 1994; Veenstra 1998; Fong & Ginsburg 2012),[28] but these implementations often do not use transformations or differ greatly from the theoretical assumptions of the publications. For example, Marcus (1980: 102–104) and Stabler (1987: 5) use special purpose rules for auxiliary inversion.[29] These rules reverse the order of *John* and *has* for the analysis of sentences such as (51a) so that we get the order in (51b), which is then parsed with the rules for non-inverted structures.

(51)   a. Has John scheduled the meeting for Wednesday?
       b. John has scheduled the meeting for Wednesday?

These rules for auxiliary inversion are very specific and explicitly reference the category of the auxiliary. This does not correspond to the analyses proposed in GB in any way. As we have seen in Section 3.1.5, there are no special transformational rules for auxiliary inversion. Auxiliary inversion is carried out by the more general transformation Move-α and the associated restrictive principles. It is not unproblematic that the explicit formulation of the rule refers to the category *auxiliary* as is clear when one views Stabler's GB-inspired phrase structure grammar:

(52)   a. s → switch(aux_verb,np), vp.
       b. s([First|L0],L,X0,X) :- aux_verb(First),
                                np(L0,L1,X0,X1),
                                vp([First|L1],L,X1,X).

The rule in (52a) is translated into the Prolog predicate in (52b). The expression [First|L0] after the s corresponds to the string, which is to be processed. The '|'-operator divides the

---

[26] See e.g., Kuhns (1986: 550), Crocker & Lewin (1992: 508), Kolb & Thiersch (1991: 262), Kolb (1997: 3) and Freidin (1997: 580), Veenstra (1998: 25, 47), Lappin et al. (2000a: 888) and Stabler (2011a: 397, 399, 400) for the latter.

[27] See e.g., Kolb (1997: 4), Fanselow (2009) and the quote from Stabler on page 171.

[28] See Fordham & Crocker (1994) for a combination of a GB approach with statistical methods.

[29] Nozohoor-Farshi (1986, 1987) has shown that Marcus' parser can only parse context-free languages. Since natural languages are of a greater complexity (see Chapter 17) and grammars of corresponding complexity are allowed by current versions of Transformational Grammar, Marcus' parser can be neither an adequate implementation of the Chomskyan theory in question nor a piece of software for analyzing natural language in general.

list into a beginning and a rest. *First* is the first word to be processed and L0 contains all other words. In the analysis of (51a), First is *has* and L0 is *John scheduled the meeting for Wednesday*. In the Prolog clause, it is then checked whether First is an auxiliary (aux_- verb(First)) and if this is the case, then it will be tried to prove that the list L0 begins with a noun phrase. Since *John* is an NP, this is successful. L1 is the sublist of L0 which remains after the analysis of L0, that is *scheduled the meeting for Wednesday*. This list is then combined with the auxiliary (First) and now it will be checked whether the resulting list *has scheduled the meeting for Wednesday* begins with a VP. This is the case and the remaining list L is empty. As a result, the sentence has been successfully processed.

The problem with this analysis is that exactly one word is checked in the lexicon. Sentences such as (53) can not be analyzed:[30]

(53)   Could or should we pool our capital with that of other co-ops to address the needs of a regional "neighborhood"?[31]

In this kind of sentence, two modal verbs have been coordinated. They then form an X^0 and – following GB analyses – can be moved together. If one wanted to treat these cases as Stabler does for the simplest case, then we would need to divide the list of words to be processed into two unlimited sub-lists and check whether the first list contains an auxiliary or several coordinated auxiliaries. We would require a recursive predicate aux_verbs which somehow checks whether the sequence *could or should* is a well-formed sequence of auxiliaries. This should not be done by a special predicate but rather by syntactic rules responsible for the coordination of auxiliaries. The alternative to a rule such as (52a) would be the one in (54), which is the one that is used in theories like GPSG (Gazdar et al. 1985: 62), LFG (Falk 1984: 491), some HPSG analyses (Ginzburg & Sag 2000: 36), and Construction Grammar (Fillmore 1999):

(54)   s → v(aux+), np, vp.

This rule would have no problems with coordination data like (53) as coordination of multiple auxiliaries would produce an object with the category v(aux+) (for more on coordination see Section 21.6.2). If inversion makes it necessary to stipulate a special rule like (52a), then it is not clear why one could not simply use the transformation-less rule in (54).

In the MITRE system (Zwicky et al. 1965), there was a special grammar for the surface structure, from which the deep structure was derived via reverse application of trans- formations, that is, instead of using one grammar to create deep structures which are then transformed into other structures, one required two grammars. The deep structures that were determined by the parser were used as input to a transformational component since this was the only way to ensure that the surface structures can actually be derived from the base structure (Kay 2011: 10).

There are other implementations discussed in this chapter that differ from transfor- mation-based analyses. For example, Kolb & Thiersch (1991: 265, Section 4) arrive at

---

[30] For a discussion that shows that the coordination of lexical elements has to be an option in linguistic theories, see Abeillé (2006).

[31] http://www.cooperativegrocer.coop/articles/index.php?id=595. 28.03.2010.

the conclusion that a declarative, constraint-based approach to GB is more appropriate than a derivational one. Johnson (1989) suggests a *Parsing as Deduction* approach which reformulates sub-theories of GB ($\overline{\text{X}}$ theory, Theta-Theory, Case Theory, ...) as logical expressions.[32] These can be used independently of each other in a logical proof. In Johnson's analysis, GB theory is understood as a constraint-based system. More general restrictions are extracted from the restrictions on S- and D-structure which can then be used directly for parsing. This means that transformations are not directly carried out by the parser. As noted by Johnson, the language fragment he models is very small. It contains no description of *wh*-movement, for example (p. 114).

Probably the most detailed implementation in the tradition of GB and Barriers – the theoretical stage after GB (see Chomsky 1986a) – is Stabler's Prolog implementation (1992). Stabler's achievement is certainly impressive, but his book confirms what has been claimed thus far: Stabler has to simply stipulate many things which are not explicitly mentioned in *Barriers* (e.g., using feature-value pairs when formalizing $\overline{\text{X}}$ theory, a practice that was borrowed from GPSG) and some assumptions cannot be properly formalized and are simply ignored (see Briscoe 1997 for details).

GB analyses which fulfill certain requirements can be reformulated so that they no longer make use of transformations. These transformation-less approaches are also called *representational*, whereas the transformation-based approaches are referred to as *derivational*. For representational analyses, there are only surface structures augmented by traces but none of these structures is connected to an underlying structure by means of transformations (see e.g., Koster 1978; 1987: 235; Kolb & Thiersch 1991; Haider 1993: Section 1.4; Frey 1993: 14; Lohnstein 1993: 87–88, 177–178; Fordham & Crocker 1994: 38; Veenstra 1998: 58). These analyses can be implemented in the same way as corresponding HPSG analyses (see Chapter 9) as computer-processable fragments and this has in fact been carried out for example for the analysis of verb position in German.[33] However, such implemented analyses differ from GB analyses with regard to their basic architecture and in small, but important details such as how one deals with the interaction of long-distance dependencies and coordination (Gazdar 1981b). For a critical discussion and classification of movement analyses in Transformational Grammar, see Borsley (2012).

Following this somewhat critical overview, I want to add a comment in order to avoid being misunderstood: I do not demand that all linguistic work shall be completely formalized. There is simply no space for this in a, say, thirty page essay. Furthermore, I do not believe that all linguists should carry out formal work and implement their analyses as computational models. However, there has to be *somebody* who works out the formal details and these basic theoretical assumptions should be accepted and adopted for a sufficient amount of time by the research community in question.

---

[32] See Crocker & Lewin (1992: 511) and Fordham & Crocker (1994: 38) for another constraint-based Parsing-as-Deduction approach.

[33] This shows that ten Hacken's contrasting of HPSG with GB and LFG (ten Hacken 2007: Section 4.3) and the classification of these frameworks as belonging to different research paradigms is completely mistaken. In his classification, ten Hacken refers mainly to the model-theoretic approach that HPSG assumes. However, LFG also has a model-theoretic formalization (Kaplan 1995). Furthermore, there is also a model-theoretic variant of GB (Rogers 1998). For further discussion, see Chapter 14.

Comprehension questions

1. Give some examples of functional and lexical categories.

2. How can one represent lexical categories with binary features and what advantages does this have?

Exercises

1. Draw syntactic trees for the following examples:

(55) a. dass die   Frau   den   Mann liebt
          that the.NOM woman the.ACC man   loves

          'that the woman loves the man'

     b. dass der   Mann geliebt wird
          that the.NOM man loved   is

          'that the man is loved'

     c. Der   Mann wird geliebt.
         the.NOM man is   loved

         'The man is loved.'

     d. dass der   Mann der   Frau   hilft
          that the.NOM man the.DAT woman helps

          'that the man helps the woman'

     e. Der Mann   hilft der   Frau.
         the man.NOM helps the.DAT woman

         'The man is helping the woman.'

For the passive sentences, use the analysis where the subject noun phrase is moved from the object position, that is, the analysis without an empty expletive as the subject.

Further reading

For Sections 3.1–3.5, I used material from Peter Gallmann from 2003 (Gallmann 2003). This has been modified, however, at various points. I am solely responsible for any mistakes or inadequacies. For current materials by Peter Gallmann, see http://www.syntax-theorie.de.

In the book *Syntaktische Analyseperspektiven*, Lohnstein (2014) presents a variant of GB which more or less corresponds to what is discussed in this chapter (CP/IP, movement-based analysis of the passive). The chapters in said book have been written by proponents of various theories and all analyze the same newspaper article. This book is extremely interesting for all those who wish to compare the various theories out there.

Haegeman (1994) is a comprehensive introduction to GB. Those who do read German may consider the textbooks by Fanselow & Felix (1987), von Stechow & Sternefeld (1988) and Grewendorf (1988) since they are also addressing the phenomena that are covered in this book.

In many of his publications, Chomsky discusses alternative, transformation-less approaches as "notational variants". This is not appropriate, as analyses without transformations can make different predictions to transformation-based approaches (e.g., with respect to coordination and extraction. See Section 5.5 for a discussion of GPSG in this respect). In Gazdar (1981a), one can find a comparison of GB and GPSG as well as a discussion of the classification of GPSG as a notational variant of Transformational Grammar with contributions from Noam Chomsky, Gerald Gazdar and Henry Thompson.

Borsley (1999) and Kim & Sells (2008) have parallel textbooks for GB and HPSG in English. For the comparison of Transformational Grammar and LFG, see Bresnan & Kaplan (1982). Kuhn (2007) offers a comparison of modern derivational analyses with constraint-based LFG and HPSG approaches. Borsley (2012) contrasts analyses of long-distance dependencies in HPSG with movement-based analyses as in GB/Minimalism. Borsley discusses four types of data which are problematic for movement-based approaches: extraction without fillers, extraction with multiple gaps (see also the discussion of (57) on p. 166 and of (55) on p. 193 of this book), extractions where fillers and gaps do not match and extraction without gaps.

4 Transformational Grammar – Minimalism

Like the Government & Binding framework that was introduced in the previous chapter, the Minimalist framework was initiated by Noam Chomsky at the MIT in Boston. Chomsky (1993, 1995b) argued that the problem of language evolution should be taken seriously and that the question of how linguistic knowledge could become part of our genetic endowment should be answered. To that end he suggested refocusing the theoretical developments towards models that have to make minimal assumptions regarding the machinery that is needed for linguistic analyses and hence towards models that assume less language specific innate knowledge.

Like GB, Minimalism is wide-spread: theoreticians all over the world are working in this framework, so the following list of researchers and institutions is necessarily incomplete. *Linguistic Inquiry* and *Syntax* are journals that almost exclusively publish Minimalist work and the reader is referred to these journals to get an idea about who is active in this framework. The most prominent researchers in Germany are Artemis Alexiadou, Humboldt University Berlin; Günther Grewendorf (2002), Frankfurt am Main; Joseph Bayer, Konstanz; and Gereon Müller, Leipzig.

While innovations like $\overline{\text{X}}$ theory and the analysis of clause structure in GB are highly influential and can be found in most of the other theories that are discussed in this book, this is less so for the technical work done in the Minimalist framework. It is nevertheless useful to familiarize with the technicalities since Minimalism is a framework in which a lot of work is done and understanding the basic machinery makes it possible to read empirically interesting work in that framework.

While the GB literature of the 1980s and 1990s shared a lot of assumptions, there was an explosion of various approaches in the Minimalist framework that is difficult to keep track of. The presentation that follows is based on David Adger's textbook (Adger 2003).

4.1 General remarks on the representational format

The theories that are developed in the framework of the Minimalist Program build on the work done in the GB framework. So a lot of things that were explained in the previous chapter can be taken over to this chapter. However, there have been some changes in fundamental assumptions. The general parametrized principles were dropped from the theory and instead the relevant distinctions live in features. Languages differ in the values that certain features may have and in addition to this, features may be strong or weak and feature strength is also a property that may vary from language to language.

Strong features make syntactic objects move to higher positions. The reader is familiar with this feature-driven movement already since it was a component of the movement-based analysis of the passive in Section 3.4. In the GB analysis of passive, the object had to move to the specifier position of IP in order to receive case. Such movements that are due to missing feature values are a key component in Minimalist proposals.

4.1.1 Basic architecture

Chomsky assumes that there are just two operations (rules) for combining linguistic objects: External and Internal Merge. External Merge simply combines two elements like *the* and *book* and results in a complex phrase. Internal Merge is used to account for movement of constituents. It applies to one linguistic object and takes some part of this linguistic object and adjoins it to the left of the respective object. The application of External Merge and Internal Merge can apply in any order. For instance, two objects can be combined with External Merge and then one of the combined items is moved to the left by applying Internal Merge. The resulting object can be externally merged with another object and so on. As an example consider the NP in (1):

(1)   the man who we know

To derive this NP the verb *know* is externally merged with its object *who*. After several intermediate merges that will be discussed below, *know who* will be merged with *we* and finally the *who* is moved to the left by Internal Merge, resulting in *who we know*. This relative clause can be externally merged with *man* and so on.

So, Minimalist theories differ from GB in not assuming a Deep Structure that is generated by some $\overline{\text{X}}$ grammar and a Surface Structure that is derived from the Deep Structure by Move-α. Instead, it is assumed that there is a phase in which External and Internal Merge (combination and movement) apply in any order to derive a certain structure that is then said to be spelled out. It is said that the structure is sent to the interfaces: the articulatory-perceptual system (AP) on the one hand and the conceptual-intentional system (CI) on the other side. AP corresponds to the level of Phonological Form (PF) and CI to the level of Logical Form (LF) in GB. The new architecture is depicted in Figure 4.1 on the following page. Overt syntax stands for syntactic operations that usually have a visible effect. After overt syntax the syntactic object is sent off to the interfaces and some transformations may take place after this Spell-Out point. Since such transformations do not affect pronunciation, this part of syntax is called *covert syntax*. Like in GB's LF, the covert syntax can be used to derive certain scope readings.

This architecture was later modified to allow Spell-Out at several points in the derivation. It is now assumed that there are *phases* in a derivation and that a completed phase is spelled out once it is used in a combination with a head (Chomsky 2008). For instance, a subordinated sentence like *that Peter comes* in (2) is one phase and is sent to the interfaces before the whole sentence is completed.[1]

---

[1] Andreas Pankau (p. c. 2015) pointed out to me that there is a fundamental problem with such a conception of phases, since if it is the case that only elements that are in a relation to a head are send off to the interface then the topmost phrase in a derivation would never be sent to the interfaces, since it does not depend on any head.

lexicon

overt syntax

←— Spell-Out

covert syntax

LF/CI   PF/AP
(meaning)   (sound)

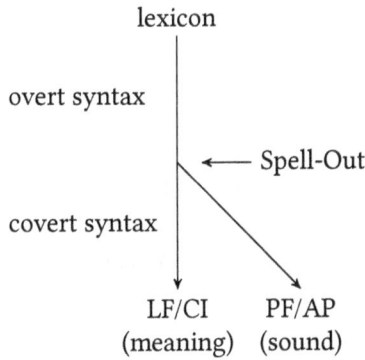

Figure 4.1: Architecture assumed in Minimalist theories before the Phase model

(2)   He believes that Peter comes.

There are different proposals as to what categories form complete phases. Since the concept of phases is not important for the following introduction, I will ignore this concept in the following. See Section 15.1 on the psycholinguistic plausibility of phases in particular and the Minimalist architecture in general.

4.1.2 Valence, feature checking, and agreement

The basic mechanism in Minimalist theories is feature checking. For instance, the noun *letters* may have a P feature, which means that it has to combine with a PP in order to form a complete phrase.

(3)   letters to Peter

It is assumed that there are interpretable and uninterpretable features. An example of an interpretable feature is the number feature of nouns. The singular/plural distinction is semantically relevant. The category features for part of speech information are purely syntactic and hence cannot be interpreted semantically. Minimalism assumes that all uninterpretable features have to be used up during the derivation of a complex linguistic object. This process of eating up the features is called *checking*. As an example, let us consider the noun *letters* again. The analysis of (3) is depicted in Figure 4.2 on the following page. The fact that the P feature of *letters* is uninterpretable is represented by the little *u* in front of the P. The uninterpretable P feature of *letters* can be checked against the P feature of *to Peter*. All checked features are said to delete automatically. The deletion is marked by striking the features out in the figures. Strings like (4) are ruled out as complete derivations since the N feature of P is not checked. This situation is shown in Figure 4.3 on the next page.

(4)   * letters to

N

letters [N, pl, uP]   P

to [P, uN]   Peter [N]

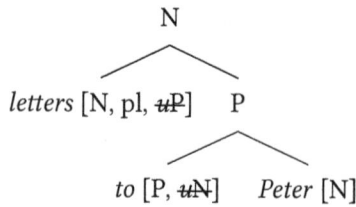

Figure 4.2: Valence representation via uninterpretable features

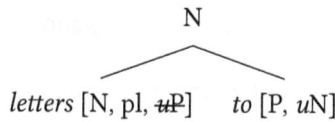

N

letters [N, pl, uP]   to [P, uN]

Figure 4.3: Illegitimate syntactic object due to an uninterpretable feature

If this structure would be used in a larger structure that is spelled out, the derivation would *crash* since the conceptual system could not make sense of the N feature that is still present at the P node.

Selectional features are atomic, that is, the preposition cannot select an NP[*acc*] as in GB and the other theories in this book unless NP[*acc*] is assumed to be atomic. There- fore, an additional mechanism is assumed that can check other features in addition to selectional features. This mechanism is called *Agree*.

(5) a. * letters to he
     b.   letters to him

The analysis of (5b) is shown in Figure 4.4. There is an interesting difference between the

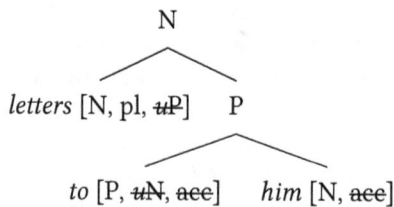

N

letters [N, pl, uP]   P

to [P, uN, acc]   him [N, acc]

Figure 4.4: Feature checking via Agree

checking of selectional features and the checking of features via Agree. The features that are checked via Agree do not have to be at the top node of the object that is combined with a head. This will play a role later in the analysis of the passive and local reordering.

4.1.3 Phrase structure and $\overline{\text{X}}$ theory

The projections of $\overline{\text{X}}$ structures were given in Figure 2.9 on page 76. According to early versions of the $\overline{\text{X}}$ theory, there could be arbitrarily many complements that were combined with X^0 to form an $\overline{\text{X}}$. Arbitrarily many adjuncts could attach to $\overline{\text{X}}$ and then at most one specifier could be combined with the $\overline{\text{X}}$ yielding an XP. Minimalist theories assume binary branching and hence there is at most one complement, which is the first-merged item. Furthermore, it is not assumed that there is a unique specifier position. Chomsky rather assumes that all items that are not complements are specifiers. That is, he distinguishes between first-merged (complements) and later-merged items (specifiers). Figure 4.5 shows an example with two specifiers. It is also possible to have just

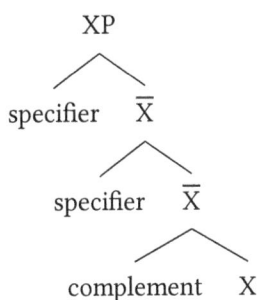

XP

specifier $\overline{\text{X}}$

specifier $\overline{\text{X}}$

complement X

Figure 4.5: Complements and specifiers in Minimalist theories

a complement and no specifier or to have one or three specifiers. What structures are ultimately licensed depends on the features of the items that are involved in the Merge operations. Whether a phrasal projection counts as an $\overline{\text{X}}$ or an XP depends on whether the phrase is used as a complement or specifier of another head or whether it is used as head in further Merge operations. If a phrase is used as specifier or complement its status is fixed to be a phrase (XP), otherwise the projectional status of resulting phrases is left underspecified. Lexical head daughters in Merge operations have the category X and complex head daughters in Merge operations have the category $\overline{\text{X}}$. This solves the problem that standard $\overline{\text{X}}$ theoretic approaches had with pronouns and proper names: a lot of unary branching structure had to be assumed (See left picture in Figure 2.9). This is not necessary any longer in current Minimalist theories.[2]

4.1.4 Little *v*

In Section 3.4, I used $\overline{\text{X}}$ structures in which a ditransitive verb was combined with its accusative object to form a $\overline{\text{V}}$, which was then combined with the dative object to form a further $\overline{\text{V}}$. Such binary branching structures and also flat structures in which both objects are combined with the verb to form a $\overline{\text{V}}$ are rejected by many practitioners of

---

[2] For problems with this approach see Broszewski (2003: Chapter 2.1).

GB and Minimalism since the branching does not correspond to branchings that would be desired for phenomena like the binding of reflexives and negative polarity items. A binding in which *Benjamin* binds *himself* in (6a) is impossible:

(6) a. *Emily showed himself Benjamin in the mirror.
     b.   Peter showed himself Benjamin in the mirror.

What is required for the analysis of Binding and NPI phenomena in theories that analyze these phenomena in terms of tree configurations is that the reflexive pronoun is "higher" in the tree than the proper name *Benjamin*. More precisely, the reflexive pronoun *himself* has to c-command *Benjamin*. c-command is defined as follows (Adger 2003: 117):[3]

(7) A node A c-commands B if, and only if A's sister either:
     a. is B, or
     b. contains B

In the trees to the left and in the middle of Figure 4.6 the c-command relations are not as desired: in the left-most tree both NPs c-command each other and in the middle one *Benjamin* c-commands *himself* rather than the other way round. Hence it is assumed

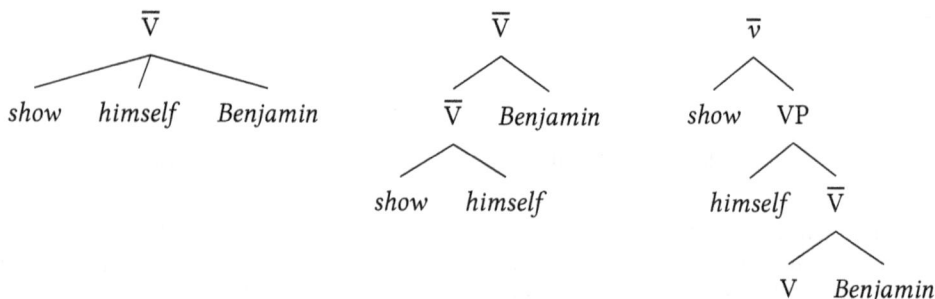

Figure 4.6: Three possible analyses of ditransitives

that the structures at the left and in the middle are inappropriate and that there is some additional structure involving the category *v*, which is called *little v* (Adger 2003: Section 4.4). The sister of *himself* is $\overline{V}$ and $\overline{V}$ contains *Benjamin*, hence *himself* c-commands *Benjamin*. Since the sister of *Benjamin* is V and V neither is nor contains *himself*, *Benjamin* does not c-command *himself*.

The analysis of ditransitives involving an additional verbal head goes back to Larson (1988). Hale & Keyser (1993: 70) assume that this verbal head contributes a causative semantics. The structure in Figure 4.7 is derived by assuming that the verb *show* starts out in the V position and then moves to the *v* position. *show* is assumed to mean *see* and in the position of little *v* it picks up the causative meaning, which results in a *cause-see'* meaning (Adger 2003: 133).

---

[3] c-command also plays a prominent role in GB. In fact, one part of Government & Binding is the Binding Theory, which was not discussed in the previous chapter since binding phenomena do not play a role in this book.

```
                      vP
                     /  \
                Peter    v̄
                        /  \
                 v + show   VP
                           /  \
                     himself   V̄
                              /  \
                    ⟨ show ⟩ [V]   Benjamin
```

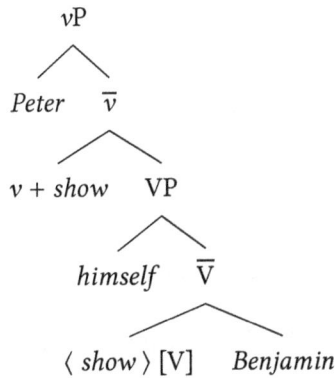

Figure 4.7: Analysis of ditransitives involving movement to little *v*

While the verb shell analysis with an empty verbal head was originally invented by Larson (1988) for the analysis of ditransitive verbs, it is now also used for the analysis of strictly transitive and even intransitive verbs.

Adger (2003: Section 4.5) argues that semantic roles are assigned uniformly in certain tree configurations:

(8) a. NP daughter of *v*P → interpreted as agent
     b. NP daughter of VP → interpreted as theme
     c. PP daughter of *v̄* → interpreted as goal

Adger assumes that such uniformly assigned semantic roles help in the process of language acquisition and from this, it follows that little *v* should also play a role in the analysis of examples with strictly transitive and intransitive verbs. The Figures 4.8 and 4.9 show the analysis of sentences containing the verbs *burn* and *laugh*, respectively.[4]

Adger (2003: 164) assumes that intransitive and transitive verbs move from V to little *v* as well. This will be reflected in the following figures.

4.1.5 CP, TP, *v*P, VP

Section 3.1.5 dealt with the CP/IP system in GB. In the course of the development of Minimalism, the Inflectional Phrase was split into several functional projections (Chomsky 1989) of which only the Tense Phrase is assumed in current Minimalist analyses. So, the TP of Minimalism corresponds to IP in the GB analysis. Apart from this change, the core ideas of the CP/IP analysis have been transferred to the Minimalist analysis of English. This subsection will first discuss special features that are assumed to trigger movement (Subsection 4.1.5.1) and then case assignment (Subsection 4.1.5.2).

---

[4] If all intransitive verbs of this type are supposed to have agents as subjects, a very broad conception of agent has to be assumed that also subsumes the subject of verbs like *sleep*. Usually sleeping is not an activity that is performed intentionally.

vP

Agent $\bar{v}$ [u̶D̶]

v   VP

burn [V, u̶D̶]   Theme

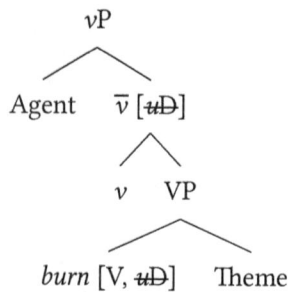

Figure 4.8: Analysis of strictly transitives involving little v

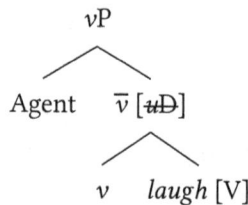

vP

Agent $\bar{v}$ [u̶D̶]

v   laugh [V]

Figure 4.9: Analysis of intransitives involving little v

4.1.5.1 Features as triggers for movement: The EPP feature on T

In GB approaches, the modals and auxiliaries were analyzed as members of the category
I and the subjects as specifiers of IP. In the previous section, I showed how subjects
are analyzed as specifiers of vP. Now, if one assumes that a modal verb combines with
such a vP, the subject follows the modal, which does not correspond to the order that
is observable in English. This problem is solved by assuming a strong uninterpretable D
feature at T. Since the feature is strong, a suitable D has to move to the specifier of T and
check the D locally. Figure 4.10 on the following page shows the TP that plays a role in
the analysis of (9):

(9)   Anna will read the book.

The DP *the book* is the object of *read* and checks the D feature of *read*. little v selects for
the subject *Anna*. Since T has a strong D feature (marked by an asterisk "*"), *Anna* must
not remain inside of the vP but moves on to the specifier position of TP.

  Full sentences are CPs. For the analysis of (9), an empty C head is assumed that is
combined with the TP. The empty C contributes a clause type feature Decl. The full
analysis of (9) is shown in Figure 4.11.

  The analysis of the question in (10) involves an unvalued clause-type feature on T for
the sentence type *question.*

(10)   What will Anna read?

TP
Anna [D]   T̄[*uD**]
will T[pres]   vP
⟨ Anna ⟩   v̄ [*uD*]
v   VP
read   v   ⟨ read ⟩ [V, *uD*]   DP
the book

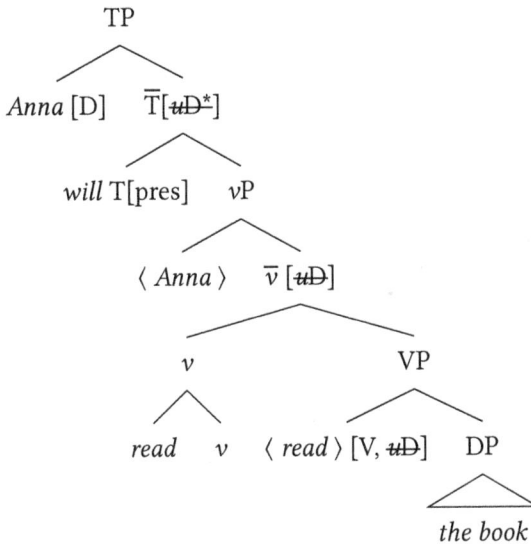

Figure 4.10: Analysis of *Anna will read the book.* involving a modal and movement of the subject from v to T

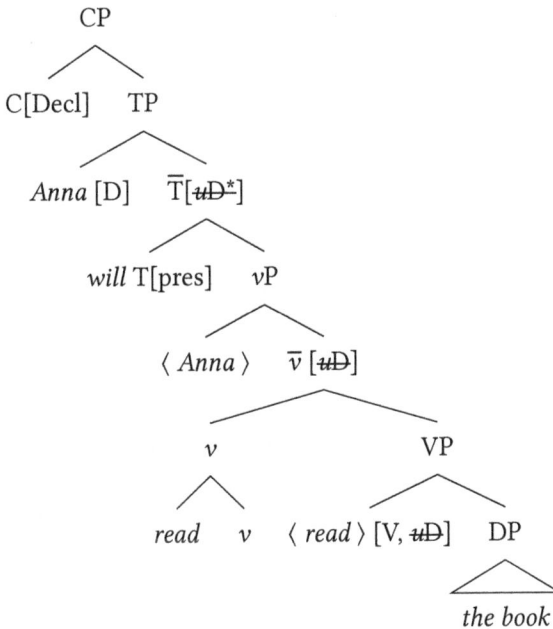

CP
C[Decl]   TP
Anna [D]   T̄[*uD**]
will T[pres]   vP
⟨ Anna ⟩   v̄ [*uD*]
v   VP
read   v   ⟨ read ⟩ [V, *uD*]   DP
the book

Figure 4.11: Analysis of *Anna will read the book.* as CP with an empty C with the clause-type feature Decl

The empty complementizer C has a Q feature that can value the clause-type feature on T. Since clause-type features on T that have the value Q are stipulated to be strong, the T element has to move to C to check the feature locally. In addition, the *wh* element is moved. This movement is enforced by a strong wh feature on C. The analysis of (10) is given in Figure 4.12.

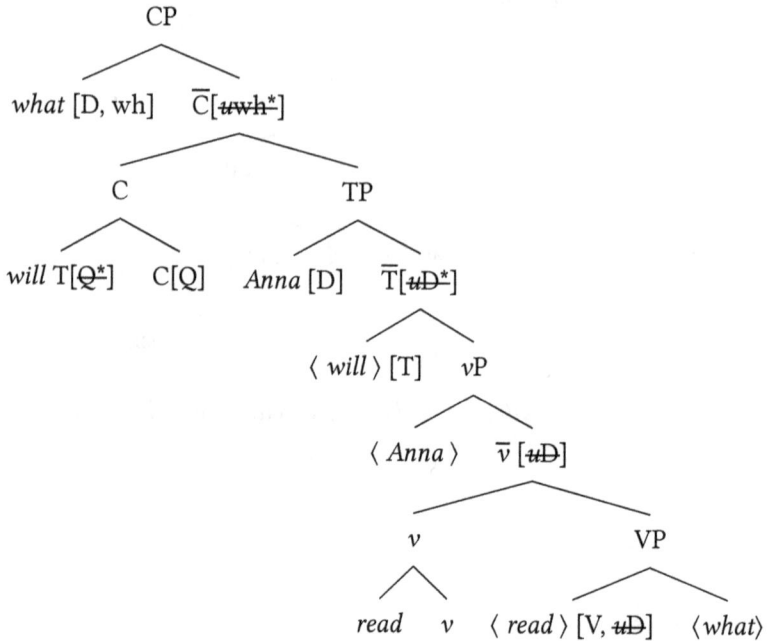

Figure 4.12: Analysis of *What will Anna read?* with an empty C with a strong wh feature

4.1.5.2 Case assignment

In the GB analysis that was presented in Chapter 3, nominative was assigned by (finite) I and the other cases by the verb (see Section 3.4.2). The assignment of nominative is taken over to Minimalist analyses, so it is assumed that nominative is assigned by (finite) T. However, in the Minimalist theory under consideration, there is not a single verb projection, but there are two verbal projections: *v*P and VP. Now, one could assume that V assigns accusative to its complement or that *v* assigns accusative to the complement of the verb it dominates. Adger (2003: Section 6.3.2, Section 6.4) assumes the latter approach, since it is compatible with the analysis of so-called unaccusative verbs and the passive. Figure 4.13 on the following page shows the TP for (11):

(11)   Anna reads the book.

The two NPs *Anna* and *the book* start out with unvalued uninterpretable case features: [ucase:]. The features get valued by T and *v*. It is assumed that only one feature is

TP

Anna [D, ~~nom~~]   T̄[~~uD*~~, ~~nom~~]

T[pres]   vP

⟨ Anna ⟩   v̄ [~~uD~~]

v   VP

read   v [~~acc~~]   ⟨ read ⟩ [V, ~~uD~~]   DP[~~acc~~]

the book

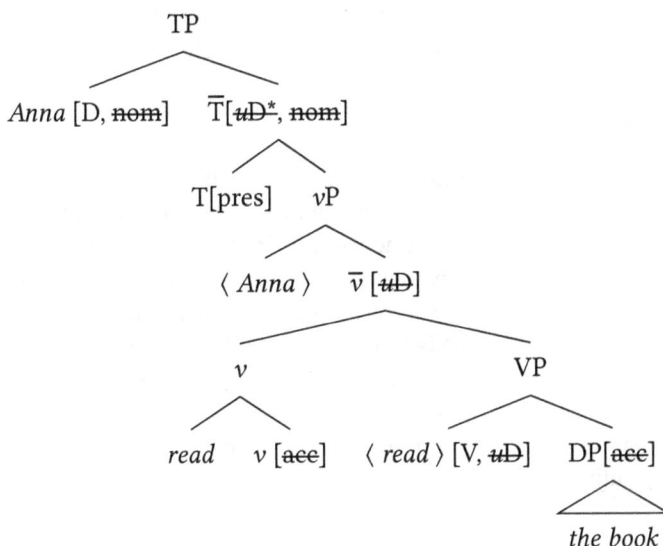

Figure 4.13: Case assignment by T and v in the TP for of *Anna reads the book*.

checked by Merge, so this would be the D feature on T, leaving the case feature for the other available checking mechanism: Agree. Agree can be used to check features in sister nodes, but also features further away in the tree. The places that are possible candidates for Agree relations have to stand in a certain relation to each other. The first node has to c-command the node it Agrees with. c-command roughly means: one node up and then arbitrarily many nodes down. So v c-commands VP, V, the DP *the book*, and all the nodes within this DP. Since Agree can value features of c-commanded nodes, the accusative on v can value the case feature of the DP *the book*.

The non-locality that is build into Agree raises a problem: why is it that (12) is ungrammatical?

(12)   * Him likes she.

The accusative of v could be checked with its subject and the nominative of T with the object of *likes*. Both DPs stand in the necessary c-command relations to T and v. This problem is solved by requiring that all Agree relations have to involve the closest possible element. Adger (2003: 218) formulates this constraint as follows:

(13)   Locality of matching: Agree holds between a feature F on X and a matching feature F on Y if and only if there is no intervening Z[F].

Intervention is defined as in (14):

(14)   Intervention: In a structure [X ... Z ... Y], Z intervenes between X and Y iff X c-commands Y.

So, since T may Agree with *Anna* it must not Agree with *the book*. Hence nominative assignment to *she* in (12) is impossible and (12) is correctly ruled out.

4.1.6 Adjuncts

Adger (2003: Section 4.2.3) assumes that adjuncts attach to XP and form a new XP. He calls this operation *Adjoin*. Since this operation does not consume any features it is different from External Merge and hence a new operation would be introduced into the theory, contradicting Chomsky's claim that human languages use only Merge as a structure building operation. There are proposals to treat adjuncts as elements in special adverbial phrases with empty heads (see Section 4.6.1) that are also assumed to be part of a hierarchy of functional projections. Personally, I prefer Adger's solution that corresponds to what is done in many other frameworks: there is a special rule or operation for the combination of adjuncts and heads (see for instance Section 9.1.7 on the HPSG schema for head adjunct combinations).

4.2 Verb position

The analysis of verb first sentences in German is straightforward, given the machinery that was introduced in the previous section. The basic idea is the same as in GB: the finite verb moves from V to *v* to T and then to C. The movement to T is forced by a strong tense feature on T and the movement of the T complex to C is enforced by a clause-type feature on T that is valued as a strong Decl by C. The analysis of (15) is shown in Figure 4.14 on the following page.

(15) Kennt jeder   diesen Mann?
      knows everybody this   man
      'Does everybody know this man?'

4.3 Long-distance dependencies

Having explained the placement of the verb in initial position, the analysis of V2 sentences does not come with a surprise: Adger (2003: 331) assumes a feature that triggers the movement of a constituent to a specifier position of C. Adger calls this feature top, but this is a misnomer since the initial position in German declarative sentences is not restricted to topics. Figure 4.15 on page 136 shows the analysis of (16):

(16) Diesen Mann kennt jeder.
      this   man knows everybody
      'Everbody knows this man.'

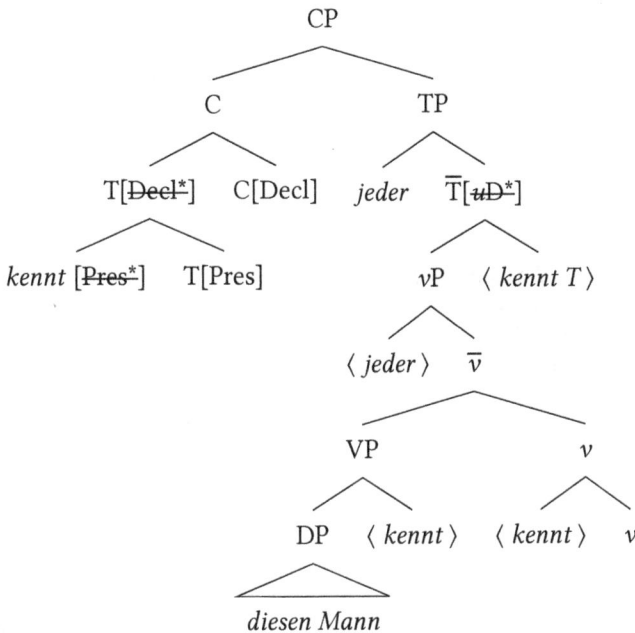

Figure 4.14: Analysis of *Kennt jeder diesen Mann?* 'Does everybody know this man?' following the analysis of Adger (2003)

4.4 Passive

Adger (2003) suggests an analysis for the passive in English, which I adapted here to German. Like in the GB analysis that was discussed in Section 3.4 it is assumed that the verb does not assign accusative to the object of *schlagen* 'to beat'. In Minimalist terms, this means that little *v* does not have an acc feature that has to be checked. This special version of little *v* is assumed to play a role in the analysis of sentences of so-called unaccusative verbs (Perlmutter 1978). Unaccusative verbs are a subclass of intransitive verbs that have many interesting properties. For instance, they can be used as adjectival participles although this is usually not possible with intransitive verbs:

(17) a. * der getanzte Mann
          the danced   man

      b.   der gestorbene Mann
          the died   man
          'the dead man'

The explanation of this difference is that adjectival participles predicate over what is the object in active sentences:

```
                              CP
                    ┌──────────┴──────────┐
            diesen Mann [top]         C̄[u̶t̶o̶p̶*]
                               ┌───────────┴───────────┐
                               C                       TP
                        ┌──────┴──────┐          ┌──────┴──────┐
                   T[D̶e̶c̶l̶*]   C[Decl]       jeder      T̄[u̶D̶*]
                  ┌──────┴──────┐                    ┌─────┴─────┐
            kennt [P̶r̶e̶s̶*]    T[Pres]               vP      ⟨ kennt T ⟩
                                                ┌────┴────┐
                                          ⟨ jeder ⟩      v̄
                                                    ┌─────┴──────┐
                                                   VP            v
                                             ┌──────┴──────┐  ┌──┴──┐
                                   ⟨ diesen Mann ⟩[D]  ⟨ kennt ⟩ ⟨ kennt ⟩  v
```

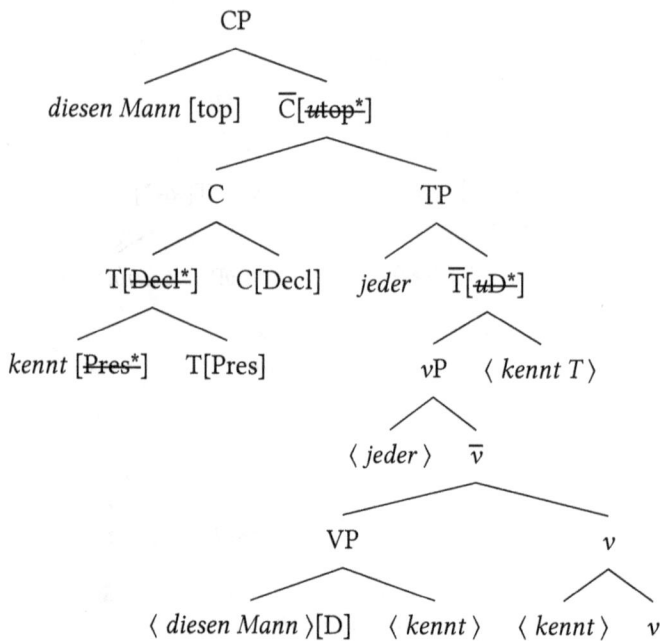

Figure 4.15: Analysis of *Diesen Mann kennt jeder.* 'This man, everybody knows.' following the analysis of Adger (2003: 331)

(18) a. dass der Mann das Buch gelesen hat
          that the man   the book read   has
          'that the man read the book'
      b. das gelesene Buch
          the read   book

Now the assumption is that the argument of *gestorben* 'died' behaves like an object, while the argument of *getanzt* 'danced' behaves like a subject. If adjectival passives predicate over the object it is explained why (17b) is possible, while (17a) is not.

Adger (2003: 140) assumes the structure in Figure 4.16 on the following page for vPs with unaccusative verbs. It is assumed that this unaccusative variant of little *v* plays a role in the analysis of the passive. Unaccusative verbs are similar to passivized verbs in that they do have a subject that somehow also has object properties. The special version of little *v* is selected by the Passive head *werden* 'be', which forms a Passive Phrase (abbreviated as PassP). See Figure 4.17 for the analysis of the example in (19):

(19) dass er geschlagen wurde
      that he beaten   was
      'that he was beaten'

vP
├── v
└── VP
    ├── fall[V, uN]
    └── Theme

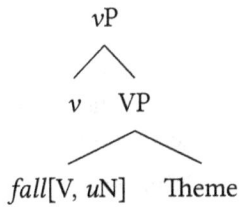

Figure 4.16: Structure of vP with unaccusative verbs like *fall, collapse, wilt* according to Adger (2003: 140)

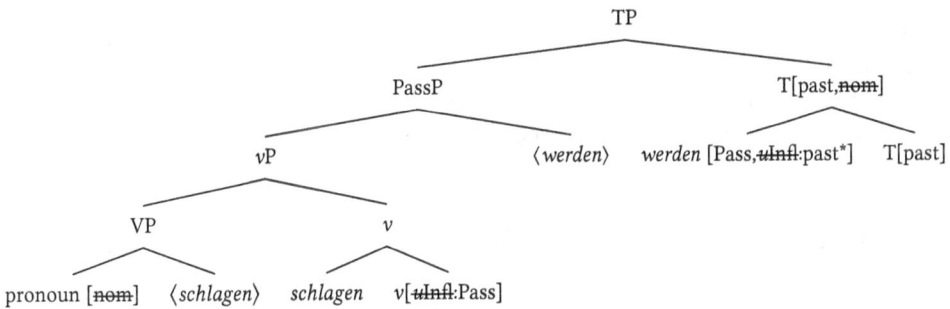

TP
├── PassP
│   ├── vP
│   │   ├── VP
│   │   │   ├── pronoun [nom]
│   │   │   └── ⟨schlagen⟩
│   │   └── v
│   │   ├── schlagen
│   │   └── v[uInfl:Pass]
│   └── ⟨werden⟩
└── T[past,nom]
    ├── werden [Pass,uInfl:past*]
    └── T[past]

Figure 4.17: Minimalist analysis of the passive without movement but with nonlocal case assignment via Agree

The Pass head requires the Infl feature of little *v* to have the value Pass, which results in participle morphology at spellout. Hence the form that is used is *geschlagen* 'beaten'. The auxiliary moves to T to check the strong Infl feature at T and since the Infl feature is past, the past form of *werden* 'be', namely *wurde* 'was', is used at spellout. T has a nom feature that has to be checked. Interestingly, the Minimalist approach does not require the object of *schlagen* to move to the specifier position of T in order to assign case, since case assignment is done via Agree. Hence in principle, the pronominal argument of *schlagen* could stay in its object position and nevertheless get nominative from T. This would solve the problem of the GB analysis that was pointed out by Lenerz (1977: Section 4.4.3). See page 109 for Lenerz' examples and discussion of the problem. However, Adger (2003: 332) assumes that German has a strong EPP feature on T. If this assumption is upheld, all problems of the GB account will carry over to the Minimalist analysis: all objects have to move to T even when there is no reordering taking place. Furthermore, impersonal passives of the kind in (20) would be problematic, since there is no noun phrase that could be moved to T in order to check the EPP feature:

(20)   weil   getanzt wurde
       because danced was

       'because there was dancing there'

4.5 Local reordering

Adger (2003) does not treat local reordering. But there are several other suggestions in the literature. Since all reorderings in Minimalist theories are feature-driven, there must be an item that has a feature that triggers reorderings like those in (21b):

(21) a. [weil] jeder diesen Mann kennt
because everyone this man knows

'because everyone knows this man'

   b. [weil] diesen Mann jeder kennt
because this man everyone knows

There have been various suggestions involving functional projections like Topic Phrase (Laenzlinger 2004: 222) or AgrS and AgrO (Meinunger 2000: Chapter 4) that offer places to move to. G. Müller (2014a: Section 3.5) offers a leaner solution, though. In his approach, the object simply moves to a second specifier position of little *v*. The analysis is depicted in Figure 4.18.[5]

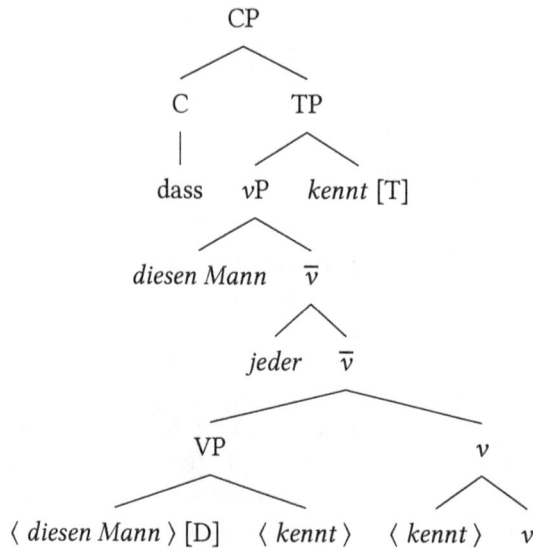

Figure 4.18: Analysis of *dass diesen Mann jeder kennt* 'that everybody knows this man' as movement of the object to a specifier position of *v*

An option that was suggested by Laenzlinger (2004: 229–230) is to assume several Object Phrases for objects that may appear in any order. The objects move to the specifier positions of these projections and since the order of the Object Phrases is not restricted, both orders in (22) can be analyzed:

---

[5] G. Müller assumes optional features on *v* and V that trigger local reorderings (p. 48). These are not given in the figure.

(22) a. dass Hans diesen Brief meinem Onkel gibt
       that Hans this   letter my   uncle gives

      'that Hans gives this letter to my uncle'

   b. dass Hans meinem Onkel diesen Brief gibt
       that Hans my   uncle this   letter gives

      'that Hans gives to my uncle this letter'

4.6 New developments and theoretical variants

At the start of the 90s, Chomsky suggested a major rethink of the basic theoretical assumptions of GB and only keeping those parts of the theory which are absolutely necessary. In the *Minimalist Program*, Chomsky gives the central motivations for the far-reaching revisions of GB theory (Chomsky 1993, 1995b). Until the beginning of the 90s, it was assumed that Case Theory, the Theta-Criterion, $\overline{\text{X}}$ theory, Subjacency, Binding Theory, Control Theory etc. all belonged to the innate faculty for language (Richards 2015: 804). This, of courses, begs the question of how this very specific linguistic knowledge made its way into our genome. The Minimalist Program follows up on this point and attempts to explain properties of language through more general cognitive principles and to reduce the amount of innate language-specific knowledge postulated. The distinction between Deep Structure and Surface Structure, for example, was abandoned. Move still exists as an operation, but can be used directly to build sub-structures rather than after a complete D-structure has been created. Languages differ with regard to whether this movement is visible or not.

Although Chomsky's Minimalist Program should be viewed as a successor to GB, advocates of Minimalism often emphasize the fact that Minimalism is not a theory as such, but rather a research program (Chomsky 2007: 4; 2013: 6). The actual analyses suggested by Chomsky (1995b) when introducing the research program have been reviewed by theoreticians and have sometimes come in for serious criticism (Kolb 1997; Johnson & Lappin 1997, 1999; Lappin, Levine & Johnson 2000a,b, 2001; Seuren 2004; Pinker & Jackendoff 2005), however, one should say that some criticisms overshoot the mark.

There are various strains of Minimalism. In the following sections, I will discuss some of the central ideas and explain which aspects are regarded problematic.

4.6.1 Move, Merge, feature-driven movement and functional projections

Johnson, Lappin and Kolb have criticized the computational aspects of Chomsky's system. Chomsky suggested incorporating principles of economy into the theory. In certain cases, the grammatical system can create an arbitrary number of structures, but only the most economical, that is, the one which requires the least effort to produce, will be accepted as grammatical (transderivational economy). This assumption does not necessarily have to be taken too seriously and, in reality, does not play a role in many works in the Minimalist framework (although see Richards (2015) for recent approaches with derivations which are compared in terms of economy). Nevertheless, there are other aspects of Chomsky's theory which can be found in many recent works. For example, Chomsky has proposed reducing the number of basic, structure building operations which license structures to two: Move and Merge (that is, Internal and External Merge). Move corresponds to the operation Move-α, which was already discussed in Chapter 3, and Merge is the combination of (two) linguistic objects.

It is generally assumed that exactly two objects can be combined (Chomsky 1995b: 226). For Move, it is assumed that there must be a reason for a given movement operation. The reason for movement is assumed to be that an element can check some feature in the position it is moved to. This idea was already presented in the analysis of the passive in Section 3.4: the accusative object does not bear case in passive sentences and therefore has to be moved to a position where it can receive case. This kind of approach is also used in newer analyses for a range of other phenomena. For example, it is assumed that there are phrases whose heads have the categories focus and topic. The corresponding functional heads are always empty in languages like German and English. Nevertheless, the assumption of these heads is motivated by the fact that other languages possess markers which signal the topic or focus of a sentence morphologically. This argumentation is only possible if one also assumes that the inventory of categories is the same for all languages. Then, the existence of a category in one language would suggest the existence of the same category in all other languages. This assumption of a shared universal component (Universal Grammar, UG) with detailed language-specific knowledge is, however, controversial and is shared by few linguists outside of the Chomskyan tradition. Even for those working in Chomskyan linguistics, there have been questions raised about whether it is permissible to argue in this way since if it is only the ability to create recursive structures that is responsible for the human-specific ability to use language (faculty of language in the narrow sense) – as Hauser, Chomsky & Fitch (2002) assume –, then the individual syntactic categories are not part of UG and data from other languages cannot be used to motivate the assumption of invisible categories in another language.

4.6.1.1 Functional projections and modularization of linguistic knowledge

The assumption that movement must be licensed by feature checking has led to an inflation of the number of (silent) functional heads.[6] Rizzi (1997: 297) suggests the structure in Figure 4.19 on the following page (see also Grewendorf 2002: 85, 240; 2009).

---

[6] The assumption of such heads is not necessary since features can be 'bundled' and then they can be checked together. For an approach in this vein, which is in essence similar to what theories such as HPSG assume, see Sternefeld (2006: Section II.3.3.4, Section II.4.2).

In so-called cartographic approaches, it is assumed that every morphosyntactic feature corresponds to an independent syntactic head (Cinque & Rizzi 2010: 54, 61). For an explicitly formalized proposal in which exactly one feature is consumed during a combination operation see Stabler (2001: 335). Stabler's *Minimalist Grammars* are discussed in more detail in Section 4.6.4.

ForceP
Force'
Force⁰   TopP*
Top'
Top⁰   FocP
Foc'
Foc⁰   TopP*
Top'
Top⁰   FinP
Fin'
Fin⁰   IP

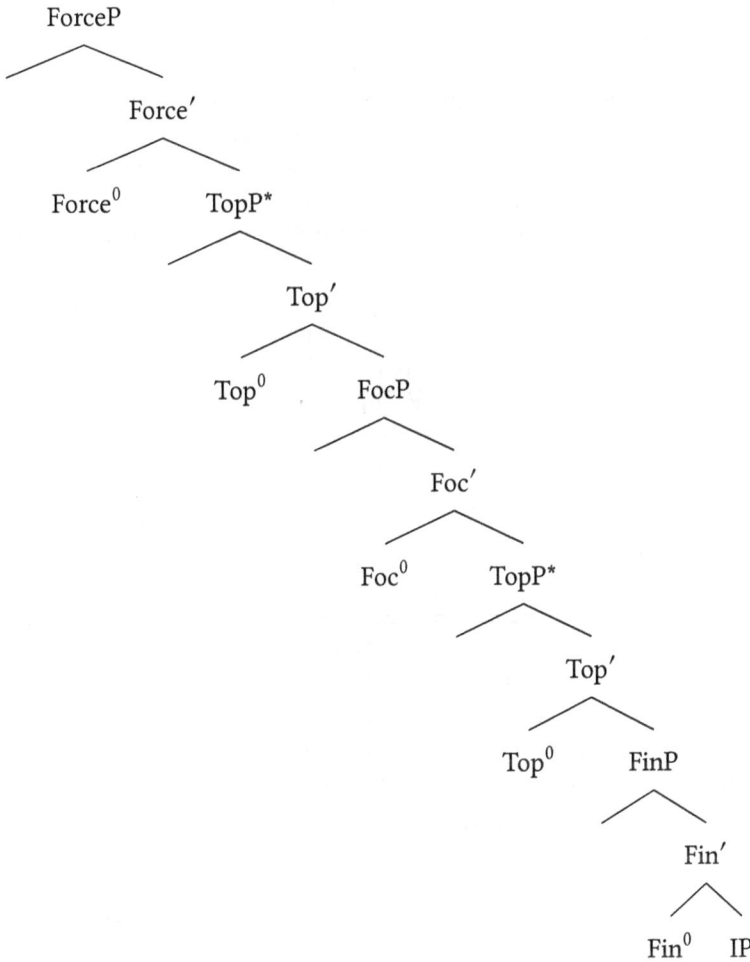

Figure 4.19: Syntactic structure of sentences following Rizzi (1997: 297)

The functional categories Force, Top, Foc and Fin correspond to clause type, topic, focus and finiteness. It is assumed that movement always targets a specifier position. Topics and focused elements are always moved to the specifier position of the corresponding phrase. Topics can precede or follow focused elements, which is why there are two topic projections: one above and one below FocP. Topic phrases are recursive, that is, an arbitrary number of TopPs can appear at the positions of TopP in the figure. Following Grewendorf (2002: 70), topic and focus phrases are only realized if they are required for particular information structural reasons, such as movement.[7] Chomsky (1995b: 147)

---

[7] There are differing opinions as to whether functional projections are optional or not. Some authors assume that the complete hierarchy of functional projections is always present but functional heads can remain empty (e.g., Cinque 1999: 106 and Cinque & Rizzi 2010: 55).

follows Pollock (1989) in assuming that all languages have functional projections for subject and object agreement as well as negation (AgrS, AgrO, Neg).[8] Sternefeld (1995: 78), von Stechow (1996: 103) and Meinunger (2000: 100–101, 124) differentiate between two agreement positions for direct and indirect objects (AgrO, AgrIO). As well as AgrS, AgrO and Neg, Beghelli & Stowell (1997) assume the functional heads Share and Dist in order to explain scope phenomena in English as feature-driven movements at LF. For a treatment of scope phenomena without empty elements or movement, see Section 19.3. Błaszczak & Gärtner (2005: 13) assume the categories −PolP, +PolP and %PolP for their discussion of polarity.

Webelhuth (1995: 76) gives an overview of the functional projections that had been proposed up to 1995 and offers references for AgrA, AgrN, AgrV, Aux, Clitic Voices, Gender, Honorific, μ, Number, Person, Predicate, Tense, Z.

In addition to AdvP, NegP, AgrP, FinP, TopP and ForceP, Wiklund, Hrafnbjargarson, Bentzen & Hróarsdóttir (2007) postulate an OuterTopP. Poletto (2000: 31) suggests both a HearerP and a SpeakerP for the position of clitics in Italian.

Cinque (1999: 106) adopts the 32 functional heads in Table 4.1 in his work. He assumes

Table 4.1: Functional heads following Cinque (1999: 106)

1. $Mood_{Speech\ Act}$	2. $Mood_{Evaluative}$	3. $Mood_{Evidential}$	4. $Mood_{Epistemic}$
5. T(Past)	6. T(Future)	7. $Mood_{Irrealis}$	8. $Mod_{Necessity}$
9. $Mod_{Possibility}$	10. $Mod_{Volitional}$	11. $Mod_{Obligation}$	12. $Mod_{Ability/permission}$
13. $Asp_{Habitual}$	14. $Asp_{Repetitive(I)}$	15. $Asp_{Frequentative(I)}$	16. $Asp_{Celerative(I)}$
17. T(Anterior)	18. $Asp_{Terminative}$	19. $Asp_{Continuative}$	20. $Asp_{Perfect(?)}$
21. $Asp_{Retrospective}$	22. $Asp_{Proximative}$	23. $Asp_{Durative}$	24. $Asp_{Generic/progressive}$
25. $Asp_{Prospective}$	26. $Asp_{SgCompletive(I)}$	27. $Asp_{PlCompletive}$	28. Asp_{Voice}
29. $Asp_{Celerative(II)}$	30. $Asp_{SgCompletive(II)}$	31. $Asp_{Repetitive(II)}$	32. $Asp_{Frequentative(II)}$

that all sentences contain a structure with all these functional heads. The specifier positions of these heads can be occupied by adverbs or remain empty. Cinque claims that these functional heads and the corresponding structures form part of Universal Grammar, that is, knowledge of these structures is innate (page 107).[9] Laenzlinger (2004) follows Cinque in proposing this sequence of functional heads for German. He also follows Kayne (1994), who assumes that all syntactic structures have the order specifier head complement cross-linguistically, even if the surface order of the constituents seems to contradict this.

---

[8] See Chomsky (1995b: Section 4.10.1), however.

[9] Table 4.1 shows only the functional heads in the clausal domain. Cinque (1994: 96, 99) also accounts for the order of adjectives with a cascade of projections: Quality, Size, Shape, Color, Nationality. These categories and their ordering are also assumed to belong to UG (p. 100).

Cinque (1994: 96) claims that a maximum of seven attributive adjectives are possible and explains this with the fact that there are a limited number of functional projections in the nominal domain. As was shown on page 65, with a fitting context it is possible to use several adjectives of the same kind, which is why some of Cinque's functional projections would have to be subject to iteration.

The constituent orders that are visible in the end are derived by leftward-movement.[10] Figure 4.20 on the following page shows the analysis of a verb-final clause where the functional adverbial heads have been omitted.[11] Subjects and objects are generated as arguments inside of vP and VP, respectively. The subject is moved to the specifier of the subject phrase and the object is moved to the specifier of the object phrase. The verbal projection (VP_k) is moved in front of the auxiliary into the specifier position of the phrase containing the auxiliary. The only function of SubjP and ObjP is to provide a landing site for the respective movements. For a sentence in which the object precedes the subject, Laenzlinger assumes that the object moves to the specifier of a topic phrase. Figure 4.20 contains only a ModP and an AspP, although Laenzlinger assumes that all the heads proposed by Cinque are present in the structure of all German clauses. For ditransitive verbs, Laenzlinger assumes multiple object phrases (page 230). A similar analysis with movement of object and subject from verb-initial VPs to Agr positions was suggested by Zwart (1994) for Dutch.

For general criticism of Kayne's model, see Haider (2000). Haider shows that a Kayne-like theory makes incorrect predictions for German (for instance regarding the position of selected adverbials and secondary predicates and regarding verbal complex formation) and therefore fails to live up to its billing as a theory which can explain all languages. Haider (1997a: Section 4) has shown that the assumption of an empty Neg head, as assumed by Pollock (1989), Haegeman (1995) and others, leads to problems. See Bobaljik (1999) for problems with the argumentation for Cinque's cascade of adverb-projections.

Furthermore, it has to be pointed out that SubjP and ObjP, TraP (Transitive Phrase) and IntraP (Intransitive Phrase) (Karimi-Doostan 2005: 1745) and TopP (topic phrase), DistP (quantifier phrase), AspP (aspect phrase) (Kiss 2003: 22; Karimi 2005: 35), PathP and PlaceP (Svenononius 2004: 246) encode information about grammatical function, valence, information structure and semantics in the category symbols.[12] In a sense, this is a misuse of category symbols, but such a misuse of information structural and se-

---

[10] This also counts for extraposition, that is, the movement of constituents into the postfield in German. Whereas this would normally be analyzed as rightward-movement, Kayne (1994: Chapter 9) analyzes it as movement of everything else to the left. Kayne assumes that (i.b) is derived from (i.a) by moving part of the NP:

(i)   a. just walked into the room [NP someone who we don't know].

      b. Someone*i* just walked into the room [NP *−i* who we don't know].

(i.a) must have to be some kind of derived intermediate representation, otherwise English would not be SV(O) underlyingly but rather V(O)S. (i.a) is therefore derived from (ii) by fronting the VP *just walked into the room*.

(ii) Someone who we don't know just walked into the room

Such analyses have the downside that they cannot be easily combined with performance models (see Chapter 15).

[11] These structures do not correspond to $\overline{\text{X}}$ theory as it was presented in Section 2.5. In some cases, heads have been combined with complements to form an XP rather than an X′. For more on $\overline{\text{X}}$ theory in the Minimalist Program, see Section 4.6.3.

[12] For further examples and references, see Newmeyer (2004a: 194; 2005: 82). Newmeyer references also works which stipulate a projection for each semantic role, e.g., Agent, Reciprocal, Benefactive, Instrumental, Causative, Comitative, and Reversive Phrase.

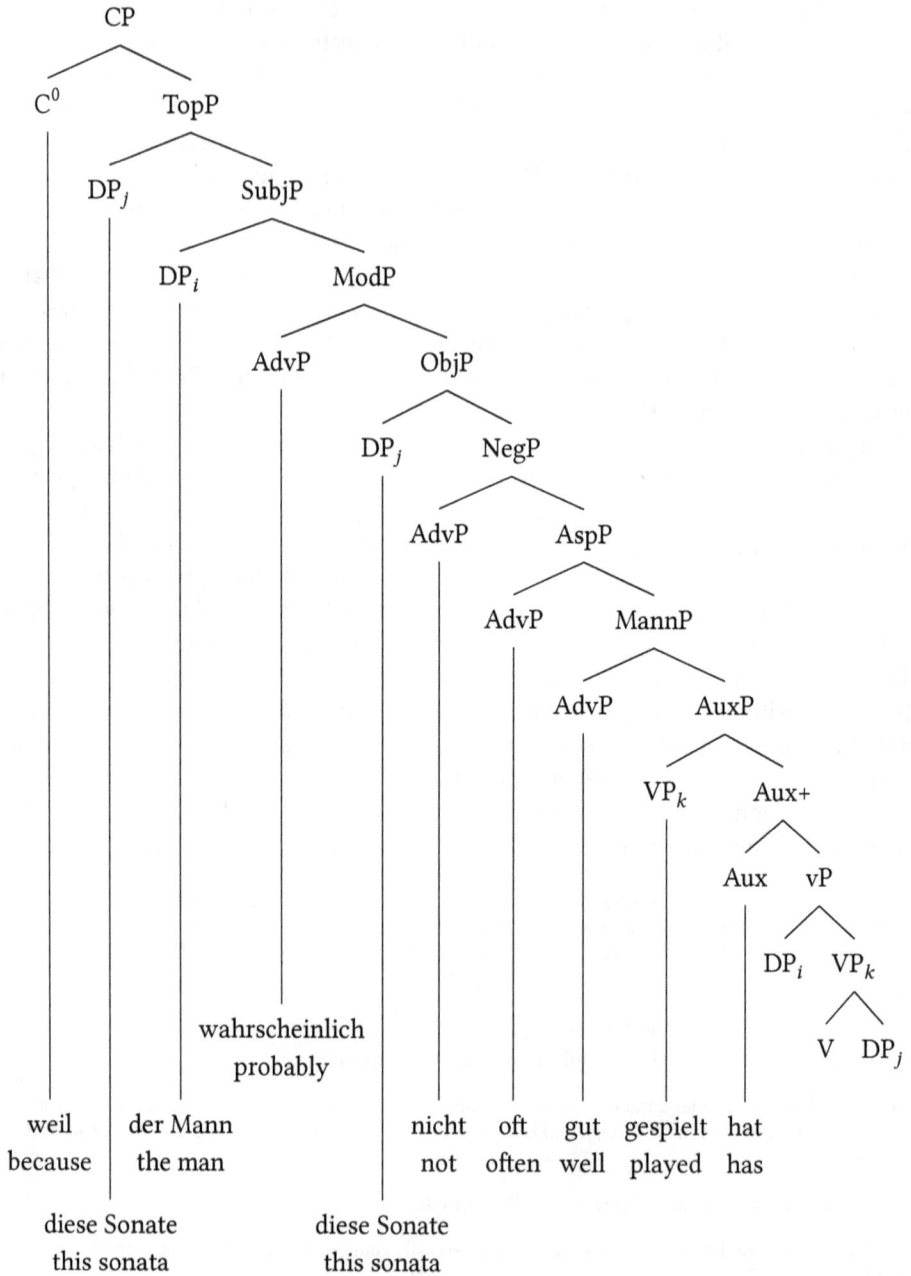

Figure 4.20: Analysis of sentence structure with leftward remnant movement and functional heads following Laenzlinger (2004: 224)

mantic categories is necessary since syntax, semantics, and information structure are tightly connected and since it is assumed that the semantics interprets the syntax, that is, it is assumed that semantics comes after syntax (see Figure 3.2 and Figure 4.1). By using semantically and pragmatically relevant categories in syntax, there is no longer a clean distinction between the levels of morphology, syntax, semantics and pragmatics: everything has been 'syntactified'. Felix Bildhauer (p. c. 2012) has pointed out to me that approaches which assume a cascade of functional projections where the individual aspects of meaning are represented by nodes are actually very close to phrasal approaches in Construction Grammar (see Adger 2013: 470 also for a similar view). One simply lists configurations and these are assigned a meaning (or features which are interpreted post-syntactically, see Cinque & Rizzi (2010: 62) for the interpretation of TopP, for example).

4.6.1.2 Feature checking in specifier positions

If one takes the theory of feature checking in Specifier-Head relations to its logical conclusion, then one arrives at an analysis such as the one suggested by Radford (1997: 452). Radford assumes that prepositions are embedded in an Agreement Phrase in addition to the structure in (23), which is usually assumed, and that the preposition adjoins to the head of the Agreement Phrase and the argument of the preposition is moved to the specifier position of the Agreement Phrase.

(23) [$_{PP}$ P DP]

The problem here is that the object now precedes the preposition. In order to rectify this, Radford assumes a functional projection p (read *little p*) with an empty head to which the preposition then adjoins. This analysis is shown in Figure 4.21 on the next page. This machinery is only necessary in order to retain the assumption that feature checking takes place in specifier-head relations. If one were to allow the preposition to determine the case of its object locally, then all this theoretical apparatus would not be necessary and it would be possible to retain the well-established structure in (23).

Sternefeld (2006: 549–550) is critical of this analysis and compares it to Swiss cheese (being full of holes). The comparison to Swiss cheese is perhaps even too positive since, unlike Swiss cheese, the ratio of substance to holes in the analysis is extreme (2 words vs. 5 empty elements). We have already seen an analysis of noun phrases on page 69, where the structure of an NP, which only consisted of an adjective *klugen* 'clever', contained more empty elements than overt ones. The difference to the PP analysis discussed here is that empty elements are only postulated in positions where overt determiners and nouns actually occur. The little p projection, on the other hand, is motivated entirely theory-internally. There is no theory-external motivation for any of the additional assumptions made for the analysis in Figure 4.21 (see Sternefeld 2006: 549–550).

A variant of this analysis has been proposed by Hornstein, Nunes & Grohmann (2005: 124). The authors do without little p, which makes the structure less complex. They assume the structure in (24), which corresponds to the AgrOP-subtree in Figure 4.21.

(24) [$_{AgrP}$ DP$_k$ [$_{Agr'}$ P$_i$+Agr [$_{PP}$ t$_i$ t$_k$]]]

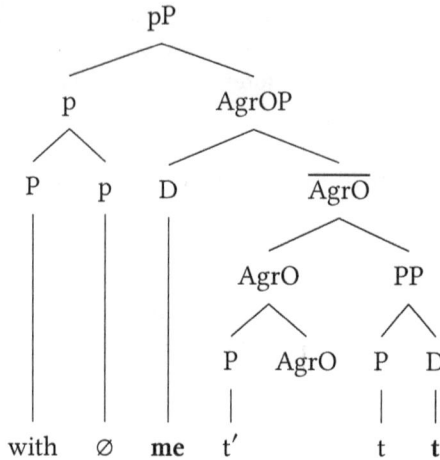

Figure 4.21: PP analysis following Radford with case assignment in specifier position and little p

The authors assume that the movement of the DP to SpecAgrP happens invisibly, that is, covert. This solves Radford's problem and makes the assumption of pP redundant.

The authors motivate this analysis by pointing out agreement phenomena in Hungarian: Hungarian postpositions agree with the preceding noun phrase in person and number. That is, the authors argue that English prepositional and Hungarian postpositional phrases have the same structure derived by movement, albeit the movement is covert in English.

In this way, it is possible to reduce the number and complexity of basic operations and, in this sense, the analysis is minimal. These structures are, however, still incredibly complex. No other kind of theory discussed in this book needs the amount of inflated structure to analyze the combination of a preposition with a noun phrase. The structure in (24) cannot be motivated by reference to data from English and it is therefore impossible to acquire it from the linguistic input. A theory which assumes this kind of structures would have to postulate a Universal Grammar with the information that features can only be checked in (certain) specifier positions (see Chapters 13 and 16 for more on Universal Grammar and language acquisition). For general remarks on (covert) movement see Haider (2014: Section 2.3).

4.6.1.3 Locality of selection and functional projections

Another problem arises from the use of functional heads to encode linear order. In the classic CP/IP-system and all other theories discussed here, a category stands for a class of objects with the same distribution, that is, NP (or DP) stands for pronouns and complex noun phrases. Heads select phrases with a certain category. In the CP/IP-system, I selects a VP and an NP, whereas C selects an IP. In newer analyses, this kind of selectional mechanism does not work as easily. Since movement has taken place in (25b), we are dealing with a TopP or FocP in *das Buch dem Mann zu geben* 'the book the man to give'. Therefore, *um* cannot simply select an non-finite IP, but rather has to disjunctively be able to select a TopP, FocP or IP. It has to be ensured that TopPs and FocPs are marked with regard to the form of the verb contained inside them, since *um* can only be combined with *zu*-infinitives.

(25) a. um dem Mann das Buch zu geben
           for the man the book to give
           'to give the man the book'

      b. um das Buch dem Mann zu geben
           for the book the man to give
           'to give the book to the man'

The category system, selectional mechanisms and projection of features would therefore have to be made considerably more complicated when compared to a system which simply base generates the orders or a system in which a constituent is moved out of the IP, thereby creating a new IP.

Proposals that follow Cinque (1999) are problematic for similar reasons: Cinque assumes the category AdverbP for the combination of an adverb and a VP. There is an empty functional head, which takes the verbal projection as its complement and the adverb surfaces in the specifier of this projection. In these systems, adverb phrases have to pass on inflectional properties of the verb since verbs with particular inflectional properties (finiteness, infinitives with *zu*, infinitives without *zu*, participles) have to be selected by higher heads (see page 177 and Section 9.1.4). There is of course the alternative to use Agree for this, but then all selection would be nonlocal and after all selection is not agreement. For further, more serious problems with this analysis like modification of adverbs by adverbs in connection with partial fronting and restrictions on non-phrasality of preverbal adverbials in English, see Haider (1997a: Section 5).

A special case of the adverb problem is the negation problem: Ernst (1992) studied the syntax of negation more carefully and pointed out that negation can attach to several different verbal projections (26a,b), to adjectives (26c) and adverbs (26d).

(26) a. Ken could not have heard the news.

      b. Ken could have not heard the news.

      c. a [not unapproachable] figure

      d. [Not always] has she seasoned the meat.

If all of these projections are simply NegPs without any further properties (about verb form, adjective part of speech, adverb part of speech), it would be impossible to account for their different syntactic distributions. Negation is clearly just a special case of the more general problem, since adverbs may attach to adjectives forming adjectival phrases in the traditional sense and not adverb phrases in Chinque's sense. For instance, the adverb *oft* 'often' in (27) modifies *lachender* 'laughing' forming the adjectival phrase *oft lachender*, which behaves like the unmodified adjectival participle *lachender*: it modifies *Mann* 'man' and it precedes it.

(27)   a. ein lachender Mann
          a   laughing man

          'a laughing man'

     b. ein oft   lachender Mann
          a   often laughing man

          'a man that laughs often'

Of course one could imagine solutions to the last three problems that use the Agree relation to enforce selectional constraints nonlocally, but such accounts would violate locality of selection (see Ernst 1992: 110 and the discussion in Section 18.2 of this book) and would be much more complicated than accounts that assume a direct selection of dependents.

Related to the locality issues that were discussed in the previous paragraph is the assumption of special functional projections for the placement of clitics: if one uses SpeakerP so that a clitic for first person singular can be moved to the correct specifier positions and a HearerP so that the clitic for second person can be moved to the correct position (Poletto 2000: 31), then what one has are special projections which need to encode in addition all features that are relevant for clauses (alternatively one could of course assume nonlocal Agree to be responsible for distributional facts). In addition to these features, the category labels contain information that allows higher heads to select clauses containing clitics. In other approaches and earlier variants of transformational grammar, selection was assumed to be strictly local so that higher heads only have access to those properties of embedded categories that are directly relevant for selection (Abraham 2005: 223; Sag 2007) and not information about whether an argument of a head within the clause is the speaker or the hearer or whether some arguments in the clause are realized as clitics. Locality will be discussed further in Section 18.2.

4.6.1.4 Feature-driven movement

Finally, there is a conceptual problem with feature-driven movement, which has been pointed out by Gisbert Fanselow: Frey (2004a: 27) assumes a KontrP (contrastive phrase) and Frey (2004b) a TopP (topic phrase) (see Rizzi (1997) for TopP and FocP (focus phrase) in Italian and Haftka (1995), Grewendorf (2002: 85, 240); 2009, Abraham (2003: 19), Laenzlinger (2004: 224) and Hinterhölzel (2004: 18) for analyses of German with TopP and/or FocP). Constituents have to move to the specifier of these functional heads depending on their information structural status. Fanselow (2003a) has shown that such movement-based theories for the ordering of elements in the middle field are not compatible with current assumptions of the Minimalist Program. The reason for this is that sometimes movement takes place in order to create space for other elements (altruistic movement). If the information structure of a sentence requires that the closest object to a verb is neither focused nor part of the focus, then the object closest to the verb should not receive the main stress in the clause. This can be achieved by deaccentuation, that is, by moving the accent to another constituent or even, as shown in (28b), by moving the object to a different position from the one in which it receives structural stress.

(28) a. dass die Polizei gestern   Linguisten verhaftete
           that the police yesterday linguists   arrested

      'that the police arrested linguists yesterday'

      b. dass die Polizei Linguisten gestern   verhaftete
          that the police linguists   yesterday arrested

      'that the police arrested linguists yesterday'

In Spanish, partial focus can be achieved not by special intonation, but rather only by altruistic movement in order to move the object out of the focus. See also Bildhauer & Cook (2010: p. 72) for a discussion of 'altruistic' multiple frontings in German.

It is therefore not possible to assume that elements are moved to a particular position in the tree in order to check some feature motivated by information structural properties. Since feature checking is a prerequisite for movement in current minimalist theory, one would have to postulate a special feature, which only has the function of triggering altruistic movement. Fanselow (2003a: Section 4; 2006: 8) has also shown that the ordering constraints that one assumes for topic, focus and sentence adverbs can be adequately described by a theory which assumes firstly, that arguments are combined (in minimalist terminology: *merged*) with their head one after the other and secondly, that adjuncts can be adjoined to any projection level. The position of sentence adverbs directly before the focused portion of the sentence receives a semantic explanation: since sentence adverbs behave like focus-sensitive operators, they have to directly precede elements that they refer to. It follows from this that elements which do not belong to the focus of an utterance (topics) have to occur in front of the sentence adverb. It is therefore not necessary to assume a special topic position to explain local reorderings in the middle field. This analysis is also pursued in LFG and HPSG. The respective analyses are discussed in more detail in the corresponding chapters.

4.6.2 Labeling

In the Minimalist Program, Chomsky tries to keep combinatorial operations and mechanisms as simple as possible. He motivates this with the assumption that the existence of a UG with less language-specific knowledge is more plausible from a evolutionary point of view than a UG which contains a high degree of language-specific knowledge (Chomsky 2008: 135).

For this reason, he removes the projection levels of $\overline{X}$ theory, traces, indices and "similar descriptive technology" (Chomsky 2008: 138). All that remains is Merge and Move, that is, Internal and External Merge. Internal and External Merge combine two syntactic objects α and β into a larger syntactic object which is represented as a set { α, β }. α and β can be either lexical items or internally complex syntactic objects. Internal Merge

moves a part of an object to its periphery.[13] The result of internally merging an element
is a set { α, β } where α was a part of β. External Merge also produces a set with two
elements. However, two independent objects are merged. The objects that are created
by Merge have a certain category (a set of features). For instance, if one combines the
elements α and β, one gets { l, { α, β } }, where l is the category of the resulting object.
This category is also called a *label*. Since it is assumed that all constituents are headed,
the category that is assigned to { α, β } has to be either the category of α or the category
of β. Chomsky (2008: 145) discusses the following two rules for the determination of the
label of a set.

(29)   a. In { H, α }, H an LI, H is the label.

     b. If α is internally merged to β, forming { α, β } then the label of β is the label
of { α, β }.

As Chomsky notes, these rules are not unproblematic since the label is not uniquely determined in all cases. An example is the combination of two lexical elements. If both H
and α in (29a) are lexical items (LI), then both H and α can be the label of the resulting
structure. Chomsky notices that this could result in deviant structures, but claims that
this concern is unproblematic and ignores it. Chomsky offered a treatment of the combination of two lexical items in his 2013 paper. The solution to the problem is to assume that
all combinations of lexical elements consist of a functional element and a root (Marantz
1997; Borer 2005). Roots are not considered as labels per definition[14] and hence the category of the functional element determines the category of the combination (Chomsky
2013: 47). Such an analysis can only be rejected: the goal of the Minimalist Program is to
simplify the theoretical proposals to such an extent that the models of language acquisition and language evolution become plausible, but in order to simplify basic concepts it
is stipulated that a noun cannot simply be a noun but needs a functional element to tell
the noun what category it has. Given that the whole point of Chomsky's Bare Phrase
Structure (Chomsky 1995a) was the elimination of the unary branching structures in $\overline{X}$
theory, it is unclear why they are reintroduced now through the backdoor, only more
complex with an additional empty element.[15] Theories like Categorial Grammar and
HPSG can combine lexical items directly without assuming any auxiliary projections or
empty elements. See also Rauh (2013) for a comparison of the treatment of syntactic categories in earlier versions of Transformational Grammar, HPSG, Construction Grammar,
Role and Reference Grammar and root-based Neo-Constructivist proposals like the one

---

[13] To be more specific, part of a syntactic object is copied and the copy is placed at the edge of the entire
object. The original of this copy is no longer relevant for pronunciation (*Copy Theory of Movement*).
[14] Another category that is excluded as label per definition is *Conj*, which stands for conjunction (Chomsky
2013: 45–46). This is a stipulation that is needed to get coordination to work. See below.
[15] The old $\overline{X}$ rule in (i.a) corresponds to the binary combination in (i.b).

(i)   a. N′ → N

    b. N → N-func root

In (i.a) a lexical noun is projected to an N′ and in (i.b), a root is combined with a functional nominal head
into a nominal category.

assumed by Chomsky (2013). Rauh concludes that the direct connection of syntactic and semantic information is needed and that the Neo-Constructivism of Marantz and Borer has to be rejected. For further criticism of Neo-Constructivist approaches see Wechsler (2008a) and Müller & Wechsler (2014a: Sections 6.1 and 7).

The combination of a pronoun with a verbal projection poses a problem that is related to what has been said above. In the analysis of *He left*, the pronoun *he* is a lexical element and hence would be responsible for the label of *He left*, since *left* is an internally complex verbal projection in Minimalist theories. The result would be a nominal label rather than a verbal one. To circumvent this problem, Chomsky (2013: 46) assumes that *he* has a complex internal structure: 'perhaps D-pro', that is, *he* is (perhaps) composed out of an invisible determiner and a pronoun.

The case in which two non-LIs are externally merged (for instance a nominal and a verbal phrase) is not discussed in Chomsky (2008). Chomsky (2013: 43–44) suggests that a phrase XP is irrelevant for the labeling of { XP, YP } if XP is moved (or rather copied in the Copy Theory of Movement) in a further step. Chomsky assumes that one of two phrases in an { XP, YP } combination has to move, since otherwise labeling would be impossible (p. 12).[16] The following coordination example will illustrate this: Chomsky assumes that the expression *Z and W* is analyzed as follows: first, Z and W are merged. This expression is combined with Conj (30a) and in the next step Z is raised (30b).

(30) a. $[_\alpha$ Conj $[_\beta$ Z W]]
      b. $[_\gamma$ Z $[_\alpha$ Conj $[_\beta$ Z W]]]

Since Z in β is only a copy, it does not count for labeling and β can get the label of W. It is stipulated for the combination of Z and α that Conj cannot be the label and hence the label of the complete structure is Z.[17]

A special case that is discussed by Chomsky is the Internal Merge of an LI α with a non LI β. According to rule (29a) the label would be α. According to (29b), the label would be β (see also Donati (2006)). Chomsky discusses the combination of the pronoun *what* with *you wrote* as an example.

---

[16] His explanation is contradictory: on p. 11 Chomsky assumes that a label of a combination of two entities with the same category is this category. But in his treatment of coordination, he assumes that one of the conjuncts has to be raised, since otherwise the complete structure could not be labeled.

[17] As Bob Borsley (p.c. 2013) pointed out to me, this makes wrong predictions for coordinations of two singular noun phrases with *and*, since the result of the coordination is a plural NP and not a singular one like the first conjunct. Theories like HPSG can capture this by grouping features in bundles that can be shared in coordinated structures (syntactic features and nonlocal features, see Pollard & Sag (1994: 202)).
 Furthermore the whole account cannot explain why (i.b) is ruled out.

(i) a. both Kim and Lee
    b. * both Kim or Lee

The information about the conjunction has to be part of the representation for *or Lee* in order to be able to contrast it with *and Lee*.
 A further problem is that the label of α should be the label of W since Conj does not count for label determination. This would lead to a situation in which we have to choose between Z and W to determine the label of γ. Following Chomsky's logic, either Z or W would have to move on to make it possible to label γ. Chomsky (2013) mentions this problem in footnote 40, but does not provide a solution.

(31) what [C [you wrote *t*]]

If the label is determined according to (29b), one then has a syntactic object that would be called a CP in the GB framework; since this CP is, moreover, interrogative, it can function as the complement of *wonder* as in (32a). If the label is determined according to (29a), one gets an object that can function as the accusative object of *read* in (32b), that is, something that corresponds to a DP in GB terminology.

(32) a. I wonder what you wrote.

     b. I read what you wrote.

what you wrote in (32b) is a so-called free relative clause.

    Chomsky's approach to free relative clauses is interesting but is unable to describe the phenomenon in full breadth. The problem is that the phrase that contains the relative pronoun may be complex (contrary to Donati's claims, see also Citko (2008: 930–932)).[18] (33) provides an English example from Bresnan & Grimshaw (1978: 333). German examples from Bausewein (1990: 155) and Müller (1999b: 78) are given in (34).

(33) I'll read [whichever book] you give me.

(34) a. Ihr könnt beginnen, [mit *wem*] ihr wollt.[19]
        you can   start   with whom you want

        'You can start with whoever you like.'

     b. [*Wessen* Birne]   noch halbwegs in der Fassung steckt, pflegt solcherlei
        whose bulb/head yet   halfway in the socket   is   uses   such
        Erloschene zu meiden;[20]
        extinct   to avoid

        'Those who still have their wits half way about them tend to avoid such vacant characters;'

     c. [*Wessen* Schuhe] „danach" besprenkelt sind, hat keinen Baum gefunden und
        whose shoes   after.that speckled   are has no   tree found   and
        war nicht zu einem Bogen in der Lage.[21]
        was not to a   bow   in the position

        'Those whose shoes are spattered afterwards couldn't find a tree and were incapable of peeing in an arc.'

Since *wessen Schuhe* 'whose shoes' is not a lexical item, rule (29b) has to be applied, provided no additional rules are assumed to deal with such cases. This means that the whole free relative clause *wessen Schuhe danach besprenkelt sind* is labeled as CP. For the free relatives in (33) and (34) the labeling as a CP is an unwanted result, since they

---

[18] Chomsky (2013: 47) admits that there are many open questions as far as the labeling in free relative clauses is concerned and hence admits that there remain many open questions with labeling as such.

[19] Bausewein (1990: 155).

[20] Thomas Gsella, taz, 12.02.1997, p. 20.

[21] taz, taz mag, 08./09.08.1998, p. XII.

function as subjects or objects of the matrix predicates and hence should be labelled DP. However, since *wessen Schuhe* is a complex phrase and not a lexical item, (29a) does not apply and hence there is no analysis of the free relative clause as a DP. Therefore, it seems one must return to something like the GB analysis proposed by Groos & van Riemsdijk (1981), at least for the German examples. Gross and van Riemsdijk assume that free relatives consist of an empty noun that is modified by the relative clause like a normal noun. In such an approach, the complexity of the relative phrase is irrelevant. It is only the empty head that is relevant for labeling the whole phrase.[22] However, once empty heads are countenanced in the analysis, the application of (29a) to (31) is undesirable since the application would result in two analyses for (32b): one with the empty nominal head and one in which (31) is labeled as NP directly. One might argue that in the case of several possible derivations, the most economical one wins, but the assumption of transderivational constraints leads to undesired consequences (Pullum 2013: Section 5).

Chomsky (2013) abandons the labeling condition in (29b) and replaces it with general labeling rules that hold for both internal and external Merge of two phrases. He distinguishes two cases. In the first case, labeling becomes possible since one of the two phrases of the set { XP, YP } is moved away. This case was already discussed above.

---

[22] Assuming an empty head is problematic since it may be used as an argument only in those cases in which it is modified by an adjunct, namely the relative clause (Müller 1999b: 97). See also Ott (2011: 187) for a later rediscovery of this problem. It can be solved in HPSG by assuming a unary projection that projects the appropriate category from a relative clause. I also use the unary projection to analyze so-called *non-matching* free relative clauses (Müller 1999b). In constructions with nonmatching free relative clauses, the relative clause fills an argument slot that does not correspond to the properties of the relative phrase (Bausewein 1990). Bausewein discusses the following example, in which the relative phrase is a PP but the free relative fills the accusative slot of *kocht* 'cooks'.

(i) Sie kocht, worauf   sie Appetit hat.
     she cooks where.on she appetite has

     'She cooks what she feels like eating.'

See Müller (1999b: 60–62) for corpus examples.

Minimalist theories do not employ unary projections. Ott (2011) develops an analysis in which the category of the relative phrase is projected, but he does not have a solution for nonmatching free relative clauses (p. 187). The same is true for Citko's analysis, in which an internally merged XP can provide the label.

Many other proposals for labeling or, rather, non-labeling exist. For instance, some Minimalists want to eliminate labeling altogether and argue for a label-free syntax. As was pointed out by Osborne, Putnam & Groß (2011), such analyses bring Minimalism closer to Dependency Grammar. It is unclear how any of these models could deal with non-matching free relative clauses. Groß & Osborne (2009: Section 5.3.3) provide an analysis of free relatives in their version of Dependency Grammar, but deny the existence of nonmatching ones (p. 78). They suggest an analysis in which the relative phrase is the root/label of the free relative clause and hence they have the same problem as Minimalist proposals have with non-matching free relative clauses. As Groß & Osborne (2009: 73) and Osborne et al. (2011: 327) state: empty heads are usually not assumed in (their version of) Dependency Grammar. Neither are unary branching projections. This seems to make it impossible to state that free relative clauses with a relative phrase YP can function as XP, provided XP is a category that is higher in the obliqueness hierarchy of Keenan & Comrie (1977), a generalization that was discovered by Bausewein (1990) (see also Müller 1999b: 60–62 and Vogel 2001: 4). In order to be able to express the relevant facts, an element or a label has to exist that is different from the label of *worauf* in (i).

Chomsky writes about the other case: *X and Y are identical in a relevant respect, provid-
ing the same label, which can be taken as the label of the SO* (p. 11). He sketches an analysis
of interrogative clauses on p. 13 in which the interrogative phrase has a Q feature and
the remaining sentence from which the Q phrase was extracted has a Q feature as well.
Since the two constituents share this property, the label of the complete clause will be Q.
This kind of labeling will "perhaps" also be used for labeling normal sentences consisting
of a subject and a verb phrase agreeing in person and number. These features would be
responsible for the label of the sentence. The exact details are not worked out, but almost
certainly will be more complex than (29b).

A property that is inherent in both Chomsky (2005) and Chomsky (2013) is that the
label is exclusively determined from one of the merged objects. As Bob Borsley pointed
out to me, this is problematic for interrogative/relative phrases like (35).

(35)   with whom

The phrase in (35) is both a prepositional phrase (because the first word is a preposition) and an interrogative/relative phrase (because the second word is an interroga-
tive/relative word). So, what is needed for the correct labeling of PPs like the one in (35)
is a well-defined way of percolating different properties from daughters to the mother
node.[23]

For further problems concerning labeling and massive overgeneration by recent for-
mulations of Merge see Fabregas et al. (2016).

Summarizing, one can say that labeling, which was introduced to simplify the theory
and reduce the amount of language specific innate knowledge that has to be assumed,
can only be made to function with a considerable amount of stipulations. For instance,
the combination of lexical elements requires the assumption of empty functional heads,
whose only purpose is determining the syntactic category of a certain lexical element.
If this corresponded to linguistic reality, knowledge about labeling, the respective functional categories, and information about those categories that have to be ignored for
the labeling would have to be part of innate language specific knowledge and nothing
would be gained. One would be left with bizarre analyses with an enormous degree
of complexity without having made progress in the Minimalist direction. Furthermore,
there are empirical problems and a large number of unsolved cases.

---

[23] HPSG solves this problem by distinguishing head features including part of speech information and nonlocal features containing information about extraction and interrogative/relative elements. Head features
are projected from the head, the nonlocal features of a mother node are the union of the nonlocal features
of the daughters minus those that are bound off by certain heads or in certain configurations.

Citko (2008: 926) suggests an analysis in which both daughters can contribute to the mother node. The
result is a complex label like { P, { D, N }}. This is a highly complex data structure and Citko does not provide
any information on how the relevant information that it contains is accessed. Is an object with the label
{ P, { D, N }} a P, a D or an N? One could say that P has priority since it is in the least embedded set, but D
and N are in one set. What about conflicting features? How does a preposition that selects for a DP decide
whether { D, N } is a D or an N? In any case it is clear that a formalization will involve recursive relations
that dig out elements of subsets in order to access their features. This adds to the overall complexity of
the proposal and is clearly dispreferred over the HPSG solution, which uses one part of speech value per
linguistic object.

The conclusion is that the label of a binary combination should not be determined in the ways suggested by Chomsky (2008, 2013). An alternative option for computing the label is to use the functor of a functor argument structure as the label (Berwick & Epstein 1995: 145). This is the approach taken by Categorial Grammar (Ajdukiewicz 1935; Steedman 2000) and in Stabler's Minimalist Grammars (2011b).[24] Stabler's formalization of Merge will be discussed in Section 4.6.4.

4.6.3 Specifiers, complements, and the remains of $\overline{\text{X}}$ theory

Chomsky (2008: 146) assumes that every head has exactly one complement but an arbitrary number of specifiers. In standard $\overline{\text{X}}$ theory, the restriction that there can be at most one complement followed from the general $\overline{\text{X}}$ schema and the assumption that structures are at most binary branching: in standard $\overline{\text{X}}$ theory a lexical head was combined with all its complements to form an X′. If there are at most two daughters in a phrase, it follows that there can be only one complement (Sentences with ditransitive verbs have been analyzed with an empty head licensing an additional argument; see Larson (1988) for the suggestion of an empty verbal head and Müller & Wechsler (2014a: Sections 6.1 and 7) for a critical assessment of approaches involving little *v*). In standard $\overline{\text{X}}$ theory there was just one specifier. This restriction has now been abandoned. Chomsky writes that the distinction between specifier and complement can now be derived from the order in which elements are merged with their head: elements that are *first-merged* are complements and all others – those which are *later-merged* – are specifiers.

Such an approach is problematic for sentences with monovalent verbs: according to Chomsky's proposal, subjects of monovalent verbs would not be specifiers but complements.[25] This problem will be discussed in more detail in Section 4.6.4.

---

[24] For the Categorial Grammar approach to work, it is necessary to assign the category x/x to an adjunct, where x stands for the category of the head to which the adjunct attaches. For instance, an adjective combines with a nominal object to form a nominal object. Therefore its category is n/n rather than adj.

Similarly, Stabler's approach does not extend to adjuncts unless he is willing to assign the category noun to attributive adjectives. One way out of this problem is to assume a special combination operation for adjuncts and their heads (see Frey & Gärtner 2002: Section 3.2). Such a combination operation is equivalent to the Head-Adjunct Schema of HPSG.

[25] Pauline Jacobson (p.c. 2013) pointed out that the problem with intransitive verbs could be solved by assuming that the last-merged element is the specifier and all non-last-merged elements are complements. This would solve the problems with intransitive verbs and with the coordination of verbs in (36) but it would not solve the problem of coordination in head-final languages as in (39). Furthermore, current Minimalist approaches make use of multiple specifiers and this would be incompatible with the Jacobsonian proposal unless one would be willing to state more complicated restrictions on the status of non-first-merged elements.

Apart from this, theories assuming that syntactic objects merged with word groups are specifiers do not allow for analyses in which two lexical verbs are directly coordinated, as in (36):[26]

(36)   He [knows and loves] this record.

For example, in an analysis suggested by Steedman (1991: 264), *and* (being the head) is first merged with *loves* and then the result is merged with *knows*. The result of this combination is a complex object that has the same syntactic properties as the combined parts: the result is a complex verb that needs a subject and an object. After the combination of the conjunction with the two verbs, the result has to be combined with *this record* and *he*. *this record* behaves in all relevant respects like a complement. Following Chomsky's definition, however, it should be a specifier, since it is combined with the third application of Merge. The consequences are unclear. Chomsky assumes that Merge does not specify constituent order. According to him, the linearization happens at the level of Phonological Form (PF). The restrictions that hold there are not described in his recent papers. However, if the categorization as complement or specifier plays a role for linearization as in Kayne's work (2011: 2, 12) and in Stabler's proposal (see Section 4.6.4), *this record* would have to be serialized before *knows and loves*, contrary to the facts. This means that a Categorial Grammar-like analysis of coordination is not viable and the only remaining option would seem to assume that *knows* is combined with an object and then two VPs are coordinated. Kayne (1994: 61, 67) follows Wexler & Culicover (1980: 303) in suggesting such an analysis and assumes that the object in the first VP is deleted. However, Borsley (2005: 471) shows that such an analysis makes wrong predictions, since (37a) would be derived from (37b) although these sentences differ in meaning.[27]

(37)   a. Hobbs whistled and hummed the same tune.
       b. Hobbs whistled the same tune and hummed the same tune.

---

[26] Chomsky (2013: 46) suggests the coordination analysis in (30): according to this analysis, the verbs would be merged directly and one of the verbs would be moved around the conjunction in a later step of the derivation. As was mentioned in the previous section, such analyses do not contribute to the goal of making minimal assumptions about innate language specific knowledge since it is absolutely unclear how such an analysis of coordination would be acquired by language learners. Hence, I will not consider this coordination analysis here.

Another innovation of Chomsky's 2013 paper is that he eliminates the concept of specifier. He writes in footnote 27 on page 43: *There is a large and instructive literature on problems with Specifiers, but if the reasoning here is correct, they do not exist and the problems are unformulable.* This is correct, but this also means that everything that was explained with reference to the notion of specifier in the Minimalist framework until now does not have an explanation any longer. If one follows Chomsky's suggestion, a large part of the linguistic research of the past years becomes worthless and has to be redone.

Chomsky did not commit himself to a particular view on linearization in his earlier work, but somehow one has to ensure that the entities that were called specifier are realized in a position in which constituents are realized that used to be called specifier. This means that the following remarks will be relevant even under current Chomskyan assumptions.

[27] See also Bartsch & Vennemann (1972: 102), Jackendoff (1977: 192–193), Dowty (1979: 143), den Besten (1983: 104–105), Klein (1985: 8–9) and Eisenberg (1994b) for similar observations and criticism of similar proposals in earlier versions of Transformational Grammar.

Since semantic interpretation cannot see processes such as deletion that happen at the level of Phonological Form (Chomsky 1995b: Chapter 3), the differences in meaning cannot be explained by an analysis that deletes material.

In a further variant of the VP coordination analysis, there is a trace that is related to *this record*. This would be a *Right-Node-Raising* analysis. Borsley (2005) has shown that such analyses are problematic. Among the problematic examples that he discusses is the following pair (see also Bresnan 1974: 615).

(38)   a.   He tried to persuade and convince him.

   b.   * He tried to persuade, but couldn't convince, him.

The second example is ungrammatical if *him* is not stressed. In contrast, (38a) is well-formed even with unstressed *him*. So, if (38a) were an instance of Right-Node-Raising, the contrast would be unexpected. Borsley therefore excludes a Right-Node-Raising analysis.

The third possibility to analyze sentences like (36) assumes discontinuous constituents and uses material twice: the two VPs *knows this record* and *loves this record* are coordinated with the first VP being discontinuous. (See Crysmann (2001) and Beavers & Sag (2004) for such proposals in the framework of HPSG.) However, discontinuous constituents are not usually assumed in the Minimalist framework (see for instance Kayne (1994: 67)). Furthermore, Abeillé (2006) showed that there is evidence for structures in which lexical elements are coordinated directly. This means that one needs analyses like the CG analysis discussed above, which would result in the problems with the specifier/complement status just discussed.

Furthermore, Abeillé has pointed out that NP coordinations in head-final languages like Korean and Japanese present difficulties for Merge-based analyses. (39) shows a Japanese example.

(39)   Robin-to   Kim
   Robin-and Kim
   'Kim and Robin'

In the first step *Robin* is merged with *to*. In a second step *Kim* is merged. Since *Kim* is a specifier, one would expect that *Kim* is serialized before the head as it is the case for other specifiers in head-final languages.

Chomsky tries to get rid of the unary branching structures of standard $\overline{\text{X}}$ theory, which were needed to project lexical items like pronouns and determiners into full phrases, referring to work by Muysken (1982). Muysken used the binary features MIN and MAX to classify syntactic objects as minimal (words or word-like complex objects) or maximal (syntactic objects that stand for complete phrases). Such a feature system can be used to describe pronouns and determiners as [+MIN, +MAX]. Verbs like *give*, however, are classified as [+MIN, −MAX]. They have to project in order to reach the [+MAX]-level. If specifiers and complements are required to be [+MAX], then determiners and pronouns fulfill this requirement without having to project from X^0 via X' to the XP-level.

In Chomsky's system, the MIN/MAX distinction is captured with respect to the completeness of heads (complete = phrase) and to the property of being a lexical item. However, there is a small but important difference between Muysken's and Chomsky's proposal: the predictions with regard to the coordination data that was discussed above. Within the category system of $\overline{\text{X}}$ theory, it is possible to combine two X^0s to get a new, complex X^0. This new object has basically the same syntactic properties that simple X^0s have (see Jackendoff 1977: 51 and Gazdar, Klein, Pullum & Sag 1985). In Muysken's system, the coordination rule (or the lexical item for the conjunction) can be formulated such that the coordination of two +MIN items is a +MIN item. In Chomsky's system an analogous rule cannot be defined, since the coordination of two lexical items is not a lexical item any longer.

Like Chomsky in his recent Minimalist work, Categorial Grammar (Ajdukiewicz 1935) and HPSG (Pollard and Sag 1987; 1994: 39–40) do not (strictly) adhere to $\overline{\text{X}}$ theory. Both theories assign the symbol NP to pronouns (for CG see Steedman & Baldridge (2006: p. 615), see Steedman (2000: Section 4.4) for the incorporation of lexical type raising in order to accommodate quantification). The phrase *likes Mary* and the word *sleeps* have the same category in Categorial Grammar (s\np). In both theories it is not necessary to project a noun like *tree* from N^0 to $\overline{\text{N}}$ in order to be able to combine it with a determiner or an adjunct. Determiners and monovalent verbs in controlled infinitives are not projected from an X^0 level to the XP level in many HPSG analyses, since the valence properties of the respective linguistic objects (an empty SUBCAT or COMPS list) are sufficient to determine their combinatoric potential and hence their distribution (Müller 1996d; Müller 1999a). If the property of being minimal is needed for the description of a phenomenon, the binary feature LEX is used in HPSG (Pollard and Sag 1987: 172; 1994: 22). However, this feature is not needed for the distinction between specifiers and complements. This distinction is governed by principles that map elements of an argument structure list (ARG-ST) onto valence lists that are the value of the SPECIFIER and the COMPLEMENTS feature (abbreviated as SPR and COMPS respectively).[28] Roughly speaking, the specifier in a verbal projection is the least oblique argument of the verb for configurational languages like English. Since the argument structure list is ordered according to the obliqueness hierarchy of Keenan & Comrie (1977), the first element of this list is the least oblique argument of a verb and this argument is mapped to the SPR list. The element in the SPR list is realized to the left of the verb in SVO languages like English. The elements in the COMPS list are realized to the right of their head. Approaches like the one by Ginzburg & Sag (2000: 34, 364) that assume that head-complement phrases combine a word with its arguments have the same problem with coordinations like (36) since the head of the VP is not a word.[29] However, this restriction for the head can be replaced by one that refers to the LEX feature rather than to the property of being a word or lexical item.

---

[28] Some authors assume a three-way distinction between subjects, specifiers, and complements.

[29] As mentioned above, a multidomination approach with discontinuous constituents is a possible solution for the analysis of (36) (see Crysmann 2001 and Beavers & Sag 2004). However, the coordination of lexical items has to be possible in principle as Abeillé (2006) has argued. Note also that the HPSG approach to coordination cannot be taken over to the MP. The reason is that the HPSG proposals involve special grammar rules for coordination and MP comes with the claim that there is only Merge. Hence the additional introduction of combinatorial rules is not an option within the MP.

Pollard & Sag as well as Sag & Ginzburg assume flat structures for English. Since one of the daughters is marked as lexical, it follows that the rule does not combine a head with a subset of its complements and then apply a second time to combine the result with further complements. Therefore, a structure like (40a) is excluded, since *gave John* is not a word and hence cannot be used as the head daughter in the rule.

(40) a. [[gave John] a book]

  b. [gave John a book]

Instead of (40a), only analyses like (40b) are admitted; that is, the head is combined with all its arguments all in one go. The alternative is to assume binary branching structures (Müller 2015c; Müller & Ørsnes 2015: Section 1.2.2). In such an approach, the head complement schema does not restrict the word/phrase status of the head daughter. The binary branching structures in HPSG correspond to External Merge in the MP.

In the previous two sections, certain shortcomings of Chomsky's labeling definition and problems with the coordination of lexical items were discussed. In the following section, I discuss Stabler's definition of Merge in Minimalist Grammar, which is explicit about labeling and in one version does not have the problems discussed above. I will show that his formalization corresponds rather directly to HPSG representations.

4.6.4 Minimalism, Categorial Grammar, and HPSG

In this section, I will relate Minimalism, Categorial Grammar and HPSG to one another. Readers who are not yet familiar with Categorial Grammar and HPSG should skim this section or consult the Chapters 6, 8 and 9 and return here afterwards.

In Section 4.6.2, it was shown that Chomsky's papers leave many crucial details about labeling unspecified. Stabler's work is relatively close to recent Minimalist approaches, but is worked out much more precisely (see also Stabler (2011a: 397, 399, 400) on formalization of post GB approaches). Stabler (2001) shows how Kayne's theory of remnant movement can be formalized and implemented. Stabler refers to his particular way of formalizing Minimalist theories as *Minimalist Grammars* (MG). There are a number of interesting results with regard to the weak capacity of Minimalist Grammars and variants thereof (Michaelis 2001). It has been shown, for instance, that the number of possible languages one could create with MGs includes the set of those which can be created by Tree Adjoining Grammars (see Chapter 12). This means that it is possible to assign a greater number of word strings to structures with MGs, however, the structures derived by MGs are not necessarily always the same as the structures created by TAGs. For more on the generative capacity of grammars, see Chapter 17.

Although Stabler's work can be regarded as a formalization of Chomsky's Minimalist ideas, Stabler's approach differs from Chomsky's in certain matters of detail. Stabler assumes that the results of the two Merge operations are not sets but pairs. The head in a pair is marked by a pointer ('<' or '>'). Bracketed expressions like $\{ \alpha, \{ \alpha, \beta \} \}$ (discussed in Section 4.6.2) are replaced by trees like the one in (41).

(41)

$$
\begin{array}{c}
> \\
\diagup\diagdown \\
3 \quad < \\
\diagup\diagdown \\
1 \quad 2
\end{array}
$$

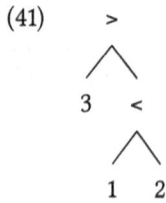

1 is the head in (41), 2 is the complement and 3 the specifier. The pointer points to the part of the structure that contains the head. The daughters in a tree are ordered, that is, 3 is serialized before 1 and 1 before 2.

Stabler (2011a: 402) defines External Merge as follows:

(42) $\text{em}(t_1[=f], t_2[f]) = \begin{cases} \begin{array}{c} < \\ \diagup\diagdown \\ t_1 \quad t_2 \end{array} & \text{if } t_1 \text{ has exactly 1 node} \\ \\ \begin{array}{c} > \\ \diagup\diagdown \\ t_2 \quad t_1 \end{array} & \text{otherwise} \end{cases}$

=f is a selection feature and f the corresponding category. When $t_1[=f]$ and $t_2[f]$ are combined, the result is a tree in which the selection feature of t_1 and the respective category feature of t_2 are deleted. The upper tree in (42) represents the combination of a (lexical) head with its complement. t_1 is positioned before t_2. The condition that t_1 has to have exactly one node corresponds to Chomsky's assumption that the first Merge is a Merge with a complement and that all further applications of Merge are Merges with specifiers (Chomsky 2008: 146).

Stabler defines Internal Merge as follows:[30]

(43) $\text{im}(t_1[+f]) =$

$$
\begin{array}{c}
> \\
\diagup\overline{}\diagdown \\
t_2^{>} \quad t_1\{t_2[-f]^{>} \mapsto \epsilon\}
\end{array}
$$

t_1 is a tree with a subtree t_2 which has the feature f with the value '−'. This subtree is deleted ($t_2[-f]^{>} \mapsto \epsilon$) and a copy of the deleted subtree without the −f feature ($t_2^{>}$) is positioned in specifier position. The element in specifier position has to be a maximal projection. This requirement is visualized by the raised '>'.

Stabler provides an example derivation for the sentence in (44).

(44) who Marie praises

---

[30] In addition to what is shown in (43), Stabler's definition contains a variant of the *Shortest Move Constraint* (SMC), which is irrelevant for the discussion at hand and hence will be omitted.

praises is a two-place verb with two =D features. This encodes the selection of two determiner phrases. *who* and *Marie* are two Ds and they fill the object and subject position of the verb. The resulting verbal projection *Marie praises who* is embedded under an empty complementizer which is specified as +WH and hence provides the position for the movement of *who*, which is placed in the specifier position of CP by the application of Internal Merge. The −WH feature of *who* is deleted and the result of the application of Internal Merge is *who Marie praises*.

This analysis has a problem that was pointed out by Stabler himself in unpublished work cited by Veenstra (1998: 124): it makes incorrect predictions in the case of monovalent verbs. If a verb is combined with an NP, the definition of External Merge in (42) treats this NP as a complement[31] and serializes it to the right of the head. Instead of analyses of sentences like (45a) one gets analyses of strings like (45b).

(45) a. Max sleeps.
      b. * Sleeps Max.

To solve this problem, Stabler assumes that monovalent verbs are combined with a nonovert object (see Veenstra (1998: 61, 124) who, quoting Stabler's unpublished work, also adopts this solution). With such an empty object, the resulting structure contains the empty object as a complement. The empty object is serialized to the right of the verb and *Max* is the specifier and hence serialized to the left of the verb as in (46)).

(46) Max sleeps _.

Of course, any analysis of this kind is both stipulative and entirely ad hoc, being motivated only by the wish to have uniform structures. Moreover, it exemplifies precisely one of the methodological deficiencies of Transformational Generative Grammar discussed at length by Culicover & Jackendoff (2005: Section 2.1.2): the excessive appeal to uniformity.

An alternative is to assume an empty verbal head that takes *sleeps* as complement and *Max* as subject. Such an analysis is often assumed for ditransitive verbs in Minimalist theories which assume Larsonian verb shells (Larson 1988). Larsonian analyses usually assume that there is an empty verbal head that is called little *v* and that contributes a causative meaning. As was discussed in Section 4.1.4, Adger (2003) adopts a little *v*-based analysis for intransitive verbs. Omitting the TP projection, his analysis is provided in Figure 4.22 on the following page. Adger argues that the analysis of sentences with unergative verbs involves a little *v* that selects an agent, while the analysis of unaccusative verbs involves a little *v* that does not select an N head. For unaccusatives, he assumes that the verb selects a theme. He states that little *v* does not necessarily have a causative meaning but introduces the agent. But note that in the example at hand the subject of *sleep* is neither causing an event, nor is it necessarily deliberately doing something. So it is rather an undergoer than an agent. This means that the assumption of the empty *v* head is made for purely theory-internal reasons without any semantic motivation in the case of intransitives. If the causative contribution of little *v* in ditransitive

---

[31] Compare also Chomsky's definition of specifier and complement in Section 4.6.3.

vP

Max　$\overline{v}$

v　*sleep*

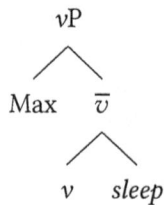

Figure 4.22: Little *v*-based analysis of *Max sleeps*

constructions is assumed, this would mean that one needs two little *v*s, one with and one without a causative meaning. In addition to the lack of theory-external motivation for little *v*, there are also empirical problems for such analyses (for instance with coordination data). The reader is referred to Müller & Wechsler (2014a: Sections 6.1 and 7) for further details.

Apart from the two operations that were defined in (42) and (43), there are no other operations in MG.[32] Apart from the problems with monovalent verbs, this results in the problem that was discussed in Section 4.6.3: there is no analysis with a direct combination of verbs for (36) – repeated here as (47).

(47)   He [knows and loves] this record.

The reason is that the combination of *knows, and* and *loves* consists of three nodes and the Merge of *knows and loves* with *this record* would make *this record* the specifier of the structure. Therefore *this record* would be serialized before *knows and loves*, contrary to the facts. Since the set of languages that can be generated with MGs contains the languages that can be generated with certain TAGs and with Combinatorial Categorial Grammar (Michaelis 2001), the existence of a Categorial Grammar analysis implies that the coordination examples can be derived in MGs somehow. But for linguists, the fact that it is possible to generate a certain string at all (the weak capacity of a grammar) is of less significance. It is the actual structures that are licensed by the grammar that are important (the strong capacity).

4.6.4.1 Directional Minimalist Grammars and Categorial Grammar

Apart from reintroducing X^0 categories, the coordination problem can be solved by changing the definition of Merge in a way that allows heads to specify the direction of combination with their arguments: Stabler (2011b: p. 635) suggests marking the position of an argument relative to its head together with the selection feature and gives the following redefinition of External Merge.

---

[32] For extensions see Frey & Gärtner (2002: Section 3.2).

$$(48) \quad \text{em}(t_1[\alpha], t_2[x]) = \begin{cases} \begin{array}{c} < \\ \wedge \\ t_1 \quad t_2 \end{array} & \text{if } \alpha \text{ is } =x \\[2em] \begin{array}{c} > \\ \wedge \\ t_2 \quad t_1 \end{array} & \text{if } \alpha \text{ is } x= \end{cases}$$

The position of the equal sign specifies on which side of the head an argument has to be realized. This corresponds to forward and backward Application in Categorial Grammar (see Section 8.1.1). Stabler calls this form of grammar Directional MG (DMG). This variant of MG avoids the problem with monovalent verbs and the coordination data is unproblematic as well if one assumes that the conjunction is a head with a variable category that selects for elements of the same category to the left and to the right of itself. *know* and *love* would both select an object to the right and a subject to the left and this requirement would be transferred to *knows and loves*.[33] See Steedman (1991: 264) for the details of the CG analysis and Bouma & van Noord (1998: 52) for an earlier HPSG proposal involving directionality features along the lines suggested by Stabler for his DMGs.

4.6.4.2 Minimalist Grammars and Head-Driven Phrase Structure Grammar

The notation for marking the head of a structure with '>' and '<' corresponds directly to the HPSG representation of heads. Since HPSG is a sign-based theory, information about all relevant linguistic levels is represented in descriptions (phonology, morphology, syntax, semantics, information structure). (49) gives an example: the lexical item for the word *grammar*.

$$(49) \quad \begin{bmatrix} word \\ \text{PHON} & \langle \text{ 'gram}\partial r \rangle \\ \text{SYNSEM} | \text{LOC} & \begin{bmatrix} loc \\ \text{CAT} & \begin{bmatrix} cat \\ \text{HEAD} & noun \\ \text{SPR} & \langle \text{ DET } \rangle \end{bmatrix} \\ \text{CONT} & \dots \begin{bmatrix} grammar \\ \text{INST} & X \end{bmatrix} \end{bmatrix} \end{bmatrix}$$

The part of speech of *grammar* is *noun*. In order to form a complete phrase, it requires a determiner. This is represented by giving the SPR feature the value ⟨ DET ⟩. Semantic information is listed under CONT. For details see Chapter 9.

---

[33] Note however, that this transfer makes it necessary to select complex categories, a fact that I overlooked in Müller (2013c). The selection of simplex features vs. complex categories will be discussed in Section 4.6.5.

Since we are dealing with syntactic aspects exclusively, only a subset of the used features is relevant: valence information and information about part of speech and certain morphosyntactic properties that are relevant for the external distribution of a phrase is represented in a feature description under the path SYNSEM|LOC|CAT. The features that are particularly interesting here are the so-called head features. Head features are shared between a lexical head and its maximal projection. The head features are located inside CAT and are grouped together under the path HEAD. Complex hierarchical structure is also modelled with feature value pairs. The constituents of a complex linguistic object are usually represented as parts of the representation of the complete object. For instance, there is a feature HEAD-DAUGHTER the value of which is a feature structure that models a linguistic object that contains the head of a phrase. The Head Feature Principle (50) refers to this daughter and ensures that the head features of the head daughter are identical with the head features of the mother node, that is, they are identical to the head features of the complete object.

(50) *headed-phrase* $\Rightarrow$ $\begin{bmatrix} \text{SYNSEM|LOC|CAT|HEAD} \;\boxed{1} \\ \text{HEAD-DTR|SYNSEM|LOC|CAT|HEAD} \;\boxed{1} \end{bmatrix}$

Identity is represented by boxes with the same number.

Ginzburg & Sag (2000: 30) represent all daughters of a linguistic object in a list that is given as the value of the DAUGHTERS attribute. The value of the feature HEAD-DAUGHTER is identified with one of the elements of the DAUGHTERS list:

(51) a. $\begin{bmatrix} \text{HEAD-DTR} \;\boxed{1} \\ \text{DTRS} \quad \left\langle \boxed{1}\; \alpha, \beta \right\rangle \end{bmatrix}$

b. $\begin{bmatrix} \text{HEAD-DTR} \;\boxed{1} \\ \text{DTRS} \quad \left\langle \alpha, \boxed{1}\; \beta \right\rangle \end{bmatrix}$

α and β are shorthands for descriptions of linguistic objects. The important point about the two descriptions in (51) is that the head daughter is identical to one of the two daughters, which is indicated by the $\boxed{1}$ in front of α and β, respectively. In the first feature description, the first daughter is the head and in the second description, the second daughter is the head. Because of the Head Feature Principle, the syntactic properties of the whole phrase are determined by the head daughter. That is, the syntactic properties of the head daughter correspond to the label in Chomsky's definition. This notation corresponds exactly to the one that is used by Stabler: (51a) is equivalent to (52a) and (51b) is equivalent to (52b).

(52) a.   <   b.   >

         α β α β

An alternative structuring of this basic information, discussed by Pollard & Sag (1994: Chapter 9), uses the two features HEAD-DAUGHTER and NON-HEAD-DAUGHTERS rather than HEAD-DAUGHTER and DAUGHTERS. This gives rise to feature descriptions like (53a), which corresponds directly to Chomsky's set-based representations, discussed in Section 4.6.2 and repeated here as (53b).

(53) a. $\begin{bmatrix} \text{HEAD-DTR} & \alpha \\ \text{NON-HEAD-DTRS} & \langle \beta \rangle \end{bmatrix}$

  b. $\{\alpha, \{\alpha, \beta\}\}$

The representation in (53a) does not contain information about linear precedence of α and β. Linear precedence of constituents is constrained by linear precedence rules, which are represented independently from constraints regarding (immediate) dominance.

The definition of Internal Merge in (43) corresponds to the Head-Filler Schema in HPSG (Pollard & Sag 1994: 164). Stabler's derivational rule deletes the subtree $t_2[-f]^>$. HPSG is monotonic, that is, nothing is deleted in structures that are licensed by a grammar. Instead of deleting t_2 inside of a larger structure, structures containing an empty element (NB – not a tree) are licensed directly.[34] Both in Stabler's definition and in the HPSG schema, t_2 is realized as filler in the structure. In Stabler's definition of Internal Merge, the category of the head daughter is not mentioned, but Pollard & Sag (1994: 164) restrict the head daughter to be a finite verbal projection. Chomsky (2007: 17) assumes that all operations but External Merge operate on phase level. Chomsky assumes that CP and v*P are phases. If this constraint is incorporated into the definition in (43), the restrictions on the label of t_1 would have to be extended accordingly. In HPSG, sentences like (54) have been treated as VPs, not as CPs and hence Pollard & Sag's requirement that the head daughter in the Head Filler Schema be verbal corresponds to Chomsky's restriction.

(54) Bagels, I like.

Hence, despite minor presentational differences, we may conclude that the formalization of Internal Merge and that of the Head-Filler Schema are very similar.

An important difference between HPSG and Stabler's definition is that 'movement' is not feature driven in HPSG. This is an important advantage since feature-driven movement cannot deal with instances of so-called altruistic movement (Fanselow 2003a), that is, movement of a constituent that happens in order to make room for another constituent in a certain position (see Section 4.6.1.4).

A further difference between general $\overline{\text{X}}$ theory and Stabler's formalization of Internal Merge on the one hand and HPSG on the other is that in the latter case there is no restriction regarding the completeness (or valence 'saturation') of the filler daughter. Whether the filler daughter has to be a maximal projection (English) or not (German), follows from restrictions that are enforced locally when the trace is combined with its head. This makes it possible to analyze sentences like (55) without remnant movement.[35]

(55) Gelesen$_i$ hat$_j$ das Buch keiner $_{-i}$ $_{-j}$.
    read   has the book nobody

---

[34] See Bouma, Malouf & Sag (2001a) for a traceless analysis of extraction in HPSG and Müller (2015b: Chapter 7) and Chapter 19 of this book for a general discussion of empty elements.

[35] See also Müller & Ørsnes (2013b) for an analysis of object shift in Danish that can account for verb fronting without remnant movement. The analysis does not have any of the problems that remnant movement analyses have.

In contrast, Stabler is forced to assume an analysis like the one in (56b) (see also G. Müller (1998) for a remnant movement analysis). In a first step, *das Buch* is moved out of the VP (56a) and in a second step, the emptied VP is fronted as in (56b).

(56) a. Hat [das Buch]$_j$ [keiner [$_{VP}$ $_{-j}$ gelesen]].

   b. [$_{VP}$ $_{-j}$ Gelesen]$_i$ hat [das Buch]$_j$ [keiner $_{-i}$].

Haider (1993: 281), De Kuthy & Meurers (2001: Section 2) and Fanselow (2002) showed that this kind of remnant movement analysis is problematic for German. The only phenomenon that Fanselow identified as requiring a remnant movement analysis is the problem of multiple fronting (see Müller (2003a) for an extensive discussion of relevant data). Müller (2005b,c, 2015b) develops an alternative analysis of these multiple frontings which uses an empty verbal head in the *Vorfeld*, but does not assume that adjuncts or arguments like *das Buch* in (56b) are extracted from the *Vorfeld* constituent. Instead of the remnant movement analysis, the mechanism of argument composition from Categorial Grammar (Geach 1970; Hinrichs & Nakazawa 1994) is used to ensure the proper realization of arguments in the sentence. Chomsky (2007: 20) already uses argument composition as part of his analysis of TPs and CPs. Hence both remnant movement and argument composition are assumed in recent Minimalist proposals. The HPSG alternative, however, would appear to need less theoretical apparatus and hence has to be preferred for reasons of parsimony.

Finally, it should be mentioned that all transformational accounts have problems with Across the Board extraction like (57a) and (57) in which one element corresponds to several gaps.

(57) a. Bagels, I like and Ellison hates.[36]

   b. The man who$_i$ [Mary loves $_{-i}$] and [Sally hates $_{-i}$] computed my tax.

This problem was solved for GPSG by Gazdar (1981b) and the solution carries over to HPSG. The Minimalist community tried to address these problems by introducing operations like sideward movement (Nunes 2004) where constituents can be inserted into sister trees. So in the example in (57a), *Bagels* is copied from the object position of *hates* into the object position of *like* and then these two copies are related to the fronted element. Kobele criticized such solutions since they overgenerate massively and need complicated filters. What he suggests instead is the introduction of a GPSG-style SLASH mechanism into Minimalist theories (Kobele 2008).

Furthermore, movement paradoxes (Bresnan 2001: Chapter 2) can be avoided by not sharing all information between filler and gap, a solution that is not available for transformational accounts, which usually assume identity of filler and gap or – as under the Copy Theory of Movement – assume that a derivation contains multiple copies of one object only one of which is spelled out. See also Borsley (2012) for further puzzles for, and problems of, movement-based approaches.

A further difference between MG and HPSG is that the Head-Filler Schema is not the only schema for analyzing long-distance dependencies. As was noted in footnote 10 on page 143, there is dislocation to the right (extraposition) as well as fronting. Although

---

[36] Pollard & Sag (1994: 205).

these should certainly be analyzed as long-distance dependencies, they differ from other long-distance dependencies in various respects (see Section 13.1.5). For analyses of extraposition in the HPSG framework, see Keller (1995), Bouma (1996), and Müller (1999a).

Apart from the schema for long-distance dependencies, there are of course other schemata in HPSG which are not present in MG or Minimalism. These are schemata which describe constructions without heads or are necessary to capture the distributional properties of parts of constructions, which cannot be easily captured in lexical analyses (e.g., the distribution of *wh-* and relative pronouns). See Section 21.10.

Chomsky (2010) has compared a Merge-based analysis of auxiliary inversion to a HPSG analysis and critiqued that the HPSG analysis uses ten schemata rather than one (Merge). Ginzburg & Sag (2000) distinguish three types of construction with moved auxiliaries: inverted sentences such as those with fronted adverbial and with *wh*-questions (58a,b), inverted exclamatives (58c) and polar interrogatives (58d):

(58) a. Under no circumstances *did she think they would do that.*
      b. Whose book *are you reading*?
      c. Am I tired!
      d. Did Kim leave?

Fillmore (1999) captures various different usage contexts in his Construction Grammar analysis of auxiliary inversion and shows that there are semantic and pragmatic differences between the various contexts. Every theory must be able to account for these. Furthermore, one does not necessarily require ten schemata. It is possible to determine this – as Categorial Grammar does – in the lexical entry for the auxiliary or on an empty head (see Chapter 21 for a more general discussion of lexical and phrasal analyses). Regardless of this, every theory has to somehow account for these ten differences. If one wishes to argue that this has nothing to do with syntax, then somehow this has to be modelled in the semantic component. This means that there is no reason to prefer one theory over another at this point.

4.6.5 Selection of atomic features vs. selection of complex categories

Berwick & Epstein (1995) pointed out that Minimalist theories are very similar to Categorial Grammar and I have discussed the similarities between Minimalist theories and HPSG in Müller (2013c) and in the previous subsections. However, I overlooked one crucial difference between the usual assumptions about selection in Minimalist proposals on the one hand and Categorial Grammar, Dependency Grammar, LFG, HPSG, TAG, and Construction Grammar on the other hand: what is selected in the former type of theory is a single feature, while the latter theories select for feature bundles. This seems to be a small difference, but the consequences are rather severe. Stabler's definition of External Merge that was given on page 160 removes the selection feature (=f) and the corresponding feature of the selected element (f). In some publications and in the introduction in this book, the selection features are called uninterpretable features and are marked with a *u*. The uninterpretable features have to be checked and then they are removed from the linguistic object as in Stabler's definition. The fact that they have been checked is represented by striking them out. It is said that all uninterpretable features have to be checked before a syntactic object is send to the interfaces (semantics and pronunciation). If uninterpretable features are not checked, the derivation crashes. Adger (2003: Section 3.6) explicitly discusses the consequences of these assumptions: a selecting head checks a feature of the selected object. It is not possible to check features of elements that are contained in the object that a head combines with. Only features at the topmost node, the so-called root node, can be checked with external merge. The only way features inside complex objects can be checked is by means of movement. This means that a head may not combine with a partially saturated linguistic object, that is, with a linguistic object that has an unchecked selection feature. I will discuss this design decision with reference to an example provided by Adger (2003: 95). The noun *letters* selects for a P and Ps select for an N. The analysis of (59a) is depicted left in Figure 4.23.

(59)   a.   letters to Peter
       b.   * letters to

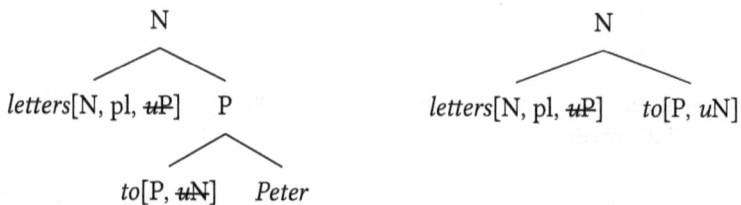

Figure 4.23: The analysis of *letters to Peter* according to Adger (2003: 95)

The string in (59b) is ruled out since the uninterpretable N feature of the preposition *to* is not checked. So this integrates the constraint that all dependent elements have to be maximal into the core mechanism. This makes it impossible to analyze examples like (60) in the most straightforward way, namely as involving a complex preposition and a noun that is lacking a determiner:

(60)   vom   Bus
       from.the bus

In theories in which complex descriptions can be used to describe dependants, the dependent may be partly saturated. So for instance in HPSG, fused prepositions like *vom* 'from.the' can select an N̄, which is a nominal projection lacking a specifier:

(61)   N[SPR ⟨ DET ⟩]

The description in (61) is an abbreviation for an internally structured set of feature-value pairs (see Section 9.6.1). The example here is given for the illustration of the differences only, since there may be ways of accounting for such cases in a single-feature-Merge system. For instance, one could assume a DP analysis and have the complex preposition select a complete NP (something of category N with no uninterpretable features). Alternatively, one can assume that there is indeed a full PP with all the structure that is usually assumed and the fusion of preposition and determiner happens during pronunciation. The first suggestion eliminates the option of assuming an NP analysis as it was suggested by Bruening (2009) in the Minimalist framework.

Apart from this illustrative example with a fused preposition, there are other cases in which one may want to combine unsaturated linguistic objects. I already discussed coordination examples above. Another example is the verbal complex in languages like German, Dutch, and Japanese. Of course there are analyses of these languages that do not assume a verbal complex (G. Müller 1998; Wurmbrand 2003a), but these are not without problems. Some of the problems were discussed in the previous section as well.

Summing up this brief subsection, it has to be said that the feature checking mechanism that is built into the conception of Merge is more restrictive than the selection that is used in Categorial Grammar, Lexical Functional Grammar, HPSG, Construction Grammar, and TAG. In my opinion, it is too restrictive.

4.6.6 Summary

In sum, one can say that the computational mechanisms of the Minimalist Program (e.g., transderivational constraints and labeling), as well as the theory of feature-driven movement are problematic and the assumption of empty functional categories is sometimes ad hoc. If one does not wish to assume that these categories are shared by all languages, then proposing two mechanisms (Merge and Move) does not represent a simplification of grammar since every single functional category which must be stipulated constitutes a complication of the entire system.

The labeling mechanism is not yet worked out in detail, does not account for the phenomena it was claimed to provide accounts for, and hence should be replaced by the head/functor-based labeling that is used in Categorial Grammar and HPSG.

4.7 Summary and classification

This section is similar to Section 3.6. I first comment on language acquisition and then on formalization.

4.7.1 Explaining language acquisition

Chomsky (2008: 135) counts theories in the MP as Principle & Parameter analyses and identifies MP parameters as being in the lexicon. Also, see Hornstein (2013: 396). UG is defined as possibly containing non-language-specific components, which are genetically determined (Chomsky 2007: 7). UG consists of unbounded Merge and the condition that expressions derived by a grammar must fulfill the restrictions imposed by the phonological and conceptual-intentional interfaces. In addition, a specific repertoire of features is assumed to be part of UG (Chomsky 2007: 6–7). The exact nature of these features has not been explained in detail and, as a result, the power of UG is somewhat vague. However, there is a fortunate convergence between various linguistic camps as Chomsky does not assume that the swathes of functional projections which we encountered in Section 4.6.1 also form part of UG (however, authors like Cinque & Rizzi (2010) do assume that a hierarchy of functional projections is part of UG). Since there are still parameters, the same arguments used against GB approaches to language acquisition that were mentioned in Section 3.6.1 are still relevant for theories of language acquisition in the Minimalist Program. See Chapter 16 for an in-depth discussion of approaches to language acquisition and the Principles & Parameters model as well as input-based approaches.

Chomsky's main goal in the Minimalist Program is to simplify the theoretical assumptions regarding formal properties of language and the computational mechanisms that are used so much as to make it plausible that they or relevant parts of them are part of our genetic endowment. But if we recapitulate what was assumed in this chapter, it is difficult to believe that Minimalist theories achieve this goal. To derive a simple sentence with an intransitive verb, one needs several empty heads and movements. Features can be strong or weak, Agree operates nonlocally in trees across several phrase boundaries. And in order to make correct predictions, it has to be made sure that Agree can only see the closest possible element (13)–(14). This is a huge machinery in comparison to a Categorial Grammar that just combines adjacent things. Categorial Grammars can be acquired from input (see Section 13.8.3), while it is really hard to imagine how the fact that there are features that trigger movement when they are strong, but do not trigger it when they are weak, should be acquired from data alone.

4.7.2 Formalization

Section 3.6.2 commented on the lack of formalization in transformational grammar up until the 1990s. The general attitude towards formalization did not change in the minimalist era and hence there are very few formalizations and implementations of Minimalist theories.

Stabler (2001) shows how it is possible to formalize and implement Kayne's theory of remnant movement. In Stabler's implementation[37], there are no transderivational constraints, no numerations[38], he does not assume Agree (see Fong 2014: 132) etc. The fol-

---

[37] His system is available at: http://www.linguistics.ucla.edu/people/stabler/coding.html. 05.03.2016.

[38] There is a numeration lexicon in Veenstra (1998: Chapter 9). This lexicon consists of a set of numerations, which contain functional heads, which can be used in sentences of a certain kind. For example, Veenstra assumes numerations for sentences with bivalent verbs and subjects in initial position, for embeded sentences with monovalent verbs, for wh-questions with monovalent verbs, and for polar interrogatives with monovalent verbs. An element from this set of numerations corresponds to a particular configuration and a phrasal construction in the spirit of Construction Grammar. Veenstra's analysis is not a formalization of the concept of the numeration that one finds in Minimalist works. Normally, it is assumed that a numeration contains all the lexical entries which are needed for the derivation of a sentence. As (i) shows, complex sentences can consist of combinations of sentences with various different sentence types:

(i) Der Mann, der behauptet hat, dass Maria gelacht hat, steht neben der Palme,   die   im letzten
    the man who claimed   has that Maria laughed has stands next.to the palm.tree which in last
    Jahr gepflanzt wurde.
    year planted   was

   'The man who claimed Maria laughed is standing next to the palm tree that was planted last year.'

In (i), there are two relative clauses with verbs of differing valence, an embedded sentence with a monovalent verb and the matrix clause. Under a traditional understanding of numerations, Veenstra would have to assume an infinite numeration lexicon containing all possible combinations of sentence types.

lowing is also true of Stabler's implementation of Minimalist Grammars and GB systems: there are no large grammars. Stabler's grammars are small, meant as a proof of concept and purely syntactic. There is no morphology[39], no treatment of multiple agreement (Stabler 2011b: Section 27.4.3) and above all no semantics. PF and LF processes are not modelled.[40] The grammars and the computational system developed by Sandiway Fong are of similar size and faithfulness to the theory (Fong & Ginsburg 2012; Fong 2014): the grammar fragments are small, encode syntactic aspects such as labeling directly in the phrase structure (Fong & Ginsburg 2012: Section 4) and therefore, fall behind $\overline{X}$ theory. Furthermore, they do not contain any morphology. Spell-Out is not implemented, so in the end it is not possible to parse or generate any utterances.[41] The benchmark here has been set by implementations of grammars in constraint-based theories; for example, the HPSG grammars of German, English and Japanese that were developed in the 90s as part of Verbmobil (Wahlster 2000) for the analysis of spoken language or the LFG or CCG systems with large coverage. These grammars can analyze up to 83 % of utterances in spoken language (for Verbmobil from the domains of appointment scheduling and trip planning) or written language. Linguistic knowledge is used to generate and analyze linguistic structures. In one direction, one arrives at a semantic representation of a string of words and in the other one can create a string of words from a given semantic representation. A morphological analysis is indispensable for analyzing naturally occurring data from languages with elaborated morphological marking systems. In the remainder of this book, the grammars and computational systems developed in other theories will be discussed at the beginning of the respective chapters.

The reason for the lack of larger fragments inside of GB/MP could have to do with the fact that the basic assumptions of Minimalist community change relatively quickly:

> In Minimalism, the triggering head is often called a *probe*, the moving element is called a *goal*, and there are various proposals about the relations among the features that trigger syntactic effects. Chomsky (1995b: p. 229) begins with the assumption that features represent requirements which are checked and deleted when the requirement is met. The first assumption is modified almost immediately so that only

---

[39] The test sentences have the form as in (i).

(i) a. the king will -s eat

b. the king have -s eat -en

c. the king be -s eat -ing

d. the king -s will -s have been eat -ing the pie

[40] See Sauerland & Elbourne (2002) for suggestions of PF and LF-movement and the deletion of parts of copies (p. 285). The implementation of this would be far from trivial.

[41] The claim by Berwick, Pietroski, Yankama & Chomsky (2011: 1221) in reference to Fong's work is just plain wrong: *But since we have sometimes adverted to computational considerations, as with the ability to "check" features of a head/label, this raises a legitimate concern about whether our framework is computationally realizable. So it is worth noting that the copy conception of movement, along with the locally oriented "search and labeling" procedure described above, can be implemented computationally as an efficient parser; see Fong, 2011, for details.* If one has a piece of software which cannot parse a single sentence, then one cannot claim that it is efficient since one does not know whether the missing parts of the program could make it extremely inefficient. Furthermore, one cannot compare the software to other programs. As has already been discussed, labeling is not carried out by Fong as was described in Chomsky's work, but instead he uses a phrase structure grammar of the kind described in Chapter 2.

a proper subset of the features, namely the 'formal', 'uninterpretable' features are deleted by checking operations in a successful derivation (Collins, 1997; Chomsky 1995b: §4.5). Another idea is that certain features, in particular the features of certain functional categories, may be initially unvalued, becoming valued by entering into appropriate structural configurations with other elements (Chomsky 2008; Hiraiwa, 2005). And some recent work adopts the view that features are never deleted (Chomsky 2007: p. 11). These issues remain unsolved. (Stabler 2011a: 397)

In order to fully develop a grammar fragment, one needs at least three years (compare the time span between the publication of *Barriers* (1986) and Stabler's implementation (1992)). Particularly large grammars require the knowledge of several researchers working in international cooperation over the space of years or even decades. This process is disrupted if fundamental assumptions are repeatedly changed at short intervals.

Further reading

This chapter heavily draws from Adger (2003). Other textbooks on Minimalism are Radford (1997), Grewendorf (2002), and Hornstein, Nunes & Grohmann (2005).

Kuhn (2007) offers a comparison of modern derivational analyses with constraint-based LFG and HPSG approaches. Borsley (2012) contrasts analyses of long-distance dependencies in HPSG with movement-based analyses as in GB/Minimalism. Borsley discusses four types of data which are problematic for movement-based approaches: extraction without fillers, extraction with multiple gaps, extractions where fillers and gaps do not match and extraction without gaps.

The discussion of labeling, abandonment of $\overline{\text{X}}$ theory and a comparison between Stabler's Minimalist Grammars and HPSG from Sections 4.6.2–4.6.4 can be found in Müller (2013c).

Intonational Phrasing, Discontinuity, and the Scope of Negation by Błaszczak & Gärtner (2005) is recommended for the more advanced reader. The authors compare analyses of negated quantifiers with wide scope in the framework of Minimalism (following Kayne) as well as Categorial Grammar (following Steedman).

Sternefeld (2006) is a good, detailed introduction to syntax (839 pages) which develops a Transformational Grammar analysis of German which (modulo transformations) almost matches what is assumed in HPSG (feature descriptions for arguments ordered in a valence list according to a hierarchy). Sternefeld's structures are minimal since he does not assume any functional projections if they cannot be motivated for the language under discussion. Sternefeld is critical regarding certain aspects which some other analyses take for granted. Sternefeld views his book explicitly as a textbook from which one can learn how to argue coherently when creating theories. For this reason, this book is not just recommended for students and PhD students.

Sternefeld & Richter (2012) discuss the situation in theoretical linguistics with particular focus on the theories described in this and the previous chapter. I can certainly understand the frustration of the authors with regard to the vagueness of analyses, argumentation style, empirical base of research, rhetorical clichés, immunization attempts and general respect for scientific standards: a current example of this is the article *Problems of Projection* by Chomsky (2013).[42] I, however, do not share the general, pessimistic tone of this article. In my opinion, the patient's condition is critical, but he is not dead yet. As a reviewer of the Sternefeld and Richter paper pointed out, the situation in linguistics has changed so much that now having a dissertation from MIT does not necessarily guarantee you a position (footnote 16) later on. One could view a reorientation of certain scientists with regard to certain empirical questions, adequate handling of data (Fanselow 2004b; 2009: 137) and improved communication between theoretical camps as a way out of this crisis.

Since the 90s, it is possible to identify an increased empirical focus (especially in Germany), which manifests itself, for example, in the work of linguistic Collaborative Research Centers (SFBs) or the yearly *Linguistic Evidence* conference. As noted by the reviewer cited above, in the future, it will not be enough to focus on Chomsky's problems in determining the syntactic categories in sentences such as *He left* (see Section 4.6.2). Linguistic dissertations will have to have an empirical section, which shows that the author actually understands something about language. Furthermore, dissertations, and of course other publications, should give an indication that the author has not just considered theories from a particular framework but is also aware of the broad range of relevant descriptive and theoretical literature.

As I have shown in Section 4.6.4 and in Müller (2013c) and will also show in the following chapters and the discussion chapters in particular, there are most certainly similarities between the various analyses on the market and they do converge in certain respects. The way of getting out of the current crisis lies with the empirically-grounded and theoretically broad education and training of following generations.

In short: both teachers and students should read the medical record by Sternefeld and Richter. I implore the students not to abandon their studies straight after reading it, but rather to postpone this decision at least until after they have read the remaining chapters of this book.

---

[42] Vagueness: in this article, *perhaps* occurs 19 times, *may* 17 as well as various *if*s. Consistency: the assumptions made are inconsistent. See footnote 16 on page 151 of this book. Argumentation style: the term specifier is abolished and it is claimed that the problems associated with this term can no longer be formulated. Therefore, they are now not of this world. See footnote 26 on page 156 of this book. Immunization: Chomsky writes the following regarding the Empty Category Principle: *apparent exceptions do not call for abandoning the generalization as far as it reaches, but for seeking deeper reasons to explain where and why it holds* p. 9. This claim is most certainly correct, but one wonders how much evidence one needs in a specific case in order to disregard a given analysis. In particular regarding the essay *Problems of Projection*, one has to wonder why this essay was even published only five years after *On phases*. The evidence against the original approach is overwhelming and several points are taken up by Chomsky (2013) himself. If Chomsky were to apply his own standards (for a quote of his from 1957, see page 6) as well as general scientific methods (Occam's Razor), the consequence would surely be a return to head-based analyses of labeling.

For detailed comments on this essay, see Sections 4.6.2 and 4.6.3.

5 Generalized Phrase Structure Grammar

Generalized Phrase Structure Grammar (GPSG) was developed as an answer to Transformational Grammar at the end of the 1970s. The book by Gazdar, Klein, Pullum & Sag (1985) is the main publication in this framework. Hans Uszkoreit has developed a largish GPSG fragment for German (1987). Analyses in GPSG were so precise that it was possible to use them as the basis for computational implementations. The following is a possibly incomplete list of languages with implemented GPSG fragments:

- German (Weisweber 1987; Weisweber & Preuss 1992; Naumann 1987, 1988; Volk 1988)

- English (Evans 1985; Phillips & Thompson 1985; Phillips 1992; Grover, Carroll & Briscoe 1993)

- French (Emirkanian, Da Sylva & Bouchard 1996)

- Persian (Bahrani, Sameti & Manshadi 2011)

As was discussed in Section 3.1.1, Chomsky (1957) argued that simple phrase structure grammars are not well-suited to describe relations between linguistic structures and claimed that one needs transformations to explain them. These assumptions remained unchallenged for two decades (with the exception of publications by Harman (1963) and Freidin (1975)) until alternative theories such as LFG and GPSG emerged, which addressed Chomsky's criticisms and developed non-transformational explanations of phenomena for which there were previously only transformational analyses or simply none at all. The analysis of local reordering of arguments, passives and long-distance dependencies are some of the most important phenomena that have been discussed in this framework. Following some introductory remarks on the representational format of GPSG in Section 5.1, I will present the GPSG analyses of these phenomena in some more detail.

5.1 General remarks on the representational format

This section has three parts. The general assumptions regarding features and the representation of complex categories is explained in Section 5.1.1, the assumptions regarding the linearization of daughters in a phrase structure rule is explained in Section 5.1.2. Section 5.1.3 introduces metarules, Section 5.1.4 deals with semantics, and Section 5.1.5 with adjuncts.

5.1.1 Complex categories, the Head Feature Convention, and $\overline{\text{X}}$ rules

In Section 2.2, we augmented our phrase structure grammars with features. GPSG goes one step further and describes categories as sets of feature-value pairs. The category in (1a) can be represented as in (1b):

(1)   a.   NP(3,sg,nom)

     b.   { CAT n, BAR 2, PER 3, NUM sg, CASE nom }

It is clear that (1b) corresponds to (1a). (1a) differs from (1b) with regard to the fact that the information about part of speech and the $\overline{\text{X}}$ level (in the symbol NP) are prominent, whereas in (1b) these are treated just like the information about case, number or person.

Lexical entries have a feature SUBCAT. The value is a number which says something about the kind of grammatical rules in which the word can be used. (2) shows examples for grammatical rules and lists some verbs which can occur in these rules.[1]

(2)   V2 → H[5]   (*kommen* 'come', *schlafen* 'sleep')
      V2 → H[6], N2[CASE acc]   (*kennen* 'know', *suchen* 'search')
      V2 → H[7], N2[CASE dat]   (*helfen* 'help', *vertrauen* 'trust')
      V2 → H[8], N2[CASE dat], N2[CASE acc] (*geben* 'give', *zeigen* 'show')
      V2 → H[9], V3[+dass]   (*wissen* 'know', *glauben* 'believe')

These rules license VPs, that is, the combination of a verb with its complements, but not with its subject. The numbers following the category symbols (V or N) indicate the $\overline{\text{X}}$ projection level. For Uszkoreit, the maximum number of projections of a verbal projection is three rather than two as is often assumed.

The H on the right side of the rule stands for *head*. The *Head Feature Convention* (HFC) ensures that certain features of the mother node are also present on the node marked with H (for details see Gazdar, Klein, Pullum & Sag 1985: Section 5.4 and Uszkoreit 1987: 67):

Principle 1 (Head Feature Convention)
The mother node and the head daughter must bear the same head features unless indicated otherwise.

In (2), examples for verbs which can be used in the rules are given in brackets. As with ordinary phrase structure grammars, one also requires corresponding lexical entries for verbs in GPSG. Two examples are provided in (3):

(3)   V[5, VFORM *inf*] → einzuschlafen
      V[6, VFORM *inf*] → aufzuessen

The first rule states that *einzuschlafen* 'to fall asleep' has a SUBCAT value of 5 and the second indicates that *aufzuessen* 'to finish eating' has a SUBCAT value of 6. It follows, then, that *einzuschlafen* can only be used in the first rule (2) and *aufzuessen* can only be

---

[1] The analyses discussed in the following are taken from Uszkoreit (1987).

used in the second. Furthermore, (3) contains information about the form of the verb (*inf* stands for infinitives with *zu* 'to').

If we analyze the sentence in (4) with the second rule in (2) and the second rule in (3), then we arrive at the structure in Figure 5.1.

(4)   Karl hat versucht, [den Kuchen aufzuessen].
    Karl has tried   the cake   to.eat.up

   'Karl tried to finish eating the cake.'

$$V2[\text{vform } \mathit{inf}]$$

$$N2 \qquad V[6, \text{vform } \mathit{inf}]$$

den Kuchen aufzuessen
the cake   to.eat.up

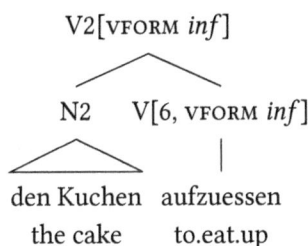

Figure 5.1: Projection of head features in GPSG

The rules in (2) say nothing about the order of the daughters which is why the verb (H[6]) can also be in final position. This aspect will be discussed in more detail in Section 5.1.2. With regard to the HFC, it is important to bear in mind that information about the infinitive verb form is also present on the mother node. Unlike simple phrase structure rules such as those discussed in Chapter 2, this follows automatically from the Head Feature Convention in GPSG. In (3), the value of vform is given and the HFC ensures that the corresponding information is represented on the mother node when the rules in (2) are applied. For the phrase in (4), we arrive at the category V2[vform *inf*] and this ensures that this phrase only occurs in the contexts it is supposed to:

(5)   a.   [Den Kuchen aufzuessen] hat er nicht gewagt.
       the cake   to.eat.up   has he not   dared

      'He did not dare to finish eating the cake.'

   b.   * [Den Kuchen aufzuessen] darf   er nicht.
        the cake   to.eat.up   be.allowed.to he not

      Intended: 'He is not allowed to finish eating the cake.'

   c.   * [Den Kuchen aufessen] hat er nicht gewagt.
        the cake   eat.up   has he not dared

      Intended: 'He did not dare to finish eating the cake.'

   d.   [Den Kuchen aufessen] darf '   er nicht.
        the cake   eaten.up be.allowed.to he not

     'He is not allowed to finish eating the cake.'

gewagt 'dared' selects for a verb or verb phrase with an infinitive with *zu* 'to' but not a bare infinitive, while *darf* 'be allowed to' takes a bare infinitive.

This works in an analogous way for noun phrases: there are rules for nouns which do not take an argument as well as for nouns with certain arguments. Examples of rules for nouns which either require no argument or two PPs are given in (6) (Gazdar, Klein, Pullum & Sag 1985: 127):

(6) N1 → H[30]   (*Haus* 'house', *Blume* 'flower')
     N1 → H[31], PP[*mit*], PP[*über*] (*Gespräch* 'talk', *Streit* 'argument')

The rule for the combination of $\overline{\text{N}}$ and a determiner is as follows:

(7) N2 → Det, H1

N2 stands for NP, that is, for a projection of a noun phrase on bar level two, whereas H1 stands for a projection of the head daughter on the bar level one. The Head Feature Convention ensures that the head daughter is also a nominal projection, since all features on the head daughter apart from the $\overline{\text{X}}$ level are identified with those of the whole NP. When analyzing (8), the second rule in (6) licenses the $\overline{\text{N}}$ *Gesprächs mit Maria über Klaus*. The fact that *Gesprächs* 'conversation' is in the genitive is represented in the lexical item of *Gesprächs* and since *Gesprächs* is the head, it is also present at $\overline{\text{N}}$, following the Head Feature Convention.

(8) des   Gespräch-s   mit Maria über Klaus
     the.GEN conversation-GEN with Maria about Klaus

     'the conversation with Maria about Klaus'

For the combination of $\overline{\text{N}}$ with the determiner, we apply the rule in (7). The category of the head determines the word class of the element on the left-hand side of the rule, which is why the rule in (7) corresponds to the classical $\overline{\text{X}}$ rules that we encountered in (65c) on page 73. Since *Gesprächs mit Maria über Klaus* is the head daughter, the information about the genitive of $\overline{\text{N}}$ is also present at the NP node.

5.1.2 Local reordering

The first phenomenon to be discussed is local reordering of arguments. As was already discussed in Section 3.5, arguments in the middle field can occur in an almost arbitrary order. (9) gives some examples:

(9) a. [weil] der   Mann der   Frau   das   Buch gibt
         because the.NOM man the.DAT woman the.ACC book gives

         'because the man gives the book to the woman'

     b. [weil] der   Mann das   Buch der   Frau   gibt
         because the.NOM man the.ACC book the.DAT woman gives

     c. [weil] das   Buch der   Mann der   Frau   gibt
         because the.ACC book the.NOM man the.DAT woman gives

   d. [weil]   das   Buch der   Frau   der   Mann gibt
        because the.ACC book the.DAT woman the.NOM man gives

   e. [weil]   der   Frau   der   Mann das   Buch gibt
        because the.DAT woman the.NOM man the.ACC book gives

   f. [weil]   der   Frau   das   Buch der   Mann gibt
        because the.DAT woman the.ACC book the.NOM man gives

In the phrase structure grammars in Chapter 2, we used features to ensure that verbs occur with the correct number of arguments. The following rule in (10) was used for the sentence in (9a):

(10) S → NP[nom] NP[dat] NP[acc] V_nom_dat_acc

If one wishes to analyze the other orders in (9), then one requires an additional five rules, that is, six in total:

(11) S → NP[nom] NP[dat] NP[acc] V_nom_dat_acc
       S → NP[nom] NP[acc] NP[dat] V_nom_dat_acc
       S → NP[acc] NP[nom] NP[dat] V_nom_dat_acc
       S → NP[acc] NP[dat] NP[nom] V_nom_dat_acc
       S → NP[dat] NP[nom] NP[acc] V_nom_dat_acc
       S → NP[dat] NP[acc] NP[nom] V_nom_dat_acc

In addition, it is necessary to postulate another six rules for the orders with verb-initial order:

(12) S → V_nom_dat_acc NP[nom] NP[dat] NP[acc]
       S → V_nom_dat_acc NP[nom] NP[acc] NP[dat]
       S → V_nom_dat_acc NP[acc] NP[nom] NP[dat]
       S → V_nom_dat_acc NP[acc] NP[dat] NP[nom]
       S → V_nom_dat_acc NP[dat] NP[nom] NP[acc]
       S → V_nom_dat_acc NP[dat] NP[acc] NP[nom]

Furthermore, one would also need parallel rules for transitive and intransitive verbs with all possible valences. Obviously, the commonalities of these rules and the generalizations regarding them are not captured. The point is that we have the same number of arguments, they can be realized in any order and the verb can be placed in initial or final position. As linguists, we find it desirable to capture this property of the German language and represent it beyond phrase structure rules. In Transformational Grammar, the relationship between the orders is captured by means of movement: the Deep Structure corresponds to verb-final order with a certain order of arguments and the surface order is derived by means of Move-α. Since GPSG is a non-transformational theory, this kind of explanation is not possible. Instead, GPSG imposes restrictions on *immediate dominance* (ID), which differ from those which refer to *linear precedence* (LP): rules such as (13) are to be understood as dominance rules, which do not have anything to say about the order of the daughters (Pullum 1982).

(13)   S → V, NP[nom], NP[acc], NP[dat]

The rule in (13) simply states that S dominates all other nodes. Due to the abandonment of ordering restrictions for the right-hand side of the rule, we only need one rule rather than twelve.

Nevertheless, without any kind of restrictions on the right-hand side of the rule, there would be far too much freedom. For example, the following order would be permissible:

(14)   * Der Frau   der   Mann gibt ein   Buch.
        the woman.DAT the.NOM man   gives the.ACC book

Such orders are ruled out by so-called *Linear Precedence Rules* or LP-rules. LP-constraints are restrictions on local trees, that is, trees with a depth of one. It is, for example, possible to state something about the order of V, NP[nom], NP[acc] and NP[dat] in Figure 5.2 using linearization rules.

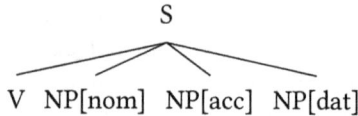

Figure 5.2: Example of a local tree

The following linearization rules serve to exclude orders such as those in (14):

(15)   V[+MC] < X
        X   < V[−MC]

MC stands for *main clause*. The LP-rules ensure that in main clauses (+MC), the verb precedes all other constituents and follows them in subordinate clauses (−MC). There is a restriction that says that all verbs with the MC-value '+' also have to be (+FIN). This will rule out infinitive forms in initial position.

These LP rules do not permit orders with an occupied prefield or postfield in a local tree. This is intended. We will see how fronting can be accounted for in Section 5.4.

5.1.3 Metarules

We have previously encountered linearization rules for sentences with subjects, however our rules have the form in (16), that is, they do not include subjects:

(16)   V2 → H[7], N2[CASE dat]
        V2 → H[8], N2[CASE dat], N2[CASE acc]

These rules can be used to analyze the verb phrases *dem Mann das Buch zu geben* 'to give the man the book' and *das Buch dem Mann zu geben* 'to give the book to the man' as they appear in (17), but we cannot analyze sentences like (9), since the subject does not occur on the right-hand side of the rules in (16).

(17) a. Er verspricht, [dem   Mann das   Buch zu geben].
         he promises   the.DAT man   the.ACC book to give

      'He promises to give the man the book.'

      b. Er verspricht, [das   Buch dem   Mann zu geben].
         he promises   the.ACC book the.DAT man to give

      'He promises to give the book to the man.'

A rule with the format of (18) does not make much sense for a GPSG analysis of German since it cannot derive all the orders in (9) as the subject can occur between the elements of the VP as in (9c).

(18) S → N2 V2

With the rule in (18), it is possible to analyze (9a) as in Figure 5.3 and it would also be possible to analyze (9b) with a different ordering of the NPs inside the VP. The remaining examples in (9) cannot be captured by the rule in (18), however. This has to do with the

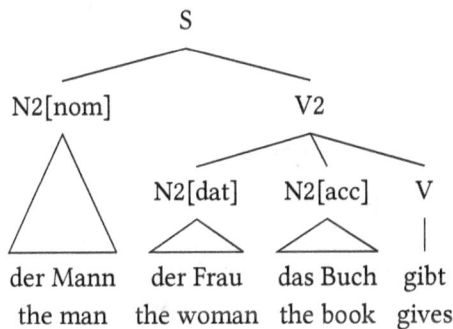

Figure 5.3: VP analysis for German (not appropriate in the GPSG framework)

fact that only elements in the same local tree, that is, elements which occur on the right-hand side of a rule, can be reordered. While we can reorder the parts of the VP and thereby derive (9b), it is not possible to place the subject at a lower position between the objects. Instead, a metarule can be used to analyze sentences where the subject occurs between other arguments of the verb. This rule relates phrase structure rules to other phrase structure rules. A metarule can be understood as a kind of instruction that creates another rule for each rule with a certain form and these newly created rules will in turn license local trees.

For the example at hand, we can formulate a metarule which says the following: if there is a rule with the form "V2 consists of something" in the grammar, then there also has to be another rule "V3 consists of whatever V2 consists + an NP in the nominative". In formal terms, this looks as follows:

(19) V2 → W ↦
      V3 → W, N2[CASE nom]

W is a variable which stands for an arbitrary number of categories (W = *whatever*). The metarule creates the following rule in (20) from the rules in (16):

(20)   V3 → H[7], N2[CASE dat], N2[CASE nom]
      V3 → H[8], N2[CASE dat], N2[CASE acc], N2[CASE nom]

Now, the subject and other arguments both occur in the right-hand side of the rule and can therefore be freely ordered as long as no LP rules are violated.

5.1.4 Semantics

The semantics adopted by Gazdar, Klein, Pullum & Sag (1985: Chapter 9–10) goes back to Richard Montague (1974). Unlike a semantic theory which stipulates the combinatorial possibilities for each rule (see Section 2.3), GPSG uses more general rules. This is possible due to the fact that the expressions to be combined each have a semantic type. It is customary to distinguish between entities (e) and truth values (t). Entities refer to an object in the world (or in a possible world), whereas entire sentences are either true or false, that is, they have a truth value. It is possible to create more complex types from the types e and t. Generally, the following holds: if a and b are types, then $\langle a, b \rangle$ is also a type. Examples of complex types are $\langle e, t \rangle$ and $\langle e, \langle e, t \rangle \rangle$. We can define the following combinatorial rule for this kind of typed expressions:

(21)   If α is of type $\langle b, a \rangle$ and β of type b, then $\alpha(\beta)$ is of type a.

This type of combination is also called *functional application*. With the rule in (21), it is possible that the type $\langle e, \langle e, t \rangle \rangle$ corresponds to an expression which still has to be combined with two expressions of type e in order to result in an expression of t. The first combination step with e will yield $\langle e, t \rangle$ and the second step of combination with a further e will give us t. This is similar to what we saw with λ-expressions on page 62: $\lambda y \lambda x$ *like*$'(x, y)$ has to combine with a y and an x. The result in this example was *mögen*$'(max',$ *lotte*$')$, that is, an expression that is either true or false in the relevant world.

    In Gazdar et al. (1985), an additional type is assumed for worlds in which an expression is true or false. For reasons of simplicity, I will omit this here. The types that we need for sentences, NPs and N′s, determiners and VPs are given in (22):

(22)   a. TYP(S) = t
      b. TYP(NP) = $\langle \langle e, t \rangle, t \rangle$
      c. TYP(N′) = $\langle e, t \rangle$
      d. TYP(Det) = $\langle$ TYP(N′), TYP(NP) $\rangle$
      e. TYP(VP) = $\langle e, t \rangle$

A sentence is of type t since it is either true or false. A VP needs an expression of type e to yield a sentence of type t. The type of the NP may seem strange at first glance, however, it is possible to understand it if one considers the meaning of NPs with quantifiers. For sentences such as (23a), a representation such as (23b) is normally assumed:

(23)   a. All children laugh.
      b. $\forall x\ child'(x) \rightarrow laugh'(x)$

The symbol ∀ stands for the universal quantifier. The formula can be read as follows. For every object, for which it is the case that it has the property of being a child, it is also the case that it is laughing. If we consider the contribution made by the NP, then we see that the universal quantifier, the restriction to children and the logical implication come from the NP:

(24) $\forall x\ child'(x) \rightarrow P(x)$

This means that an NP is something that must be combined with an expression which has exactly one open slot corresponding to the x in (24). This is formulated in (22b): an NP corresponds to a semantic expression which needs something of type ⟨ e, t ⟩ to form an expression which is either true or false (that is, of type *t*).

An N′ stands for a nominal expression for the kind λx child(x). This means if there is a specific individual which one can insert in place of the x, then we arrive at an expression that is either true or false. For a given situation, it is the case that either John has the property of being a child or he does not. An N′ has the same type as a VP.

TYP(N′) and TYP(NP) in (22d) stand for the types given in (22c) and (22b), that is, a determiner is semantically something which has to be combined with the meaning of N′ to give the meaning of an NP.

Gazdar, Klein, Pullum & Sag (1985: 209) point out a redundancy in the semantic specification of grammars which follow the rule-to-rule hypothesis (see Section 2.3) since, instead of giving rule-by-rule instructions with regard to combinations, it suffices in many cases simply to say that the functor is applied to the argument. If we use types such as those in (22), it is also clear which constituent is the functor and which is the argument. In this way, a noun cannot be applied to a determiner, but rather only the reverse is possible. The combination in (25a) yields a well-formed result, whereas (25b) is ruled out.

(25)   a. Det′(N′)
       b. N′(Det′)

The general combinatorial principle is then as follows:

(26)   Use functional application for the combination of the semantic contribution of the daughters to yield a well-formed expression corresponding to the type of the mother node.

The authors of the GPSG book assume that this principle can be applied to the vast majority of GPSG rules so that only a few special cases have to be dealt with by explicit rules.

5.1.5 Adjuncts

For nominal structures in English, Gazdar et al. (1985: 126) assume the $\overline{\overline{X}}$ analysis and, as we have seen in Section 2.4.1, this analysis is applicable to nominal structures in German. Nevertheless, there is a problem regarding the treatment of adjuncts in the verbal domain if one assumes flat branching structures, since adjuncts can freely occur between arguments:

(27) a. weil   der Mann der Frau   das Buch *gestern*   gab
         because the man   the woman the book yesterday gave

         'because the man gave the book to the woman yesterday'

      b. weil   der Mann der Frau   *gestern*   das Buch gab
         because the man   the woman yesterday the book gave

      c. weil   der Mann *gestern*   der Frau   das Buch gab
         because the man   yesterday the woman the book gave

      d. weil   *gestern*   der Mann der Frau   das Buch gab
         because yesterday the man   the woman the book gave

For (27), one requires the following rule:

(28) V3 → H[8], N2[CASE dat], N2[CASE acc], N2[CASE nom], AdvP

Of course, adjuncts can also occur between the arguments of verbs from other valence classes:

(29) weil   (oft) die Frau   (oft) dem Mann (oft)   hilft
      because often the woman often the man   often helps

      'because the woman often helps the man'

Furthermore, adjuncts can occur between the arguments of a VP:

(30) Der Mann hat versucht, der Frau   heimlich das Buch zu geben.
      the man   has tried   the woman secretly the book to give

      'The man tried to secretly give the book to the woman.'

In order to analyze these sentences, we can use a metarule which adds an adjunct to the right-hand side of a V2 (Uszkoreit 1987: 146).

(31) V2 → W ↦
      V2 → W, AdvP

By means of the subject introducing metarule in (19), the V3-rule in (28) is derived from a V2-rule. Since there can be several adjuncts in one sentence, a metarule such as (31) must be allowed to apply multiple times. The recursive application of metarules is often ruled out in the literature due to reasons of generative capacity (see Chapter 17) (Thompson 1982; Uszkoreit 1987: 146). If one uses the Kleene star, then it is possible to formulate the adjunct metarule in such as way that it does not have to apply recursively (Uszkoreit 1987: 146):

(32) V2 → W ↦
      V2 → W, AdvP*

If one adopts the rule in (32), then it is not immediately clear how the semantic con-tribution of the adjuncts can be determined.[2] For the rule in (31), one can combine the semantic contribution of the AdvP with the semantic contribution of the V2 in the in-put rule. This is of course also possible if the metarule is applied multiple times. If this metarule is applied to (33a), for example, the V2-node in (33a) contains the semantic contribution of the first adverb.

(33)   a. V2 → V, NP, AdvP

      b. V2 → V, NP, AdvP, AdvP

The V2-node in (33b) receives the semantic representation of the adverb applied to the V2-node in (33a).

Weisweber & Preuss (1992) have shown that it is possible to use metarules such as (31) if one does not use metarules to compute a set of phrase structure rules, but rather directly applies the metarules during the analysis of a sentence. Since sentences are always of finite length and the metarule introduces an additional AdvP to the right-hand side of the newly licensed rule, the metarule can only be applied a finite number of times.

5.2 Passive as a metarule

The German passive can be described in an entirely theory-neutral way as follows:[3]

- The subject is suppressed.

- If there is an accusative object, this becomes the subject.

This is true for all verb classes which can form the passive. It does not make a difference whether the verbs takes one, two or three arguments:

(34)   a. weil   er   noch gearbeitet hat
          because he.NOM still worked   has

          'because he has still worked'

      b. weil   noch gearbeitet wurde
          because still worked   was

          'because there was still working there'

---

[2] In LFG, an adjunct is entered into a set in the functional structure (see Section 7.1.6). This also works with the use of the Kleene Star notation. From the f-structure, it is possible to compute the semantic denotation with corresponding scope by making reference to the c-structure. In HPSG, Kasper (1994) has made a proposal which corresponds to the GPSG proposal with regard to flat branching structures and an arbitrary number of adjuncts. In HPSG, however, one can make use of so-called relational constraints. These are similar to small programs which can create relations between values inside complex structures. Using such relational constraints, it is then possible to compute the meaning of an unrestricted number of adjuncts in a flat branching structure.

[3] This characterization does not hold for other languages. For instance, Icelandic allows for dative subjects. See Zaenen, Maling & Thráinsson (1985).

(35) a. weil   er   an Maria gedacht hat
         because he.NOM on Maria thought has

         'because he thought of Maria'

      b. weil   an Maria gedacht wurde
         because on Maria thought was

         'because Maria was thought of'

(36) a. weil   sie   ihn   geschlagen hat
         because she.NOM him.ACC beaten   has

         'because she has beaten him'

      b. weil   er   geschlagen wurde
         because he.NOM beaten   was

         'because he was beaten'

(37) a. weil   er   ihm   den   Aufsatz gegeben hat
         because he.NOM him.DAT the.ACC essay   given   has

         'because he has given him the essay'

      b. weil   ihm   der   Aufsatz gegeben wurde
         because him.DAT the.NOM essay   given   was

         'because he was given the essay'

In a simple phrase structure grammar, we would have to list two separate rules for each pair of sentences making reference to the valence class of the verb in question. The characteristics of the passive discussed above would therefore not be explicitly stated in the set of rules. In GPSG, it is possible to explain the relation between active and passive rules using a metarule: for each active rule, a corresponding passive rule with suppressed subject is licensed. The link between active and passive clauses can therefore be captured in this way.

An important difference to Transformational Grammar/GB is that we are not creating a relation between two trees, but rather between active and passive rules. The two rules license two unrelated structures, that is, the structure of (38b) is not derived from the structure of (38a).

(38) a. weil   sie   ihn   geschlagen hat
         because she.NOM him.ACC beaten   has

         'because she has beaten him'

      b. weil   er   geschlagen wurde
         because he.NOM beaten   was

         'because he was beaten'

The generalization with regard to active/passive is captured nevertheless.

In what follows, I will discuss the analysis of the passive given in Gazdar, Klein, Pullum & Sag (1985) in some more detail. The authors suggest the following metarule for English (p. 59):[4]

(39) VP → W, NP ↦

  VP[PAS] → W, (PP[*by*])

This rule states that verbs which take an object can occur in a passive VP without this object. Furthermore, a *by*-PP can be added. If we apply this metarule to the rules in (40), then this will yield the rules listed in (41):

(40) VP → H[2], NP

  VP → H[3], NP, PP[*to*]

(41) VP[PAS] → H[2], (PP[*by*])

  VP[PAS] → H[3], PP[*to*], (PP[*by*])

It is possible to use the rules in (40) to analyze verb phrases in active sentences:

(42) a. [$_S$ The man [$_{VP}$ devoured the carcass]].

  b. [$_S$ The man [$_{VP}$ handed the sword to Tracy]].

The combination of a VP with the subject is licensed by an additional rule (S → NP, VP).

With the rules in (41), one can analyze the VPs in the corresponding passive sentences in (43):

(43) a. [$_S$ The carcass was [$_{VP[PAS]}$ devoured (by the man)]].

  b. [$_S$ The sword was [$_{VP[PAS]}$ handed to Tracy (by the man)]].

At first glance, this analysis may seem odd as an object is replaced inside the VP by a PP which would be the subject in an active clause. Although this analysis makes correct predictions with regard to the syntactic well-formedness of structures, it seems unclear how one can account for the semantic relations. It is possible, however, to use a lexical rule that licenses the passive participle and manipulates the semantics of the output lexical item in such a way that the *by*-PP is correctly integrated semantically (Gazdar et al. 1985: 219).

We arrive at a problem, however, if we try to apply this analysis to German since the impersonal passive cannot be derived by simply suppressing an object. The V2-rules for verbs such as *arbeiten* 'work' and *denken* 'think' as used for the analysis of (34a) and (35a) have the following form:

(44) V2 → H[5]

  V2 → H[13], PP[*an*]

---

[4] See Weisweber & Preuss (1992: 1114) for a parallel rule for German which refers to accusative case on the left-hand side of the metarule.

There is no NP on the right-hand side of these rules which could be turned into a *von*-PP. If the passive is to be analyzed as suppressing an NP argument in a rule, then it should follow from the existence of the impersonal passive that the passive metarule has to be applied to rules which license finite clauses, since information about whether there is a subject or not is only present in rules for finite clauses.[5] In this kind of system, the rules for finite sentences (V3) are the basic rules and the rules for V2 would be derived from these.

It would only make sense to have a metarule which applies to V3 for German since English does not have V3 rules which contain both the subject and its object on the right-hand side of the rule.[6] For English, it is assumed that a sentence consists of a subject and a VP (see Gazdar et al. 1985: 139). This means that we arrive at two very different analyses for the passive in English and German, which do not capture the descriptive insight that the passive is the suppression of the subject and the subsequent promotion of the object in the same way. The central difference between German and English seems to be that English obligatorily requires a subject,[7] which is why English does not have an impersonal passive. This is a property independent of passives, which affects the possibility of having a passive structure, however.

The problem with the GPSG analysis is the fact that valence is encoded in phrase structure rules and that subjects are not present in the rules for verb phrases. In the following chapters, we will encounter approaches from LFG, Categorial Grammar, HPSG, Construction Grammar, and Dependency Grammar which encode valence separately from phrase structure rules and therefore do not have a principled problem with impersonal passive.

See Jacobson (1987b: 394–396) for more problematic aspects of the passive analysis in GPSG and for the insight that a lexical representation of valence – as assumed in Categorial Grammar, GB, LFG and HPSG – allows for a lexical analysis of the phenomenon, which is however unformulable in GPSG for principled reasons having to do with the fundamental assumptions regarding valence representations.

5.3 Verb position

Uszkoreit (1987) analyzed verb-initial and verb-final order as linearization variants of a flat tree. The details of this analysis have already been discussed in Section 5.1.2.

An alternative suggestion in a version of GPSG comes from Jacobs (1986: 110): Jacobs's analysis is a rendering of the verb movement analysis in GB. He assumes that there is an

---

[5] GPSG differs from GB in that infinitive verbal projections do not contain nodes for empty subjects. This is also true for all other theories discussed in this book with the exception of Tree-Adjoining Grammar.

[6] Gazdar et al. (1985: 62) suggest a metarule similar to our subject introduction metarule on page 181. The rule that is licensed by their metarule is used to analyze the position of auxiliaries in English and only licenses sequences of the form AUX NP VP. In such structures, subjects and objects are not in the same local tree either.

[7] Under certain conditions, the subject can also be omitted in English. For more on imperatives and other subject-less examples, see page 516.

empty verb in final position and links this to the verb in initial position using technical means which we will see in more detail in the following section.

5.4 Long-distance dependencies as the result of local dependencies

One of the main innovations of GPSG is its treatment of long-distance dependencies as a sequence of local dependencies (Gazdar 1981b). This approach will be explained taking constituent fronting to the prefield in German as an example. Until now, we have only seen the GPSG analysis for verb-initial and verb-final position: the sequences in (45) are simply linearization variants.

(45)   a. [dass] der Mann der Frau   das Buch gibt
            that the man   the woman the book gives

         'that the man gives the book to the woman'
       b. Gibt der Mann der Frau   das Buch?
          gives the man   the woman the book

         'Does the man give the book to the woman?'

What we want is to derive the verb-second order in the examples in (46) from V1 order in (45b).

(46)   a. Der Mann gibt   der Frau   das Buch.
            the man   gives the woman the book

         'The man gives the woman the book.'
       b. Der Frau   gibt der Mann das Buch.
            the woman gives the man   the book

         'The man gives the woman the book.'

For this, the metarule in (47) has to be used. This metarule removes an arbitrary category X from the set of categories on the right-hand side of the rule and represents it on the left-hand side with a slash ('/'):[8]

(47)   V3 → W, X ↦
       V3/X → W

This rule creates the rules in (49) from (48):

(48)   V3 → H[8], N2[CASE dat], N2[CASE acc], N2[CASE nom]

(49)   V3/N2[CASE nom] → H[8], N2[CASE dat], N2[CASE acc]
       V3/N2[CASE dat]   → H[8], N2[CASE acc], N2[CASE nom]
       V3/N2[CASE acc]   → H[8], N2[CASE dat], N2[CASE nom]

---

[8] An alternative to Uszkoreit's trace-less analysis (1987: 77), which is explained here, consists of using a trace for the extracted element as in GB.

The rule in (50) connects a sentence with verb-initial order with a constituent which is missing in the sentence:

(50)   V3[+FIN] → X[+TOP], V3[+MC]/X

In (50), X stands for an arbitrary category which is marked as missing in V3 by the '/'. X is referred to as a *filler*.

The interesting cases of values for X with regard to our examples are given in (51):

(51)   V3[+FIN] → N2[+TOP, CASE nom], V3[+MC]/N2[CASE nom]
       V3[+FIN] → N2[+TOP, CASE dat],   V3[+MC]/N2[CASE dat]
       V3[+FIN] → N2[+TOP, CASE acc],   V3[+MC]/N2[CASE acc]

(51) does not show actual rules. Instead, (51) shows examples for insertions of specific categories into the X-position, that is, different instantiations of the rule.

The following linearization rule ensures that a constituent marked by [+TOP] in (50) precedes the rest of the sentence:

(52)   [+TOP] < X

TOP stands for *topicalized*. As was mentioned on page 103, the prefield is not restricted to topics. Focused elements and expletives can also occur in the prefield, which is why the feature name is not ideal. However, it is possible to replace it with something else, for instance *prefield*. This would not affect the analysis. X in (52) stands for an arbitrary category. This is a new X and it is independent from the one in (50).

Figure 5.4 shows the interaction of the rules for the analysis of (53).[9]

(53)   Dem   Mann gibt er   das   Buch.
       the.DAT man   gives he,NOM the.ACC book
       'He gives the man the book.'

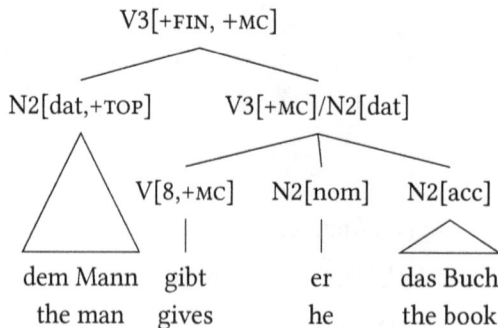

Figure 5.4: Analysis of fronting in GPSG

---

[9] The FIN feature has been omitted on some of the nodes since it is redundant: +MC-verbs always require the FIN value '+'.

The metarule in (47) licenses a rule which adds a dative object into slash. This rule now licenses the subtree for *gibt er das Buch* 'gives he the book'. The linearization rule V[+MC] < X orders the verb to the very left inside of the local tree for V3. In the next step, the constituent following the slash is bound off. Following the LP-rule [+TOP] < X, the bound constituent must be ordered to the left of the V3 node.

The analysis given in Figure 5.4 may seem too complex since the noun phrases in (53) all depend on the same verb. It is possible to invent a system of linearization rules which would allow one to analyze (53) with an entirely flat structure. One would nevertheless still need an analysis for sentences such as those in (37) on page 104 – repeated here as (54) for convenience:

(54) a. [Um zwei Millionen Mark]$_i$ soll er versucht haben, [eine
around two million Deutsche.Marks should he tried have an
Versicherung _$_i$ zu betrügen].[10]
insurance.company to deceive

'He apparently tried to cheat an insurance company out of two million Deutsche Marks.'

b. „Wer$_i$, glaubt er, daß er _$_i$ ist?" erregte sich ein Politiker vom Nil.[11]
who believes he that he is retort REFL a politician from.the Nile

'"Who does he think he is?", a politician from the Nile exclaimed.'

c. Wen$_i$ glaubst du, daß ich _$_i$ gesehen habe?[12]
who believe you that I seen have

'Who do you think I saw?'

d. [Gegen ihn]$_i$ falle es den Republikanern hingegen schwerer,
against him fall it the Republicans however more.difficult
[[Angriffe _$_i$] zu lancieren].[13]
attacks to launch

'It is, however, more difficult for the Republicans to launch attacks against him.'

The sentences in (54) cannot be explained by local reordering as the elements in the prefield are not dependent on the highest verb, but instead originate in the lower clause. Since only elements from the same local tree can be reordered, the sentences in (54) cannot be analyzed without postulating some kind of additional mechanism for long-distance dependencies.[14]

---

[10] taz, 04.05.2001, p. 20.
[11] Spiegel, 8/1999, p. 18.
[12] Scherpenisse (1986: 84).
[13] taz, 08.02.2008, p. 9.
[14] One could imagine analyses that assume the special mechanism for nonlocal dependencies only for sentences that really involve dependencies that are nonlocal. This was done in HPSG by Kathol (1995) and Wetta (2011) and by Groß & Osborne (2009) in Dependency Grammar. I discuss the Dependency Grammar analyses in detail in Section 11.7.1 and show that analyses that treat simple V2 sentences as ordering variants of non-V2 sentences have problems with the scope of fronted adjuncts, with coordination of simple sentences and sentences with nonlocal dependencies and with so-called multiple frontings.

Before I conclude this chapter, I will discuss yet another example of fronting, namely one of the more complex examples in (54). The analysis of (54c) consists of several steps: the introduction, percolation and finally binding off of information about the long-dis-tance dependency. This is shown in Figure 5.5. Simplifying somewhat, I assume that

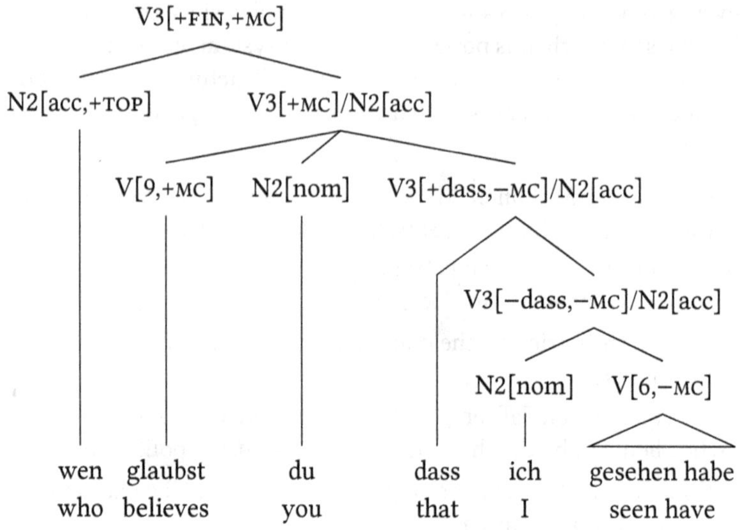

V3[+FIN,+MC]

N2[acc,+TOP]   V3[+MC]/N2[acc]

V[9,+MC]   N2[nom]   V3[+dass,−MC]/N2[acc]

V3[−dass,−MC]/N2[acc]

N2[nom]   V[6,−MC]

wen	glaubst	du	dass	ich	gesehen habe
who	believes	you	that	I	seen have

Figure 5.5: Analysis of long-distance dependencies in GPSG

gesehen habe 'have seen' behaves like a normal transitive verb.[15] A phrase structure rule licensed by the metarule in (47) licenses the combination of *ich* 'I' and *gesehen habe* 'has seen' and represents the missing accusative object on the V3 node. The complementizer *dass* 'that' is combined with *ich gesehen habe* 'I have seen' and the information about the fact that an accusative NP is missing is percolated up the tree. This percolation is controlled by the so-called *Foot Feature Principle*, which states that all foot features of all the daughters are also present on the mother node. Since the SLASH feature is a foot feature, the categories following the '/' percolate up the tree if they are not bound off in the local tree. In the final step, the V3/N2[acc] is combined with the missing N2[acc]. The result is a complete finite declarative clause of the highest projection level.

5.5 Summary and classification

Some twenty years after Chomsky's criticism of phrase structure grammars, the first large grammar fragment in the GPSG framework appeared and offered analyses of phe-nomena which could not be described by simple phrase structure rules. Although works in GPSG essentially build on Harman's 1963 idea of a transformation-less grammar, they also go far beyond this. A special achievement of GPSG is, in particular, the treatment of

---

[15] See Nerbonne (1986a) and Johnson (1986), for analyses of verbal complexes in GPSG.

long-distance dependencies as worked out by Gazdar (1981b). By using the SLASH-mech-
anism, it was possible to explain the simultaneous extraction of elements from conjuncts
(Across the Board Extraction, Ross 1967). The following examples from Gazdar (1981b:
173) show that gaps in conjuncts must be identical, that is, a filler of a certain category
must correspond to a gap in every conjunct:

(55) a. The kennel which Mary made and Fido sleeps in has been stolen.
         (= S/NP & S/NP)

     b. The kennel in which Mary keeps drugs and Fido sleeps has been stolen.
         (= S/PP & S/PP)

     c. * The kennel (in) which Mary made and Fido sleeps has been stolen.
         (= S/NP & S/PP)

GPSG can plausibly handle this with mechanisms for the transmission of information
about gaps. In symmetric coordination, the SLASH elements in each conjunct have to
be identical. On the one hand, a transformational approach is not straightforwardly
possible since one normally assumes in such analyses that there is a tree and something
is moved to another position in the tree thereby leaving a trace. However, in coordinate
structures, the filler would correspond to two or more traces and it cannot be explained
how the filler could originate in more than one place.

While the analysis of Across the Board extraction is a true highlight of GPSG, there
are some problematic aspects that I want to address in the following: the interaction
between valence and morphology, the representation of valence and partial verb phrase
fronting, and the expressive power of the GPSG formalism.

5.5.1 Valence and morphology

The encoding of valence in GPSG is problematic for several reasons. For example, morphological processes take into account the valence properties of words. Adjectival derivation with the suffix *-bar* '-able' is only productive with transitive verbs, that is, with verbs
with an accusative object which can undergo passivization:

(56) a. lös-bar   (nominative, accusative)
         solv-able

     b. vergleich-bar   (nominative, accusative, PP[mit])
         compar-able

     c. * schlaf-bar   (nominative)
         sleep-able

     d. * helf-bar   (nominative, dative)
         help-able

A rule for derivations with *-bar-* '-able' must therefore make reference to valence information. This is not possible in GPSG grammars since every lexical entry is only assigned
a number which says something about the rules in which this entry can be used. For *-bar-*

derivations, one would have to list in the derivational rule all the numbers which correspond to rules with accusative objects, which of course does not adequately describe the phenomenon. Furthermore, the valence of the resulting adjective also depends on the valence of the verb. For example, a verb such as *vergleichen* 'compare' requires a *mit* (with)-PP and *vergleichbar* 'comparable' does too (Riehemann 1993: 7, 54; 1998: 68). In the following chapters, we will encounter models which assume that lexical entries contain information as to whether a verb selects for an accusative object or not. In such models, morphological rules which need to access the valence properties of linguistic objects can be adequately formulated.

The issue of interaction of valence and derivational morphology will be taken up in Section 21.2.2 again, where approaches in LFG and Construction Grammar are discussed that share assumptions about the encoding of valence with GPSG.

5.5.2 Valence and partial verb phrase fronting

Nerbonne (1986a) and Johnson (1986) investigate fronting of partial VPs in the GPSG framework. (57) gives some examples: in (57a) the bare verb is fronted and its arguments are realized in the middle field, in (57b) one of the objects is fronted together with the verb and in (57c) both objects are fronted with the verb.

(57)   a. Erzählen wird er seiner Tochter ein Märchen können.
           tell   will he his   daughter a   fairy.tale can

       b. Ein Märchen erzählen wird er seiner Tochter können.
           a   fairy.tale tell   will he his   daughter can

       c. Seiner Tochter ein Märchen erzählen wird er können.
           his   daughter a   fairy.tale tell   will he can

           'He will be able to tell his daughter a fairy tale.'

The problem with sentences such as those in (57) is that the valence requirements of the verb *erzählen* 'to tell' are realized in various positions in the sentence. For fronted constituents, one requires a rule which allows a ditransitive to be realized without its arguments or with one or two objects. Furthermore, it has to be ensured that the arguments that are missing in the prefield are realized in the remainder of the clause. It is not legitimate to omit obligatory arguments or realize arguments with other properties like a different case, as the examples in (58) show:

(58)   a.   Verschlungen hat er   es   nicht.
            devoured   has he.NOM it.ACC not

            'He did not devour it.'

       b. * Verschlungen hat er   nicht.
            devoured   has he.NOM not

       c. * Verschlungen hat er   ihm   nicht.
            devoured   has he.NOM him.DAT not

The obvious generalization is that the fronted and unfronted arguments must add up to the total set belonging to the verb. This is scarcely possible with the rule-based valence representation in GPSG. In theories such as Categorial Grammar (see Chapter 8), it is possible to formulate elegant analyses of (58) (Geach 1970). Nerbonne and Johnson both suggest analyses for sentences such as (58) which ultimately amount to changing the representation of valence information in the direction of Categorial Grammar.

Before I turn to the expressive power of the GPSG formalism, I want to note that the problems that we discussed in the previous subsections are both related to the representation of valence in GPSG. We already run into valence-related problems when discussing the passive in Section 5.2: since subjects and objects are introduced in phrase structure rules and since there are some languages in which subject and object are not in the same local tree, there seems to be no way to describe the passive as the suppression of the subject in GPSG.

5.5.3 Generative capacity

In GPSG, the system of linearization, dominance and metarules is normally restricted by conditions we will not discuss here in such a way that one could create a phrase structure grammar of the kind we saw in Chapter 2 from the specification of a GPSG grammar. Such grammars are also called context-free grammars. In the mid-80s, it was shown that context-free grammars are not able to describe natural language in general, that is it could be shown that there are languages that need more powerful grammar formalisms than context-free grammars (Shieber 1985; Culy 1985; see Pullum (1986) for a historical overview). The so-called *generative capacity* of grammar formalisms is discussed in Chapter 17.

Following the emergence of constraint-based models such as HPSG (see Chapter 9) and unification-based variants of Categorial Grammar (see Chapter 8 and Uszkoreit 1986a), most authors previously working in GPSG turned to other frameworks. The GPSG analysis of long-distance dependencies and the distinction between immediate dominance and linear precedence are still used in HPSG and variants of Construction Grammar to this day. See also Section 12.2 for a Tree Adjoining Grammar variant that separates dominance from precedence.

Comprehension questions

1. What does it mean for a grammar to be in an ID/LP format?

2. How are linear variants of constituents in the middle field handled by GPSG?

3. Think of some phenomena which have been described by transformations and consider how GPSG has analyzed these data using other means.

Exercises

1. Write a small GPSG grammar which can analyze the following sentences:

(59) a. [dass] der   Mann ihn   liest
           that the.NOM man   him.ACC reads

          'that the man reads it'

  b. [dass] ihn   der   Mann liest
           that him.ACC the.NOM man   reads

          'that the man reads it'

  c. Der   Mann liest ihn.
          the.NOM man   reads him.ACC

          'The man reads it.'

Include all arguments in a single rule without using the metarule for introducing subjects.

Further reading

The main publication in GPSG is Gazdar, Klein, Pullum & Sag (1985). This book has been critically discussed by Jacobson (1987b). Some problematic analyses are contrasted with alternatives from Categorial Grammar and reference is made to the heavily Categorial Grammar influenced work of Pollard (1984), which counts as one of the predecessors of HPSG. Some of Jacobson's suggestions can be found in later works in HPSG.

Grammars of German can be found in Uszkoreit (1987) and Busemann (1992). Gazdar (1981b) developed an analysis of long-distance dependencies, which is still used today in theories such as HPSG.

A history of the genesis of GPSG can be found in Pullum (1989b).

6 Feature descriptions

In the previous chapter, we talked about sets of feature-value pairs, which can be used to describe linguistic objects. In this chapter, we will introduce feature descriptions which play a role in theories such as LFG, HPSG, Construction Grammar, versions of Categorial Grammar and TAG (and even some formalizations of Minimalist theories (Veenstra 1998)). This chapter will therefore lay some of the groundwork for the chapters to follow.

Feature structures are complex entities which can model properties of a linguistic object. Linguists mostly work with feature descriptions which describe only parts of a given feature structure. The difference between models and descriptions will be explained in more detail in Section 6.7.

Alternative terms for feature structures are:

- feature-value structure

- attribute-value structure

Other terms for feature description are the following:

- *attribute-value matrix* (AVM)

- *feature matrix*

In what follows, I will restrict the discussion to the absolutely necessary details in order to keep the formal part of the book as short as possible. I refer the interested reader to Shieber (1986), Pollard & Sag (1987: Chapter 2), Johnson (1988), Carpenter (1992), King (1994) and Richter (2004). Shieber's book is an accessible introduction to Unification Grammars. The works by King and Richter, which introduce important foundations for HPSG, would most probably not be accessible for those without a good grounding in mathematics. However, it is important to know that these works exist and that the corresponding linguistic theory is build on a solid foundation.

6.1 Feature descriptions

When describing linguistic signs, we have to say something about their properties. For a noun, we can say that it has case, gender, number and person features. For a word such as *Mannes* 'man', we can say that these features have the values *genitive, masculine, singular* and *3*. If we were to write these as a list of feature-value pairs, we would arrive at the following feature description:

(1) Feature-value pair for *Mannes*:

$$\begin{bmatrix} \text{CASE} & genitive \\ \text{GENDER} & masculine \\ \text{NUMBER} & singular \\ \text{PERSON} & 3 \end{bmatrix}$$

It is possible to describe a variety of different things using feature descriptions. For example, we can describe a person as in (2):

(2) $\begin{bmatrix} \text{FIRSTNAME} & max \\ \text{LASTNAME} & meier \\ \text{DATE-OF-BIRTH} & 10.10.1985 \end{bmatrix}$

People are related to other people – a fact that can also be expressed in feature-value pairs. For example, the fact that Max Meier has a father called Peter Meier can be captured by expanding (2) as follows:

(3) $\begin{bmatrix} \text{FIRSTNAME} & max \\ \text{LASTNAME} & meier \\ \text{DATE-OF-BIRTH} & 10.10.1985 \\ \text{FATHER} & \begin{bmatrix} \text{FIRSTNAME} & peter \\ \text{LASTNAME} & meier \\ \text{DATE-OF-BIRTH} & 10.05.1960 \\ \text{FATHER} & \dots \\ \text{MOTHER} & \dots \end{bmatrix} \\ \text{MOTHER} & \dots \end{bmatrix}$

The value of the FATHER feature is another feature description containing the same features as (2).

In feature descriptions, a *path* is a sequence of features which immediately follow each other. The *value of a path* is the feature description at the end of the path. Therefore, the value of FATHER|DATE-OF-BIRTH is *10.05.1960*.

One can think of many different features that could be included in representations such as (3). One may wonder how to integrate information about offspring into (3).

An obvious solution would be to add features for DAUGHTER und SON:

(4) $\begin{bmatrix} \text{FIRSTNAME} & max \\ \text{LASTNAME} & meier \\ \text{DATE-OF-BIRTH} & 10.10.1985 \\ \text{FATHER} & \dots \\ \text{MOTHER} & \dots \\ \text{DAUGHTER} & \dots \end{bmatrix}$

This solution is not satisfactory as it is not immediately clear how one could describe a person with several daughters. Should one really introduce features such as DAUGHTER-1 or DAUGHTER-3?

(5)
$$
\begin{bmatrix}
\text{FIRSTNAME} & \textit{max} \\
\text{LASTNAME} & \textit{meier} \\
\text{DATE-OF-BIRTH} & \textit{10.10.1985} \\
\text{FATHER} & \dots \\
\text{MOTHER} & \dots \\
\text{DAUGHTER-1} & \dots \\
\text{DAUGHTER-2} & \dots \\
\text{DAUGHTER-3} & \dots
\end{bmatrix}
$$

How many features do we want to assume? Where is the limit? What would the value of DAUGHTER-32 be?

For this case, it makes much more sense to use a list. Lists are indicated with angle brackets. Any number of elements can occur between these brackets. A special case is when no element occurs between the brackets. A list with no elements is also called *empty list*. In the following example, Max Meier has a daughter called Clara, who herself has no daughter.

(6)
$$
\begin{bmatrix}
\text{FIRSTNAME} & \textit{max} \\
\text{LASTNAME} & \textit{meier} \\
\text{DATE-OF-BIRTH} & \textit{10.10.1985} \\
\text{FATHER} & \dots \\
\text{MOTHER} & \dots \\
\text{DAUGHTER} & \left\langle
\begin{bmatrix}
\text{FIRSTNAME} & \textit{clara} \\
\text{LASTNAME} & \textit{meier} \\
\text{DATE-OF-BIRTH} & \textit{10.10.2004} \\
\text{FATHER} & \dots \\
\text{MOTHER} & \dots \\
\text{DAUGHTER} & \langle\rangle
\end{bmatrix}
\right\rangle
\end{bmatrix}
$$

Now, we are left with the question of sons. Should we add another list for sons? Do we want to differentiate between sons and daughters? It is certainly the case that the gender of the children is an important property, but these are properties of the objects themselves, since every person has a gender. The description in (7) therefore offers a more adequate representation.

At this point, one could ask why the parents are not included in a list as well. In fact, we find similar questions also in linguistic works: how is information best organized for the job at hand? One could argue for the representation of descriptions of the parents under separate features, by pointing out that with such a representation it is possible to make certain claims about a mother or father without having to necessarily search for the respective descriptions in a list.

If the order of the elements is irrelevant, then we could use sets rather than lists. Sets are written inside curly brackets.[1]

---

[1] The definition of a set requires many technicalities. In this book, I would use sets only for collecting semantic information. This can be done equally well using lists, which is why I do not introduce sets here and instead use lists.

(7)
$$
\begin{bmatrix}
\text{FIRSTNAME} & max \\
\text{LASTNAME} & meier \\
\text{DATE-OF-BIRTH} & 10.10.1985 \\
\textbf{GENDER} & \textbf{\textit{male}} \\
\text{FATHER} & \ldots \\
\text{MOTHER} & \ldots \\
\text{CHILDREN} & \left\langle
\begin{bmatrix}
\text{FIRSTNAME} & clara \\
\text{LASTNAME} & meier \\
\text{DATE-OF-BIRTH} & 10.10.2004 \\
\textbf{GENDER} & \textbf{\textit{female}} \\
\text{FATHER} & \ldots \\
\text{MOTHER} & \ldots \\
\text{CHILDREN} & \langle\rangle
\end{bmatrix}
\right\rangle
\end{bmatrix}
$$

6.2 Types

In the previous section, we introduced feature descriptions consisting of feature-value pairs and showed that it makes sense to allow for complex values for features. In this section, feature descriptions will be augmented to include types. Feature descriptions which are assigned a type are also called *typed feature descriptions*. Types say something about which features can or must belong to a particular structure. The description previously discussed describes an object of the type *person*.

(8)
$$
\begin{bmatrix}
person & \\
\text{FIRSTNAME} & max \\
\text{LASTNAME} & meier \\
\text{DATE-OF-BIRTH} & 10.10.1985 \\
\text{GENDER} & male \\
\text{FATHER} & \ldots \\
\text{MOTHER} & \ldots \\
\text{CHILDREN} & \langle \ldots, \ldots \rangle
\end{bmatrix}
$$

Types are written in *italics*.

The specification of a type determines which properties a modelled object has. It is then only possible for a theory to say something about these properties. Properties such as OPERATING VOLTAGE are not relevant for objects of the type *person*. If we know the type of a given object, then we also know that this object must have certain properties even if we do not yet know their exact values. In this way, (9) is still a description of Max Meier even though it does not contain any information about Max' date of birth:

(9)
$$
\begin{bmatrix}
person & \\
\text{FIRSTNAME} & max \\
\text{LASTNAME} & meier \\
\text{GENDER} & male
\end{bmatrix}
$$

We know, however, that Max Meier must have been born on some day since this is a description of the type *person*. The question *What is Max' date of birth?* makes sense for a structure such as (9) in a way that the question *Which operating voltage does Max have?* does not. If we know that an object is of the type *person*, then we have the following basic structure:

(10)
$$\begin{bmatrix} person \\ \text{FIRSTNAME} & firstname \\ \text{LASTNAME} & lastname \\ \text{DATE-OF-BIRTH} & date \\ \text{GENDER} & gender \\ \text{FATHER} & person \\ \text{MOTHER} & person \\ \text{CHILDREN} & list\ of\ person \end{bmatrix}$$

In (10) and (9), the values of features such as FIRSTNAME are in italics. These values are also types. They are different from types such as *person*, however, as no features belong to them. These kinds of types are called *atomic*.

Types are organized into hierarchies. It is possible to define the subtypes *woman* and *man* for *person*. These would determine the gender of a given object. (11) shows the feature structure for the type *woman*, which is analogous to that of *man*.

(11)
$$\begin{bmatrix} female\ person \\ \text{FIRSTNAME} & firstname \\ \text{LASTNAME} & lastname \\ \text{DATE-OF-BIRTH} & date \\ \text{GENDER} & female \\ \text{FATHER} & person \\ \text{MOTHER} & person \\ \text{CHILDREN} & list\ of\ person \end{bmatrix}$$

At this point, we could ask ourselves if we really need the feature GENDER. The necessary information is already represented in the type *woman*. The question if specific information is represented by special features or whether it is stored in a type without a corresponding individual feature will surface again in the discussion of linguistic analyses. Both alternatives differ mostly in the fact that the information which is modelled by types is not immediately accessible for structure sharing, which is discussed in Section 6.4.

Type hierarchies play an important role in capturing linguistic generalizations, which is why type hierarchies and the inheritance of constraints and information will be explained with reference to a further example in what follows. One can think of type hierarchies as an effective way of organizing information. In an encyclopedia, the individual entries are linked in such a way that the entries for monkey and mouse will each contain a pointer to mammal. The description found under mammal does therefore not have to be repeated for the subordinate concepts. In the same way, if one wishes to

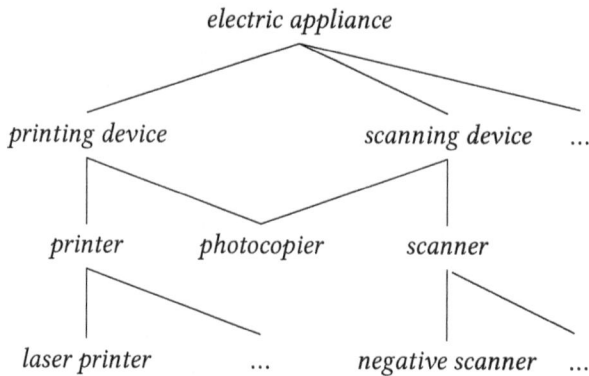

Figure 6.1: Non-linguistic example of multiple inheritance

describe various electric appliances, one can use the hierarchy in Figure 6.1. The most general type *electrical device* is the highest in Figure 6.1. Electrical devices have certain properties, e.g., a power supply with a certain power consumption. All subtypes of *electrical device* "inherit" this property. In this way, *printing device* and *scanning device* also have a power supply with a specific power consumption. A *printing device* can produce information and a *scanning device* can read in information. A *photocopier* can both produce information and read it. Photocopiers have both the properties of scanning and printing devices. This is expressed by the connection between the two superordinate types and *photocopier* in Figure 6.1. If a type is at the same time the subtype of several superordinate types, then we speak of *multiple inheritance*. If devices can print, but not scan, they are of type *printer*. This type can have further more specific subtypes, which in turn may have particular properties, e.g., *laser printer*. New features can be added to subtypes, but it is also possible to make values of inherited features more specific. For example, the material that can be scanned with a *negative scanner* is far more restricted than that of the supertype *scanner*, since negative scanners can only scan negatives.

The objects that are modeled always have a maximally specific type. In the example above, this means that we can have objects of the type *laser printer* and *negative scanner* but not of the type *printing device*. This is due to the fact that *printing device* is not maximally specific since this type has two subtypes.

Type hierarchies with multiple inheritance are an important means for expressing linguistic generalizations (Flickinger, Pollard & Wasow 1985; Flickinger 1987; Sag 1997). Types of words or phrases which occur at the very top of these hierarchies correspond to constraints on linguistic objects, which are valid for linguistic objects in all languages. Subtypes of such general types can be specific to certain languages or language classes.

6.3 Disjunction

Disjunctions can be used if one wishes to express the fact that a particular object can have various different properties. If one were to organize a class reunion twenty years after leaving school and could not recall the exact names of some former classmates, it would be possible to search the web for "Julia (Warbanow or Barbanow)". In feature descriptions, this "or" is expressed by a '∨'.

$$(12) \quad \begin{bmatrix} person \\ \text{FIRSTNAME } julia \\ \text{LASTNAME } warbanow \lor barbanow \end{bmatrix}$$

Some internet search engines do not allow for searches with 'or'. In these cases, one has to carry out two distinct search operations: one for "Julia Warbanow" and then another for "Julia Barbanow". This corresponds to the two following disjunctively connected descriptions:

$$(13) \quad \begin{bmatrix} person \\ \text{FIRSTNAME } julia \\ \text{LASTNAME } warbanow \end{bmatrix} \lor \begin{bmatrix} person \\ \text{FIRSTNAME } julia \\ \text{LASTNAME } barbanow \end{bmatrix}$$

Since we have type hierarchies as a means of expression, we can sometimes do without disjunctive specification of values and instead state the supertype: for *printer* ∨ *photocopier*, one can simply write *printing device* if one assumes the type hierarchy in Figure 6.1 on the preceeding page.

6.4 Structure sharing

Structure sharing is an important part of the formalism. It serves to express the notion that certain parts of a structure are identical. A linguistic example for the identity of values is agreement. In sentences such as (14), the number value of the noun phrase has to be identical to that of the verb:

(14)   a.   Der Mann schläft.
            the man   sleeps
            'The man is sleeping.'

       b.   Die Männer schlafen.
            the men   sleep
            'The men are sleeping.'

       c. * Der Mann schlafen.
            the man   sleep
            Intended: 'The man are sleeping.'

The identity of values is indicated by boxes containing numbers. The boxes can also be viewed as variables.

When describing objects we can make claims about equal values or claims about identical values. A claim about the identity of values is stronger. Let us take the following feature description containing information about the children that Max's father and mother have as an example:

$$(15)\quad \begin{bmatrix} person \\ \text{FIRSTNAME} & max \\ \text{LASTNAME} & meier \\ \text{DATE-OF-BIRTH} & 10.10.1985 \\ \text{FATHER} & \begin{bmatrix} person \\ \text{FIRSTNAME} & peter \\ \text{LASTNAME} & meier \\ \text{CHILDREN} & \left\langle \begin{bmatrix} person \\ \text{FIRSTNAME} & klaus \end{bmatrix}, \ldots \right\rangle \end{bmatrix} \\ \text{MOTHER} & \begin{bmatrix} person \\ \text{FIRSTNAME} & anna \\ \text{LASTNAME} & meier \\ \text{CHILDREN} & \left\langle \begin{bmatrix} person \\ \text{FIRSTNAME} & klaus \end{bmatrix}, \ldots \right\rangle \end{bmatrix} \end{bmatrix}$$

Notice that under the paths FATHER|CHILDREN and MOTHER|CHILDREN, we find a list containing a description of a person with the first name Klaus. The question of whether the feature description is of one or two children of Peter and Anna cannot be answered. It is certainly possible that we are dealing with two different children from previous partnerships who both happen to be called Klaus.

By using structure sharing, it is possible to specify the identity of the two values as in (16). In (16), Klaus is a single child that belongs to both parents. Everything inside

$$(16)\quad \begin{bmatrix} person \\ \text{FIRSTNAME} & max \\ \text{LASTNAME} & meier \\ \text{DATE-OF-BIRTH} & 10.10.1985 \\ \text{FATHER} & \begin{bmatrix} person \\ \text{FIRSTNAME} & peter \\ \text{LASTNAME} & meier \\ \text{CHILDREN} & \left\langle \boxed{1} \begin{bmatrix} person \\ \text{FIRSTNAME} & klaus \end{bmatrix}, \ldots \right\rangle \end{bmatrix} \\ \text{MOTHER} & \begin{bmatrix} person \\ \text{FIRSTNAME} & anna \\ \text{LASTNAME} & meier \\ \text{CHILDREN} & \left\langle \boxed{1}, \ldots \right\rangle \end{bmatrix} \end{bmatrix}$$

the brackets which immediately follow $\boxed{1}$ is equally present in both positions. One can think of $\boxed{1}$ as a pointer or reference to a structure which has only been described once. One question still remains open: what about Max? Max is also a child of his parents and should therefore also occur in a list of the children of his parents. There are two points in (16) where there are three dots. These ellipsis marks stand for information about the other children of Peter and Anna Meier. Our world knowledge tells us that both of them must have the same child namely Max Meier himself. In the following section, we will see how this can be expressed in formal terms.

6.5 Cyclic structures

We have introduced structure sharing in order to be able to express the fact that Max's parents both have a son Klaus together. It would not be enough to list Max in the child-lists of his parents separately. We want to capture the fact that it is the same Max which appears in each of these lists and furthermore, we have to ensure that the child being described is identical to the entire object being described. Otherwise, the description would permit a situation where Max's parents could have a second child also called Max. The description given in (17) can capture all facts correctly. Structures such as

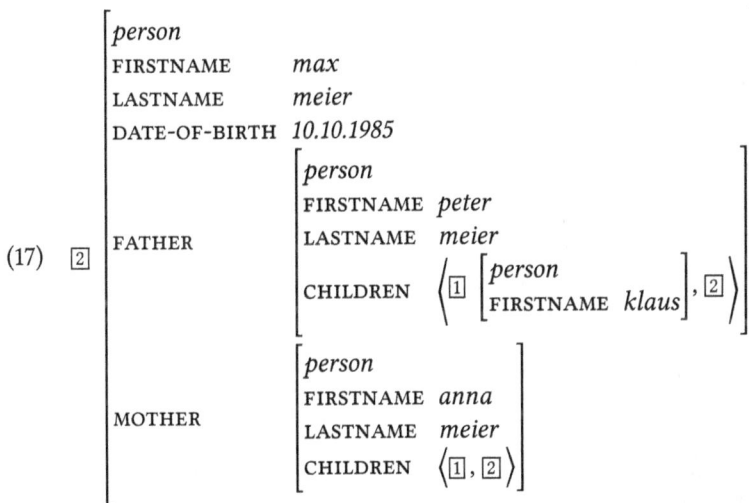

$$
(17) \quad \boxed{2} \;
\begin{bmatrix}
\textit{person} \\
\text{FIRSTNAME} & \textit{max} \\
\text{LASTNAME} & \textit{meier} \\
\text{DATE-OF-BIRTH} & \textit{10.10.1985} \\
\text{FATHER} &
\begin{bmatrix}
\textit{person} \\
\text{FIRSTNAME} & \textit{peter} \\
\text{LASTNAME} & \textit{meier} \\
\text{CHILDREN} & \left\langle \boxed{1}\begin{bmatrix}\textit{person} \\ \text{FIRSTNAME} & \textit{klaus}\end{bmatrix}, \boxed{2} \right\rangle
\end{bmatrix} \\
\text{MOTHER} &
\begin{bmatrix}
\textit{person} \\
\text{FIRSTNAME} & \textit{anna} \\
\text{LASTNAME} & \textit{meier} \\
\text{CHILDREN} & \left\langle \boxed{1}, \boxed{2} \right\rangle
\end{bmatrix}
\end{bmatrix}
$$

those described in (17) are called cyclic because one ends up going in a circle if one follows a particular path: e.g., the path FATHER|CHILDREN|...|FATHER|CHILDREN|...[2] can be potentially repeated an infinite number of times.

6.6 Unification

Grammatical rules are written exactly like lexical entries in HPSG and Construction Grammar and are done so with the help of feature descriptions. For a word or a larger phrasal entity to be usable as daughter in a phrase licensed by some grammatical rule,

---

[2] The dots here stand for the path to [2] in the list which is the value of CHILDREN. See Exercise 3.

the word or phrase must have properties which are compatible with the description of the daughters in the grammatical rule. If this kind of compatibility exists, then we can say that the respective items are *unifiable*.[3] If one unifies two descriptions, the result is a description which contains information from both descriptions but no additional information.

The way unification works can be demonstrated with feature descriptions describing people. One can imagine that Bettina Kant goes to the private detective Max Müller and wants to find a specific person. Normally, those who go to a detective's office only come with a partial description of the person they are looking for, e.g., the gender, hair color or date of birth. Perhaps even the registration number of the car belonging to the person is known.

It is then expected of the detective that he or she provides information fitting the description. If we are looking for a blonde female named Meier (18a), then we do not want to get descriptions of a male red-head (18b). The descriptions in (18) are incompatible and cannot be unified:

(18) a.
$$\begin{bmatrix} person \\ \text{LASTNAME} & meier \\ \text{GENDER} & female \\ \text{HAIRCOLOR} & blonde \end{bmatrix}$$

b.
$$\begin{bmatrix} person \\ \text{LASTNAME} & meier \\ \text{GENDER} & male \\ \text{HAIRCOLOR} & red \end{bmatrix}$$

The description in (19) would be a possible result for a search for a blonde, female individual called Meier:

(19)
$$\begin{bmatrix} person \\ \text{FIRSTNAME} & katharina \\ \text{LASTNAME} & meier \\ \text{GENDER} & female \\ \text{DATE-OF-BIRTH} & 15.10.1965 \\ \text{HAIRCOLOR} & blonde \end{bmatrix}$$

Katharina Meier could also have other properties unknown to the detective. The important thing is that the properties known to the detective match those that the client is

---

[3] The term *unification* should be used with care. It is only appropriate if certain assumptions with regard to the formal basis of linguistic theories are made. Informally, the term is often used in formalisms where unification is not technically defined. In HPSG, it mostly means that the constraints of two descriptions lead to a single description. What one wants to say here, intuitively, is that the objects described have to satisfy the constraints of both descriptions at the same time (*constraint satisfaction*). Since the term *unification* is so broadly-used, it will also be used in this section. The term will not play a role in the remaining discussions of theories with the exception of explicitly unification-based approaches. In contrast, the concept of constraint satisfaction presented here is very important for the comprehension of the following chapters.

looking for. Furthermore, it is important that the detective uses reliable information and does not make up any information about the sought object. The unification of the search in (18a) and the information accessible to the detective in (19) is in fact (19) and not (20), for example:

$$(20) \quad \begin{bmatrix} person \\ \text{FIRSTNAME} & katharina \\ \text{LASTNAME} & meier \\ \text{GENDER} & female \\ \text{DATE-OF-BIRTH} & 15.10.1965 \\ \text{HAIRCOLOR} & blond \\ \text{CHILDREN} & \langle \rangle \end{bmatrix}$$

(20) contains information about children, which is neither contained in (18a) nor in (19). It could indeed be the case that Katharina Meier has no children, but there are perhaps several people called Katharina Meier with otherwise identical properties. With this invented information, we might exclude one or more possible candidates.

It is possible that our detective Max Müller does not have any information about hair color in his files. His files could contain the following information:

$$(21) \quad \begin{bmatrix} person \\ \text{FIRSTNAME} & katharina \\ \text{LASTNAME} & meier \\ \text{GENDER} & female \\ \text{DATE-OF-BIRTH} & 15.10.1965 \end{bmatrix}$$

These data are compatible with the search criteria. If we were to unify the descriptions in (18a) and (21), we would get (19). If we assume that the detective has done a good job, then Bettina Kant now knows that the person she is looking for has the properties of her original search plus the newly discovered properties.

6.7 Phenomena, models and formal theories

In the previous sections, we introduced feature descriptions with types. These feature descriptions describe typed feature structures, which are models of observable linguistic structures. In the definitions of types, one determines which properties of linguistic objects should be described. The type hierarchy together with type definitions is also referred to as a *signature*. As a grammarian, one typically uses types in feature descriptions. These descriptions contain constraints which must hold for linguistic objects. If no constraints are given, all values that are compatible with the specification in the signature are possible values. For example, one can omit the case description of a linguistic object such as *Frau* 'woman' since *Frau* can – as shown in (22) – appear in all four cases:

(22) a. Die   Frau   schläft.   (nominative)
          the.NOM woman sleeps

      b. Wir gedenken   der   Frau.   (genitive)
          we commemorate the.GEN woman

      c. Er hilft der   Frau.   (dative)
          he helps the.DAT woman

      d. Er liebt die   Frau.   (accusative)
          he loves the.ACC woman

In a given model, there are only fully specified representations, that is, the model contains four forms of *Frau*, each with a different case. For masculine nouns such as *Mann* 'man', one would have to say something about case in the description since the genitive-singular form *Mann-es* differs from other singular forms, which can be seen by adding *Mann* into the examples in (22). (23) shows the feature descriptions for *Frau* 'woman' and *Mann* 'man':

(23) a. Frau 'woman':
          $\begin{bmatrix} \text{GENDER} & \textit{fem} \end{bmatrix}$

      b. Mann 'man':
          $\begin{bmatrix} \text{GENDER} & \textit{mas} \\ \text{CASE} & \textit{nominative} \lor \textit{dative} \lor \textit{accusative} \end{bmatrix}$

Unlike (23b), (23a) does not contain a case feature since we do not need to say anything special about case in the description of *Frau*. Since all nominal objects require a case feature, it becomes clear that the structures for *Frau* must actually also have a case feature. The value of the case feature is of the type *case*. *case* is a general type which subsumes the subtypes *nominative*, *genitive*, *dative* and *accusative*. Concrete linguistic objects always have exactly one of these maximally specified types as their case value. The feature structures belonging to (23) are given in Figure 6.2 and Figure 6.3.

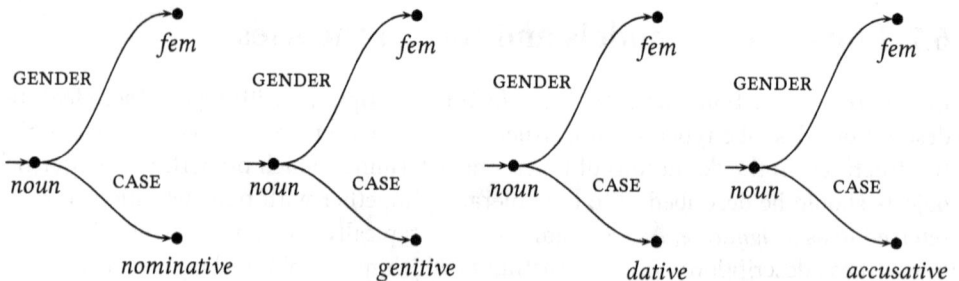

Figure 6.2: Feature structures for the description of *Frau* 'woman' in (23a)

In these representations, each node has a certain type (*noun, fem, nominative, ...*) and the types in feature structures are always maximally specific, that is, they do not have any further subtypes. There is always an entry node (*noun* in the example above) and

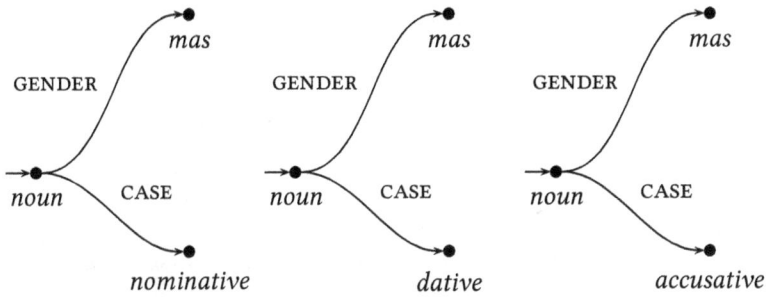

Figure 6.3: Feature structures for the description of *Mann* 'man' in (23b)

the other nodes are connected with arrows that are annotated with the feature labels (GENDER, CASE).

If we return to the example with people from the previous sections, we can capture the difference between a model and a description as follows: if we have a model of people that includes first name, last name, date of birth, gender and hair color, then it follows that every object we model also has a birthday. We can, however, decide to omit these details from our descriptions if they do not play a role for stating constraints or formulating searches.

The connection between linguistic phenomena, the model and the formal theory is shown in Figure 6.4. The model is designed to model linguistic phenomena. Further-

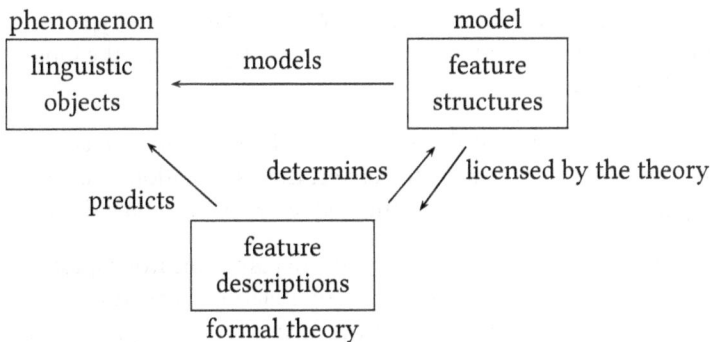

Figure 6.4: Phenomenon, model and formal theory

more, it must be licensed by our theory. The theory determines the model and makes predictions with regard to possible phenomena.

Comprehension questions

1. What are the reasons for using types?

2. What is inheritance? What is special about multiple inheritance?

3. Are the following structures compatible, that is, can they be used to describe the same object?

(24)
$$
\begin{bmatrix}
\text{FIRSTNAME } max \\
\text{LASTNAME } meier \\
\text{FATHER } \begin{bmatrix} person \\ \text{FIRSTNAME } peter \\ \text{LASTNAME } \quad meier \end{bmatrix}
\end{bmatrix}
\quad
\begin{bmatrix}
\text{FIRSTNAME } max \\
\text{LASTNAME } meier \\
\text{FATHER } \begin{bmatrix} person \\ \text{FIRSTNAME } peter \\ \text{LASTNAME } \quad müller \end{bmatrix}
\end{bmatrix}
$$

(25)
$$
\begin{bmatrix}
\text{FIRSTNAME } max \\
\text{LASTNAME } meier \\
\text{FATHER } \begin{bmatrix} person \\ \text{FIRSTNAME } peter \\ \text{LASTNAME } \quad meier \end{bmatrix}
\end{bmatrix}
\quad
\begin{bmatrix}
\text{FIRSTNAME } max \\
\text{LASTNAME } meier \\
\text{MOTHER } \begin{bmatrix} person \\ \text{FIRSTNAME } ursula \\ \text{LASTNAME } \quad müller \end{bmatrix}
\end{bmatrix}
$$

Exercises

1. Think about how one could describe musical instruments using feature descriptions.

2. Come up with a type hierarchy for the word classes (*det, comp, noun, verb, adj, prep*). Think about the ways in which one can organize the type hierachy so that one can express the generalizations that where captured by the binary features in Table 3.1 on page 92.

3. In this chapter, we introduced lists. This may look like an extension of the formalism, but it is not as it is possible to convert the list notation into a notation which only requires feature-value pairs. Think about how one could do this.

4. (Additional exercise) The relation *append* will play a role in Chapter 9. This relation serves to combine two lists to form a third. Relational constraints such as *append* do in fact constitute an expansion of the formalism. Using relational constraints, it is possible to relate any number of feature values to other values, that is, one can write programs which compute a particular value depending on other values. This poses the question as to whether one needs such powerful descriptive tools in a linguistic theory and if we do allow them, what kind of complexity we afford them. A theory which can do without relational constraints should be preferred over one that uses relational constraints (see Müller 2007b: Chapter 20 for a comparison of theories).

   For the concatenation of lists, there is a possible implementation in feature structures without recourse to relational constraints. Find out how this can be done. Give your sources and document how you went about finding the solution.

Further reading

This chapter was designed to give the reader an easy-to-follow introduction to typed feature structures. The mathematical properties of the structures, type hierarchies and the combinatorial possibilities of such structures could not be discussed in detail here, but knowledge of at least part of these properties is important for work in computational linguistics and in developing one's own analyses. For more information, I refer the interested reader to the following publications: Shieber (1986) is a short introduction to the theory of Unification Grammar. It offers a relatively general overview followed by the discussion of important grammar types such as DCG, LFG, GPSG, HPSG, PATR-II. Johnson (1988) describes the formalism of untyped feature structures in a mathematically precise way. Carpenter (1992) goes into the detail about the mathematical aspects of typed feature structures. The formalism developed by King (1999) for HPSG-grammars forms the basis for the formalism by Richter (2004), which currently counts as the standard formalism for HPSG.

7 Lexical Functional Grammar

Lexical Functional Grammar (LFG) was developed in the 80s by Joan Bresnan and Ron Kaplan (Bresnan & Kaplan 1982). LFG forms part of so-called West-Coast linguistics: unlike MIT, where Chomsky works and teaches, the institutes of researchers such as Joan Bresnan and Ron Kaplan are on the west coast of the USA (Joan Bresnan in Stanford and Ron Kaplan at Xerox in Palo Alto and now at the language technology firm Nuance Communications in the Bay Area in California).

Bresnan & Kaplan (1982) view LFG explicitly as a psycholinguistically plausible alternative to transformation-based approaches. For a discussion of the requirements regarding the psycholinguistic plausibility of linguistics theories, see Chapter 15.

The more in-depth works on German are Berman (1996, 2003a) and Cook (2001).

LFG has well-designed formal foundations (Kaplan & Bresnan 1982; Kaplan 1995), and hence first implementations were available rather quickly (Frey & Reyle 1983a,b; Yasukawa 1984; Block & Hunze 1986; Eisele & Dorre 1986; Wada & Asher 1986; Delmonte 1990; Her, Higinbotham & Pentheroudakis 1991; Kohl 1992; Kohl, Gardent, Plainfossé, Reape & Momma 1992; Kaplan & Maxwell III 1996; Mayo 1997, 1999; Boullier & Sagot 2005a,b; Clément 2009; Clément & Kinyon 2001).

The following is a list of languages with implemented LFG fragments, probably incomplete:

- Arabic (Attia 2008),

- Arrernte (Dras, Lareau, Börschinger, Dale, Motazedi, Rambow, Turpin & Ulinski 2012),

- Bengali (Sengupta & Chaudhuri 1997),

- Danish (Ørsnes 2002; Ørsnes & Wedekind 2003, 2004),

- English (Her, Higinbotham & Pentheroudakis 1991; Butt, Dipper, Frank & King 1999a; Riezler, King, Kaplan, Crouch, Maxwell III & Johnson 2002; King & Maxwell III 2007),

- French (Zweigenbaum 1991; Frank 1996; Frank & Zaenen 2002; Butt, Dipper, Frank & King 1999a; Clément & Kinyon 2001; Boullier, Sagot & Clément 2005; Schwarze & de Alencar 2016),

- Georgian (Meurer 2009),

- German (Rohrer 1996; Berman 1996; Kuhn & Rohrer 1997; Butt et al. 1999a; Dipper 2003; Rohrer & Forst 2006; Forst 2006; Frank 2006; Forst & Rohrer 2009),

- Hungarian (Laczkó et al. 2010),

- Indonesian (Arka, Andrews, Dalrymple, Mistica & Simpson 2009),

- Italian (Delmonte 1990; Mayo 1999; Quaglia 2014),

- Irish (Sulger 2009, 2010),

- Japanese (Her, Higinbotham & Pentheroudakis 1991; Masuichi & Ohkuma 2003; Umemoto 2006),

- Korean (Her, Higinbotham & Pentheroudakis 1991),

- Malagasy (Randriamasimanana 2006; Dalrymple, Liakata & Mackie 2006),

- Mandarin Chinese (Her, Higinbotham & Pentheroudakis 1991; Fang & King 2007),

- Murrinh-Patha (Seiss & Nordlinger 2012),

- Norwegian (Dyvik, Meurer & Rosén 2005),

- Polish (Patejuk & Przepiórkowski 2012),

- Portuguese (de Alencar 2004, 2013),

- Spanish (Mayo 1999),

- Tigrinya (Kifle 2012),

- Turkish (Çetinoğlu & Oflazer 2006),

- Hungarian (Laczkó, Rákosi & Tóth 2010; Rákosi, Laczkó & Csernyi 2011),

- Urdu/Hindi (Butt, King & Roth 2007; Bögel, Butt & Sulger 2008),

- Welsh (Mittendorf & Sadler 2005) and

- Wolof (Dione 2014, 2013).

Many of theses grammars were developed in the ParGram consortium[1] (Butt, King, Niño & Segond 1999b; Butt, Dyvik, King, Masuichi & Rohrer 2002). Apart from these grammars there is a small fragment of Northern Sotho, which is currently being expanded (Faaß 2010).

Many of the LFG systems combine linguistically motivated grammars with a statistical component. Such a component can help to find preferred readings of a sentence first, it can increase the efficiency of processing and make the complete processing robust (for instance Kaplan et al. 2004; Riezler et al. 2002). Josef van Genabith's group in Dublin is working on the induction of LFG grammars from corpora (e.g., Johnson et al. 1999; O'Donovan et al. 2005; Cahill et al. 2005; Chrupala & van Genabith 2006; Guo et al. 2007; Cahill et al. 2008; Schluter & van Genabith 2009).

---

[1] http://pargram.b.uib.no/research-groups/. 01.10.2015.

Some of the systems can be tested online:

- http://iness.uib.no/xle-web/xle-web

- http://lfg-demo.computing.dcu.ie/lfgparser.html

- http://www.xlfg.org/

7.1 General remarks on the representational format

LFG assumes multiple levels of representation.[2] The most important are c-structure and f-structure. c-structure is the constituent structure and it is licensed by a phrase structure grammar. This phrase structure grammar uses $\overline{X}$ structures for languages for which this is appropriate. f-structure stands for functional structure. Functional structure contains information about the predicates involved and about the grammatical functions (subject, object, ...) which occur in a constituent. Mappings mediate between these representational levels.

7.1.1 Functional structure

In LFG, grammatical functions such as subject and object play a very important role. Unlike in most other theories discussed in this book, they are primitives of the theory. A sentence such as (1a) will be assigned a functional structure as in (1b):

(1) a. David devoured a sandwich.

    b.
$$\begin{bmatrix} \text{PRED} & \text{'DEVOUR} \langle \text{SUBJ, OBJ} \rangle \text{'} \\ \text{SUBJ} & \begin{bmatrix} \text{PRED} & \text{'DAVID'} \end{bmatrix} \\ \text{OBJ} & \begin{bmatrix} \text{SPEC} & \text{A} \\ \text{PRED} & \text{'SANDWICH'} \end{bmatrix} \end{bmatrix}$$

All lexical items that have a meaning (e.g., nouns, verbs, adjectives) contribute a PRED feature with a corresponding value. The grammatical functions governed by a head (government = subcategorization) are determined in the specification of PRED.[3] Corresponding functions are called *governable grammatical functions*. Examples of this are shown in Table 7.1 on the next page (Dalrymple 2006). The PRED specification corresponds to the theta grid in GB theory. The valence of a head is specified by the PRED value.

The non-governable grammatical functions are given in Table 7.2 on the following page. Topic and focus are information-structural terms. There are a number of works on

---

[2] The English examples and their analyses discussed in this section are taken from Dalrymple (2001) and Dalrymple (2006).

[3] In the structure in (1b), the SUBJ and OBJ in the list following *devour* are identical to the values of SUBJ and OBJ in the structure. For reasons of presentation, this will not be explicitly indicated in this structure and following structures.

Table 7.1: Governable grammatical functions

SUBJ:	subject
OBJ:	object
COMP:	sentential complement or closed (non-predicative) infinitival complement
XCOMP:	open (predicative) complement, often infinitival, the SUBJ function is externally controlled
OBJ$_\theta$:	secondary OBJ functions that are related to a special, language specific set of grammatical roles; English has OBJ$_{THEME}$ only.
OBL$_\theta$:	a group of thematically restricted oblique functions, as for instance OBL$_{GOAL}$ or OBL$_{AGENT}$. These often correspond to adpositional phrases in c-structure.

Table 7.2: Non-governable grammatical functions

ADJ:	adjuncts
TOPIC:	the topic of an utterance
FOCUS:	the focus of an utterance

their exact definition, which differ to varying degrees (Kruijff-Korbayová & Steedman 2003: 253–254), but broadly speaking, one can say that the focus of an utterance constitutes new information and that the topic is old or given information. Bresnan (2001: 97) uses the following question tests in order to determine topic and focus:

(2) Q: What did you name your cat?
A: Rosie I named her. (*Rosie* = FOCUS)

(3) Q: What did you name your pets?
A: My dog, I named Harold. My cat, I named Rosie. (*my dog, my cat* = TOPIC)

f-structures are characterized using functional descriptions, for example, one can refer to a value of the feature TENSE in the functional structure f using the following expression:

(4) $(f$ TENSE$)$

It is possible to say something about the value which this feature should have in the feature description. The following descriptions express the fact that in the structure f, the feature TENSE must have the value PAST.

(5) $(f$ TENSE$)$ = PAST

The value of a feature may also be a specific f-structure. The expression in (6) ensures that the SUBJ feature in f is the f-structure g:

(6) $(f \text{ SUBJ}) = g$

For the analysis of (7a), we get the constraints in (7b):

(7) a. David sneezed.

   b. $(f \text{ PRED}) = \text{'SNEEZE}\langle\text{SUBJ}\,\rangle\text{'}$
      $(f \text{ TENSE}) = \text{PAST}$
      $(f \text{ SUBJ}) = g$
      $(g \text{ PRED}) = \text{'DAVID'}$

The description in (7b) describes the following structure:

(8) $f:$ $\begin{bmatrix} \text{PRED} & \text{'SNEEZE}\langle\text{SUBJ}\,\rangle\text{'} \\ \text{TENSE} & \text{PAST} \\ \text{SUBJ} & g: \begin{bmatrix} \text{PRED 'DAVID'} \end{bmatrix} \end{bmatrix}$

But (7b) also describes many other structures which contain further features. We are only interested in minimal structures that contain the information provided in the description.

(9) shows how a node in the c-structure can be connected to the f-structure for the entire sentence:

(9)

The function ϕ from the NP-node to the f-structure corresponding to the NP is depicted with an arrow marked ϕ.

A phrase and its head always correspond to the same f-structure:

(10)

In LFG grammars of English, the CP/IP system is assumed as in GB theory (see Section 3.1.5). IP, I′ and I (and also VP) are mapped onto the same f-structure.

(11) a. David is yawning.

b.

$$
\begin{array}{c}
\text{IP}\\
\overset{\displaystyle\frown}{\text{NP} \quad \text{I}'}\\
\;\;| \qquad \overset{\displaystyle\frown}{\text{I} \;\; \text{VP}}\\
\text{N}' \quad | \quad |\\
\;| \qquad \text{is} \quad \text{V}'\\
\text{N} \qquad\qquad |\\
\;| \qquad\qquad \text{V}\\
\text{David} \qquad\;\; |\\
\qquad\qquad \text{yawning}
\end{array}
\qquad
\begin{bmatrix}
\text{PRED} & \text{'YAWN}\langle\text{SUBJ}\,\rangle\text{'}\\
\text{TENSE} & \text{PRES}\\[4pt]
\text{SUBJ} & \begin{bmatrix}\text{PRED 'DAVID'}\end{bmatrix}
\end{bmatrix}
$$

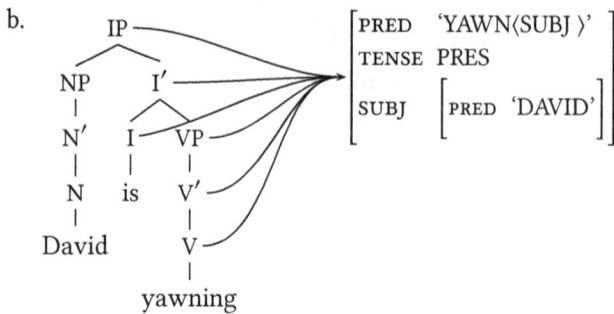

f-structures have to fulfill two well-formedness conditions: they have to be both *complete* and *coherent*. Both these conditions will be discussed in the following sections.

7.1.2 Completeness

Every head adds a constraint of the PRED value of the corresponding f-structure. In determining completeness, one has to check that the elements required in the PRED value are actually realized. In (12b), OBJ is missing a value, which is why (12a) is ruled out by the theory.

(12)   a. * David devoured.

b.
$$
\begin{bmatrix}
\text{PRED} & \text{'DEVOUR}\langle\text{SUBJ,OBJ}\rangle\text{'}\\[4pt]
\text{SUBJ} & \begin{bmatrix}\text{PRED 'DAVID'}\end{bmatrix}
\end{bmatrix}
$$

7.1.3 Coherence

The Coherence Condition requires that all argument functions in a given f-structure have to be selected in the value of the local PRED attribute. (13a) is ruled out because COMP does not appear under the arguments of *devour*.

(13)   a. * David devoured a sandwich that Peter sleeps.

b.
$$
\begin{bmatrix}
\text{PRED} & \text{'DEVOUR}\langle\text{SUBJ,OBJ}\rangle\text{'}\\
\text{SUBJ} & [\,\text{PRED 'DAVID'}\,]\\[4pt]
\text{OBJ} & \begin{bmatrix}\text{SPEC} & \text{A}\\ \text{PRED} & \text{'SANDWICH'}\end{bmatrix}\\[8pt]
\text{COMP} & \begin{bmatrix}\text{PRED} & \text{'SLEEP}\langle\text{SUBJ}\rangle\text{'}\\ \text{SUBJ} & \begin{bmatrix}\text{PRED 'PETER'}\end{bmatrix}\end{bmatrix}
\end{bmatrix}
$$

The constraints on completeness and coherence together ensure that all and only those arguments required in the PRED specification are actually realized. Both of those constraints taken together correspond to the Theta-Criterion in GB theory (see page 90).[4]

---

[4] For the differences between predicate-argument structures in LFG and the Deep Structure oriented Theta Criterion, see Bresnan & Kaplan (1982: xxvi–xxviii).

7.1.4 Restrictions on the c-structure/f-structure relation

Symbols in c-structures are assigned restrictions for f-structures. The following symbols are used: '↑' refers to the f-structure of the immediately dominating node and '↓' refers to the f-structure of the c-structure node bearing the annotation. A common annotation is '↑ = ↓'. This constraint states that the f-structure of the mother node is identical to that of the annotated category:

(14) V' →   V

                                        ↑ = ↓

            f-structure of the mother = own f-structure

The annotation '↑ = ↓' is below the head of a structure.

Phrases which are licensed by the annotated c-structure in (14) can be visualized as follows:

(15)

(16) shows a V' rule with an object:

(16) V' →   V   NP
                  ↑ = ↓   (↑ OBJ) = ↓

The annotation on the NP signals that the OBJ value in the f-structure of the mother (↑ OBJ) is identical to the f-structure of the NP node, that is, to everything that is contributed from the material below the NP node (↓). This is shown in the figure in (17):

(17)

In the equation (↑ OBJ) = ↓, the arrows '↑' and '↓' correspond to feature structures. '↑' and '↓' stand for the *f* and *g* in equations such as (6).

(18) is an example with an intransitive verb and (19) is the corresponding visualization:

(18) *sneezed* V   (↑ PRED) = 'SNEEZE⟨SUBJ ⟩'
                     (↑ TENSE) = PAST

(19)

7.1.5 Semantics

Following Dalrymple (2006: 90–92), *glue semantics* is the dominant approach to semantic interpretation in LFG (Dalrymple, Lamping & Saraswat 1993; Dalrymple 2001: Chapter 8). There are, however, other variants where Kamp's discourse representation structures (Kamp & Reyle 1993) are used (Frey & Reyle 1983a,b).

In the following, glue semantics will be presented in more detail.[5] Under a glue-based approach, it is assumed that f-structure is the level of syntactic representation which is crucial for the semantic interpretation of a phrase, that is, unlike GB theory, it is not the position of arguments in the tree which play a role in the composition of meaning, but rather functional relations such as SUBJ and OBJ. Glue semantics assumes that each substructure of the f-structure corresponds to a semantic resource connected to a meaning and furthermore, that the meaning of a given f-structure comes from the sum of these parts. The way the meaning is assembled is regulated by certain instructions for the combination of semantic resources. These instructions are given as a set of logic premises written in linear logic as *glue language*. The computation of the meaning of an utterance corresponds to a logical conclusion.

This conclusion is reached on the basis of logical premises contributed by the words in an expression or possibly even by a syntactic construction itself. The requirements on how the meaning of the parts can be combined to yield the full meaning are expressed in linear logic, a resource-based logic. Linear logic is different from classic logic in that it does not allow that premises of conclusions are not used at all or more than once in a derivation. Hence, in linear logic, premises are resources which have to be used. This corresponds directly to the use of words in an expression: words contribute to the entire meaning exactly once. It is not possible to ignore them or to use their meaning more than once. A sentence such as *Peter knocked twice.* does not mean the same as *Peter knocked.* The meaning of *twice* must be included in the full meaning of the sentences. Similarly, the sentence cannot mean the same as *Peter knocked twice twice.*, since the semantic contribution of a given word cannot be used twice.

The syntactic structure for the sentence in (20a) together with its semantic representation is given in (20b):

(20)   a.   David yawned.

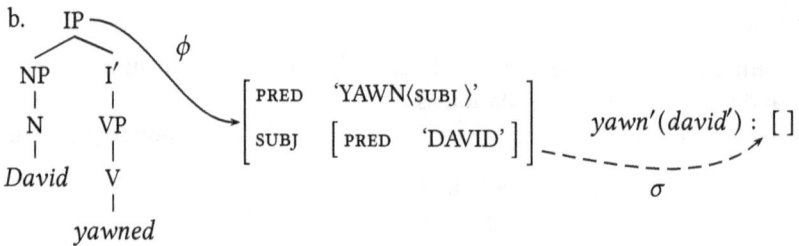

The semantic structure of this sentence is connected to the f-structure via the correspondence function σ (depicted here as a dashed line). The semantic representation is derived from the lexical information for the verb *yawned*, which is given in (21).

(21) $\lambda x.yawn'(x) : (\uparrow \text{SUBJ})_\sigma \multimap \uparrow_\sigma$

This formula is referred to as the *meaning constructor*. Its job is to combine the meaning of *yawned* – a one place predicate $\lambda x.yawn'(x)$ – with the formula $(\uparrow \text{SUBJ})_\sigma \multimap \uparrow_\sigma$ in

---

[5] The following discussion heavily draws from the corresponding section of Dalrymple (2006). (It is a translation of my translation of the original material into German.)

linear logic. Here, the connective ⊸ is the *linear implication* symbol of linear logic. The symbol contains the meaning that *if* a semantic resource (↑ SUBJ)$_\sigma$ for the meaning of the subject is available, *then* a semantic resource for ↑$_\sigma$ must be created which will stand for the entire meaning of the sentence. Unlike the implication operator of classic logic, the linear implication must consume and produce semantic resources: the formula (↑ SUBJ)$_\sigma$ ⊸ ↑$_\sigma$ states that if a semantic resource (↑ SUBJ)$_\sigma$ is found, it is consumed and the semantic resource ↑$_\sigma$ is produced.

Furthermore, it is assumed that a proper name such as *David* contributes its own semantic structure as a semantic resource. In an utterance such as *David yawned*, this resource is consumed by the verb *yawned*, which requires a resource for its SUBJ in order to produce the resource for the entire sentence. This corresponds to the intuition that a verb in any given sentence requires the meaning of its arguments in order for the entire sentence to be understood.

The f-structure of *David yawned* with the instantiated meaning construction contributed by *David* and *yawned* is given in (22):

(22)
$$y : \begin{bmatrix} \text{PRED} & \text{'YAWN} \langle \text{SUBJ} \rangle \text{'} \\ \text{SUBJ} & d : \begin{bmatrix} \text{PRED} & \text{'DAVID'} \end{bmatrix} \end{bmatrix}$$

    [David] $david' : d_\sigma$

    [yawn] $\lambda x.yawn'(x) : d_\sigma \multimap y_\sigma$

The left side of the meaning constructor marked by [David] is the meaning of the proper name *David*, *david'* to be precise. The left-hand side of the meaning constructor [yawn] is the meaning of the intransitive verb – a one-place predicate $\lambda x.yawn'(x)$.

Furthermore, one must still postulate further rules to determine the exact relation between the right-hand side (the glue) of the meaning constructors in (22) and the left-hand side (the meaning). For simple, non-implicational meaning constructors such as [David] in (22), the meaning on the left is the same as the meaning of the semantic structure on the right. Meaning constructors such as [yawn] have a λ-expression on the left, which has to be combined with another expression via functional application (see Section 2.3). The linear implication on the right-hand side must be applied in parallel. This combined process is shown in (23).

(23)
$$\frac{x : f_\sigma \quad P : f_\sigma \multimap g_\sigma}{P(x) : g_\sigma}$$

The right-hand side of the rule corresponds to a logical conclusion following the *modus ponens* rule. With these correspondences between expressions in linear logic and the meanings themselves, we can proceed as shown in (24), which is based on Dalrymple (2006: 92). After combining the respective meanings of *yawned* and *David* and then carrying out β-reduction, we arrive at the desired result of $yawn'(david')$ as the meaning of *David yawned*.

(24) $david' : d_\sigma$ The meaning $david'$ is associated with the semantic structure of SUBJ d_σ.

$\lambda x.yawn'(x) : d_\sigma \multimap y_\sigma$ If we find the semantic resource for the SUBJ
d_σ on the glue side, this resource is con-
sumed and the semantic resource for the entire sentence y_σ is produced. On the meaning side, we apply the function $\lambda x.yawn'(x)$
to the meaning associated with d_σ.

$yawn'(david') : y_\sigma$ We have created the semantic structure y_σ
for the entire sentence, associated with the
meaning of $yawn'(david')$.

Glue analyses of quantification, modification and other phenomena have been investi-
gated in a volume on glue semantics (Dalrymple 1999). Particularly problematic for these
approaches are cases where there appear to be too many or too few resources for the
production of utterances. These kinds of cases have been discussed by Asudeh (2004).

7.1.6 Adjuncts

Adjuncts are not selected by their head. The grammatical function ADJ is a non-governable grammatical function. Unlike arguments, where every grammatical function can
only be realized once, a sentence can contain multiple adjuncts. The value of ADJ in the
f-structure is therefore not a simple structure as with the other grammatical functions,
but rather a set. For example, the f structure for the sentence in (25a) contains an ADJ set
with two elements: one for *yesterday* and one for *at noon*.

(25)   a.   David devoured a sandwich at noon yesterday.

b.
$$\begin{bmatrix} \text{PRED 'DEVOUR}\langle\text{SUBJ,OBJ}\rangle' \\ \text{SUBJ} \begin{bmatrix} \text{PRED 'DAVID'} \end{bmatrix} \\ \text{OBJ} \begin{bmatrix} \text{SPEC A} \\ \text{PRED 'SANDWICH'} \end{bmatrix} \\ \text{ADJ} \left\{ \begin{bmatrix} \text{PRED 'YESTERDAY'} \end{bmatrix}, \begin{bmatrix} \text{PRED 'AT}\langle\text{OBJ}\rangle' \\ \text{OBJ} \begin{bmatrix} \text{PRED 'NOON'} \end{bmatrix} \end{bmatrix} \right\} \end{bmatrix}$$

The annotation on the c-structure rule for adjuncts requires that the f-structure of the
adjuncts be part of the ADJ set of the mother's f-structure:

(26) V′ →   V′   PP
              ↑ = ↓   ↓ ∈ (↑ ADJ)

The representation of adjuncts in a set is not sufficient to characterize the meaning of an utterance containing scope-bearing adjuncts (as for instance the negation in sentences like (31) on page 101). In order to determine scopal relations, one has to refer to the linear order of the adjuncts, that is, the c-structure. For linearization restrictions in LFG, see Zaenen & Kaplan (1995).

7.2 Passive

Bresnan & Mchombo (1995) argue that one should view words as "atoms" of which syntactic structure is comprised (*lexical integrity*[6]).

Syntactic rules cannot create new words or make reference to the internal structure of words. Every terminal node (each "leaf" of the tree) is a word. It follows from this that analyses such as the GB analysis of Pollock (1989) in Figure 7.1 on the next page for the French example in (27) are ruled out (the figure is taken from Kuhn 2007: 617):

(27) Marie ne parlerait   pas
     Marie NEG speak.COND.3SG NEG

     'Marie would not speak.'

In Pollock's analysis, the various morphemes are in specific positions in the tree and are combined only after certain movements have been carried out.

The assumption of lexical integrity is made by all theories discussed in this book with the exception of GB and Minimalism. However, formally, this is not a must as it is also possible to connect morphemes to complex syntactic structures in theories such as Categorial Grammar, GPSG, HPSG, CxG, DG and TAG. As far as I know, this kind of analysis has never been proposed.

Bresnan noticed that, as well as passivized verbs, there are passivized adjectives which show the same morphological idiosyncrasies as the corresponding participles (Bresnan 1982b: 21; Bresnan 2001: 31). Some examples are given in (28):

(28) a. a well-written novel (write – written)
      b. a recently given talk (give – given)
      c. my broken heart (break – broken)
      d. an uninhabited island (inhabit – inhabited)
      e. split wood (split – split)

If one assumes lexical integrity, then adjectives would have to be derived in the lexicon. If the verbal passive were not a lexical process, but rather a phrase-structural one, then the form identity would remain unexplained.

In LFG, grammatical functions are primitives, that is, they are not derived from a position in the tree (e.g., Subject = SpecIP). Words (fully inflected word-forms) determine the

---

[6] See Anderson (1992: 84) for more on lexical integrity.

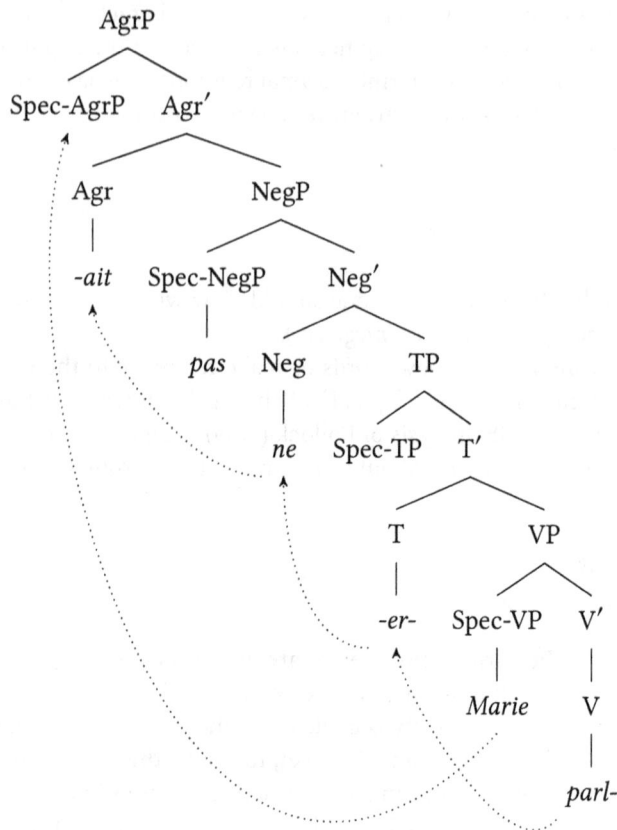

Figure 7.1: Pollock's analysis of *Marie ne parlerait pas* 'Marie would not speak.' according to Kuhn (2007: 617)

grammatical function of their arguments. Furthermore, there is a hierarchy of grammatical functions. During participle formation in morphology, the highest verbal argument is suppressed. The next highest argument moves up and is not realized as the OBJECT but rather as the SUBJECT. This was explicitly encoded in earlier work (Bresnan 1982b: 8):

(29) Passivization rule:
$$(\text{SUBJ}) \mapsto \emptyset/(\text{OBL})$$
$$(\text{OBJ}) \mapsto (\text{SUBJ})$$

The first rule states that the subject is either not realized ($\emptyset$) or it is realized as an oblique element (the *by*-PP in English). The second rule states that if there is an accusative object, this becomes the subject.

In later work, the assignment of grammatical functions was taken over by Lexical Mapping Theory (Bresnan & Kanerva 1989). It is assumed that thematic roles are ordered in a universally valid hierarchy (Bresnan & Kanerva 1989; Bresnan 2001: 307): agent >

beneficiary > experiencer/goal > instrument > patient/theme > locative. Patient-like roles are marked as unrestricted ($[-r]$) in a corresponding representation, the so-called a-structure. Secondary patient-like roles are marked as *objective* ($[+o]$) and all other roles are marked as non-objective ($[-o]$). For the transitive verb *schlagen* 'to beat', we have the following:

(30)

			Agent	Patient
a-structure	*schlagen* 'beat'	⟨ x	y ⟩
			$[-o]$	$[-r]$

The mapping of a-structure to f-structure is governed by the following restrictions:

(31) a. Subject-Mapping-Principle: The most prominent role marked with $[-o]$ is mapped to SUBJ if it is initial in the a-structure. Otherwise, the role marked with $[-r]$ is mapped to SUBJ.

 b. The argument roles are connected to grammatical functions as shown in the following table. Non-specified values for o and r are to be understood as '+':

	$[-r]$	$[+r]$
$[-o]$	SUBJ	OBL$_\theta$
$[+o]$	OBJ	OBJ$_\theta$

 c. Function-Argument Biuniqueness: Every a-structure role must be associated to exactly one function and vice versa.

For the argument structure in (30), the principle in (31a) ensures that the agent x receives the grammatical function SUBJ. (31b) adds an o-feature with the value '+' so that the patient y is associated with OBJ:

(32)

			Agent	Patient
a-structure	*schlagen* 'beat'	⟨ x	y ⟩
			$[-o]$	$[-r]$
			SUBJ	OBJ

Under passivization, the most prominent role is suppressed so that only the $[-r]$ marked patient role remains. Following (31a), this role will then be mapped to the subject.

(33)

			Agent	Patient
a-structure	*schlagen* 'beat'	⟨ x	y ⟩
			$[-o]$	$[-r]$
			Ø	SUBJ

Unlike the objects of transitive verbs, the objects of verbs such as *helfen* 'help' are marked as $[+o]$ (Berman 1999). The lexical case of the objects is given in the a-structure, since this case (dative) is linked to a semantic role (Zaenen, Maling & Thráinsson 1985: 465). The corresponding semantic roles are obligatorily mapped to the grammatical function OBJ$_\theta$.

(34)   Agent   Beneficiary
    a-structure   *helfen* 'help'   ⟨ x   y ⟩
                                 [−o]   [+o]/DAT
                                 SUBJ OBJ_θ

Passivization will yield the following:

(35)   Agent   Beneficiary
    a-structure   *helfen* 'help'   ⟨ x   y ⟩
                                 [−o]   [+o]/DAT
                                 ∅ OBJ_θ

Since there is neither a [−o] nor a [−r] argument, no argument is connected to the subject function. The result is an association of arguments and grammatical functions that corresponds to the one found in impersonal passives.

These mapping principles may seem complex at first glance, but they play a role in analyzing an entire range of phenomena, e.g., the analysis of unaccusative verbs (Bresnan & Zaenen 1990). For the analysis of the passive, we can now say that the passive suppresses the highest [−o] role. Mentioning an eventual object in the passive rule is no longer necessary.

7.3 Verb position

There are two possibilities for the analysis of verb placement in German.

- a trace in verb-final position (as in GB) (see Choi 1999, Berman 1996: Section 2.1.4) and

- so-called *extended head domains* (see Berman 2003a).

In the analysis of extended head domains, the verb is simply omitted from the verb phrase. The following preliminary variant of the VP rule is used:[7]

(36)   VP → (NP) (NP) (NP) (V)

All components of the VP are optional as indicated by the brackets. As in GB analyses, the verb in verb-first clauses is in C. No I projection is assumed – as in a number of GB works (Haider 1993, 1995, 1997a; Sternefeld 2006: Section IV.3), since it is difficult to motivate its existence for German (Berman 2003a: Section 3.2.2). The verb contributes its f-structure information from the C position. Figure 7.2 on the following page contains a simplified version of the analysis proposed by Berman (2003a: 41).

After what we learned about phrase structure rules in Chapters 2 and 5, it may seem strange to allow VPs without V. This is not a problem in LFG, however, since for the analysis of a given sentence, it only has to be ensured that all the necessary parts (and

---

[7] See Bresnan (2001: 110) and Dalrymple (2006: Section 2.2) for a corresponding rule with optional constituents on the right-hand side of the rule.

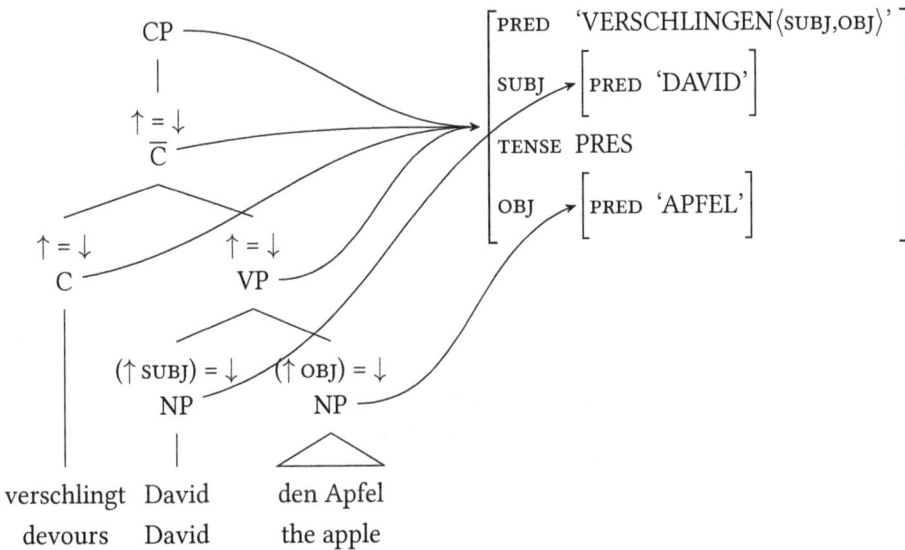

Figure 7.2: Analysis of verb placement following Berman (2003a: 41)

only these) are present. This is ensured by the constraints on completeness and coherence. Where exactly the information comes from is not important. In Figure 7.2, the verb information does not come from the VP, but rather from the C node. C′ is licensed by a special rule:

(37) C′ → C VP
          ↑ = ↓ ↑ = ↓

In LFG rules, there is normally only one element annotated with '↑ = ↓', namely the head. In (37), there are two such elements, which is why both equally contribute to the f-structure of the mother. The head domain of V has been extended to C. The information about SUBJ and OBJ comes from the VP and the information about PRED from C.

7.4 Local reordering

Two possibilities for treating local reordering have been discussed in the literature:[8]

- movement of arguments from a base configuration as in GB (see Choi 1999)

- direct licensing by phrase structure rules (see Berman 1996: Section 2.1.3.1; 2003a)

If one assumes that traces are relevant for the semantic interpretation of a given structure, then the first option has the same problems as movement-based GB analyses. These have already been discussed in Section 3.5.

---

[8] Kaplan (1995: 20–21) shows how one can write grammars in the ID/LP format in LFG. A GPSG-like analysis of German constituent order has not been proposed in the LFG framework.

In what follows, I will present the analysis proposed by Berman (1996: Section 2.1.3) in a somewhat simplified form. Case and grammatical functions of verbal arguments are determined in the lexicon (Berman 1996: 22). (38) shows the lexical entry for the verb *verschlingen* 'devour':[9, 10]

(38) *verschlingt* V   ($\uparrow$ PRED) = 'VERSCHLINGEN⟨SUBJ, OBJ ⟩'
                           ($\uparrow$ SUBJ AGR CAS) = NOM
                           ($\uparrow$ OBJ AGR CAS) = ACC
                           ($\uparrow$ TENSE) = PRES

Berman proposes an analysis that does not combine the verb with all its arguments and adjuncts at the same time, as was the case in GPSG. Instead, she chooses the other extreme and assumes that the verb is not combined with an adjunct or an argument, but rather forms a VP directly. The rule for this is shown in (39):

(39) VP $\rightarrow$ (V)
                        $\uparrow$ = $\downarrow$

---

[9] The four cases in German can be represented using two binary features (GOV, OBL) (Berman 1996: 22). Nominative corresponds to GOV– and OBL– and accusative to GOV+ and OBL–. This kind of encoding allows one to leave case partially underspecified. If one does not provided a value for GOV, then an element with OBL– is compatible with both nominative and accusative. Since this underspecification is not needed in the following discussion, I will omit this feature decomposition and insert the case values directly.

[10] Alternative analyses derive the grammatical function of an NP from its case (Berman 2003a: 37 for German; Bresnan 2001: 187, 201 for German and Russian).

   (i)   ($\downarrow$ CASE) = ACC $\Rightarrow$ ($\uparrow$ OBJ) = $\downarrow$

Karttunen (1989: Section 2.1) makes a similar suggestion for Finnish in the framework of Categorial Grammar. Such analyses are not entirely unproblematic as case cannot always be reliably paired with grammatical functions. In German, as well as temporal accusatives (ii.a), there are also verbs with two accusative objects (ii.b–c) and predicative accusatives (ii.d).

   (ii)   a. Er arbeitete den   ganzen   Tag.
             he worked   the.ACC whole.ACC day

          b. Er lehrte ihn   den   Ententanz.
             he taught him.ACC the.ACC duck.dance

          c. Das kostet ihn   einen Taler.
             that costs him.ACC a.ACC taler

          d. Sie nannte ihn   einen Lügner.
             she called him.ACC a.ACC liar

All of these accusatives can occur in long-distance dependencies (see Section 7.5):

   (iii) Wen glaubst du, dass ich getroffen habe.
          who believe you that I   met   have
          'Who do you think I met?'

wen is not the object of *glauben* 'believe' and as such cannot be included in the f-structure of *glauben* 'believe'. One would have to reformulate the implication in (i) as a disjunction of all possible grammatical functions of the accusative and in addition account for the fact that accusatives can come from a more deeply embedded f-structure.

At first sight, this may seem odd since a V such as *verschlingen* 'devour' does not have the same distribution as a verb with its arguments. However, one should recall that the constraints pertaining to coherence and completeness of f-structures play an important role so that the theory does not make incorrect predictions.

Since the verb can occur in initial position, it is marked as optional in the rule in (39) (see Section 7.3).

The following rule can be used additionally to combine the verb with its subject or object.

(40) VP →   NP   VP
                ($\uparrow$ SUBJ |OBJ |OBJ$_\theta$) = $\downarrow$ $\uparrow$ = $\downarrow$

The '|' here stands for a disjunction, that is, the NP can either be the subject or the object of the superordinate f-structure. Since VP occurs both on the left and right-hand side of the rule in (40), it can be applied multiple times. The rule is not complete, however. For instance, one has to account for prepositional objects, for clausal arguments, for adjectival arguments and for adjuncts. See footnote 12 on page 233.

Figure 7.3 shows the analysis for (41a).

(41) a. [dass] David den Apfel verschlingt
              that David the apple devours

          'that David is devouring the apple'

      b. [dass] den Apfel David verschlingt
              that the apple David devours

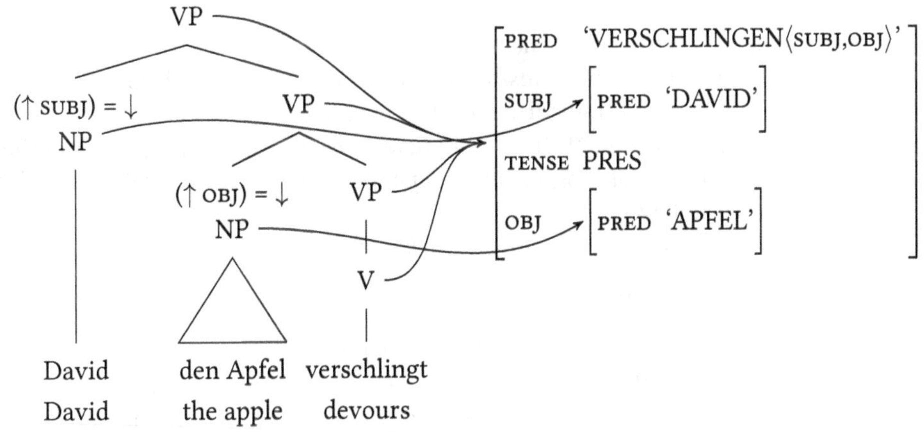

Figure 7.3: Analysis of SOV order following Berman (1996)

The analysis of (41b) is shown in Figure 7.4 on the following page. The analysis of (41b) differs from the one of (41a) only in the order of the replacement of the NP node by the subject or object.

One further fact must be discussed: in the rule (39), the verb is optional. If it is omitted, the VP is empty. In this way, the VP rule in (40) can have an empty VP on the right-hand

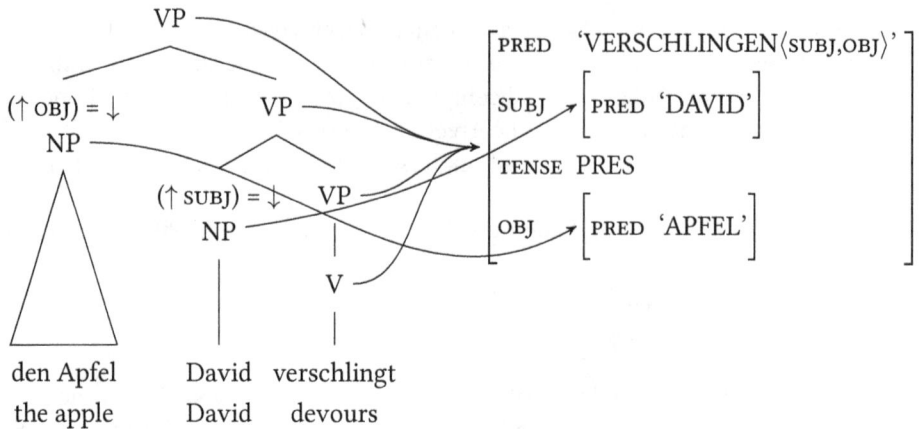

Figure 7.4: Analysis of OSV order following Berman (1996)

side of the rule. This VP is also simply omitted even though the VP symbol in the right-hand side of rule (40) is not marked as optional. That is, the corresponding symbol then also becomes optional as a result of taking the rest of the grammar into consideration as well as possible interactions with other rules.

7.5 Long-distance dependencies and functional uncertainty

We have seen that LFG can explain phenomena such as passivization, local reordering as well as verb placement without transformations. In Chapter 5 on GPSG, we already saw that the development of a transformation-less analysis for long-distance dependencies constitutes a real achievement. In LFG, Kaplan & Zaenen (1989) proposed another transformation-less analysis of long-distance dependencies, which we will consider in further detail in what follows.

In example (42), the displaced constituent *Chris* is characterized by two functions:

(42)   Chris, we think that David saw.

For one, it has an argument function which is normally realized in a different position (the OBJ function of *saw* in the above example) and additionally it has a discourse function: a certain emphasis of the information-structural status in this construction (TOPIC in the matrix clause). In LFG, TOPIC and FOCUS are assumed to be grammaticalized discourse functions (furthermore, SUBJ is classified as the default discourse function). Only grammaticalized discourse functions are represented on the level of f-structure, that is, those that are created by a fixed syntactic mechanism and that interact with the rest of the syntax.

Unlike argument functions, the discourse functions TOPIC and FOCUS are not lexically subcategorized and are therefore not subject to the completeness and coherence conditions. The values of discourse function features like TOPIC and FOCUS are identified with an f-structure that bears an argument function. (43) gives the f-structure for the sentence in (42):

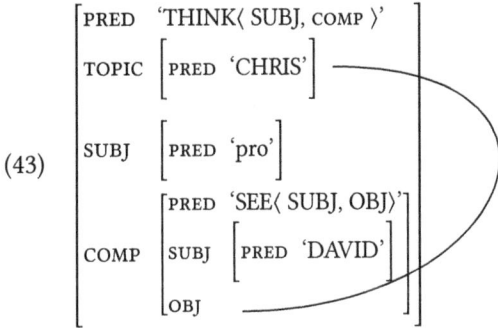

(43)
$$
\begin{bmatrix}
\text{PRED} & \text{'THINK}\langle \text{SUBJ, COMP} \rangle\text{'} \\
\text{TOPIC} & \begin{bmatrix} \text{PRED} & \text{'CHRIS'} \end{bmatrix} \\
\text{SUBJ} & \begin{bmatrix} \text{PRED} & \text{'pro'} \end{bmatrix} \\
\text{COMP} & \begin{bmatrix} \text{PRED} & \text{'SEE}\langle \text{SUBJ, OBJ} \rangle\text{'} \\ \text{SUBJ} & \begin{bmatrix} \text{PRED} & \text{'DAVID'} \end{bmatrix} \\ \text{OBJ} & \end{bmatrix}
\end{bmatrix}
$$

The connecting line means that the value of TOPIC is identical to the value of COMP|OBJ. In Chapter 6 on feature descriptions, I used boxes for structure sharing rather than connecting lines, since boxes are more common across frameworks. It is possible to formulate the structure sharing in (43) as an f-structure constraint as in (44):

(44)   (↑ TOPIC) = (↑ COMP OBJ)

Fronting operations such as (42) are possible from various levels of embedding: for instance, (45a) shows an example with less embedding. The object is located in the same f-structure as the topic. However, the object in (42) comes from a clause embedded under *think*.

The f-structure corresponding to (45a) is given in (45b):

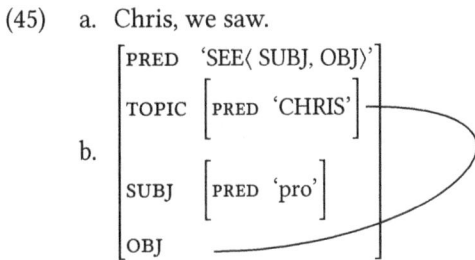

(45)   a. Chris, we saw.

   b.
$$
\begin{bmatrix}
\text{PRED} & \text{'SEE}\langle \text{SUBJ, OBJ} \rangle\text{'} \\
\text{TOPIC} & \begin{bmatrix} \text{PRED} & \text{'CHRIS'} \end{bmatrix} \\
\text{SUBJ} & \begin{bmatrix} \text{PRED} & \text{'pro'} \end{bmatrix} \\
\text{OBJ} &
\end{bmatrix}
$$

The identity restriction for TOPIC and object can be formulated in this case as in (46):

(46)   (↑ TOPIC) = (↑ OBJ)

Example (47a) shows a case of even deeper embedding than in (42) and (47b,c) show the corresponding f-structure and the respective restriction.

(47)   a.   Chris, we think Anna claims that David saw.

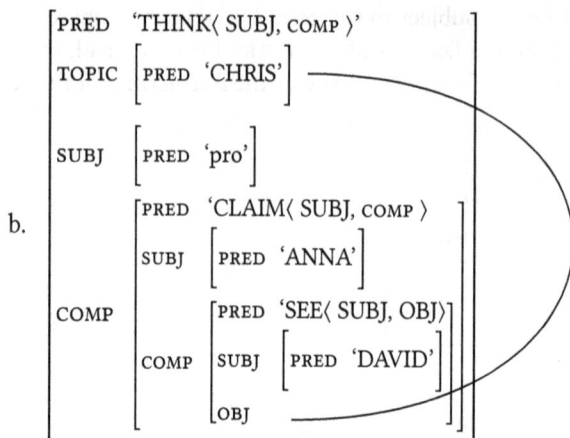

b.
$$\begin{bmatrix} \text{PRED} & \text{'THINK}\langle\text{ SUBJ, COMP }\rangle\text{'} \\ \text{TOPIC} & \begin{bmatrix} \text{PRED} & \text{'CHRIS'} \end{bmatrix} \\ \text{SUBJ} & \begin{bmatrix} \text{PRED} & \text{'pro'} \end{bmatrix} \\ \text{COMP} & \begin{bmatrix} \text{PRED} & \text{'CLAIM}\langle\text{ SUBJ, COMP }\rangle \\ \text{SUBJ} & \begin{bmatrix} \text{PRED} & \text{'ANNA'} \end{bmatrix} \\ \text{COMP} & \begin{bmatrix} \text{PRED} & \text{'SEE}\langle\text{ SUBJ, OBJ}\rangle \\ \text{SUBJ} & \begin{bmatrix} \text{PRED} & \text{'DAVID'} \end{bmatrix} \\ \text{OBJ} & \quad \end{bmatrix} \end{bmatrix} \end{bmatrix}$$

c.   (↑ TOPIC) = (↑ COMP COMP OBJ)

The restrictions in (44), (46) and (47c) are c-structure constraints. The combination of a c-structure with (44) is given in (48):

(48)   CP   →   XP   C′
                  (↑ TOPIC) = ↓   ↑ = ↓
                  (↑ TOPIC) = (↑ COMP OBJ)

(48) states that the first constituent contributes to the TOPIC value in the f-structure of the mother and furthermore that this topic value has to be identical to that of the object in the complement clause. We have also seen examples of other embeddings of various depths. We therefore need restrictions of the following kind as in (49):

(49)   a.   (↑ TOPIC) = (↑ OBJ)
       b.   (↑ TOPIC) = (↑ COMP OBJ)
       c.   (↑ TOPIC) = (↑ COMP COMP OBJ)
       d.   ...

The generalization emerging from these equations is given in (50):

(50)   (↑ TOPIC) = (↑ COMP* OBJ)

Here, '*' stands for an unrestricted number of occurrences of COMP. This means of leaving the possible identification of discourse and grammatical function open is known as *functional uncertainty*, see Kaplan & Zaenen (1989).

   As was shown in the discussion of examples (2) and (3) on page 216, it is not the case that only a TOPIC can be placed in the specifier position of CP in English as FOCUS can occur there too. One can use disjunctions in LFG equations and express the corresponding condition as follows:

(51)   (↑ TOPIC|FOCUS) = (↑ COMP* OBJ)

One can introduce a special symbol for TOPIC|FOCUS, which stands for a disjunction of discourse functions: DF. (51) can then be abbreviated as in (52):

(52) (↑ DF) = (↑ COMP* OBJ)

The final version of the c-structure rule for fronting in English will therefore have the form of (53):[11]

(53) CP →   XP   C'
              (↑ DF) = ↓   ↑ = ↓
              (↑ DF) = (↑ COMP* OBJ)

In German, as well as objects, nearly any other constituent (e.g., subjects, sentential complements, adjuncts) can be fronted. The c-structure rule for this is shown in (54):[12]

(54) CP →   XP   C'
              (↑ DF) = ↓   ↑ = ↓
              (↑ DF) = (↑ COMP* GF)

Here, GF is an abbreviation for a disjunction of grammatical functions which can occur in the prefield.

7.6 Summary and classification

LFG is a constraint-based theory and utilizes feature descriptions and PSG rules. Grammatical functions are treated as primitives of the theory, which sets LFG apart from most of the other theories covered in this book. They are not defined structurally (as in GB). LFG is a lexicalist theory. Like GPSG, LFG can do without transformations. Processes affecting argument structure such as passivization are analyzed by means of lexical rules. Whereas GPSG treated long-distance dependencies using the percolation of information in trees, LFG uses functional uncertainty: a part of the f-structure is identified with another f-structure that can be embedded to an arbitrary depth. Coherence and completeness ensure that the long-distance dependency can be correctly resolved, that is, it ensures that a fronted object is not assigned to an f-structure which already contains an object or one in which no object may occur.

While LFG does contain a phrase-structural component, this plays a significantly less important role compared to other models of grammar. There are rules in which all constituents are optional and it has even been proposed for some languages that there are

---

[11] Note that the two disjunctions that are abbreviated by the respective occurrences of DF are independent in principle. This is unwanted. We want to talk about either a topic or a focus not about a topic and a focus in the mother f-structure. So additional machinery is needed to ensure that both occurrences of DF refer to the same discourse function.

[12] Berman (1996) uses the symbol ZP for symbols in the prefield rather than XP in (54). She formulates various phrase structure rules for ZPs, which replace ZP with NP, PP, AP and various adjuncts. Following Berman, ZPs can also be combined with the verb in the middle field. For reasons of exposition, I refrained from using ZP symbols in the formulation of the VP rule (40) in Section 7.4 and instead used NP directly.

rules where the part of speech of the constituents is not specified (see Section 13.1.2). In these kinds of grammars, f-structure, coherence and completeness work together to ensure that the grammar only allows well-formed structures.

LFG differs from other theories such as HPSG and variants of Construction Grammar in that feature structures are untyped. Generalizations can therefore not be represented in type hierarchies. Until a few years ago, the hierarchical organization of knowledge in inheritance hierarchies did not form part of theoretical analyses. In computer implementations, there were macros but these were viewed as abbreviations without any theoretical status. It is possible to organize macros into hierarchies and macros were discussed explicitly in Dalrymple, Kaplan & King (2004) with reference to capturing linguistic generalizations. Asudeh, Dalrymple & Toivonen (2008) suggest using macros not only for the organization of lexical items but also for capturing generalizations regarding c-structure annotations. Because of these developments, there was a greater convergence between LFG and other theories such as HPSG and CxG.

Williams (1984) compares analyses in LFG with GB. He shows that many analyses are in fact transferable: the function that f-structure has in LFG is handled by the Theta-Criterion and Case Theory in GB. LFG can explicitly differentiate between subjects and non-subjects. In GB, on the other hand, a clear distinction is made between external and internal arguments (see Williams 1984: Section 1.2). In some variants of GB, as well as in HPSG and CxG, the argument with subject properties (if there is one) is marked explicitly (Haider 1986a; Heinz & Matiasek 1994; Müller 2003b; Michaelis & Ruppenhofer 2001). This special argument is referred to as the *designated argument*. In infinitival constructions, subjects are often not expressed inside the infinitival phrase. Nevertheless, the unexpressed subject is usually coreferential with an argument of the matrix verb:

(55)   a. Er versucht, [das Buch zu lesen].
           he tries   the book to read
           'He is trying to read the book.'

       b. Er zwingt ihn, [das Buch zu lesen].
           he forces him the book to read
           'He is forcing him to read the book.'

This is a fact that every theory needs to be able to capture, that is, every theory must be able to differentiate between subjects and non-subjects.

For a comparison of GB/Minimalism and LFG/HPSG, see Kuhn (2007).

Comprehension questions

1. What do the terms *coherence* and *completeness* mean?

2. What are extended head domains?

3. What does lexical integrity mean?

Exercises

1. Give the lexical entry for *kannte* 'knew'.

2. How could one analyze the following sentence?

   (56) Den Apfel verschlingt David.
         the apple devours   David

   'David devours the apple.'

   Provide the necessary c-structure rules. What kind of f-structure is licensed? Draw a syntactic tree with corresponding references to the f-structure. For fronted constituents, simply write NP rather than expanding the XP node. The c-structure rule for the NP can also be omitted and a triangle can be drawn in the tree.

Further reading

Section 7.1 was based extensively on the textbook and introductory article of Dalrymple (2001, 2006). Additionally, I have drawn from teaching materials of Jonas Kuhn from 2007. Bresnan (2001) is a comprehensive textbook in English for the advanced reader. Some of the more in-depth analyses of German in LFG are Berman (1996, 2003a). Schwarze & de Alencar (2016) is an introduction to LFG that uses French examples. The authors demonstrate how the XLE system can be used for the development of a French LFG grammar. The textbook also discusses the Finite State Morphology component that comes with the XLE system.

Levelt (1989) developed a model of language production based on LFG. Pinker (1984) – one of the best-known researchers on language acquisition – used LFG as the model for his theory of acquisition. For another theory on first and second language acquisition that uses LFG, see Pienemann (2005).

8 Categorial Grammar

Categorial Grammar is the second oldest of the approaches discussed in this book. It was developed in the 30s by the Polish logician Kazimierz Ajdukiewicz (Ajdukiewicz 1935). Since syntactic and semantic descriptions are tightly connected and all syntactic combinations correspond to semantic ones, Categorial Grammar is popular amongst logicians and semanticists. Some stellar works in the field of semantics making use of Categorial Grammar are those of Richard Montague (1974). Other important works come from David Dowty in Columbus, Ohio (1979), Michael Moortgat in Utrecht (1989), Glyn Morrill in Barcelona (1994), Bob Carpenter in New York (1998) and Mark Steedman in Edinburgh (1991; 1997; 2000). A large fragment for German using Montague Grammar has been developed by von Stechow (1979). The 2569-page grammar of the *Institut für Deutsche Sprache* in Mannheim (Eroms, Stickel & Zifonun 1997) contains Categorial Grammar analyses in the relevant chapters. Fanselow (1981) worked on morphology in the framework of Montague Grammar. Uszkoreit (1986a), Karttunen (1986, 1989) and Calder, Klein & Zeevat (1988) developed combinations of unification-based approaches and Categorial Grammar.

The basic operations for combining linguistic objects are rather simple and well-understood so that it is no surprise that there are many systems for the development and processing of Categorial Grammars (Yampol & Karttunen 1990; Carpenter 1994; Bouma & van Noord 1994; Lloré 1995; König 1999; Moot 2002; White & Baldridge 2003; Baldridge, Chatterjee, Palmer & Wing 2007; Morrill 2012). An important contribution has been made by Mark Steedman's group (see for instance Clark, Hockenmaier & Steedman 2002; Clark & Curran 2007).

Implemented fragments exist for the following languages:

- German (Uszkoreit 1986a; König 1999; Vierhuff, Hildebrandt & Eikmeyer 2003; Vancoppenolle, Tabbert, Bouma & Stede 2011)

- English (Villavicencio 2002; Baldridge 2002; Beavers 2003, 2004)

- Finish (Karttunen 1989)

- French (Baschung, Bes, Corluy & Guillotin 1987)

- Dutch (Bouma & van Noord 1994; Baldridge 2002)

- Tagalog (Baldridge 2002)

- Turkish (Hoffman 1995; Baldridge 2002)

In addition, Baldridge, Chatterjee, Palmer & Wing (2007: 15) mention an implementation for Classical Arabic.

Some of the systems for the processing of Categorial Grammars have been augmented by probabilistic components so that the processing is robust (Osborne & Briscoe 1997; Clark, Hockenmaier & Steedman 2002). Some systems can derive lexical items from corpora, and Briscoe (2000) and Villavicencio (2002) use statistical information in their UG-based language acquisition models.

8.1 General remarks on the representational format

In what follows I introduce some basic assumptions of Categorial Grammar. After these introductory remarks, I will discuss specific analyses that were developed by Steedman (1997) in the framework of Combinatory Categorial Grammar. There are other variants of Categorial Grammar as for instance type-logical CG, the variety espoused by Morrill (1994), Dowty (1997), Moortgat (2011), and others, which cannot be discussed here.

8.1.1 Representation of valence information

In Categorial Grammar, complex categories replace the SUBCAT feature that is used in GPSG to ensure that a head can only be used with suitable grammatical rules. Simple phrase structure rules can be replaced with complex categories as follows:

(1) Rule   Category in the lexicon
     vp → v(ditrans) np np   (vp/np)/np
     vp → v(trans) np   vp/np
     vp → v(np_and_pp) np pp(to)   (vp/pp)/np

vp/np stands for something that needs an np in order for it to form a vp.

In Categorial Grammar, there are only a few very abstract rules. One of these is forward application, also referred to as the multiplication rule:

(2) forward application:
     X/Y * Y = X

This rule combines an X looking for a Y with a Y and requires that Y occurs to the right of X/Y. The result of this combination is an X that no longer requires a Y. X/Y is called the *functor* and Y is the *argument* of the functor.

As in GB theory, valence is encoded only once in Categorial Grammar, in the lexicon. In GPSG, valence information was present in grammatical rules and in the SUBCAT feature of the lexical entry.

Figure 8.1 on the following page shows how a lexical entry for a transitive verb is combined with its object. A derivation in CG is basically a binary branching tree; it is, however, mostly represented as follows: an arrow under a pair of categories indicates

$$\frac{\overline{chased} \quad \overline{Mary}}{\frac{vp/np \qquad np}{vp}} \text{->}$$

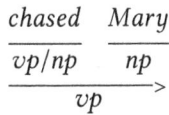

Figure 8.1: Combination of a verb and its object (preliminary)

that these have been combined via a combinatorial rule. The direction of this arrow indicates the direction of this combination. The result is given beneath the arrow. Figure 8.2 shows the tree corresponding to Figure 8.1.

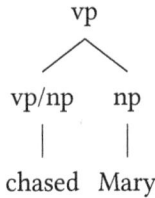

```
            vp
          /    \
     vp/np      np
       |         |
    chased     Mary
```

Figure 8.2: Derivation in Figure 8.1 as a tree diagram

One usually assumes left associativity for '/'; that is, (vp/pp)/np = vp/pp/np.

If we look at the lexical entries in (1), it becomes apparent that the category v does not appear. The lexicon only determines what the product of combination of a lexical entry with its arguments is. The symbol for vp can also be eliminated: an (English) vp is something that requires an NP to its left in order to form a complete sentence. This can be represented as s\np. Using the rule for backward application, it is possible to compute derivations such as the one in Figure 8.3.

(3) Backward application:
   Y * X\Y = X

$$\frac{\dfrac{\overline{the} \quad \overline{cat}}{\dfrac{np/n \quad n}{np} \text{->}} \qquad \dfrac{\overline{chased} \quad \overline{Mary}}{\dfrac{(s\backslash np)/np \quad np}{s\backslash np} \text{->}}}{s} \text{<}$$

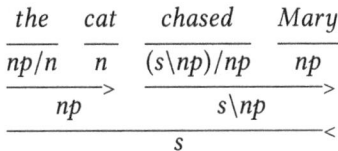

Figure 8.3: Analysis of a sentence with a transitive verb

In Categorial Grammar, there is no explicit difference made between phrases and words: an intransitive verb is described in the same way as a verb phrase with an object: s\np. Equally, proper nouns are complete noun phrases, which are assigned the symbol np.

8.1.2 Semantics

As already mentioned, Categorial Grammar is particularly popular among semanticists as syntactic combinations always result in parallel semantic combinations and even for complex combinations such as those we will discuss in more detail in the following sections, there is a precise definition of meaning composition. In the following, we will take a closer look at the representational format discussed in Steedman (1997: Section 2.1.2).

Steedman proposes the following lexical entry for the verb *eats*:[1]

(4) eats := (s: $eat'(x, y)\backslash np_{3S}$:x)/np:y

In (4), the meaning of each category is given after the colon. Since nothing is known about the meaning of the arguments in the lexical entry of *eat*, the meaning is represented by the variables x and y. When the verb combines with an NP, the denotation of the NP is inserted. An example is given in (5):[2]

(5) $$\frac{(s : eat'(x, y)\backslash np_{3S} : x)/np : y \quad np : apples'}{s : eat'(x, apples')\backslash np_{3S} : x} {\scriptstyle >}$$

When combining a functor with an argument, it must be ensured that the argument fits the functor, that is, it must be unifiable with it (for more on unification see Section 6.6). The unification of np:y with np: *apples'* results in np: *apples'* since *apples'* is more specific than the variable y. Apart from its occurrence in the term np:y, y occurs in the description of the verb in another position (s: eat'(x, y)$\backslash np_{3S}$:x) and therefore also receives the value *apples'* there. Thus, the result of this combination is s: eat'(x, $apples'$)$\backslash np_{3S}$:x as shown in (5).

Steedman notes that this notation becomes less readable with more complex derivations and instead uses the more standard λ-notation:

(6) eats := (s\np$_{3S}$)/np: $\lambda y.\lambda x.eat'(x, y)$

Lambdas are used to allow access to open positions in complex semantic representations (see Section 2.3). A semantic representation such as $\lambda y.\lambda x.eat'(x, y)$ can be combined with the representation of *apples* by removing the first lambda expression and inserting the denotation of *apples* in all the positions where the corresponding variable (in this case, y) appears (see Section 2.3 for more on this point):

(7) $\lambda y.\lambda x.eat'(x, y)$ *apples'*
$\lambda x.eat'(x, apples')$

This removal of lambda expressions is called β-reduction.

If we use the notation in (6), the combinatorial rules must be modified as follows:

(8) X/Y:f * Y:a   = X: f a
Y:a   * X\Y:f = X: f a

---

[1] I have adapted his notation to correspond to the one used in this book.

[2] The assumption that *apples* means *apples'* and not *apples'*(z) minus the quantifier contribution is a simplification here.

In such rules, the semantic contribution of the argument (a) is written after the semantic denotation of the functor (f). The open positions in the denotation of the functor are represented using lambdas. The argument can be combined with the first lambda expression using β-reduction.

Figure 8.4 shows the derivation of a simple sentence with a transitive verb. After forward and backward application, β-reduction is immediately applied.

$$
\begin{array}{ccc}
\underline{\textit{Jacob}} & \underline{\textit{eats}} & \underline{\textit{apples}} \\
np : jacob' & (s\backslash np)/np : \lambda y.\lambda x.eat'(x,y) & np : apples'
\end{array}
$$

$$
\cfrac{
\cfrac{
s\backslash np : \lambda y.\lambda x.eat'(x,y)\ apples' \\
= \lambda x.eat'(x, apples')
}{}
}{
\begin{array}{c}
s : \lambda x.eat'(x, apples')\ jacob' \\
= eat'(jacob', apples')
\end{array}
}
$$

Figure 8.4: Meaning composition in Categorial Grammar

8.1.3 Adjuncts

As noted in Section 1.6, adjuncts are optional. In phrase structure grammars, this can be captured, for example, by rules that have a certain element (for instance a VP) on the left-hand side of the rule and the same element and an adjunct on the right-hand side of the rule. Since the symbol on the left is the same as the one on the right, this rule can be applied arbitrarily many times. (9) shows some examples of this:

(9) a. VP → VP PP
     b. Noun → Noun PP

One can analyze an arbitrary amount of PPs following a VP or noun using these rules.

In Categorial Grammar, adjuncts have the following general form: X\X or X/X. Adjectives are modifiers, which must occur before the noun. They have the category n/n. Modifiers occurring after nouns (prepositional phrases and relative clauses) have the category n\n instead.[3] For VP-modifiers, X is replaced by the symbol for the VP (s\np) and this yields the relatively complex expression (s\np)\(s\np). Adverbials in English are VP-modifiers and have this category. Prepositions that can be used in a PP modifying a verb require an NP in order to form a complete PP and therefore have the category ((s\np)\(s\np))/np. Figure 8.5 on the next page gives an example of an adverb (*quickly*) and a preposition (*round*). Note that the result of the combination of *round* and *the garden* corresponds to the category of the adverb ((s\np)\(s\np)). In GB theory, adverbs and prepositions were also placed into a single class (see page 92). This overarching class was then divided into subclasses based on the valence of the elements in question.

---

[3] In Categorial Grammar, there is no category symbol like $\overline{X}$ for intermediate projections of $\overline{X}$ theory. So rather than assuming $\overline{N}/\overline{N}$, CG uses n/n. See Exercise 2.

The	small	cat	chased	Mary	quickly	round	the	garden
np/n	n/n	n	$(s\backslash np)/np$	np	$(s\backslash np)\backslash(s\backslash np)$	$(s\backslash np)\backslash(s\backslash np)/np$	np/n	n

$$\text{---} \xrightarrow{}$$
$$n$$
$$\text{---} \xrightarrow{}$$
$$np$$

$$\xrightarrow{}$$
$$s\backslash np$$

$$\xleftarrow{}$$
$$s\backslash np$$

$$\xrightarrow{}$$
$$np$$

$$\xrightarrow{}$$
$$(s\backslash np)\backslash(s\backslash np)$$

$$\xleftarrow{}$$
$$(s\backslash np)$$

$$\xleftarrow{}$$
$$s$$

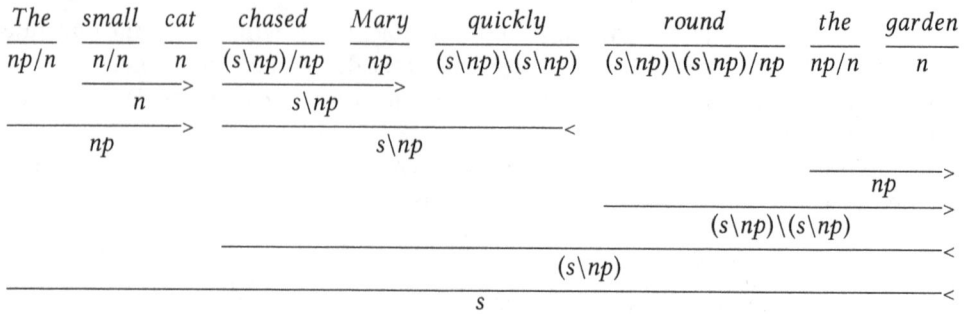

Figure 8.5: Example of an analysis with adjuncts in Categorial Grammar

8.2 Passive

In Categorial Grammar, the passive is analyzed by means of lexical rule (Dowty 1978: 412; Dowty 2003: Section 3.4). (10) shows the rule in Dowty (2003: 49).

(10) Syntax: $\alpha \in (s\backslash np)/np \rightarrow \text{PST-PART}(\alpha) \in \text{PstP}/np_{by}$
     Semantics: α' $\rightarrow \lambda y \lambda x \alpha'(y)(x)$

Here, PstP stands for past participle and np_{by} is an abbreviation for a verb phrase modifier of the form vp\vp or rather $(s\backslash np)\backslash(s\backslash np)$. The rule says the following: if a word belongs to the set of words with the category $(s\backslash np)/np$, then the word with past participle morphology also belongs in the set of words with the category PstP/np_{by}.

(11a) shows the lexical entry for the transitive verb *touch* and (11b) the result of rule application:

(11)   a. touch: $(s\backslash np)/np$
       b. touched: PstP/np_{by}

The auxiliary *was* has the category $(s\backslash np)/\text{PstP}$ and the preposition *by* has the category np_{by}/np, or its unabbreviated form $((s\backslash np)\backslash(s\backslash np))/np$. In this way, (12) can be analyzed as in Figure 8.6 on the following page.

(12)   John was touched by Mary.

The question as to how to analyze the pair of sentences in (13) still remains unanswered.[4]

(13)   a. He gave the book to Mary.
       b. The book was given to Mary.

gave has the category $((s\backslash np)/pp)/np$, that is, the verb must first combine with an NP (*the book*) and a PP (*to Mary*) before it can be combined with the subject. The problem is that the rule in (10) cannot be applied to *gave* with a *to*-PP since the pp argument is sandwiched between both np arguments in $((s\backslash np)/pp)/np$. One would have to generalize the rule in (10) somehow by introducing new technical means[5] or assume additional rules for cases such as (13b).

---

[4] Thanks to Roland Schäfer (p. m., 2009) for pointing out these data to me.
[5] Baldridge (p. M. 2010) suggests using regular expressions in a general lexical rule for passive.

$$
\begin{array}{ccccc}
\textit{John} & \textit{was} & \textit{touched} & \textit{by} & \textit{Mary.} \\
\hline
np & (s\backslash np)/PstP & \overline{PstP/np_{by}}^{\text{-LR}} & np_{by}/np & np
\end{array}
$$

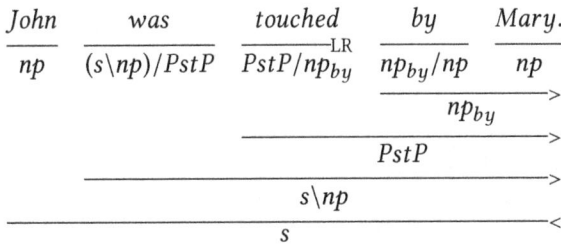

Figure 8.6: Analysis of the passive using a lexical rule

8.3 Verb position

Steedman (2000: 159) proposed an analysis with variable branching for Dutch, that is, there are two lexical entries for *at* 'eat': an initial one with its arguments to the right, and another occupying final position with its arguments to its left.

(14)   a.   *at* 'eat' in verb-final position: $(s_{+\text{SUB}}\backslash np)\backslash np$
       b.   *at* 'eat' in verb-initial position: $(s_{-\text{SUB}}/np)/np$

Steedman uses the feature SUB to differentiate between subordinate and non-subordinate sentences. Both lexical items are related via lexical rules.

One should note here that the NPs are combined with the verb in different orders. The normal order is:

(15)   a.   in verb-final position: $(s_{+\text{SUB}}\backslash np[nom])\backslash np[acc]$
       b.   in verb-initial position: $(s_{-\text{SUB}}/np[acc])/np[nom]$

The corresponding derivations for German sentences with a bivalent verb are shown in Figures 8.7 and 8.8.

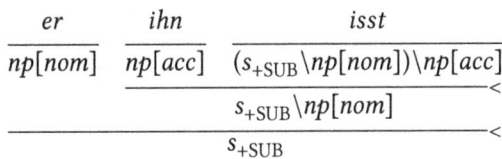

$$
\begin{array}{ccc}
\textit{er} & \textit{ihn} & \textit{isst} \\
\hline
np[nom] & np[acc] & (s_{+\text{SUB}}\backslash np[nom])\backslash np[acc]
\end{array}
$$

Figure 8.7: Analysis of verb-final sentences following Steedman

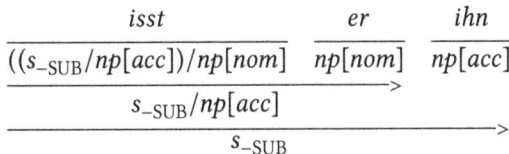

$$
\begin{array}{ccc}
\textit{isst} & \textit{er} & \textit{ihn} \\
\hline
((s_{-\text{SUB}}/np[acc])/np[nom] & np[nom] & np[acc]
\end{array}
$$

Figure 8.8: Analysis of verb-initial sentences following Steedman

In Figure 8.7, the verb is first combined with an accusative object, whereas in Figure 8.8, the verb is first combined with the subject. For criticism of these kinds of analyses with variable branching, see Netter (1992) and Müller (2005b, 2015b).

Jacobs (1991) developed an analysis which corresponds to the verb movement analysis in GB. He assumes verb-final structures, that is, there is a lexical entry for verbs where arguments are selected to the left of the verb. A transitive verb would therefore have the entry in (16a). Additionally, there is a trace in verb-final position that requires the arguments of the verb and the verb itself in initial position. (16b) shows what the verb trace looks like for a transitive verb in initial position:

(16)   a.   Verb in final position:
       (s\np[nom])\np[acc]

     b.   Verb trace for the analysis of verb-first:
       ((s\((s\np[nom])\np[acc]))\np[nom])\np[acc]

The entry for the verb trace is very complex. It is probably simpler to examine the analysis in Figure 8.9.

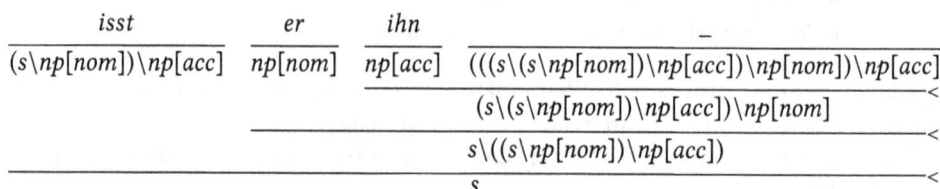

isst	*er*	*ihn*	_
(s\np[nom])\np[acc]	np[nom]	np[acc]	(((s\(s\np[nom])\np[acc])\np[nom])\np[acc]
			(s\(s\np[nom])\np[acc])\np[nom] <
			s\((s\np[nom])\np[acc]) <
		s	<

Figure 8.9: Analysis of verb-initial sentences following Jacobs (1991)

The trace is the head in the entire analysis: it is first combined with the accusative object and then with the subject. In a final step, it is combined with the transitive verb in initial-position.[6] A problem with this kind of analysis is that the verb *isst* 'eats', as well as *er* 'he' and *ihn* 'him'/'it', are arguments of the verb trace in (17).

(17)   Morgen   [isst [er [ihn _]]]
      tomorrow   eats   he   him

      'He will eat it/him tomorrow.'

Since adjuncts can occur before, after or between arguments of the verb in German, one would expect that *morgen* 'tomorrow' can occur before the verb *isst*, since *isst* is just a normal argument of the verbal trace in final position. As adjuncts do not change the categorial status of a projection, the phrase *morgen isst er ihn* 'tomorrow he eats him' should be able to occur in the same positions as *isst er ihn*. This is not the case, however. If we replace *isst er ihn* by *morgen isst er ihn* in (18a), the result is (18b), which is ungrammatical.

---

[6] See Netter (1992) for a similar analysis in HPSG.

(18) a. Deshalb isst er ihn.
          therefore eats he him

          'Therefore he eats it/him.'

      b. * Deshalb morgen   isst er ihn.
          therefore tomorrow eats he him

An approach which avoids this problem comes from Kiss & Wesche (1991) (see Section 9.3). Here, the authors assume that there is a verb in initial position which selects a projection of the verb trace. If adverbials are only combined with verbs in final-position, then a direct combination of *morgen* 'tomorrow' and *isst er ihn* 'eats he it' is ruled out. If one assumes that the verb in first-position is the functor, then it is possible to capture the parallels between complementizers and verbs in initial position (Höhle 1997): finite verbs in initial position differ from complementizers only in requiring a projection of a verb trace, whereas complementizers require projections of overt verbs:

(19) a. dass [er ihn isst]
          that he it   eats

      b. Isst [er ihn _]
          eats he it

This description of verb position in German captures the central insights of the GB analysis in Section 3.2.

8.4 Local reordering

Up to now, we have seen combinations of functors and arguments where the arguments were either to the left or to the right of the functor. The saturation of arguments always took place in a fixed order: the argument furthest to the right was combined first with the functor, e.g., (s\np)/pp first combined with the PP, and the result of this combination was combined with the NP.

There are a number of possibilities to analyze ordering variants in German: Uszkoreit (1986b) suggests accounting for possible orders lexically; that is, that each possible order corresponds to a lexical item. One would therefore have at least six lexical items for a ditransitive verb. Briscoe (2000: 257) and Villavicencio (2002: 96–98) propose a variant of this analysis where the order of arguments is modified in the syntax: a syntactic rule can, for example, change the order (S/PRT)/NP into (S/NP)/PRT.

A different approach is suggested by Steedman & Baldridge (2006). They discuss various options for ordering arguments attested in the languages of the world. This includes languages in which the order of combination is free, as well as languages where the direction of combination is free. Steedman and Baldridge introduce the following convention for representing categories: elements in curly brackets can be discharged in any order. '|' in place of '\' or '/' serves to indicate that the direction of combination is free. Some prototypical examples are shown in (20):

(20) English   (S\NP)/NP   S(VO)
      Latin   S{|NP[nom], |NP[acc] }   free order
      Tagalog   S{/NP[nom], /NP[acc] }   free order, verb-initial
      Japanese   S{\NP[nom], \NP[acc] }   free order, verb-final

Hoffman (1995: Section 3.1) has proposed an analysis analogous to that of Japanese for Turkish and this could also be used in conjunction with an analysis of verb position for German. This would correspond to the GB/MP analysis of Fanselow (2001) or the HPSG analysis presented in Section 9.4.

8.5 Long-distance dependencies

Steedman (1989: Section 1.2.4) proposes an analysis of long-distance dependencies without movement or empty elements. For examples such as (21), he assumes that the category of *Harry must have been eating* or *Harry devours* is s/np.

(21) a. These apples, Harry must have been eating.
      b. apples which Harry devours

The fronted NP *these apples* and the relative pronoun *which* are both functors in the analysis of (21) which take s/np as their argument. Using the machinery introduced up to now, we cannot assign the category s/np to the strings *Harry must have been eating* and *Harry devours* in (21) although it is intuitively the case that *Harry devours* is a sentence missing an NP. We still require two further extensions of Categorial Grammar: type raising and forward and backward composition. Both of these operations will be introduced in the following sections.

8.5.1 Type Raising

The category np can be transformed into the category (s/(s\np)) by *type raising*. If we combine this category with (s\np), then we get the same result as if we had combined np and (s\np) with the forward application rule in (2). (22a) shows the combination of an NP with a VP (a sentence missing an NP to its left). The combination of the type-raised NP with the VP is given in (22b).

(22) a. np * s\np = s
      b. s/(s\np) * s\np = s

In (22a), a verb or verb phrase selects an NP to its left (s\np). In (22b), an NP having undergone type raising selects a verb or verb phrase to its right which requires an NP to its left (s\np).

Type raising simply reverses the direction of selection: the VP in (22a) is the functor and the NP is the argument, whereas in (22b), it is the type raised NP which acts as the functor, and the VP is the argument. In each case, the result of the combination is the same. This change of selectional direction may just seem like a trick at first glance, but as we will see, this trick can be extremely useful. First, however, we will introduce forward and backward composition.

8.5.2 Forward and backward composition

(23) shows the rules for forward and backward composition.

(23)   a. Forward composition (> B)
           X/Y * Y/Z = X/Z
       b. Backward composition (< B)
           Y\Z * X\Y = X\Z

These rules will be explained using forward composition as an example. (23a) can be understood as follows: X/Y more or less means; if I find a Y, then I am a complete X. In the combinatorial rule, X/Y is combined with Y/Z. Y/Z stands for a Y that is not yet complete and is still missing a Z. The requirement that Y must find a Z in order to be complete is postponed: we pretend that Y is complete and use it anyway, but we still bear in mind that something is actually still missing. Hence, if we combine X/Y with Y/Z, we get something which becomes an X when combined with a Z.

8.5.3 Analysis of long-distance dependencies

By using forward composition, we can assign *Harry must have been eating* the category s/np. Figure 8.10 shows how this works. *must* is a verb which requires an unmarked

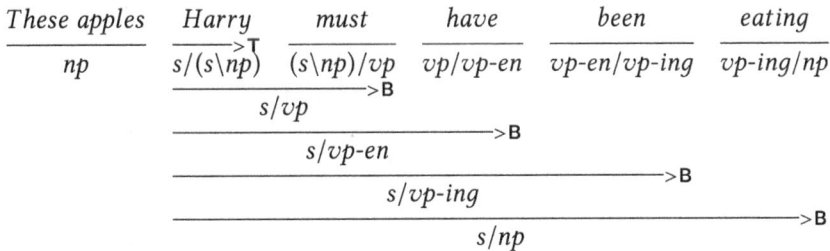

Figure 8.10: Application of forward composition to VP-chains

infinitive form, *have* requires a participle and *been* must combine with a gerund. In the above figure, the arrow with a small 'T' stands for type raising, whereas the arrows with a 'B' indicate composition. The direction of composition is shown by the direction of the arrow.

For the analysis of (21a), we are still missing one small detail, a rule that turns the NP at the beginning of the sentence into a functor which can be combined with s/np. Normal type raising cannot handle this because it would produce s/(s\np) when s/(s/np) is required.

Steedman (1989: 217) suggests the rule in (24):

(24) Topicalization (↑):
      X ⇒ st/(s/X)
      where X ∈ { np, pp, vp, ap, s′ }

st stands for a particular type of sentence (s), namely one with topicalization (t). The ⇒ expresses that one can type raise any X into an st/(s/X).

If we replace X with np, we can turn *these apples* into st/(s/np) and complete the analysis of (21a) as shown in Figure 8.11.

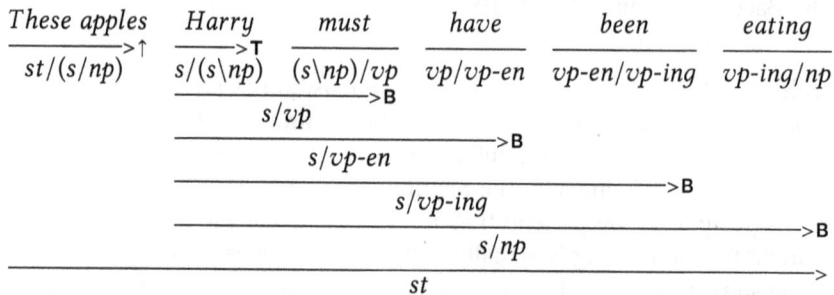

These apples	Harry	must	have	been	eating
st/(s/np) →↑	s/(s\np) →T	(s\np)/vp	vp/vp-en	vp-en/vp-ing	vp-ing/np

$$s/vp \quad \text{>B}$$
$$s/vp\text{-}en \quad \text{>B}$$
$$s/vp\text{-}ing \quad \text{>B}$$
$$s/np \quad \text{>B}$$
$$st \quad \text{>}$$

Figure 8.11: Analysis of long-distance dependencies in Categorial Grammar

The mechanism presented here will of course also work for dependencies that cross sentence boundaries. Figure 8.12 shows the analysis for (25):

(25) Apples, I believe that Harry eats.

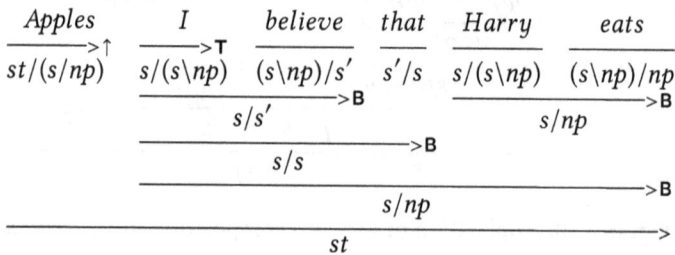

Apples	I	believe	that	Harry	eats
st/(s/np) →↑	s/(s\np) →T	(s\np)/s′	s′/s	s/(s\np)	(s\np)/np

$$s/s' \quad \text{>B}$$
$$s/np \quad \text{>B}$$
$$s/s \quad \text{>B}$$
$$s/np \quad \text{>B}$$
$$st \quad \text{>}$$

Figure 8.12: Analysis of long-distance dependencies across sentence boundaries

Using the previously described tools, it is, however, only possible to describe extractions where the fronted element in the sentence would have occurred at the right edge of the phrase without fronting. This means it is not possible to analyze sentences where the middle argument of a ditransitive verb has been extracted (Steedman 1985: 532). Pollard (1988: 406) provides the derivation in Figure 8.13 on the following page for (26).

(26) Fido we put downstairs.

Fido	we	put	downstairs
$(st/pp)/((s/pp)/np)$	$s/(s\backslash np)$	$((s\backslash np)/pp)/np$	pp

Fido ->⇈ we ->T put ((s\np)/pp)/np ->BB

$(s/pp)/np$

st/pp ->

st ->

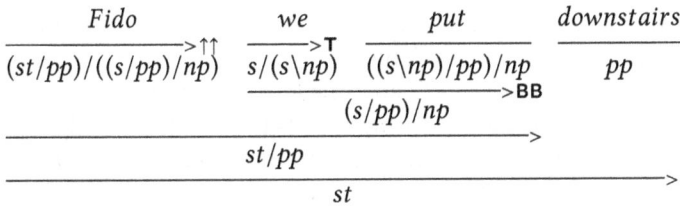

Figure 8.13: Analysis of long-distance dependencies across sentence boundaries

In this analysis, it is not possible to combine *we* and *put* using the rule in (23a) since $(s\backslash np)$ is not directly accessible: breaking down $((s\backslash np)/pp)/np$ into functor and argument gives us $((s\backslash np)/pp)$ and np. In order to deal with such cases, we need another variant of composition:

(27) Forward composition for n=2 (> BB)
$X/Y * (Y/Z1)/Z2 = (X/Z1)/Z2$

With this addition, it is now possible to combine the type-raised *we* with *put*. The result is $(s/pp)/np$. The topicalization rule in (24), however, requires an element to the right of st with the form (s/X). This is not the case in Figure 8.13. For the NP *Fido*, we need a functor category which allows that the argument itself is complex. The rule which is needed for the case in (26) is given in (28).

(28) Topicalization for n=2 (⇈):
$X2 \Rightarrow (st/X1)/((s/X1)/X2)$
where X1 and X2 $\in$ { NP, PP, VP, AP, S' }

If we assume that verbs can have up to four arguments (z. B. *buy*: buyer, seller, goods, price), then it would be necessary to assume a further rule for composition as well as another topicalization rule. Furthermore, one requires a topicalization rule for subject extraction (Pollard 1988: 405). Steedman has developed a notation which provides a compact notation of the previously discussed rules, but if one considers what exactly these representations stand for, one still arrives at the same number of rules that have been discussed here.

8.6 Summary and classification

The operations of Combinatory Categorial Grammar, which go beyond those of standard Categorial Grammar, allow for so much flexibility that it is even possible to assign a category to sequences of words that would not normally be treated as a constituent. This is an advantage for the analysis of coordination (see Section 21.6.2) and furthermore, Steedman (1991) has argued that intonation data support the constituent status of these strings. See also Section 15.2 for a direct model of incremental language processing in

Categorial Grammar. In phrase structure grammars, it is possible to use GPSG mechanisms to pass information about relative pronouns contained in a phrase up the tree. These techniques are not used in CG and this leads to a large number of recategorization rules for topicalization and furthermore leads to inadequate analyses of pied-piping constructions in relative clauses. As the topicalization analysis was already discussed in Section 8.5, I will briefly elaborate on relative clauses here.

Steedman & Baldridge (2006: 614) present an analysis of long-distance dependencies using the following relative clause in (29):

(29)   the man that Manny says Anna married

The relative pronoun is the object of *married* but occurs outside the clause *Anna married*. Steedman assumes the lexical entry in (30) for relative pronouns:

(30)   (n\n)/(s/np)

This means the following: if there is a sentence missing an NP to the right of a relative pronoun, then the relative pronoun can form an N-modifier (n\n) with this sentence. The relative pronoun is the head (functor) in this analysis.

Utilizing both additional operations of type raising and composition, the examples with relative clauses can be analyzed as shown in Figure 8.14. The lexical entry for the

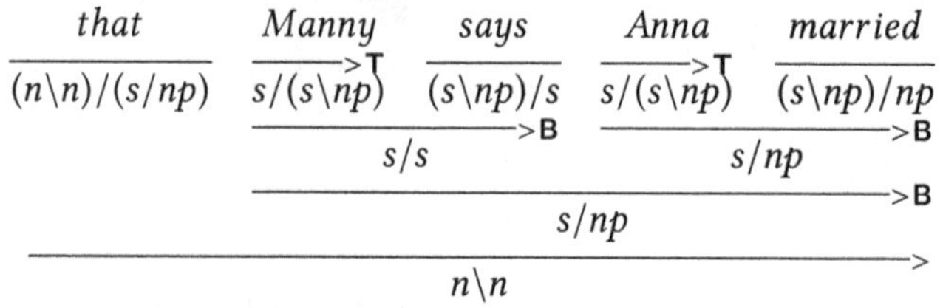

$$
\begin{array}{ccccc}
\textit{that} & \textit{Manny} & \textit{says} & \textit{Anna} & \textit{married} \\
\hline
(n\backslash n)/(s/np) & s/(s\backslash np) & (s\backslash np)/s & s/(s\backslash np) & (s\backslash np)/np \\
 & \text{>T} & \text{>T} & \text{>T} & \text{>B} \\
\end{array}
$$

Figure 8.14: Categorial Grammar analysis of a relative clause with long-distance dependency

verbs corresponds to what was discussed in the preceding sections: *married* is a normal transitive verb and *says* is a verb that requires a sentential complement and forms a VP (s\np) with it. This VP yields a sentence when combined with an NP. The noun phrases in Figure 8.14 have been type raised. Using forward composition, it is possible to combine *Anna* and *married* to yield s/np. This is the desired result: a sentence missing an NP to its right. *Manny* and *says* and then *Manny says* and *Anna married* can also be combined via forward composition and we then have the category s/np for *Manny says Anna married*. This category can be combined with the relative pronoun using forward application and we then arrive at n\n, which is exactly the category for postnominal modifiers.

However, the assumption that the relative pronoun constitutes the head is problematic since one has to then go to some lengths to explain pied-piping constructions such as those in (31).

(31)   a. Here's the minister [[in [the middle [of [whose sermon]]]] the dog barked].[7]

      b. Reports [the height of the lettering on the covers of which] the government prescribes should be abolished.[8]

In (31), the relative pronoun is embedded in a phrase that has been extracted from the rest of the relative clause. The relative pronoun in (31a) is the determiner of *sermon*. Depending on the analysis, *whose* is the head of the phrase *whose sermon*. The NP is embedded under *of* and the phrase *of whose sermon* depends on *middle*. The entire NP *the middle of the sermon* is a complement of the preposition *in*. It would be quite a stretch to claim that *whose* is the head of the relative clause in (31a). The relative pronoun in (31b) is even more deeply embedded. Steedman (1997: 50) gives the following lexical entries for *who*, *whom* and *which*:

(32)   a. ((n\n)/(s\np))\(np/np)   (complex subject-relative phrase)

      b. ((n\n)/(s/pp))\(pp/np)   (complex extracted PP-relative phrase)

      c. ((n\n)/(s/np))\(np/np)   (complex extracted NP-relative phrase)

Using (32b) and (32c), it is possible to analyze (33a) and (33b):

(33)   a. a report the cover of which Keats (expects that Chapman) will design

      b. a subject on which Keats (expects that Chapman) will speak

In the analysis of (33b), *which* requires a preposition to its left (pp/np) so it can form the category (n\n)/(s/pp). This category needs a sentence lacking a PP to its right in order to form a post-nominal modifier (n\n). In the analysis of (33a), *the cover of* becomes np/np by means of composition and *which* with the lexical entry (32c) can combine with *the cover of* to its left. The result is the category (n\n)/(s/np), that is, something that requires a sentence missing an NP.

Ross' examples (31b) can also be analyzed as follows (32c):

(34)   reports [the height of the lettering on the covers of]$_{np/np}$ which$_{(n\backslash n)/(s/np)}$ the government prescribes

The complex expression *the height of the lettering on the covers of* becomes np/np after composition and the rest of the analysis proceeds as that of (33a).

In addition to entries such as those in (32), we also need further entries to analyze sentences such as (35), where the relative phrase has been extracted from the middle of the clause (see Pollard 1988: 410):

(35)   Fido is the dog which we put downstairs.

The problem here is similar to what we saw with topicalization: *we put* does not have the cateory s/np but rather (s/pp)/np and as such, cannot be directly combined with the relative pronoun in (30).

---

[7] Pollard & Sag (1994: 212).

[8] Ross (1967: 109).

Morrill (1995: 204) discusses the lexical entry in (32b) for the relative pronoun in (36):

(36) about which John talked

In the lexical entry (32b), *which* requires something to the left of it, which requires a noun phrase in order to form a complete prepositional phrase; that is, *which* selects a preposition. Morrill noted that there is a need to postulate further lexical items for cases like (37) in which the relative pronoun occurs in the middle of the fronted phrase.

(37) the contract [the loss of which after so much wrangling] John would finally have to pay for

These and other cases could be handled by additional lexical stipulations. Morrill instead proposes additional types of the combination of functors and arguments, which allow a functor B ↑ A to enclose its argument A and produce B, or a functor A ↓ B to enclose its argument to then yield B (p. 190). Even with these additional operations, he still needs the two lexical items in (38) for the derivation of a pied-piping construction with an argument NP or a PP:

(38) a. (NP ↑ NP) ↓ (N\N)/(S/NP)
      b. (PP ↑ NP) ↓ (N\N)/(S/PP)

These lexical items are still not enough, however, as (38b) contains a PP but this PP corresponds to an argument PP, which is required for (36). To analyze (31a), which involves a PP adjunct, we need to assume the category (s\np)/(s\np) for the prepositional phrase *in the middle of whose sermon*. We, therefore, also require at least three additional items for relative pronouns.

By introducing new operations, Morrill manages to reduce the number of lexical entries for *which*; however, the fact remains that he has to mention the categories which can occur in pied-piping constructions in the lexical entry of the relative pronoun.

Furthermore, the observation that relative clauses consist of a phrase with a relative pronoun plus a sentence missing a relative phrase is lost. This insight can be kept if one assumes a GPSG-style analysis where information about whether there is a relative pronoun in the relative phrase can be passed up to the highest node of the relative phrase. The relative clause can then be analyzed as the combination of a sentence with a gap and an appropriately marked relative phrase. For the discussion of such analyses in the framework of GB theory and HPSG/CxG, see Section 21.10.3.

Comprehension questions

1. Identify the functors and arguments in Figures 8.1 and 8.3.

2. Which combination operations do you know?

3. What is composition used for?

Exercises

1. Analyze the following sentence:

   (39)   The children in the room laugh loudly.

2. Analyze the noun phrase in (40):

   (40)   the picture of Mary

   Compare the resulting analysis with the structure given in Figure 2.4 on page 67 and think about which categories of $\overline{\text{X}}$ syntax the categories in Categorial Grammar correspond to.

Further reading

Mark Steedman discusses a variant of Categorial Grammar, *Combinatory Categorial Grammar*, in a series of books and articles: Steedman (1991, 2000); Steedman & Baldridge (2006).

Lobin (2003) compares Categorial Grammar with Dependency Grammar and Pickering & Barry (1993) suggest a combination of Dependency Grammar and Categorial Grammar, which they call Dependency Categorial Grammar.

Briscoe (2000) and Villavicencio (2002) discuss UG-based acquisition models in the framework of Categorial Grammar.

9 Head-Driven Phrase Structure Grammar

Head-Driven Phrase Structure Grammar (HPSG) was developed by Carl Pollard and Ivan Sag in the mid-80's in Stanford and in the Hewlett-Packard research laboratories in Palo Alto (Pollard & Sag 1987, 1994). Like LFG, HPSG is part of so-called West Coast linguistics. Another similarity to LFG is that HPSG aims to provide a theory of competence which is compatible with performance (Sag & Wasow 2011, 2015, see also Chapter 15).

The formal properties of the description language for HPSG grammars are well-understood and there are many systems for processing such grammars (Dörre & Seiffert 1991; Dörre & Dorna 1993; Popowich & Vogel 1991; Uszkoreit, Backofen, Busemann, Diagne, Hinkelman, Kasper, Kiefer, Krieger, Netter, Neumann, Oepen & Spackman 1994; Erbach 1995; Schütz 1996; Schmidt, Theofilidis, Rieder & Declerck 1996b; Schmidt, Rieder & Theofilidis 1996a; Uszkoreit, Backofen, Calder, Capstick, Dini, Dörre, Erbach, Estival, Manandhar, Mineur & Oepen 1996; Müller 1996c, 2004c; Carpenter & Penn 1996; Penn & Carpenter 1999; Götz, Meurers & Gerdemann 1997; Copestake 2002; Callmeier 2000; Dahllöf 2003; Meurers, Penn & Richter 2002; Penn 2004; Müller 2007a; Sato 2008; Kaufmann 2009).[1] Currently, the LKB system by Ann Copestake and the TRALE system, that was developed by Gerald Penn (Meurers, Penn & Richter 2002; Penn 2004), have the most users. The DELPH-IN consortium – whose grammar fragments are based on the LKB – and various TRALE users have developed many small and some large grammar fragments of various languages. The following is a list of implementations in different systems:

- Arabic (Haddar, Boukedi & Zalila 2010; Hahn 2011; Masum, Islam, Rahman & Ahmed 2012; Boukedi & Haddar 2014; Loukam, Balla & Laskri 2015; Arad Greshler, Herzig Sheinfux, Melnik & Wintner 2015),

- Bengali (Paul 2004; Islam, Hasan & Rahman 2012),

- Bulgarian (Simov, Osenova, Simov & Kouylekov 2004; Osenova 2010a,b, 2011),

- Cantonese (Fan, Song & Bond 2015),

- Danish (Ørsnes 1995, 2009b; Neville & Paggio 2004; Müller 2009c; Müller & Ørsnes 2011; Müller 2012a; Müller & Ørsnes 2015),

---

[1] Uszkoreit et al. (1996) and Bolc et al. (1996) compare systems that were available or were developed at the beginnings of the 1990s. Melnik (2007) compares LKB and TRALE. See also Müller (2015a: Section 5.1).

- German (Kiss 1991; Netter 1993, 1996; Meurers 1994; Hinrichs et al. 1997; Kordoni 1999; Tseng 2000; Geißler & Kiss 1994; Keller 1994; Müller 1996c, 1999a; Müller & Kasper 2000; Crysmann 2003, 2005b,c; Müller 2007b; Kaufmann & Pfister 2007, 2008; Kaufmann 2009; Fokkens 2011),

- English (Copestake & Flickinger 2000; Flickinger, Copestake & Sag 2000; Flickinger 2000; Dahllöf 2002, 2003; De Kuthy & Meurers 2003a; Meurers, De Kuthy & Metcalf 2003; De Kuthy, Metcalf & Meurers 2004),

- Esperanto (Li 1996),

- French (Tseng 2003),

- Ga (Kropp Dakubu, Hellan & Beermann 2007; Hellan 2007),

- Georgian (Abzianidze 2011),

- Greek (Kordoni & Neu 2005),

- Hausa (Crysmann 2005a, 2009, 2011, 2012),

- Hebrew (Melnik 2007; Haugereid, Melnik & Wintner 2013; Arad Greshler, Herzig Sheinfux, Melnik & Wintner 2015),

- Japanese (Siegel 2000; Siegel & Bender 2002; Bender & Siegel 2005),

- Yiddish (Müller & Ørsnes 2011),

- Korean (Kim & Yang 2003, 2004, 2006, 2009; Kim, Sells & Yang 2007; Song, Kim, Bond & Yang 2010; Kim, Yang, Song & Bond 2011),

- Maltese (Müller 2009b),

- Mandarin Chinese (Liu 1997; Ng 1997; Müller & Lipenkova 2009, 2013; Fan, Song & Bond 2015),

- Dutch (van Noord & Bouma 1994; Bouma, van Noord & Malouf 2001b; Fokkens 2011),

- Norwegian (Hellan & Haugereid 2003; Beermann & Hellan 2004; Hellan & Beermann 2006),

- Persian (Müller 2010b; Müller & Ghayoomi 2010),

- Polish (Przepiórkowski, Kupść, Marciniak & Mykowiecka 2002; Mykowiecka, Marciniak, Przepiórkowski & Kupść 2003),

- Portuguese (Branco & Costa 2008a,b; Costa & Branco 2010),

- Russian (Avgustinova & Zhang 2009),

- Sahaptin (Drellishak 2009),

- Spanish (Pineda & Meza 2005a,b; Bildhauer 2008; Marimon 2013),

- Sign Language (German, French, British, Greek!) (Sáfár & Marshall 2002; Marshall & Sáfár 2004; Sáfár & Glauert 2010),

- South African Sign Language (Bungeroth 2002),

- Turkish (Fokkens, Poulson & Bender 2009),

- Wambaya (Bender 2008a,c, 2010).

The first implemented HPSG grammar was a grammar of English developed in the Hewlett-Packard labs in Palo Alto (Flickinger, Pollard & Wasow 1985; Flickinger 1987). Grammars for German were developed in Heidelberg, Stuttgart and Saarbrücken in the LILOG project. Subsequently, grammars for German, English and Japanese were developed in Heidelberg, Saarbrücken and Stanford in the Verbmobil project. Verbmobil was the largest ever AI project in Germany. It was a machine translation project for spoken language in the domains of trip planning and appointment scheduling (Wahlster 2000).

Currently there are two larger groups that are working on the development of grammars: the DELPH-IN consortium (Deep Linguistic Processing with HPSG)[2] and the network CoGETI (Constraintbasierte Grammatik: Empirie, Theorie und Implementierung)[3]. Many of the grammar fragments that are listed above were developed by members of DELPH-IN and some were derived from the Grammar Matrix which was developed for the LKB to provide grammar writers with a typologically motivated initial grammar that corresponds to the properties of the language under development (Bender, Flickinger & Oepen 2002). The CoreGram project[4] is a similar project that is being run at the Freie Universität Berlin. It is developing grammars for German, Danish, Persian, Maltese, Mandarin Chinese, Spanish, French and Yiddish that share a common core. Constraints that hold for all languages are represented in one place and used by all grammars. Furthermore there are constraints that hold for certain language classes and again they are represented together and used by the respective grammars. So while the Grammar Matrix is used to derive grammars that individual grammar writers can use, adapt and modify to suit their needs, CoreGram really develops grammars for various languages that are used simultaneously and have to stay in sync. A description of the CoreGram can be found in Müller (2013a, 2015a).

There are systems that combine linguistically motivated analyses with statistics components (Brew 1995; Miyao et al. 2005; Miyao & Tsujii 2008) or learn grammars or lexica from corpora (Fouvry 2003; Cramer & Zhang 2009).

The following URLs point to pages on which grammars can be tested:

- http://www.delph-in.net/erg/

- http://hpsg.fu-berlin.de/Demos/

[2] http://www.delph-in.net/. 13.11.2015.
[3] http://wwwuser.gwdg.de/~cogeti/. 13.11.2015. Supported by the DFG under the grant number HO3279/3-1.
[4] http://hpsg.fu-berlin.de/Projects/CoreGram.html. 11.03.2016.

9.1 General remarks on the representational format

HPSG has the following characteristics: it is a lexicon-based theory, that is, the majority of linguistic constraints are situated in the descriptions of words or roots. HPSG is sign-based in the sense of Saussure (1916a): the form and meaning of linguistic signs are always represented together. Typed feature structures are used to model all relevant information.[5] These structures can be described with feature descriptions such as in (1). Lexical entries, phrases and principles are always modeled and described with the same formal means. Generalizations about word classes or rule schemata are captured with inheritance hierarchies (see Section 6.2). Phonology, syntax and semantics are represented in a single structure. There are no separate levels of representation such as PF or LF in Government & Binding Theory. (1) shows an excerpt from the representation of a word such as *Grammatik* 'grammar'.

(1) Lexical item for the word *Grammatik* 'grammar':

$$
\begin{bmatrix}
word \\
\text{PHONOLOGY} \quad \langle\, Grammatik\, \rangle \\
\text{SYNTAX-SEMANTICS} \ \dots
\begin{bmatrix}
local \\
\text{CATEGORY}
\begin{bmatrix}
category \\
\text{HEAD}
\begin{bmatrix}
noun \\
\text{CASE } \boxed{1}
\end{bmatrix} \\
\text{SUBCAT } \langle\, \text{DET[CASE } \boxed{1}]\, \rangle
\end{bmatrix} \\
\text{CONTENT} \ \dots
\begin{bmatrix}
grammatik \\
\text{INST } X
\end{bmatrix}
\end{bmatrix}
\end{bmatrix}
$$

One can see that this feature description contains information about the phonology, syntactic category and semantic content of the word *Grammatik*. To keep things simple, the value of PHONOLOGY (PHON) is mostly given as an orthographic representation. In fully fleshed-out theories, the PHON value is a complex structure that contains information about metrical grids and weak or strong accents. See Bird & Klein (1994), Orgun (1996), Höhle (1999), Walther (1999), Crysmann (2002: Chapter 6), and Bildhauer (2008) for phonology in the framework of HPSG. The details of the description in (1) will be explained in the following sections.

HPSG has adopted various insights from other theories and newer analyses have been influenced by developments in other theoretical frameworks. Functor-argument structures, the treatment of valence information and function composition have been adopted from Categorial Grammar. Function composition plays an important role in the analysis of verbal complexes in languages like German and Korean. The Immediate Dominance/Linear Precedence format (ID/LP format, see Section 5.1.2) as well as the Slash

---

[5] Readers who read this book non-sequentially and who are unfamiliar with typed feature descriptions and typed feature structures should consult Chapter 6 first.

mechanism for long-distance dependencies (see Section 5.4) both come from GPSG. The analysis assumed here for verb position in German is inspired by the one that was developed in the framework of Government & Binding (see Section 3.2).

9.1.1 Representation of valence information

The phrase structure grammars discussed in Chapter 2 have the disadvantage that one requires a great number of different rules for the various valence types. (2) shows some examples of this kind of rules and the corresponding verbs.

(2) S → NP[*nom*], V   *X schläft* 'X is sleeping'
     S → NP[*nom*], NP[*acc*], V   *X Y erwartet* 'X expects Y'
     S → NP[*nom*], PP[*über*], V   *X über Y spricht* 'X talks about Y'
     S → NP[*nom*], NP[*dat*], NP[*acc*], V   *X Y Z gibt* 'X gives Z to Y'
     S → NP[*nom*], NP[*dat*], PP[*mit*], V   *X Y mit Z dient* 'X serves Y with Z'

In order for the grammar not to create any incorrect sentences, one has to ensure that verbs are only used with appropriate rules.

(3) a. * dass Peter das Buch schläft
         that Peter the book sleeps

     b. * dass Peter erwartet
         that Peter expects

     c. * dass Peter über   den Mann erwartet
         that Peter about the man   expects

Therefore, verbs (and heads in general) have to be divided into valence classes. These valence classes have to then be assigned to grammatical rules. One must therefore further specify the rule for transitive verbs in (2) as follows:

(4) S → NP[*nom*], NP[*acc*], V[*nom_acc*]

Here, valence has been encoded twice. First, we have said something in the rules about what kind of elements can or must occur, and then we have stated in the lexicon which valence class the verb belongs to. In Section 5.5, it was pointed out that morphological processes need to refer to valence information. Hence, it is desirable to remove redundant valence information from grammatical rules. For this reason, HPSG – like Categorial Grammar – includes descriptions of the arguments of a head in the lexical entry of that head. There is a feature with a list-value, the SUBCAT feature, which contains descriptions of the objects that must combine with a head in order to yield a complete phrase. (5) gives some examples for the verbs in (2):

(5) Verb   SUBCAT
     schlafen 'to sleep'   ⟨ NP[*nom*] ⟩
     erwarten 'to expect'   ⟨ NP[*nom*], NP[*acc*] ⟩
     sprechen 'to speak'   ⟨ NP[*nom*], PP[*über*] ⟩
     geben 'to give'   ⟨ NP[*nom*], NP[*dat*], NP[*acc*] ⟩
     dienen 'to serve'   ⟨ NP[*nom*], NP[*dat*], PP[*mit*] ⟩

SUBCAT is an abbreviation for subcategorization. It is often said that a head subcategorizes for certain arguments. See page 89 for more on the term *subcategorization*.

Figure 9.1 shows the analysis for (6a) and the analysis for (6b) is in Figure 9.2 on the following page:

(6)   a.   [dass] Peter schläft
    that Peter sleeps

   b.   [dass] Peter Maria erwartet
     that Peter Maria expects

    'that Peter expects Maria'

$$V[\text{SUBCAT } \langle \rangle]$$

1 NP[*nom*] V[SUBCAT ⟨ 1 ⟩]

  Peter   schläft
  Peter   sleeps

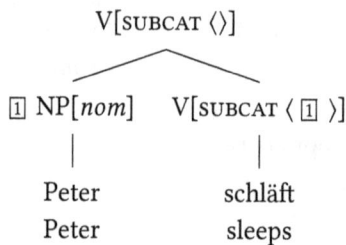

Figure 9.1: Analysis of *Peter schläft* 'Peter sleeps' in *dass Peter schläft* 'that Peter sleeps'

In Figures 9.1 and 9.2, one element of the SUBCAT list is combined with its head in each local tree. The elements that are combined with the selecting head are then no longer present in the SUBCAT list of the mother node. V[SUBCAT ⟨ ⟩] corresponds to a complete phrase (VP or S). The boxes with numbers show the structure sharing (see Section 6.4). Structure sharing is the most important means of expression in HPSG. It plays a central role for phenomena such as valence, agreement and long-distance dependencies. In the examples above, 1 indicates that the description in the SUBCAT list is identical to another daughter in the tree. The descriptions contained in valence lists are usually partial descriptions, that is, not all properties of the argument are exhaustively described. Therefore, it is possible that a verb such as *schläft* 'sleeps' can be combined with various kinds of linguistic objects: the subject can be a pronoun, a proper name or a complex noun phrase, it only matters that the linguistic object in question has an empty SUBCAT list and bears the correct case.[6]

9.1.2 Representation of constituent structure

As already noted, feature descriptions in HPSG serve as the sole descriptive inventory of morphological rules, lexical entries and syntactic rules. The trees we have seen thus far are only visualizations of the constituent structure and do not have any theoretical status. There are also no rewrite rules in HPSG.[7] The job of phrase structure rules

---

[6] Furthermore, it must agree with the verb. This is not shown here.

[7] However, phrase structure rules are used in some computer implementations of HPSG in order to improve the efficiency of processing.

V[SUBCAT ⟨⟩]

⟨1⟩ NP[*nom*]   V[SUBCAT ⟨ ⟨1⟩ ⟩]

⟨2⟩ NP[*acc*]   V[SUBCAT ⟨ ⟨1⟩, ⟨2⟩ ⟩]

Peter   Maria   erwartet
Peter   Maria   expects

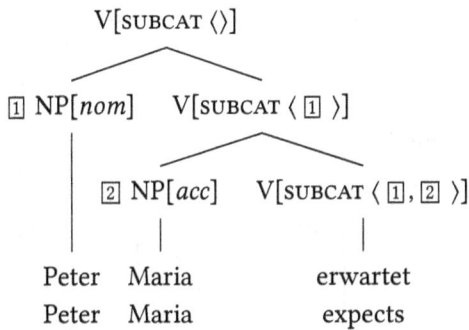

Figure 9.2: Analysis of *Peter Maria erwartet* 'Peter expects Maria.'

is handled by feature descriptions. Information about dominance is represented using
DTR features (head daughter and non-head daughter), information about precedence is
implicitly contained in PHON. (7) shows the representation of PHON values in a feature
description corresponding to the tree in Figure 9.3.

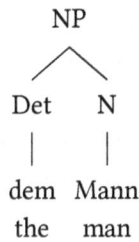

NP

Det   N

dem   Mann
the   man

Figure 9.3: Analysis of *dem Mann* 'the man'

(7)
$$\begin{bmatrix} \text{PHON} & \langle \textit{dem Mann} \rangle \\ \text{HEAD-DTR} & [\text{PHON} \langle \textit{Mann} \rangle] \\ \text{NON-HEAD-DTRS} & \langle [\text{PHON} \langle \textit{dem} \rangle] \rangle \end{bmatrix}$$

In (7), there is exactly one head daughter (HEAD-DTR). The head daughter is always the
daughter containing the head. In a structure with the daughters *das* 'the' and *Bild von
Maria* 'picture of Maria', the latter would be the head daughter. In principle, there can be
multiple non-head daughters. If we were to assume a flat structure for a sentence with a
ditransitive verb, as in Figure 2.1 on page 54, we would have three non-head daughters.
It also makes sense to assume binary branching structures without heads (see Müller
2007b: Chapter 11 for an analysis of relative clauses). In such structures we would also
have more than one non-head daughter, namely exactly two.

Before it is shown how it is ensured that only those head-argument structures are
licensed in which the argument matches the requirements of the head, I will present the

general structure of feature descriptions in HPSG. The structure presented at the start of this chapter is repeated in (8) with all the details relevant to the present discussion:

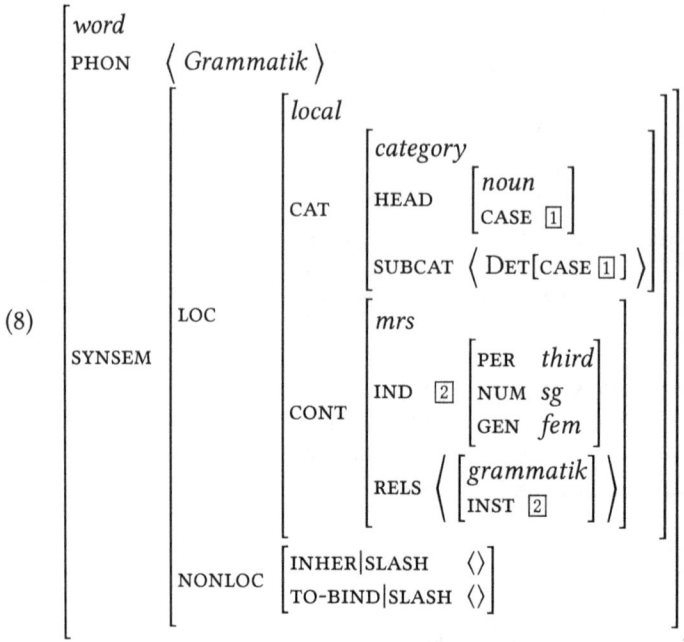

$$
(8)\ \begin{bmatrix} word \\ \text{PHON} \quad \langle\ Grammatik\ \rangle \\ \text{SYNSEM}\ \begin{bmatrix} \text{LOC}\ \begin{bmatrix} local \\ \text{CAT}\ \begin{bmatrix} category \\ \text{HEAD}\ \begin{bmatrix} noun \\ \text{CASE}\ \boxed{1} \end{bmatrix} \\ \text{SUBCAT}\ \langle\ \text{DET}[\text{CASE}\ \boxed{1}]\ \rangle \end{bmatrix} \\ \text{CONT}\ \begin{bmatrix} mrs \\ \text{IND}\ \boxed{2}\ \begin{bmatrix} \text{PER}\ third \\ \text{NUM}\ sg \\ \text{GEN}\ fem \end{bmatrix} \\ \text{RELS}\ \langle\ \begin{bmatrix} grammatik \\ \text{INST}\ \boxed{2} \end{bmatrix}\ \rangle \end{bmatrix} \end{bmatrix} \\ \text{NONLOC}\ \begin{bmatrix} \text{INHER}|\text{SLASH}\quad \langle\rangle \\ \text{TO-BIND}|\text{SLASH}\ \langle\rangle \end{bmatrix} \end{bmatrix} \end{bmatrix}
$$

In the outer layer, there are the features PHON and SYNSEM. As previously mentioned, PHON contains the phonological representation of a linguistic object. The value of SYN-SEM is a feature structure which contains syntactic and semantic information that can be selected by other heads. The daughters of phrasal signs are represented outside of SYN-SEM. This ensures that there is a certain degree of locality involved in selection: a head cannot access the internal structure of the elements which it selects (Pollard und Sag 1987: 143–145; 1994: 23). See also Sections 10.6.2.1 and 18.2 for a discussion of locality. Inside SYNSEM, there is information relevant in local contexts (LOCAL, abbreviated to LOC) as well as information important for long-distance dependencies (NONLOCAL or NON-LOC for short). Locally relevant information includes syntactic (CATEGORY or CAT), and semantic (CONTENT or CONT) information. Syntactic information encompasses information that determines the central characteristics of a phrase, that is, the head information. This is represented under HEAD. Further details of this will be discussed in Section 9.1.4. Among other things, the part of speech of a linguistic object belongs to the head properties of a phrase. As well as HEAD, SUBCAT belongs to the information contained inside CAT. The semantic content of a sign is present under CONT. The type of the CONT value is *mrs*, which stands for *Minimal Recursion Semantics* (Copestake, Flickinger, Pollard & Sag 2005). An MRS structure is comprised of an index and a list of relations which restrict this index. Of the NONLOCAL features, only SLASH is given here. There are further features for dealing with relative and interrogative clauses (Pollard & Sag 1994; Sag 1997; Ginzburg & Sag 2000; Holler 2005), which will not be discussed here.

As can be seen, the description of the word *Grammatik* 'grammar' becomes relatively complicated. In theory, it would be possible to list all properties of a given object directly in a single list of feature-value pairs. This would, however, have the disadvantage that the identity of groups of feature-value pairs could not be expressed as easily. Using the feature geometry in (8), one can express the fact that the CAT values of both conjuncts in symmetric coordinations such as those in (9) are identical.

(9)   a. [der Mann] und [die Frau]
         the man and the woman

      b. Er   [kennt] und [liebt] diese   Schallplatte.
         he.NOM knows and loves this.ACC record

      c. Er ist [dumm] und [arrogant].
         he is   dumb and arrogant

(9b) should be compared with the examples in (10). In (10a), the verbs select for an accusative and a dative object, respectively and in (10b), the verbs select for an accusative and a prepositional object:

(10)   a. * Er   kennt und hilft dieser Frau   / diese   Frau.
         he.NOM knows and helps this.DAT woman   this.ACC woman

         Intended: 'He knows and helps this woman.'

      b. * weil   er auf Maria kennt und wartet
         because he for Maria knows and waits

         Intended: 'because he knows Maria and waits for her'

While the English translation of (10a) is fine, since both *knows* and *helps* take an accusative, (10a) is out, since *kennt* 'knows' takes an accusative and *hilft* 'helps' a dative object. Similarly, (10b) is out since *kennt* 'knows' selects an accusative object and *wartet* 'waits' selects for a prepositional phrase containing the preposition *auf* 'for'.

If valence and the part of speech information were not represented in one common sub-structure, we would have to state separately that utterances such as (9) require that both conjuncts have the same valence and part of speech.

After this general introduction of the feature geometry that is assumed here, we can now turn to the head-argument schema:

Schema 1 (Head-Argument Schema (binary branching, preliminary version))

head-argument-phrase $\Rightarrow$
$$\begin{bmatrix} \text{SYNSEM}|\text{LOC}|\text{CAT}|\text{SUBCAT}\ \boxed{1} \\ \text{HEAD-DTR}|\text{SYNSEM}|\text{LOC}|\text{CAT}|\text{SUBCAT}\ \boxed{1}\ \oplus\ \langle\ \boxed{2}\ \rangle \\ \text{NON-HEAD-DTRS}\ \big\langle\ [\ \text{SYNSEM}\ \boxed{2}\ ]\ \big\rangle \end{bmatrix}$$

Schema 1 states the properties a linguistic object of the type *head-argument-phrase* must have. The arrow in Schema 1 stands for a logical implication and not for the arrow of rewrite rules as we know it from phrase structure grammars. '⊕' (*append*) is a relation which combines two lists. (11) shows possible splits of a list that contains two elements:

(11) $\langle\, x, y\,\rangle = \langle\, x\,\rangle \oplus \langle\, y\,\rangle$ or
$\quad\quad \langle\rangle \oplus \langle\, x, y\,\rangle$ or
$\quad\quad \langle\, x, y\,\rangle \oplus \langle\rangle$

The list $\langle\, x, y\,\rangle$ can be subdivided into two lists each containing one element, or alternatively into the empty list and $\langle\, x, y\,\rangle$.

Schema 1 can be read as follows: if an object is of the type *head-argument-phrase* then it must have the properties on the right-hand side of the implication. In concrete terms, this means that these objects always have a valence list which corresponds to ①, that they have a head daughter with a valence list that can be divided into two sublists ① and $\langle$ ② $\rangle$ and also that they have a non-head daughter whose syntactic and semantic properties (SYNSEM value) are compatible with the last element of the SUBCAT list of the head daughter (②). (12) provides the corresponding feature description for the example in (6a).

(12)
$$
\begin{bmatrix}
\textit{head-argument-phrase} \\
\text{PHON } \langle\, \textit{Peter schläft}\,\rangle \\
\text{SYNSEM|LOC|CAT|SUBCAT } \langle\rangle \\[4pt]
\text{HEAD-DTR } \begin{bmatrix}
\text{PHON } \langle\, \textit{schläft}\,\rangle \\
\text{SYNSEM|LOC|CAT|SUBCAT } \langle\, ① \text{ NP[}\textit{nom}\text{]} \,\rangle
\end{bmatrix} \\[14pt]
\text{NON-HEAD-DTRS } \left\langle\, \begin{bmatrix}
\text{PHON } \langle\, \textit{Peter}\,\rangle \\
\text{SYNSEM } ①
\end{bmatrix} \,\right\rangle
\end{bmatrix}
$$

NP[*nom*] is an abbreviation for a complex feature description. Schema 1 divides the SUBCAT list of the head daughter into a single-element list and what is left. Since *schläft* 'sleeps' only has one element in its SUBCAT list, what remains is the empty list. This remainder is also the SUBCAT value of the mother.

9.1.3 Linearization rules

Dominance schemata do not say anything about the order of the daughters. As in GPSG, linearization rules are specified separately. Linearization rules can make reference to the properties of daughters, their function in a schema (head, argument, adjunct, ...) or both. If we assume a feature INITIAL for all heads, then heads which precede their arguments would have the INITIAL value '+' and heads following their arguments would have the value '−'. The linearization rules in (13) ensure that ungrammatical orders such as (14b,d) are ruled out.[8]

---

[8] Noun phrases pose a problem for (13): determiners have been treated as argument until now and were included in the SUBCAT list of the head noun. Determiners occur to the left of noun, whereas all other arguments of the noun are to the right. This problem can be solved either by refining linearization rules (Müller 1999a: 164–165) or by introducing a special valence feature for determiners (Pollard & Sag 1994: Section 9.4). For an approach using such a feature, see Section 9.6.1.

(13) a. Head[INITIAL +] < Argument
      b. Argument < Head[INITIAL−]

Prepositions have an INITIAL value '+' and therefore have to precede arguments. Verbs in final position bear the value '−' and have to follow their arguments.

(14) a. [in [den Schrank]]
          in the cupboard

      b. * [[den Schrank] in]
             the cupboard in

      c. dass [er [ihn umfüllt]]
          that he it   decants

      d. * dass [er [umfüllt ihn]]
            that he decants it

9.1.4 Projection of head properties

As was explained in Section 1.5 certain properties of heads are important for the distribution of the whole phrase. For instance, the verb form belongs to the features that are important for the distribution of verbal projections. Certain verbs require a verbal argument with a particular form:

(15) a. [Dem Mann helfen] will   er nicht.
          the man help   wants he not

          'He doesn't want to help the man.'

      b. [Dem Mann geholfen] hat er nicht.
          the man helped   has he not

          'He hasn't helped the man.'

      c. * [Dem Mann geholfen] will   er nicht.
            the man helped   wants he not

      d. * [Dem Mann helfen] hat er nicht.
            the man help   has he not

wollen 'to want' always requires an infinitive without *zu* 'to', while *haben* 'have' on the other hand requires a verb in participle form. *glauben* 'believe' can occur with a finite clause, but not with an infinitive without *zu*:

(16) a. Ich glaube, Peter kommt morgen.
          I   believe Peter comes tomorrow

          'I think Peter is coming tomorrow.'

      b. * Ich glaube, Peter morgen   kommen.
            I   believe Peter tomorrow come

      c. * Ich glaube, morgen   kommen.
            I   believe tomorrow come

This shows that projections of verbs must not only contain information about the part of speech but also information about the verb form. Figure 9.4 shows this on the basis of the finite verb *gibt* 'gives'.

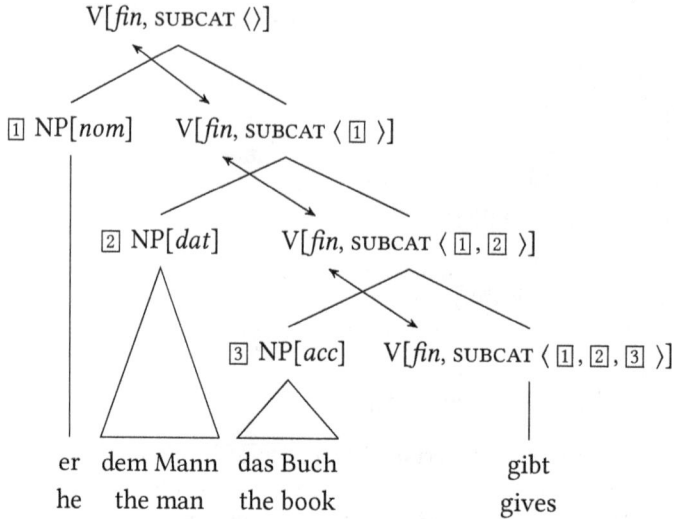

Figure 9.4: Projection of the head features of the verb

GPSG has the Head Feature Convention that ensures that head features on the mother node are identical to those on the node of the head daughter. In HPSG, there is a similar principle. Unlike GPSG, head features are explicitly contained as a group of features in the feature structures. They are listed under the path SYNSEM|LOC|CAT|HEAD. (17) shows the lexical item for *gibt* 'gives':

(17)   *gibt* 'gives':

$$
\begin{bmatrix}
word \\
\text{PHON} \left\langle\, gibt \,\right\rangle \\
\text{SYNSEM|LOC|CAT}
\begin{bmatrix}
\text{HEAD}
\begin{bmatrix}
verb \\
\text{VFORM } fin
\end{bmatrix} \\
\text{SUBCAT } \left\langle\, NP[nom], NP[dat], NP[acc] \,\right\rangle
\end{bmatrix}
\end{bmatrix}
$$

The *Head Feature Principle* takes the following form:

Principle 1 (*Head Feature Principle*)
The HEAD value of any headed phrase is structure-shared with the HEAD value of the head daughter.

Figure 9.5 on the following page is a variant of Figure 9.4 with the structure sharing made explicit.

$$
\begin{bmatrix} \text{HEAD} & \boxed{1} \\ \text{SUBCAT} & \langle \ \rangle \end{bmatrix}
$$

$\boxed{2}$ NP[*nom*] $\begin{bmatrix} \text{HEAD} & \boxed{1} \\ \text{SUBCAT} & \langle \boxed{2} \ \rangle \end{bmatrix}$

$\boxed{3}$ NP[*dat*] $\begin{bmatrix} \text{HEAD} & \boxed{1} \\ \text{SUBCAT} & \langle \boxed{2}, \boxed{3} \ \rangle \end{bmatrix}$

$\boxed{4}$ NP[*acc*] $\begin{bmatrix} \text{HEAD} & \boxed{1} & \begin{bmatrix} \textit{verb} \\ \text{VFORM} & \textit{fin} \end{bmatrix} \\ \text{SUBCAT} & \langle \boxed{2}, \boxed{3}, \boxed{4} \ \rangle \end{bmatrix}$

er	dem Mann	das Buch	gibt
he	the man	the book	gives

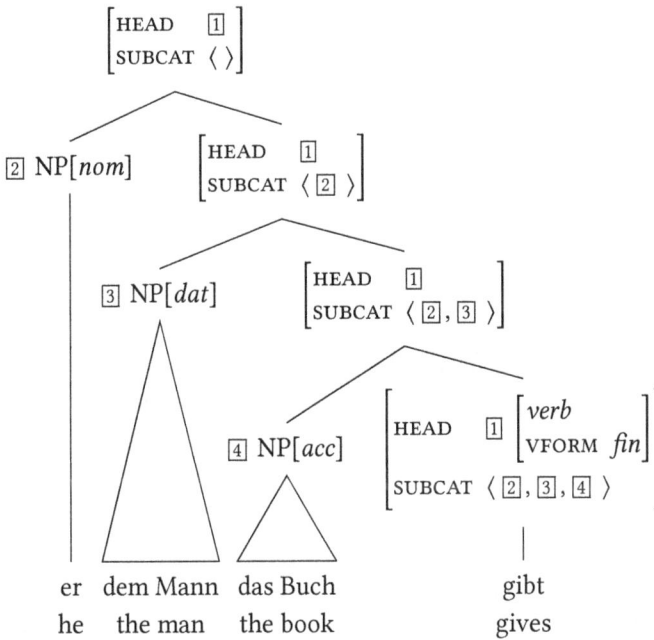

Figure 9.5: Projection of head features of a verb with structure sharing

The following section will deal with how this principle is formalized as well as how it can be integrated into the architecture of HPSG.

9.1.5 Inheritance hierarchies and generalizations

Up to now, we have seen one example of a dominance schema and more will follow in the coming sections, e.g., schemata for head-adjunct structures as well as for the binding off of long-distance dependencies. The Head Feature Principle is a general principle which must be met by all structures licensed by these schemata. As mentioned above, it must be met by all structures with a head. Formally, this can be captured by categorizing syntactic structures into those with and those without heads and assigning the type *headed-phrase* to those with a head. The type *head-argument-phrase* – the type which the description in Schema 1 on page 263 has – is a subtype of *headed-phrase*. Objects of a certain type x always have all properties that objects have that are supertypes of x. Recall the example from Section 6.2: an object of the type *female person* has all the properties of the type *person*. Furthermore, objects of type *female person* have additional, more specific properties not shared by other subtypes of *person*.

If one formulates a restriction on a supertype, this automatically affects all of its subtypes. The Head Feature Principle hence can be formalized as follows:

(18) *headed-phrase* $\Rightarrow \begin{bmatrix} \text{SYNSEM|LOC|CAT|HEAD} & \boxed{1} \\ \text{HEAD-DTR|SYNSEM|LOC|CAT|HEAD} & \boxed{1} \end{bmatrix}$

The arrow corresponds to a logical implication, as mentioned above. Therefore, (18) can be read as follows: if a structure is of type *headed-phrase*, then it must hold that the value of SYNSEM|LOC|CAT|HEAD is identical to the value of HEAD-DTR|SYNSEM|LOC|CAT|HEAD.

An extract from the type hierarchy under *sign* is given in Figure 9.6.

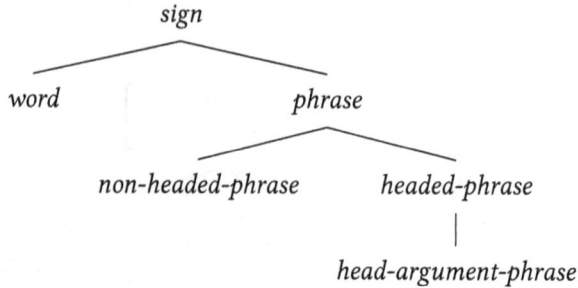

Figure 9.6: Type hierarchy for *sign*: all subtypes of *headed-phrase* inherit constraints

word and *phrase* are subclasses of linguistic signs. Phrases can be divided into phrases with heads (*headed-phrase*) and those without (*non-headed-phrase*). There are also subtypes for phrases of type *non-headed-phrase* and *headed-phrase*. We have already discussed *head-argument-phrase*, and other subtypes of *headed-phrase* will be discussed in the later sections. As well as *word* and *phrase*, there are the types *root* and *stem*, which play an important role for the structure of the lexicon and the morphological component. Due to space considerations, it is not possible to further discuss these types here, but see Chapter 22.

The description in (19) shows the Head-Argument Schema from page 263 together with the restrictions that the type *head-argument-phrase* inherits from *headed-phrase*.

(19) Head-Argument Schema + Head Feature Principle:

$$
\begin{bmatrix}
\textit{head-argument-phrase} \\
\text{SYNSEM|LOC|CAT}
\begin{bmatrix}
\text{HEAD} & \boxed{1} \\
\text{SUBCAT} & \boxed{2}
\end{bmatrix} \\[2ex]
\text{HEAD-DTR|SYNSEM|LOC|CAT}
\begin{bmatrix}
\text{HEAD} & \boxed{1} \\
\text{SUBCAT} & \boxed{2} \oplus \langle\, \boxed{3}\, \rangle
\end{bmatrix} \\[2ex]
\text{NON-HEAD-DTRS}\ \big\langle\, [\ \text{SYNSEM}\ \boxed{3}\ ]\, \big\rangle
\end{bmatrix}
$$

(20) gives a description of a structure licensed by Schema 1. As well as valence information, the head information is specified in (20) and it is also apparent how the Head Feature Principle ensures the projection of features: the head value of the entire structure ($\boxed{1}$) corresponds to the head value of the verb *gibt* 'gives'.

$$
(20) \quad \begin{bmatrix} \textit{head-argument-phrase} \\ \text{PHON} \left\langle \textit{das Buch gibt} \right\rangle \\[4pt] \text{SYNSEM|LOC|CAT} \begin{bmatrix} \text{HEAD} & \boxed{1} \\ \text{SUBCAT} & \boxed{2} \left\langle \text{NP}[\textit{nom}], \text{NP}[\textit{dat}] \right\rangle \end{bmatrix} \\[18pt] \text{HEAD-DTR} \begin{bmatrix} \textit{word} \\ \text{PHON} \left\langle \textit{gibt} \right\rangle \\[4pt] \text{SYNSEM|LOC|CAT} \begin{bmatrix} \text{HEAD} & \boxed{1} \begin{bmatrix} \textit{verb} \\ \text{VFORM} \textit{ fin} \end{bmatrix} \\[4pt] \text{SUBCAT} & \boxed{2} \oplus \langle \boxed{3} \rangle \end{bmatrix} \end{bmatrix} \\[30pt] \text{NON-HEAD-DTRS} \left\langle \begin{bmatrix} \text{PHON} \left\langle \textit{das Buch} \right\rangle \\[4pt] \text{SYNSEM} \boxed{3} \begin{bmatrix} \text{LOC|CAT} \begin{bmatrix} \text{HEAD} & \begin{bmatrix} \textit{noun} \\ \text{CAS } \textit{acc} \end{bmatrix} \\ \text{SUBCAT} \langle \rangle \end{bmatrix} \end{bmatrix} \\[12pt] \text{HEAD-DTR} \ldots \\ \text{NON-HEAD-DTRS} \ldots \end{bmatrix} \right\rangle \end{bmatrix}
$$

For the entire sentence *er das Buch dem Mann gibt* 'he the book to the man gives', we arrive at a structure (already shown in Figure 9.5) described by (21):

$$
(21) \quad \begin{bmatrix} \text{SYNSEM|LOC|CAT} \begin{bmatrix} \text{HEAD} & \begin{bmatrix} \textit{verb} \\ \text{VFORM} \textit{ fin} \end{bmatrix} \\[4pt] \text{SUBCAT} \langle \rangle \end{bmatrix} \end{bmatrix}
$$

This description corresponds to the sentence symbol S in the phrase structure grammar on page 53, however (21) additionally contains information about the form of the verb.

Using dominance schemata as an example, we have shown how generalizations about linguistic objects can be captured, however, we also want to be able to capture generalizations in other areas of the theory: like Categorial Grammar, the HPSG lexicon contains a very large amount of information. Lexical entries (roots and words) can also be divided into classes, which can then be assigned types. In this way, it is possible to capture what all verbs, intransitive verbs and transitive verbs, have in common. See Figure 22.1 on page 656.

Now that some fundamental concepts of HPSG have been introduced, the following section will show how the semantic contribution of words is represented and how the meaning of a phrase can be determined compositionally.

9.1.6 Semantics

An important difference between theories such as GB, LFG and TAG, on the one hand, and HPSG and CxG on the other is that the semantic content of a linguistic object is modeled in a feature structure just like all its other properties. As previously mentioned, semantic information is found under the path SYNSEM|LOC|CONT. (22) gives an example of the CONT value for *Buch* 'book'. The representation is based on Minimal Recursion Semantics (MRS):[9]

$$
(22) \quad
\begin{bmatrix}
mrs \\[2pt]
\text{IND} \quad \boxed{1} \begin{bmatrix} \text{PER} & 3 \\ \text{NUM} & sg \\ \text{GEN} & neu \end{bmatrix} \\[10pt]
\text{RELS} \quad \left\langle \begin{bmatrix} buch \\ \text{INST} & \boxed{1} \end{bmatrix} \right\rangle
\end{bmatrix}
$$

IND stands for index and RELS is a list of relations. Features such as person, number and gender are part of a nominal index. These are important in determining reference or coreference. For example, *sie* 'she' in (23) can refer to *Frau* 'woman' but not to *Buch* 'book'. On the other hand, *es* 'it' cannot refer to *Frau* 'woman'.

(23) Die Frau$_i$ kauft ein Buch$_j$. Sie$_i$ liest es$_j$.
       the woman buys a   book   she reads it

'The woman buys a book. She reads it.'

In general, pronouns have to agree in person, number and gender with the element they refer to. Indices are then identified accordingly. In HPSG, this is done by means of structure sharing. It is also common to speak of *coindexation*. (24) provides some examples of coindexation of reflexive pronouns:

(24)   a. Ich$_i$ sehe mich$_i$.
           I   see myself

       b. Du$_i$ siehst dich$_i$.
           you see   yourself

       c. Er$_i$ sieht sich$_i$.
           he sees himself

       d. Wir$_i$ sehen uns$_i$.
           we   see   ourselves

       e. Ihr$_i$ seht euch$_i$.
           you see yourselves

       f. Sie$_i$ sehen sich$_i$.
           they see   themselves

---

[9] Pollard & Sag (1994) and Ginzburg & Sag (2000) make use of Situation Semantics (Barwise & Perry 1983; Cooper, Mukai & Perry 1990; Devlin 1992). An alternative approach which has already been used in HPSG is Lexical Resource Semantics (Richter & Sailer 2004). For an early underspecification analysis in HPSG, see Nerbonne (1993).

The question of which instances of coindexation are possible and which are necessary is determined by Binding Theory. Pollard & Sag (1992, 1994) have shown that Binding Theory in HPSG does not have many of the problems that arise when implementing binding in GB with reference to tree configurations. There are, however, a number of open questions for Binding Theory in HPSG (Müller 1999a: Section 20.4).

(25) shows the CONT value for the verb *geben* 'give':

$$
(25) \quad
\begin{bmatrix}
\textit{mrs} \\
\text{IND} \quad \boxed{1} \ \textit{event} \\
\text{RELS} \quad \left\langle
\begin{bmatrix}
\textit{geben} \\
\text{EVENT} \ \boxed{1} \\
\text{AGENT} \ \textit{index} \\
\text{GOAL} \quad \textit{index} \\
\text{THEME} \ \textit{index}
\end{bmatrix}
\right\rangle
\end{bmatrix}
$$

It is assumed that verbs have an event variable of the type *event*, which is represented under IND just as with indices for nominal objects. Until now, we did not assign elements in the valence list to argument roles in the semantic representation. This connection is referred to as *linking*. (26) shows how linking works in HPSG. The referential indices of the argument noun phrases are structure-shared with one of the semantic roles of the relation contributed by the head.

(26) *gibt* 'gives':

$$
\begin{bmatrix}
\text{CAT}
\begin{bmatrix}
\text{HEAD}
\begin{bmatrix}
\textit{verb} \\
\text{VFORM} \ \textit{fin}
\end{bmatrix} \\
\text{SUBCAT} \ \left\langle \text{NP}[\textit{nom}]_{\boxed{1}}, \text{NP}[\textit{dat}]_{\boxed{2}}, \text{NP}[\textit{acc}]_{\boxed{3}} \right\rangle
\end{bmatrix} \\
\text{CONT}
\begin{bmatrix}
\textit{mrs} \\
\text{IND} \ \boxed{4} \ \textit{event} \\
\text{RELS} \ \left\langle
\begin{bmatrix}
\textit{geben} \\
\text{EVENT} \ \boxed{4} \\
\text{AGENT} \ \boxed{1} \\
\text{GOAL} \quad \boxed{2} \\
\text{THEME} \ \boxed{3}
\end{bmatrix}
\right\rangle
\end{bmatrix}
\end{bmatrix}
$$

Since we use general terms such as AGENT and PATIENT for argument roles, it is possible to state generalizations about valence classes and the realization of argument roles. For example, one can divide verbs into verbs taking an agent, verbs with an agent and theme, verbs with agent and patient etc. These various valence/linking patterns can be represented in type hierarchies and these classes can be assigned to the specific lexical entries, that is, one can have them inherit constraints from the respective types. A type constraint for verbs with agent, theme and goal takes the form of (27):

$$(27) \begin{bmatrix} \text{CAT}|\text{SUBCAT} \left\langle \;[\,]_{\boxed{1}},\; [\,]_{\boxed{2}},\; [\,]_{\boxed{3}} \;\right\rangle \\ \text{CONT} \begin{bmatrix} mrs \\ \text{IND} \quad \boxed{4}\; event \\ \text{RELS} \left\langle \begin{bmatrix} agent\text{-}goal\text{-}theme\text{-}rel \\ \text{EVENT} \quad \boxed{4} \\ \text{AGENT} \quad \boxed{1} \\ \text{GOAL} \quad \boxed{2} \\ \text{THEME} \quad \boxed{3} \end{bmatrix} \right\rangle \end{bmatrix} \end{bmatrix}$$

$[\,]_{\boxed{1}}$ stands for an object of unspecified syntactic category with the index $\boxed{1}$. The type for the relation *geben'* is a subtype of *agent-goal-theme-rel*. The lexical entry for the word *geben* 'give' or rather the root *geb-* has the linking pattern in (27). For more on theories of linking in HPSG, see Davis (1996), Wechsler (1991) und Davis & Koenig (2000).

Up to now, we have only seen how the meaning of lexical entries can be represented. The Semantics Principle determines the computation of the semantic contribution of phrases: the index of the entire expression corresponds to the index of the head daughter, and the RELS value of the entire sign corresponds to the concatenation of the RELS values of the daughters plus any relations introduced by the dominance schema. The last point is important because the assumption that schemata can add something to meaning can capture the fact that there are some cases where the entire meaning of a phrase is more than simply the sum of its parts. Pertinent examples are often discussed as part of Construction Grammar. Semantic composition in HPSG is organized such that meaning components that are due to certain patterns can be integrated into the complete meaning of an utterance. For examples, see Section 21.10.

The connection between the semantic contribution of the verb and its arguments is established in the lexical entry. As such, we ensure that the argument roles of the verb are assigned to the correct argument in the sentence. This is, however, not the only thing that the semantics is responsible for. It has to be able to generate the various readings associated with quantifier scope ambiguities (see page 88) as well as deal with semantic embedding of predicates under other predicates. All these requirements are fulfilled by MRS. Due to space considerations, we cannot go into detail here. The reader is referred to the article by Copestake, Flickinger, Pollard & Sag (2005) and to Section 19.3 in the discussion chapter.

9.1.7 Adjuncts

Analogous to the selection of arguments by heads via SUBCAT, adjuncts can also select their heads using a feature (MODIFIED). Adjectives, prepositional phrases that modify nouns, and relative clauses select an almost complete nominal projection, that is, a noun that only still needs to be combined with a determiner to yield a complete NP. (28) shows a description of the respective *synsem* object. The symbol $\overline{\text{N}}$, which is familiar from $\overline{\text{X}}$ theory (see Section 2.5), is used as abbreviation for this feature description.

(28)   AVM that is abbreviated as $\overline{\text{N}}$:

$$\left[\text{CAT} \begin{bmatrix} \text{HEAD} & \textit{noun} \\ \text{SUBCAT} & \langle \text{DET} \rangle \end{bmatrix} \right]$$

(29) shows part of the lexical item for *interessantes* 'interesting':

(29)   CAT value for *interessantes* 'interesting':

$$\begin{bmatrix} \text{HEAD} & \begin{bmatrix} \textit{adj} \\ \text{MOD} & \overline{\text{N}} \end{bmatrix} \\ \text{SUBCAT} & \langle \rangle \end{bmatrix}$$

interessantes is an adjective that does not take any arguments and therefore has an empty SUBCAT list. Adjectives such as *treu* 'loyal' would have a dative NP in their SUBCAT list.

(30)   ein dem   König treues Mädchen
       a   the.DAT king   loyal girl
       'a girl loyal to the king'

The CAT value is given in (31):

(31)   CAT value for *treues* 'loyal':

$$\begin{bmatrix} \text{HEAD} & \begin{bmatrix} \textit{adj} \\ \text{MOD} & \overline{\text{N}} \end{bmatrix} \\ \text{SUBCAT} & \langle \text{NP}[\textit{dat}] \rangle \end{bmatrix}$$

dem König treues 'loyal to the king' forms an adjective phrase, which modifies *Mädchen*.

Unlike the selectional feature SUBCAT that belongs to the features under CAT, MOD is a head feature. The reason for this is that the feature that selects the modifying head has to be present on the maximal projection of the adjunct. The $\overline{\text{N}}$-modifying property of the adjective phrase *dem König treues* 'loyal to the king' has to be included in the representation of the entire AP just as it is present in the lexical entry for adjectives in (29) at the lexical level. The adjectival phrase *dem König treues* has the same syntactic properties as the basic adjective *interessantes* 'interesting':

(32)   CAT value für *dem König treues*:

$$\begin{bmatrix} \text{HEAD} & \begin{bmatrix} \textit{adj} \\ \text{MOD} & \overline{\text{N}} \end{bmatrix} \\ \text{SUBCAT} & \langle \rangle \end{bmatrix}$$

Since MOD is a head feature, the Head Feature Principle (see page 266) ensures that the MOD value of the entire projection is identical to the MOD value of the lexical entry for *treues* 'loyal'.

As an alternative to the selection of the head by the modifier, one could assume a description of all possible adjuncts on the head itself. This was suggested by Pollard & Sag (1987: 161). Pollard & Sag (1994: Section 1.9) revised the earlier analysis since the semantics of modification could not be captured.[10]

Figure 9.7 demonstrates selection in head-adjunct structures.

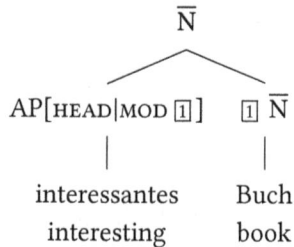

$$\overline{N}$$

$$AP[\text{HEAD}|\text{MOD} \;\boxed{1}] \qquad \boxed{1} \; \overline{N}$$

interessantes	Buch
interesting	book

Figure 9.7: Head-adjunct structure (selection)

Head-adjunct structures are licensed by the Schema 2.

Schema 2 (Head-Adjunct Schema (preliminary version))

head-adjunct-phrase ⇒

$$\begin{bmatrix} \text{HEAD-DTR}|\text{SYNSEM} \; \boxed{1} \\ \\ \text{NON-HEAD-DTRS} \; \left\langle \begin{bmatrix} \text{SYNSEM}|\text{LOC}|\text{CAT} \begin{bmatrix} \text{HEAD}|\text{MOD} \; \boxed{1} \\ \text{SUBCAT} \quad \langle\rangle \end{bmatrix} \end{bmatrix} \right\rangle \end{bmatrix}$$

The value of the selectional feature on the adjunct ($\boxed{1}$) is identified with the SYNSEM value of the head daughter, thereby ensuring that the head daughter has the properties specified by the adjunct. The SUBCAT value of the non-head daughter is the empty list, which is why only completely saturated adjuncts are allowed in head-adjunct structures. Phrases such as (33b) are therefore correctly ruled out:

(33) a. die Wurst in der Speisekammer
          the sausage in the pantry

      b. * die Wurst in
           the sausage in

Example (33a) requires some further explanation. The preposition *in* (as used in (33a)) has the following CAT value:

---

[10] See Bouma, Malouf & Sag (2001a), however. Bouma, Malouf & Sag (2001a) pursue a hybrid analysis where there are adjuncts which select heads and also adjuncts that are selected by a head. Minimal Recursion Semantics is the semantic theory underlying this analysis. Using this semantics, the problems arising for Pollard & Sag (1987) with regard to the semantics of modifiers are avoided.

(34)   CAT value of *in*:

$$
\begin{bmatrix}
\text{HEAD} & \begin{bmatrix} prep \\ \text{MOD } \overline{\text{N}} \end{bmatrix} \\
\text{SUBCAT} & \langle \text{ NP}[dat] \rangle
\end{bmatrix}
$$

After combining *in* with the nominal phrase *der Speisekammer* 'the pantry' one gets:

(35)   CAT value for *in der Speisekammer* 'in the pantry':

$$
\begin{bmatrix}
\text{HEAD} & \begin{bmatrix} prep \\ \text{MOD } \overline{\text{N}} \end{bmatrix} \\
\text{SUBCAT} & \langle \rangle
\end{bmatrix}
$$

This representation corresponds to that of the adjective *interessantes* 'interesting' and can – ignoring the position of the PP – also be used in the same way: the PP modifies a $\overline{\text{N}}$.

Heads that can only be used as arguments but do not modify anything have a MOD value of *none*. They can therefore not occur in the position of the non-head daughter in head-adjunct structures since the MOD value of the non-head daughter has to be compatible with the SYNSEM value of the head daughter.

9.2 Passive

HPSG follows Bresnan's argumentation (see Section 7.2) and takes care of the passive in the lexicon.[11] A lexical rule takes the verb stem as its input and licenses the participle form and the most prominent argument (the so-called designated argument) is suppressed.[12] Since grammatical functions are not part of theory in HPSG, we do not require any mapping principles that map objects to subjects. Nevertheless, one still has to explain the change of case under passivization. If one fully specifies the case of a particular argument in the lexical entries, one has to ensure that the accusative argument of a transitive verb is realized as nominative in the passive. (36) shows what the respective lexical rule would look like:

---

[11] Some exceptions to this are analyses influenced by Construction Grammar such as Tseng (2007) and Haugereid (2007). These approaches are problematic, however, as they cannot account for Bresnan's adjectival passives. For other problems with Haugereid's analysis, see Müller (2007c) and Section 21.3.6.

[12] For more on the designated argument, see Haider (1986a). HPSG analyses of the passive in German have been considerably influenced by Haider. Haider uses the designated argument to model the difference between so-called unaccusative and unergative verbs (Perlmutter 1978): unaccusative verbs differ from unergatives and transitives in that they do not have a designated argument. We cannot go into the literature on unaccusativity here. The reader is referred to the original works by Haider and the chapter on the passive in Müller (2007b).

(36) Lexical rule for personal passives adapted from Kiss (1992):

$$
\begin{bmatrix} stem \\ \text{PHON } \boxed{1} \\ \text{SYNSEM|LOC|CAT } \begin{bmatrix} \text{HEAD} & verb \\ \text{SUBCAT} & \left\langle \text{NP}[nom], \text{NP}[acc]_{\boxed{2}} \right\rangle \oplus \boxed{3} \end{bmatrix} \end{bmatrix} \mapsto
$$

$$
\begin{bmatrix} word \\ \text{PHON } f(\boxed{1}) \\ \text{SYNSEM|LOC|CAT } \begin{bmatrix} \text{HEAD} & \begin{bmatrix} \text{VFORM } passive\text{-}part \end{bmatrix} \\ \text{SUBCAT} & \left\langle \text{NP}[nom]_{\boxed{2}} \right\rangle \oplus \boxed{3} \end{bmatrix} \end{bmatrix}
$$

This lexical rule takes a verb stem[13] as its input, which requires a nominative argument, an accusative argument and possibly further arguments (if $\boxed{3}$ is not the empty list) and licenses a lexical entry that requires a nominative argument and possibly the arguments in $\boxed{3}$.[14] The output of the lexical rule specifies the VFORM value of the output word. This is important as the auxiliary and the main verb must go together. For example, it is not possible to use the perfect participle instead of the passive participle since these differ in their valence in Kiss' approach:

(37) a. Der Mann hat den Weltmeister geschlagen.
          the man   has the world.champion beaten

          'The man has beaten the world champion.'

      b. * Der Mann wird den Weltmeister geschlagen.
          the man   is   the world.champion beaten

      c. Der Weltmeister wird geschlagen.
          the world.champion is beaten

          'The world champion is (being) beaten.'

There are a few conventions for the interpretation of lexical rules: all information that is not mentioned in the output sign is taken over from the input sign. Thus, the meaning

---

[13] The term *stem* includes roots (*helf-* 'help-'), products of derivation (*besing-* 'to sing about') and compounds. The lexical rule can therefore also be applied to stems like *helf-* and derived forms such as *besing-*.

[14] This rule assumes that arguments of ditransitive verbs are in the order nominative, accusative, dative. Throughout this chapter, I assume a nominative, dative, accusative order, which corresponds to the unmarked order of arguments in the German clause. Kiss (2001) argued that a representation of the unmarked order is needed to account for scope facts in German. Furthermore, the order of the arguments corresponds to the order one would assume for English, which has the advantage that cross-linguistic generalizations can be captured. In earlier work I assumed that the order is nominative, accusative, dative since this order encodes a prominence hierarchy that is relevant in a lot of areas in German grammar. Examples are: ellipsis (Klein 1985), Topic Drop (Fries 1988), free relatives (Bausewein 1990; Pittner 1995; Müller 1999b), depictive secondary predicates (Müller 2004d, 2002a, 2008), Binding Theory (Grewendorf 1985; Pollard und Sag: 1992; 1994: Chapter 6). This order also corresponds to the Obliqueness Hierarchy suggested by Keenan & Comrie (1977) and Pullum (1977). In order to capture this hierarchy, a special list with nominative, accusative, dative order would have to be assumed.

The version of the passive lexical rule that will be suggested below is compatible with both orders of arguments.

of the verb is not mentioned in the passive rule, which makes sense as the passive rule is a meaning preserving rule. The CONT values of the input and output are not mentioned in the rule and hence are identical. It is important here that the linking information its retained. As an example consider the application of the rule to the verb stem *schlag-* 'beat':

(38) a. Input *schlag-* 'beat' :

$$
\begin{bmatrix}
\text{PHON} \ \langle \ schlag \ \rangle \\
\text{SYNSEM|LOC}
\begin{bmatrix}
\text{CAT}
\begin{bmatrix}
\text{HEAD} & verb \\
\text{SUBCAT} & \langle \ \text{NP}[nom]_{\boxed{1}}, \ \text{NP}[acc]_{\boxed{2}} \ \rangle
\end{bmatrix} \\
\text{CONT}
\begin{bmatrix}
\text{IND} & \boxed{3} \ event \\
\text{RELS} & \left\langle
\begin{bmatrix}
schlagen \\
\text{EVENT} & \boxed{3} \\
\text{AGENT} & \boxed{1} \\
\text{PATIENT} & \boxed{2}
\end{bmatrix}
\right\rangle
\end{bmatrix}
\end{bmatrix}
\end{bmatrix}
$$

  b. Output *geschlagen* 'beaten':

$$
\begin{bmatrix}
\text{PHON} \ \langle \ geschlagen \ \rangle \\
\text{SYNSEM|LOC}
\begin{bmatrix}
\text{CAT}
\begin{bmatrix}
\text{HEAD}
\begin{bmatrix}
verb \\
\text{VFORM} & passive\text{-}part
\end{bmatrix} \\
\text{SUBCAT} & \langle \ \text{NP}[nom]_{\boxed{2}} \ \rangle
\end{bmatrix} \\
\text{CONT}
\begin{bmatrix}
\text{IND} & \boxed{3} \ event \\
\text{RELS} & \left\langle
\begin{bmatrix}
schlagen \\
\text{EVENT} & \boxed{3} \\
\text{AGENT} & \boxed{1} \\
\text{PATIENT} & \boxed{2}
\end{bmatrix}
\right\rangle
\end{bmatrix}
\end{bmatrix}
\end{bmatrix}
$$

The agent role is connected to the subject of *schlag-*. After passivization, the subject is suppressed and the argument connected to the patient role of *schlag-* becomes the subject of the participle. Argument linking is not affected by this and thus the nominative argument is correctly assigned to the patient role.

As Meurers (2001) has shown, lexical rules can also be captured with feature descriptions. (39) shows the feature description representation of (36). What is on the left-hand side of the rule in (36), is contained in the value of LEX-DTR in (39). Since this kind of lexical rule is fully integrated into the formalism, feature structures corresponding to these lexical rules also have their own type. If the result of the application of a given rule is an inflected word, then the type of the lexical rule (*acc-passive-lexical-rule* in our example) is a subtype of *word*. Since lexical rules have a type, it is possible to state generalizations over lexical rules.

The lexical rules discussed thus far work well for the personal passive. For the impersonal passive, however, we would require a second lexical rule. Furthermore, we would

(39)

$$\begin{bmatrix} acc\text{-}passive\text{-}lexical\text{-}rule \\ \text{PHON } f(\boxed{1}) \\ \text{SYNSEM|LOC|CAT} \begin{bmatrix} \text{HEAD} & \begin{bmatrix} \text{VFORM } passive\text{-}part \end{bmatrix} \\ \text{SUBCAT} & \langle \text{NP}[nom]_{\boxed{2}} \rangle \oplus \boxed{3} \end{bmatrix} \\ \text{LEX-DTR} \begin{bmatrix} stem \\ \text{PHON } \boxed{1} \\ \text{SYNSEM|LOC|CAT} \begin{bmatrix} \text{HEAD} & verb \\ \text{SUBCAT} & \langle \text{NP}[nom], \text{NP}[acc]_{\boxed{2}} \rangle \oplus \boxed{3} \end{bmatrix} \end{bmatrix} \end{bmatrix}$$

have two different lexical items for the passive and the perfect, although the forms are always identical in German. In the following, I will discuss the basic assumptions that are needed for a theory of the passive that can sufficiently explain both personal and impersonal passives and thereby only require one lexical item for the participle form.

9.2.1 Valence information and the Case Principle

In Section 3.4.1, the difference between structural and lexical case was motivated. In the HPSG literature, it is assumed following Haider (1986a) that the dative is a lexical case. For arguments marked with a lexical case, their case value is directly specified in the description of the argument. Arguments with structural case are also specified in the lexicon as taking structural case, but the actual case value is not provided. In order for the grammar not to make any false predictions, it has to be ensured that the structural cases receive a unique value dependent on their environment. This is handled by the Case Principle:[15]

Principle 2 (Case Principle)

- *In a list containing the subject as well as complements of a verbal head, the first element with structural case receives nominative.*

- *All other elements in the list with structural case receive accusative.*

- *In nominal environments, elements with structural case are assigned genitive.*

(40) shows prototypical valence lists for finite verbs:

---

[15] The Case Principle has been simplified here. Cases of so-called 'raising' require special treatment. For more details, see Meurers (1999c), Przepiórkowski (1999a) and Müller (2007b: Chapter 14, Chapter 17). The Case Principle given in these publications is very similar to the one proposed by Yip, Maling & Jackendoff (1987) and can therefore also explain the case systems of the languages discussed in their work, notably the complicated case system of Icelandic.

(40) a. *schläft* 'sleeps':   SUBCAT $\langle$ NP[*str*]$_j$ $\rangle$

  b. *unterstützt* 'supports': SUBCAT $\langle$ NP[*str*]$_j$, NP[*str*]$_k$ $\rangle$

  c. *hilft* 'helps':   SUBCAT $\langle$ NP[*str*]$_j$, NP[*ldat*]$_k$ $\rangle$

  d. *schenkt* 'gives':   SUBCAT $\langle$ NP[*str*]$_j$, NP[*ldat*]$_k$, NP[*str*]$_l$ $\rangle$

str stands for *structural* and *ldat* for *lexical dative*. The Case Principle ensures that the subjects of the verbs listed above have to be realized in the nominative and also that objects with structural case are assigned accusative.

With the difference between structural and lexical case, it is possible to formulate a passive-lexical rule that can account for both the personal and the impersonal passive:

(41) Lexical rule for personal and impersonal passive (simplified):

$$
\begin{bmatrix} stem \\ \text{PHON } \boxed{1} \\ \text{SYNSEM|LOC|CAT} \begin{bmatrix} \text{HEAD} & verb \\ \text{SUBCAT} & \langle \text{NP}[str] \rangle \oplus \boxed{2} \end{bmatrix} \end{bmatrix} \mapsto
$$

$$
\begin{bmatrix} word \\ \text{PHON } f(\boxed{1}) \\ \text{SYNSEM|LOC|CAT} \begin{bmatrix} \text{HEAD} & \begin{bmatrix} \text{VFORM} & ppp \end{bmatrix} \\ \text{SUBCAT} & \boxed{2} \end{bmatrix} \end{bmatrix}
$$

This lexical rule does exactly what we expect it to do from a pretheoretical perspective on the passive: it suppresses the most prominent argument with structural case, that is, the argument that corresponds to the subject in the active clause. The standard analysis of verb auxiliary constructions assumes that the main verb and the auxiliary forms a verbal complex (Hinrichs & Nakazawa 1994; Pollard 1994; Müller 1999a, 2002a; Meurers 2000; Kathol 2000). The arguments of the embedded verb are taken over by the auxiliary. After combining the participle with the passive auxiliary, we arrive at the following SUBCAT lists:

(42) a. *geschlafen wird* 'slept is':   SUBCAT $\langle$ $\rangle$

  b. *unterstützt wird* 'supported is': SUBCAT $\langle$ NP[*str*]$_k$ $\rangle$

  c. *geholfen wird*: 'helped is'   SUBCAT $\langle$ NP[*ldat*]$_k$ $\rangle$

  d. *geschenkt wird*: 'given is'   SUBCAT $\langle$ NP[*ldat*]$_k$, NP[*str*]$_l$ $\rangle$

(42) differs from (40) in that a different NP is in first position. If this NP has structural case, it will receive nominative case. If there is no NP with structural case, as in (42c), the case remains as it was, that is, lexically specified.

We cannot go into the analysis of the perfect here. It should be noted, however, that the same lexical item for the participle is used for (43).

(43) a. Er hat den Weltmeister   geschlagen.
          he has the world.champion beaten

          'He has beaten the world champion.'

      b. Der Weltmeister   wurde geschlagen.
          the world.champion was   beaten

          'The world champion was beaten.'

It is the auxiliary that determines which arguments are realized (Haider 1986a; Müller 2007b: Chapter 17). The lexical rule in (41) licenses a form that can be used both in passive and perfect. Therefore, the VFORM value is of *ppp*, which stands for *participle perfect passive*.

One should note that this analysis of the passive works without movement of constituents. The problems with the GB analysis do not arise here. Reordering of arguments (see Section 9.4) is independent of passivization. The accusative object is not mentioned at all unlike in GPSG, Categorial Grammar or Bresnan's LFG analysis from before the introduction of Lexical Mapping Theory (see page 224). The passive can be analyzed directly as the suppression of the subject. Everything else follows from interaction with other principles of grammar.

9.3 Verb position

The analysis of verb position that I will present here is based on the GB-analysis. In HPSG, there are a number of different approaches to describe the verb position, however in my opinion, the HPSG variant of the GB analysis is the only adequate one (Müller 2005b,c, 2015b). The analysis of (44) can be summarized as follows: in the verb-initial clauses, there is a trace in verb-final position. There is a special form of the verb in initial position that selects a projection of the verb trace. This special lexical item is licensed by a lexical rule. The connection between the verb and the trace is treated like long-distance dependencies in GPSG via identification of information in the tree or feature structure (structure sharing).

(44) Kennt$_k$ jeder   diesen Mann $_{-k}$?
      knows everyone this   man

      'Does everyone know this man?'

Figure 9.8 on the following page gives an overview of this. The verb trace in final position behaves just like the verb both syntactically and semantically. The information about the missing word is represented as the value of the feature DOUBLE SLASH (abbreviated: DSL). This is a head feature and is therefore passed up to the maximal projection (VP). The verb in initial position has a VP in its SUBCAT list which is missing a verb (VP//V). This is the same verb that was the input for the lexical rule and that would normally occur in final position. In Figure 9.8, there are two maximal verb projections: *jeder diesen Mann* $_{-k}$ with the trace as the head and *kennt jeder diesen Mann* $_{-k}$ with *kennt* as the head.

This analysis will be explained in more detail in what follows. For the trace in Figure 9.8, one could assume the lexical entry in (45).

VP

V ⟨ VP//V ⟩   VP//V

V   NP   V'//V

NP   V//V

kennt$_k$ jeder   diesen Mann $_{-k}$
knows   everyone   this man

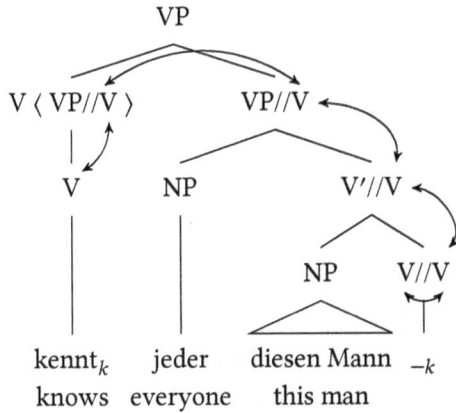

Figure 9.8: Analysis of verb position in HPSG

(45) Verb trace for *kennt* 'knows':

$$
\begin{bmatrix}
\text{PHON } \langle\rangle \\
\text{SYNSEM}|\text{LOC}
\begin{bmatrix}
\text{CAT}
\begin{bmatrix}
\text{HEAD} \begin{bmatrix} verb \\ \text{VFORM } fin \end{bmatrix} \\
\text{SUBCAT } \langle \text{NP}[nom]_{\boxed{1}}, \text{NP}[acc]_{\boxed{2}} \rangle
\end{bmatrix} \\
\text{CONT}
\begin{bmatrix}
\text{IND } \boxed{3} \\
\text{RELS } \left\langle
\begin{bmatrix}
kennen \\
\text{EVENT} \quad \boxed{3} \\
\text{EXPERIENCER } \boxed{1} \\
\text{THEME} \quad \boxed{2}
\end{bmatrix}
\right\rangle
\end{bmatrix}
\end{bmatrix}
\end{bmatrix}
$$

This lexical entry differs from the normal verb *kennt* only in its PHON value. The syntactic aspects of an analysis with this trace are represented in Figure 9.9 on the next page.

The combination of the trace with *diesen Mann* 'this man' and *jeder* 'everbody' follows the rules and principles that we have encountered thus far. This begs the immediate question as to what licenses the verb *kennt* in Figure 9.9 and what status it has.

If we want to capture the fact that the finite verb in initial position behaves like a complementizer (Höhle 1997), then it makes sense to give head status to *kennt* in Figure 9.9 and have *kennt* select a saturated, verb-final verbal projection. Finite verbs in initial position differ from complementizers in that they require a projection of a verb trace, whereas complementizers need projections of overt verbs:

(46) a. dass [jeder   diesen Mann kennt]
          that everybody this   man   knows
          'that everybody knows this man'

V[SUBCAT ⟨⟩]

V   V[SUBCAT ⟨⟩]

3 NP[*nom*]   V[SUBCAT ⟨ 3 ⟩]

4 NP[*acc*]   [V[SUBCAT ⟨ 3 , 4 ⟩]

kennt   jeder   diesen Mann   –
knows everyone   this man

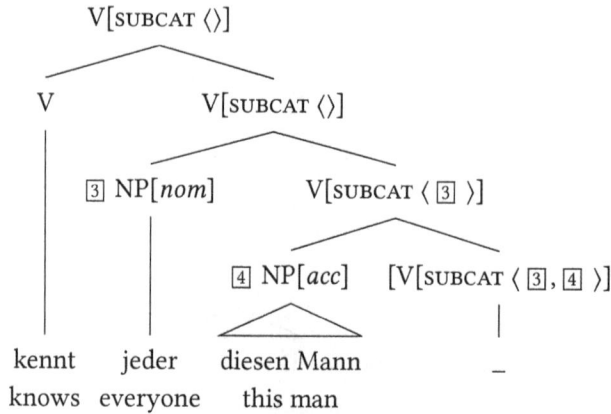

Figure 9.9: Analysis of *Kennt jeder diesen Mann?* 'Does everyone know this man?'

    b. Kennt [jeder   diesen Mann _]
       knows everybody this   man

      'Does everybody know this man?'

It is normally not the case that *kennen* 'know' selects a complete sentence and nothing else as would be necessary for the analysis of *kennt* as the head in (46b). Furthermore, we must ensure that the verbal projection with which *kennt* is combined contains the verb trace belonging to *kennt*. If it could contain a trace belonging to *gibt* 'gives', for example, we would be able to analyze sentences such as (47b):

(47) a. Gibt [der Mann der Frau   das Buch $_{-gibt}$]?
         gives the man the woman the book

       'Does the man give the woman the book?'

    b. * Kennt [der Mann der Frau   das Buch $_{-gibt}$]?
       knows the man the woman the book

In the preceding discussion, the dependency between the fronted verb and the verb trace was expressed by coindexation. In HPSG, identity is always enforced by structure sharing. The verb in initial position must therefore require that the trace has exactly those properties of the verb that the verb would have had, were it in final position. The information that must be shared is therefore all locally relevant syntactic and semantic information, that is, all information under LOCAL. Since PHON is not part of the LOCAL features, it is not shared and this is why the PHON values of the trace and verb can differ. Up to now, one crucial detail has been missing in the analysis: the LOCAL value of the trace cannot be directly structure-shared with a requirement of the initial verb since the verb *kennt* can only select the properties of the projection of the trace and the SUBCAT list of the selected projection is the empty list. This leads us to the problem that was pointed out in the discussion of (47b). It must therefore be ensured that all information about the verb trace is available on the highest node of its projection. This can be achieved by introducing a head feature whose value is identical to the LOCAL value of the trace. This feature is referred to as DSL. As was already mentioned above, DSL stands for *double slash*. It is called so because it has a similar function to the SLASH feature, which we will encounter in the following section.[16] (48) shows the modified entry for the verb trace:

(48) Verb trace of *kennt* (preliminary version):

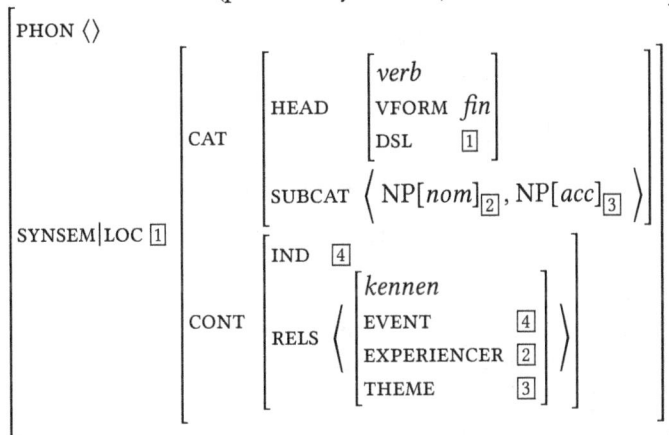

$$
\begin{bmatrix}
\text{PHON } \langle \rangle \\[2pt]
\text{SYNSEM}|\text{LOC } \boxed{1}
\begin{bmatrix}
\text{CAT}
\begin{bmatrix}
\text{HEAD}
\begin{bmatrix}
verb \\
\text{VFORM } \mathit{fin} \\
\text{DSL} \quad \boxed{1}
\end{bmatrix} \\[6pt]
\text{SUBCAT } \left\langle \text{NP}[nom]_{\boxed{2}}, \text{NP}[acc]_{\boxed{3}} \right\rangle
\end{bmatrix} \\[10pt]
\text{CONT}
\begin{bmatrix}
\text{IND} \quad \boxed{4} \\[2pt]
\text{RELS } \left\langle
\begin{bmatrix}
kennen \\
\text{EVENT} \quad \boxed{4} \\
\text{EXPERIENCER } \boxed{2} \\
\text{THEME} \quad \boxed{3}
\end{bmatrix}
\right\rangle
\end{bmatrix}
\end{bmatrix}
\end{bmatrix}
$$

Through sharing of the LOCAL value and the DSL value in (48), the syntactic and semantic information of the verb trace is present at its maximal projection, and the verb in initial position can check whether the projection of the trace is compatible.[17]

The special lexical item for verb-initial position is licensed by the following lexical rule:[18]

---

[16] The feature DSL was proposed by Jacobson (1987a) in the framework of Categorial Grammar to describe head movement in English inversions. Borsley (1989) adopted this idea and translated it into HPSG terms, thereby showing how head movement in a HPSG variant of the CP/IP system can be modeled using DSL. The introduction of the DSL feature to describe head movement processes in HPSG is motivated by the fact that, unlike long-distance dependencies as will be discussed in Section 9.5, this kind of movement is local.

The suggestion to percolate information about the verb trace as part of the head information comes from Oliva (1992).

[17] Note that the description in (48) is cyclic since the tag $\boxed{1}$ is used inside itself. See Section 6.5 on cyclic feature descriptions. This cyclic description is the most direct way to express that a linguistic object with certain local properties is missing and to pass this information on along the head path as the value of the DSL feature. This will be even clearer when we look at the final version of the verb trace in (50) on page 285.

[18] The lexical rule analysis cannot explain sentences such as (i):

(i) Karl kennt und liebt diese Schallplatte.
     Karl knows and loves this record

This has to do with the fact that the lexical rule cannot be applied to the result of coordination, which constitutes a complex syntactic object. If we apply the lexical rule individually to each verb, then we arrive at variants of the verbs which would each select verb traces for *kennen* 'to know' and *lieben* 'to love'. Since the CAT values of the conjuncts are identified with each other in coordinations, coordinations involving the V1 variants of *kennt* and *liebt* would be ruled out since the DSL values of the selected VPs contain the meaning of the respective verbs and are hence not compatible (Müller 2005b: 13). Instead of a lexical rule, one must assume a unary syntactic rule that applies to the phrase *kennt und liebt* 'knows and loves'. As we have seen, lexical rules in the HPSG formalization assumed here correspond to unary rules such that the difference between (49) and a corresponding syntactic rule is mostly a difference in representation.

(49) Lexical rule for verbs in initial position:

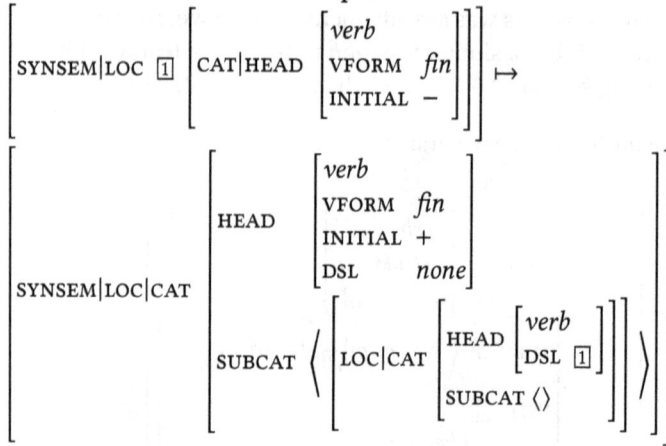

$$
\begin{bmatrix} \text{SYNSEM}|\text{LOC} & \boxed{1} \begin{bmatrix} \text{CAT}|\text{HEAD} & \begin{bmatrix} \textit{verb} \\ \text{VFORM} & \textit{fin} \\ \text{INITIAL} & - \end{bmatrix} \end{bmatrix} \end{bmatrix} \mapsto
$$

$$
\begin{bmatrix} \text{SYNSEM}|\text{LOC}|\text{CAT} & \begin{bmatrix} \text{HEAD} & \begin{bmatrix} \textit{verb} \\ \text{VFORM} & \textit{fin} \\ \text{INITIAL} & + \\ \text{DSL} & \textit{none} \end{bmatrix} \\ \text{SUBCAT} & \left\langle \begin{bmatrix} \text{LOC}|\text{CAT} & \begin{bmatrix} \text{HEAD} & \begin{bmatrix} \textit{verb} \\ \text{DSL} & \boxed{1} \end{bmatrix} \\ \text{SUBCAT} & \langle\rangle \end{bmatrix} \end{bmatrix} \right\rangle \end{bmatrix} \end{bmatrix}
$$

The verb licensed by this lexical rule selects a maximal projection of the verb trace which has the same local properties as the input verb. This is achieved by the coindexation of the LOCAL values of the input verb and the DSL values of the selected verb projection. Only finite verbs in final position (INITIAL−) can be the input for this rule. The output is a verb in initial-position (INITIAL+). The corresponding extended analysis is given in Figure 9.10. V1-LR stands for the verb-initial lexical rule.

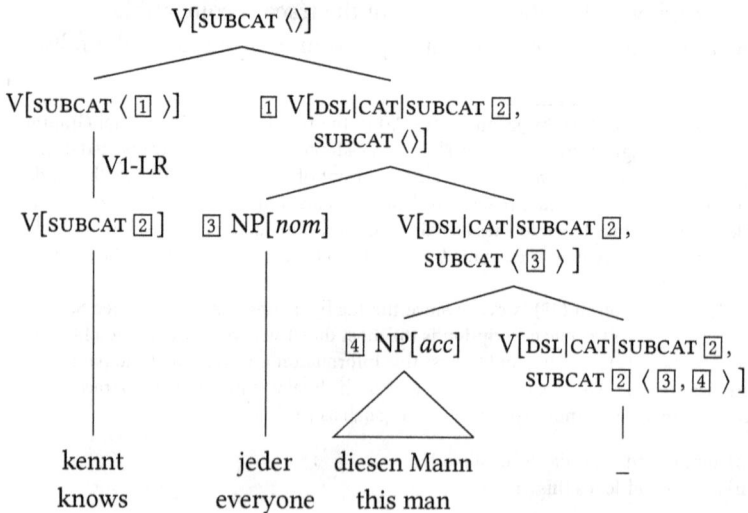

Figure 9.10: Visualization of the analysis of *Kennt jeder diesen Mann?* 'Does everyone know this man?'

The lexical rule in (49) licenses a verb that selects a VP (\boxed{1} in Figure 9.10). The DSL value of this VP corresponds to the LOCAL value of the verb that is the input of the lexical

rule. Part of the DSL value is also the valence information represented in Figure 9.10 (2).
Since DSL is a head feature, the DSL value of the VP is identical to that of the verb trace
and since the LOCAL value of the verb trace is identified with the DSL value, the SUBCAT
information of the verb *kennen* is also available at the trace. The combination of the trace
with its arguments proceeds exactly as with an ordinary verb.

It would be unsatisfactory if we had to assume a special trace for every verb. Fortunately, this is not necessary as a general trace as in (50) will suffice for the analysis of
sentences with verb movement.

(50) General verb trace following Meurers (2000: 206–208):

$$\begin{bmatrix} \text{PHON } \langle \rangle \\ \text{SYNSEM}|\text{LOC } \boxed{1} \; \begin{bmatrix} \text{CAT}|\text{HEAD}|\text{DSL } \boxed{1} \end{bmatrix} \end{bmatrix}$$

This may seem surprising at first glance, but if we look closer at the interaction of the
lexical rule (49) and the percolation of the DSL feature in the tree, then it becomes clear
that the DSL value of the verb projection and therefore the LOCAL value of the verb trace
is determined by the LOCAL value of the input verb. In Figure 9.10, *kennt* is the input
for the verb movement lexical rule. The relevant structure sharing ensures that, in the
analysis of (44), the LOCAL value of the verb trace corresponds exactly to what is given
in (48).

The most important points of the analysis of verb position are summarized below:

- A lexical rule licenses a special lexical item for each finite verb.

- This lexical item occupies the initial position and requires as its argument a complete projection of a verb trace.

- The projection of the verb trace must have a DSL value corresponding to the LOCAL
value of the input verb of the lexical rule.

- Since DSL is a head feature, the selected DSL value is also present on the trace.

- As the DSL value of the trace is identical to its LOCAL value, the LOCAL value of the
trace is identical to the LOCAL value of the input verb in the lexical rule.

After discussing the analysis of verb-first sentences, we will now turn to local reordering.

9.4 Local reordering

There are several possibilities for the analysis of constituent order in the middle field:
one can assume completely flat structures as in GPSG (Kasper 1994), or instead assume
binary branching structures and allow for arguments to be saturated in any order. A
compromise was proposed by Kathol (2001) and Müller (1999a, 2002a, 2004c): binary
branching structures with a special list that contains the arguments and adjuncts belonging to one head. The arguments and adjuncts are allowed to be freely ordered inside

such lists. See Reape (1994) and Section 11.7.2.2 of this book for the formal details of these approaches. Both the completely flat analysis and the compromise have proved to be on the wrong track (see Müller 2005b, 2014c and Müller 2007b: Section 9.5.1) and therefore, I will only discuss the analysis with binary branching structures.

Figure 9.11 shows the analysis of (51a).

(51) a. [weil]   jeder   diesen Mann kennt
          because everyone this   man   knows

     b. [weil]   diesen Mann jeder   kennt
          because this   man   everyone knows

        'because everyone knows this man'

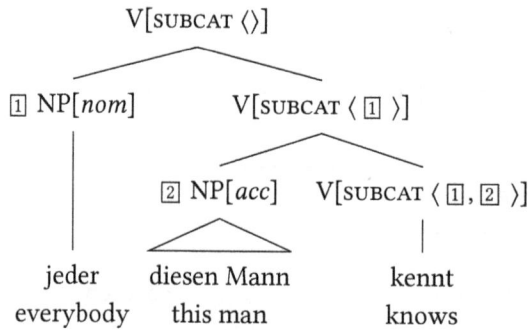

Figure 9.11: Analysis of constituent order in HPSG: unmarked order

The arguments of the verb are combined with the verb starting with the last element of the SUBCAT list, as explained in Section 9.1.2. The analysis of the marked order is shown in Figure 9.12. Both trees differ only in the order in which the elements are taken off

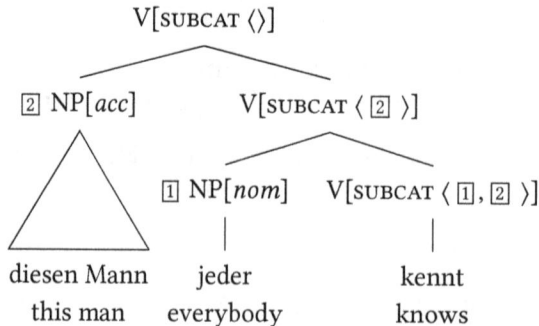

Figure 9.12: Analysis of constituent order in HPSG: marked order

from the SUBCAT list: in Figure 9.11, the last element of the SUBCAT list is discharged first and in Figure 9.12 the first one is.

The following schema is a revised version of the Head-Argument Schema:

Schema 3 (Head-Argument Schema (binary branching))

head-argument-phrase $\Rightarrow$
$$\begin{bmatrix} \text{SYNSEM|LOC|CAT|SUBCAT} \boxed{1} \oplus \boxed{3} \\ \text{HEAD-DTR|SYNSEM|LOC|CAT|SUBCAT} \boxed{1} \oplus \langle\, \boxed{2}\, \rangle \oplus \boxed{3} \\ \text{NON-HEAD-DTRS} \, \langle\, [\, \text{SYNSEM} \boxed{2}\,]\, \rangle \end{bmatrix}$$

Whereas in the first version of the Head-Argument Schema it was always the last element from the SUBCAT list that was combined with the head, the SUBCAT list is divided into three parts using *append*: a list of arbitrary length ($\boxed{1}$), a list consisting of exactly one element ($\langle\, \boxed{2}\, \rangle$) and a further list of arbitrary length ($\boxed{3}$). The lists $\boxed{1}$ and $\boxed{3}$ are combined and the result is the SUBCAT value of the mother node.

Languages with fixed constituent order (such as English) differ from languages such as German in that they discharge the arguments starting from one side (for more on the subject in English, see Section 9.6.1), whereas languages with free constituent order can combine arguments with the verb in any order. In languages with fixed constituent order, either $\boxed{1}$ or $\boxed{3}$ is always the empty list. Since German structures are not restricted with regard to $\boxed{1}$ or $\boxed{3}$, that is $\boxed{1}$ and $\boxed{3}$ can either be the empty list or contain elements, the intuition is captured that there are less restrictions in languages with free constituent order than in languages with fixed order. We can compare this to the Kayneian analysis from Section 4.6.1, where it was assumed that all languages are derived from the base order [specifier [head complement]] (see Figure 4.20 on page 144 for Laenzlinger's analysis of German as an SVO-language (Laenzlinger 2004)). In these kinds of analyses, languages such as English constitute the most basic case and languages with free ordering require some considerable theoretical effort to get the order right. In comparison to that, the analysis proposed here requires more theoretical restrictions if the language has more restrictions on permutations of its constituents. The complexity of the licensed structures does not differ considerably from language to language under an HPSG approach. Languages differ only in the type of branching they have.[19, 20]

The analysis presented here utilizing the combination of arguments in any order is similar to that of Fanselow (2001) in the framework of GB/MP as well as the Categorial Grammar analyses of Hoffman (1995: Section 3.1) and Steedman & Baldridge (2006). Gunji proposed similar HPSG analyses for Japanese as early as 1986.

---

[19] This does not exclude that the structures in question have different properties as far as their processability by humans is concerned. See Gibson (1998); Hawkins (1999) and Chapter 15.

[20] Haider (1997b: 18) has pointed out that the branching type of VX languages differs from those of XV languages in analyses of the kind that is proposed here. This affects the c-command relations and therefore has implications for Binding Theory in GB/MP. However, the direction of branching is irrelevant for HPSG analyses as Binding Principles are defined using o-command (Pollard & Sag 1994: Chapter 6) and o-command makes reference to the Obliqueness Hierarchy, that is, the order of elements in the SUBCAT list rather than the order in which these elements are combined with the head.

9.5 Long-distance dependencies

The analysis of long-distance dependencies utilizes techniques that were originally developed in GPSG: information about missing constituents is passed up the tree (or feature structure).[21] There is a trace at the position where the fronted element would normally occur. Figure 9.13 shows the analysis of (52).

(52) [Diesen Mann]$_j$ kennt$_i$ $\_j$ jeder $\_i$.
     this   man   knows   everyone

     'Everyone knows this man.'

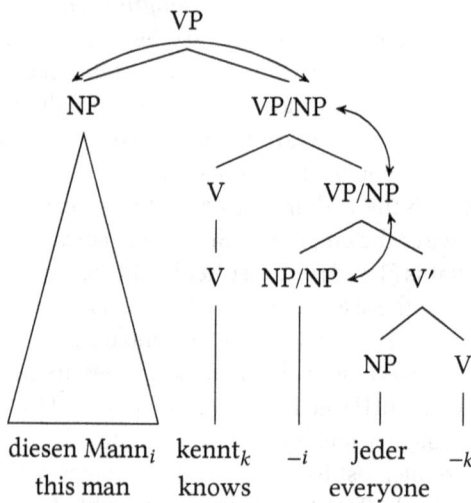

Figure 9.13: Analysis of long-distance dependencies in HPSG

In principle, one could also assume that the object is extracted from its unmarked position (see Section 3.5 on the unmarked position). The extraction trace would then follow the subject:

(53) [Diesen Mann]$_j$ kennt$_i$ jeder $\_j$ $\_i$.
     this   man   knows everyone

     'Everyone knows this man.'

---

[21] In HPSG, nothing is actually 'passed up' in a literal sense in feature structures or trees. This could be seen as one of the most important differences between deterministic (e.g., HPSG) and derivational theories like transformational grammars (see Section 15.1). Nevertheless, it makes sense for expository purposes to explain the analysis as if the structure were built bottom-up, but linguistic knowledge is independent of the direction of processing. In recent computer implementations, structure building is mostly carried out bottom-up but there were other systems which worked top-down. The only thing that is important in the analysis of nonlocal dependencies is that the information about the missing element on all intermediate nodes is identical to the information in the filler and the gap.

Fanselow (2004c) argues that certain phrases can be placed in the Vorfeld without having a special pragmatic function. For instance, (expletive) subjects in active sentences (54a), temporal adverbials (54b), sentence adverbials (54c), dative objects of psychological verbs (54d) and objects in passives (54e) can be placed in the Vorfeld, even though they are neither topic nor focus.

(54) a. Es regnet.
          it rains
          'It rains.'

      b. Am Sonntag hat ein Eisbär   einen Mann gefressen.
          on Sunday has a   polar.bear a   man eaten
          'On Sunday, a polar bear ate a man.'

      c. Vielleicht hat der Schauspieler seinen Text vergessen.
          perhaps   has the actor   his   text forgotten
          'Perhaps, the actor has forgotton his text.'

      d. Einem Schauspieler ist der   Text entfallen.
          a.DAT actor   is the.NOM text forgotten
          'An actor forgot the text.'

      e. Einem Kind wurde das   Fahrrad gestohlen.
          a.DAT child was the.NOM bike   stolen
          'A bike was stolen from a child.'

Fanselow argues that information structural effects can be due to reordering in the Mittelfeld. So by ordering the accusative object as in (55), one can reach certain effects:

(55) Kennt diesen Mann jeder?
      knows this   man everybody
      'Does everybody know this man?'

If one assumes that there are frontings to the *Vorfeld* that do not have information structural constraints attached to them and that information structural constraints are associated with reorderings in the Mittelfeld, then the assumption that the initial element in the Mittelfeld is fronted explains why the examples in (54) are not information structurally marked. The elements in the Vorfeld are unmarked in the initial position in the Mittelfeld as well:

(56) a. Regnet es?
          rains it
          'Does it rains?'

      b. Hat am Sonntag ein Eisbär   einen Mann gefressen?
          has on Sunday a   polar.bear a   man eaten
          'Did a polar bear eat a man on Sunday?'

    c. Hat vielleicht der Schauspieler seinen Text vergessen?
       has perhaps the actor   his   text forgotten

      'Has the actor perhaps forgotton his text?'

    d. Ist einem Schauspieler der   Text entfallen?
       is a.DAT actor   the.NOM text forgotten

      'Did an actor forget the text?'

    e. Wurde einem Kind das   Fahrrad gestohlen?
       was   a.DAT child the.NOM bike   stolen

      'Was a bike stolen from a child?'

So, I assume that the trace of a fronted argument that would not be Mittelfeld-initial in the unmarked order is combined with the head last, as described in Section 9.4. Of course, the same applies to all extracted arguments that would be Mittelfeld-initial in the unmarked order anyway: the traces are combined last with the head as for instance in (57):

(57) [Jeder]$_j$ kennt$_i$ $_{-j}$ diesen Mann $_{-i}$.
      everybody knows   this   man

    'Everyone knows this man.'

After this rough characterization of the basic idea, we now turn to the technical details: unlike verb movement, which was discussed in Section 9.3, constituent movement is nonlocal, which is why the two movement types are modeled with different features (SLASH vs. DSL). DSL is a head feature and, like all other head features, projects to the highest node of a projection (for more on the Head Feature Principle, see page 266). SLASH, on the other hand, is a feature that belongs to the NONLOC features represented under SYNSEM|NONLOC. The value of the NONLOC feature is a structure with the features INHERITED (or INHER for short) and TO-BIND. The value of INHER is a structure containing information about elements involved in a long-distance dependency. (58) gives the structure assumed by Pollard & Sag (1994: 163):[22]

(58)
$$
\begin{bmatrix}
\textit{nonloc} \\
\text{QUE} & \textit{list of npros} \\
\text{REL} & \textit{list of indices} \\
\text{SLASH} & \textit{list of local structures}
\end{bmatrix}
$$

QUE is important for the analysis of interrogative clauses as is REL for the analysis of relative clauses. Since these will not feature in this book, they will be omitted in what follows. The value of SLASH is a list of *local* objects.

    As with the analysis of verb movement, it is assumed that there is a trace in the position where the accusative object would normally occur and that this trace shares the properties of that object. The verb can therefore satisfy its valence requirements locally.

---

[22] Pollard & Sag assume that the values of QUE, REL, and SLASH are sets rather than lists. The math behind sets is rather complicated, which is why I assume lists here.

Information about whether there has been combination with a trace and not with a genuine argument is represented inside the complex sign and passed upward in the tree. The long-distance dependency can then be resolved by an element in the prefield higher in the tree.

Long-distance dependencies are introduced by the trace, which has a feature corresponding to the LOCAL value of the required argument in its SLASH list. (59) shows the description of the trace as is required for the analysis of (52):

(59)   Trace of the accusative object of *kennen* (preliminary):

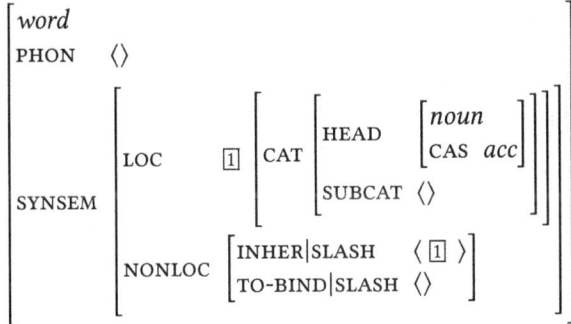

$$
\begin{bmatrix}
word \\
\text{PHON} \quad \langle\rangle \\
\text{SYNSEM} \begin{bmatrix}
\text{LOC} \quad \boxed{1} \begin{bmatrix}
\text{CAT} \begin{bmatrix}
\text{HEAD} \begin{bmatrix} noun \\ \text{CAS } acc \end{bmatrix} \\
\text{SUBCAT } \langle\rangle
\end{bmatrix}
\end{bmatrix} \\
\text{NONLOC} \begin{bmatrix}
\text{INHER|SLASH} \quad \langle \boxed{1} \rangle \\
\text{TO-BIND|SLASH} \quad \langle\rangle
\end{bmatrix}
\end{bmatrix}
\end{bmatrix}
$$

Since traces do not have internal structure (no daughters), they are of type *word*. The trace has the same properties as the accusative object. The fact that the accusative object is not present at the position occupied by the trace is represented by the value of SLASH.

The following principle is responsible for ensuring that NONLOC information is passed up the tree.

Principle 3 (Nonlocal Feature Principle)
In a headed phrase, for each nonlocal feature, the INHERITED *value of the mother is a list that is the concatenation of the* INHERITED *values of the daughters minus the elements in the* TO-BIND *list of the head daughter.*

The Head-Filler Schema (Schema 4) licenses the highest node in Figure 9.14 on the next page. The schema combines a finite, verb-initial clause (INITIAL+) that has an element in SLASH with a non-head daughter whose LOCAL value is identical to the SLASH element. In this structure, no arguments are saturated. Nothing can be extracted from the filler daughter itself, which is ensured by the specification of the SLASH value of the non-head daughter. Figure 9.14 shows a more detailed variant of the analysis of fronting to the prefield. The verb movement trace for *kennt* 'knows' is combined with a nominative NP and an extraction trace. The extraction trace stands for the accusative object in our example. The accusative object is described in the SUBCAT list of the verb ($\boxed{4}$). Following the mechanism for verb movement, the valence information that was originally contained in the entry for *kennt* ($\langle \boxed{3}, \boxed{4} \rangle$) is present on the verb trace. The combination of the projection of the verb trace with the extraction trace works in exactly the same way as for non-fronted arguments. The SLASH value of the extraction trace is passed up the tree and bound off by the Head-Filler Schema.

Schema 4 (Head-Filler Schema)

head-filler-phrase ⇒

$$
\begin{bmatrix}
\text{HEAD-DTR|SYNSEM} & \begin{bmatrix} \text{LOC|CAT} & \begin{bmatrix} \text{HEAD} & \begin{bmatrix} verb \\ \text{VFORM} & fin \\ \text{INITIAL} & + \end{bmatrix} \\ \text{SUBCAT} \langle \rangle \end{bmatrix} \\ \text{NONLOC} & \begin{bmatrix} \text{INHER|SLASH} & \langle \boxed{1} \rangle \\ \text{TO-BIND|SLASH} & \langle \boxed{1} \rangle \end{bmatrix} \end{bmatrix} \\
\text{NON-HEAD-DTRS} & \left\langle \begin{bmatrix} \text{SYNSEM} & \begin{bmatrix} \text{LOC} \; \boxed{1} \\ \text{NONLOC|INHER|SLASH} \langle \rangle \end{bmatrix} \end{bmatrix} \right\rangle
\end{bmatrix}
$$

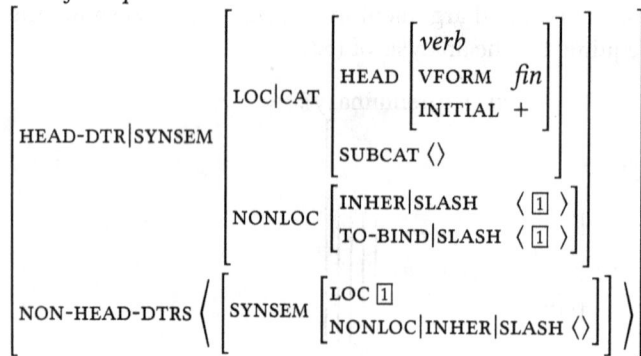

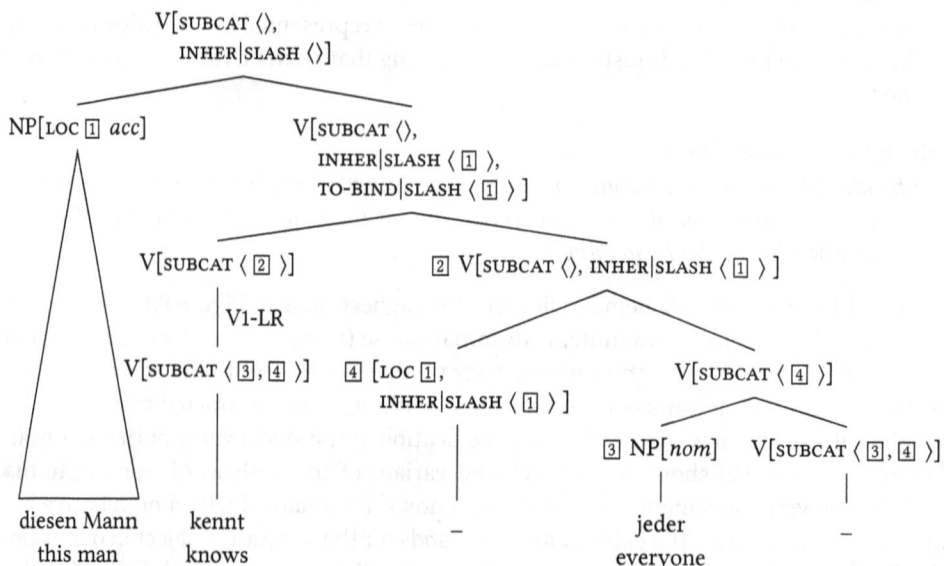

Figure 9.14: Analysis of *Diesen Mann kennt jeder.* 'Everyone knows this man.' combined with the verb movement analysis for verb-initial order

(59) provides the lexical entry for a trace that can function as the accusative object of *kennen* 'to know'. As with the analysis of verb movement, it is not necessary to have numerous extraction traces with differing properties listed in the lexicon. A more general entry such as the one in (60) will suffice:

(60)   Extraction trace:

$$
\begin{bmatrix}
word \\
\text{PHON} \quad \langle\rangle \\
\text{SYNSEM} \begin{bmatrix} \text{LOC} \quad \boxed{1} \\ \text{NONLOC} \begin{bmatrix} \text{INHER|SLASH} \quad \langle \boxed{1} \rangle \\ \text{TO-BIND|SLASH} \quad \langle\rangle \end{bmatrix} \end{bmatrix}
\end{bmatrix}
$$

This has to do with the fact that the head can satisfactorily determine the LOCAL properties of its arguments and therefore also the local properties of the traces that it combines with. The identification of the object in the SUBCAT list of the head with the SYNSEM value of the trace coupled with the identification of the information in SLASH with information about the fronted element serves to ensure that the only elements that can be realized in the prefield are those that fit the description in the SUBCAT list of the head. The same holds for fronted adjuncts: since the LOCAL value of the constituent in the prefield is identified with the LOCAL value of the trace via the SLASH feature, there is then sufficient information available about the properties of the trace.

The central points of the preceding analysis can be summarized as follows: information about the local properties of a trace is contained in the trace itself and then present on all nodes dominating it until one reaches the filler. This analysis can offer an explanation for so-called extraction path marking languages where certain elements show inflection depending on whether they are combined with a constituent out of which something has been extracted in a long-distance dependency. Bouma, Malouf & Sag (2001a) cite Irish, Chamorro, Palauan, Icelandic, Kikuyu, Ewe, Thompson Salish, Moore, French, Spanish, and Yiddish as examples of such languages and provide corresponding references. Since information is passed on step-by-step in HPSG analyses, all nodes intervening in a long-distance dependency can access the elements in that dependency.

9.6 New developments and theoretical variants

This section discusses refinements of the representation of valence information in Subsection 9.6.1 and briefly mentions an important variant of HPSG, namely Linearization-based HPSG in Subsection 9.6.2.

9.6.1 Specifier, complements and argument structure

In this chapter, SUBCAT was assumed as the only valence feature. This corresponds to the state of theory in Pollard & Sag (1994: Chapter 1–8). It has turned out to be desirable to assume at least one additional valence feature and a corresponding schema for the combination of constituents. This additional feature is called SPECIFIER (SPR) and is used in grammars of English (Pollard & Sag 1994: Chapter 9) and German (Müller 2007b: Section 9.3) for the combination of a determiner with a noun. It is assumed that the noun selects its determiner. For the noun *Zerstörung* 'destruction', we have the following CAT value:

$$
(61) \quad
\begin{bmatrix}
\text{HEAD} & \begin{bmatrix} noun \\ \text{INITIAL } + \end{bmatrix} \\
\text{SPR} & \langle \text{DET} \rangle \\
\text{SUBCAT} & \langle \text{NP[GEN], PP[}durch\text{] } \rangle
\end{bmatrix}
$$

Schema 5 can be used just like the Head-Argument Schema for the combination of noun and determiner.

Schema 5 (Specifier-Head Schema)

$$
head\text{-}specifier\text{-}phrase \Rightarrow
\begin{bmatrix}
\text{SYNSEM|LOC|CAT|SPR} \; \boxed{1} \\
\text{HEAD-DTR|SYNSEM|LOC|CAT} \begin{bmatrix} \text{SPR} & \boxed{1} \oplus \langle \boxed{2} \rangle \\ \text{SUBCAT} & \langle \rangle \end{bmatrix} \\
\text{NON-HEAD-DTRS} \; \langle \; [\text{SYNSEM} \; \boxed{2} \;] \; \rangle
\end{bmatrix}
$$

The analysis of the NP in (62) with the Specifier Schema is shown in Figure 9.15 on the following page.

(62)   die Zerstörung der   Stadt durch die Soldaten
       the destruction of.the city   by   the soldiers

Following the linearization rules discussed in Section 9.1.3, it is ensured that the noun occurs before the complements as the INITIAL value of the noun is '+'. The LP-rule in (63) leads to the determiner being ordered to the left of the noun.

(63)   specifier < head

In grammars of English, the SPR feature is also used for the selection of the subject of verbs (Sag, Wasow & Bender 2003: Section 4.3). In a sentence such as (64), the verb is first combined with all its complements (the elements in the SUBCAT or COMPS in newer works) and is then combined with the subject in a second step by applying Schema 5.

(64)   Max likes ice cream.

As we have seen in Section 9.4, it makes sense to represent subjects and arguments in the same valence list for the analysis of finite sentences. In this way, the fact can be captured that the order in which a verb is combined with its arguments is not fixed. While the different orders could also be captured by assuming that the subject is selected via

N[SPR ⟨ ⟩,
    SUBCAT ⟨ ⟩]

[1] Det

N[SPR ⟨ [1] ⟩,
    SUBCAT ⟨ ⟩]

N[SPR ⟨ [1] ⟩,
    SUBCAT ⟨ [2] ⟩]

[2] PP[*durch*]

N[SPR ⟨ [1] ⟩,
    SUBCAT ⟨ [2], [3] ⟩]

[3] NP[*gen*]

| die | Zerstörung | der Stadt | durch die Soldaten |
| the | destruction | of the city | by the soldiers |

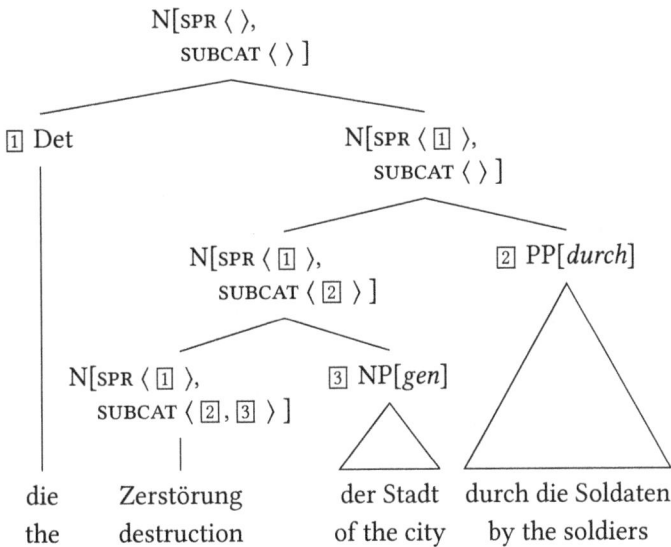

Figure 9.15: NP analysis with valence features SPR

SPR, the fact that scrambling is a phenomenon that affects all arguments in the same way would not be covered in a SPR-based analysis. Furthermore, the extraction out of subjects is impossible in languages like English, but it is possible in German (for references and attested examples see p. 530). This difference can be captured by assuming that subjects are selected via SPR in English and that extraction out of elements in the SPR list is prohibited. Since subjects in German are represented on the COMPS list, the fact that they pattern with the objects in terms of possible extractions is captured.

A further expansion from Pollard & Sag (1994: Chapter 9) is the introduction of an additional list that is called ARG-ST in newer works. ARG-ST stands for Argument Structure. The ARG-ST list corresponds to what we encountered as SUBCAT list in this chapter. It contains the arguments of a head in an order corresponding to the Obliqueness Hierarchy. The elements of the list are linked to argument roles in the semantic content of the head (see Section 9.1.6). Binding Theory operates on the ARG-ST list. This level of representation is probably the same for most languages: in every language there are semantic predicates and semantic arguments. Most languages make use of syntactic categories that play a role in selection, so there is both syntactic and semantic selection.[23] Languages differ with regard to how these arguments are realized. In English, the first element in the valence list is mapped to the SPR list and the remaining arguments to the SUBCAT (or COMPS list in more recent work). In German, the SPR list of verbs remains empty. (65) shows some relevant examples for German and English.

---

[23] Koenig & Michelson (2012) argue for an analysis of Oneida (a Northern Iroquoian language) that does not include a representation of syntactic valence. If this analysis is correct, syntactic argument structure would not be universal, but would be characteristic for a large number of languages.

(65) a.

$$
\begin{bmatrix}
\text{PHON} \ \langle \ schlag \ \rangle \\
\text{SYNSEM|LOC}
\begin{bmatrix}
\text{CAT}
\begin{bmatrix}
\text{HEAD} & verb \\
\text{SPR} & \langle\rangle \\
\text{SUBCAT} & \boxed{1} \\
\text{ARG-ST} & \boxed{1} \ \langle \ \text{NP}[str]_{\boxed{2}}, \text{NP}[str]_{\boxed{3}} \ \rangle
\end{bmatrix} \\
\text{CONT}
\begin{bmatrix}
\text{IND} & \boxed{4} \ event \\
\text{RELS} & \left\langle
\begin{bmatrix}
schlagen \\
\text{EVENT} & \boxed{4} \\
\text{AGENT} & \boxed{2} \\
\text{PATIENT} & \boxed{3}
\end{bmatrix}
\right\rangle
\end{bmatrix}
\end{bmatrix}
\end{bmatrix}
$$

b.

$$
\begin{bmatrix}
\text{PHON} \ \langle \ beat \ \rangle \\
\text{SYNSEM|LOC}
\begin{bmatrix}
\text{CAT}
\begin{bmatrix}
\text{HEAD} & verb \\
\text{SPR} & \langle \ \boxed{1} \ \rangle \\
\text{SUBCAT} & \boxed{2} \\
\text{ARG-ST} & \langle \ \boxed{1} \ \text{NP}[str]_{\boxed{3}} \ \rangle \oplus \boxed{2} \ \langle \ \text{NP}[str]_{\boxed{4}} \ \rangle
\end{bmatrix} \\
\text{CONT}
\begin{bmatrix}
\text{IND} & \boxed{5} \ event \\
\text{RELS} & \left\langle
\begin{bmatrix}
beat \\
\text{EVENT} & \boxed{5} \\
\text{AGENT} & \boxed{3} \\
\text{PATIENT} & \boxed{4}
\end{bmatrix}
\right\rangle
\end{bmatrix}
\end{bmatrix}
\end{bmatrix}
$$

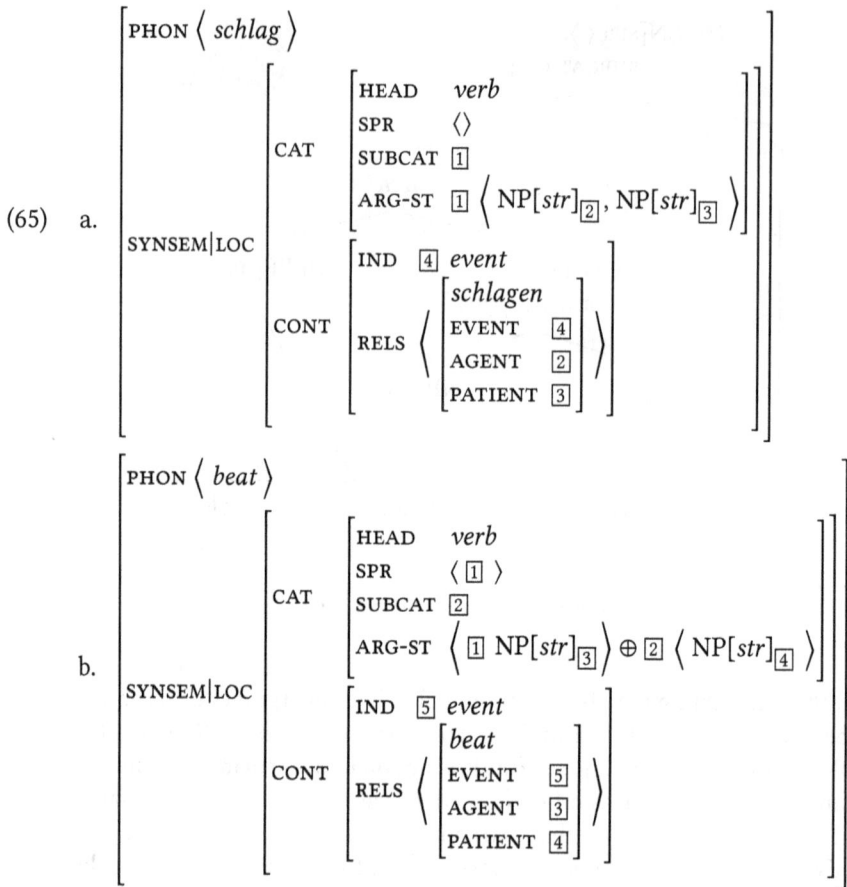

One can view the ARG-ST list as the equivalent to Deep Structure in GB theory: semantic roles are assigned with reference to this list. The difference is that there is no ordered tree that undergoes transformations. The question of whether all languages can be derived from either VO or OV order therefore becomes irrelevant.

9.6.2 Linearization-based HPSG

The schemata that were presented in this chapter combine adjacent constituents. The assumption of adjacency can be dropped and discontinuous constituents maybe permitted. Variants of HPSG that allow for discontinuous constituents are usually referred to as *Linearization-based HPSG*. The first formalization was developed by Mike Reape (1991, 1992, 1994). Proponents of linearization approaches are for instance Kathol (1995, 2000); Donohue & Sag (1999); Richter & Sailer (1999b); Crysmann (2008); Beavers & Sag (2004); Sato (2006); Wetta (2011). I also suggested linearization-based analyses (Müller 1999a, 2002a) and implemented a large-scale grammar fragment based on Reape's ideas (Müller 1996c). Linearization-based approaches to the German sentence structure are similar to the GPSG approach in that it is assumed that verb and arguments and adjuncts are members of the same linearization domain and hence may be realized in any order. For instance, the verb may precede arguments and adjuncts or follow them. Hence, no empty element for the verb in final position is necessary. While this allows for grammars without empty elements for the analysis of the verb position, it is unclear how examples with apparent multiple frontings can be accounted for, while such data can be captured directly in the proposal suggested in this chapter. The whole issue is discussed in more detail in Müller (2015b). I will not explain Reape's formalization here, but defer its discussion until Section 11.7.2.2, where the discontinuous, non-projective structures of some Dependency Grammars are compared to linearization-based HPSG approaches. Apparent multiple frontings and the problems they pose for simple linearization-based approaches are discussed in Section 11.7.1.

9.7 Summary and classification

In HPSG, feature descriptions are used to model all properties of linguistic objects: roots, words, lexical rules and dominance schemata are all described using the same formal tools. Unlike GPSG and LFG, there are no separate phrase structure rules. Thus, although HPSG stands for Head-Driven Phrase Structure Grammar, it is not a phrase structure grammar. In HPSG implementations, a phrase structure backbone is often used to increase the efficiency of processing. However, this is not part of the theory and linguistically not necessary.

HPSG differs from Categorial Grammar in that it assumes considerably more features and also in that the way in which features are grouped plays an important role for the theory.

Long-distance dependencies are not analyzed using function composition as in Categorial Grammar, but instead as in GPSG by appealing to the percolation of information in the tree. In this way, it is possible to analyze pied-piping constructions such as those discussed in Section 8.6 with just one lexical item per relative pronoun, whose relevant local properties are identical to those of the demonstrative pronoun. The relative clause in (66) would be analyzed as a finite clause from which a PP has been extracted:

(66) der Mann, [RS [PP an den] [S/PP wir gedacht haben]]
      the man   on who   we thought have
      'the man we thought of'

For relative clauses, it is required that the first daughter contains a relative pronoun. This can, as shown in the English examples on page 251, be in fact very deeply embedded. Information about the fact that *an den* 'of whom' contains a relative pronoun is provided in the lexical entry for the relative pronoun *den* by specifying the value of NONLOC| INHER|REL. The Nonlocal Feature Principle passes this information on upwards so that the information about the relative pronoun is contained in the representation of the phrase *an den*. This information is bound off when the relative clause is put together (Pollard & Sag 1994: Chapter 5; Sag 1997). It is possible to use the same lexical entry for *den* in the analyses of both (66) and (67) as – unlike in Categorial Grammar – the relative pronoun does not have to know anything about the contexts in which it can be used.

(67) der Mann, [$_{RS}$ [$_{NP}$ den] [$_{S/NP}$ wir kennen]]
      the man   that   we know

'the man that we know'

Any theory that wants to maintain the analysis sketched here will have to have some mechanism to make information available about the relative pronoun in a complex phrase. If we have such a mechanism in our theory – as is the case in LFG and HPSG – then we can also use it for the analysis of long-distance dependencies. Theories such as LFG and HPSG are therefore more parsimonious with their descriptive tools than other theories when it comes to the analysis of relative phrases.

In the first decade of HPSG history (Pollard & Sag 1987, 1994; Nerbonne, Netter & Pollard 1994), despite the differences already mentioned here, HPSG was still very similar to Categorial Grammar in that it was a strongly lexicalized theory. The syntactic make-up and semantic content of a phrase was determined by the head (hence the term *head-driven*). In cases where head-driven analyses were not straight-forwardly possible, because no head could be identified in the phrase in question, then it was commonplace to assume empty heads. An example of this is the analysis of relative clauses in Pollard & Sag (1994: Chapter 5). Since an empty head can be assigned any syntactic valence and an arbitrary semantics (for discussion of this point, see Chapter 19), one has not really explained anything as one needs very good reasons for assuming an empty head, for example that this empty position can be realized in other contexts. This is, however, not the case for empty heads that are only proposed in order to save theoretical assumptions. Therefore, Sag (1997) developed an analysis of relative clauses without any empty elements. As in the analyses sketched for (66) and (67), the relative phrases are combined directly with the partial clause in order to form the relative clause. For the various observable types of relative clauses in English, Sag proposes different dominance rules. His analysis constitutes a departure from strong lexicalism: in Pollard & Sag (1994), there are six dominance schemata, whereas there are 23 in Ginzburg & Sag (2000).

The tendency to a differentiation of phrasal schemata can also be observed in the proceedings of recent conferences. The proposals range from the elimination of empty elements to radically phrasal analyses (Haugereid 2007, 2009).[24]

Even if this tendency towards phrasal analyses may result in some problematic analyses, it is indeed the case that there are areas of grammar where phrasal analyses are required (see Section 21.10). For HPSG, this means that it is no longer entirely head-driven and is therefore neither Head-Driven nor Phrase Structure Grammar.

HPSG makes use of typed feature descriptions to describe linguistic objects. Generalizations can be expressed by means of hierarchies with multiple inheritance. Inheritance also plays an important role in Construction Grammar. In theories such as GPSG, Categorial Grammar and TAG, it does not form part of theoretical explanations. In implementations, macros (abbreviations) are often used for co-occurring feature-value pairs

---

[24] For discussion, see Müller (2007c) and Section 21.3.6.

(Dalrymple, Kaplan & King 2004). Depending on the architecture assumed, such macros are not suitable for the description of phrases since, in theories such as GPSG and LFG, phrase structure rules are represented differently from other feature-value pairs (however, see Asudeh, Dalrymple & Toivonen (2008, 2013) for macros and inheritance used for c-structure annotations). Furthermore, there are further differences between types and macros, which are of a more formal nature: in a typed system, it is possible under certain conditions to infer the type of a particular structure from the presence of certain features and of certain values. With macros, this is not the case as they are only abbreviations. The consequences for linguistic analyses made by this differences are, however, minimal.

HPSG differs from GB theory and later variants in that it does not assume transformations. In the 80s, representational variants of GB were proposed, that is, it was assumed that there was no D-structure from which an S-structure is created by simultaneous marking of the original position of moved elements. Instead, one assumed the S-structure with traces straight away and the assumption that there were further movements in the mapping of S-structure to Logical Form was also abandoned (Koster 1978; Haider 1993: Section 1.4; Frey 1993: 14). This view corresponds to the view in HPSG and many of the analyses in one framework can be translated into the other.

In GB theory, the terms subject and object do not play a direct role: one can use these terms descriptively, but subjects and objects are not marked by features or similar devices. Nevertheless it is possible to make the distinction since subjects and objects are usually realized in different positions in the trees (the subject in specifier position of IP and the object as the complement of the verb). In HPSG, subject and object are also not primitives of the theory. Since valence lists (or ARG-ST lists) are ordered, however, this means that it is possible to associate the ARG-ST elements to grammatical functions: if there is a subject, this occurs in the first position of the valence list and objects follow.[25] For the analysis of (68b) in a transformation-based grammar, the aim is to connect the base order in (68a) and the derived order in (68b). Once one has recreated the base order, then it is clear what is the subject and what is the object. Therefore, transformations applied to the base structure in (68a) have to be reversed.

(68) a. [weil]   jeder   diesen Mann kennt
          because everyone this   man   knows

      'because everyone knows this man'

      b. [weil]   diesen Mann jeder   kennt
          because this   man   everyone knows

In HPSG and also in other transformation-less models, the aim is to assign arguments in the order in (68b) to descriptions in the valence list. The valence list (or ARG-ST in newer approaches) corresponds in a sense to Deep Structure in GB. The difference is that the

---

[25] When forming complex predicates, an object can occur in first position. See Müller (2002a: 157) for the long passive with verbs such as *erlauben* 'allow'. In general, the following holds: the subject is the first argument with structural case.

head itself is not included in the argument structure, whereas this is the case with D-structure.

Bender (2008c) has shown how one can analyze phenomena from non-configurational languages such as Wambaya by referring to the argument structure of a head. In Wambaya, words that would normally be counted as constituents in English or German can occur discontinuously, that is an adjective that semantically belongs to a noun phrase and shares the same case, number and gender values with other parts of the noun phrase can occur in a position in the sentence that is not adjacent to the remaining noun phrase. Nordlinger (1998) has analyzed the relevant data in LFG. In her analysis, the various parts of the constituent refer to the f-structure of the sentence and thus indirectly ensure that all parts of the noun phrase have the same case. Bender adopts a variant of HPSG where valence information is not removed from the valence list after an argument has been combined with its head, but rather this information remains in the valence list and is passed up towards the maximal projection of the head (Meurers 1999c; Przepiórkowski 1999b; Müller 2007b: Section 17.4). Similar proposals were made in GB by Higginbotham (1985: 560) and Winkler (1997). By projecting the complete valence information, it remains accessible in the entire sentence and discontinuous constituents can refer to it (e.g., via MOD) and the respective constraints can be formulated.[26] In this analysis, the argument structure in HPSG corresponds to f-structure in LFG. The extended head domains of LFG, where multiple heads can share the same f-structure, can also be modeled in HPSG. To this end, one can utilize function composition as it was presented in the chapter on Categorial Grammar (see Chapter 8.5.2). The exact way in which this is translated into HPSG cannot be explained here due to space restrictions. The reader is referred to the original works by Hinrichs & Nakazawa (1994) and the explanation in Müller (2007b: Chapter 15).

Valence information plays an important role in HPSG. The lexical item of a verb in principle predetermines the set of structures in which the item can occur. Using lexical rules, it is possible to relate one lexical item to other lexical items. These can be used in other sets of structures. So one can see the functionality of lexical rules in establishing a relation between sets of possible structures. Lexical rules correspond to transformations in Transformational Grammar. This point is discussed in more detail in Section 19.5. The effect of lexical rules can also be achieved with empty elements. This will also be the matter of discussion in Section 19.5.

In GPSG, metarules were used to license rules that created additional valence patterns for lexical heads. In principle, metarules could also be applied to rules without a lexical head. This is explicitly ruled out by Flickinger (1983) and Gazdar et al. (1985: 59) using a special constraint. Flickinger, Pollard & Wasow (1985: 265) pointed out that this kind of constraint is unnecessary if one uses lexical rules rather than metarules since the former can only be applied to lexical heads.

For a comparison of HPSG and Stabler's Minimalist Grammars, see Section 4.6.4.

---

[26] See also Müller (2008) for an analysis of depictive predicates in German and English that makes reference to the list of realized or unrealized arguments of a head, respectively. This analysis is also explained in Section 18.2.

Comprehension questions

1. What status do syntactic trees have in HPSG?

2. How does case assignment take place in the analysis of example (69)?

    (69)   Dem   Mann wurde ein   Buch geschenkt.
            the.DAT man was   a.NOM book given
            'The man was given a book.'

3. What is *linking* and how is it accounted for in HPSG?

Exercises

1. Give a feature description for (70) ignoring *dass*.

    (70)   [dass] Max lacht
            that Max laughs

2. The analysis of the combination of a noun with a modifying adjective in Section 9.1.7 was just a sketch of an analysis. It is, for example, not explained how one can ensure that the adjective and noun agree in case. Consider how it would be possible to expand such an analysis so that the adjective-noun combination in (71a) can be analyzed, but not the one in (71b):

    (71)   a.   eines   interessanten   Mannes
                 an.GEN interesting.GEN man.GEN

         b. * eines   interessanter   Mannes
                 an.GEN interesting.NOM man.GEN

Further reading

Here, the presentation of the individual parts of the theory was – as with other theories – kept relatively short. For a more comprehensive introduction to HPSG, including motivation of the feature geometry, see Müller (2007b). In particular, the analysis of the passive was sketched in brief here. The entire story including the analysis of unaccusative verbs, adjectival participles, modal infinitives as well as diverse passive variants and the long passive can be found in Müller (2002a: Chapter 3) and Müller (2007b: Chapter 17).

Overviews of HPSG can be found in Levine & Meurers (2006), Przepiórkowski & Kupść (2006), Bildhauer (2014) and Müller (2015c).

10 Construction Grammar

Like LFG and HPSG, *Construction Grammar* (CxG) forms part of West Coast linguistics. It has been influenced considerably by Charles Fillmore, Paul Kay and George Lakoff (all three at Berkeley) and Adele Goldberg (who completed her PhD in Berkeley and is now in Princeton) (Fillmore 1988; Fillmore, Kay & O'Connor 1988; Kay & Fillmore 1999; Kay 2002, 2005; Goldberg 1995, 2006).

Fillmore, Kay, Jackendoff and others have pointed out the fact that, to a large extent, languages consist of complex units that cannot straightforwardly be described with the tools that we have seen thus far. In frameworks such as GB, an explicit distinction is made between core grammar and the periphery (Chomsky 1981a: 8), whereby the periphery is mostly disregarded as uninteresting when formulating a theory of Universal Grammar. The criticism leveled at such practices by CxG is justified since what counts as the 'periphery' sometimes seems completely arbitrary (Müller 2014d) and no progress is made by excluding large parts of the language from the theory just because they are irregular to a certain extent.

In Construction Grammar, idiomatic expressions are often discussed with regard to their interaction with regular areas of grammar. Kay & Fillmore (1999) studied the *What's X doing Y?*-construction in their classic essay. (1) contains some examples of this construction:

(1)   a.   What is this scratch doing on the table?
      b.   What do you think your name is doing in my book?

The examples show that we are clearly not dealing with the normal meaning of the verb *do*. As well as the semantic bleaching here, there are particular morphosyntactic properties that have to be satisfied in this construction. The verb *do* must always be present and also in the form of the present participle. Kay and Fillmore develop an analysis explaining this construction and also capturing some of the similarities between the WXDY-construction and the rest of the grammar.

There are a number of variants of Construction Grammar:

- Berkeley Construction Grammar (Fillmore 1988; Kay & Fillmore 1999; Fried 2015)

- Goldbergian/Lakovian Construction Grammar (Lakoff 1987; Goldberg 1995, 2006)

- Cognitive Grammar (Langacker 1987, 2000, 2008; Dąbrowska 2004)

- Radical Construction Grammar (Croft 2001)

- Embodied Construction Grammar (Bergen & Chang 2005)

- Fluid Construction Grammar (Steels & De Beule 2006; Steels 2011)

- Sign-Based Construction Grammar (Sag 2010, 2012)

The aim of Construction Grammar is to both describe and theoretically explore language in its entirety. In practice, however, irregularities in language are often given far more importance than the phenomena described as 'core grammar' in GB. Construction Grammar analyses usually analyze phenomena as phrasal patterns. These phrasal patterns are represented in inheritance hierarchies (e.g., Croft 2001; Goldberg 2003b). An example for the assumption of a phrasal construction is Goldberg's analysis of resultative constructions. Goldberg (1995) and Goldberg & Jackendoff (2004) argue for the construction status of resultatives. In their view, there is no head in (2) that determines the number of arguments.

(2) Willy watered the plants flat.

The number of arguments is determined by the construction instead, that is, by a rule or schema saying that the subject, verb, object and a predicative element must occur together and that the entire complex has a particular meaning. This view is fundamentally different from analyses in GB, Categorial Grammar, LFG[1] and HPSG. In the aforementioned theories, it is commonly assumed that arguments are always selected by lexical heads and not independently licensed by phrasal rules. See Simpson (1983), Neeleman (1994), Wunderlich (1997), Wechsler (1997), and Müller (2002a) for corresponding work in LFG, GB, Wunderlich's Lexical Decomposition Grammar and HPSG.

Like the theories discussed in Chapters 5–9, CxG is also a non-transformational theory. Furthermore, no empty elements are assumed in most variants of the theory and the assumption of lexical integrity is maintained as in LFG and HPSG. It can be shown that these assumptions are incompatible with phrasal analyses of resultative constructions (see Section 21.2.2 and Müller 2006, 2007c). This point will not be explained further here. Instead, I will discuss the work of Fillmore and Kay to prepare the reader to be able to read the original articles and subsequent publications. Although the literature on Construction Grammar is now relatively vast, there is very little work on the basic formal assumptions or analyses that have been formalized precisely. Examples of more formal works are Kay & Fillmore (1999), Kay (2002), Michaelis & Ruppenhofer (2001), and Goldberg (2003b). Another formal proposal was developed by Jean-Pierre Koenig (1999) (formerly Berkeley). This work is coached in the framework of HPSG, but it has been heavily influenced by CxG. Fillmore and Kay's revisions of their earlier work took place in close collaboration with Ivan Sag. The result was a variant of HPSG known as Sign-Based Construction Grammar (SBCG) (Sag 2010, 2012). See Section 10.6.2 for further discussion.

John Bryant, Nancy Chang, Eva Mok have developed a system for the implementation of Embodied Construction Grammar[2]. Luc Steels is working on the simulation of language evolution and language acquisition (Steels 2003). Steels works experimentally

---

[1] See Alsina (1996) and Asudeh, Dalrymple & Toivonen (2008, 2013), however. For more discussion of this point, see Sections 21.1.3 and 21.2.2.

[2] See http://www.icsi.berkeley.edu/~jbryant/old-analyzer.html and Bryant (2003).

modeling virtual communities of interacting agents. Apart from this he uses robots that
interact in language games (Steels 2015). In personal communication (p. c. 2007) Steels
stated that is is a long way to go until robots finally will be able to learn to speak but
the current state of the art is already impressive. Steels can use robots that have a visual system (camera and image processing) and use visual information paired with au-
dio information in simulations of language acquisition. The implementation of Fluid
Construction Grammar is documented in Steels (2011) and Steels (2012). The second
book contains parts about German, in which the implementation of German declarative
clauses and *w* interrogative clauses is explained with respect to topological fields (Micelli 2012). The FCG system, various publications and example analyses are available
at: http://www.fcg-net.org/. Jurafsky (1996) developed a Construction Grammar for English that was paired with a probabilistic component. He showed that many performance
phenomena discussed in the literature (see Chapter 15 on the Competence/Performance
Distinction) can be explained with recourse to probabilities of phrasal constructions and
valence properties of words. Bannard, Lieven & Tomasello (2009) use a probabilistic context-free grammar to model grammatical knowledge of two and three year old children.

10.1 General remarks on the representational format

In this section, I will discuss the mechanisms of Berkeley Construction Grammar (BCG).
As I pointed out in Müller (2006), there are fundamental problems with the formalization
of BCG. The details will be given in Section 10.6.1. While the framework was developed
further into Sign-Based Construction Grammar (see Section 10.6.2) by its creators Kay
and Fillmore, there are still authors working in the original framework (for instance
Fried 2013). I will therefore present the basic mechanisms here to make it possible to
understand the original ideas and put them into a broader context.

As we saw in Section 9.1.2, dominance relations in HPSG are modeled like other properties of linguistic objects using feature-value pairs. In general, CxG uses feature-value
pairs to describe linguistic objects, but dominance relations are represented by boxes
(Kay & Fillmore 1999; Goldberg 2003b):

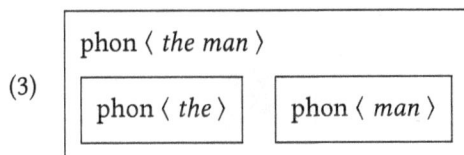

(3)
| phon ⟨ *the man* ⟩ |
| phon ⟨ *the* ⟩   phon ⟨ *man* ⟩ |

The structure can be written using feature-value pairs as follows:

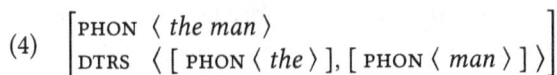

(4)
$$\begin{bmatrix} \text{PHON} & \langle \textit{the man} \rangle \\ \text{DTRS} & \langle\, [\, \text{PHON} \, \langle \textit{the} \rangle \,], [\, \text{PHON} \, \langle \textit{man} \rangle \,] \,\rangle \end{bmatrix}$$

10.1.1 The head-complement construction

Kay & Fillmore (1999) assume the following construction for the combination of heads
with their complements:

(5) Head plus Complements Construction (HC)

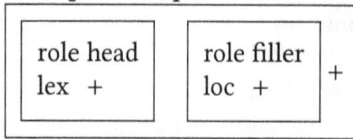

role head	role filler	
lex +	loc +	+

A head is combined with at least one complement (the '+' following the box stands for at least one sign that fits the description in that box). LOC+ means that this element must be realized locally. The value of ROLE tells us something about the role that a particular element plays in a construction. Unfortunately, here the term *filler* is used somewhat differently than in GPSG and HPSG. Fillers are not necessarily elements that stand in a long-distance dependency to a gap. Instead, a *filler* is a term for a constituent that fills the argument slot of a head.

The verb phrase construction is a sub-construction of the head-complement construction:

(6) Verb phrase Construction:

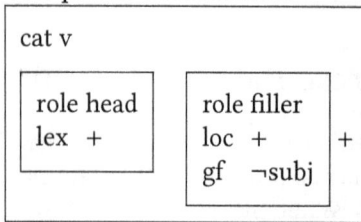

cat v

role head	role filler	
lex +	loc +	+
	gf ¬subj	

The syntactic category of the entire construction is V. Its complements cannot have the grammatical function subject.

The VP construction is a particular type of head-complement construction. The fact that it has much in common with the more general head-complement construction is represented as follows:

(7) Verb phrase Construction with inheritance statement:

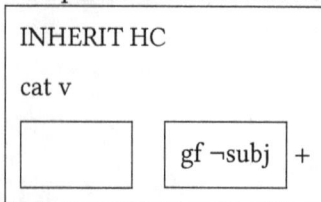

INHERIT HC

cat v

	gf ¬subj	+

This representation differs from the one in HPSG, aside from the box notation, only in the fact that feature descriptions are not typed and as such it must be explicitly stated in the representation from which superordinate construction inheritance takes place. HPSG – in addition to the schemata – has separate type hierarchies specifying the inheritance relation between types.

10.1.2 Representation of valence information

In Kay and Fillmore, valence information is represented in a set (VAL). The Valence Principle states that local filler-daughters have to be identified with an element in the valence set of the mother.[3] The Subset Principle states that the set values of the head-daughter are subsets of the corresponding sets of the mother. This is the exact opposite approach to the one taken in Categorial Grammar and HPSG. In HPSG grammars, valence lists at the mother nodes are shorter, whereas in Berkeley CxG at least as many elements are present on the mother node as on the head-daughter.

10.1.3 Semantics

Semantics in CxG is handled exactly the same way as in HPSG: semantic information is contained in the same feature structure as syntactic information. The relation between syntax and semantics is captured by using the same variable in the syntactic and semantic description. (8) contains a feature description for the verb *arrive*:

(8)   Lexical entry for *arrive* following Kay & Fillmore (1999: 11):

$$
\begin{bmatrix}
\text{cat} \ \ \text{v} \\[4pt]
\text{sem} \ \ \left\{ \begin{bmatrix} ^{\text{I}} \ \text{FRAME} \ \ \text{ARRIVE} \\ \ \ \text{ARGS} \ \ \ \{\,A\,\} \end{bmatrix} \right\} \\[8pt]
\text{val} \ \ \{\,[\,\text{SEM}\,\{\,A\,\}\,]\,\}
\end{bmatrix}
$$

Kay & Fillmore (1999: 9) refer to their semantic representations as a notational variant of the Minimal Recursion Semantics of Copestake, Flickinger, Pollard & Sag (2005). In later works, Kay (2005) explicitly uses MRS. As the fundamentals of MRS have already been discussed in Section 9.1.6, I will not repeat them here. For more on MRS, see Section 19.3.

10.1.4 Adjuncts

For the combination of heads and modifiers, Kay and Fillmore assume further phrasal constructions that are similar to the verb phrase constructions discussed above and create a relation between a head and a modifier. Kay and Fillmore assume that adjuncts also contribute something to the VAL value of the mother node. In principle, VAL is nothing more than the set of all non-head daughters in a tree.

10.2 Passive

The passive has been described in CxG by means of so-called linking constructions, which are combined with lexical entries in inheritance hierarchies. In the base lexicon, it is only listed which semantic roles a verb fulfils and the way in which these are realized is determined by the respective linking constructions with which the basic lexical entry is combined. Figure 10.1 on the next page gives an example of a relevant inheritance hierarchy. There is a linking construction for both active and passive as well as lexical entries for *read* and *eat*. There is then a cross-classification resulting in an active and a passive variant of each verb.

---

[3] Sets in BCG work differently from those used in HPSG. A discussion of this is deferred to Section 10.6.1.

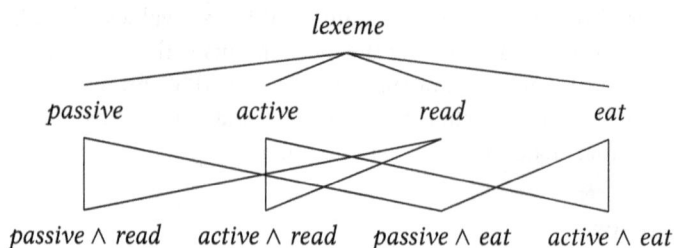

$$\textit{lexeme}$$

passive   active   read   eat

passive ∧ read   active ∧ read   passive ∧ eat   active ∧ eat

Figure 10.1: Passive and linking constructions

The idea behind this analysis goes back to work by Fillmore and Kay between 1995 and 1997[4], but variants of this analysis were first published in Koenig (1999: Chapter 3) and Michaelis & Ruppenhofer (2001: Chapter 4). Parallel proposals have been made in TAG (Candito 1996; Clément & Kinyon 2003: 188; Kallmeyer & Osswald 2012: 171–172) and HPSG (Koenig 1999; Davis & Koenig 2000; Kordoni 2001).

Michaelis & Ruppenhofer (2001: 55–57) provide the following linking constructions:[5]

(9) a. *Transitive Construction:*

$$\begin{bmatrix} \text{SYN} & \begin{bmatrix} \text{CAT} & v \\ \text{VOICE} & \textit{active} \end{bmatrix} \\ \text{VAL} & \left\{ \begin{bmatrix} \text{ROLE} & \begin{bmatrix} \text{GF} & \textit{obj} \\ \text{DA} & - \end{bmatrix} \end{bmatrix} \right\} \end{bmatrix}$$

  b. the *Subject Construction:*

$$\begin{bmatrix} \text{SYN} & \begin{bmatrix} \text{CAT} & v \end{bmatrix} \\ \text{VAL} & \left\{ \begin{bmatrix} \text{ROLE} & \begin{bmatrix} \text{GF} & \textit{subj} \end{bmatrix} \end{bmatrix} \right\} \end{bmatrix}$$

  c. the *Passive Construction:*

$$\begin{bmatrix} \text{SYN} & \begin{bmatrix} \text{CAT} & v \\ \text{FORM} & \textit{PastPart} \end{bmatrix} \\ \text{VAL} & \left\{ \begin{bmatrix} \text{ROLE} & \begin{bmatrix} \text{GF} & \textit{obl} \\ \text{DA} & + \end{bmatrix} \\ \text{SYN} & P[\textit{von}]/\textit{zero} \end{bmatrix} \right\} \end{bmatrix}$$

The structure in (9a) says that the valence set of a linguistic object that is described by the transitive construction has to contain an element that has the grammatical function *object* and whose DA value is '−'. The DA value of the argument that would be the subject in an active clause is '+' and '−' for all other arguments. The subject construction states

---

[4] http://www.icsi.berkeley.edu/~kay/bcg/ConGram.html. 03.05.2010.
[5] In the original version of the transitive construction in (9a), there is a feature θ that has the value DA−, however, DA is a feature itself and − is the value. I have corrected this in (9a) accordingly.

  In the following structures, GF stands for *grammatical function* and DA for *distinguished argument*. The distinguished argument usually corresponds to the subject in an active clause.

that an element of the valence set must have the grammatical function *subject*. In the passive construction, there has to be an element with the grammatical function *oblique* that also has the DA value '+'. In the passive construction the element with the DA value '+' is realized either as a *by*-PP or not at all (*zero*).

The interaction of the constructions in (9) will be explained on the basis of the verb *schlagen* 'to beat':

(10) Lexical entry for *schlag-* 'beat':

$$
\begin{bmatrix}
\text{SYN} & \begin{bmatrix} \text{CAT } v \end{bmatrix} \\
\text{VAL} & \left\{ \begin{bmatrix} \text{ROLE} & \begin{bmatrix} \theta & agent \\ \text{DA} & + \end{bmatrix} \end{bmatrix}, \begin{bmatrix} \text{ROLE} & \begin{bmatrix} \theta & patient \end{bmatrix} \end{bmatrix} \right\}
\end{bmatrix}
$$

If we combine this lexical entry with the transitive and subject constructions, we arrive at (11a) following Fillmore, Kay, Michaelis, and Ruppenhofer, whereas combining it with the subject and passive construction yields (11b):[6]

(11) a. *schlag-* + Subject and Transitive Construction:

$$
\begin{bmatrix}
\text{SYN} & \begin{bmatrix} \text{CAT} & v \\ \text{VOICE} & active \end{bmatrix} \\
\text{VAL} & \left\{ \begin{bmatrix} \text{ROLE} & \begin{bmatrix} \theta & agent \\ \text{GF} & subj \\ \text{DA} & + \end{bmatrix} \end{bmatrix}, \begin{bmatrix} \text{ROLE} & \begin{bmatrix} \theta & patient \\ \text{GF} & obj \\ \text{DA} & - \end{bmatrix} \end{bmatrix} \right\}
\end{bmatrix}
$$

b. *schlag-* + Subject and Passive Construction:

$$
\begin{bmatrix}
\text{SYN} & \begin{bmatrix} \text{CAT} & v \\ \text{FORM} & PastPart \end{bmatrix} \\
\text{VAL} & \left\{ \begin{bmatrix} \text{ROLE} & \begin{bmatrix} \theta & agent \\ \text{GF} & obl \\ \text{DA} & + \end{bmatrix} \\ \text{SYN} & P[von]/zero \end{bmatrix}, \begin{bmatrix} \text{ROLE} & \begin{bmatrix} \theta & patient \\ \text{GF} & subj \end{bmatrix} \end{bmatrix} \right\}
\end{bmatrix}
$$

Using the entries in (11), it is possible to analyze the sentences in (12):

(12) a. Er schlägt den Weltmeister.
      he beats the world.champion

      'He is beating the world champion.'

    b. Der Weltmeister   wird (von ihm) geschlagen.
      the world.champion is   by him beaten

      'The world champion is being beaten (by him).'

This analysis is formally inconsistent as set unification cannot be formalized in such a way that the aforementioned constructions can be unified (Müller 2006; Müller 2007b:

---

[6] This assumes a particular understanding of set unification. For criticism of this, see Section 10.6.1.

Section 7.5.2, see also Section 10.6.1 below). It is, however, possible to fix this analysis by using the HPSG formalization of sets (Pollard & Sag 1987; Pollard & Moshier 1990). The Subject, Transitive and Passive Constructions must then be modified such that they can say something about what an element in VAL looks like, rather than specifying the VAL value of a singleton set.

(13) The *Subject Construction* with Pollard & Moschier's definition of sets:

$$\begin{bmatrix} \text{SYN}|\text{CAT V} \\ \text{VAL } \boxed{1} \end{bmatrix} \wedge \left\{ \begin{bmatrix} \text{ROLE} \begin{bmatrix} \text{GF } subj \end{bmatrix} \end{bmatrix} \right\} \subset \boxed{1}$$

The restriction in (13) states that the valence set of a head has to contain an element that has the grammatical function *subj*. By these means, it is possible to suppress arguments (by specifying SYN as *zero*), but it is not possible to add any additional arguments to the fixed set of arguments of *schlagen* 'to beat'.[7] For the analysis of Middle Constructions such as (14), inheritance-based approaches do not work as there is no satisfactory way to add the reflexive pronoun to the valence set:[8]

(14) Das Buch liest sich gut.
      the book reads REFL good
      'The book reads well / is easy to read.'

If we want to introduce additional arguments, we require auxiliary features. An analysis using auxiliary features has been suggested by Koenig (1999). Since there are many argument structure changing processes that interact in various ways and are linked to particular semantic side-effects, it is inevitable that one ends up assuming a large number of syntactic and semantic auxiliary features. The interaction between the various linking constructions becomes so complex that this analysis also becomes cognitively implausible and has to be viewed as technically unusable. For a more detailed discussion of this point, see Müller (2007b: Section 7.5.2).

The following empirical problem is much more serious: some processes like passivization, impersonalization and causativization can be applied in combination or even allow for multiple application, but if the grammatical function of a particular argument is determined once and for all by unification, additional unifications cannot change the initial assignment. We will first look at languages which allow for a combination of

---

[7] Rather than requiring that *schlagen* 'to beat' has exactly two arguments as in HPSG, one could also assume that the constraint on the main lexical item would be of the kind in (11a). One would then require that *schlagen* has at least the two members in its valence set. This would complicate everything considerably and furthermore it would not be clear that the subject referred to in (13) would be one of the arguments that are referred to in the description of the lexical item for *schlagen* in (11a).

[8] One technically possible solution would be the following: one could assume that verbs that occur in middle constructions always have a description of a reflexive pronoun in their valence set. The Transitive Construction would then have to specify the SYN value of the reflexive pronoun as *zero* so that the additional reflexive pronoun is not realized in the Transitive Construction. The middle construction would suppress the subject, but realizes the object and the reflexive.

This solution cannot be applied to the recursive processes we will encounter in a moment such as causativization in Turkish, unless one wishes to assume infinite valence sets.

passivization and impersonalization, such as Lithuanian (Timberlake 1982: Section 5), Irish (Noonan 1994), and Turkish (Özkaragöz 1986; Knecht 1985: Section 2.3.3). I will use Özkaragöz's Turkish examples in (15) for illustration (1986: 77):

(15)   a. Bu şato-da   boğ-ul-un-ur.
           this château-LOC strangle-PASS-PASS-AOR
           'One is strangled (by one) in this château.'

       b. Bu oda-da   döv-ül-ün-ür.
           this room-LOC hit-PASS-PASS-AOR
           'One is beaten (by one) in this room.'

       c. Harp-te vur-ul-un-ur.
           war-LOC shoot-PASS-PASS-AOR
           'One is shot (by one) in war.'

-In, *-n*, and *-Il* are allomorphs of the passive/impersonal morpheme.[9]

Approaches that assume that the personal passive is the unification of some general structure with some passive-specific structure will not be able to capture double passivization or passivization + impersonalization since they have committed themselves to a certain structure too early. The problem for nontransformational approaches that state syntactic structure for the passive is that such a structure, once stated, cannot be modified. That is, we said that the underlying object is the subject in the passive sentence. But in order to get the double passivization/passivization + impersonalization, we have to suppress this argument as well. What is needed is some sort of process (or description) that takes a representation and relates it to another representation with a suppressed subject. This representation is related to a third representation which again suppresses the subject resulting in an impersonal sentence. In order to do this one needs different strata as in Relational Grammar (Timberlake 1982; Özkaragöz 1986), metarules (Gazdar, Klein, Pullum & Sag 1985), lexical rules (Dowty, 1978: 412; 2003: Section 3.4; Bresnan 1982b; Pollard & Sag 1987; Blevins 2003; Müller 2003b), transformations (Chomsky 1957), or just a morpheme-based morphological analysis that results in items with different valence properties when the passivization morpheme is combined with a head (Chomsky 1981a).

The second set of problematic data that will be discussed comes from causativization in Turkish (Lewis 1967: 146):

(16)   öl-dür-t-tür-t-
       'to cause someone to cause someone to cause someone to kill someone'
       (kill = cause someone to die)

The causative morpheme *-t* is combined four times with the verb (*tür* is an allomorph of the causative morpheme). This argument structure-changing process cannot be modeled

---

[9] According to Özkaragöz, the data is best captured by an analysis that assumes that the passive applies to a passivized transitive verb and hence results in an impersonal passive. The cited authors discussed their data as instances of double passivization, but it was argued by Blevins (2003) that these and similar examples from other languages are impersonal constructions that can be combined with personal passives.

in an inheritance hierarchy since if we were to say that a word can inherit from the causative construction three times, we would still not have anything different to what we would have if the inheritance via the causative construction had applied only once. For this kind of phenomenon, we would require rules that relate a linguistic object to another, more complex object, that is, lexical rules (unary branching rules which change the phonology of a linguistic sign) or binary rules that combine a particular sign with a derivational morpheme. These rules can semantically embed the original sign (that is, add *cause* to *kill*).

The problem of repeated combination with causativization affixes is an instance of a more general problem: derivational morphology cannot be handled by inheritance as was already pointed out by Krieger & Nerbonne (1993) with respect to cases like *preprepreversion*.

If we assume that argument alternations such as passive, causativization and the Middle Construction should be described with the same means across languages, then evidence from Lithuanian and Turkish form an argument against inheritance-based analyses of the passive (Müller 2006, 2007c; Müller & Wechsler 2014a). See also Section 21.2.2 for the discussion of an inheritance-based approach to passive in LFG and Section 21.4.2 for the discussion of an inheritance-based approach in Simpler Syntax.

10.3 Verb position

At present, I only know of one article in the framework of CxG that has dealt with the sentence structure in German. This is the article by Vanessa Micelli (2012), where she describes a computer implementation of a German grammar in Fluid Construction Grammar. This fragment is restricted to declarative V2-clauses and *wh*-questions. In her analysis, the middle field forms a constituent comprising exactly two constituents (the direct and indirect object).[10] The right sentence bracket and the postfield are empty. Long-distance dependencies are not discussed. It is only possible for arguments of the verb in the left sentence bracket to occur in the prefield. Micelli's work is an interesting starting point but one has to wait and see how the analysis will be modified when the grammar fragment is expanded.

In the following, I will not discuss Micelli's analysis further, but instead explore some of the possibilities for analyzing German sentence structure that are at least possible in principle in a CxG framework. Since there are neither empty elements nor transformations, the GB and HPSG analyses as well as their variants in Categorial Grammar are ruled out. The following options remain:

- an analysis similar to LFG with an optional verb

- an entirely flat analysis as proposed in GPSG

- an analysis with binary branching but variable verb position like that of Steedman (2000: 159)

---

[10] Note that none of the constituent tests that were discussed in Section 1.3 justifies such an analysis and that no other theory in this book assumes the *Mittelfeld* to be a constituent.

Different variants of CxG make different assumptions about how abstract constructions can be. In Categorial Grammar, we have very general combinatorial rules which combine possibly complex signs without adding any meaning of their own (see rule (2) on page 238 for example). (17) shows an example in which the abstract rule of forward application was used:

(17) [[[[Gibt] der Mann] der Frau]   das Buch]
          give   the man   the woman the book
      'Does the man give the woman the book?'

If we do not want these kinds of abstract combinatorial rules, then this analysis must be excluded.

The LFG analysis in Section 7.3 is probably also unacceptable on a CxG view as it is assumed in this analysis that *der Mann der Frau das Buch* forms a VP although only three NPs have been combined. CxG has nothing like the theory of extended head domains that was presented in Section 7.3.

Thus, both variants with binary-branching structures are ruled out and only the analysis with flat branching structures remains. Sign-based CxG, which is a variant of HPSG (Sag 2010: 486), as well as Embodied Construction Grammar (Bergen & Chang 2005: 156) allow for a separation of immediate dominance and linear order so that it would be possible to formulate a construction which would correspond to the dominance rule in (18) for transitive verbs:[11]

(18) S → V, NP, NP

Here, we have the problem that adjuncts in German can occur between any of the arguments. In GPSG, adjuncts are introduced by metarules. In formal variants of CxG, lexical rules, but not metarules, are used.[12] If one does not wish to expand the formalism to include metarules, then there are three options remaining:

- Adjuncts are introduced in the lexicon (van Noord & Bouma 1994; Bouma, Malouf & Sag 2001a) and treated as arguments in the syntax,

- Constructions always have slots available for an arbitrary number of adjuncts, or

- Constructions can be discontinuous

Kasper (1994) has proposed an analysis of the first type in HPSG: adjuncts and arguments are combined with the head in a flat structure. This corresponds to the dominance rule in (19), where the position of adjuncts is not stated by the dominance rule.

(19) S → V, NP, NP, Adj*

---

[11] In principle, this is also Micelli's analysis, but she assumed that the middle field forms a separate constituent.

[12] Goldberg (2014: 116) mentions metarule-like devices and refers to Cappelle (2006). The difference between metarules and their CxG variant as envisioned by Cappelle and Goldberg is that in CxG two constructions are related without one construction being basic and the other one derived. Rather there exists a mutual relation between two constructions.

If we want to say something about the meaning of the entire construction, then one has to combine the original construction (transitive, in the above example) with the semantics contributed by each of the adjuncts. These computations are not trivial and require relational constraints (small computer programs), which should be avoided if there are conceptually simpler solutions for describing a particular phenomenon.

The alternative would be to use discontinuous constructions. Analyses with discontinuous constituents have been proposed in both HPSG (Reape 1994) and Embodied Construction Grammar (Bergen & Chang 2005). If we apply Bergen and Chang's analysis to German, the italicized words in (20) would be part of a ditransitive construction.

(20)   *Gibt der Mann* morgen   *der Frau*   unter der Brücke *das Geld?*
     gives the man   tomorrow the woman under the bridge the money

     'Is the man going to give the woman the money under the bridge tomorrow?'

The construction has been realized discontinuously and the adjuncts are inserted into the gaps. In this kind of approach, one still has to explain how the scope of quantifiers and adjuncts is determined. While this may be possible, the solution is not obvious and has not been worked out in any of the CxG approaches to date. For further discussions of approaches that allow for discontinuous constituents see Section 11.7.2.2.

10.4 Local reordering

If we assume flat branching structures, then it is possible to use the GPSG analysis for the order of arguments. However, Kay (2002) assumes a phrasal construction for so-called Heavy-NP-Shift in English, which means that there is a new rule for the reordering of heavy NPs in English rather than one rule and two different ways to linearize the daughters.

In CxG, it is often argued that the usage contexts of certain orders differ and we therefore must be dealing with different constructions. Accordingly, one would have to assume six constructions to capture the ordering variants of sentences with ditransitive verbs in final position (see also page 179). An alternative would be to assume that the ordering variants all have a similar structure and that the information-structural properties are dependent on the position of constituents in the respective structure (see De Kuthy 2000 for German and Bildhauer 2008 for Spanish).

10.5 Long-distance dependencies

Kay & Fillmore (1999: Section 3.10) discuss long-distance dependencies in their article. Since the number of arguments is not specified in the verb phrase construction, it is possible that an argument of the verb is not locally present. Like the LFG and GPSG analyses in previous chapters, there are no empty elements assumed for the analysis of long-distance dependencies. In the *Left Isolation Construction* that licenses the entire sentence, there is a left daughter and a right daughter. The left daughter corresponds to whatever was extracted from the right daughter. The connection between the fronted element and the position where it is missing is achieved by the operator VAL. VAL provides all elements of the valence set of a linguistic object as well as all elements in the valence set of these elements and so on. It is thereby possible to have unrestricted access to an argument or adjunct daughter of any depth of embedding, and then identify the fronted constituent with an open valence slot.[13] This approach corresponds to the LFG analysis of Kaplan & Zaenen (1989) based on functional uncertainty.

10.6 New developments and theoretical variants

Berkeley Construction Grammar was already discussed in the main part of this chapter. The discussion of the formal underpinnings was deferred until the theoretical variants section, since it is more advanced. I made some comments on set unification in Müller (2006: 858), but the longer discussion is only available in Müller (2007b: Section 7.5.2), which is in German. Therefore, I include Section 10.6.1 here, which discusses the formal underpinnings of Berkeley Construction Grammar in more detail and shows that they are not suited for what they were intended to do.

Section 10.6.2 discusses Sign-Based Construction Grammar, which was developed in joint work by Charles Fillmore, Paul Kay and Ivan Sag. It embodies ideas from BCG without having its formal flaws. Section 10.6.3 deals with Embodied Construction Grammar, which is based on work by Charles Fillmore, Paul Kay and George Lakoff. Section 10.6.4 deals with Fluid Construction Grammar.

10.6.1 Berkeley Construction Grammar

Section 10.2 discussed the valence representation in BCG and linking constructions for active and passive. Kay & Fillmore (1999) represent valence information in sets and I deferred the discussion of the formal properties of sets in BCG to this section. Fillmore and Kay's assumptions regarding set unification differ fundamentally from those that are made in HPSG. Kay and Fillmore assume that the unification of the set { a } with the set { b }, where a and b do not unify, results in the union of the two sets, that is { a, b }. Due to this special understanding of sets it is possible to increase the number of elements in a set by means of unification. The unification of two sets that contain compatible elements is the disjunction of sets that contain the respective unifications of the compatible elements. This sounds complicated, but we are only interested in a specific case: the unification of an arbitrary set with a singleton set:

(21) { NP[*nom*], NP[*acc*] } ∧ { NP[*nom*] } = { NP[*nom*], NP[*acc*] }

According to Fillmore & Kay the unification of a set with another set that contains a compatible element does not result in an increase of the number of list elements.

---

[13] Note again, that there are problems with the formalization of this proposal in Kay & Fillmore's paper. The formalization of VAL, which was provided by Andreas Kathol, seems to presuppose a formalization of sets as the one that is used in HPSG, but the rest of Fillmore & Kay's paper assumes a different formalization, which is inconsistent. See Section 10.6.1.

(22) illustrates another possible case:

(22)   { NP, NP[*acc*] } ∧ { NP[*nom*] } = { NP[*nom*], NP[*acc*] }

The first NP in (22) is underspecified with respect to its case. The case of the NP in the second set is specified as nominative. NP[*nom*] does not unify with NP[*acc*] but with NP.

This particular conception of unification has consequences. Unification is usually defined as follows:

(23)   The unification of two structures FS_1 and FS_2 is the structure FS_3 that is subsumed by both FS_1 and FS_2 where there is no other structure that subsumes FS_1 and FS_2 and is subsumed by FS_3.

A structure FS_1 is said to subsume FS_3 iff FS_3 contains all feature value pairs and structure sharings from FS_1. FS_3 may contain additional feature value pairs or structure sharings. The consequence is that the subsumption relations in (24b,c) have to hold if unification of valence sets works as in (24a):

(24)   Properties of the set unification according to Kay & Fillmore (1999):
a. { NP[*nom*] } ∧ { NP[*acc*] } = { NP[*nom*], NP[*acc*] }
b. { NP[*nom*] } ≥ { NP[*nom*], NP[*acc*] }
c. { NP[*acc*] } ≥ { NP[*nom*], NP[*acc*] }

(24b) means that a feature structure with a valence set that contains just one NP[*nom*] is more general than a feature structure that contains both an NP[*nom*] and an NP[*acc*]. Therefore the set of transitive verbs is a subset of the intransitive verbs. This is rather unintuitive, but compatible with Fillmore & Kay's system for the licensing of arguments. However, there are problems with the interaction of valence specifications and linking constructions, which we turn to now.

We have seen the result of combining lexical items with linking constructions in (11a) and (11b), but the question of how these results are derived has not been addressed so far. Kay (2002) suggests an automatic computation of all compatible combinations of maximally specific constructions. Such a procedure could be used to compute the lexical representations we saw in Section 10.2 and these could be then used to analyze the well-formed sentences in (12).

However, problems would result for ungrammatical sentences like (25b). *grauen* 'to dread' is a subjectless verb. If one would simply combine all compatible linking constructions with *grauen*, the Kay & Fillmoreian conception of set unification would cause the introduction of a subject into the valence set of *grauen*. (25b) would be licensed by the grammar:

(25)   a.   Dem   Student graut vor   der Prüfung.
             the.DAT student dreads before the exam

             'The student dreads the exam.'

       b. * Ich graue dem   Student vor   der Prüfung.
            I   dread the.DAT student before the exam

One could solve this problem by specifying an element with the grammatical function *subject* in the lexical entry of *grauen* 'to dread'. In addition, it would have to be stipulated that this subject can only be realized as an overt or covert expletive (The covert expletive would be SYN *zero*). For the covert expletive, this means it has neither a form nor a meaning. Such expletive pronouns without phonological realization are usually frowned upon in Construction Grammar and analyses that can do without such abstract entities are to be preferred.

Kay & Fillmore (1999) represent the semantic contribution of signs as sets as well. This excludes the possibility of preventing the unwanted unification of linking constructions by referring to semantic constraints since we have the same effect as we have with valence sets: if the semantic descriptions are incompatible, the set is extended. This means that in an automatic unification computation all verbs are compatible with the Transitive Construction in (9a) and this would license analyses for (26) in addition to those of (25b).

(26)   a. * Der Mann schläft das Buch.
          the man   sleeps the book

       b. * Der Mann denkt an die Frau   das Buch.
          the man   thinks at the woman the book

An intransitive verb was unified with the Transitive Construction in the analysis of (26a) and in (26b) a verb that takes a prepositional object was combined with the Transitive Construction. This means that representations like (11) cannot be computed automatically as was intended by Kay (2002). Therefore one would have to specify subconstructions for all argument structure possibilities for every verb (active, passive, middle, ...). This does not capture the fact that speakers can form passives after acquiring new verbs without having to learn about the fact that the newly learned verb forms one.

Michaelis & Ruppenhofer (2001) do not use sets for the representation of semantic information. Therefore they could use constraints regarding the meaning of verbs in the Transitive Construction. To this end, one needs to represent semantic relations with feature descriptions as it was done in Section 9.1.6. Adopting such a representation, it is possible to talk about two-place relations in an abstract way. See for instance the discussion of (27) on page 271. However, the unification with the Subject Construction cannot be blocked with reference to semantics since there exist so-called raising verbs that take a subject without assigning a semantic role to it. As is evidenced by subject verb agreement, *du* 'you' is the subject in (27), but the subject does not get a semantic role. The referent of *du* is not the one who *seems*.

(27)   Du scheinst gleich einzuschlafen.
       you seem.2SG soon   in.to.sleep

       'You seem like you will fall asleep soon.'

This means that one is forced to either assume an empty expletive subject for verbs like *grauen* or to specify explicitly which verbs may inherit from the subject construction and which may not.

In addition to (27), there exist object raising constructions with accusative objects that can be promoted to subject in passives. The subject in the passive construction does not get a semantic role from the finite verb:

(28) a. Richard lacht   ihn an.
          Richard laughs   him towards

          'Richard smiles at him.'

      b. Richard fischt den Teich leer.
          Richard fishes the pond empty

The objects in (28) are semantic arguments of *an* 'towards' and *leer* 'empty', respectively, but not semantic arguments of the verbs *lacht* 'laughs' and *fischt* 'fishes', respectively. If one wants to explain these active forms and the corresponding passive forms via the linking constructions in (9), one cannot refer to semantic properties of the verb. Therefore, one is forced to postulate specific lexical entries for all possible verb forms in active and passive sentences.

10.6.2 Sign-Based Construction Grammar

In more recent work by Fillmore, Kay, Michaelis and Sag, the Kay & Fillmore formalization of the description of valence using the Kay & Fillmore version of sets was abandoned in favor of the HPSG formalization (Kay 2005; Michaelis 2006; Sag 2012; Sag, Boas & Kay 2012: 10–11). Sign-Based Construction Grammar was developed from the Berkeley variant of CxG. Sign-Based Construction Grammar is a variant of HPSG (Sag 2010: 486) and as such uses the formal apparatus of HPSG (typed feature structures). Valence and saturation are treated in exactly the same way as in standard HPSG. Changes in valence are also analyzed as in HPSG using lexical rules (Sag, Boas & Kay 2012: Section 2.3). The analysis of long-distance dependencies was adopted from HPSG (or rather GPSG). Minimal Recursion Semantics (MRS; Copestake, Flickinger, Pollard & Sag 2005) is used for the description of semantic content. The only difference to works in standard HPSG is the organization of the features in feature structures. A new feature geometry was introduced to rule out constructions that describe daughters of daughters and therefore have a much larger locality domain in contrast to rules in phrase structure grammars, LFG, and GPSG. I do not view this new feature geometry as particularly sensible as it can be easily circumvented and serves to complicate the theory. This will be discussed in Section 10.6.2.1. Other changes regard the omission of the LOCAL feature and the omission of valence features. These changes are discussed in Section 10.6.2.2 and 10.6.2.4, respectively.

10.6.2.1 Locality and MOTHER

Sag, Wasow & Bender (2003: 475–489) and Sag (2007, 2012) suggest using a MOTHER feature in addition to daughter features. The Head-Complement Construction would then have the form in (29):

(29) Head-Complement Construction following Sag, Wasow & Bender (2003: 481):

head-comp-cx →

$$
\begin{bmatrix}
\text{MOTHER|SYN|VAL|COMPS } \langle \rangle \\
\text{HEAD-DTR } \boxed{0} \begin{bmatrix} word \\ \text{SYN|VAL|COMPS } \boxed{A} \end{bmatrix} \\
\text{DTRS } \langle \boxed{0} \rangle \oplus \boxed{A} \; nelist
\end{bmatrix}
$$

The value of COMPS is then a list of the complements of a head (see Section 9.6.1). Unlike in standard HPSG, it is not *synsem* objects that are selected with valence lists, but rather signs. The analysis of the phrase *ate a pizza* takes the form in (30).[14]

(30)

$$
\begin{bmatrix}
\textit{head-comp-cx} \\
\text{MOTHER} \begin{bmatrix}
phrase \\
\text{FORM } \langle \textit{ate, a, pizza} \rangle \\
\text{SYN} \begin{bmatrix} \text{HEAD} & verb \\ \text{SPR} & \langle \text{NP[\textit{nom}]} \rangle \\ \text{COMPS} & \langle \rangle \end{bmatrix} \\
\text{SEM} \quad \dots
\end{bmatrix} \\
\text{HEAD-DTR } \boxed{1} \begin{bmatrix}
word \\
\text{FORM } \langle \textit{ate} \rangle \\
\text{SYN} \begin{bmatrix} \text{HEAD} & verb \\ \text{SPR} & \langle \text{NP[\textit{nom}]} \rangle \\ \text{COMPS} & \langle \boxed{2} \text{ NP[\textit{acc}]} \rangle \end{bmatrix} \\
\text{SEM} \quad \dots
\end{bmatrix} \\
\text{DTRS} \quad \langle \boxed{1}, \boxed{2} \rangle
\end{bmatrix}
$$

The difference to HPSG in the version of Pollard & Sag (1994) is that for Sag, Wasow & Bender, signs do not have daughters and this makes the selection of daughters impossible. As a result, the SYNSEM feature becomes superfluous (selection of the PHON value and of the value of the newly introduced FORM feature is allowed in Sag, Wasow & Bender (2003) and Sag (2012)). The information about the linguistic objects that contribute to a complex sign is only represented in the very outside of the structure. The sign represented under MOTHER is of the type *phrase* but does not contain any information about the daughters. The object described in (30) is of course also of another type than the phrasal or lexical signs that can occur as its daughters. We therefore need the following extension so that the grammar will work (Sag, Wasow & Bender 2003: 478):[15]

(31) Φ is a Well-Formed Structure according to a grammar *G* if and only if:

---

[14] SBCG uses a FORM feature in addition to the PHON feature, which is used for phonological information as in earlier versions of HPSG (Sag 2012: Section 3.1, Section 3.6). The FORM feature is usually provided in example analyses.

[15] A less formal version of this constraint is given as the Sign Principle by Sag (2012: 105): "Every sign must be listemically or constructionally licensed, where: a sign is listemically licensed only if it satisfies some listeme, and a sign is constructionally licensed if it is the mother of some well-formed construct."

1. there is a construction C in G, and
2. there is a feature structure I that is an instantiation of C, such that Φ is the value of the MOTHER feature of I.

For comparison, a description is given in (32) with the feature geometry that was assumed in Section 9.6.1.

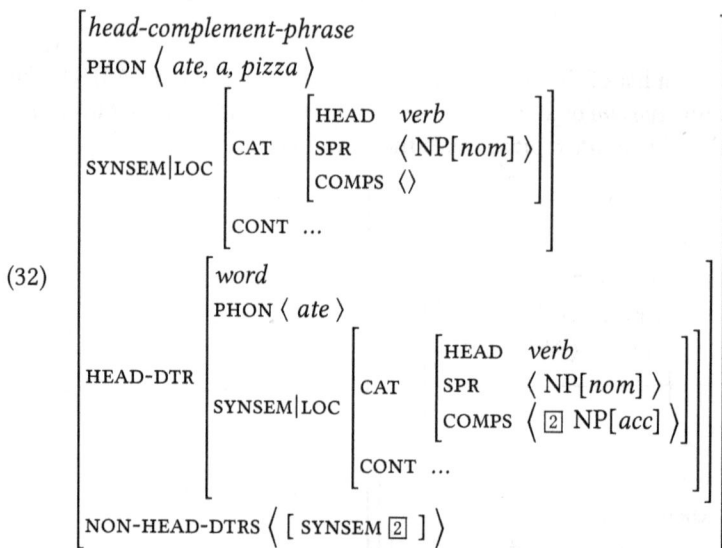

$$
(32) \quad
\begin{bmatrix}
\textit{head-complement-phrase} \\
\text{PHON} \left\langle \textit{ate, a, pizza} \right\rangle \\[2ex]
\text{SYNSEM}|\text{LOC}
\begin{bmatrix}
\text{CAT}
\begin{bmatrix}
\text{HEAD} & \textit{verb} \\
\text{SPR} & \left\langle \text{NP}[\textit{nom}] \right\rangle \\
\text{COMPS} & \left\langle \right\rangle
\end{bmatrix} \\[3ex]
\text{CONT} \ ...
\end{bmatrix} \\[6ex]
\text{HEAD-DTR}
\begin{bmatrix}
\textit{word} \\
\text{PHON} \left\langle \textit{ate} \right\rangle \\[2ex]
\text{SYNSEM}|\text{LOC}
\begin{bmatrix}
\text{CAT}
\begin{bmatrix}
\text{HEAD} & \textit{verb} \\
\text{SPR} & \left\langle \text{NP}[\textit{nom}] \right\rangle \\
\text{COMPS} & \left\langle \boxed{2}\ \text{NP}[\textit{acc}] \right\rangle
\end{bmatrix} \\[3ex]
\text{CONT} \ ...
\end{bmatrix}
\end{bmatrix} \\[6ex]
\text{NON-HEAD-DTRS} \left\langle [\ \text{SYNSEM}\ \boxed{2}\ ] \right\rangle
\end{bmatrix}
$$

In (32), the features HEAD-DTR and NON-HEAD-DTRS belong to those features that phrases of type *head-complement-phrase* have. In (30), however, the phrase corresponds only to the value of the MOTHER feature and therefore has no daughters represented in the sign itself. Using the feature geometry in (32), it is in principle possible to formulate restrictions on the daughters of the object in the NON-HEAD-DTRS list, which would be completely ruled out under the assumption of the feature geometry in (30) and the restriction in (31).

There are several arguments against this feature geometry, which will be discussed in the following subsections. The first one is an empirical one: there may be idioms that span clauses. The second argument concerns the status of the meta statement in (31) and the third one computational complexity.

10.6.2.1.1 Idioms that cross constituent boundaries

In Müller (2007b: Chapter 12) I conjectured that the locality restrictions may be too strong since there may be idioms that require one to make reference to daughters of daughters for their description. Richter & Sailer (2009) discuss the following idioms as examples:

(33) a. nicht wissen, wo   X_Dat der Kopf steht
      not   know   where X   the head stands

    'to not know where x's head is at'

b. glauben, X_Acc tritt   ein Pferd
   believe X   kicks a   horse

   'be utterly surprised'

c. aussehen, als hätten X_Dat die Hühner das Brot   weggefressen
   look   as.if had   X   the chicken the bread away.eaten

   'to look confused/puzzled'

d. look as if butter wouldn't melt [in X's mouth]

   'to look absolutely innocent'

In sentences containing the idioms in (33a–c), the X-constituent has to be a pronoun that refers to the subject of the matrix clause. If this is not the case, the sentences become ungrammatical or lose their idiomatic meaning.

(34) a. Ich glaube, mich   / # dich   tritt ein Pferd.
          I   believe me.ACC   you.ACC kicks a   horse

     b. Jonas glaubt, ihn tritt ein Pferd.[16]
          Jonas believes him kicks a   horse

       'Jonas is utterly surprised.'

     c. # Jonas glaubt, dich tritt ein Pferd.
          Jonas believes you kicks a   horse

       'Jonas believes that a horse kicks you.'

In order to enforce this co-reference, a restriction has to be able to refer to both the subject of *glauben* 'believe' and the object of *treten* 'kick' at the same time. In SBCG, there is the possibility of referring to the subject since the relevant information is also available on maximal projections (the value of a special feature (XARG) is identical to the subject of a head). In (33a–c), we are dealing with accusative and dative objects. Instead of only making information about one argument accessible, one could represent the complete argument structure on the maximal projection (as is done in some versions of HPSG, see page 300 and pages 544–546). This would remove locality of selection, however, since if all heads project their argument structure, then it is possible to determine the properties of arguments of arguments by looking at the elements present in the argument structure. Thus, the argument structure of *wissen* 'to know' in (35) would contain the description of a *dass* clause.

(35) Peter weiß, dass Klaus kommt.
      Peter knows that Klaus comes

     'Peter knows that Klaus is coming.'

Since the description of the *dass* clause contains the argument structure of *dass*, it is possible to access the argument of *dass*. *wissen* 'to know' can therefore access *Klaus kommt*. As such, *wissen* also has access to the argument structure of *kommt* 'to come',

---

[16] http://www.machandel-verlag.de/der-katzenschatz.html, 06.07.2015.

which is why *Klaus* is also accessible to *wissen*. However, the purpose of the new, more restrictive feature geometry was to rule out such nonlocal access to arguments.

An alternative to projecting the complete argument structure was suggested by Kay et al. (2015: Section 6): instead of assuming that the subject is the XARG in idiomatic constructions like those in (33), they assume that the accusative or dative argument is the XARG. This is an interesting proposal that could be used to fix the cases under discussion, but the question is whether it scales up if interaction with other phenomena are considered. For instance, Bender & Flickinger (1999) use XARG in their account of question tags in English. So, if English idioms can be found that require a non-subject XARG in embedded sentences while also admitting the idiom parts in the embedded sentence to occur as full clause with question tag, we would have conflicting demands and would have to assume different XARGs for root and embedded clauses, which would make this version of the lexical theory rather unattractive, since we would need two lexical items for the respective verb.

(33d) is especially interesting, since here the X that refers to material outside the idiom is in an adjunct. If such cases existed, the XARG mechanism would be clearly insufficient since XARG is not projected from adjuncts. However, as Kay et al. (2015) point out the X does not necessarily have to be a pronoun that is coreferent with an element in a matrix clause. They provide the following example:

(36)   Justin Bieber—Once upon a time Ø butter wouldn't melt in little Justin's mouth. Now internationally famous for being a weapons-grade petulant brat ...

So, whether examples of the respective kind can be found is an open question.

Returning to our *horse* examples, Richter & Sailer (2009: 313) argue that the idiomatic reading is only available if the accusative pronouns is fronted and the embedded clause is V2. The examples in (37) do not have the idiomatic reading:

(37)   a. Ich glaube, dass mich ein Pferd tritt.
          I   believe that me   a   horse kicks

          'I believe that a horse kicks me.'

       b. Ich glaube, ein Pferd tritt   mich.
          I   believe a   horse kicks me

          'I believe that a horse kicks me.'

Richter & Sailer assume a structure for *X_Acc tritt ein Pferd* in (33b) that contains, among others, the constraints in (38).

The feature geometry in (38) differs somewhat from what was presented in Chapter 9 but that is not of interest here. It is only of importance that the semantic contribution of the entire phrase is *surprised'*($x_{\boxed{2}}$). The following is said about the internal structure of the phrase: it consists of a filler-daughter (an extracted element) and also of a head daughter corresponding to a sentence from which something has been extracted. The head daughter means 'a horse kicks $x_{\boxed{2}}$' and has an internal head somewhere whose

(38)

$$
\begin{bmatrix}
phrase \\
\text{SYNSEM}|\text{LOC} \begin{bmatrix} \text{CAT}|\text{LISTEME} & \textit{very-surprised} \\ \text{CONT}|\text{MAIN} & \textit{surprised}'(x_{\boxed{2}}) \end{bmatrix} \\
\text{DTRS} \begin{bmatrix}
\text{FILLER-DTR} \begin{bmatrix} word \\ \text{SYNSEM}|\text{LOC} & \boxed{1} \end{bmatrix} \\
\text{H-DTR} \begin{bmatrix}
\text{LF}|\text{EXC} & \text{'a horse kicks } x_{\boxed{2}} \text{'} \\
(\text{DTRS}|\text{H-DTR})^+ \begin{bmatrix}
word \\
\text{SYNSEM}|\text{LOC}|\text{CAT} \begin{bmatrix} \text{HEAD} & [\text{TENSE } \textit{pres}] \\ \text{LISTEME} & \textit{treten} \end{bmatrix} \\
\text{ARG-ST} \left\langle \text{NP}[\text{LISTEME } \textit{pferd}, \text{DEF } -, \textit{sg}], \begin{bmatrix} \text{LOC} \boxed{1} & \begin{bmatrix} \text{CAT}|\text{HEAD}|\text{CASE } \textit{acc} \\ \text{CONT} \begin{bmatrix} \textit{ppro} \\ \text{INDEX} & \boxed{2} \end{bmatrix} \end{bmatrix} \end{bmatrix} \right\rangle
\end{bmatrix}
\end{bmatrix}
\end{bmatrix}
\end{bmatrix}
$$

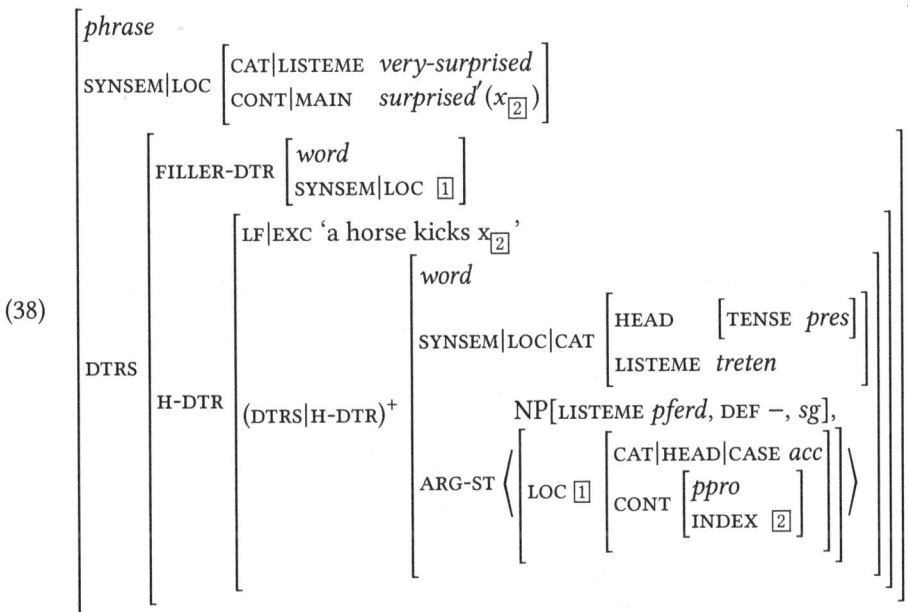

argument structure list contains an indefinite NP with the word *Pferd* 'horse' as its head. The second element in the argument structure is a pronominal NP in the accusative whose LOCAL value is identical to that of the filler ($\boxed{1}$). The entire meaning of this part of the sentence is *surprised'*($x_{\boxed{2}}$), whereby $\boxed{2}$ is identical to the referential index of the pronoun. In addition to the constraints in (38), there are additional ones that ensure that the partial clause appears with the relevant form of *glauben* 'to believe' or *denken* 'to think'. The exact details are not that important here. What is important is that one can specify constraints on complex syntactic elements, that is, it must be possible to refer to daughters of daughters. This is possible with the classical HPSG feature geometry, but not with the feature geometry of SBCG. For a more general discussion of locality, see Section 18.2.

The restrictions on *Pferd* clauses in (38) are too strict, however, since there are variants of the idiom that do not have the accusative pronoun in the *Vorfeld*:

(39)   a. ich glaub es   tritt mich ein Pferd wenn ich einen derartigen Unsinn
           I   believe EXPL kicks me   a   horse when I   a   such   nonsense
           lese.[17]
           read

      'I am utterly surprised when I read such nonsense.'

---

[17] http://www.welt.de/wirtschaft/article116297208/Die-verlogene-Kritik-an-den-Steuerparadiesen.html, commentary section, 10.12.2015.

    b. omg dieser xBluuR der nn ist wieder da   ey nein ich glaub es   tritt
       omg this   XBluuR he   is again there   no I   believe EXPL kicks
       mich ein Pferd!![18]
       me   a   horse

       'OMG, this xBluuR, the nn, he is here again, no, I am utterly surprised.'

    c. ich glaub   jetzt tritt   mich ein pferd[19]
       I   believe now kicks me   a   horse

       'I am utterly surprised now.'

In (40a–b) the *Vorfeld* is filled by an expletive and in (40c) an adverb fills the *Vorfeld* position. While these forms of the idiom are really rare, they do exist and should be allowed for by the description of the idiom. So, one would have to make sure that *ein Pferd* 'a horse' is not fronted, but this can be done in the lexical item of *tritt* 'kicks'. This shows that the cases at hand cannot be used to argue for models that allow for the representation of (underspecified) trees of depth greater one, but I still believe that such idioms can be found. Of course this is an open empirical question.

What is not an open empirical question though is whether humans store chunks with complex internal structure or not. It is clear that we do and much Construction Grammar literature emphasizes this. Constructional HPSG can represent such chunks, but SBCG cannot since linguistic signs do not have daughters. So here Constructional HPSG and TAG are the theories that can represent complex chunks of linguistic material with its internal structure, while other theories like GB, Minimalism, CG, LFG and DG can not.

10.6.2.1.2 Complicated licensing of constructions

In addition to these empirical problems, there is a conceptual problem with (31): (31) is not part of the formalism of typed feature structures but rather a meta-statement. Therefore, grammars which use (31) cannot be described with the normal formalism. The formalization given in Richter (2004) cannot be directly applied to SBCG, which means that the formal foundations of SBCG still have to be worked out.[20] Furthermore, the original problem that (31) was designed to solve is not solved by introducing the new feature geometry and the meta statement. Instead, the problem is just moved to another level since we now need a theory about what is a permissible meta-statement and what is not. As such, a grammarian could add a further clause to the meta statement stating that Φ is only a well-formed structure if it is true of the daughters of a relevant construction C that they are the MOTHER value of a construction C′. It would be possible to formulate constraints in the meta-statement about the construction C′ or individual values inside

---

[18] http://forum.gta-life.de/index.php?user/3501-malcolm/, 10.12.2015.

[19] http://www.castingshow-news.de/menowin-frhlich-soll-er-zum-islam-konvertieren-7228/, 10.12.2015.

[20] A note of caution is necessary since there were misunderstandings in the past regarding the degree of formalizations of SBCG: in comparison to most other theories discussed in this book, SBCG is well-formalized. For instance it is easy to come up with a computer implementation of SBCG fragments. I implemented one in the TRALE system myself. The reader is referred to Richter (2004) to get an idea what kind of deeper formalization is talked about here.

the corresponding feature structures. In this way, locality would have been abandoned since it is possible to refer to daughters of daughters. By assuming (31), the theoretical inventory has been increased without any explanatory gain.

10.6.2.1.3 Computational complexity

One motivation behind restrictions on locality was to reduce the computational complexity of the formalism (Ivan Sag, p. c. 2011, See Chapter 17 on computational complexity and generative power). However, the locality restrictions of SBCG can be circumvented easily by structure sharing (Müller 2013b: Section 9.6.1). To see this consider a construction with the following form:

$$
(40) \quad \begin{bmatrix} \text{MOTHER} & \begin{bmatrix} sign \\ \text{PHON} & phonological\text{-}object \\ \text{FORM} & morphological\text{-}object \\ \text{SYN} & syntactic\ information \\ \text{SEM} & semantic\ information \\ \text{NASTY} & \boxed{1} \end{bmatrix} \\ \text{DTRS} & \boxed{1}\ list\ of\ signs \end{bmatrix}
$$

The feature NASTY in the MOTHER sign refers to the value of DTRS and hence all the internal structure of the sign that is licensed by the constructional schema in (40) is available. Of course one could rule out such things by stipulation – if one considered it to be empirically adequate, but then one could as well continue to use the feature geometry of Constructional HPSG (Sag 1997) and stipulate constraints like "Do not look into the daughters." An example of such a constraint given in prose is the Locality Principle of Pollard & Sag (1987: 143–144).

10.6.2.2 Lexical extraction and the LOCAL feature

A main theme in Ivan Sag's work was to eliminate empty elements from grammar. He co-developed a lexical analysis of extraction that did not use empty elements (van Noord & Bouma 1994; Bouma, Malouf & Sag 2001a). Rather than assuming a trace as in earlier versions of HPSG (see Section 9.5) a lexical rule (lexical construction) or a special mapping between list-valued features (for instance ARG-ST and VALENCE) is assumed so that a lexical item is licensed that has an element in the GAP list (SLASH in earlier versions of HPSG). The LOCAL feature in Standard HPSG is used to bundle all those information that is shared between a filler and the gap. The lexical entry for the trace was given as (60) on page 293 and is repeated as (41) for convenience. For the trace-based analysis of extraction it is crucial that only information under CATEGORY and CONT is shared between filler and gap. This information is bundled under LOCAL. Information about daughters and phonology of the filler is not shared. Since traces are not pronounced, their PHONOLOGY value would be incompatible with any PHONOLOGY value of a filler.

(41) Extraction trace:

$$
\begin{bmatrix}
word \\
\text{PHON} & \langle \rangle \\
\text{SYNSEM} & \begin{bmatrix} \text{LOC} & \boxed{1} \\ \text{NONLOC} & \begin{bmatrix} \text{INHER|SLASH} & \langle \boxed{1} \rangle \\ \text{TO-BIND|SLASH} & \langle \rangle \end{bmatrix} \end{bmatrix}
\end{bmatrix}
$$

In a lexical approach, one would assume an additional lexical item with an element in SLASH or GAP.

(42) Lexical introduction of nonlocal dependencies according to Sag (2012: 163):

$$
\begin{bmatrix}
\text{FORM} & \langle\, like\, \rangle \\
\text{ARG-ST} & \left\langle \boxed{1} \begin{bmatrix} \text{NP} \\ \text{GAP} \langle \rangle \end{bmatrix}, \boxed{2} \begin{bmatrix} \text{NP} \\ \text{GAP} \langle \rangle \end{bmatrix} \right\rangle \\
\text{SYN} & \begin{bmatrix} \text{VAL} & \langle \boxed{1} \rangle \\ \text{GAP} & \langle \boxed{2} \rangle \end{bmatrix}
\end{bmatrix}
$$

The analysis of (43) then results in a linguistic object in which the second element of the ARG-ST list of *like* has the FORM value ⟨ *bagels* ⟩.

(43) Bagels, I like.

In a trace-based account, the FORM value of the extracted element would be the empty list.

Now, the problem is that not everybody agrees with the traceless analysis of unbounded dependencies. For instance, Levine & Hukari (2006) wrote a monograph discussing various versions of traceless accounts of extraction and argue against them. Chaves (2009) suggested solutions to some of the puzzles, but does not solve them entirely. While feature geometries that include a LOCAL feature allow researchers to assume trace-based analyses, the SBCG geometry makes this impossible. So those who use traces in their theories will never adopt the SBCG geometry. See Section 19 for more on empty elements.

A further advantage of having a package of information that is shared in nonlocal dependencies is that some information can be excluded from sharing by specifying it outside of such a package. This was used by Höhle (1994), Müller (1996d, 2002a), and Meurers (1999a) to account for partial verb phrase fronting in German. The generalization about partial verb phrase fronting in German is that verbs can be fronted together with some or all of their objects even though the verb does not form a VP in other contexts. For instance, *erzählen* 'tell' and *wird* 'will' in (44a) usually form a complex that may not be separated by scrambling a projection of *erzählen* to the left.

(44) a. dass er seiner Tochter ein Märchen erzählen wird
      that he his daughter a fairy.tale tell will
      'that he will tell his daughter a fairy tale'

b. * dass er seiner Tochter   ein Märchen erzählen nie   wird
that he his   daughter a   fairy.tale tell   never will

Hinrichs & Nakazawa (1994) account for this by assuming a special schema for verbal complexes and by assuming that such verbal complexes are marked in a certain way (later this was encoded with the LEX feature with the value '+') and that heads that form a verbal complex select for appropriately marked elements. So in the analysis of (44a) *wird* 'will' selects a LEX + element and the word *erzählen* 'tell' satisfies this requirement.

The problem for many accounts of nonlocal dependencies is that the fronted material is not necessarily a single verb:

(45) a. Erzählen wird er   seiner Tochter ein   Märchen.
       tell   will he.NOM his.DAT daughter a.ACC fairytale

       'He will tell his daughter a fairytale.'

   b. Ein Märchen   erzählen wird er   seiner   Tochter.
      a   fairytale.ACC tell   will he.NOM his.DAT daughter

   c. Seiner Tochter erzählen wird er   das   Märchen.
      his.DAT daughter tell   will he.NOM the.ACC fairytale

   d. Seiner Tochter ein   Märchen erzählen wird er.
      his.DAT daughter a.ACC fairytale tell   will he.NOM

If the local requirement of *wird* would be shared between filler and gap, the sentences in (45b)–(45d) would be ruled out, since the projections in the *Vorfeld* are not lexical elements but complex phrasal projections that are LEX −. Now, as pointed out by the authors mentioned above, this turns into a non-issue if not all information is shared between filler and gap. If LEX is outside LOCAL, the filler maybe LEX −, while the local constraints on the extracted element require the LEX value +. If all information is shared as in SBCG, no such solution is possible. Of course one could stick to the SBCG feature geometry and say that not the entire ARG-ST element is shared with the GAP element, but then one would end up with single structure sharings of all the features at the outermost level of a sign, that is, PHON, FORM, SYN, SEM, and CNTXT (see Sag 2012: 98 for these features)[21] and the whole point of grouping features is to avoid such multiple individual structure sharings in situations in which there is a systematic relation between feature values.

10.6.2.3 Selection of PHON and FORM values

The feature geometry of constructional HPSG has the PHON value outside of SYNSEM. Therefore verbs can select for syntactic and semantic properties of their arguments but not for their phonology. For example, they can require that an object has accusative

---

[21] Note that these structure sharings are necessary. It is not an option to leave the values of these features unspecified in the argument structure list. Since we have a model-theoretic view on things, an unspecified value would make the respective structures infinitely ambiguous, since infinitely many instantiation of these features are possible.

case but not that it starts with a vowel. SBCG allows for the selection of phonological information (the feature is called FORM here) and one example of such a selection is the indefinite article in English, which has to be either *a* or *an* depending on whether the noun or nominal projection it is combined with starts with a vowel or not (Flickinger, Mail to the HPSG mailing list, 01.03.2016):

(46) a. an institute
      b. a house

The distinction can be modeled by assuming a selection feature for determiners.[22] An alternative would be of course to capture all phonological phenomena by formulating constraints on phonology on the phrasal level (see Bird & Klein 1994 and Walther 1999 for phonology in HPSG).

Note also that the treatment of raising and nonlocal dependencies in SBCG admits nonlocal selection of phonology values, since the FORM value of the filler is present at the ARG-ST list of the head from which the argument is extracted. In earlier HPSG versions only LOCAL information is shared and elements in valence lists do not have a PHON feature. In principle, SBCG could be used to model languages in which the phonology of a filler is relevant for a head from which it is extracted. So for instance *likes* can see the phonology of *bagels* in (47):

(47) Bagels, I think that Peter likes.

It would be possible to state constraints saying that the filler has to contain a vowel or two vowels or that it ends with a consonant. In addition all elements on the extraction path (*that* and *think*) can see the phonology of the filler as well. While there are languages that mark the extraction path, I doubt that there are languages that have phonological effects across long distances.

Similarly, the analysis of raising in SBCG assumes that the element on the valence list of the embedded verb is identical to an element in the ARG-ST list of the matrix verb (Sag 2012: 159). Hence, both verbs in (48) can see the phonology of the subject:

(48) Kim can eat apples.

In principle there could be languages in which the form of the downstairs verb depends on the presence of an initial consonant in phonology of the subject. English allows for long chains of raising verbs and one could imagine languages in which all the verbs on the way are sensitive to the phonology of the subject. Such languages probably do not exist.

Now, is this a problem? Not for me, but if one develops a general setup in a way to exclude everything that is not attested in the languages of the world (as for instance the selection of arguments of arguments of arguments), then it is a problem that heads can see the phonology of elements that are far away.

---

[22] In Standard HPSG there is mutual selection between the determiner and the noun. The noun selects the determiner via SPR and the determiner selects the noun via a feature called SPECIFIED. This feature is similar to the MOD feature, which was explained in Section 9.1.7.

There are two possible conclusions for practitioners of SBCG: either the MOTHER feature could be given up since one agrees that theories that do not make wrong predictions are sufficiently constraint and one does not have to explicitly state what cannot occur in languages or one would have to react to the problem with nonlocally selected phonology values and therefore assume a SYNSEM or LOCAL feature that bundles information that is relevant in raising and nonlocal dependencies and does not include the phonology.[23] This supports the arguments I made on MOTHER and LOCAL in the previous subsections.

10.6.2.4 The VALENCE list

Another change from Constructional HPSG to SBCG involves the use of a single valence feature rather then three features SPR, SUBJ and COMPS that were suggested by Borsley (1987) to solve problems in earlier HPSG versions that used a single valence feature (SUBCAT). Borseley's suggestion was taken up by Pollard & Sag (1994: Chapter 9) and has been used in some version or other in other HPSG versions since then.

Sag (2012: 85) assumes that VPs are described by the following feature description:

(49) $\left[\text{SYN} \left[\text{VAL} \langle \text{NP} \rangle \right] \right]$

The problem with such an approach is that VPs differ from other phrasal projections in having an element on their VALENCE list. APs, NPs, and (some) PPs have an empty VALENCE list. In other versions of HPSG the complements are represented on the COMPS list and generalizations about phrases with fully saturated COMPS lists can be expressed directly. One such generalization is that projections with an empty COMPS list (NPs, PPs, VPs, adverbs, CPs) can be extraposed in German (Müller 1999a: Section 13.1.2).

10.6.2.5 Conclusion

Due to the conceptual problems with meta-statements and the relatively simple ways of getting around locality restrictions, the reorganization of features (MOTHER vs. SYN-SEM) does not bring with it any advantages. Since the grammar becomes more complex due to the meta-constraint, we should reject this change.[24] Other changes in the fea-

---

[23] If SYNSEM is reintroduced, the elements in the valence lists could be of type *synsem*. Information about phonology would not be part of the description of the selected elements. This would not solve the problem of partial verb phrase fronting though, since the LEX feature is selected for (hence part of the information under SYNSEM) but not shared with the filler. One would need a LOCAL feature in addition to SYNSEM. See Section 10.6.2.2.

[24] In Müller (2013b: 253) I claimed that SBCG uses a higher number of features in comparison to other variants of HPSG because of the assumption of the MOTHER feature. As Van Eynde (2015) points out this is not true for more recent variants of HPSG since they have the SYNSEM feature, which is not needed if MOTHER is assumed. (Van Eynde refers to the LOCAL feature, but the LOCAL feature was eliminated because it was considered superfluous because of the lexical analysis of extraction, see Section 10.6.2.2.) If one simply omits the MOTHER feature from SBCG one is back to the 1987 version of HPSG (Pollard & Sag 1987), which also used a SYN and a SEM feature. What would be missing would be the locality of selection (Sag 2012: 149) that was enforced to some extent by the SYNSEM feature. Note that the locality of selection that is enforced by SYNSEM can be circumvented by the use of relational constraints as well (see Frank Richter and Manfred Sailer's work on collocations (Richter & Sailer 1999a; Soehn & Sailer 2008)). So in principle, we end up with style guides in this area of grammar as well.

ture geometry (elimination of the LOCAL feature and use of a single valence feature) are problematic as well. However, if we do reject the revised feature geometry and revert to the feature geometry that was used before, then Sign-Based Construction Grammar and Constructional HPSG (Sag 1997) are (almost) indistinguishable.

10.6.3 Embodied Construction Grammar

Embodied Construction Grammar was developed by Bergen & Chang (2005) and there are some implementations of fragments of German that use this format (Porzel et al. 2006). In the following, I will briefly present the formalism using an example construction. (50) gives the DetNoun construction:[25]

(50)

Construction DetNoun
subcase of RefExp
constructional
d:Determiner
c:CommonNoun
self.case   ↔ d.case
self.number ↔ c.number
d.gender   ↔ c.gender
d.case   ↔ c.case
d.number   ↔ c.number
form
d.f **before** c.f
meaning
self.m   ↔ c.m

This representational form is reminiscent of PATR-II grammars (Shieber, Uszkoreit, Pereira, Robinson & Tyson 1983): as in PATR-II, the daughters of a construction are given names. As such, (50) contains the daughters c and d. d is a determiner and c is a common noun. It is possible to refer to the construction itself via the object **self**. Constructions (and also their daughters) are feature-value descriptions. Structure sharing is represented by path equations. For example, d.gender ↔ c.gender states that the value of the gender feature of the determiner is identical to the gender feature of the noun. As well as restrictions on features, there are restrictions on the form. d.f **before** c.f states that the form contribution of the determiner must occur before that of the noun. Bergen & Chang (2005) differentiate between immediate (**meets**) and non-immediate precedence (**before**). Part of the information represented under f is the orthographic form (f.orth). The inheritance relation is given explicitly in the construction as in Kay & Fillmore (1999).

The construction in (50) can be represented in a similar way to the format used in Chapter 6: (51) shows how this is done. The structure in (51) corresponds to a construction where the determiner directly precedes the noun because the form contribution of the

---

[25] For a similar construction, see Bergen & Chang (2005: 162).

$$(51) \quad \begin{bmatrix} \text{DetNoun} \\ \text{F|ORTH} \quad \boxed{1} \oplus \boxed{2} \\ \text{CASE} \quad \boxed{3} \\ \text{NUMBER} \quad \boxed{4} \\ \text{M} \quad \boxed{5} \\ \\ \text{DTRS} \quad \left\langle \begin{bmatrix} \text{Determiner} \\ \text{F|ORTH} \quad \boxed{1} \\ \text{CASE} \quad \boxed{3} \\ \text{NUMBER} \quad \boxed{4} \\ \text{GENDER} \quad \boxed{6} \end{bmatrix}, \begin{bmatrix} \text{CommonNoun} \\ \text{F|ORTH} \quad \boxed{2} \\ \text{CASE} \quad \boxed{3} \\ \text{NUMBER} \quad \boxed{4} \\ \text{GENDER} \quad \boxed{6} \\ \text{M} \quad \boxed{5} \end{bmatrix} \right\rangle \end{bmatrix}$$

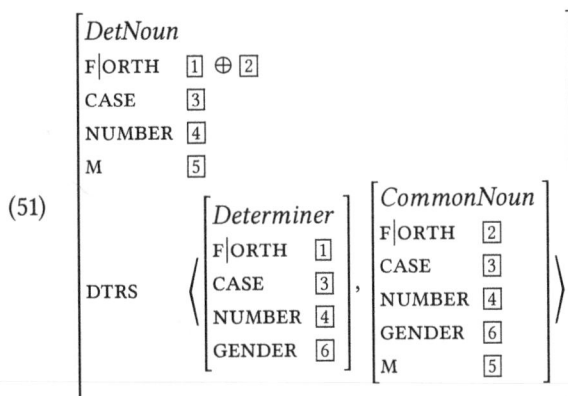

determiner has been combined with that of the noun. This strict adjacency constraint makes sense as the claim that the determiner must precede the noun is not restrictive enough since sequences such as (52b) would be allowed:

(52)   a.   [dass] die Frauen Türen öffnen
            that   the women doors open

            'that the woman open doors'

     b.   * die   Türen   öffnen
             Frauen

If discontinuous phrases are permitted, *die Türen* 'the doors' can be analyzed with the DetNoun Construction although another noun phrase intervenes between the determiner and the noun (Müller 1999a: 424; 1999c). The order in (52b) can be ruled out by linearization constraints or constraints on the continuity of arguments. If we want the construction to require that the determiner and noun be adjacent, then we would simply use **meets** instead of **before** in the specification of the construction.

This discussion has shown that (51) is more restrictive than (50). There are, however, contexts in which one could imagine using discontinuous constituents such as the deviant one in (52b). For example, discontinuous constituents have been proposed for verbal complexes, particle verbs and certain coordination data (Wells 1947). Examples for analyses with discontinuous constituents in the framework of HPSG are Reape (1994), Kathol (1995), Kathol (2000), Crysmann (2008), and Beavers & Sag (2004).[26] These analyses, which are discussed in Section 11.7.2.2 in more detail, differ from those previously presented in that they use a feature DOMAIN instead of or in addition to the daughters features. The value of the DOMAIN feature is a list containing the head and the elements dependent on it. The elements do not have to necessarily be adjacent in the utterance, that is, discontinuous constituents are permitted. Which elements are entered into this list in which way is governed by the constraints that are part of the linguistic theory. This differs from the simple **before** statement in ECG in that it is much more flexible

---

[26] Crysmann, Beaver and Sag deal with coordination phenomena. For an analysis of coordination in TAG that also makes use of discontinuous constituents, see Sarkar & Joshi (1996) and Section 21.6.2.

and in that one can also restrict the area in which a given element can be ordered since elements can be freely ordered inside their domain only.

There is a further difference between the representation in (50) and the general HPSG schemata: in the ECG variant, linearization requirements are linked to constructions. In HPSG and GPSG, it is assumed that linearization rules hold generally, that is, if we were to assume the rules in (53), we would not have to state for each rule explicitly that shorter NPs tend to precede longer ones and that animate nouns tend to occur before inanimate ones.

(53) a. S → NP[nom], NP[acc], V
      b. S → NP[nom], NP[dat], V
      c. S → NP[nom], NP[dat], NP[acc], V
      d. S → NP[nom], NP[acc], PP, V

It is possible to capture these generalizations in ECG if one specifies linearization constraints for more general constructions and more specific constructions inherit them from these. As an example, consider the Active-Ditransitive Construction discussed by Bergen & Chang (2005: 170):

(54)
> **Construction** Active-Ditransitive
> **subcase of** Pred-Expr
> **constructional**
> agent:Ref-Expr
> action:Verb
> recipient:Ref-Expr
> theme:Ref-Expr
>
> ...
>
> **form**
> agent.f **before** action.f
> action.f **meets** recipient.f
> recipient.f **meets** theme.f
> **meaning**
>   ...

These restrictions allow the sentences in (55a,b) and rule out those in (55c):

(55) a. Mary tossed me a drink.
      b. Mary happily tossed me a drink.
      c. * Mary tossed happily me a drink.

The restriction agent.f **before** action.f forces an order where the subject occurs before the verb but also allows for adverbs to occur between the subject and the verb. The other constraints on form determine the order of the verb and its object: the recipient must be adjacent to the verb and the theme must be adjacent to the recipient. The requirement that an agent in the active must occur before the verb is not specific to ditransitive constructions. This restriction could therefore be factored out as follows:

(56)

> **Construction** Active-Agent-Verb
>   **subcase of** Pred-Expr
>   **constructional**
>   agent:Ref-Expr
>   action:Verb
> **form**
>   agent.f **before** action.f

The Active-Ditransitive Construction in (54) would then inherit the relevant information from (56).

In addition to the descriptive means used in (50), there is the evokes operator (Bergen & Chang 2005: 151–152). An interesting example is the representation of the term hypotenuse: this concept can only be explained by making reference to a right-angled triangle (Langacker 1987: Chapter 5). Chang (2008: 67) gives the following formalization:

(57)

> **Schema** hypotenuse
>   **subcase of** line-segment
>   **evokes** right-triangle **as** rt
> **constraints**
>   **self** ↔ rt.long-side

This states that a hypotenuse is a particular line segment, namely the longest side of a right-angled triangle. The concept of a right-angled triangle is activated by means of the evokes operator. Evokes creates an instance of an object of a certain type (in the example, *rt* of type *right-triangle*). It is then possible to refer to the properties of this object in a schema or in a construction.

The feature description in (58) is provided in the notation from Chapter 6. It is the equivalent to (57).

(58) $\boxed{1}$
$$\begin{bmatrix} hypotenuse \\ \text{EVOKES} \quad \left\langle \begin{bmatrix} right\text{-}triangle \\ \text{LONG-SIDE} \quad \boxed{1} \end{bmatrix} \right\rangle \end{bmatrix}$$

The type *hypotenuse* is a subtype of *line-segment*. The value of EVOKES is a list since a schema or construction can evoke more than one concept. The only element in this list in (58) is an object of type *right-triangle*. The value of the feature LONG-SIDE is identified with the entire structure. This essentially means the following: I, as a hypotenuse, am the long side of a right-angled triangle.

Before turning to FCG in the next subsection, we can conclude that ECG and HPSG are notational variants.

10.6.4 Fluid Construction Grammar

Van Trijp (2013, 2014) claims that SBCG and HPSG are fundamentally different from Fluid Construction Grammar (FCG). He claims that the former approaches are generative ones while the latter is a cognitive-functional one. I think that it is not legitimate to draw these distinctions on the basis of what is done in FCG.[27] I will comment on this at various places in this section. I first deal with the representations that are used in FCG, talk about argument structure constructions, the combination operations fusion and merging that are used in FCG and then provide a detailed comparison of FCG and SBCG/HPSG.

10.6.4.1 General remarks on the representational format

Fluid Construction Grammar (FCG, Steels 2011) is similar to HPSG in that it uses attribute value matrices to represent linguistic objects. However, these AVMs are untyped as in LFG. Since there are no types, there are no inheritance hierarchies that can be used to capture generalizations, but one can use macros to reach similar effects. Constructions can refer to more general constructions (van Trijp 2013: 105). Every AVM comes with a name and can be depicted as follows:

(59)
$$\begin{bmatrix} \textit{unit-name} \\ \begin{bmatrix} \text{FEATURE}_1 & \textit{value}_1 \\ \dots \\ \text{FEATURE}_n & \textit{value}_n \end{bmatrix} \end{bmatrix}$$

Linguistic objects have a form and a meaning pole. The two poles could be organized into a single feature description by using a SYN and a SEM feature, but in FCG papers the two poles are presented separately and connected via a double arrow. (60) is an example:

(60) The name *Kim* according to van Trijp (2013: 99):

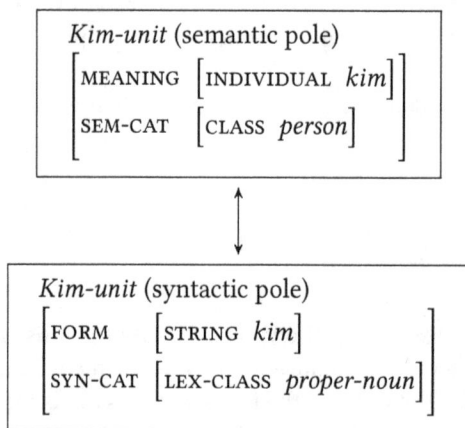

$$\begin{bmatrix} \textit{Kim-unit} \text{ (semantic pole)} \\ \begin{bmatrix} \text{MEANING} & \begin{bmatrix} \text{INDIVIDUAL} & \textit{kim} \end{bmatrix} \\ \text{SEM-CAT} & \begin{bmatrix} \text{CLASS} & \textit{person} \end{bmatrix} \end{bmatrix} \end{bmatrix}$$

$$\updownarrow$$

$$\begin{bmatrix} \textit{Kim-unit} \text{ (syntactic pole)} \\ \begin{bmatrix} \text{FORM} & \begin{bmatrix} \text{STRING} & \textit{kim} \end{bmatrix} \\ \text{SYN-CAT} & \begin{bmatrix} \text{LEX-CLASS} & \textit{proper-noun} \end{bmatrix} \end{bmatrix} \end{bmatrix}$$

Depending on the mode in which the lexical items are used, the syntactic pole or the semantic pole is used first. The first processing step is a matching phase in which it is checked whether the semantic pole (for generation) or the syntactic pole (for parsing)

---

[27] Steels (2013: 153) emphasizes the point that FCG is a technical tool for implementing constructionist ideas rather than a theoretical framework of its own. However, authors working with the FCG system publish linguistic papers that share a certain formal background and certain linguistic assumptions. So this section addresses some of the key assumptions made and some of the mechanisms used.

matches the structure that was build so far. After this test for unification, the actual unification, which is called merging, is carried out. After this step, the respective other pole (syntax for generation and semantics for parsing) is merged. This is illustrated in Figure 10.2.

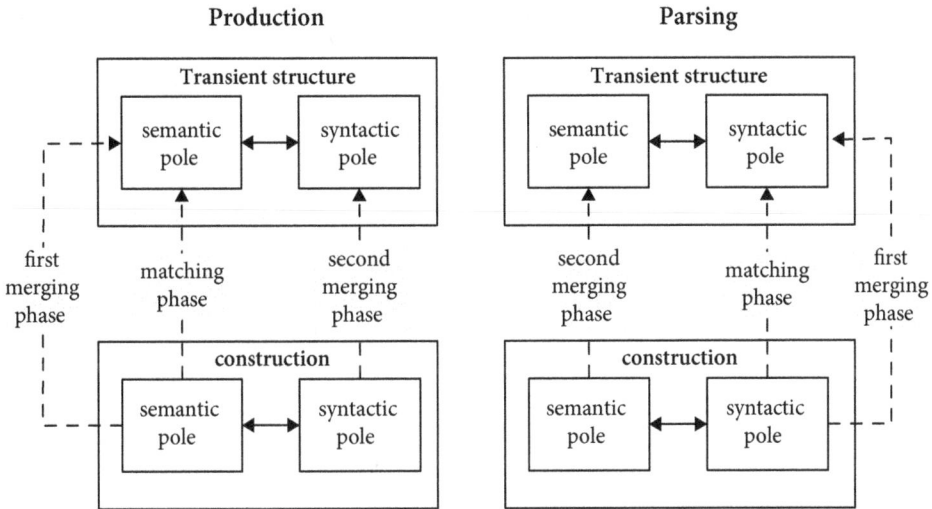

Figure 10.2: Generation and parsing in FCG (van Trijp 2013: 99)

10.6.4.2 Argument Structure Constructions

Fluid Construction Grammar assumes a phrasal approach to argument structure, that is, it is assumed that lexical items enter into phrasal configurations that contribute independent meaning (van Trijp 2011). The FCG approach is one version of implementing Goldberg's plugging approach to argument structure constructions (Goldberg 1995). Van Trijp suggests that every lexical item comes with a representation of potential argument roles like Agent, Patient, Recipient, and Goal. Phrasal argument structure constructions are combined with the respective lexical items and realize a subset of the argument roles, that is they assign them to grammatical functions. Figure 10.3 on the next page shows an example: the verb *sent* has the semantic roles Agent, Patient, Recipient, and Goal. Depending on the argument structure construction that is chosen, a subset of these roles is selected for realization.[28]

Note that under such an approach, it is necessary to have a passive variant of every active construction. For languages that allow for the combination of passive and imper-

---

[28] It is interesting to note here that van Trijp (2011: 141) actually suggests a lexical account since every lexical item is connected to various phrasal constructions via coapplication links. So every such pair of a lexical item and a phrasal construction corresponds to a lexical item in Lexicalized Tree Adjoining Grammar (LTAG). See also Müller & Wechsler (2014a: 25) on Goldberg's assumption that every lexical item is associated with phrasal constructions.

Note that such coapplication links are needed since without them the approach cannot account for cases in which two or more argument roles can only be realized together but not in isolation or in any other combination with other listed roles.

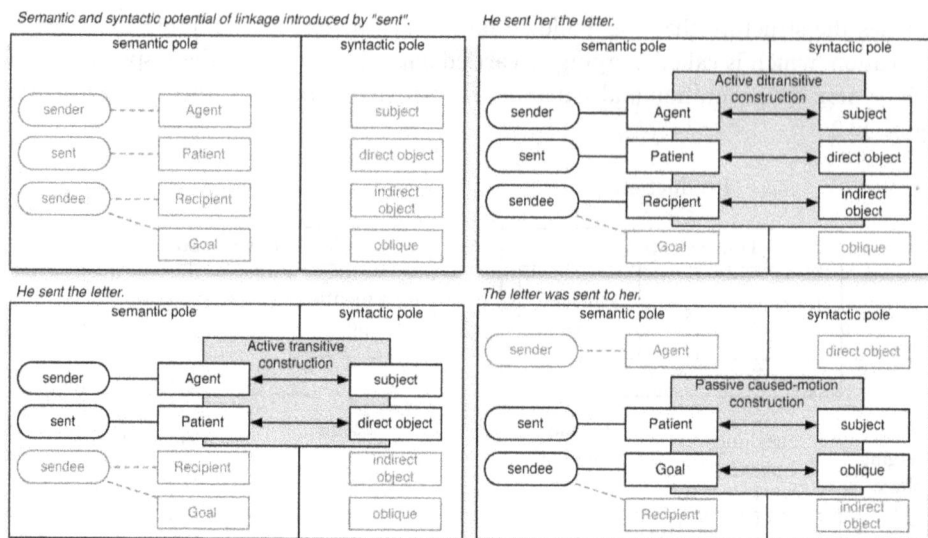

Figure 10.3: Lexical items and phrasal constructions. Figure from van Trijp (2011: 122)

sonal constructions, one would be forced to assume a transitive-passive-impersonal construction. As was argued in Müller (2006: Section 2.6) free datives (commodi/incommodi) in German can be added to almost any construction. They interact with the dative passive and hence should be treated as arguments. So, for the resultative construction one would need an active variant, a passive variant, a variant with dative argument, a variant with dative argument and dative passive, and a middle variant. While it is technically possible to list all these patterns and it is imaginable that we store all this information in our brains, the question is whether such listings really reflect our linguistic knowledge. If a new construction comes into existence, lets say an active sentence pattern with a nominative and two datives in German, wouldn't we expect that this pattern can be used in the passive? While proposals that establish relations between active and passive constructions would predict this, alternative proposals that just list the attested possibilities do not.

The issue of how such generalizations should be captured was discussed in connection with the organization of the lexicon in HPSG (Flickinger 1987; Meurers 2001). In the lexical world, one could simply categorize all verbs according to their valence and say that *loves* is a transitive verb and the passive variant *loved* is an intransitive verb. Similarly *gives* would be categorized as a ditransitive verb and *given* as a transitive one. Obviously this misses the point that *loved* and *given* share something: they both are related to their active form in a systematic way. This kind of generalization was called a horizontal generalization as compared to vertical generalizations, which describe classes in an inheritance hierarchy.

The issue is independent of the lexical organization of knowledge, it can be applied to phrasal representations as well. Phrasal constructions can be organized in hierarchies (vertical), but the relation between certain variants is not covered by this. The analog to the lexical rules in a lexical approach are GPSG-like metarules in a phrasal approach. So what seems to be missing in FCG is something that relates phrasal patterns, e.g., allo-constructions (Cappelle 2006; Goldberg 2014: 116, see also footnote 12).

10.6.4.3 Fusion, matching and merging

As was pointed out by Dowty (1989: 89–90), checking for semantic compatibility is not sufficient when deciding whether a verb may enter (or be fused with) a certain construction. The example is the contrast between *dine, eat,* and *devour.* While the thing that is eaten may not be realized with *dine*, its realization is optional with *eat* and obligatory with *devour*. So the lexical items have to come with some information about this.

Van Trijp (2011) and Steels & van Trijp (2011) make an interesting suggestion that could help here: every verb comes with a list of potential roles and argument structure constructions can pick subsets of these roles (see Figure 10.3). This is called *matching*: introducing new argument roles is not allowed. This would make it possible to account for *dine*: one could say that there is something that is eaten, but that no Theme role is made available for linking to grammatical functions. To account for the extension of argument roles as it is observed in the Caused-Motion Construction (Goldberg 1995: Chapter 7), Steels & van Trijp (2011) suggest a process called *merging*. Merging is seen as a repair strategy: if an utterance involves an intransitive verb and some other material, the utterance cannot be processed with matching alone. For example, when processing Goldberg's example in (61), *he sneezed* could be parsed, but *the foam* and *off the cappuccino* would be unintegrated (see Chapter 21 for an extended discussion of such constructions).

(61)   He sneezed the foam off the cappuccino.[29]

So, Steels & van Trijp (2011: 319–320) suggest that only if regular constructions cannot apply, merging is allowed. The problem with this is that human language is highly ambiguous and in the case at hand this could result in situations in which there is a reading for an utterance, so that the repair strategy would never kick in. Consider (62):[30]

(62)   Schlag den Mann tot!
       beat   the man dead
       'Beat the man to death!' or 'Beat the dead man!'

(62) has two readings: the resultative reading in which *tot* 'dead' expresses the result of the beating and another reading in which *tot* is a depictive predicate. The second reading is dispreferred, since the activity of beating dead people is uncommon, but the structure is parallel to other sentences with depictive predicates:

(63)   Iss den Fisch roh!
       eat the fish raw

---

[29] Goldberg (2006: 42).
[30] I apologize for these examples ...

The depictive reading can be forced by coordinating *tot* with a predicate that is not a plausible result predicate:

(64) Schlag ihn tot   oder lebendig!
      beat   him dead or   alive

   'Beat him when he is dead or while he is alive!'

So, the problem is that (62) has a reading which does not require the invocation of the repair mechanism: *schlug* 'beat' is used with the transitive construction and *tot* is an adjunct (see Winkler 1997). However, the more likely analysis of (64) is the one with the resultative analysis, in which the valence frame is extended by an oblique element. So this means that one has to allow the application of merging independent of other analyses that might be possible. As Steels & van Trijp (2011: 320) note, if merging is allowed to apply freely, utterances like (65a) will be allowed and of course (65b) as well.

(65)   a. * She sneezed her boyfriend.

       b. * She dined a steak.

In (65) *sneeze* and *dined* are used in the transitive construction.

   The way out of this dilemma is to establish information in lexical items that specifies in which syntactic environments a verb can be used. This information can be weighted and for instance the probability of *dine* to be used transitively would be extremely low. Steels and van Trijp would connect their lexical items to phrasal constructions via so-called coapplication links and the strength of the respective link would be very low for *dine* and the transitive construction and reasonably high for *sneeze* and the Caused-Motion Construction. This would explain the phenomena (and in a usage-based way), but it would be a lexical approach, as it is common in CG, HPSG, SBCG, and DG.

10.6.4.4 Long-distance dependencies

Van Trijp (2014) compares the SLASH-based approaches that are used in GPSG, HPSG, and SBCG with the approach that he suggests within the framework of FCG. He claims that there are fundamental differences between SBCG and FCG and assigns SBCG to the class of generative grammars, while placing FCG in the class of cognitive-functional approaches. He claims that his cognitive-functional approach is superior in terms of completeness, explanatory adequacy, and theoretical parsimony (p. 2). What van Trijp (2014) suggests is basically an analysis that was suggested by Reape (2000) in unpublished work (see Reape (1994) for a published version of an linearization-based approach and Kathol (2000); Müller (1996c, 1999a, 2002a) for linearization-based approaches that despite of being linearization-based assume the SLASH approach for nonlocal dependencies). Van Trijp develops a model of grammar that allows for discontinuous constituents and just treats the serialization of the object in sentences like (66) as an alternative linearization option.

(66)   a. This book, I read.

       b. What did the boy hit?

Van Trijp's analysis involves several units that do not normally exist in phrase structure grammars, but can be modeled via adjacency constraints or represent relations between items which are part of lexical representations in HPSG/SBCG anyway. An example is the subject-verb anchor that connects the subject and the verb to represent the fact that these two items play an important functional role. Figure 10.4 shows the analysis of (67).

(67)   What did the boy hit?

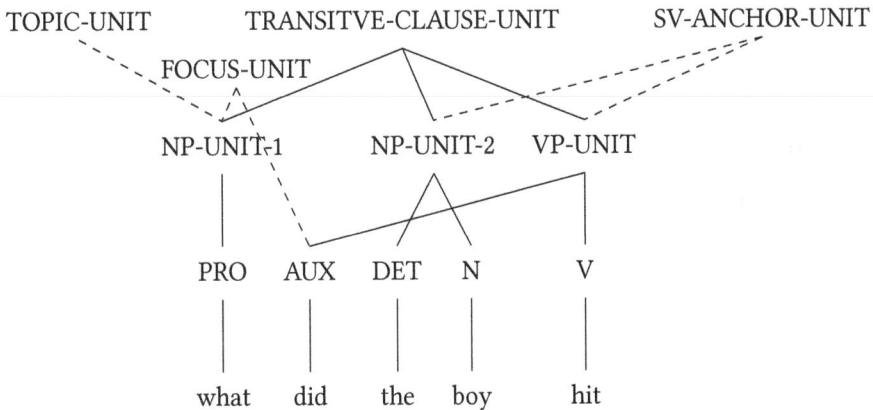

Figure 10.4: The analysis of *What did the boy hit?* according to van Trijp (2014: 265)

As can be seen in the figure, van Trijp also refers to information structural terms like topic and focus. It should be noted here that the analysis of information structure has quite some history in the framework of HPSG (Engdahl & Vallduví 1996; Kuhn 1995, 1996; Günther et al. 1999; Wilcock 2001; De Kuthy 2002; Paggio 2005; Bildhauer 2008; Bildhauer & Cook 2010). The fact that information structure is not talked about in syntax papers like Sag (2012) does not entail that information structure is ignored or should be ignored in theories like HPSG and SBCG. So much for completeness. The same holds of course for explanational adequacy. This leaves us with theoretical parsimony, but before I comment on this, I want to discuss van Trijp's analysis in a little bit more detail in order to show that many of his claims are empirically problematic and that his theory therefore cannot be explanatory since empirical correctness is a precondition for explanatory adequacy.

Van Trijp claims that sentences with nonlocal dependency constructions in English start with a topic.[31] Bresnan's sentences in (2) and (3) were discussed on page 216 (Bresnan 2001: 97) and are repeated below for convenience:

(68)   Q: What did you name your cat?
       A: Rosie I named her. (*Rosie* = FOCUS)

---

[31] Van Trijp (2014: 256) uses the following definitions for topic and focus: "Topicality is defined in terms of aboutness: the topic of an utterance is what the utterance is 'about'. Focality is defined in terms of salience: focus is used for highlighting the most important information given the current communicative setting."

(69)   Q: What did you name your pets?
        A: My dog, I named Harold. My cat, I named Rosie. (*my dog, my cat* = TOPIC)

These sentences show that the pre-subject position is not unambiguously a topic or a focus position. So, a statement saying that the fronted element is a topic is empirically not correct. If this position is to be associated with an information structural function, this association has to be a disjunction admitting both topics and focused constituents.

   A further problematic aspect of van Trijp's analysis is that he assumes that the auxiliary *do* is an object marker (p. 10, 22) or a non-subject marker (p. 23). It is true that *do* support is not necessary in subject questions like (70a), but only in (70b), but this does not imply that all items that are followed by *do* are objects.

(70)   a. Who saw the man?
        b. Who did John see?

First, *do* can be used to emphasize the verb:

(71)   Who *did* see the man?

Second, all types of other grammatical functions can precede the verb:

(72)   a. Where did you see the man?   (adverbial)
        b. How tall is the man?   (predicative)
        c. What did John consider Peter?   (predicative)
        d. What does this book cost?   (adverbial)
        e. About what did you talk?   (prepositional object)

And finally, even a subject can appear in front of *do* if it is extracted from another clause:

(73)   Who does he think saw this man?   (subject)

   There is a further empirical problem: approaches that assume that a filler is related to its origin can explain scope ambiguities that only arise when an element is extracted. Compare for instance the sentence in (74a) with the sentences in (74b, c): although the order of *oft* 'often' and *nicht* 'not' in (74a) and (74c) is the same, (74a) is ambiguous but (74c) is not.

(74)   a. Oft   liest er das Buch nicht.
            often reads he the book not
            'It is often that he does not read the book.' or 'It is not the case that he reads the book often.'

        b. dass er das Buch nicht oft   liest
            that he the book not often reads
            'that it is not the case that he reads the book often'

        c. dass er das Buch oft   nicht liest
            that he the book often not reads
            'that it is often that he does not read the book'

(74a) has the two readings that correspond to (74b) and (74c). A purely linearization-based approach probably has difficulties to explain this. A SLASH-based approach can assume that (74a) has a gap (or some similar means for the introduction of nonlocal dependencies) at the position of *oft* in (74b) or (74c). The gap information is taken into account in the semantic composition at the site of the gap. This automatically accounts for the observed readings.

Another empirical problem that has to be solved is the existence of extraction path marking languages. Bouma, Malouf & Sag (2001a) list a number of languages in which elements vary depending on the existence or absence of a gap in a constituent they attach to. For instance, Irish has complementizers that have one form if the clause they attach to has an element extracted and another form if it does not. SLASH-based proposals can account for this in a straight-forward way: the fact that a constituent is missing in a phrase is represented in the SLASH value of the trace and this information is percolated up the tree. So even complex structures contain the information that there is a constituent missing inside them. Complementizers that are combined with sentences therefore can select sentences with SLASH values that correspond to their inflection. Van Trijp's answer to this challenge is that all languages are different (van Trijp 2014: 263) and that the evidence from one language does not necessarily mean that the analysis for that language is also appropriate for another language. While I agree with this view in principle (see Section 13.1), I do think that extraction is a rather fundamental property of languages and that nonlocal dependencies should be analyzed in parallel for those languages that have it.

Van Trijp points out that SBCG does not have a performance model and contrasts this with FCG. On page 252 he states:

> So parsing starts by segmenting the utterance into discrete forms, which are then categorized into words by morphological and lexical constructions, and which can then be grouped together as phrases (see Steels, 2011b, for a detailed account of lexico-phrasal processing in FCG). So the parser will find similar constituents for all four utterances, as shown in examples (21–24). Since auxiliary-*do* in example (24) falls outside the immediate domain of the VP, it is not yet recognized as a member of the VP.
>
> All of these phrases are disconnected, which means that the grammar still has to identify the relations between the phrases. (van Trijp 2014: 252)

Van Trijp provides several tree fragments that contain NPs for subject and object and states that these have to be combined in order to analyze the sentences he discusses. This is empirically inadequate: if FCG does not make the competence/performance distinction, then the way utterances are analyzed should reflect the way humans process language (and this is what is usually claimed about FCG). However, all we know about human language processing points towards an incremental processing, that is, we process information as soon as it is available. We start to process the first word taking into account all of the relevant aspects (phonology, stress, part of speech, semantics, information structure) and come up with an hypothesis about how the utterance could proceed.

As soon as we have two words processed (in fact even earlier: integration already happens during the processing of words) we integrate the second word into what we know already and continue to follow our hypothesis, or revise it, or simply fail. See Section 15.2 for details on processing and the discussion of experiments that show that processing is incremental. So, we have to say that van Trijp's analysis fails on empirical grounds: his modeling of performance aspects is not adequate.

The parsing scheme that van Trijp describes is pretty much similar to those of HPSG parsers, but these usually come without any claims about performance. Modeling performance is rather complex since a lot of factors play a role. It is therefore reasonable to separate competence and performance and continue to work the way it is done in HPSG and FCG. This does not mean that performance aspects should not be modeled, in fact psycholinguistic models using HPSG have been developed in the past (Konieczny 1996), but developing both a grammar with large coverage and the performance model that combines with it demands a lot of resources.

I now turn to parsimony: van Trijp uses a subject-verb anchor construction that combines the subject and the main verb. Because of examples like (75) it must be possible to have discontinuous subject-verb constructions:[32]

(75)   Peter often reads books.

But if such constructions can be discontinuous one has to make sure that (76b) cannot be an instantiation of the subject-verb construction:

(76)   a.   The boy I think left.
        b.   * I the boy think left.

Here it is required to have some adjacency between the subject and the verb it belongs to, modulo some intervening adverbials. This is modelled quite nicely in phrase structure grammars that have a VP node. Whatever the internal structure of such a VP node may be, it has to be adjacent to the subject in sentences like the ones above. The dislocated element has to be adjacent to the complex consisting of subject and VP. This is what the Filler-Head Schema does in HPSG and SBCG. Van Trijp criticizes SBCG for having to stipulate such a schema, but I cannot see how his grammar can be complete without a statement that ensures the right order of elements in sentences with fronted elements.

Van Trijp stated that FCG differs from what he calls generative approaches in that it does not want to characterize only the well-formed utterances of a language. According to him, the parsing direction is much more liberal in accepting input than other theories. So it could well be that he is happy to find a structure for (76b). Note though that this is incompatible with other claims made by van Trijp: he argued that FCG is superior to other theories in that it comes with a performance model (or rather in not

---

[32] Unless modals and tense auxiliaries are treated as main verbs (which they should not in English), constructions with modals seem to be another case where the subject and the main verb are not adjacent:

(i)   a.   Peter will read the book.
       b.   Peter has read the book.

separating competence from performance at all). But then (76b) should be rejected both on competence and performance grounds. It is just unacceptable and speakers reject it for whatever reasons. Any sufficiently worked out theory of language has to account for this.

One of the success stories of non-transformational grammar is the SLASH-based analysis of nonlocal dependencies by Gazdar (1981b). This analysis made it possible for the first time to explain Ross's Across the Board Extraction (Ross 1967). The examples were already discussed on page 193 and are repeated here for convenience:

(77) a. The kennel which Mary made and Fido sleeps in has been stolen.

(= S/NP & S/NP)

  b. The kennel in which Mary keeps drugs and Fido sleeps has been stolen.

(= S/PP & S/PP)

  c. * The kennel (in) which Mary made and Fido sleeps has been stolen.

(= S/NP & S/PP)

The generalization is that two (or more) constituents can be coordinated if they have identical syntactic categories and identical SLASH values. This explains why *which* and *in which* in (77a,b) can fill two positions in the respective clauses. Now, theories that do not use a SLASH feature for the percolation of information about missing elements have to find different ways to make sure that all argument slots are filled and that the correct correspondence between extracted elements and the respective argument role is established. Note that this is not straightforward in models like the one suggested by van Trijp, since he has to allow the preposition *in* to be combined with some material to the left of it that is simultaneously also the object of *made*. Usually an NP cannot simply be used by two different heads as their argument. As an example consider (78a):

(78) a. * John said about the cheese that I like.

  b. John said about the cheese that I like it.

If it would be possible to use material several times, a structure for (78a) would be possible in which *the cheese* is the object of the preposition *about* and of the verb *like*. This sentence, however, is totally out: the pronoun *it* has to be used to fill the object slot.

There is a further problem related to discontinuity. If one does not restrict continuity, then constituent orders like (79b) are admitted by the grammar:

(79) a. Deshalb klärt,   dass Peter kommt, ob   Klaus spielt.
         therefore resolves that Peter comes   whether Klaus plays

      'Therefore that Peter comes resolves whether Klaus will play.'

  b. * Deshalb klärt   dass ob   Peter Klaus kommt spielt.
         therefore resolves that whether Peter Klaus comes plays

The interesting thing about the word salad in (79b) is that the constituent order within the *dass* clause and within the *ob* clause is correct. That is, the complementizer precedes the subject, which in turn precedes the verb. The problem is that the constituents of the two clauses are mixed.

In a model that permits discontinuous constituents, one cannot require that all parts of an argument have to be arranged after all parts that belong to another argument since discontinuity is used to account for nonlocal dependencies. So, it must be possible to have *Klaus* before other arguments (or parts of other arguments) since *Klaus* can be extracted. An example of mixing parts of phrases is given in (80):

(80)   Dieses Buch hat der Mann mir versprochen, seiner Frau zu geben, der gestern
        this   book has the man me promised   his   wife to give   who yesterday
        hier aufgetreten ist.
        here performed is

        'The man who performed here yesterday promised me to give this book to his wife.'

We see that material that refers to *der Mann* 'the man', namely the relative clause *der gestern hier aufgetreten ist* 'who performed here yesterday', appears to the right. And the object of *geben* 'to give', which would normally be part of the phrase *dieses Buch seiner Frau zu geben* 'this book his wife to give' appears to the left. So, in general it is possible to mix parts of phrases, but this is possible in a very restricted way only. Some dependencies extend all the way to the left of certain units (fronting) and others all the way to the right (extraposition). Extraposition is clause-bound, while extraction is not. In approaches like GPSG, HPSG and SBCG, the facts are covered by assuming that constituents for a complete clause are continuous apart from constituents that are fronted or extraposed. The fronted and extraposed constituents are represented in SLASH and EXTRA (Keller 1995; Müller 1999a), respectively, rather than in valence features, so that it is possible to require of constituents that have all their valents saturated to be continuous.

Summing up the discussion of parsimony, it has to be said that van Trijp has to provide the details on how continuity is ensured. The formalization of this is not trivial and only after this is done can FCG be compared with the SLASH-based approach.

In addition to all the points discussed so far, there is a logical flaw in van Trijp's argumentation. He states that:

> whereas the filler-gap analysis cannot explain WHY *do*-support does not occur in *wh*-questions where the subject is assigned questioning focus, this follows naturally from the interaction of different linguistic perspectives in this paper's approach. (van Trijp 2014: 263)

The issue here is whether a filler-gap analysis or an analysis with discontinuous constituents is suited better for explaining the data. A correct argumentation against the filler-gap analysis would require a proof that information structural or other functional constraints cannot be combined with this analysis. This proof was not provided and in fact I think it cannot be provided since there are approaches that integrate information structure. Simply pointing out that a theory is incomplete does not falsify a theory. This point was already made in my review of Boas (2003) and in a reply to Boas (2014). See

Müller (2005a: 655–656), Müller (2007b: Chapter 20), and Müller & Wechsler (2014b: Footnote 15).

The conclusion about the FCG analysis of nonlocal dependencies is that there are some empirical flaws that can be easily fixed or assumptions that can simply be dropped (role of *do* as object marker, claim that the initial position in English fronting construction is the topic), some empirical shortcomings (coordination, admittance of illformed utterances with discontinuous constituents), some empirical problems when the analysis is extended to other languages (scope of adjuncts in German), and the parsimony of the analyses is not really comparable since the restrictions on continuity are not really worked out (or at least not published). If the formalization of restrictions on continuity in FCG turns out to be even half as complex as the formalization that is necessary for accounts of nonlocal dependencies (extraction and extraposition) in linearization-based HPSG that Reape (2000) suggested,[33] the SLASH-based analysis would be favorable.

In any case, I do not see how nonlocal dependencies could be used to drive a wedge between SBCG and FCG. If there are functional considerations that have to be taken into account, they should be modeled in both frameworks. In general, FCG should be more restrictive than SBCG since FCG claims to integrate a performance model, so both competence and performance constraints should be operative. I will come back to the competence/performance distinction in the following section, which is a more general comparison of SBCG and FCG.

10.6.4.5 Comparison to Sign-Based Construction Grammar/HPSG

According to van Trijp (2013), there are the differences shown in Table 10.1. These differences will be discussed in the following subsections.

Table 10.1: Differences between SBCG and FCG according to van Trijp (2013: 112)

Scientific model	Theoretical physics (abstract calculus)	Evolutionary theory (complex adaptive system)
Linguistic approach	Generative (competence model)	Cognitive-functional (parsing and production)
Formalization	Mathematical (amenable for implementation)	Computational (implemented)
Constructions	Static type constraints	Dynamic mappings
Constructicon	Signature and grammar	Open-ended inventory
Processing	Assumption of processing-independence	Bidirectional processing model

---

[33] See Kathol & Pollard (1995) for a linearization-based account of extraposition. This account is implemented in the Babel System (Müller 1996c). See (Müller 1999d) on restricting discontinuity. Linearization-based approaches were argued to not be able to account for apparent multiple frontings in German (Müller 2005c, 2015b) and hence linearization-based approaches were replaced by more traditional variants that allow for continuous constituents only.

10.6.4.5.1 Competence/performance distinction

As for the linguistic approach, the use of the term *generative* is confusing. What van Trijp means – and also explains in the paper – is the idea that one should separate competence and performance. We will deal with both the generative-enumerative vs. constraint-based view and with the competence/performance distinction in more detail in the Chapters 14 and 15, respectively. Concerning the cognitive-functional approach, van Trijp writes:

> The goal of a cognitive-functional grammar, on the other hand, is to explain how speakers express their conceptualizations of the world through language (= *production*) and how listeners analyze utterances into meanings (= *parsing*). Cognitive-functional grammars therefore implement both a competence and a processing model. (van Trijp 2013: 90)

It is true that HPSG and SBCG make a competence/performance distinction (Sag & Wasow 2011). HPSG theories are theories about the structure of utterances that are motivated by distributional evidence. These theories do not contain any hypothesis regarding brain activation, planning of utterance, processing of utterances (garden path effects) and similar things. In fact, none of the theories that are discussed in this book contains an explicit theory that explains all these things. I think that it is perfectly legitimate to work in this way: it is legitimate to study the structure of words without studying their semantics and pragmatics, it is legitimate to study phonology without caring about syntax, it is legitimate to deal with specific semantic problems without caring about phonology and so on, provided there are ways to integrate the results of such research into a bigger picture. So, it is wrong to develop models like those developed in current versions of Minimalism (called Biolinguistics), where it is assumed that utterances are derived in phases (NPs, CPs, depending on the variant of the theory) and then shipped to the interfaces (spell out and semantic interpretation). This is not what humans do (see Chapter 15). But if we are neutral with respect towards such issues, we are fine. In fact, there is psycholinguistic work that couples HPSG grammars to performance models (Konieczny 1996) and similar work exists for TAG (Shieber & Johnson 1993; Demberg & Keller 2008).

Finally, there is also work in Construction Grammar that abstracts away from performance considerations. For instance, Adele Goldberg's book from 1995 does not contain a worked out theory of performance facts. It contains boxes in which grammatical functions are related to semantic roles. So this basically is a competence theory as well. Of course there are statements about how this is connected to psycholinguistic findings, but this is also true for theories like HPSG, SBCG and Simpler Syntax (Jackendoff 2011: 600) that explicitly make the competence/performance distinction.

10.6.4.5.2 Mathematical formalization vs. implementation

The difference between mathematical and computational formalization is a rather strange distinction to make. I think that a formal and precise description is a prerequisite for implementation (see the discussion in Section 3.6.2 and Section 4.7.2). Apart from this, a

computer implementation of SBCG is trivial, given the systems that we have for processing HPSG grammars. In order to show this, I want to address one issue that van Trijp
discusses. He claims that SBCG cannot be directly implemented. On issues of complexity
of constraint solving systems he quotes (Levine & Meurers 2006: Section 4.2.2):

> Actual implementations of HPSG typically handle the problem by guiding the lin-
> guistic processor using a (rule-based) phrase structure backbone, but the disadvan-
> tage of this approach is that the "organization and formulation of the grammar is
> different from that of the linguistic theory" (Levine & Meurers 2006: Section 4.2.2).
> (van Trijp 2013)

He concludes:

> Applying all these observations to the operationalization of SBCG, we can con-
> clude that an SBCG grammar is certainly amenable for computational implemen-
> tation because of its formal explicitness. There are at least two computational plat-
> forms available, mostly used for implementing HPSG-based grammars, whose ba-
> sic tenets are compatible with the foundations of SBCG: LKB (Copestake 2002)
> and TRALE (Richter 2006). However, none of these platforms supports a 'direct'
> implementation of an SBCG grammar as a general constraint system, so SBCG's
> performance-independence hypothesis remains conjecture until proven otherwise.

There are two issues that should be kept apart here: efficiency and faithfulness to the theory. First, as Levine and Meurers point out, there were many constraint solving systems
at the beginning of the 90's. So there are computer systems that can and have been used
to implement and process HPSG grammars. This is very valuable since they can be used
for direct verification of specific theoretical proposals. As was discussed by Levine and
Meurers, trying to solve constraints without any guidance is not the most efficient way
to deal with the parsing/generation problem. Therefore, additional control-structure was
added. This control structure is used for instance in a parser to determine the syntactic
structure of a phrase and other constraints will apply as soon as there is sufficient information available for them to apply. For instance, the assignment of structural case
happens once the arguments of a head are realized. Now, is it bad to have a phrase
structure backbone? One can write down phrase structure grammars that use phrase
structure rules that have nothing to do with what HPSG grammars usually do. The systems TRALE (Meurers, Penn & Richter 2002; Penn 2004) and LKB will process them. But
one is not forced to do this. For instance, the grammars that I developed for the Core-
Gram project (Müller 2013a, 2015a) are very close to the linguistic theory. To see that
this is really the case, let us look at the Head-Argument Schema. The Head-Argument
Schema is basically the type *head-argument-phrase* with certain type constraints that
are partly inherited from its supertypes. The type with all the constraints was given on
page 268 and is repeated here as (81):

(81) (syntactic) constraints on *head-argument-phrase*:

$$
\begin{bmatrix}
\textit{head-argument-phrase} \\[4pt]
\text{SYNSEM|LOC|CAT} \begin{bmatrix} \text{HEAD} & \boxed{1} \\ \text{SUBCAT} & \boxed{2} \end{bmatrix} \\[12pt]
\text{HEAD-DTR|SYNSEM|LOC|CAT} \begin{bmatrix} \text{HEAD} & \boxed{1} \\ \text{SUBCAT} & \boxed{2} \oplus \langle\, \boxed{3} \,\rangle \end{bmatrix} \\[12pt]
\text{NON-HEAD-DTRS} \left\langle\, [\, \text{SYNSEM } \boxed{3} \,] \,\right\rangle
\end{bmatrix}
$$

This can be translated into a phrase structure grammar in a straight-forward way:

(82) a.
$$
\begin{bmatrix}
\textit{head-argument-phrase} \\[4pt]
\text{SYNSEM|LOC|CAT} \begin{bmatrix} \text{HEAD} & \boxed{1} \\ \text{SUBCAT} & \boxed{2} \end{bmatrix} \\[12pt]
\text{HEAD-DTR } \boxed{4} \text{ |SYNSEM|LOC|CAT} \begin{bmatrix} \text{HEAD} & \boxed{1} \\ \text{SUBCAT} & \boxed{2} \oplus \langle\, \boxed{3} \,\rangle \end{bmatrix} \\[12pt]
\text{NON-HEAD-DTRS} \left\langle\, \boxed{5}\ [\, \text{SYNSEM } \boxed{3} \,] \,\right\rangle
\end{bmatrix} \rightarrow \boxed{4}, \boxed{5}
$$

b.
$$
\begin{bmatrix}
\textit{head-argument-phrase} \\[4pt]
\text{SYNSEM|LOC|CAT} \begin{bmatrix} \text{HEAD} & \boxed{1} \\ \text{SUBCAT} & \boxed{2} \end{bmatrix} \\[12pt]
\text{HEAD-DTR } \boxed{4} \text{ |SYNSEM|LOC|CAT} \begin{bmatrix} \text{HEAD} & \boxed{1} \\ \text{SUBCAT} & \boxed{2} \oplus \langle\, \boxed{3} \,\rangle \end{bmatrix} \\[12pt]
\text{NON-HEAD-DTRS} \left\langle\, \boxed{5}\ [\, \text{SYNSEM } \boxed{3} \,] \,\right\rangle
\end{bmatrix} \rightarrow \boxed{5}, \boxed{4}
$$

The left hand side of the rule is the mother node of the tree, that is, the sign that is licensed by the schema provided that the daughters are present. The right hand side in (82a) consists of the head daughter $\boxed{4}$ followed by the non-head daughter $\boxed{5}$. We have the opposite order in (82b), that is, the head daughter follows the non-head daughter. The two orders correspond to the two orders that are permitted by LP-rules: the head precedes its argument if it is marked INITIAL+ and it follows it if it is marked INITIAL−.

The following code shows how (83b) is implemented in TRALE:

```
arg_h rule (head_argument_phrase,
            synsem:loc:cat:head:initial:minus,
            head_dtr:HeadDtr,
            non_head_dtrs:[NonHeadDtr]
            )
    ===>
cat> NonHeadDtr,
cat> HeadDtr.
```

A rule starts with an identifier that is needed for technical reasons like displaying intermediate structures in the parsing process in debugging tools. A description of the mother node follows and after the arrow we find a list of daughters, each introduced by the operator cat>.[34] Structure sharing is indicated by values with capital letters. The above TRALE rule is a computer-readable variant of (82b), but includes the explicit specification of the value of INITIAL.

Now, the translation of a parallel schema using a MOTHER feature like (83a) into a phrase structure rule is almost as simple:

(83) a.
$$\begin{bmatrix} \textit{head-argument-cx} \\ \text{MOTHER|SYNSEM|LOC|CAT} \begin{bmatrix} \text{HEAD} & \boxed{1} \\ \text{SUBCAT} & \boxed{2} \end{bmatrix} \\ \text{HEAD-DTR} \boxed{4} \text{ |SYNSEM|LOC|CAT} \begin{bmatrix} \text{HEAD} & \boxed{1} \\ \text{SUBCAT} & \boxed{2} \oplus \langle \boxed{3} \rangle \end{bmatrix} \\ \text{NON-HEAD-DTRS} \left\langle \boxed{5} \left[\text{SYNSEM} \boxed{3} \right] \right\rangle \end{bmatrix}$$

b. $\boxed{6} \rightarrow \boxed{4}, \boxed{5}$ where
$$\begin{bmatrix} \textit{head-argument-cx} \\ \text{MOTHER} \boxed{6} \text{ |SYNSEM|LOC|CAT} \begin{bmatrix} \text{HEAD} & \boxed{1} \\ \text{SUBCAT} & \boxed{2} \end{bmatrix} \\ \text{HEAD-DTR} \boxed{4} \text{ |SYNSEM|LOC|CAT} \begin{bmatrix} \text{HEAD} & \boxed{1} \\ \text{SUBCAT} & \boxed{2} \oplus \langle \boxed{3} \rangle \end{bmatrix} \\ \text{NON-HEAD-DTRS} \left\langle \boxed{5} \left[\text{SYNSEM} \boxed{3} \right] \right\rangle \end{bmatrix}$$

(83b) is only one of the two phrase structure rules that correspond to (83a), but since the other one only differs from (83b) in the ordering of $\boxed{4}$ and $\boxed{5}$, it is not given here.

For grammars in which the order of the elements corresponds to the observable order of the daughters in a DTRS list, the connection to phrase structure rules is even simpler:

(84) $\boxed{1} \rightarrow \boxed{2}$ where
$$\begin{bmatrix} \textit{construction} \\ \text{MOTHER} & \boxed{1} \\ \text{DTRS} & \boxed{2} \end{bmatrix}$$

The value of DTRS is a list and hence $\boxed{2}$ stands for the list of daughters on the right hand side of the phrase structure rule as well. The type *construction* is a supertype of all constructions and hence (84) can be used to analyze all phrases that are licensed by the grammar. In fact, (84) is one way to put the meta constraint in (31).

So, this shows that the version of SBCG that has been developed by Sag (2012) has a straightforward implementation in TRALE.[35] The question remains whether *SBCG's performance-independence hypothesis remains conjecture until proven otherwise* as van Trijp sees it. The answer is: it is not a conjecture since any of the old constraint-solving

---

[34] Other operators are possible in TRALE. For instance, sem_head can be used to guide the generator. This is control information that has nothing to do with linguistic theory and not necessarily with the way humans process natural language. There is also a cats operator, which precedes lists of daughters. This can be used to implement flat phrase structures.

[35] A toy fragment of English using a MOTHER feature and phrase structure rules with specifications of the kind given above can be downloaded at http://hpsg.fu-berlin.de/Fragments/SBCG-TRALE/.

systems of the nineties could be used to process SBCG. The question of whether this is efficient is an engineering problem that is entirely irrelevant for theoretical linguistics. Theoretical linguistics is concerned with human languages and how they are processed by humans. So whether some processing system that does not make any claims about human language processing is efficient or not is absolutely irrelevant. Phrase structure-based backbones are therefore irrelevant as well, provided they refer to the grammar as described in theoretical work.

Now, this begs the question whether there is a contradiction in my claims. On page 324 I pointed out that SBCG is lacking a formalization in Richter's framework (Richter 2004). Richter and also Levine & Meurers (2006) pointed out that there are problems with certain theoretically possible expressions and it is these expressions that mathematical linguists care about. So the goal is to be sure that any HPSG grammar has a meaning and that it is clear what it is. Therefore, this goal is much more foundational than writing a single grammar for a particular fragment of a language. There is no such foundational work for FCG since FCG is a specific toolkit that has been used to implement a set of grammars.

10.6.4.5.3 Static constraints vs. dynamic mappings and signature + grammar vs. open-endedness

The cool thing about Fluid Construction Grammar is its fluidity, that is there are certain constraints that can be adapted if there is pressure, the inventory of the theory is open-ended, so categories and features can be added if need be.

Again, this is not a fundamental difference between HPSG/SBCG and FCG. An HPSG grammar fragment of a specific language is a declarative representation of linguistic knowledge and as such it of course just represents a certain fragment and does not contain any information how this set of constraints evolved or how it is acquired by speakers. For this we need specific theories about language evolution/language change/language acquisition. This is parallel to what we said about the competence/performance distinction, in order to account for language evolution we would have to have several HPSG grammars and say something about how one developed from the other. This will involve weighted constraints, it will involve recategorization of linguistic items and lots more.[36] So basically HPSG has to be extended, has to be paired with a model about language evolution in the very same way as FCG is.

10.6.4.5.4 Theoretical physics vs. Darwinian evolutionary theory

Van Trijp compares SBCG and FCG and claims that SBCG follows the model of theoretical physics – like Chomsky does –, while FCG adopts a Darwinian model of science – like Croft does –, the difference being that SBCG makes certain assumptions that are true

---

[36] There are systems that use weighted constraints. We had a simple version of this in the German HPSG grammar that was developed in *Verbmobil* project (Müller & Kasper 2000) already. Further theoretical approaches to integrate weighted constraints are Brew (1995) and more recently Guzmán Naranjo (2015). Usually such weighted constraints are not part of theoretical papers, but there are exceptions as for instance the paper by Briscoe and Copestake about lexical rules (Briscoe & Copestake 1999).

of all languages, while FCG does not make any a priori assumptions. The fundamental assumptions made in both theories are that the objects that we model are best described by feature value pairs (a triviality). FCG assumes that there is always a syntactic and a semantic pole (fundamental assumption in the system) and researchers working in HPSG/SBCG assume that if languages have certain phenomena, they will be analyzed in similar ways. For instance, if a language has nonlocal dependencies, these will be analyzed via the SLASH mechanism. However, this does not entail that one believes that grammars of all languages have a SLASH feature. And in fact, there may even be languages that do not have valence features (Koenig & Michelson 2010), which may be a problem for FCG since it relies on the SYN-pole for the matching phase. So as far as SBCG is concerned, there is considerable freedom to choose features that are relevant in an analysis, and of course additional features and types can be assumed in case a language is found that provides evidence for this. The only example of a constraint provided by van Trijp that is possibly too strong is the locality constraint imposed by the MOTHER feature. The idea about this feature is that everything that is of relevance in a more non-local context has to be passed up explicitly. This is done for nonlocal dependencies (via SLASH) and for instance also for information concerning the form of a preposition inside of a PP (via PFORM). Certain verbs require prepositional objects and restrict the form of the preposition. For instance, *wait* has to make sure that its prepositional object has the preposition *for* in it. Since this information is usually available only at the preposition, it has to be passed up to the PP level in order to be directly selectable by the governing verb.

(85) I am waiting for my man.

So, assuming strict locality of selection requires that all phenomena that cannot be treated locally have to be analyzed by passing information up. Assuming strict locality is a design decision that does not have any empirical consequences, as far as it does not rule out any language or construction in principle. It just requires that information has to be passed up that needs to be accessed at higher nodes. As I have shown in Section 10.6.2, the locality constraint is easily circumvented even within SBCG and it makes the analysis of idioms unnecessarily complicated and unintuitive, so I suggest dropping the MOTHER feature. But even if MOTHER is kept, it is not justified to draw a distinction between SBCG and FCG along the lines suggested by van Trijp.

Independent of the MOTHER issue, the work done in the CoreGram project (Müller 2013a, 2015a) shows that one can derive generalizations in a bottom-up fashion rather than imposing constraints on grammars in a top-down way. The latter paper discusses Croft's methodological considerations and shows how methodological pitfalls are circumvented in the project. HPSG/SBCG research differs from work in Chomskyan frameworks in not trying to show that all languages are like English or Romance or German or whatever, rather languages are treated on their own as it is common in the Construction Grammar community. This does not imply that there is no interest in generalizations and universals or near universals or tendencies, but again the style of working and the rhetoric in HPSG/SBCG is usually different from the ones in Mainstream Generative Grammar. Therefore, I think that the purported difference between SBCG and FCG does not exist.

10.6.4.5.5 Permissiveness of the theories

Van Trijp claims that HPSG/SBCG is a "generative grammar" since its aim is to account for and admit only grammatical sentences. FCG on the other hand is more permissive and tries to get the most out of the input even if it is fragmentary or ungrammatical (see also Steels 2013: 166). While it is an engineering decision to be able to parse un-grammatical input – and there are most certainly systems for the robust processing of HPSG grammars (Kiefer, Krieger & Nederhof 2000; Copestake 2007), it is also clear that humans cannot parse everything. There are strong constraints whose violations cause measurable effects in the brain. This is something that a model of language (that includes competence and performance factors or does not make the difference at all) has to ex-plain. The question is what the cause of deviance is: is it processing complexity? Is it a category mismatch? A clash in information structure? So, if FCG permits structures that are not accepted by human native speakers and that do not make any sense whatsoever, additional constraints have to be added. If they are not added, the respective FCG the-ory is not an adequate theory of the language under consideration. Again, there is no difference between HPSG/SBCG and FCG.

10.6.4.5.6 A note on engineering

My biggest problem with FCG is that linguistic and engineering aspects are mixed.[37] Certain bookkeeping features that are needed only for technical reasons appear in lin-guistic papers, technical assumptions that are made to get a parser running are mixed with linguistic constraints. Bit vector encodings that are used to represent case informa-tion are part of papers about interesting case systems. There is certainly nothing wrong with bit vector encodings. They are used in HPSG implementations as well (Reape 1991: 55; Müller 1996c: 269), but this is not mixed into the theoretical papers.

It was a big breakthrough in the 80's when theoretical linguists and computational linguists started working together and developed declarative formalisms that were inde-pendent of specific parsers and processing systems. This made it possible to take over insights from a lot of linguists who were not concerned with the actual implementation but took care of finding linguistic generalizations and specifying constraints. Since this separation is given up in FCG, it will remain an engineering project without much appeal to the general linguist.

10.7 Summary and classification

There are currently three formalized variants of Construction Grammar: Sign-Based Construction Grammar, Embodied Construction Grammar, and Fluid Construction Grammar. The first two variants can be viewed as notational variants of (Constructional)

---

[37] This is not a problem if all FCG papers are read as papers documenting the FCG-system (see Footnote 27 on page 334) since then it would be necessary to include these technical details. If the FCG papers are to be read as theoretical linguistics papers that document a certain Construction Grammar analysis, the Lisp statements and the implementational details are simply an obstacle.

HPSG (for SBCG with regard to this point, see Sag (2007: 411) and Sag (2010: 486)), or put differently, sister theories of HPSG. This is also true to a large extend for FCG, although van Trijp (2013) spends 25 pages working out the alleged differences. As I have shown in Section 10.6.4, HPSG and FCG are rather similar and I would say that these theories are sister theories as well.

Due to the origins of all three theories, respective analyses can differ quite considerably: HPSG is a strongly lexicalized theory, where phrasal dominance schemata have only been increasingly more used in the last ten years under the influence of Ivan Sag. The phrasal dominance schemata that Ivan Sag uses in his work are basically refinements of schemata that were present in earlier versions of HPSG. Crucially, all phenomena that interact with valence receive a lexical analysis (Sag, Boas & Kay 2012: Section 2.3). In CxG, on the other hand, predominantly phrasal analyses are adopted due to the influence of Adele Goldberg.

As already emphasized in Chapter 9, these are only tendencies that do not apply to all researchers working in the theories in question.

Exercises

1. Find three examples of utterances whose meaning cannot be derived from the meaning of the individual words. Consider how one could analyze these examples in Categorial Grammar (yes, Categorial Grammar).

Further reading

There are two volumes on Construction Grammar in German: Fischer & Stefanowitsch (2006) and Stefanowitsch & Fischer (2008). Deppermann (2006) discusses Construction Grammar from the point of view of conversational analysis. The 37(3) volume of the *Zeitschrift für germanistische Linguistik* from 2009 was also devoted to Construction Grammar. Goldberg (2003a) and Michaelis (2006) are overview articles in English. Goldberg's books constitute important contributions to Construction Grammar (1995; 2006; 2009). Goldberg (1995) has argued against lexical analyses such as those common in GB, LFG, CG, HPSG, and DG. These arguments can be invalidated, however, as will be shown in Section 21.7.1. Sag (1997), Borsley (2006), Jacobs (2008) and Müller & Lipenkova (2009) give examples of constructions that require a phrasal analysis if one wishes to avoid postulating empty elements. Jackendoff (2008) discusses the noun-preposition-noun construction that can only be properly analyzed as a phrasal construction (see Section 21.10). The discussion on whether argument structure constructions should be analyzed phrasally or lexically (Goldberg 1995, 2006; Müller 2006) culminated in a series of papers (Goldberg 2013a) and a target article by Müller & Wechsler (2014a) with several responses in the same volume.

Tomasello's publications on language acquisition (Tomasello 2000, 2003, 2005, 2006c) constitute a Construction Grammar alternative to the Principle & Parameters theory of acquisition as it does not have many of the problems that P&P analyses have (for more on language acquisition, see Chapter 16). For more on language acquisition and Construction Grammar, see Behrens (2009).

Dąbrowska (2004) looks at psycholinguistic constraints for possible grammatical theories.

11 Dependency Grammar

Dependency Grammar is the oldest framework described in this book. Its modern version was developed by the French linguist Lucien Tesnière (1893–1954). His foundational work *Eléments de syntaxe structurale* 'Elements of structural syntax' was basically finished in 1938 only three years after Ajdukiewicz's paper on Categorial Grammar (1935), but the publication was delayed until 1959, five years after his death. Since valence is central in Dependency Grammar, it is sometimes also referred to as Valence Grammar. Tesnière's ideas are wide-spread nowadays. The conceptions of valence and dependency are present in almost all of the current theories (Ágel & Fischer 2010: 262–263, 284).

Although there is some work on English (Anderson 1971; Hudson 1984), Dependency Grammar is most popular in central Europe and especially so in Germany (Engel 1996: 56–57). Ágel & Fischer (2010: 250) identified a possible reason for this: Tesnière's original work was not available in English until very recently (Tesnière 2015), but there has been a German translation for more than 35 years now (Tesnière 1980). Since Dependency Grammar focuses on dependency relations rather than linearization of constituents, it is often felt to be more appropriate for languages with freer constituent order, which is one reason for its popularity among researchers working on Slavic languages: the New Prague School represented by Sgall, Hajičová and Panevova developed Dependency Grammar further, beginning in the 1960s (see Hajičová & Sgall 2003 for an overview). Igor A. Mel'čuk and A. K. Žolkovskij started in the 1960s in the Soviet Union to work on a model called Meaning–Text Theory, which was also used in machine translation projects (Mel'čuk 1964, 1981, 1988; Kahane 2003). Mel'čuk left the Soviet Union towards Canada in the 1970s and now works in Montréal.

Dependency Grammar is very wide-spread in Germany and among scholars of German linguistics worldwide. It is used very successfully for teaching German as a foreign language (Helbig & Buscha 1969, 1998). Helbig and Buscha, who worked in Leipzig, East Germany, started to compile valence dictionaries (Helbig & Schenkel 1969) and later researchers working at the Institut für Deutsche Sprache (Institute for German Language) in Mannheim began similar lexicographic projects (Schumacher et al. 2004).

The following enumeration is a probably incomplete list of linguists who are/were based in Germany: Vilmos Ágel (2000), Kassel; Klaus Baumgärtner (1965, 1970), Leipzig later Stuttgart; Ulrich Engel (1977, 2014), IDS Mannheim; Hans-Werner Eroms (1985, 1987, 2000), Passau; Heinz Happ, Tübingen; Peter Hellwig (1978, 2003), Heidelberg; Jürgen Heringer (1996), Augsburg; Jürgen Kunze (1968, 1975), Berlin; Henning Lobin (1993), Gießen; Klaus Schubert (1987), Hildesheim; Heinz Josef Weber (1997), Trier; Klaus Welke (1988, 2011), Humboldt University Berlin; Edeltraud Werner (1993), Halle-Wittenberg.

Although work has been done in many countries and continuously over the decades since 1959, a periodical international conference was established as late as 2011.[1,2]

From early on, Dependency Grammar was used in computational projects. Mel'čuk worked on machine translation in the Soviet Union (Mel'čuk 1964) and David G. Hays worked on machine translation in the United States (Hays & Ziehe 1960). Jürgen Kunze, based in East Berlin at the German Academy of Sciences, where he had a chair for computational linguistics, also started to work on machine translation in the 1960s. A book that describes the formal background of the linguistic work was published as Kunze (1975). Various researchers worked in the Collaborative Research Center 100 *Electronic linguistic research* (SFB 100, Elektronische Sprachforschung) from 1973–1986 in Saarbrücken. The main topic of this SFB was machine translation as well. There were projects on Russian to German, French to German, English to German, and Esperanto to German translation. For work from Saarbrücken in this context see Klein (1971), Rothkegel (1976), and Weissgerber (1983). Muraki et al. (1985) used Dependency Grammar in a project that analyzed Japanese and generated English. Richard Hudson started to work in a dependency grammar-based framework called Word Grammar in the 1980s (Hudson 1984, 2007) and Sleator and Temperly have been working on Link Grammar since the 1990s (Sleator & Temperley 1991; Grinberg et al. 1995). Fred Karlsson's Constraint Grammars (1990) are developed for many languages (bigger fragments are available for Danish, Portuguese, Spanish, English, Swedish, Norwegian, French, German, Esperanto, Italian, and Dutch) and are used for school teaching, corpus annotation and machine translation. An online demo is available at the project website.[3]

In recent years, Dependency Grammar became more and more popular among computational linguists. The reason for this is that there are many annotated corpora (tree banks) that contain dependency information.[4] Statistical parsers are trained on such tree banks (Yamada & Matsumoto 2003; Attardi 2006; Nivre 2003; Kübler et al. 2009; Bohnet 2010). Many of the parsers work for multiple languages since the general approach is language independent. It is easier to annotate dependencies consistently since there are fewer possibilities to do so. While syntacticians working in constituency-based models may assume binary branching or flat models, high or low attachment of adjuncts, empty elements or no empty elements and argue fiercely about this, it is fairly clear what the dependencies in an utterance are. Therefore it is easy to annotate consistently and train statistical parsers on such annotated data.

Apart from statistical modeling, there are also so-called deep processing systems, that is, systems that rely on a hand-crafted, linguistically motivated grammar. I already mentioned Mel'čuk's work in the context of machine translation; Hays & Ziehe (1960) had a parser for Russian; Starosta & Nomura (1986) developed a parser that was used with an English grammar, Jäppinen, Lehtola & Valkonen (1986) developed a parser that was demoed with Finnish, Hellwig (1986, 2003, 2006) implemented grammars of German in

---

[1] http://depling.org/. 10.04.2015.

[2] A conference on Meaning–Text Theory has taken place biannually since 2003.

[3] http://beta.visl.sdu.dk/constraint_grammar. 24.07.2015.

[4] According to Kay (2000), the first treebank ever was developed by Hays and did annotate dependencies.

the framework of Dependency Unification Grammar, Hudson (1989) developed a Word Grammar for English, Covington (1990) developed a parser for Russian and Latin, which can parse discontinuous constituents, and Menzel (1998) implemented a robust parser of a Dependency Grammar of German. Other work on computational parsing to be mentioned is Kettunen (1986); Lehtola (1986); Menzel & Schröder (1998b). The following is a list of languages for which Dependency Grammar fragments exist:

- Danish (Bick 2001; Bick & Nygaard 2007)

- English (Muraki et al. 1985; Starosta & Nomura 1986; Lavoie & Rambow 1997; Hudson 1989; Sleator & Temperley 1991; Voutilainen et al. 1992; Iordanskaja et al. 1992; Coch 1996)

- Esperanto (Bick 2009)

- Estonian (Müürisep 1999; Müürisep, Puolakainen, Muischnek, Koit, Roosmaa & Uibo 2003)

- Faroese (Trosterud 2009)

- Finnish (Nelimarkka, Jäppinen & Lehtola 1984; Jäppinen, Lehtola & Valkonen 1986)

- French (Iordanskaja et al. 1992; Coch 1996; Bick 2010)

- German (Hellwig 1986; Coch 1996; Heinecke et al. 1998; Menzel & Schröder 1998a; Hellwig 2003, 2006; Gerdes & Kahane 2001)

- Irish (Dhonnchadha & van Genabith 2006)

- Japanese (Muraki, Ichiyama & Fukumochi 1985)

- Latin (Covington 1990)

- Mandarin Chinese (Liu & Huang 2006; Liu 2009)

- Norwegian (Hagen, Johannessen & Nøklestad 2000),

- Old Icelandic (Maas 1977)

- Portuguese (Bick 2003)

- Russian (Hays & Ziehe 1960; Mel'čuk 1964; Covington 1990)

- Spanish (Coch 1996; Bick 2006)

- Swahili (Hurskainen 2006)

The Constraint Grammar webpage[5] additionally lists grammars for Basque, Catalan, English, Finnish, German, Italian, Sami, and Swedish.

---

[5] http://beta.visl.sdu.dk/constraint_grammar_languages.html

11.1 General remarks on the representational format

11.1.1 Valence information, nucleus and satellites

The central concept of Dependency Grammar is valence (see Section 1.6). The central metaphor for this is the formation of stable molecules, which is explained in chemistry with reference to layers of electrons. A difference between chemical compounds and linguistic structures is that the chemical compounding is not directed, that is, it would not make sense to claim that oxygen is more important than hydrogen in forming water. In contrast to this, the verb is more important than the nominal phrases it combines with to form a complete clause. In languages like English and German, the verb determines the form of its dependents, for instance their case.

One way to depict dependencies is shown in Figure 11.1. The highest node is the verb *reads*. Its valence is a nominative NP (the subject) and an accusative NP (an object). This is

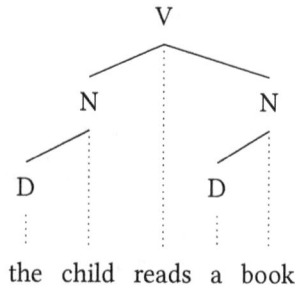

Figure 11.1: Analysis of *The child reads a book.*

depicted by the dependency links between the node representing the verb and the nodes representing the respective nouns. The nouns themselves require a determiner, which again is shown by the dependency links to *the* and *a* respectively. Note that the analysis presented here corresponds to the NP analysis that is assumed in HPSG for instance, that is, the noun selects its specifier (see Section 9.6.1). It should be noted, though, that the discussion whether an NP or a DP analysis is appropriate also took place within the Dependency Grammar community (Hudson 1984: 90; Van Langendonck 1994; Hudson 2004). See Engel (1977) for an analysis with the N as head and Welke (2011: 31) for an analysis with the determiner as head.

The verb is the head of the clause and the nouns are called *dependents*. Alternative terms for head and dependent are *nucleus* and *satellite*, respectively.

An alternative way to depict the dependencies, which is used in the Dependency Grammar variant Word Grammar (Hudson 2007), is provided in Figure 11.2 on the following page. This graph displays the grammatical functions rather than information about part of speech, but apart from this it is equivalent to the representation in Figure 11.1. The highest node in Figure 11.1 is labeled with the ROOT arrow in Figure 11.2. Downward links are indicated by the direction of the arrows.

ROOT

The child reads a book.

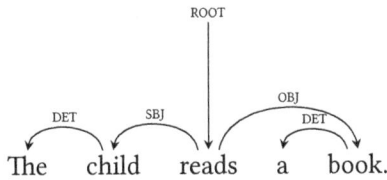

Figure 11.2: Alternative presentation of the analysis of *The child reads a book.*

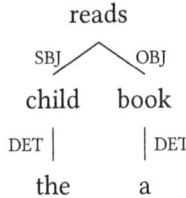

reads

SBJ OBJ

child book

DET | | DET

the a

Figure 11.3: Alternative presentation of the analysis of *The child reads a book.*

A third form of representing the same dependencies provided in Figure 11.3 has the tree format again. This tree results if we pull the root node in Figure 11.2 upwards. Since we have a clear visualization of the dependency relation that represents the nucleus above the dependents, we do not need to use arrows to encode this information. However, some variants of Dependency Grammar – for instance Word Grammar – use mutual dependencies. So for instance, some theories assume that *his* depends on *child* and *child* depends on *his* in the analysis of *his child.* If mutual dependencies have to be depicted, either arrows have to be used for all dependencies or some dependencies are represented by downward lines in hierarchical trees and other dependencies by arrows.

Of course part of speech information can be added to the Figures 11.2 and 11.3, grammatical function labels could be added to Figure 11.1, and word order can be added to Figure 11.3.

The above figures depict the dependency relation that holds between a head and the respective dependents. This can be written down more formally as an *n*-ary rule that is similar to phrase structure rules that were discussed in Chapter 2 (Gaifman 1965: 305; Hays 1964: 513; Baumgärtner 1970: 61; Heringer 1996: Section 4.1). For instance Baumgärtner suggests the rule in (1):

(1) $\chi \rightarrow \varphi_1 \ldots \varphi_i * \varphi_{i+2} \ldots \varphi_n, where\ 0 < i \leq n$

The asterisk in (1) corresponds to the word of the category χ. In our example, χ would be V, the position of the '*' would be taken by *reads*, and φ_1 and φ_3 would be N. Together with the rule in (2b) for the determiner-noun combination, the rule in (2a) would license the dependency tree in Figure 11.1.

(2)   a. V → N * N

 b. N → D *

Alternatively, several binary rules can be assumed that combine a head with its subject, direct object, or indirect object (Kahane 2009). Dependency rules will be discussed in more detail in Section 11.7.2, where dependency grammars are compared with phrase structure grammars.

11.1.2 Adjuncts

Another metaphor that was used by Tesnière is the drama metaphor. The core participants of an event are the *actants* and apart from this there is the background, the stage, the general setting. The actants are the arguments in other theories and the stage-describing entities are called *circumstants*. These circumstants are modifiers and usually analyzed as adjuncts in the other theories described in this book. As far as the representation of dependencies is concerned, there is not much of a difference between arguments and adjuncts in Dependency Grammar. Figure 11.4 shows the analysis of (3):

(3) The child often reads the book slowly.

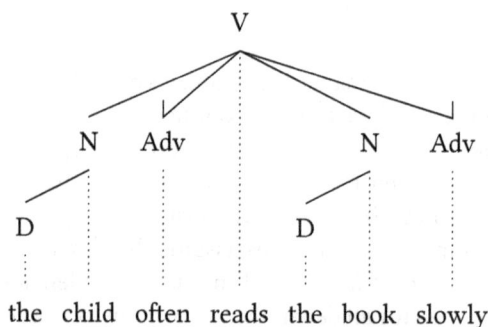

Figure 11.4: Analysis of *The child often reads the book slowly.*

The dependency annotation uses a technical device suggested by Engel (1977) to depict different dependency relations: adjuncts are marked with an additional line upwards from the adjunct node (see also Eroms 2000). An alternative way to specify the argument/adjunct, or rather the actant/circumstant distinction, is of course an explicit specification of the status as argument or adjunct. So one can use explicit labels for adjuncts and arguments as it was done for grammatical functions in the preceding. German grammars and valence dictionaries often use the labels E and A for *Ergänzung* and *Angabe*, respectively.

11.1.3 Linearization

So far we have seen dependency graphs that had connections to words that were linearized in a certain order. The order of the dependents, however, is in principle not determined by the dependency and therefore a Dependency Grammar has to contain additional statements that take care of the proper linearization of linguistic objects (stems, morphemes, words). Engel (2014: 50) assumes the dependency graph in Figure 11.5 for the sentences in (4).[6]

(4)   a. Gestern war ich bei Tom.
         yesterday was I   with Tom

       'I was with Tom yesterday.'

      b. Ich war gestern   bei Tom.
         I   was yesterday with Tom

      c. Bei Tom war ich gestern.
         with Tom was I   yesterday

      d. Ich war bei Tom gestern.
         I   was with Tom yesterday

$$V_{fin, \langle sub, sit \rangle}$$
war
was

$$E_{sub} \quad E_{sit} \quad A_{temp}$$
ich   bei Tom   gestern
I   with Tom yesterday

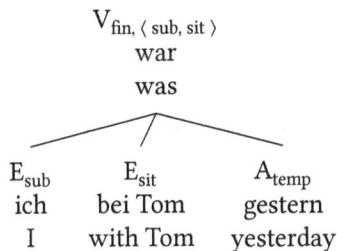

Figure 11.5: Dependency graph for several orders of *ich, war, bei Tom*, and *gestern* 'I was with Tom yesterday.' according to Engel (2014: 50)

According to Engel (2014: 50), the correct order is enforced by surface syntactic rules as for instance the rules that states that there is always exactly one element in the Vorfeld in declarative main clauses and that the finite verb is in second position.[7,8] Furthermore, there are linearization rules that concern pragmatic properties, as for instance given information before new information. Another rule ensures that weak pronouns are placed into the Vorfeld or at the beginning of the Mittelfeld. This conception of linear order is problematic both for empirical and conceptual reasons and we will turn to it again in Section 11.7.1. It should be noted here that approaches that deal with dependency alone admit discontinuous realizations of heads and their dependents. Without any further constraints, Dependency Grammars would share a problem that was already discussed on page 331 in Section 10.6.3 on Embodied Construction Grammar and in Section 10.6.4.4 with respect to Fluid Construction Grammar: one argument could interrupt another argument as in Figure 11.6 on the next page. In order to exclude such linearizations in languages in which they are impossible, it is sometimes assumed that analyses have to

---

[6] Engel uses E_{sub} for the subject and E_{acc}, E_{dat}, and E_{gen} for the objects with respective cases.

[7] "Die korrekte Stellung ergibt sich dann zum Teil aus oberflächensyntaktischen Regeln (zum Beispiel: im Vorfeld des Konstativsatzes steht immer genau ein Element; das finite Verb steht an zweiter Stelle) [...]"

[8] Engel (1970: 81) provides counterexamples to the claim that there is exactly one element in the *Vorfeld*. Related examples will be discussed in Section 11.7.1.

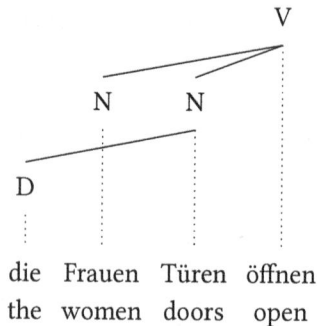

Figure 11.6: Unwanted analysis of *dass die Frauen Türen öffnen* 'that the women open doors'

be projective, that is crossing branches like those in Figure 11.6 are not allowed. This basically reintroduces the concept of constituency into the framework, since this means that all dependents of a head have to be realized close to the head unless special mechanisms for liberation are used (see for instance Section 11.5 on nonlocal dependencies).[9] Some authors explicitly use a phrase structure component to be able to formulate restrictions on serializations of constituents (Gerdes & Kahane 2001; Hellwig 2003).

11.1.4 Semantics

Tesnière already distinguished the participants of a verb in a way that was later common in theories of semantic roles. He suggested that the first actant is the agent, the second one a patient and the third a benefactive (Tesnière 2015: Chapter 106). Given that Dependency Grammar is a lexical framework, all lexical approaches to argument linking can be adopted. However, argument linking and semantic role assignment are just a small part of the problem that has to be solved when natural language expressions have to be assigned a meaning. Issues regarding the scope of adjuncts and quantifiers have to be solved and it is clear that dependency graphs representing dependencies without taking into account linear order are not sufficient. An unordered dependency graph assigns grammatical functions to a dependent of a head and hence it is similar in many respects to an LFG f-structure.[10] For a sentence like (25a) on page 222, repeated here as (5), one gets the f-structure in (25b) on page 222. This f-structure contains a subject (*David*), an object (*a sandwich*), and an adjunct set with two elements (*at noon* and *yesterday*).

---

[9] While this results in units that are also assumed in phrase structure grammars, there is a difference: the units have category labels in phrase structure grammars (for instance NP), which is not the case in Dependency Grammars. In Dependency Grammars, one just refers to the label of the head (for instance the N that belongs to *child* in Figure 11.4) or one refers to the head word directly (for instance, the word *child* in Figure 11.3). So there are fewer nodes in Dependency Grammar representations (but see the discussion in Section 11.7.2.3).

[10] Tim Osborne (p. c. 2015) reminds me that this is not true in all cases: for instance non-predicative prepositions are not reflected in f-structures, but of course they are present in dependency graphs.

(5) David devoured a sandwich at noon yesterday.

This is exactly what is encoded in an unordered dependency graph. Because of this parallel it comes as no surprise that Bröker (2003: 308) suggested to use glue semantics (Dalrymple, Lamping & Saraswat 1993; Dalrymple 2001: Chapter 8) for Dependency Grammar as well. Glue semantics was already introduced in Section 7.1.5.

There are some variants of Dependency Grammar that have explicit treatments of semantics. One example is Meaning–Text Theory (Mel'čuk 1988). Word Grammar is another one (Hudson 1991: Chapter 7; 2007: Chapter 5). The notations of these theories cannot be introduced here. It should be noted though that theories like Hudson's Word Grammar are rather rigid about linear order and do not assume that all the sentences in (4) have the same dependency structure (see Section 11.5). Word Grammar is closer to phrase structure grammar and therefore can have a semantics that interacts with constituent order in the way it is known from constituent-based theories.

11.2 Passive

Dependency Grammar is a lexical theory and valence is the central concept. For this reason, it is not surprising that the analysis of the passive is a lexical one. That is, it is assumed that there is a passive participle that has a different valence requirement than the active verb (Hudson 1990: Chapter 12; Eroms 2000: Section 10.3; Engel 2014: 53–54).

Our standard example in (6) is analyzed as shown in Figure 11.7.

(6) [dass] der Weltmeister   geschlagen wird
      that   the world.champion beaten   is

'that the world champion is (being) beaten'

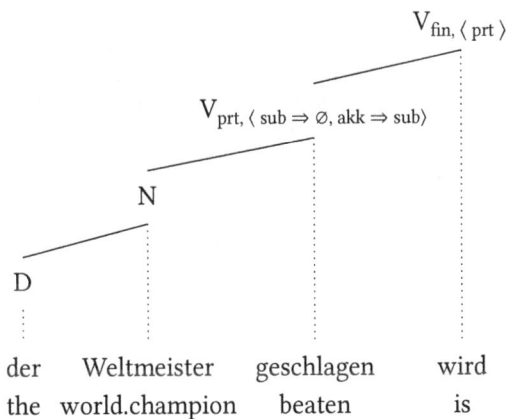

Figure 11.7: Analysis of [*dass*] *der Weltmeister geschlagen wird* 'that the world champion is (being) beaten' parallel to the analyses provided by Engel (2014: 53–54)

This figure is an intuitive depiction of what is going on in passive constructions. A formalization would probably amount to a lexical rule for the personal passive. See Hellwig (2003: 629–630) for an explicit suggestion of a lexical rule for the analysis of the passive in English.

Note that *der Weltmeister* 'the world champion' is not an argument of the passive auxiliary *wird* 'is' in Engel's analysis. This means that subject–verb agreement cannot be determined locally and some elaborated mechanism has to be developed for ensuring agreement.[11] Hudson (1990), Eroms (2000: Section 5.3) and Groß & Osborne (2009) assume that subjects depend on auxiliaries rather than on the main verb. This requires some argument transfer as it is common in Categorial Grammar (see Section 8.5.2) andH-PSG (Hinrichs & Nakazawa 1994). The adapted analysis that treats the subject of the participle as a subject of the auxiliary is given in Figure 11.8 on the following page.

11.3 Verb position

In many Dependency Grammar publications on German, linearization issues are not dealt with and authors just focus on the dependency relations. The dependency relations between a verb and its arguments are basically the same in verb-initial and verb-final sentences. If we compare the dependency graphs of the sentences in (7) given in

---

[11] This problem would get even more pressing for cases of the so-called remote passive:

(i) a. weil   der   Wagen zu reparieren versucht wurde
       because the.SG.NOM car   to repair   tried   was

   'because it was tried to repair the car'

   b. weil   die   Wagen zu reparieren versucht wurden
       because the.PL.NOM cars   to repair   tried   were

   'because it was tried to repair the cars'

Here the object of *zu reparieren*, which is the object of a verb which is embedded two levels deep, agrees with the auxiliaries *wurde* 'was' and *wurden* 'were'. However, the question how to analyze these remote passives is open in Engel's system anyway and the solution of this problem would probably involve the mechanism applied in HPSG: the arguments of *zu reparieren* are raised to the governing verb *versucht*, passive applies to this verb and turns the object into a subject which is then raised by the auxiliary. This explains the agreement between the underlying object of *zu reparieren* 'to repair' and *wurde* 'was'. Hudson (1997), working in the framework of Word Grammar, suggests an analysis of verbal complementation in German that involves what he calls *generalized raising*. He assumes that both subjects and complements may be raised to the governing head. Note that such an analysis involving generalized raising would make an analysis of sentences like (i) straightforward, since the object would depend on the same head as the subject, namely on *hat* 'has' and hence can be placed before the subject.

(ii) Gestern   hat sich der Spieler verletzt.
     yesterday has self the player injured

   'The player injured himself yesterday.'

For a discussion of Groß & Osborne's account of (ii) see page 576.

$$V_{\text{fin},\,\langle\,\text{sub, prt}\,\rangle}$$

$$N \qquad V_{\text{prt},\,\langle\,\text{sub}\,\Rightarrow\,\varnothing,\,\text{akk}\,\Rightarrow\,\text{sub}\rangle}$$

$$D$$

der	Weltmeister	geschlagen	wird
the	world.champion	beaten	is

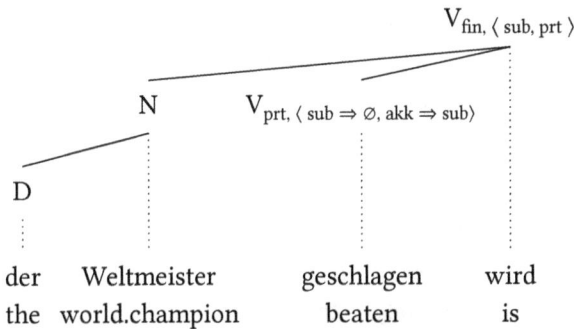

Figure 11.8: Analysis of [*dass*] *der Weltmeister geschlagen wird* 'that the world champion is (being) beaten' with the subject as dependent of the auxiliary

the Figures 11.9 and 11.10, we see that only the position of the verb is different, but the dependency relations are the same, as it should be.[12]

(7)   a.   [dass] jeder   diesen Mann kennt
           that   everybody this   man   knows

         'that everybody knows this man'

   b.   Kennt jeder   diesen Mann?
         knows everybody this   man

         'Does everybody know this man?'

    The correct ordering of the verb with respect to its arguments and adjuncts is ensured by linearization constraints that refer to the respective topological fields. See Section 11.1.3 and Section 11.7.1 for further details on linearization.

11.4 Local reordering

The situation regarding local reordering is the same. The dependency relations of the sentence in (8b) are shown in Figure 11.11 on page 367. The analysis of the sentence with normal order in (8a) has already been given in Figure 11.9.

---

[12] Eroms (2000) uses the part of speech Pron for pronouns like *jeder* 'everybody'. If information about part of speech plays a role in selection, this makes necessary a disjunctive specification of all valence frames of heads that govern nominal expressions, since they can either combine with an NP with internal structure or with a pronoun. By assigning pronouns the category N, such a disjunctive specification is avoided. A pronoun differs from a noun in its valence (it is fully saturated, while a noun needs a determiner), but not in its part of speech. Eroms & Heringer (2003: 259) use the symbol N_pro for pronouns. If the pro-part is to be understood as a special property of items with the part of speech N, this is compatible with what I have said above: heads could then select for Ns. If N_pro and N are assumed to be distinct, atomic symbols, the problem remains.

    Using N rather than Pron as part of speech for pronouns is standard in other versions of Dependency Grammar, as for instance Word Grammar (Hudson 1990: 167; Hudson 2007: 190). See also footnote 2 on page 53 on the distinction of pronouns and NPs in phrase structure grammars.

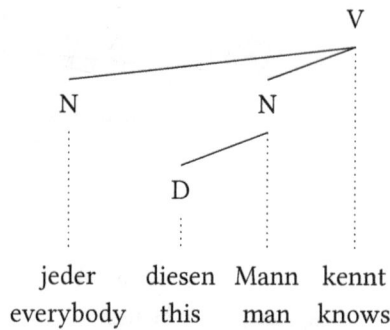

Figure 11.9: Analysis of [*dass*] *jeder diesen Mann kennt* 'that everybody knows this man'

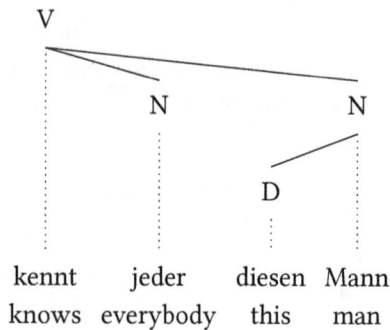

Figure 11.10: Analysis of *Kennt jeder diesen Mann?* 'Does everybody know this man?'

(8) a. [dass] jeder   diesen Mann kennt
        that everybody this   man knows
       'that everybody knows this man'
     b. [dass] diesen Mann jeder   kennt
        that this   man everybody knows
       'that everybody knows this man'

11.5 Long-distance dependencies

There are several possibilities to analyze nonlocal dependencies in Dependency Grammar. The easiest one is the one we have already seen in the previous sections. Many analyses just focus on the dependency relations and assume that the order with the verb in second position is just one of the possible linearization variants (Eroms 2000: Section 9.6.2; Groß & Osborne 2009). Figure 11.12 on the following page shows the analysis of (9):

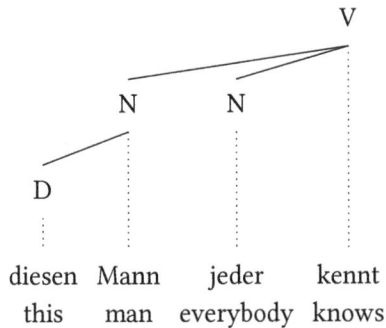

Figure 11.11: Analysis of [*dass*] *diesen Mann jeder kennt* 'that everybody knows this man'

(9) [Diesen Mann] kennt jeder.
     this   man   knows everybody

     'Everyone knows this man.'

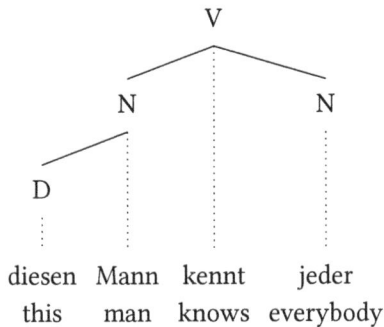

Figure 11.12: Analysis of *Diesen Mann kennt jeder.* 'This man, everybody knows.' without special treatment of fronting

Now, this is the simplest case, so let us look at the example in (10), which really involves a *nonlocal* dependency:

(10) Wen$_i$ glaubst   du,   daß ich   _$_i$ gesehen habe?[13]
     who.ACC believe.2SG you.NOM that I.NOM   seen   have

     'Who do you think I saw?'

The dependency relations are depicted in Figure 11.13 on the following page. This graph differs from most graphs we have seen before in not being projective. This means that there are crossing lines: the connection between V$_{prt}$ and the N for *wen* 'who' crosses the lines connecting *glaubst* 'believe' and *du* 'you' with their category symbols. Depending on the version of Dependency Grammar assumed, this is seen as a problem or it is not.

---

[13] Scherpenisse (1986: 84).

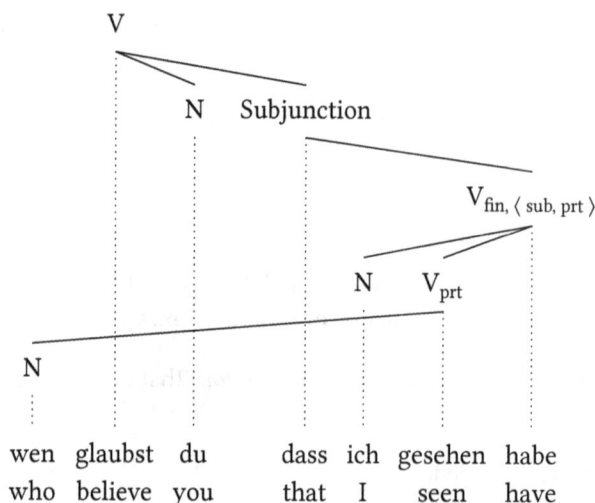

Figure 11.13: Non-projective analysis of *Wen glaubst du, dass ich gesehen habe?* 'Who do you think I saw?'

Let us explore the two options: if discontinuity of the type shown in Figure 11.13 is allowed for as in Heringer's and Eroms' grammars (Heringer 1996: 261; Eroms 2000: Section 9.6.2),[14] there has to be something in the grammar that excludes discontinuities that are ungrammatical. For instance, an analysis of (11) as in Figure 11.14 on the following page should be excluded.

(11) * Wen   glaubst   ich   du,   dass gesehen habe?
     who.ACC believe.2SG I.NOM you.NOM that seen   have
     Intended: 'Who do you think I saw?'

Note that the order of elements in (11) is compatible with statements that refer to topological fields as suggested by Engel (2014: 50): there is a *Vorfeld* filled by *wen* 'who', there is a left sentence bracket filled by *glaubst* 'believe', and there is a *Mittelfeld* filled by *ich* 'I', *du* 'you' and the clausal argument. Having pronouns like *ich* and *du* in the *Mittelfeld* is perfectly normal. The problem is that these two pronouns come from different clauses: *du* belongs to the matrix verb *glaubst* 'believe' while *ich* 'I' depends on (*gesehen* 'seen') *habe* 'have'. What has to be covered by a theory is the fact that fronting and extraposition target the left-most and right-most positions of a clause, respectively. This can be modeled in constituency-based approaches in a straightforward way, as has been shown in the previous chapters.

As an alternative to discontinuous constituents, one could assume additional mechanisms that promote the dependency of an embedded head to a higher head in the structure. Such an analysis was suggested by Kunze (1968), Hudson (1997, 2000), Kahane (1997), Kahane et al. (1998), and Groß & Osborne (2009). In what follows, I use the analy-

---

[14] However, the authors mention the possibility of raising an extracted element to a higher node. See for instance Eroms & Heringer (2003: 260).

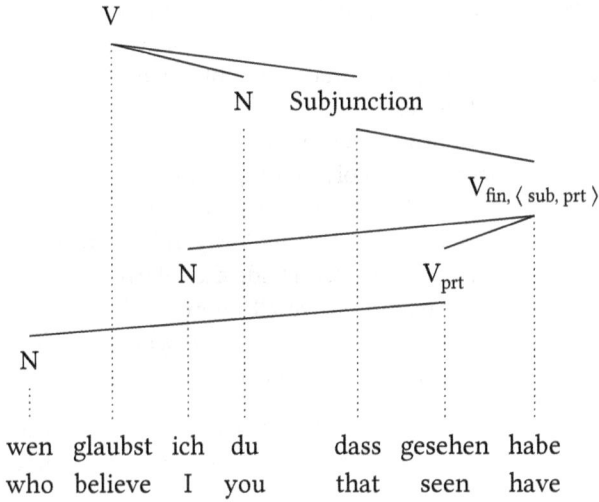

Figure 11.14: Unwanted dependency graph of * *Wen glaubst ich du, dass gesehen habe?* 'Who do you think I saw?'

sis by Groß & Osborne (2009) as an example for such analyses. Groß & Osborne depict the reorganized dependencies with a dashed line as in Figure 11.15.[15, 16] The origin of the

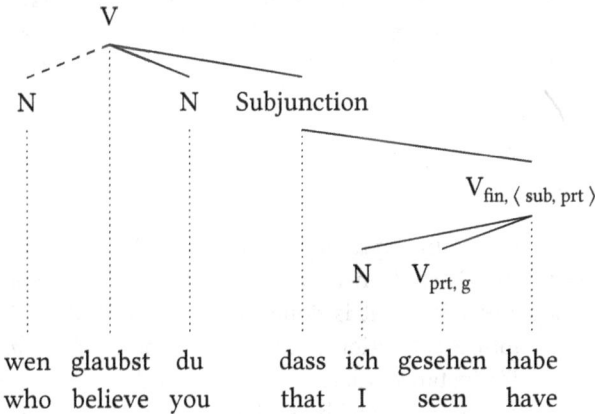

Figure 11.15: Projective analysis of *Wen glaubst du, dass ich gesehen habe?* 'Who do you think I saw?' involving rising

---

[15] Eroms & Heringer (2003: 260) make a similar suggestion but do not provide any formal details.

[16] Note that Groß & Osborne (2009) do not assume a uniform analysis of simple and complex V2 sentences. That is, for cases that can be explained as local reordering they assume an analysis without rising. Their analysis of (9) is the one depicted in Figure 11.12. This leads to problems which will be discussed in Section 11.7.1.

dependency (V_{prt}) is marked with a g and the dependent is connected to the node to which it has risen (the topmost V) by a dashed line. Instead of realizing the accusative dependent of *gesehen* 'seen' locally, information about the missing element is transferred to a higher node and realized there.

The analysis of Groß & Osborne (2009) is not very precise. There is a g and there is a dashed line, but sentences may involve multiple nonlocal dependencies. In (12) for instance, there is a nonlocal dependency in the relative clauses *den wir alle begrüßt haben* 'who we all greeted have' and *die noch niemand hier gesehen hat* 'who yet nobody here seen has': the relative pronouns are fronted inside the relative clauses. The phrase *dem Mann, den wir alle kennen* 'the man who we all know' is the fronted dative object of *gegeben* 'given' and *die noch niemand hier gesehen hat* 'who yet nobody here seen has' is extraposed from the NP headed by *Frau* 'woman'.

(12) Dem Mann, den wir alle begrüßt haben, hat die Frau   das Buch gegeben, die
      the man who we all greeted have   has the woman the book given   who
      noch niemand hier gesehen hat.
      yet nobody here seen   has

      'The woman who nobody ever saw here gave the book to the man, who all of us greeted.'

So this means that the connections (dependencies) between the head and the dislocated element have to be made explicit. This is what Hudson (1997, 2000) does in his Word Grammar analysis of nonlocal dependencies: in addition to dependencies that relate a word to its subject, object and so on, he assumes further dependencies for extracted elements. For example, *wen* 'who' in (10) – repeated here as (13) for convenience – is the object of *gesehen* 'seen' and the extractee of *glaubst* 'believe' and *dass* 'that':

(13) Wen glaubst du, dass ich gesehen habe?
      who believe you that I   seen   have

      'Who do you believe that I saw?'

Hudson states that the use of multiple dependencies in Word Grammar corresponds to structure sharing in HPSG (Hudson 1997: 15). Nonlocal dependencies are modeled as a series of local dependencies as it is done in GPSG and HPSG. This is important since it allows one to capture extraction path marking effects (Bouma, Malouf & Sag 2001a: 1–2, Section 3.2): for instance, there are languages that use a special form of the complementizer for sentences from which an element is extracted. Figure 11.16 on the following page shows the analysis of (13) in Word Grammar. The links above the words are the usual dependency links for subjects (s) and objects (o) and other arguments (r is an abbreviation for *sharer*, which refers to verbal complements, l stands for *clausal complement*) and the links below the words are links for extractees (x<). The link from *gesehen* 'seen' to *wen* 'who' is special since it is both an object link and an extraction link (x<o). This link is an explicit statement which corresponds to both the little g and the N that is marked by the dashed line in Figure 11.15. In addition to what is there in Figure 11.15, Figure 11.16 also has an extraction link from *dass* 'that' to *wen* 'who'. One could use the graphic representation of Engel, Eroms, and Gross & Osborne to display

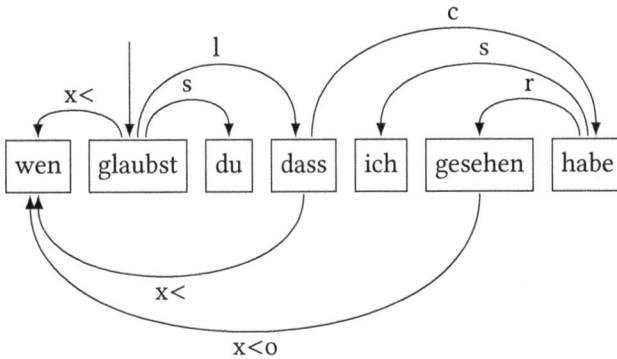

Figure 11.16: Projective analysis of *Wen glaubst du, dass ich gesehen habe?* 'Who do you think I saw?' in Word Grammar involving multiple dependencies

the Word Grammar dependencies: one would simply add dashed lines from the V_{prt} node and from the Subjunction node to the N node dominating *wen* 'who'.

While this looks simple, I want to add that Word Grammar employs further principles that have to be fulfilled by well-formed structures. In the following I explain the *No-tangling Principle*, the *No-dangling Principle* and the *Sentence-root Principle*.

Principle 1 (The No-tangling Principle) *Dependency arrows must not tangle.*

Principle 2 (The No-dangling Principle) *Every word must have a parent.*

Principle 3 (The Sentence-root Principle) *In every non-compound sentence there is just one word whose parent is not a word but a contextual element.*

The No-tangling Principle ensures that there are no crossing dependency lines, that is, it ensures that structures are projective (Hudson 2000: 23). Since non-local dependency relations are established via the specific dependency mechanism, one wants to rule out the non-projective analysis. This principle also rules out (14b), where *green* depends on *peas* but is not adjacent to *peas*. Since *on* selects *peas* the arrow from *on* to *peas* would cross the one from *peas* to *green*.

(14)   a.   He lives on green peas.

      b.   * He lives green on peas.

The No-dangling Principle makes sure that there are no isolated word groups that are not connected to the main part of the structure. Without this principle (14b) could be analyzed with the isolated word *green* (Hudson 2000: 23).

The Sentence-root Principle is needed to rule out structures with more than one highest element. *glaubst* 'believe' is the root in Figure 11.16. There is no other word that dominates it and selects for it. The principle makes sure that there is no other root. So the principle rules out situations in which all elements in a phrase are roots, since otherwise the No-dangling Principle would lose its force as it could be fulfilled trivially (Hudson 2000: 25).

I added this rather complicated set of principles here in order to get a fair comparison with phrase structure-based proposals. If continuity is assumed for phrases in general, the three principles do not have to be stipulated. So, for example, LFG and HPSG do not need these three principles.

Note that Hudson (1997: 16) assumes that the element in the *Vorfeld* is extracted even for simple sentences like (9). I will show in Section 11.7.1 why I think that this analysis has to be preferred over analyses assuming that simple sentences like (9) are just order variants of corresponding verb-initial or verb-final sentences.

11.6 New developments and theoretical variants

This section mainly deals with Tesnière's variant of Dependency Grammar. Section 11.6.1 deals with Tesnière's part of speech system and Section 11.6.2 describes the modes of combinations of linguistics objects assumed by Tesnière.

11.6.1 Tesnière's part of speech classification

As mentioned in the introduction, Tesnière is a central figure in the history of Dependency Grammar as it was him who developed the first formal model (Tesnière 1959, 1980, 2015). There are many versions of Dependency Grammar today and most of them use the part of speech labels that are used in other theories as well (N, P, A, V, Adv, Conj, ...). Tesnière had a system of four major categories: noun, verb, adjective, and adverb. The labels for these categories were derived from the endings that are used in Esperanto, that is, they are O, I, A, and E, respectively. These categories were defined semantically as specified in Table 11.1.[17] Tesnière assumed these categories to be universal and suggested

Table 11.1: Semantically motivated part of speech classification by Tesnière

	substance	process
concrete	noun	verb
abstract	adjective	adverb

that there are constraints in which way these categories may depend on others.

According to Tesnière, nouns and adverbs may depend on verbs, adjectives may depend on nouns, and adverbs may depend on adjectives or adverbs. This situation is

---

[17] As Weber (1997: 77) points out this categorization is not without problems: in what sense is *Angst* 'fear' a substance? Why should *glauben* 'believe' be a concrete process? See also Klein (1971: Section 3.4) for the discussion of *schlagen* 'to beat' and *Schlag* 'the beat' and similar cases. Even if one assumes that *Schlag* is derived from the concrete process *schlag-* by a transfer into the category O, the assumption that such Os stand for concrete substances is questionable.

depicted in the general dependency graph in Figure 11.17. The '*' means that there can be
an arbitrary number of dependencies between Es. It is of course easy to find examples

Figure 11.17: Universal configuration for dependencies according to Tesnière
(I = verb, O = noun, A = adjective, E = adverb)

in which adjectives depend on verbs and sentences (verbs) depend on nouns. Such cases
are handled via so-called *transfers* in Tesnière's system. Furthermore, conjunctions, determiners, and prepositions are missing from this set of categories. For the combination
of these elements with their dependents Tesnière used special combinatoric relations:
junction and transfer. We will deal with these in the following subsection.

11.6.2 Connection, junction, and transfer

Tesnière (1959) suggested three basic relations between nodes: connection, junction, and
transfer. Connection is the simple relation between a head and its dependents that we
have already covered in the previous sections. Junction is a special relation that plays a
role in the analysis of coordination and transfer is a tool that allows one to change the
category of a lexical item or a phrase.

11.6.2.1 Junction

Figure 11.18 on the next page illustrates the junction relation: the two conjuncts *John* and
Mary are connected with the conjunction *and*. It is interesting to note that both of the
conjuncts are connected to the head *laugh*.

In the case of two coordinated nouns we get dependency graphs like the one in Figure 11.19 on the following page. Both nouns are connected to the dominating verb and
both nouns dominate the same determiner.

An alternative to such a special treatment of coordination would be to treat the conjunction as the head and the conjuncts as its dependents.[18] The only problem of such a
proposal would be the category of the conjunction. It cannot be Conj since the governing
verb does not select a Conj, but an N. The trick that could be applied here is basically the

---

[18] I did not use Tesnière's category labels here to spare the reader the work of translating I to V and O to N.

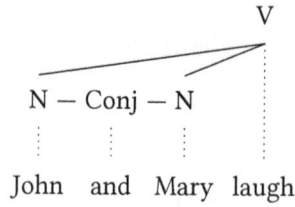

Figure 11.18: Analysis of coordination using the special relation *junction*

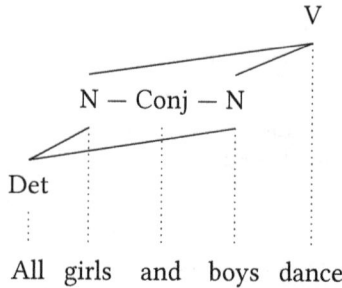

Figure 11.19: Analysis of coordination using the special relation *junction*

same trick as in Categorial Grammar (see Section 21.6.2): the category of the conjunction in Categorial Grammar is (X\X)/X. We have a functor that takes two arguments of the same category and the result of the combination is an object that has the same category as the two arguments. Translating this approach to Dependency Grammar, one would get an analysis as the one depicted in Figure 11.20 rather than the ones in Figure 11.18 and Figure 11.19. The figure for *all girls and boys* looks rather strange since both the

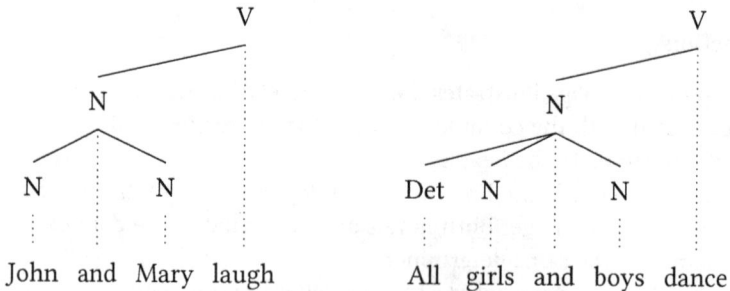

Figure 11.20: Analysis of coordination without *junction* and the conjunction as head

determiner and the two conjuncts depend on the conjunction, but since the two Ns are selecting a Det, the same is true for the result of the coordination. In Categorial Grammar notation, the category of the conjunction would be ((NP\Det)\(NP\Det))/(NP\Det) since X is instantiated by the nouns which would have the category (NP\Det) in an analysis in which the noun is the head and the determiner is the dependent.

Note that both approaches have to come up with an explanation of subject–verb agreement. Tesnière's original analysis assumes two dependencies between the verb and the individual conjuncts.[19] As the conjuncts are singular and the verb is plural, agreement cannot be modeled in tandem with dependency relations in this approach. If the second analysis finds ways of specifying the agreement properties of the coordination in the conjunction, the agreement facts can be accounted for without problems.

The alternative to a headed approach as depicted in Figure 11.20 is an unheaded one. Several authors working in phrase structure-based frameworks suggested analyses of coordination without a head. Such analyses are also assumed in Dependency Grammar (Hudson 1988; Kahane 1997). Hudson (1988) and others who make similar assumptions assume a phrase structure component for coordination: the two nouns and the conjunction are combined to form a larger object which has properties which do not correspond to the properties of any of the combined words.

Similarly, the junction-based analysis of coordination poses problems for the interpretation of the representations. If semantic role assignment happens in parallel to dependency relations, there would be a problem with graphs like the one in Figure 11.18, since the semantic role of *laugh* cannot be filled by *John* and *Mary* simultaneously. Rather it is filled by one entity, namely the one that refers to the set containing John and Mary. This semantic representation would belong to the phrase *John and Mary* and the natural candidate for being the topmost entity in this coordination is *and*, as it embeds the meaning of *John* and the meaning of *Mary*: $and'(John', Mary')$.

Such junctions are also assumed for the coordination of verbs. This is, however, not without problems, since adjuncts can have scope over the conjunct that is closest to them or over the whole coordination. An example is the following sentence from Levine (2003: 217):

(15) Robin came in, found a chair, sat down, and whipped off her logging boots in exactly thirty seconds flat.

The adjunct *in exactly thirty seconds flat* can refer either to *whipped off her logging boots* as in (16a) or scope over all three conjuncts together as in (16b):

(16) a. Robin came in, found a chair, sat down, and [[pulled off her logging boots] in exactly thirty seconds flat].

b. Robin [[came in, found a chair, sat down, and pulled off her logging boots] in exactly thirty seconds flat].

The Tesnièreian analysis in Figure 11.21 on the following page corresponds to (17), while an analysis that treats the conjunction as the head as in Figure 11.22 on the next page corresponds to (16b).

---

[19] Eroms (2000: 467) notes the agreement problem and describes the facts. In his analysis, he connects the first conjunct to the governing head, although it seems to be more appropriate to assume an internally structured coordination structure and then connect the highest conjunction.

(17) Robin came in in exactly thirty seconds flat and Robin found a chair in exactly thirty seconds flat and Robin pulled off her logging boots in exactly thirty seconds flat.

The reading in (17) results when an adjunct refers to each conjunct individually rather then referring to a cumulative event that is expressed by a verb phrase as in (16b).

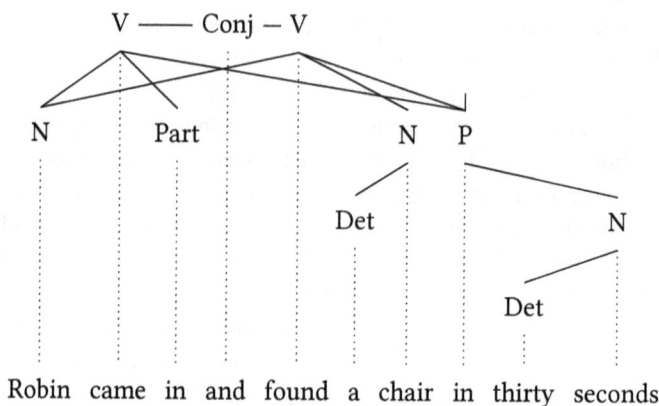

Figure 11.21: Analysis of verb coordination involving the junction relation

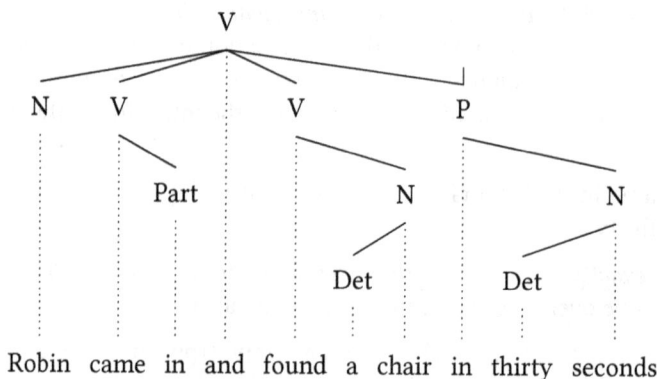

Figure 11.22: Analysis of verb coordination involving the connection relation

Levine (2003: 217) discusses these sentences in connection to the HPSG analysis of extraction by Bouma, Malouf & Sag (2001a). Bouma, Malouf & Sag suggest an analysis in which adjuncts are introduced lexically as dependents of a certain head. Since adjuncts are introduced lexically, the coordination structures basically have the same structure as the ones assumed in a Tesnièreian analysis. It may be possible to come up with a way to get the semantic composition right even though the syntax does not correspond to the semantic dependencies (see Chaves 2009 for suggestions), but it is clear that it is simpler to derive the semantics from a syntactic structure which corresponds to what is going on in semantics.

11.6.2.2 Transfer

Transfers are used in Tesnière's system for the combination of words or phrases with a head of one of the major categories (for instance nouns) with words in minor categories (for instance prepositions). In addition, transfers can transfer a word or phrase into another category without any other word participating.

Figure 11.23 shows an example of a transfer. The preposition *in* causes a category

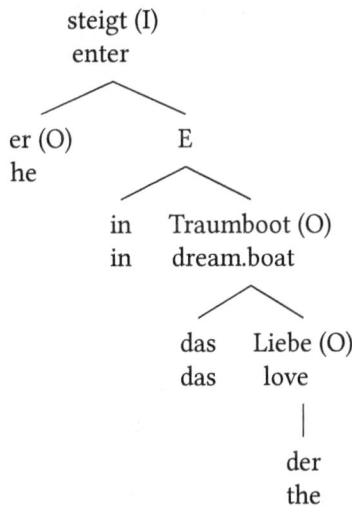

```
                        steigt (I)
                         enter
                    ╱            ╲
          er (O)                E
          he                ╱         ╲
                      in      Traumboot (O)
                      in      dream.boat
                              ╱        ╲
                        das      Liebe (O)
                        das       love
                                   │
                                  der
                                  the
```

Figure 11.23: Transfer with an example adapted from Weber (1997: 83)

change: while *Traumboot* 'dream boat' is an O (noun), the combination of the preposition and the noun is an E. The example shows that Tesnière used the grammatical category to encode grammatical functions. In theories like HPSG there is a clear distinction: there is information about part of speech on the one hand and the function of elements as modifiers and predicates on the other hand. The modifier function is encoded by the selectional feature MOD, which is independent of the part of speech. It is therefore possible to have modifying and non-modifying adjectives, modifying and non-modifying prepositional phrases, modifying and non-modifying noun phrases and so on. For the example at hand, one would assume a preposition with directional semantics that selects for an NP. The preposition is the head of a PP with a filled MOD value.

Another area in which transfer is used is morphology. For instance, the derivation of French *frappant* 'striking' by suffixation of *-ant* to the verb stem *frapp* is shown in Figure 11.24 on the following page. Such transfers can be subsumed under the general

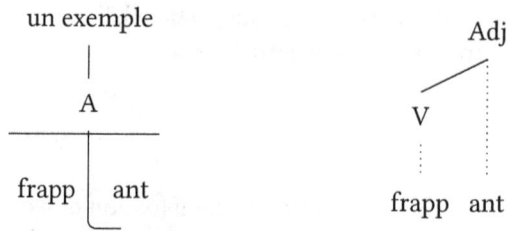

Figure 11.24: Transfer in morphology and its reconceptualization as normal dependency

connection relation if the affix is treated as the head. Morphologists working in realizational morphology and construction morphology argue against such morpheme-based analyses since they involve a lot of empty elements for conversions as for instance the conversion of the verb *play* into the noun *play* (see Figure 11.25). Consequently, lexical

Figure 11.25: Conversion as transfer from I (verb) to O (substantive) and as dependency with an empty element of the category N as head

rules are assumed for derivations and conversions in theories like HPSG. HPSG lexical rules are basically equivalent to unary branching rules (see the discussion of (39) on page 278 and Section 19.5). The affixes are integrated into the lexical rules or into realization functions that specify the morphological form of the item that is licensed by the lexical rule.

Concluding it can be said that transfer corresponds to

- binary-branching phrase structure rules, if a word or phrase is combined with another word,

- unary phrase structure rules or binary branching phrase structure rules together with an empty head if a phrase is converted to another category without any additional element present or

- a (unary) lexical rule if a word or stem is mapped to a word or a stem.

For further discussion of the relation between Tesnière's transfer rules and constituency rules see Osborne & Kahane (2015: Section 4.9.1–4.9.2). Osborne & Kahane point out that transfer rules can be used to model exocentric constructions, that is, constructions in which there is no single part that could be identified as the head. For more on headless constructions see Section 11.7.2.4.

11.6.3 Scope

As Osborne & Kahane (2015: lix) point out, Tesnière uses so-called polygraphs to represent scopal relations. So, since *that you saw yesterday* in (18) refers to *red cars* rather than *cars* alone, this is represented by a line that starts at the connection between *red* and *cars* rather than on one of the individual elements (Tesnière 2015: 150, Stemma 149).

(18)   red cars that you saw yesterday

Tesnière's analysis is depicted in the left representation in Figure 11.26. It is worth noting that this representation corresponds to the phrase structure tree on the right of Figure 11.26. The combination B between *red* and *cars* corresponds to the B node in the right-

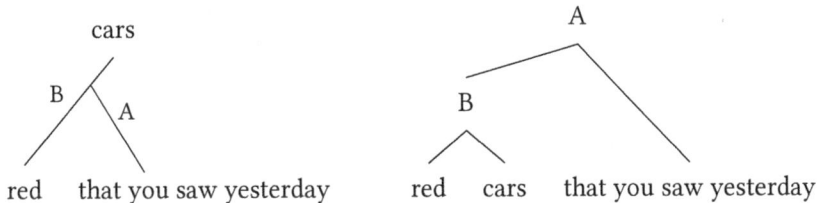

Figure 11.26: Tesnière's way of representing scope and the comparison with phrase structure-based analyses by Osborne & Kahane (2015: lix)

hand figure and the combination A of *red cars* and *that you saw yesterday* corresponds to the A node. So, what is made explicit and is assigned a name in phrase structure grammars remains nameless in Tesnière's analysis, but due to the assumption of polygraphs, it is possible to refer to the combinations. See also the discussion of Figure 11.46, which shows additional nodes that Hudson assumes in order to model semantic relations.

11.7 Summary and classification

Proponents of Dependency Grammar emphasize the point that Dependency Grammar is much simpler than phrase structure grammars, since there are fewer nodes and the general concept is more easy to grasp (see for instance Osborne 2014: Section 3.2, Section 7). This is indeed true: Dependency Grammar is well-suited for teaching grammar in introductory classes. However, as Sternefeld & Richter (2012: 285) point out in a rather general discussion, simple syntax has the price of complex semantics and vice versa. So, in addition to the dependency structure that is described in Dependency Syntax, one needs other levels. One level is the level of semantics and another one is linearization. As far as linearization is concerned, Dependency Grammar has two options: assuming continuous constituents, that is, projective structures, or allowing for discontinuous constituents. These options will be discussed in the following subsections. Section 11.7.2 compares dependency grammars with phrase structure grammars and shows that projective Dependency Grammars can be translated into phrase structure grammars. It also shows that non-projective structures can be modeled in theories like HPSG. The integration of semantics is discussed in Section 11.7.2.3 and it will become clear that once other levels are taken into account, Dependency Grammars are not necessarily simpler than phrase structure grammars.

11.7.1 Linearization

We have seen several approaches to linearization in this chapter. Many just assume a dependency graph and some linearization according to the topological fields model. As has been argued in Section 11.5, allowing discontinuous serialization of a head and its dependents opens up Pandora's box. I have discussed the analysis of nonlocal dependencies by Kunze (1968), Hudson (1997, 2000), Kahane, Nasr & Rambow (1998), and Groß & Osborne (2009). With the exception of Hudson those authors assume that dependents of a head rise to a dominating head only in those cases in which a discontinuity would arise otherwise. However, there seems to be a reason to assume that fronting should be treated by special mechanisms even in cases that allow for continuous serialization. For instance, the ambiguity or lack of ambiguity of the examples in (19) cannot be explained in a straightforward way:

(19)   a. Oft   liest er das Buch nicht.
           often reads he the book not

       'It is often that he does not read the book.' or
       'It is not the case that he reads the book often.'

       b. dass er das Buch nicht oft   liest
           that he the book not often reads

       'It is not the case that he reads the book often.'

       c. dass er das Buch oft   nicht liest
           that he the book often not   reads

       'It is often that he does not read the book.'

The point about the three examples is that only (19a) is ambiguous. Even though (19c) has the same order as far as *oft* 'often' and *nicht* 'not' are concerned, the sentence is not ambiguous. So it is the fronting of an adjunct that is the reason for the ambiguity. The dependency graph for (19a) is shown in Figure 11.27 on the following page. Of course the dependencies for (19b) and (19c) do not differ. The graphs would be the same, only differing in serialization. Therefore, differences in scope could not be derived from the dependencies and complicated statements like (20) would be necessary:

(20)   If a dependent is linearized in the *Vorfeld* it can both scope over and under all other
       adjuncts of the head it is a dependent of.

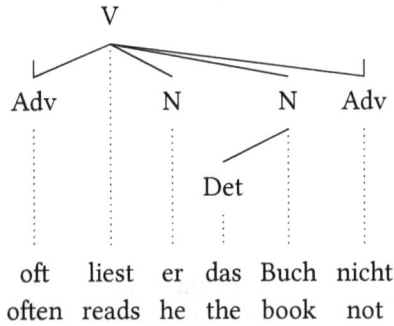

Figure 11.27: Dependency graph for *Oft liest er das Buch nicht.* 'He does not read the book often.'

Eroms (1985: 320) proposes an analysis of negation in which the negation is treated as the head; that is, the sentence in (21) has the structure in Figure 11.28.[20]

(21)   Er kommt nicht.
       he comes not
       'He does not come.'

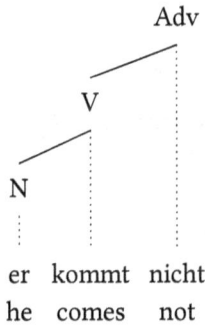

Figure 11.28: Analysis of negation according to Eroms (1985: 320)

This analysis is equivalent to analyses in the Minimalist Program assuming a NegP and it has the same problem: the category of the whole object is Adv, but it should be V. This is a problem since higher predicates may select for a V rather than an Adv.[21]

The same is true for constituent negation or other scope bearing elements. For example, the analysis of (22) would have to be the one in Figure 11.29 on the next page.

(22)   der angebliche Mörder
       the alleged   murderer

---

[20] But see Eroms (2000: Section 11.2.3).
[21] See for instance the analysis of embedded sentences like (23) below.

Adj

N

Det

der   angebliche   Mörder
the   alleged   murderer

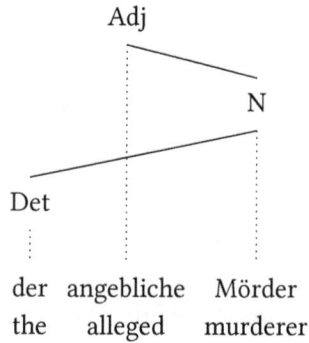

Figure 11.29: Analysis that would result if one considered all scope-bearing adjuncts to be heads

This structure would have the additional problem of being non-projective. Eroms does treat the determiner differently from what is assumed here, so this type of non-projectivity may not be a problem for him. However, the head analysis of negation would result in non-projectivity in so-called coherent constructions in German. The sentence in (23) has two readings: in the first reading, the negation scopes over *singen* 'sing' and in the second one over *singen darf* 'sing may'.

(23)   dass er nicht singen darf
       that he not   sing   may

       'that he is not allowed to sing' or 'that he is allowed not to sing'

The reading in which *nicht* 'not' scopes over the whole verbal complex would result in the non-projective structure that is given in Figure 11.30. Eroms also considers an

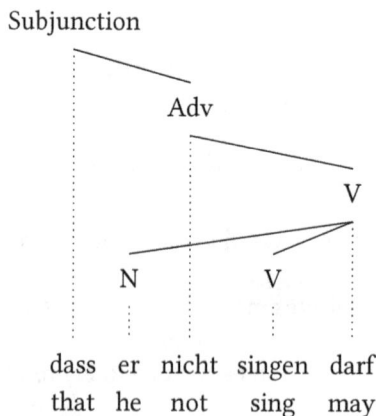

Subjunction

Adv

V

N   V

dass   er   nicht singen darf
that   he   not   sing   may

Figure 11.30: Analysis that results if one assumes the negation to be a head

analysis in which the negation is a word part ('Wortteiläquivalent'). This does, however, not help here since first the negation and the verb are not adjacent in V2 contexts like (19a) and even in verb-final contexts like (23). Eroms would have to assume that the object to which the negation attaches is the whole verbal complex *singen darf* 'sing may', that is, a complex object consisting of two words.

This leaves us with the analysis provided in Figure 11.27 and hence with a problem since we have one structure with two possible adjunct realizations that correspond to different readings. This is not predicted by an analysis that treats the two possible linearizations simply as alternative orderings.

Thomas Groß (p. c. 2013) suggested an analysis in which *oft* does not depend on the verb but on the negation. This corresponds to constituent negation in phrase structure approaches. The dependency graph is shown on the left-hand side in Figure 11.31. The

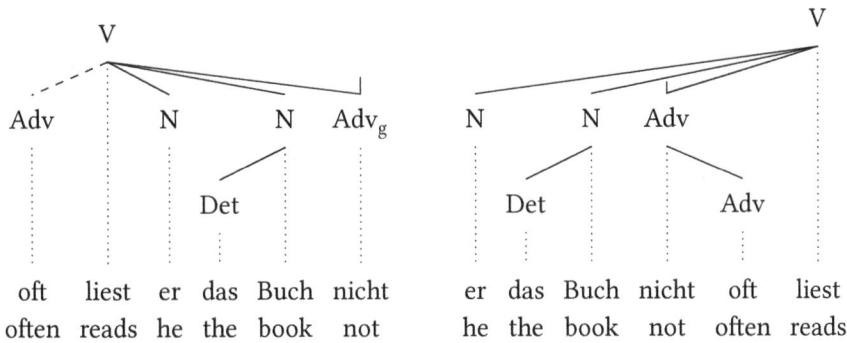

Figure 11.31: Dependency graph for *Oft liest er das Buch nicht.* 'He does not read the book often.' according to Groß and verb-final variant

figure on the right-hand side shows the graph for the corresponding verb-final sentence. The reading corresponding to constituent negation can be illustrated with contrastive expressions. While in (24a) it is only *oft* 'often' which is negated, it is *oft gelesen* 'often read' that is in the scope of negation in (24b).

(24) a. Er hat das Buch nicht oft   gelesen, sondern selten.
          he has the book not   often read   but   seldom

      'He did not read the book often, but seldom.'

      b. Er hat das Buch nicht oft   gelesen, sondern selten gekauft.
          he has the book not   often read   but   seldom bought

      'He did not read the book often but rather bought it seldom.'

These two readings correspond to the two phrase structure trees in Figure 11.32 on the following page. Note that in an HPSG analysis, the adverb *oft* would be the head of the phrase *nicht oft* 'not often'. This is different from the Dependency Grammar analysis suggested by Groß. Furthermore, the Dependency Grammar analysis has two structures: a flat one with all adverbs depending on the same verb and one in which *oft* depends on the negation. The phrase structure-based analysis has three structures: one with the order *oft* before *nicht*, one with the order *nicht* before *oft* and the one with direct combination of *nicht* and *oft*. The point about the example in (19a) is that one of the first two structures is missing in the Dependency Grammar representations. This probably

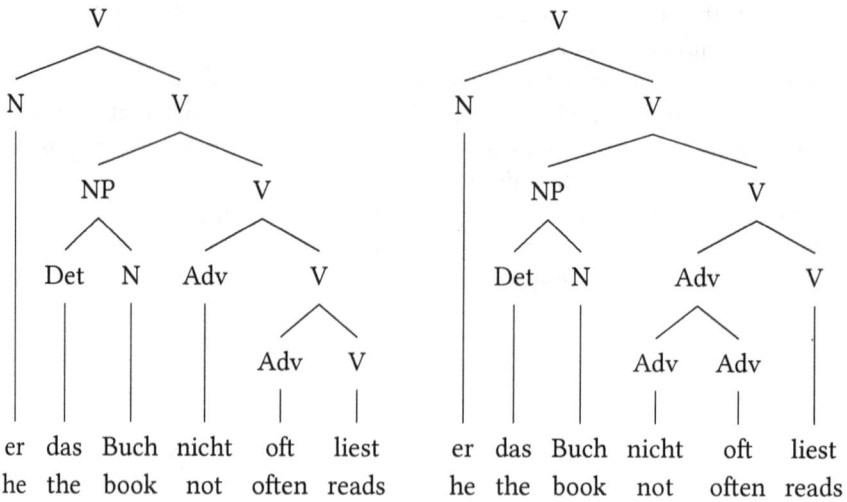

Figure 11.32: Possible syntactic analyses for *er das Buch nicht oft liest* 'he does not read the book often'

does not make it impossible to derive the semantics, but it is more difficult than it is in constituent-based approaches.

Furthermore, note that models that directly relate dependency graphs to topological fields will not be able to account for sentences like (25).

(25)   Dem Saft eine kräftige Farbe geben Blutorangen.[22]
       the juice a   strong color give blood.oranges

       'Blood oranges give a strong color to the juice.'

The dependency graph of this sentence is given in Figure 11.33 on the following page.

Such apparent multiple frontings are not restricted to NPs. Various types of dependents can be placed in the *Vorfeld*. An extensive discussion of the data is provided in Müller (2003a). Additional data have been collected in a research project on multiple frontings and information structure (Bildhauer 2011). Any theory based on dependencies alone and not allowing for empty elements is forced to give up the restriction commonly assumed in the analysis of V2 languages, namely that the verb is in second position. In comparison, analyses like GB and those HPSG variants that assume an empty verbal head can assume that a projection of such a verbal head occupies the *Vorfeld*. This explains why the material in the *Vorfeld* behaves like a verbal projection containing a visible verb: such *Vorfelds* are internally structured topologically. They may have a filled *Nachfeld* and even a particle that fills the right sentence bracket. See Müller (2005c, 2015b) for further data, discussion, and a detailed analysis. The equivalent of the analysis in Gross & Osborne's framework (2009) would be something like the graph that is

---

[22] Bildhauer & Cook (2010) found this example in the *Deutsches Referenzkorpus* (DeReKo), hosted at Institut für Deutsche Sprache, Mannheim: http://www.ids-mannheim.de/kl/projekte/korpora

V

N N N

Det Det Adj

dem Saft eine kräftige Farbe geben Blutorangen
the juice a strong color give blood.oranges

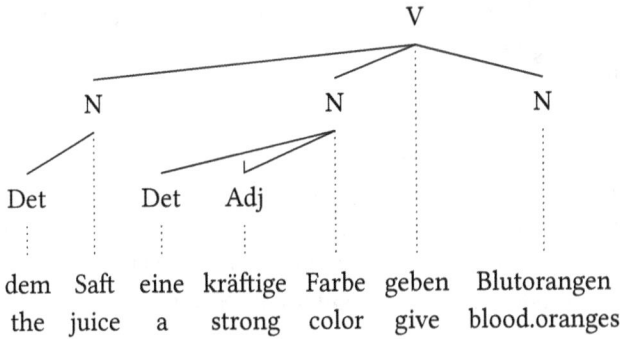

Figure 11.33: Dependency graph for *Dem Saft eine kräftige Farbe geben Blutorangen.* 'Blood oranges give the juice a strong color.'

shown in Figure 11.34, but note that Groß & Osborne (2009: 73) explicitly reject empty elements, and in any case an empty element which is stipulated just to get the multiple fronting cases right would be entirely ad hoc.[23] It is important to note that the issue is

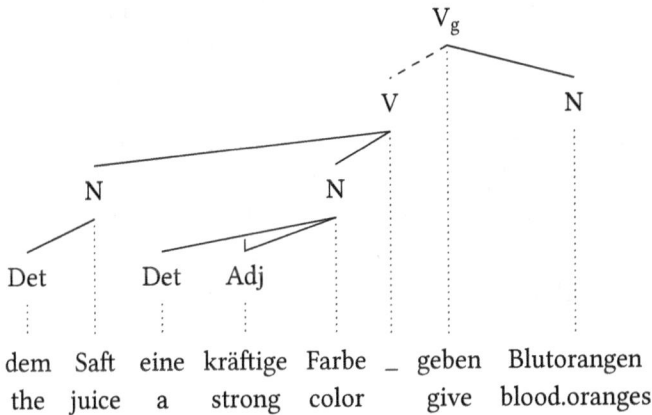

V_g

V N

N N

Det Det Adj

dem Saft eine kräftige Farbe _ geben Blutorangen
the juice a strong color give blood.oranges

Figure 11.34: Dependency graph for *Dem Saft eine kräftige Farbe geben Blutorangen.* 'Blood oranges give the juice a strong color.' with an empty verbal head for the *Vorfeld*

not solved by simply dropping the V2 constraint and allowing dependents of the finite verb to be realized to its left, since the fronted constituents do not necessarily depend on the finite verb as the examples in (26) show:

---

[23] I stipulated such an empty element in a linearization-based variant of HPSG allowing for discontinuous constituents (Müller 2002b), but later modified this analysis so that only continuous constituents are allowed, verb position is treated as head-movement and multiple frontings involve the same empty verbal head as is used in the verb movement analysis (Müller 2005c, 2015b).

(26) a. [Gezielt]   [Mitglieder] [im   Seniorenbereich]   wollen die Kendoka
        specifically members   in.the senior.citizens.sector want.to the Kendoka
        allerdings nicht werben.[24]
        however not recruit

        'However, the Kendoka do not intend to target the senior citizens sector with
        their member recruitment strategy.'

    b. [Kurz] [die Bestzeit] hatte der Berliner Andreas Klöden [...] gehalten.[25]
        briefly the best.time had the Berliner Andreas Klöden   held

        'Andreas Klöden from Berlin had briefly held the record time.'

And although the respective structures are marked, such multiple frontings can even
cross clause boundaries:

(27) Der   Maria einen Ring glaube ich nicht, daß er je   schenken wird.[26]
      the.DAT Maria a.ACC ring believe I   not   that he ever give   will

      'I don't think that he would ever give Maria a ring.'

If such dependencies are permitted it is really difficult to constrain them. The details
cannot be discussed here, but the reader is referred to Müller (2005c, 2015b).

    Note also that Engel's statement regarding the linear order in German sentences (2014:
50) referring to one element in front of the finite verb (see footnote 7) is very imprecise.
One can only guess what is intended by the word *element*. One interpretation is that it
is a continuous constituent in the classical sense of constituency-based grammars. An
alternative would be that there is a continuous realization of a head and some but not necessarily all of its dependents. This alternative would allow an analysis of extraposition
with discontinuous constituents of (28) as it is depicted in Figure 11.35 on the following
page.

(28) Ein junger Kerl stand da,   mit langen blonden Haaren, die sein Gesicht
      a   young guy stood there with long   blond hair   that his face
      einrahmten, [...][27]
      framed

      'A young guy was standing there with long blond hair that framed his face'

A formalization of such an analysis is not trivial, since one has to be precise about what
exactly can be realized discontinuously and which parts of a dependency must be realized
continuously. Kathol & Pollard (1995) developed such an analysis of extraposition in the
framework of HPSG. See also Müller (1999a: Section 13.3). I discuss the basic mechanisms
for such linearization analyses in HPSG in the following section.

---

[24] taz, 07.07.1999, p. 18. Quoted from Müller (2002b).
[25] Märkische Oderzeitung, 28./29.07.2001, p. 28.
[26] Fanselow (1993: 67).
[27] Charles Bukowski, *Der Mann mit der Ledertasche*. München: Deutscher Taschenbuch Verlag, 1994, p. 201,
translation by Hans Hermann.

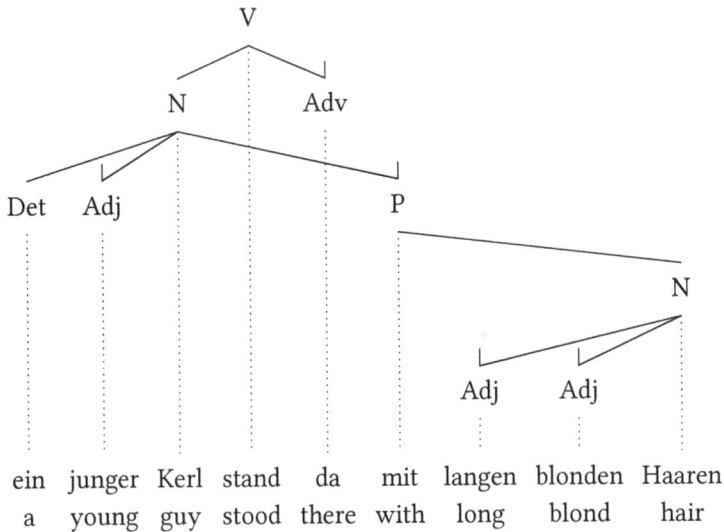

Figure 11.35: Dependency graph for *Ein junger Kerl stand da, mit langen blonden Haaren.* 'A young guy was standing there with long blond hair.' with a discontinuous constituent in the *Vorfeld*

11.7.2 Dependency Grammar vs. phrase structure grammar

This section deals with the relation between Dependency Grammars and phrase structure grammars. I first show that projective Dependency Grammars can be translated into phrase structure grammars (Section 11.7.2.1). I will then deal with non-projective DGs and show how they can be captured in linearization-based HPSG (Section 11.7.2.2). Section 11.7.2.3 argues for the additional nodes that are assumed in phrase structure-based theories and Section 11.7.2.4 discusses headless constructions, which pose a problem for all Dependency Grammar accounts.

11.7.2.1 Translating projective Dependency Grammars into phrase structure grammars

As noted by Gaifman (1965), Covington (1990: 234), Oliva (2003) and Hellwig (2006: 1093), certain projective headed phrase structure grammars can be turned into Dependency Grammars by moving the head one level up to replace the dominating node. So in an NP structure, the N is shifted into the position of the NP and all other connections remain the same. Figure 11.36 on the following page illustrates. Of course this procedure cannot be applied to all phrase structure grammars directly since some involve more elaborate structure. For instance, the rule S → NP, VP cannot be translated into a dependency rule, since NP and VP are both complex categories.

In what follows, I want to show how the dependency graph in Figure 11.1 on page 358 can be recast as headed phrase structure rules that license a similar tree, namely the one

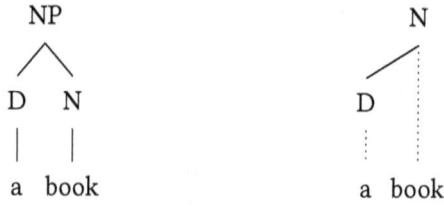

Figure 11.36: *a book* in a phrase structure and a Dependency Grammar analysis

in Figure 11.37. I did not use the labels NP and VP to keep the two figures maximally

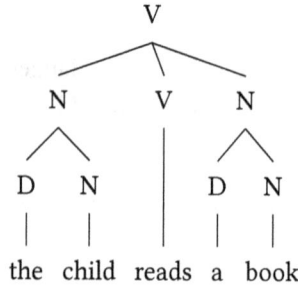

Figure 11.37: Analysis of *The child reads a book.* in a phrase structure with flat rules

similar. The P part of NP and VP refers to the saturation of a projection and is often ignored in figures. See Chapter 9 on HPSG, for example. The grammar that licenses the tree is given in (29), again ignoring valence information.

(29) N → D N   N → child   D → the   D → a
      V → N V N   N → book   V → reads

If one replaces the N and V in the right-hand side of the two left-most rules in (29) with the respective lexical items and then removes the rules that license the words, one arrives at the lexicalized variant of the grammar given in (30):

(30) N → D book   D → the
      N → D child   D → a
      V → N reads N

Lexicalized means that every partial tree licensed by a grammar rule contains a lexical element. The grammar in (30) licenses exactly the tree in Figure 11.1.[28]

---

[28] As mentioned on page 359, Gaifman (1965: 305), Hays (1964: 513), Baumgärtner (1970: 57) and Heringer (1996: 37) suggest a general rule format for dependency rules that has a special marker ('*' and '~', respectively) in place of the lexical words in (30). Heringer's rules have the form in (31):

(i) X[Y1, Y2, ~, Y3]

X is the category of the head, Y1, Y2, and Y3 are dependents of the head and '~' is the position into which the head is inserted.

One important difference between classical phrase structure grammars and Dependency Grammars is that the phrase structure rules impose a certain order on the daughters. That is, the V rule in (30) implies that the first nominal projection, the verb, and the second nominal projection have to appear in the order stated in the rule. Of course this ordering constraint can be relaxed as it is done in GPSG. This would basically permit any order of the daughters at the right hand side of rules. This leaves us with the integration of adjuncts. Since adjuncts depend on the head as well (see Figure 11.4 on page 360), a rule could be assumed that allows arbitrarily many adjuncts in addition to the arguments. So the V rule in (30) would be changed to the one in (31):[29]

(31) V → N reads N Adv*

Such generalized phrase structures would give us the equivalent of projective Dependency Grammars.[30] However, as we have seen, some researchers allow for crossing edges, that is, for discontinuous constituents. In what follows, I show how such Dependency Grammars can be formalized in HPSG.

11.7.2.2 Non-projective Dependency Grammars and phrase structure grammars with discontinuous constituents

The equivalent to non-projective dependency graphs are discontinuous constituents in phrase structure grammars. In what follows I want to provide one example of a phrase structure-based theory that permits discontinuous structures. Since, as I will show, discontinuities can be modeled as well, the difference between phrase structure grammars and Dependency Grammars boils down to the question of whether units of words are given a label (for instance NP) or not.

The technique that is used to model discontinuous constituents in frameworks like HPSG goes back to Mike Reape's work on German (1991; 1992; 1994). Reape uses a list called DOMAIN to represent the daughters of a sign in the order in which they appear at the surface of an utterance. (32) shows an example in which the DOM value of a headed-phrase is computed from the DOM value of the head and the list of non-head daughters.

$$
(32) \quad \textit{headed-phrase} \Rightarrow
\begin{bmatrix}
\text{HEAD-DTR}|\text{DOM} & \boxed{1} \\
\text{NON-HEAD-DTRS} & \boxed{2} \\
\text{DOM} & \boxed{1} \bigcirc \boxed{2}
\end{bmatrix}
$$

The symbol '◯' stands for the *shuffle* relation. *shuffle* relates three lists A, B and C iff C contains all elements from A and B and the order of the elements in A and the order of the elements of B is preserved in C. (33) shows the combination of two sets with two elements each:

---

[29] See page 184 for a similar rule in GPSG and see Kasper (1994) for an HPSG analysis of German that assumes entirely flat structures and integrates an arbitrary number of adjuncts.

[30] Sylvain Kahane (p. c. 2015) states that binarity is important for Dependency Grammars, since there is one rule for the subject, one for the object and so on (as for instance in Kahane 2009, which is an implementation of Dependency Grammar in the HPSG formalism). However, I do not see any reason to disallow for flat structures. For instance, Ginzburg & Sag (2000: 364) assumed a flat rule for subject auxiliary inversion in HPSG. In such a flat rule the specifier/subject and the other complements are combined with the verb in one go. This would also work for more than two valence features that correspond to grammatical functions like subject, direct object, indirect object. See also Footnote 28 on flat rules.

(33) $\langle a, b \rangle \bigcirc \langle c, d \rangle = \langle a, b, c, d \rangle \vee$
$$\langle a, c, b, d \rangle \vee$$
$$\langle a, c, d, b \rangle \vee$$
$$\langle c, a, b, d \rangle \vee$$
$$\langle c, a, d, b \rangle \vee$$
$$\langle c, d, a, b \rangle$$

The result is a disjunction of six lists. a is ordered before b and c before d in all of these lists, since this is also the case in the two lists $\langle a, b \rangle$ and $\langle c, d \rangle$ that have been combined. But apart from this, b can be placed before, between or after c and d. Every word comes with a domain value that is a list that contains the word itself:

(34) Domain contribution of single words, here *gibt* 'gives':

$$\boxed{1}\begin{bmatrix} \text{PHON} & \langle \textit{gibt} \rangle \\ \text{SYNSEM} & ... \\ \text{DOM} & \langle \boxed{1} \rangle \end{bmatrix}$$

The description in (34) may seem strange at first glance, since it is cyclic, but it can be understood as a statement saying that *gibt* contributes itself to the items that occur in linearization domains.

The constraint in (35) is responsible for the determination of the PHON values of phrases:

(35) $\textit{phrase} \Rightarrow$
$$\begin{bmatrix} \text{PHON} & \boxed{1} \oplus ... \oplus \boxed{n} \\ \\ \text{DOM} & \left\langle \begin{bmatrix} \textit{sign} \\ \text{PHON} \ \boxed{1} \end{bmatrix}, ..., \begin{bmatrix} \textit{sign} \\ \text{PHON} \ \boxed{n} \end{bmatrix} \right\rangle \end{bmatrix}$$

It states that the PHON value of a sign is the concatenation of the PHON values of its DOMAIN elements. Since the order of the DOMAIN elements corresponds to their surface order, this is the obvious way to determine the PHON value of the whole linguistic object.

Figure 11.38 on the following page shows how this machinery can be used to license binary branching structures with discontinuous constituents. Words or word sequences that are separated by commas stand for separate domain objects, that is, $\langle$ *das, Buch* $\rangle$ contains the two objects *das* and *Buch* and $\langle$ *das Buch, gibt* $\rangle$ contains the two objects *das Buch* and *gibt*. The important point to note here is that the arguments are combined with the head in the order accusative, dative, nominative, although the elements in the constituent order domain are realized in the order dative, nominative, accusative rather than nominative, dative, accusative, as one would expect. This is possible since the formulation of the computation of the DOM value using the shuffle operator allows for discontinuous constituents. The node for *der Frau das Buch gibt* 'the woman the book gives' is discontinuous: *ein Mann* 'a man' is inserted into the domain between *der Frau* 'the woman' and *das Buch* 'the book'. This is more obvious in Figure 11.39 on the following page, which has a serialization of NPs that corresponds to their order.

V[DOM ⟨ *der Frau, ein Mann, das Buch, gibt* ⟩]

NP[*nom*, DOM ⟨ *ein, Mann* ⟩]   V[DOM ⟨ *der Frau, das Buch, gibt* ⟩]

NP[*dat*, DOM ⟨ *der, Frau* ⟩]   V[DOM ⟨ *das Buch, gibt* ⟩]

NP[*acc*, DOM ⟨ *das, Buch* ⟩]   V[DOM ⟨ *gibt* ⟩]

ein Mann	der Frau	das Buch	gibt
a man	the woman	the book	gives

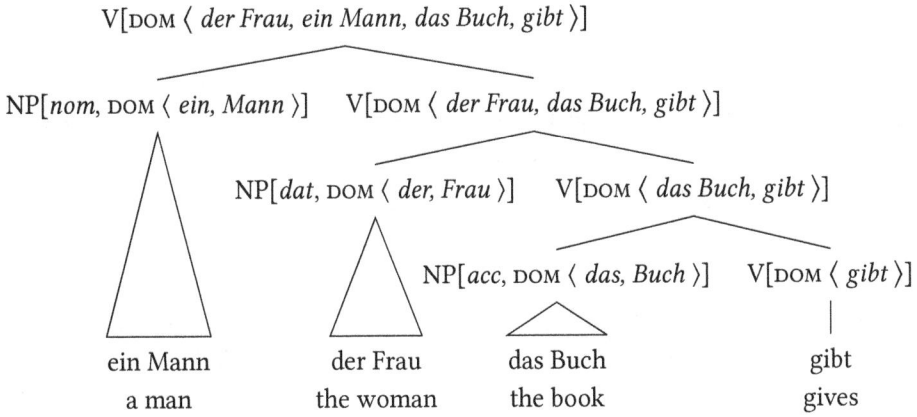

Figure 11.38: Analysis of *dass der Frau ein Mann das Buch gibt* 'that a man gives the woman the book' with binary branching structures and discontinuous constituents

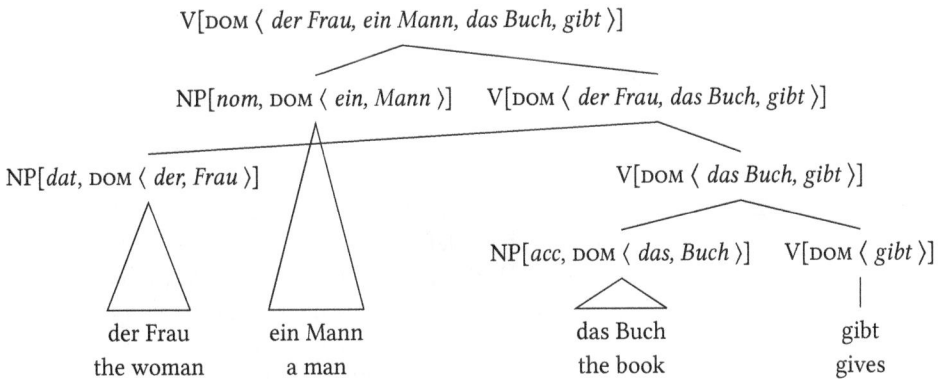

V[DOM ⟨ *der Frau, ein Mann, das Buch, gibt* ⟩]

NP[*nom*, DOM ⟨ *ein, Mann* ⟩]   V[DOM ⟨ *der Frau, das Buch, gibt* ⟩]

NP[*dat*, DOM ⟨ *der, Frau* ⟩]   V[DOM ⟨ *das Buch, gibt* ⟩]

NP[*acc*, DOM ⟨ *das, Buch* ⟩]   V[DOM ⟨ *gibt* ⟩]

der Frau	ein Mann	das Buch	gibt
the woman	a man	the book	gives

Figure 11.39: Analysis of *dass der Frau ein Mann das Buch gibt* 'that a man gives the woman the book' with binary branching structures and discontinuous constituents showing the discontinuity

Such binary branching structures were assumed for the analysis of German by Kathol (1995, 2000) and Müller (1995, 1996c, 1999a, 2002a), but as we have seen throughout this chapter, Dependency Grammar assumes flat representations (but see Footnote 30 on page 389). Schema 1 licenses structures in which all arguments of a head are realized in one go.[31]

Schema 1 (Head-Argument Schema (flat structure))
head-argument-phrase ⇒

$$\begin{bmatrix} \text{SYNSEM|LOC|CAT|SUBCAT } \langle\rangle \\ \text{HEAD-DTR|SYNSEM|LOC|CAT|SUBCAT } \boxed{1} \\ \text{NON-HEAD-DTRS } \boxed{1} \end{bmatrix}$$

To keep the presentation simple, I assume that the SUBCAT list contains descriptions of complete signs. Therefore the whole list can be identified with the list of non-head daughters.[32] The computation of the DOM value can be constrained in the following way:

(36)   *headed-phrase* ⇒
$$\begin{bmatrix} \text{HEAD-DTR} & \boxed{1} \\ \text{NON-HEAD-DTRS} & \langle \boxed{2}, ..., \boxed{n} \rangle \\ \text{DOM} & \langle \boxed{1} \rangle \bigcirc \langle \boxed{2} \rangle \bigcirc ... \bigcirc \langle \boxed{n} \rangle \end{bmatrix}$$

This constraint says that the value of DOM is a list which is the result of shuffling singleton lists each containing one daughter as elements. The result of such a shuffle operation is a disjunction of all possible permutations of the daughters. This seems to be overkill for something that GPSG already gained by abstracting away from the order of the elements on the right hand side of a phrase structure rule. Note, however, that this machinery can be used to reach even freer orders: by referring to the DOM values of the daughters rather than the daughters themselves, it is possible to insert individual words into the DOM list.

(37)   *headed-phrase* ⇒
$$\begin{bmatrix} \text{HEAD-DTR|DOM} & \boxed{1} \\ \text{NON-HEAD-DTRS} & \langle [\text{DOM } \boxed{2}] ... [\text{DOM } \boxed{n}] \rangle \\ \text{DOM} & \langle \boxed{1} \rangle \bigcirc \langle \boxed{2} \rangle \bigcirc ... \bigcirc \langle \boxed{n} \rangle \end{bmatrix}$$

Using this constraint we have DOM values that basically contain all the words in an utterance in any permutation. What we are left with is a pure Dependency Grammar without any constraints on projectivity. With such a grammar we could analyze the non-projecting structure of Figure 11.6 on page 362 and much more. The analysis in terms of domain union is shown in Figure 11.40 on the following page. It is clear that such discontinuity is unwanted and hence one has to have restrictions that enforce continuity. One

---

[31] I assume here that all arguments are contained in the SUBCAT list of a lexical head, but nothing hinges on that. One could also assume several valence features and nevertheless get a flat structure. For instance, Borsley (1989: 339) suggests a schema for auxiliary inversion in English and verb-initial sentences in Welsh that refers to both the valence feature for subjects and for complements and realizes all elements in a flat structure.

[32] Without this assumption one would need a relational constraint that maps a list with descriptions of type *synsem* onto a list with descriptions of type *sign*. See Meurers (1999c: 198) for details.

V[DOM ⟨ *die, Frauen, Türen, öffnen* ⟩]

NP[DOM ⟨ *Frauen* ⟩] NP[DOM ⟨ *die, Türen* ⟩] V[DOM ⟨ *öffnen* ⟩]

D[DOM ⟨ *die* ⟩] N[DOM ⟨ *Türen* ⟩]

die	Frauen	Türen	öffnen
the	women	doors	open

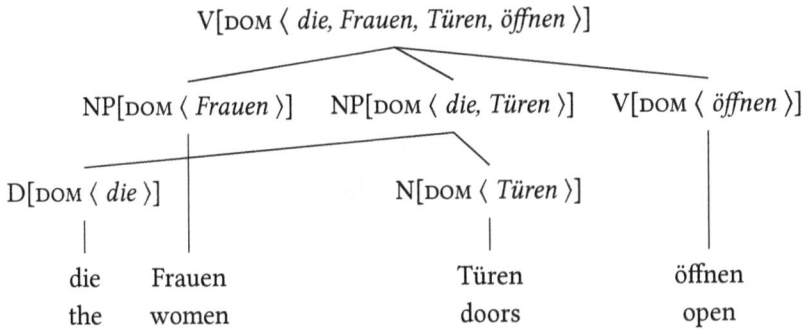

Figure 11.40: Unwanted analysis of *dass die Frauen Türen öffnen* 'that the women open doors' using Reape-style constituent order domains

possible restriction is to require projectivity and hence equivalence to phrase structure grammars in the sense that was discussed above.

There is some dispute going on about the question of whether constituency/dependency is primary/necessary to analyze natural language: while Hudson (1980) and Engel (1996) claim that dependency is sufficient, a claim that is shared by dependency grammarians (according to Engel 1996), Leiss (2003) claims that it is not. In order to settle the issue, let us take a look at some examples:

(38) Dass Peter kommt, klärt   nicht, ob   Klaus spielt.
      that Peter comes   resolves not   whether Klaus plays

      'That Peter comes does not resolve the question of whether Klaus will play.'

If we know the meaning of the utterance, we can assign a dependency graph to it. Let us assume that the meaning of (38) is something like (39):

(39) ¬ *resolve'*(*that'*(*come'*(*Peter'*)),*whether'*(*play'*(*Klaus'*)))

With this semantic information, we can of course construct a dependency graph for (38). The reason is that the dependency relation is reflected in a bi-unique way in the semantic representation in (39). The respective graph is given in Figure 11.41 on the following page. But note that this does not hold in the general case. Take for instance the example in (40):

(40) Dass Peter kommt, klärt   nicht, ob   Klaus kommt.
      that Peter comes   resolves not   whether Klaus plays

      'That Peter comes does not resolve the question of whether Klaus comes.'

Here the word *kommt* appears twice. Without any notion of constituency or restrictions regarding adjacency, linear order and continuity, we cannot assign a dependency graph unambiguously. For instance, the graph in Figure 11.42 on the next page is perfectly compatible with the meaning of this sentence: *dass* dominates *kommt* and *kommt* dominates

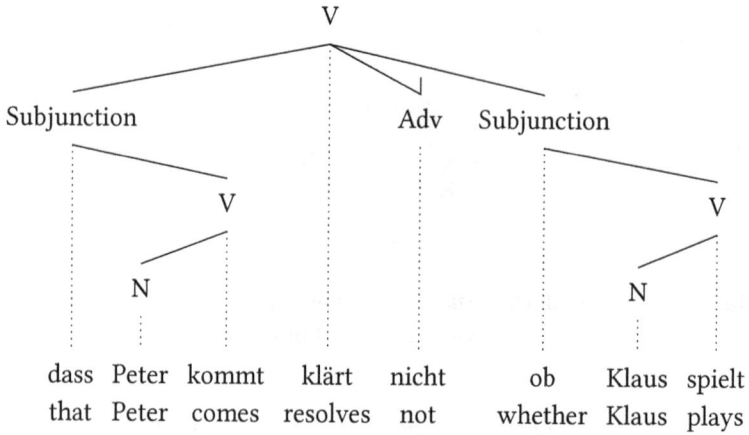

Figure 11.41: The dependency graph of *Dass Peter kommt, klärt nicht, ob Klaus spielt.* 'That Peter comes does not resolve the question of whether Klaus plays.' can be derived from the semantic representation.

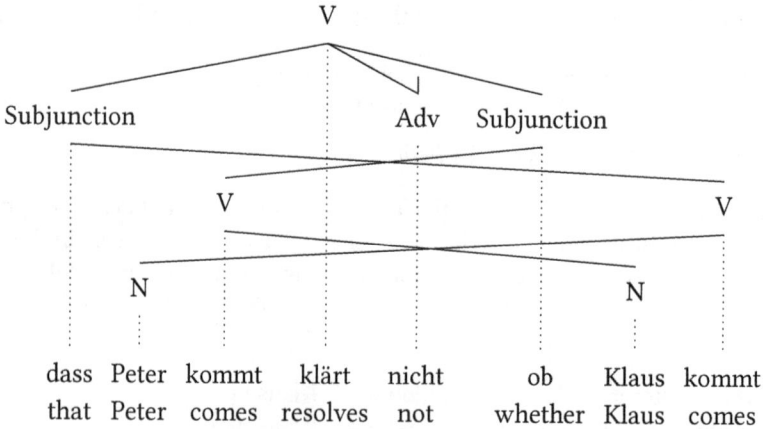

Figure 11.42: The dependency graph of *Dass Peter kommt, klärt nicht, ob Klaus kommt.* 'That Peter comes does not resolve the question of whether Klaus comes.' is not unambiguously determined by semantics.

Peter, while *ob* dominates *kommt* and *kommt* dominates *Klaus*. I used the wrong *kommt* in the dependency chains, but this is an issue of linearization and is independent of dependency. As soon as one takes linearization information into account, the dependency graph in Figure 11.42 is ruled out since *ob* 'whether' does not precede its verbal dependent *kommt* 'comes'. But this explanation does not work for the example in Figure 11.6 on page 362. Here, all dependents are linearized correctly; it is just the discontinuity of *die* and *Türen* that is inappropriate. If it is required that *die* and *Türen* are continuous, we have basically let constituents back in (see Footnote 9 on page 362).

Similarly, non-projective analyses without any constraints regarding continuity would permit the word salad in (41b):

(41) a. Deshalb klärt,   dass Peter kommt, ob   Klaus spielt.
          therefore resolves that Peter comes whether Klaus plays

      b. * Deshalb klärt   dass ob   Peter Klaus kommt spielt.
          therefore resolves that whether Peter Klaus comes plays

(41b) is a variant of (41a) in which the elements of the two clausal arguments are in correct order with respect to each other, but both clauses are discontinuous in such a way that the elements of each clause alternate. The dependency graph is shown in Figure 11.43. As was explained in Section 10.6.4.4 on the analysis of nonlocal dependencies

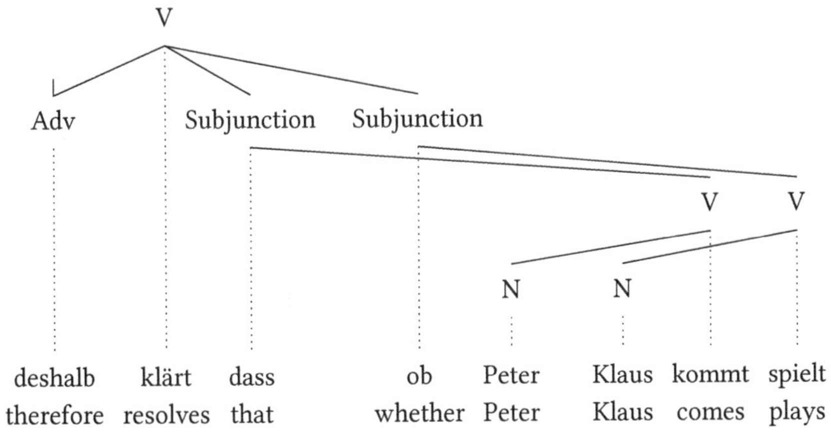

Figure 11.43: The dependency graph of the word salad *Deshalb klärt dass ob Peter Klaus kommt spielt.* 'Therefore resolves that whether Peter Klaus comes plays' which is admitted by non-projective Dependency Grammars that do not restrict discontinuity

in Fluid Construction Grammar, a grammar of languages like English and German has to constrain the clauses in such a way that they are continuous with the exception of extractions to the left. A similar statement can be found in Hudson (1980: 192). Hudson also states that an item can be fronted in English, provided all of its dependents are fronted with it (p. 184). This "item with all its dependents" is the constituent in constituent-based grammars. The difference is that this object is not given an explicit name and is not assumed to be a separate entity containing the head and its dependents in most Dependency Grammars.[33]

Summing up what has been covered in this section so far, I have shown what a phrase structure grammar that corresponds to a certain Dependency Grammar looks like. I have also shown how discontinuous constituents can be allowed for. However, there are issues that remained unaddressed so far: not all properties that a certain phrase has are identical to its lexical head and the differences have to be represented somewhere. I will discuss this in the following subsection.

11.7.2.3 Features that are not identical between heads and projections

As Oliva (2003) points out, the equivalence of Dependency Grammar and HPSG only holds up as far as HEAD values are concerned. That is, the node labels in dependency graphs correspond to the HEAD values in an HPSG. There are, however, additional features like CONT for the semantics and SLASH for nonlocal dependencies. These values usually differ between a lexical head and its phrasal projections. For illustration, let us have a look at the phrase *a book*. The semantics of the lexical material and the complete phrase is given in (42):[34]

(42)   a. *a:* $\lambda P \lambda Q \exists x (P(x) \wedge Q(x))$

      b. *book:* $\lambda y \, (book'(y))$

      c. *a book:* $\lambda Q \exists x (book'(x) \wedge Q(x))$

Now, the problem for the Dependency Grammar notation is that there is no NP node that could be associated with the semantics of *a book* (see Figure 11.36 on page 388), the only thing present in the tree is a node for the lexical N: the node for *book*.[35] This is not a big problem, however: the lexical properties can be represented as part of the highest node as the value of a separate feature. The N node in a dependency graph would then have a CONT value that corresponds to the semantic contribution of the complete phrase and a LEX-CONT value that corresponds to the contribution of the lexical head of the phrase. So for *a book* we would get the following representation:

(43) $\begin{bmatrix} \text{CONT} & \lambda Q \exists x (book'(x) \wedge Q(x)) \\ \text{LEXICAL-CONT} & \lambda y \, (book'(y)) \end{bmatrix}$

---

[33] See however Hellwig (2003) for an explicit proposal that assumes that there is a linguistic object that represents the whole constituent rather than just the lexical head.

[34] For lambda expressions see Section 2.3.

[35] Hudson (2003: 391–392) is explicit about this: "In dependency analysis, the dependents modify the head word's meaning, so the latter carries the meaning of the whole phrase. For example, in *long books about linguistics*, the word *books* means 'long books about linguistics' thanks to the modifying effect of the dependents." For a concrete implementation of this idea see Figure 11.44 on the following page.

    An alternative is to assume different representational levels as in Meaning–Text Theory (Mel'čuk 1981). In fact the CONT value in HPSG is also a different representational level. However, this representational level is in sync with the other structure that is build.

With this kind of representation one could maintain analyses in which the semantic contribution of a head together with its dependents is a function of the semantic contribution of the parts.

Now, there are probably further features in which lexical heads differ from their projections. One such feature would be SLASH, which is used for nonlocal dependencies in HPSG and could be used to establish the relation between the risen element and the head in an approach à la Groß & Osborne (2009). Of course we can apply the same trick again. We would then have a feature LEXICAL-SLASH. But this could be improved and the features of the lexical item could be grouped under one path. The general skeleton would then be (44):

$$(44) \quad \begin{bmatrix} \text{CONT} \\ \text{SLASH} \\ \text{LEXICAL} \begin{bmatrix} \text{CONT} \\ \text{SLASH} \end{bmatrix} \end{bmatrix}$$

But if we rename LEXICAL to HEAD-DTR, we basically get the HPSG representation.

Hellwig (2003: 602) states that his special version of Dependency Grammar, which he calls Dependency Unification Grammar, assumes that governing heads select complete nodes with all their daughters. These nodes may differ in their properties from their head (p. 604). They are in fact constituents. So this very explicit and formalized variant of Dependency Grammar is very close to HPSG, as Hellwig states himself (p. 603).

Hudson's Word Grammar (2015) is also explicitly worked out and, as will be shown, it is rather similar to HPSG. The representation in Figure 11.44 is a detailed description of what the abbreviated version in Figure 11.45 on the following page stands for. What

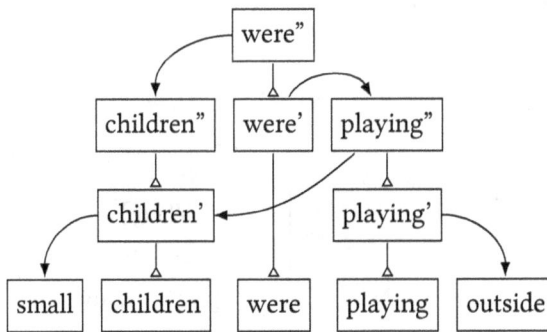

Figure 11.44: Analysis of *Small children were playing outside.* according to Hudson (2015)

is shown in the first diagram is that a combination of two nodes results in a new node. For instance, the combination of *playing* and *outside* yields *playing′*, the combination of *small* and *children* yields *children′*, and the combination of *children′* and *playing′* yields *playing″*. The combination of *were* and *playing″* results in *were′* and the combination of *children″* and *were′* yields *were″*. The only thing left to explain is why there is a node

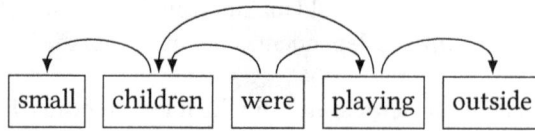

Figure 11.45: Abbreviated analysis of *Small children were playing outside.* according to Hudson (2015)

for *children* that is not the result of the combination of two nodes, namely *children''*. The line with the triangle at the bottom stands for default inheritance. That is, the upper node inherits all properties from the lower node by default. Defaults can be overridden, that is, information at the upper node may differ from information at the dominated node. This makes it possible to handle semantics compositionally: nodes that are the result of the combination of two nodes have a semantics that is the combination of the meaning of the two combined nodes. Turning to *children* again, *children'* has the property that it must be adjacent to *playing*, but since the structure is a raising structure in which *children* is raised to the subject of *were*, this property is overwritten in a new instance of *children*, namely *children''*.

The interesting point now is that we get almost a normal phrase structure tree if we replace the words in the diagram in Figure 11.44 by syntactic categories. The result of the replacement is shown in Figure 11.46. The only thing unusual in this graph (marked

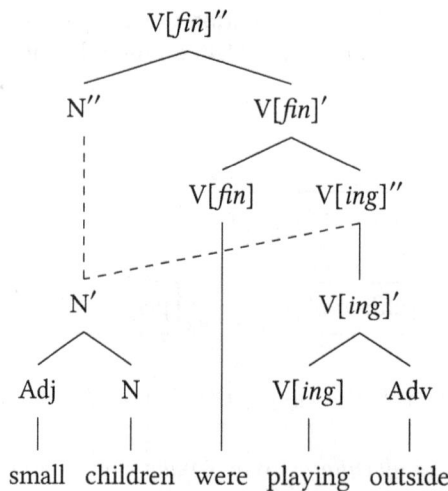

Figure 11.46: Analysis of *Small children are playing outside.* with category symbols

by dashed lines) is that N' is combined with V[*ing*]' and the mother of N', namely N'', is combined with V[*fin*]'. As explained above, this is due to the analysis of raising in Word Grammar, which involves multiple dependencies between a raised item and its heads. There are two N nodes (N′ and N″) in Figure 11.46 and two instances of *children* in Figure 11.44. Apart from this, the structure corresponds to what an HPSG grammar would license. The nodes in Hudson's diagram which are connected with lines with triangles at the bottom are related to their children using default inheritance. This too is rather similar to those versions of HPSG that use default inheritance. For instance, Ginzburg & Sag (2000: 33) use a Generalized Head Feature Principle that projects all properties of the head daughter to the mother by default.

The conclusion of this section is that the only principled difference between phrase structure grammars and Dependency Grammar is the question of how much intermediate structure is assumed: is there a VP without the subject? Are there intermediate nodes for adjunct attachment? It is difficult to decide these questions in the absence of fully worked out proposals that include semantic representations. Those proposals that are worked out – like Hudson's and Hellwig's – assume intermediate representations, which makes these approaches rather similar to phrase structure-based approaches. If one compares the structures of these fully worked out variants of Dependency Grammar with phrase structure grammars, it becomes clear that the claim that Dependency Grammars are simpler is unwarranted. This claim holds for compacted schematic representations like Figure 11.45 but it does not hold for fully worked out analyses.

11.7.2.4 Non-headed constructions

Hudson (1980: Section 4.E) discusses headless constructions like those in (45):

(45)   a.   the rich
       b.   the biggest
       c.   the longer the stem
       d.   (with) his hat over his eyes

He argues that the terms *adjective* and *noun* should be accompanied by the term *substantive*, which subsumes both terms. Then he suggests that *if a rule needs to cover the constructions traditionally referred to as noun-phrases, with or without heads, it just refers to 'nouns', and this will automatically allow the constructions to have either substantives or adjectives as heads.* (p. 195) The question that has to be asked here, however, is what the internal dependency structure of substantive phrases like *the rich* would be. The only way to connect the items seems to be to assume that the determiner is dependent on the adjective. But this would allow for two structures of phrases like *the rich man*: one in which the determiner depends on the adjective and one in which it depends on the noun. So underspecification of part of speech does not seem to solve the problem. Of course all problems with non-headed constructions can be solved by assuming empty elements.[36] This has been done in HPSG in the analysis of relative clauses (Pollard & Sag 1994: Chapter 5). English and German relative clauses consist of a phrase that contains a relative word and a sentence in which the relative phrase is missing. Pollard & Sag

---

[36] See Section 2.4.1 for the assumption of an empty head in a phrase structure grammar for noun phrases.

assume an empty relativizer that selects for the relative phrase and the clause with a gap (Pollard & Sag 1994: 216–217). Similar analyses can be found in Dependency Grammar (Eroms 2000: 291).[37] Now, the alternative to empty elements are phrasal constructions.[38] Sag (1997) working on relative clauses in English suggested a phrasal analysis of relative clauses in which the relative phrase and the clause from which it is extracted form a new phrase. A similar analysis was assumed by Müller (1996c) and is documented in Müller (1999a: Chapter 10). As was discussed in Section 8.6 it is neither plausible to assume the relative pronoun or some other element in the relative phrase to be the head of the entire relative clause, nor is it plausible to assume the verb to be the head of the entire relative clause (pace Sag), since relative clauses modify $\overline{\text{N}}$s, something that projections of (finite) verbs usually do not do. So assuming an empty head or a phrasal schema seems to be the only option.

Chapter 21 is devoted to the discussion of whether certain phenomena should be analyzed as involving phrase structural configurations or whether lexical analyses are better suited in general or for modeling some phenomena. I argue there that all phenomena interacting with valence should be treated lexically. But there are other phenomena as well and Dependency Grammar is forced to assume lexical analyses for all linguistic phenomena. There always has to be some element on which others depend. It has been argued by Jackendoff (2008) that it does not make sense to assume that one of the elements in N-P-N constructions like those in (46) is the head.

(46) a. day by day, paragraph by paragraph, country by country
      b. dollar for dollar, student for student, point for point
      c. face to face, bumper to bumper
      d. term paper after term paper, picture after picture
      e. book upon book, argument upon argument

Of course there is a way to model all the phenomena that would be modeled by a phrasal construction in frameworks like GPSG, CxG, HPSG, or Simpler Syntax: an empty head. Figure 11.47 on the following page shows the analysis of *student after student*. The lexical item for the empty N would be very special, since there are no similar non-empty lexical nouns, that is, there is no noun that selects for two bare Ns and a P.

---

[37] The Dependency Grammar representations usually have a *d-* element as the head of the relative clause. However, since the relative pronoun is also present in the clause and since the *d-* is not pronounced twice, assuming an additional *d-* head is basically assuming an empty head.

Another option is to assume that words may have multiple functions: so, a relative pronoun may be both a head and a dependent simultaneously (Tesnière 2015: Chapter 246, §8–11; Osborne & Kahane 2015: xlvi; Kahane 2009: 129–130). At least the analysis of Kahane is an instance of the Categorial Grammar analysis that was discussed in Section 8.6 and it suffers from the same problems: if the relative pronoun is a head that selects for a clause that is missing the relative pronoun, it is not easy to see how this analysis extends to cases of pied-piping like (i) in which the extracted element is a complete phrase containing the relative pronoun rather than just the pronoun itself.

(i) die Frau,   von deren Schwester ich ein Bild   gesehen habe
     the woman of whose sister   I a picture seen   have
     'the woman of whose sister I saw a picture'

[38] See Chapter 19 on empty elements in general and Subsection 21.10.3 on relative clauses in particular.

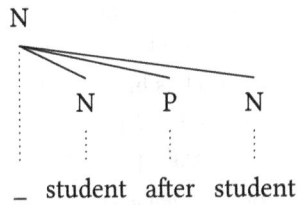

Figure 11.47: Dependency Grammar analysis of the N-P-N Construction with empty head

Bragmann (2015) pointed out an additional aspect of the N-P-N construction, which makes things more complicated. The pattern is not restricted to two nouns. There can be arbitrarily many of them:

(47) Day after day after day went by, but I never found the courage to talk to her.

So rather than an N-P-N pattern Bragmann suggests the pattern in (48), where '+' stands for at least one repetition of a sequence.

(48) N (P N)+

Now, such patterns would be really difficult to model in selection-based approaches, since one would have to assume that an empty head or a noun selects for an arbitrary number of pairs of the same preposition and noun or nominal phrase. Of course one could assume that P and N form some sort of constituent, but still one would have to make sure that the right preposition is used and that the noun or nominal projection has the right phonology. Another possibility would be to assume that the second N in N-P-N can be an N-P-N and thereby allow recursion in the pattern. But if one follows this approach it is getting really difficult to check the constraint that the involved Ns should have the same or at least similar phonologies.

One way out of these problems would of course be to assume that there are special combinatorial mechanisms that assign a new category to one or several elements. This would basically be an unheaded phrase structure rule and this is what Tesnière suggested: transfer rules (see Section 11.6.2.2). But this is of course an extension of pure Dependency Grammar towards a mixed model.

See Section 21.10 for the discussion of further cases which are probably problematic for purely selection-based grammars.

Exercises

Provide the dependency graphs for the following three sentences:

(49) a. Ich habe einen Mann getroffen, der   blonde Haare hat.
     I   have a   man   met   who blond hair has
     'I have met a man who has blond hair.'

b. Einen Mann getroffen, der   blonde Haare hat, habe ich noch nie.
   a   man met   who blond hair   has have I   yet   never

   'I have never met a man who has blond hair.'

c. Dass er morgen   kommen wird, freut   uns.
   that he tomorrow come   will   pleases us

   'That he will come tomorrow pleases us.'

You may use non-projective dependencies. For the analysis of relative clauses authors usually propose an abstract entity that functions as a dependent of the modified noun and as a head of the verb in the relative clause.

Further reading

In the section on further reading in Chapter 3, I referred to the book called *Syntaktische Analyseperspektiven* 'Syntactic perspectives on analyses'. The chapters in this book have been written by proponents of various theories and all analyze the same newspaper article. The book also contains a chapter by Engel (2014), assuming his version of Dependency Grammar, namely *Dependent Verb Grammar*.

Ágel, Eichinger, Eroms, Hellwig, Heringer & Lobin (2003, 2006) published a handbook on dependency and valence that discusses all aspects related to Dependency Grammar in any imaginable way. Many of the papers have been cited in this chapter. Papers comparing Dependency Grammar with other theories are especially relevant in the context of this book: Lobin (2003) compares Dependency Grammar and Categorial Grammar, Oliva (2003) deals with the representation of valence and dependency in HPSG, and Bangalore, Joshi & Rambow (2003) describe how valence and dependency are covered in TAG. Hellwig (2006) compares rule-based grammars with Dependency Grammars with special consideration given to parsing by computer programs.

Osborne & Groß (2012) compare Dependency Grammar with Construction Grammar and Osborne, Putnam & Groß (2011) argue that certain variants of Minimalism are in fact reinventions of dependency-based analyses.

The original work on Dependency Grammar by Tesnière (1959) is also available in parts in German (Tesnière 1980) and in full in English (Tesnière 2015).

12 Tree Adjoining Grammar

Tree Adjoining Grammar (TAG) was developed by Aravind Joshi at the University of Pennsylvania in the USA (Joshi, Levy & Takahashi 1975). Several important dissertations in TAG have been supervised by Aravind Joshi and Anthony Kroch at the University of Pennsylvania (e.g., Rambow 1994). Other research centers with a focus on TAG are Paris 7 (Anne Abeillé), Columbia University in the USA (Owen Rambow) and Düsseldorf, Germany (Laura Kallmeyer). Rambow (1994) and Gerdes (2002b) are more detailed studies of German.[1]

TAG and its variants with relevant extensions are of interest because it is assumed that this grammatical formalism can – with regard to its expressive power – relatively accurately represent what humans do when they produce or comprehend natural language. The expressive power of Generalized Phrase Structure Grammar was deliberately constrained so that it corresponds to context-free phrase structure grammars (Type-2 languages) and it has in fact been demonstrated that this is not enough (Shieber 1985; Culy 1985).[2] Grammatical theories such as HPSG and CxG can generate/describe so-called Type-0 languages and are thereby far above the level of complexity presently assumed for natural languages. The assumption is that this complexity lies somewhere between context-free and context-sensitive (Type-1) languages. This class is thus referred to as *mildly context sensitive*. Certain TAG-variants are inside of this language class and it is assumed that they can produce exactly those structures that occur in natural languages. For more on complexity, see Section 12.6.3 and Chapter 17.

There are various systems for the processing of TAG grammars (Doran, Hockey, Sarkar, Srinivas & Xia 2000; Parmentier, Kallmeyer, Maier, Lichte & Dellert 2008; Kallmeyer, Lichte, Maier, Parmentier, Dellert & Evang 2008). Smaller and larger TAG fragments have been developed for the following languages:

- Arabic (Fraj, Zribi & Ahmed 2008),

- German (Rambow 1994; Gerdes 2002a; Kallmeyer & Yoon 2004; Lichte 2007),

- English (XTAG Research Group 2001; Frank 2002; Kroch & Joshi 1987),

- French (Abeillé 1988; Candito 1996, 1998, 1999; Crabbé 2005),

- Italian (Candito 1998, 1999),

---

[1] Since my knowledge of French leaves something to be desired, I just refer to the literature in French here without being able to comment on the content.

[2] See Pullum (1986) for a historical overview of the complexity debate and G. Müller (2011) for argumentation for the non-context-free nature of German, which follows parallel to Culy with regard to the N-P-N construction (see Section 21.10.4).

- Korean (Han, Yoon, Kim & Palmer 2000; Kallmeyer & Yoon 2004),

- Vietnamese (Le, Nguyen & Roussanaly 2008)

Candito (1996) has developed a system for the representation of meta grammars which allows the uniform specification of crosslinguistic generalizations. This system was used by some of the projects mentioned above for the derivation of grammars for specific languages. For instance Kinyon, Rambow, Scheffler, Yoon & Joshi (2006) derive the verb second languages from a common meta grammar. Among those grammars for verb second languages is a grammar of Yiddish for which there was no TAG grammar until 2006.

Resnik (1992) combines TAG with a statistics component.

12.1 General remarks on representational format

12.1.1 Representation of valence information

Figure 12.1 shows so-called elementary trees. These are present in the lexicon and can be combined to create larger trees. Nodes for the insertion of arguments are specially

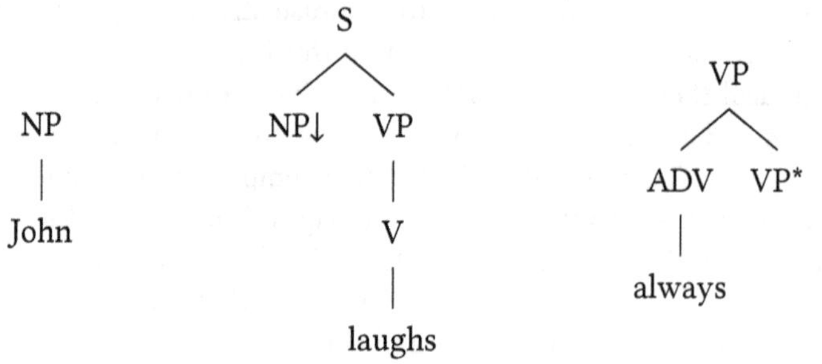

Figure 12.1: Elementary trees

marked (NP↓ in the tree for *laughs*). Nodes for the insertion of adjuncts into a tree are also marked (VP* in the tree for *always*). Grammars where elementary trees always contain at least one word are referred to as *Lexicalized Tree Adjoining Grammar* (LTAG).

12.1.2 Substitution

Figure 12.2 on the following page shows the substitution of nodes. Other subtrees have to be inserted into substitution nodes such as the NP node in the tree for *laughs*. The tree for *John* is inserted there in the example derivation.

12.1.3 Adjunction

Figure 12.3 on the following page shows an example of how the adjunction tree for *always* can be used.

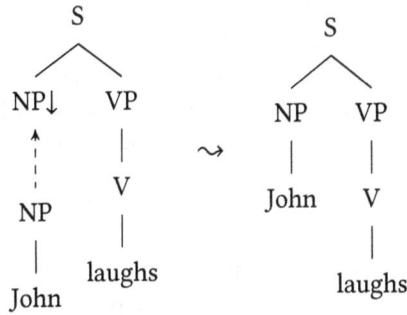

Figure 12.2: Substitution

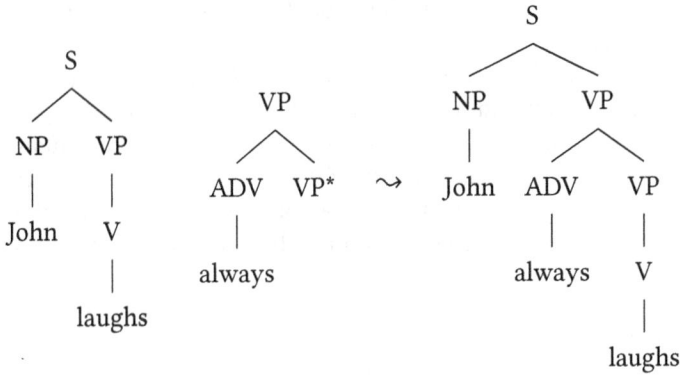

Figure 12.3: Adjunction

Adjunction trees can be inserted into other trees. Upon insertion, the target node (bearing the same category as the node marked with '*') is replaced by the adjunction tree.

TAG differs considerably from the simple phrase structure grammars we encountered in Chapter 2 in that the trees extend over a larger domain: for example, there is an NP node in the tree for *laughs* that is not a sister of the verb. In a phrase structure grammar (and of course in GB and GPSG since these theories are more or less directly built on phrase structure grammars), it is only ever possible to describe subtrees with a depth of one level. For the tree for *laughs*, the relevant rules would be those in (1):

(1) S → NP VP
     VP → V
     V → laughs

In this context, it is common to speak of *locality domains*. The extension of the locality domain is of particular importance for the analysis of idioms (see Section 18.2).

TAG differs from other grammatical theories in that it is possible for structures to be broken up again. In this way, it is possible to use adjunction to insert any amount of material into a given tree and thereby cause originally adjacent constituents to end up being arbitrarily far away from each other in the final tree. As we will see in Section 12.5, this property is important for the analysis of long-distance dependencies without movement.

12.1.4 Semantics

There are different approaches to the syntax-semantics interface in TAG. One possibility is to assign a semantic representation to every node in the tree. The alternative is to assign each elementary tree exactly one semantic representation. The semantics construction does not make reference to syntactic structure but rather the way the structure is combined. This kind of approach has been proposed by Candito & Kahane (1998) and then by Kallmeyer & Joshi (2003), who build on it. The basic mechanisms will be briefly presented in what follows.

In the literature on TAG, a distinction is made between derived trees and derivation trees. Derived trees correspond to constituent structure (the trees for *John laughs* and *John always laughs* in Figures 12.2 and 12.3). The derivation tree contains the derivational history, that is, information about how the elementary trees were combined. The elements in a derivation tree represent predicate-argument dependencies, which is why it is possible to derive a semantic derivation tree from them. This will be shown on the basis of the sentence in (2):

(2)   Max likes Anouk.

The elementary tree for (2) and the derived tree are given in Figure 12.4. The nodes in

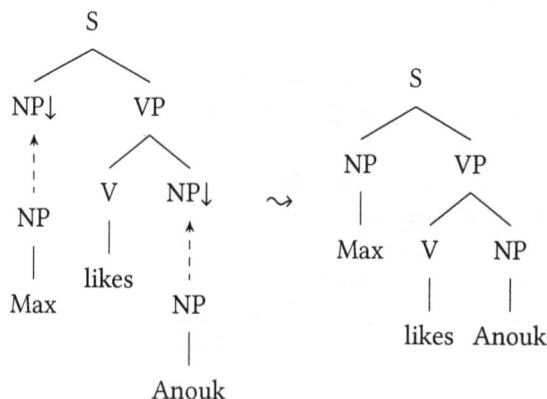

Figure 12.4: Elementary trees and derived tree for *Max likes Anouk*.

trees are numbered from top to bottom and from left to right. The result of this numbering of nodes for *likes* is shown in Figure 12.5 on the following page. The topmost node in the tree for *likes* is S and has the position 0. Beneath S, there is an NP and a VP node. These nodes are again numbered starting at 0. NP has the position 0 and VP the position 1. The VP node has in turn two daughters: V and the object NP. V receives number 0 and the object NP 1. This makes it possible to combine these numbers and then it is possible to unambiguously access individual elements in the tree. The position for the subject NP is 00 since this is a daughter of S and occurs in first position. The object NP has the numeric sequence 011 since it is below S (0), in the VP (the second daughter of S = 1) and occurs in second position (the second daughter of VP = 1).

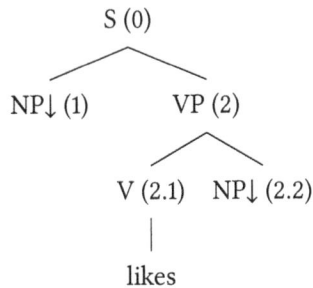

Figure 12.5: Node positions in the elementary tree for *likes*

With these tree positions, the derivation tree for (2) can be represented as in Figure 12.6. The derivation tree expresses the fact that the elementary tree for *likes* was

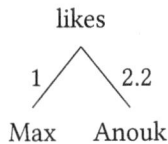

Figure 12.6: Derivation tree for *Max likes Anouk*.

combined with two arguments that were inserted into the substitution positions 00 and 011. The derivation tree also contains information about what exactly was placed into these nodes.

Kallmeyer & Joshi (2003) use a variant of *Minimal Recursion Semantics* as their semantic representational formalism (Copestake, Flickinger, Pollard & Sag 2005). I will use a considerably simplified representation here, as I did in Section 9.1.6 on semantics in HPSG. For the elementary trees *Max*, *likes* and *Anouk*, we can assume the semantic representations in (3).

(3)   Semantic representations for elementary trees:

$\max(x)$
arg: −

$\text{like}(x_1, x_2)$
arg: $\langle x_1, 1 \rangle, \langle x_2, 2.2 \rangle$

$\text{anouk}(y)$
arg: −

In a substitution operation, a variable is assigned a value. If, for example, the elementary tree for *Max* is inserted into the subject position of the tree for *likes*, then x_1 is identified with x. In the same way, x_2 is identified with y if the tree for *Anouk* is inserted into the object position. The result of these combinations is the representation in (4):

(4)   Combination of the meaning of elementary trees:

| like(x, y) |
| max(x) |
| anouk(y) |
| arg: – |

Kallmeyer & Joshi (2003) show how an extension of TAG, Multi-Component LTAG, can handle quantifier scope and discuss complex cases with embedded verbs. Interested readers are referred to the original article.

12.2 Local reordering

In TAG, there is a family of trees for each word. In order to account for ordering variants, one can assume that there are six trees corresponding to a ditransitive verb and that each of these corresponds to a different ordering of the arguments. Trees are connected to one another via lexical rules. This lexical rule-based analysis is parallel to the one developed by Uszkoreit (1986b) in Categorial Grammar.

Alternatively, one could assume a format for TAG structures similar to what we referred to as the ID/LP format in the chapter on GPSG. Joshi (1987b) defines an elementary structure as a pair that consists of a dominance structure and linearization constraints. Unlike GPSG, linearization rules do not hold for all dominance rules but rather for a particular dominance structure. This is parallel to what we saw in Section 10.6.3 on Embodied-CxG. Figure 12.7 shows a dominance tree with numbered nodes. If we com-

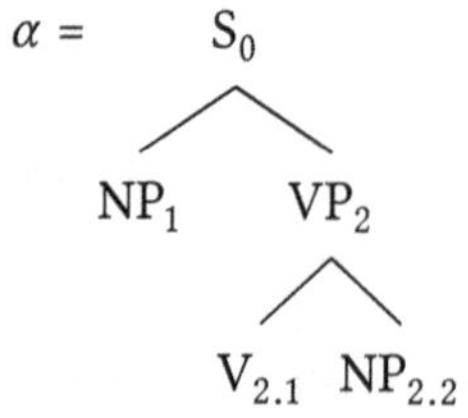

$$\alpha = \quad S_0$$

$$NP_1 \quad VP_2$$

$$V_{2.1} \quad NP_{2.2}$$

Figure 12.7: Dominance structure with numbered nodes

bine this dominance structure with the linearization rules in (5), we arrive at the exact order that we would get with ordinary phrase structure rules, namely NP_1 V NP_2.

(5) $LP_1^\alpha = \{1 < 2, 2.1 < 2.2\}$

If one specifies the linearization restrictions as in (6), all the orders in (7) are permitted, since the empty set means that we do not state any restrictions at all.

(6) $LP_2^\alpha = \{\}$

(7) a. $NP_1 \; V \; NP_2$
     b. $NP_2 \; V \; NP_1$
     c. $NP_1 \; NP_2 \; V$
     d. $NP_2 \; NP_1 \; V$
     e. $V \; NP_1 \; NP_2$
     f. $V \; NP_2 \; NP_1$

This means that it is possible to derive all orders that were derived in GPSG with flat sentence rules despite the fact that there is a constituent in the tree that consists of NP and VP. Since the dominance rules include a larger locality domain, such grammars are called LD/LP grammars (local dominance/linear precedence) rather than ID/LP grammars (immediate dominance/linear precedence) (Joshi, Shanker & Weir 1990).

Simple variants of TAG such as those presented in Section 12.1 cannot deal with reordering if the arguments of different verbs are scrambled as in (8).

(8) weil   ihm   das   Buch jemand   zu lesen versprochen hat[3]
     because him.DAT the.ACC book somebody.NOM to read promised   has

     'because somebody promised him to read the book'

In (8), *das Buch* 'the book' is the object of *zu lesen* 'to read', and *ihm* 'him' and *jemand* 'somebody' are dependent on *versprochen* and *hat*, respectively. These cases can be analyzed by LD/LP-TAG developed by Joshi (1987b) and Free Order TAG (FO-TAG) (Becker, Joshi & Rambow 1991: 21) since both of these TAG variants allow for crossing edges.

Since certain restrictions cannot be expressed in FO-TAG (Rambow 1994: 48–50), so-called Multi-Component TAG was developed. Joshi, Becker & Rambow (2000) illustrate the problem that simple LTAG grammars have with sentences such as (8) using examples such as (9):[4]

(9) a. ... daß der   Detektiv dem   Klienten [den   Verdächtigen des
           that the.NOM detective the.DAT client   the.ACC suspect   the.GEN
        Verbrechens zu überführen] versprach
        crime   to indict   promised

        'that the detective promised the client to indict the suspect of the crime'

     b. ... daß des   Verbrechens$_k$ der   Detektiv den   Verdächtigen$_j$
           that the.GEN crime   the.NOM detective the.ACC suspect
        dem   Klienten [$_j$ $_k$ zu überführen] versprach
        the.DAT client   to indict   promised

In LTAG, the elementary trees for the relevant verbs look as shown in Figure 12.8 on the following page. The verbs are numbered according to their level of embedding. The NP

---

[3] For more on this kind of examples, see Bech (1955).

[4] The authors use *versprochen hat* 'has promised' rather than *versprach* 'promised', which sounds better but does not correspond to the trees they use.

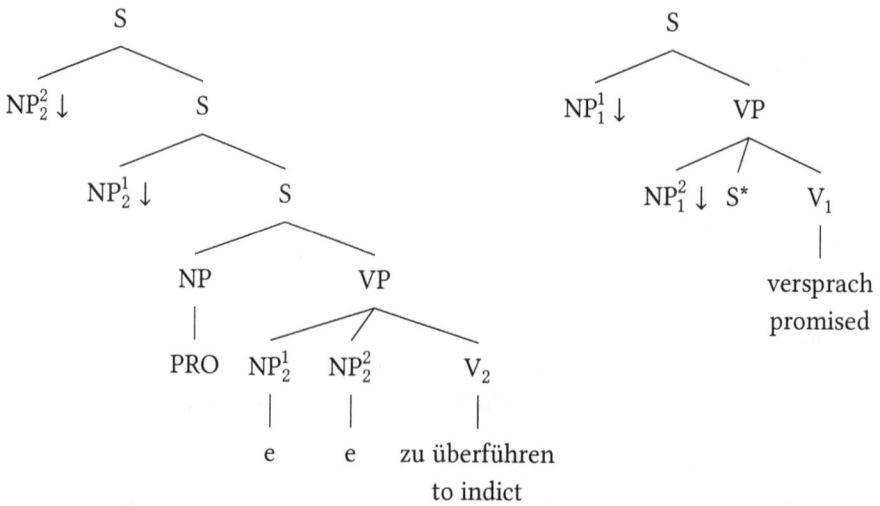

Figure 12.8: Elementary trees of an infinitive and a control verb

arguments of a verb bear the same index as that verb and each has a superscript number that distinguishes it from the other arguments. The trees are very similar to those in GB. In particular, it is assumed that the subject occurs outside the VP. For non-finite verbs, it is assumed that the subject is realized by PRO. PRO is, like *e*, a phonologically empty pronominal category that also comes from GB. The left tree in Figure 12.8 contains traces in the normal position of the arguments and the relevant NP slots in higher trees positions. An interesting difference to other theories is that these traces only exist in the tree. They are not represented as individual entries in the lexicon as the lexicon only contains words and the corresponding trees.

The tree for *versprach* 'promised' can be inserted into any S node in the tree for *zu überführen* 'to indict' and results in trees such as those in the Figures 12.9 and 12.10. In Figure 12.9, the tree for *versprach* is inserted directly above the PRO NP and in Figure 12.10 above NP_2^1.

It is clear that it is not possible to derive a tree in this way where an argument of *überführen* 'to indict' occurs between the arguments of *versprach* 'promised'. Joshi, Becker & Rambow (2000) therefore suggest an extension of the LTAG formalism. In MC-TAG, the grammar does not consist of elementary trees but rather finite sets of elementary trees. In every derivational step, a set is selected and the elements of that set are simultaneously added to the tree. Figure 12.11 on page 412 shows an elementary tree for *versprach* 'promised' consisting of multiple components. This tree contains a trace of NP_1^1 that was moved to the left. The bottom-left S node and the top-right S node are connected by a dashed line that indicates the dominance relation. However, immediate dominance is not required. Therefore, it is possible to insert the two subtrees into another tree separately from each other and thereby analyze the order in Figure 12.12 on page 413, for example.

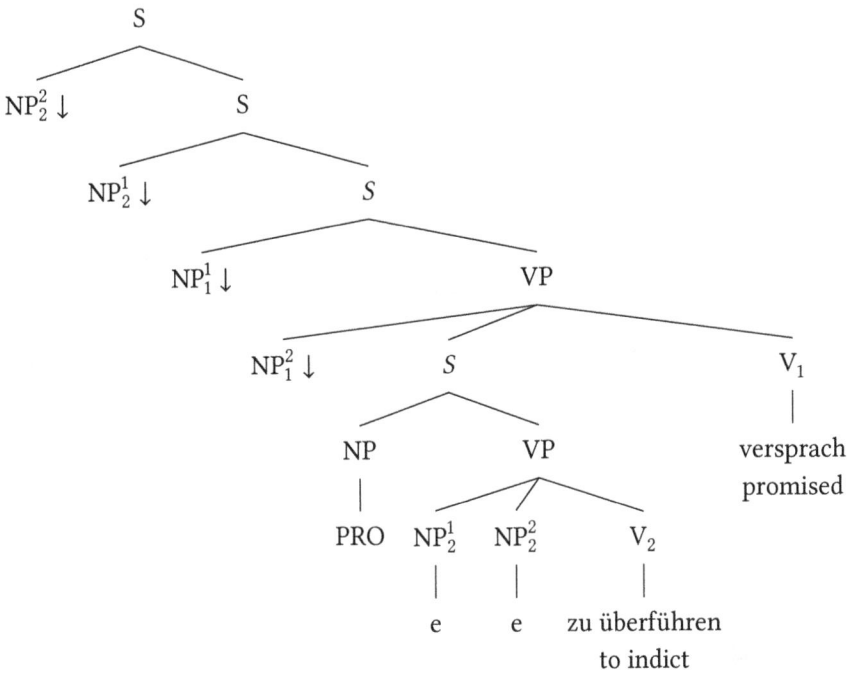

Figure 12.9: Analysis of the order $NP_2^2\ NP_2^1\ NP_1^1\ NP_1^2\ V_2V_1$: adjunction to the lowest S node

Other variants of TAG that allow for other constituent orders are V-TAG (Rambow 1994) and TT-MC-TAG (Lichte 2007).

12.3 Verb position

The position of the verb can be analyzed in a parallel way to the GPSG analysis: the verb can be realized in initial or in final position in a given linearization domain. Since the verb position has an effect on the clause type and hence on semantics, a lexical rule-based analysis would be also viable: a tree with the finite verb in initial position is licensed by a lexical rule that takes a tree with the verb in final position as input. This would be similar to the analyses in GB, Minimalism, and HPSG.

12.4 Passive

There is a possible analysis for the passive that is analogous to the transformations in Transformational Grammar: one assumes lexical rules that create a lexical item with a passive tree for every lexical item with an active tree (Kroch & Joshi 1985: 50–51).

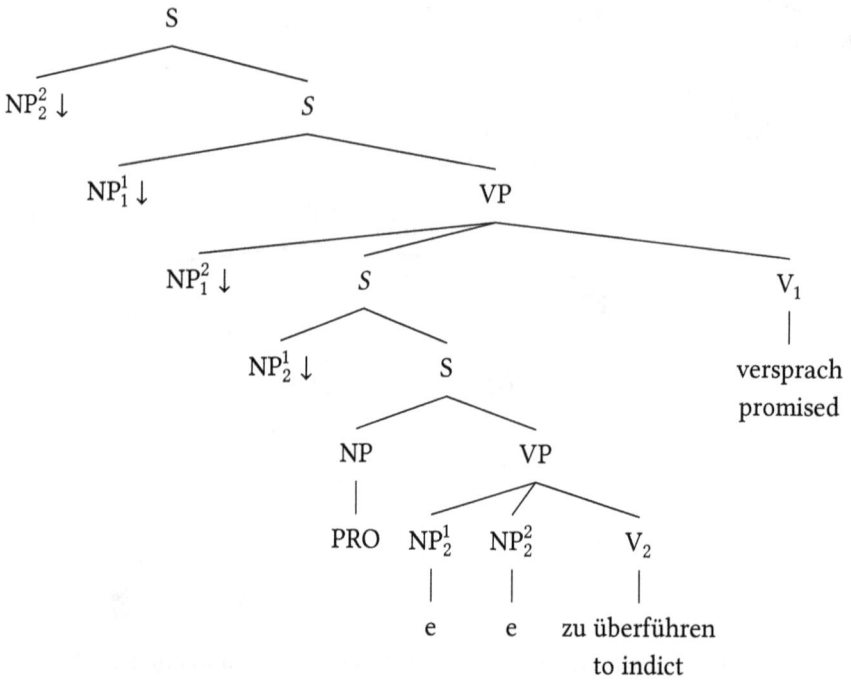

Figure 12.10: Analysis of the order NP_2^2 NP_1^1 NP_1^2 NP_2^1 V_2V_1: adjunction to the S node between NP_2^2 and NP_2^1

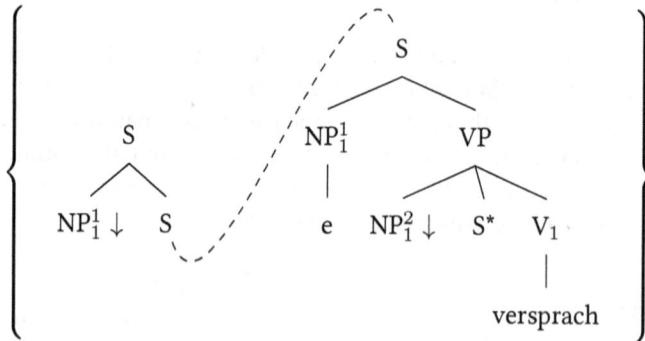

Figure 12.11: Elementary tree set for *versprach* consisting of multiple components

S

NP$_1^1$ ↓   S

NP$_2^2$ ↓   S

NP$_1^1$ VP

e   NP$_1^2$ ↓   S   V$_1$

NP$_2^1$ ↓   S   versprach
promised

NP   VP

PRO   NP$_2^1$ NP$_2^2$ V$_2$

e   e   zu überführen
to indict

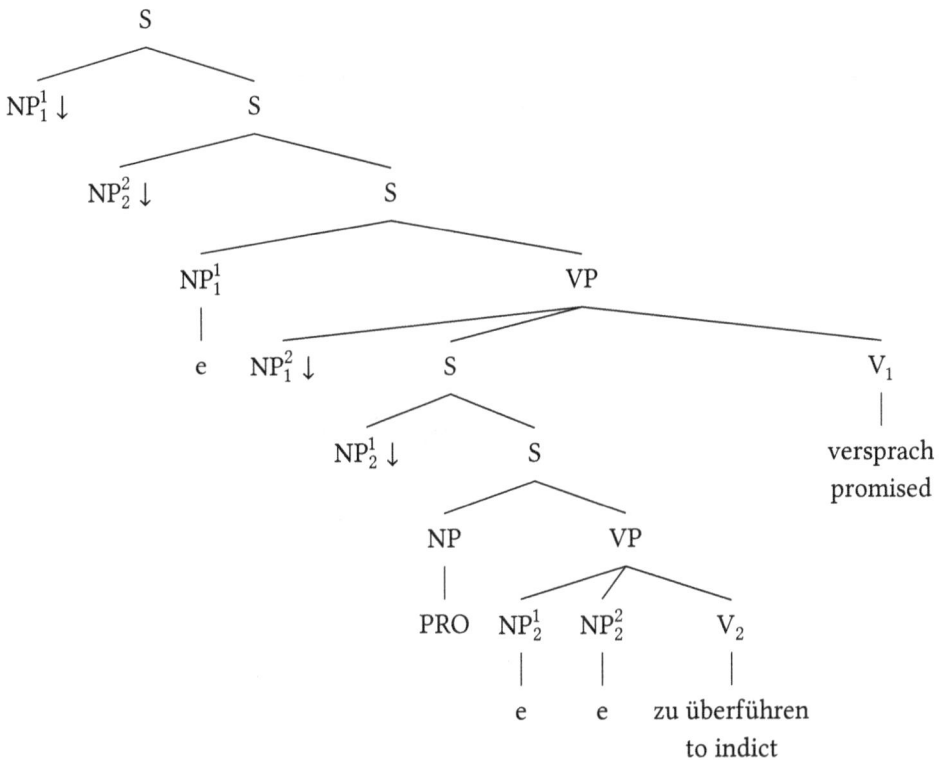

Figure 12.12: Analysis of the order NP$_1^1$ NP$_2^2$ NP$_1^2$ NP$_2^1$ V$_2$V$_1$: adjunction to the S node between NP$_2^2$ and NP$_2^1$

Kroch & Joshi (1985: 55) propose an alternative to this transformation-like approach that more adequately handles so-called raising constructions. Their analysis assumes that arguments of verbs are represented in subcategorization lists. Verbs are entered into trees that match their subcategorization list. Kroch and Joshi formulate a lexical rule that corresponds to the HPSG lexical rule that was discussed on page 275, that is, an accusative object is explicitly mentioned in the input of the lexical rule. Kroch and Joshi then suggest a complex analysis of the impersonal passive which uses a semantic null role for a non-realized object of intransitive verbs (p. 56). Such an analysis with abstract auxiliary entities can be avoided easily: one can instead use the HPSG analysis going back to Haider (1986a), which was presented in Section 9.2.

There are also proposals in TAG that use inheritance to deal with valence changing processes in general and the passive in particular (Candito 1996 and Kinyon, Rambow, Scheffler, Yoon & Joshi 2006 following Candito). As we saw in Section 10.2 of the Chapter on Construction Grammar, inheritance is not a suitable descriptive tool for valence changing processes. This is because these kinds of processes interact syntactically and semantically in a number of ways and can also be applied multiple times (Müller 2006, 2007c; 2007b: Section 7.5.2; 2013c; 2014a). See also Section 21.4 of this book.

12.5 Long-distance dependencies

The analysis of long-distance dependencies in TAG is handled with the standard apparatus: simple trees are inserted into the middle of other trees. Figure 12.13 shows an
example of the analysis of (10):

(10)   Who$_i$ did John tell Sam that Bill likes $\_i$?

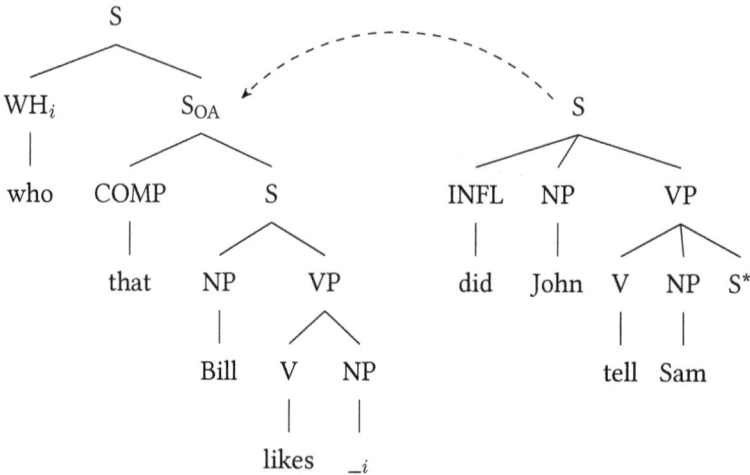

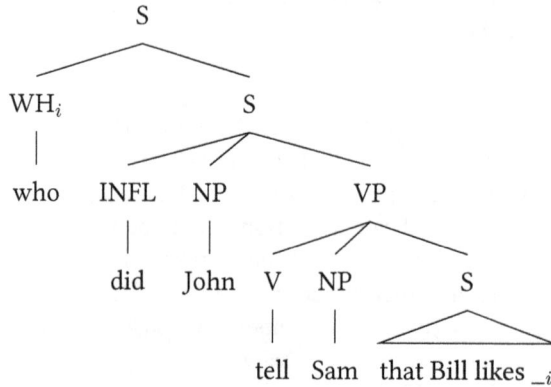

Figure 12.13: Analysis of long-distance dependencies in TAG

The tree for *WH COMP NP likes* $\_i$ belongs to the tree family of *likes* and is therefore
present in the lexicon. The tree for *tell* is adjoined to this tree, that is, this tree is inserted
in the middle of the tree for *who that Bill likes* $\_i$. Such an insertion operation can be
applied multiple times so that sentences such as (11) where *who* is moved across multiple
sentence boundaries can be analyzed:

(11) Who$_i$ did John tell Sam that Mary said that Bill likes _$_i$?

There is another important detail: although the tree for (12) has the category S, (12) is not a grammatical sentence of English.

(12) * who that Bill likes

This has to be captured somehow. In TAG, the marking OA ensures that a tree counts as incomplete. If a tree contains a node with marking OA, then an obligatory adjunction operation must take place at the relevant position.

12.6 New developments and theoretical variants

In Section 12.2, we introduced Multi-Component-TAG. There are a large number of TAG variants with different formal properties. Rambow (1994) gives an overview of the variants existing in 1994. In the following, I will discuss two interesting variants of TAG: Feature Structure-Based TAG (FTAG, Vijay-Shanker & Joshi 1988) and Vector-TAG (V-TAG, Rambow 1994).

12.6.1 FTAG

In FTAG, nodes are not atomic (N, NP, VP or S), but instead consist of feature descriptions. With the exception of substitution nodes, each node has a top structure and a bottom structure. The top structure says something about what kind of properties a given tree has inside a larger structure, and the bottom structure says something about the properties of the structure below the node. Substitution nodes only have a top structure. Figure 12.14 on the following page shows an example tree for *laughs*. A noun phrase can be combined with the tree for *laughs* in Figure 12.14. Its top structure is identified with the NP node in the tree for *laughs*. The result of this combination is shown in Figure 12.15 on the next page.

In a complete tree, all top structures are identified with the corresponding bottom structures. This way, only sentences where the subject is in third person singular can be analyzed with the given tree for *laughs*, that is, those in which the verb's agreement features match those of the subject.

For adjunction, the top structure of the tree that is being inserted must be unifiable with the top structure of the adjunction site, and the bottom structure of the node marked '*' in the inserted tree (the so-called foot node) must be unifiable with the adjunction site.

The elementary trees discussed so far only consisted of nodes where the top part matched the bottom part. FTAG allows for an interesting variant of specifying nodes that makes adjunction obligatory in order for the entire derivation to be well-formed. Figure 12.16 on page 417 shows a tree for *laughing* that contains two VP nodes with incompatible MODE values. In order for this subtree to be used in a complete structure, another tree has to be added so that the two parts of the VP node are separated. This happens by means of an auxiliary tree as shown in Figure 12.16. The highest VP node of

$$\begin{bmatrix} \text{CAT} & \text{S} \end{bmatrix}$$
$$\begin{bmatrix} \text{CAT} & \text{S} \end{bmatrix}$$

$$\begin{bmatrix} \text{CAT} & \text{NP} \\ \text{AGR} & \boxed{1} \end{bmatrix} \qquad \begin{bmatrix} \text{CAT} & \text{VP} \\ \text{AGR} & \boxed{1} & \begin{bmatrix} \text{PER} & 3 \\ \text{NUM} & sing \end{bmatrix} \end{bmatrix}$$

$$\begin{bmatrix} \text{CAT} & \text{VP} \end{bmatrix}$$

$$[\,]$$
$$\begin{bmatrix} \text{CAT} & \text{NP} \\ \text{AGR} & \begin{bmatrix} \text{PER} & 3 \\ \text{NUM} & sing \end{bmatrix} \end{bmatrix} \qquad \begin{bmatrix} \text{CAT} & \text{V} \end{bmatrix}$$
$$\begin{bmatrix} \text{CAT} & \text{V} \end{bmatrix}$$

John   laughs

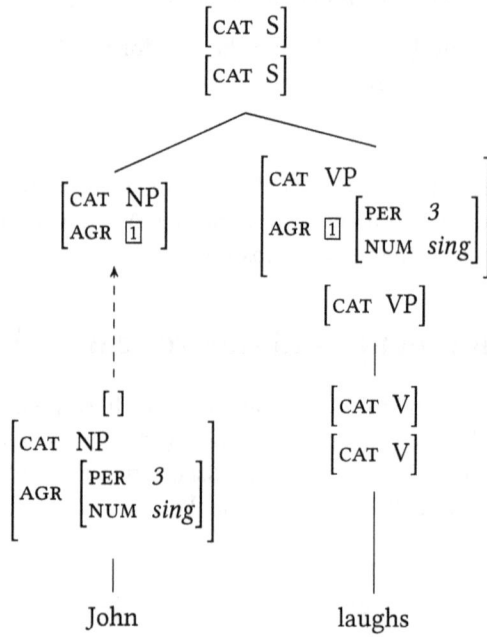

Figure 12.14: Elementary trees for *John* and *laughs* in FTAG

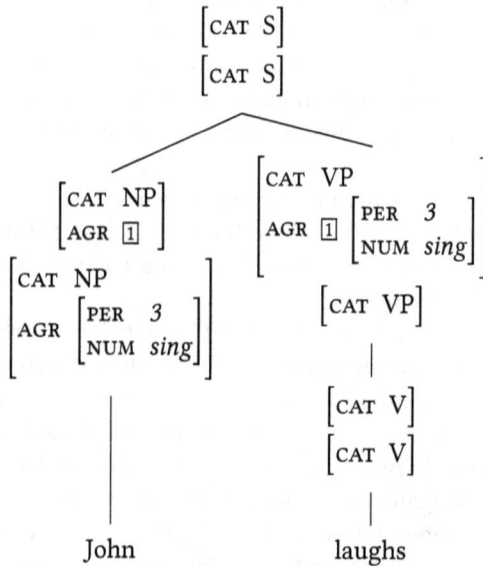

$$\begin{bmatrix} \text{CAT} & \text{S} \end{bmatrix}$$
$$\begin{bmatrix} \text{CAT} & \text{S} \end{bmatrix}$$

$$\begin{bmatrix} \text{CAT} & \text{NP} \\ \text{AGR} & \boxed{1} \end{bmatrix} \qquad \begin{bmatrix} \text{CAT} & \text{VP} \\ \text{AGR} & \boxed{1} & \begin{bmatrix} \text{PER} & 3 \\ \text{NUM} & sing \end{bmatrix} \end{bmatrix}$$

$$\begin{bmatrix} \text{CAT} & \text{NP} \\ \text{AGR} & \begin{bmatrix} \text{PER} & 3 \\ \text{NUM} & sing \end{bmatrix} \end{bmatrix} \qquad \begin{bmatrix} \text{CAT} & \text{VP} \end{bmatrix}$$

$$\begin{bmatrix} \text{CAT} & \text{V} \end{bmatrix}$$
$$\begin{bmatrix} \text{CAT} & \text{V} \end{bmatrix}$$

John   laughs

Figure 12.15: Combination of the trees for *John* and *laughs* in FTAG

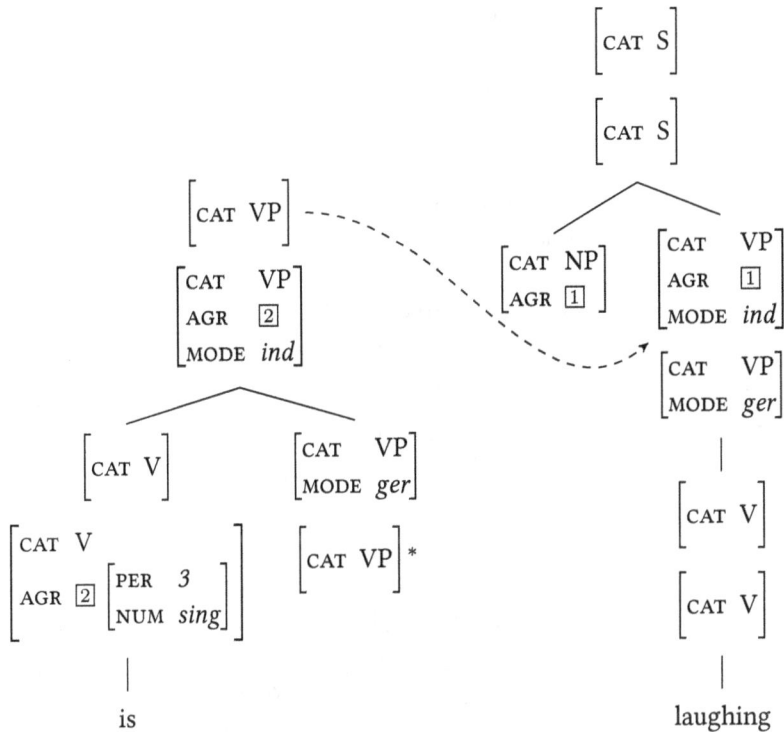

Figure 12.16: Obligatory adjunction in FTAG

the auxiliary tree is unified with the upper VP node of *laughing*. The node of the auxiliary tree marked with '*' is unified with the lower VP node of *laughing*. The result of
this is given in Figure 12.17 on the next page.

If a tree is used as a final derivation, the top structures are identified with the bottom
structures. Thus, the AGR value of the highest VP node is identified with that of the lower
one in the tree in Figure 12.17. As such, only NPs that have the same AGR value as the
auxiliary can be inserted into the NP slot.

This example shows that, instead of the marking for obligatory adjunction that we
saw in the section on long-distance dependencies, the same effect can be achieved by
using incompatible feature specifications on the top and bottom structures. If there are
incompatible top and bottom structures in a tree, then it cannot be a final derivation tree
and therefore this means that at least one adjunction operation must still take place in
order to yield a well-formed tree.

12.6.2 V-TAG

V-TAG is a variant of TAG proposed by Owen Rambow (1994) that also assumes feature
structures on nodes. In addition, like MC-TAG, it assumes that elementary trees consist

$$
\begin{bmatrix} \text{CAT} & \text{S} \end{bmatrix}
$$
$$
\begin{bmatrix} \text{CAT} & \text{S} \end{bmatrix}
$$

$$
\begin{bmatrix} \text{CAT} & \text{NP} \\ \text{AGR} & \boxed{1} \end{bmatrix}
\qquad
\begin{bmatrix} \text{CAT} & \text{VP} \\ \text{AGR} & \boxed{1} \\ \text{MODE} & ind \end{bmatrix}
$$

$$
\begin{bmatrix} \text{CAT} & \text{VP} \\ \text{AGR} & \boxed{2} \\ \text{MODE} & ind \end{bmatrix}
$$

$$
\begin{bmatrix} \text{CAT} & \text{V} \end{bmatrix}
\qquad
\begin{bmatrix} \text{CAT} & \text{VP} \\ \text{MODE} & ger \end{bmatrix}
$$

$$
\begin{bmatrix} \text{CAT} & \text{V} \\ \text{AGR} & \boxed{2} \begin{bmatrix} \text{PER} & 3 \\ \text{NUM} & sing \end{bmatrix} \end{bmatrix}
\qquad
\begin{bmatrix} \text{CAT} & \text{VP} \\ \text{MODE} & ger \end{bmatrix}
$$

is $\qquad$
$$
\begin{bmatrix} \text{CAT} & \text{V} \end{bmatrix}
$$
$$
\begin{bmatrix} \text{CAT} & \text{V} \end{bmatrix}
$$

laughing

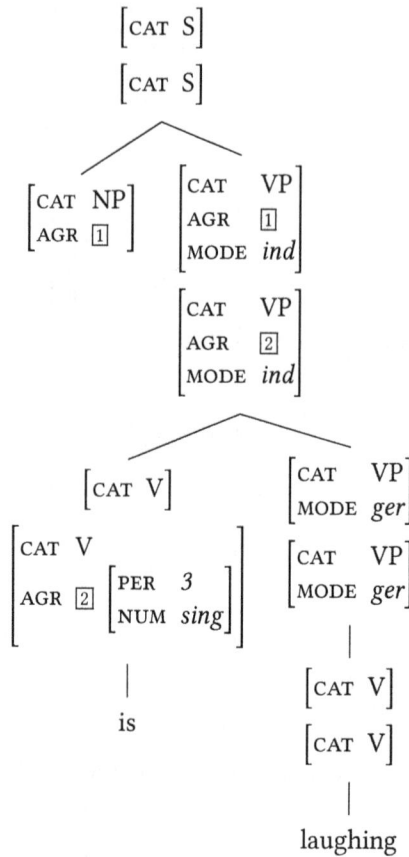

Figure 12.17: Result of obligatory adjunction in FTAG

of multiple components. Figure 12.18 on the following page shows the elementary lexical set for the ditransitive verb *geben* 'give'. The lexicon set consists of a tree for the verb, an empty element of the category VP and three trees where a VP has been combined with an NP. As in MC-TAG, dominance relations are also indicated. The dominance constraints in Figure 12.18 ensure that all lower VP nodes dominate the highest VP node of the tree further to the right. The order of the arguments of the verb as well as the position of the verb is not given. The only thing required is that lower VP in the NP trees and lower VP in the *geben* tree dominate the empty VP node. With this lexicon set, it is possible to derive all permutations of the arguments. Rambow also shows how such lexical entries can be used to analyze sentences with verbal complexes. Figure 12.19 on the following page shows a verbal complex formed from *zu reparieren* 'to repair' and *versprochen* 'promised' and the relevant dominance constraints. Both of the first NP trees have to dominate *versprochen* and the third and fourth NP tree have to dominate *zu reparieren*. The order of the NP trees is not restricted and thus all permutations of NPs can be derived.

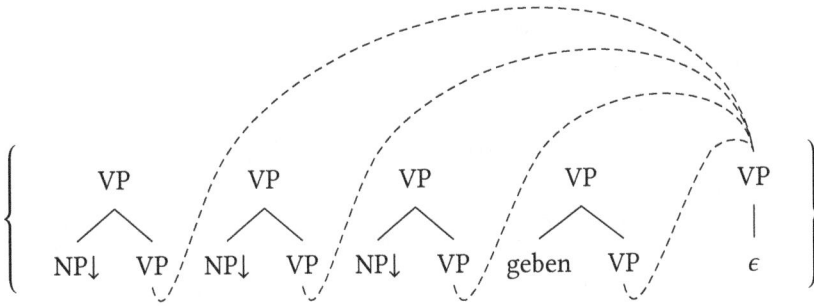

Figure 12.18: Lexicon set for *geben* 'to give' in V-TAG according to Rambow (1994: 6)

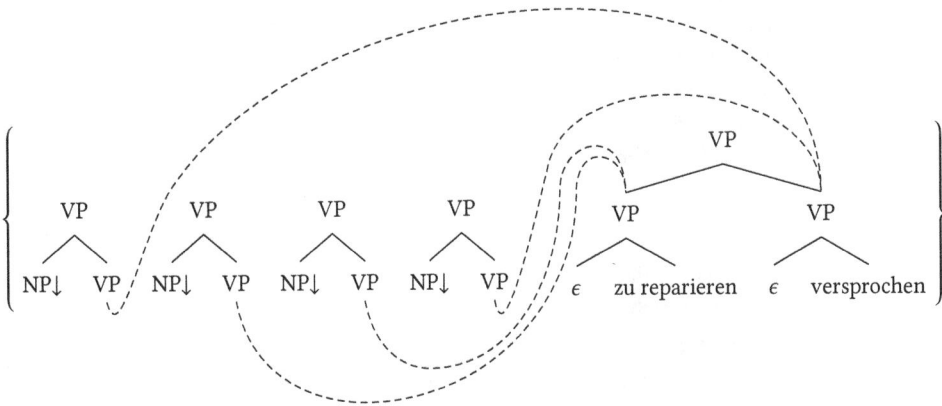

Figure 12.19: Analysis of the verbal complex *zu reparieren versprochen* in V-TAG

The interesting thing here is that this approach is similar to the one proposed by Berman (1996: Section 2.1.3) in LFG (see Section 7.4): in Berman's analysis, the verb projects directly to form a VP and the arguments are then adjoined.

A difference to other analyses discussed in this book is that there is always an empty element in the derived trees regardless of verb position.

12.6.3 The competence-performance distinction and the generative capacity of tree-local MC-LTAG

In many of the theories discussed in this book, a distinction is made between competence and performance (Chomsky 1965: Section I.1). Competence theories are supposed to describe linguistic knowledge, whereas a performance theory should explain how linguistic knowledge is used and why we make mistakes during speech production and comprehension, etc. See Chapter 15 for further discussion.

Joshi, Becker & Rambow (2000) discuss examples of center self embedding of relative clauses as those in (13b), and follow Chomsky & Miller (1963: 286) in the assumption that the fact that this kind of embedding is only possible up to three levels should not be described by grammar, but is rather due to processing problems with the hearer independent of their principle abilities with regard to grammar.

(13)   a. dass der Hund bellt, der die Katze jagt, die die Maus gefangen hat
           that the dog   barks that the cat   chases that the mouse caught   has

          'that the dog that chases the cat that caught the mouse barks'

     b. dass der Hund, [$_1$ der die Katze, [$_2$ die die Maus gefangen hat, $_2$] jagt $_1$]
           that the dog   that the cat   that the mouse caught   has   chases

           bellt
           barks

What is interesting in this context is that it is possible to construct examples of center embedding so that they are easier to process for the hearer. In this way, it is possible to increase the number of center embeddings possible to process by one and therefore to show that all grammars that formulate a restriction that there may be at most two center-embedded relative clauses are incorrect. The following example from Hans Uszkoreit is easier to process since all embedded relative clauses are isolated and the verbs are separated by material from the higher clause.

(14)   Die Bänke, [$_1$ auf denen damals   die Alten   des   Dorfes, [$_2$ die allen
      the benches   on which back.then the old.people of.the village   that all
      Kindern, [$_3$ die vorbeikamen $_3$], freundliche Blicke zuwarfen $_2$], lange Stunden
      children   that came.by   friendly   glances gave   long hours
      schweigend nebeneinander   saßen $_1$], mussten im   letzten Jahr einem
      silent   next.to.each.other sat   must   in.the last   year a
      Parkplatz weichen.
      car.park give.way.to

      'The benches on which the older residents of the village, who used to give friendly glances to all the children who came by, used to sit silently next to one another had to give way to a car park last year.'

For other factors that play a role in processing, see Gibson (1998).

    Joshi et al. (2000) discuss verbal complexes with reordered arguments. The general pattern that they discuss has the form shown in (15):

(15) $\sigma(NP_1 \; NP_2 \; ... \; NP_n) \; V_n V_{n-1} \; ... \; V_1$

Here, σ stands for any permutation of noun phrases and V_1 is the finite verb. The authors investigate the properties of Lexicalized Tree Adjoining Grammar (LTAG) with regard to this pattern and notice that LTAG cannot analyze the order in (16) if the semantics is supposed to come out correctly.

(16) $NP_2 \; NP_3 \; NP_1 \; V_3 V_2 V_1$

Since (17) is possible in German, LTAG is not sufficient to analyze all languages.

(17)   dass ihm$_2$ das Buch$_3$ niemand$_1$ zu lesen$_3$ versprechen$_2$ darf$_1$
      that him the book nobody to read promise   be.allowed.to

      'that nobody is allowed to promise him to read the book'

Therefore, they propose the extension of TAG discussed in Section 12.2; so-called *tree-local multi-component LTAG* (Tree-local MC-LTAG or TL-MCTAG). They show that TL-MCTAG can analyze (17) but not (18) with the correct semantics. They claim that these orders are not possible in German and argue that in this case, unlike the relative clause examples, one has both options, that is, the unavailability of such patterns can be explained as a performance phenomenon or as a competence phenomenon.

(18)   NP$_2$ NP$_4$ NP$_3$ NP$_1$ V$_4$V$_3$V$_2$V$_1$

If we treat this as a performance phenomenon, then we are making reference to the complexity of the construction and the resulting processing problems for the hearer. The fact that these orders do not occur in corpora can be explained with reference to the principle of cooperativeness. Speakers normally want to be understood and therefore formulate their sentences in such a way that the hearer can understand them. Verbal complexes in German with more than four verbs are hardly ever found since it is possible to simplify very complex sentences with multiple verbs in the right sentence bracket by extraposing material and therefore avoiding ambiguity (see Netter 1991: 5 and Müller 2007b: 262).

The alternative to a performance explanation would involve using a grammatical formalism which is just powerful enough to allow embedding of two verbs and reordering of their arguments, but rules out embedding of three verbs and reordering of the arguments. Joshi et al. (2000) opt for this solution and therefore attribute the impossibility of the order of arguments in (18) to competence.

In HPSG (and also in Categorial Grammar and in some GB analyses), verbal complexes are analyzed by means of argument composition (Hinrichs & Nakazawa 1989a, 1994). Under this approach, a verbal complex behaves exactly like a simplex verb and the arguments of the verbs involved can be placed in any order. The grammar does not contain any restriction on the number of verbs that can be combined, nor any constraints that ban embedding below a certain level. In the following, I will show that many reorderings are ruled out by communication rules that apply even with cases of simple two-place verbs. The conclusion is that the impossibility of embedding four or more verbs should in fact be explained as a performance issue.

Before I present arguments against a competence-based exclusion of (18), I will make a more general comment: corpora cannot help us here since one does not find any instances of verbs with four or more embeddings. Bech (1955) provides an extensive collection of material, but had to construct the examples with four embedded verbs. Meurers (1999b: 94–95) gives constructed examples with five verbs that contain multiple auxiliaries or modal verbs. These examples are barely processable and are not relevant for the discussion here since the verbs in (18) have to select their own arguments. There are therefore not that many verbs left when constructing examples. It is possible to only use subject control verbs with an additional object (e.g., *versprechen* 'to promise'), object control verbs (e.g., *zwingen* 'to force') or AcI verbs (e.g., *sehen* 'to see' or *lassen* 'to let') to construct examples. When constructing examples, it is important make sure that all the nouns involved differ as much as possible with regard to their case and their selectional restrictions (e.g., animate/inanimate) since these are features that a hearer/reader could use to possibly assign reordered arguments to their heads. If we want to have patterns such as (18) with four NPs each with a different case, then we have to choose a verb that governs the genitive. There are only a very small number of such verbs in German. Although the example constructed by Joshi et al. (2000) in (9b) fulfills these requirements, it is still very marked. It therefore becomes clear that the possibility of finding a corresponding example in a newspaper article is extremely small. This is due to the fact that there are very few situations in which such an utterance would be imaginable. Additionally, all control verbs (with the exception of *helfen* 'to help') require an infinitive with *zu* 'to' and can also be realized incoherently, that is, with an extraposed infinitival complement without verbal complex formation. As mentioned above, a cooperative speaker/author would use a less complex construction and this reduces the probability that these kinds of sentences arise even further.

Notice that tree-local MC-LTAG does not constrain the number of verbs in a sentence. The formalism allows for an arbitrary number of verbs. It is therefore necessary to assume, as in other grammatical theories, that performance constraints are responsible for the fact that we never find examples of verbal complexes with five or more verbs. Tree-local MC-LAG makes predictions about the possibility of arguments to be reordered. I consider it wrong to make constraints regarding mobility of arguments dependent on the power of the grammatical formalism since the restrictions that one finds are independent of verbal complexes and can be found with simplex verbs taking just two arguments. The problem with reordering is that it still has to be possible to assign the noun phrases to the verbs they belong to. If this assignment leads to ambiguity that cannot be resolved by case, selectional restrictions, contextual knowledge or intonation, then the unmarked constituent order is chosen. Hoberg (1981: 68) shows this very nicely with examples similar to the following:[5]

(19) a. Hanna hat immer schon gewußt, daß das Kind sie verlassen will.
Hanna has always already known that the child she leave   wants

'Hanna has always known that the child wants to leave her.'

b. # Hanna hat immer schon gewußt, daß sie das Kind verlassen will.
Hanna has always already known that she the child leave   wants

Preferred reading: 'Hanna has always known that she wants to leave the child.'

c. Hanna hat immer schon gewußt, daß sie der   Mann verlassen
Hanna has always already known that she the.NOM man   leave
will.
wants.to

'Hanna has always known that the man wants to leave her.'

---

[5] Instead of *das* 'the', Hoberg uses the possessive pronoun *ihr* 'her'. This makes the sentences more semantically plausible, but one then gets interference from the linearization requirements for bound pronouns. I have therefore replaced the pronouns with the definite article.

It is not possible to reorder (19a) to (19b) without creating a strong preference for another reading. This is due to the fact that neither *sie* 'she' nor *das Kind* 'the child' are unambiguously marked as nominative or accusative. (19b) therefore has to be interpreted as Hanna being the one that wants something, namely to leave the child. This reordering is possible, however, if at least one of the arguments is unambiguously marked for case as in (19c).

For noun phrases with feminine count nouns, the forms for nominative and accusative as well as genitive and dative are the same. For mass nouns, it is even worse. If they are used without an article, all cases are the same for feminine nouns (e.g., *Milch* 'milk') and also for masculines and neuters with exception of the genitive. In the following example from Wegener (1985: 45) it is hardly possible to switch the dative and accusative object, whereas this is possible if the nouns are used with articles as in (20c,d):

(20) a. Sie mischt Wein Wasser bei.
         she mixes wine water into

         'She mixes water into the wine.'

      b. Sie mischt Wasser Wein bei.
         she mixes water wine into

         'She mixes wine into the water.'

      c. Sie mischt dem   Wein das   Wasser bei.
         she mixes the.DAT wine the.ACC water into

         'She mixes the water into the wine.'

      d. Sie mischt das   Wasser dem   Wein bei.
         she mixes the.ACC water the.DAT wine into

         'She mixes the water into the wine.'

The two nouns can only be switched if the meaning of the sentence is clear from the context (e.g., through explicit negation of the opposite) and if the sentence carries a certain intonation.

The problem with verbal complexes is now that with four noun phrases, two of them almost always have the same case if one does not wish to resort to the few verbs governing the genitive. A not particularly nice-sounding example of morphologically unambiguously marked case is (21):

(21) weil   er   den   Mann dem   Jungen des   Freundes gedenken
      because he.NOM the.ACC man the.DAT boy   of.the.GEN friend   remember
      helfen lassen will
      help   let   wants

      'because he wants to let the man help the boy remember his friend'

Another strategy is to choose verbs that select animate and inanimate objects so that animacy of the arguments can aid interpretation. I have constructed such an example where the most deeply embedded predicate is not a verb but rather an adjective. The predicate *leer fischen* 'to fish empty' is a resultative construction that should be analyzed parallel to verbal complexes (Müller 2002a: Chapter 5).

(22) weil   niemand₁   [den   Mann]₂ [der   Frau]₃ [diesen Teich]₄ leer₄
      because nobody.NOM the.ACC man   the.DAT woman this.ACC pond   empty
      fischen₃ helfen₂ sah₁
      fish   help   saw

'because nobody saw the man help the woman fish the pond empty'

If one reads the sentences with the relevant pauses, it is comprehensible. Case is unambiguously marked on the animate noun phrases and our word knowledge helps us to interpret *diesen Teich* 'this pond' as the argument of *leer* 'empty'.

The sentence in (22) would correctly be analyzed by an appropriately written tree-local MC-LTAG and also by argument composition analyses for verbal complexes and resultative constructions. The sentence in (23) is a variant of (22) that corresponds exactly to the pattern of (18):

(23) weil   [der   Frau]₂ [diesen Teich]₄ [den   Mann]₃ niemand₁   leer₄
      because the.DAT woman this.ACC pond   the.ACC man   nobody.NOM empty
      fischen₃ helfen₂ sah₁
      fish   help   saw

'because nobody saw the man help the woman fish the pond empty'

(23) is more marked than (22), but this is always the case with local reordering (Gisbert Fanselow, p. c. 2006). This sentence should not be ruled out by the grammar. Its markedness is more due to the same factors that were responsible for the markedness of reordering of arguments of simplex verbs. Tree-local MC-LTAG can not correctly analyze sentences such as (23), which shows that this TAG variant is not sufficient for analyzing natural language.

There are varying opinions among TAG researchers as to what should be counted as competence and what should be counted as performance. For instance, Rambow (1994: 15) argues that one should not exclude reorderings that cannot be processed by means of competence grammar or the grammatical formalism. In Chapter 6, he presents a theory of performance that can explain why the reordering of arguments of various verbs in the middle field is harder to process. One should therefore opt for TAG variants such as V-TAG or TT-MC-TAG (Lichte 2007) that are powerful enough to analyze the diverse reorderings and then also use a performance model that makes it possible to explain the gradual differences in acceptability.

An alternative to looking for a grammatical formalism with minimal expressive power is to not restrict the grammatical formalism at all with regard to its expressive power and instead develop as restrictive linguistic theories as possible. For further discussion of this point, see Chapter 17.

12.7 Summary and classification

In sum, we have seen the following: LTAG is lexicalized, that is, there is at least one lexical element in every tree. There are not any trees that correspond to the rule S → NP VP since no words are mentioned in this rule. Instead, there are always complex trees that contain the subject NP and the VP. Inside the VP, there can be as much structure as is necessary to ensure that the verb is contained in the tree. As well as the head, elementary trees in LTAG always contain the arguments of the head. For transitive verbs, this means that both the subject and the object have to be components of the elementary tree. This is also true of the trees used to analyze long-distance dependencies. As shown in Figure 12.13, the object must be part of the tree. The fact that the object can be separated from the verb by multiple sentence boundaries is not represented in the elementary tree, that is, recursive parts of grammar are not contained in elementary trees. The relevant effects are achieved by adjunction, that is, by insertion of material into elementary trees. The elementary tree for extraction in Figure 12.13 differs from the elementary tree for *likes* given in Figure 12.4 for the use in normal SVO clauses. Every minimal construction, in which *likes* can occur (subject extraction, topicalization, subject relative clauses, object relative clauses, passive, ...) needs its own elementary tree (Kallmeyer & Joshi 2003: 10). The different elementary trees can be connected using lexical rules. These lexical rules map a particular tree treated as underlying to other trees. In this way, it is possible to derive a passive tree from an active tree. These lexical rules are parallel to transformations in Transformational Grammar, however, one should bear in mind that there is always a lexical element in the tree, which makes the entire grammar more restrictive than grammars with free transformations.

An interesting difference to GB and variants of LFG, CG, and HPSG that assume empty elements is that the variants of TAG presented here[6] do not contain empty elements in the lexicon. They can be used in trees but trees are listed as a whole in the lexicon.

Elementary trees can be of any size, which makes TAG interesting for the analysis of idioms (see Section 18.2). Since recursion is factored out, trees can contain elements that appear very far away from each other in the derived tree (extended domains of locality).

Kasper, Kiefer, Netter & Shanker (1995) show that it is possible to transfer HPSG grammars that fulfill certain requirements into TAG grammars. This is interesting as in this way one arrives at a grammar whose complexity behavior is known. Whereas HPSG grammars are generally in the Type-0 area, TAG grammars can, depending on the variant, fall into the realm of Type-2 languages (context-free) or even in the larger set of the mildly context-sensitive grammars (Joshi 1985). Yoshinaga, Miyao, Torisawa & Tsujii (2001) have developed a procedure for translating FB-LTAG grammars into HPSG grammars.

---

[6] See Rambow (1994) and Kallmeyer (2005: 194), however, for TAG analyses with an empty element in the lexicon.

Comprehension questions

1. How are long-distance dependencies analyzed in TAG? Does one need empty elements for this?

2. Is it possible to analyze the reordering of arguments of multiple verbs using standard TAG processes?

Exercises

1. Analyze the following string in LTAG:

   (24) der dem   König treue Diener
         the the.DAT king loyal servant

         'the servant loyal to the king'

Further reading

Some important articles are Joshi, Levy & Takahashi (1975), Joshi (1987a), and Joshi & Schabes (1997). Many works discuss formal properties of TAG and are therefore not particularly accessible for linguistically interested readers. Kroch & Joshi (1985) give a good overview of linguistic analyses. An overview of linguistic and computational linguistic works in TAG can be found in the volume edited by Abeillé and Rambow from 2000. Rambow (1994) compares his TAG variant (V-TAG) to Karttunen's *Radical Lexicalism* approach, Uszkoreit's GPSG, Combinatorial Categorial Grammar, HPSG and Dependency Grammar.

Shieber & Johnson (1993) discuss psycholinguistically plausible processing models and show that it is possible to do incremental parsing with TAG. They also present a further variant of TAG: synchronous TAG. In this TAG variant, there is a syntactic tree and a semantic tree connected to it. When building syntactic structure, the semantic structure is always built in parallel. This structure built in parallel corresponds to the level of Logical Form derived from S-Structure using transformations in GB.

Rambow (1994: Chapter 6) presents an automaton-based performance theory. He applies it to German and shows that the processing difficulties that arise when reordering arguments of multiple verbs can be explained.

Kallmeyer & Romero (2008) show how it is possible to derive MRS representations directly via a derivation tree using FTAG. In each top node, there is a reference to the semantic content of the entire structure and each bottom node makes reference to the semantic content below the node. In this way, it becomes possible to insert an adjective (e.g., *mutmaßlichen* 'suspected') into an NP tree *alle Mörder* 'all murderers' so that the adjective has scope over the nominal part of the NP (*Mörder* 'murderers'): for adjunction of the adjective to the N node, the adjective can access the semantic content of the noun. The top node of *mutmaßlichen* is then the top node of the combination *mutmaßlichen Mörder* 'suspected murderers' and this ensures that the meaning of *mut-maßlichen Mörder* is correctly embedded under the universal quantifier.

Bibliography

Abbott, Barbara. 1976. Right node raising as a test for constituenthood. *Linguistic Inquiry* 7(4). 639–642.

Abeillé, Anne. 1988. Parsing French with Tree Adjoining Grammar: Some linguistic accounts. In Dénes Vargha (ed.), *Proceedings of COLING 88*, 7–12. University of Budapest: Association for Computational Linguistics. http://www.aclweb.org/anthology/C/C88/C88-1002.pdf.

Abeillé, Anne. 2006. In defense of lexical coordination. In Olivier Bonami & Patricia Cabredo Hofherr (eds.), *Empirical issues in formal syntax and semantics*, vol. 6, 7–36. Paris: CNRS. http://www.cssp.cnrs.fr/eiss6/.

Abeillé, Anne & Owen Rambow (eds.). 2000. *Tree Adjoining Grammars: Formalisms, linguistic analysis and processing* (CSLI Lecture Notes 156). Stanford, CA: CSLI Publications.

Abeillé, Anne & Yves Schabes. 1989. Parsing idioms in Lexicalized TAG. In Harold Somers & Mary McGee Wood (eds.), *Proceedings of the Fourth Conference of the European Chapter of the Association for Computational Linguistics*, 1–9. Manchester, England: Association for Computational Linguistics.

Abney, Steven P. 1987. *The English noun phrase in its sentential aspect*. Cambridge, MA: MIT dissertation. http://www.vinartus.net/spa/87a.pdf.

Abney, Steven P. 1996. Statistical methods and linguistics. In Judith L. Klavans & Philip Resnik (eds.), *The balancing act: Combining symbolic and statistical approaches to language* (Language, Speech, and Communication), 1–26. London, England/Cambridge, MA: MIT Press.

Abney, Steven P. & Jennifer Cole. 1986. A Government-Binding parser. In S. Berman, J-W. Choe & J. McDonough (eds.), *Proceedings of NELS 16*, 1–17. University of Massachusetts, Amherst: GLSA.

Abraham, Werner. 1995. *Deutsche Syntax im Sprachenvergleich: Grundlegung einer typologischen Syntax des Deutschen* (Studien zur deutschen Grammatik 41). Tübingen: Stauffenburg Verlag.

Abraham, Werner. 2003. The syntactic link between thema and rhema: The syntax-discourse interface. *Folia Linguistica* 37(1–2). 13–34.

Abraham, Werner. 2005. *Deutsche Syntax im Sprachenvergleich: Grundlegung einer typologischen Syntax des Deutschen* (Studien zur deutschen Grammatik 41). Tübingen: Stauffenburg Verlag 2nd edn.

Abzianidze, Lasha. 2011. *An HPSG-based formal grammar of a core fragment of Georgian implemented in TRALE*. Charles University in Prague MA thesis.

Ackerman, Farrell & Gert Webelhuth. 1998. *A theory of predicates* (CSLI Lecture Notes 76). Stanford, CA: CSLI Publications.

Adams, Marianne. 1984. Multiple interrogation in Italian. *The Linguistic Review* 4(1). 1–27.

Ades, Anthony E. & Mark J. Steedman. 1982. On the order of words. *Linguistics and Philosophy* 4(4). 517–558.

Adger, David. 2003. *Core syntax: A Minimalist approach* (Oxford Core Linguistics 1). Oxford: Oxford University Press Oxford.

Adger, David. 2010. A Minimalist theory of feature structure. In Anna Kibort & Greville G. Corbett (eds.), *Features: Perspectives on a key notion in linguistics* (Oxford Linguistics), 185–218. Oxford: Oxford University Press.

Adger, David. 2013. Constructions and grammatical explanation: Comments on Goldberg. *Mind and Language* 28(4). 466–478.

Ágel, Vilmos. 2000. *Valenztheorie* (Narr Studienbücher). Tübingen: Gunter Narr Verlag.

Ágel, Vilmos, Ludwig M. Eichinger, Hans Werner Eroms, Peter Hellwig, Hans Jürgen Heringer & Henning Lobin (eds.). 2003. *Dependenz und Valenz / Dependency and valency: Ein internationales Handbuch der zeitgenössischen Forschung / An international handbook of contemporary research*, vol. 25.1 (Handbücher zur Sprach- und Kommunikationswissenschaft). Berlin: Walter de Gruyter.

Ágel, Vilmos, Ludwig M. Eichinger, Hans Werner Eroms, Peter Hellwig, Hans Jürgen Heringer & Henning Lobin (eds.). 2006. *Dependenz und Valenz / Dependency and valency: Ein internationales Handbuch der zeitgenössischen Forschung / An international handbook of contemporary research*, vol. 25.2 (Handbücher zur Sprach- und Kommunikationswissenschaft). Berlin: Walter de Gruyter.

Ágel, Vilmos & Klaus Fischer. 2010. 50 Jahre Valenztheorie und Dependenzgrammatik. *Zeitschrift für Germanistische Linguistik* 38(2). 249–290.

Ajdukiewicz, Kasimir. 1935. Die syntaktische Konnexität. *Studia Philosophica* 1. 1–27.

de Alencar, Leonel. 2004. Complementos verbais oracionais – uma análise léxicofuncional. *Lingua(gem)* 1(1). 173–218.

de Alencar, Leonel. 2013. BrGram: uma gramática computacional de um fragmento do português brasileiro no formalismo da LFG. In *Proceedings of the 9th Brazilian Symposium in Information and Human Language Technology. Fortaleza, Ceará, Brazil, October 20–24*, 183–188. Fortaleza, Ceará: Sociedade Brasileira de Computação. http://www.aclweb.org/anthology/W13-4823.

Alsina, Alex. 1996. Resultatives: A joint operation of semantic and syntactic structures. In Miriam Butt & Tracy Holloway King (eds.), *Proceedings of the LFG '96 conference, Rank Xerox, Grenoble*, Stanford, CA: CSLI Publications. http://csli-publications.stanford.edu/LFG/1/.

Alsina, Alex, KP Mohanan & Tara Mohanan. 2005. How to get rid of the COMP. In Miriam Butt & Tracy Holloway King (eds.), *Proceedings of the LFG 2005 conference*, Stanford, CA: CSLI Publications. http://csli-publications.stanford.edu/LFG/10/lfg05amm.pdf.

Altmann, Hans & Ute Hofman. 2004. *Topologie fürs Examen: Verbstellung, Klammer-struktur, Stellungsfelder, Satzglied- und Wortstellung* (Linguistik fürs Examen 4). Wiesbaden: VS Verlag für Sozialwissenschaften/GWV Fachverlage GmbH.

Ambridge, Ben & Adele E. Goldberg. 2008. The island status of clausal complements: Evidence in favor of an information structure explanation. *Cognitive Linguistics* 19. 349–381.

Ambridge, Ben & Elena V. M. Lieven. 2011. *Child language acquisition: Contrasting theoretical approaches.* Cambridge, UK: Cambridge University Press.

Ambridge, Ben, Caroline F. Rowland & Julian M. Pine. 2008. Is structure dependence an innate constraint? New experimental evidence from children's complex-question production. *Cognitive Science: A Multidisciplinary Journal* 32(1). 222–255.

Anderson, John M. 1971. *The grammar of case: Towards a localistic theory*, vol. 4 (Cambridge Studies in Linguistics). Cambridge, UK: Cambridge University Press.

Anderson, Stephen R. 1992. *A-morphous morphology* (Cambridge Studies in Linguistics 62). Cambridge: Cambridge University Press.

Aoun, Joseph & David W. Lightfoot. 1984. Government and contraction. *Linguistic Inquiry* 15(3). 465–473.

Aoun, Joseph & Dominique Sportiche. 1983. On the formal theory of government. *The Linguistic Review* 2(3). 211–236.

Arad Greshler, Tali, Livnat Herzig Sheinfux, Nurit Melnik & Shuly Wintner. 2015. Development of maximally reusable grammars: Parallel development of Hebrew and Arabic grammars. In Stefan Müller (ed.), *Proceedings of the 22nd International Conference on Head-Driven Phrase Structure Grammar, Nanyang Technological University (NTU), Singapore*, 27–40. Stanford, CA: CSLI Publications. http://csli-publications.stanford.edu/HPSG/2015/ahmw.pdf.

Arends, Jacques. 2008. A demographic perspective on Creole formation. In Silvia Kouwenberg & John Victor Singler (eds.), *The handbook of pidgin and creole studies*, 309–331. Oxford/Cambridge: Blackwell Publishing Ltd.

Arka, I Wayan, Avery Andrews, Mary Dalrymple, Meladel Mistica & Jane Simpson. 2009. A linguistic and computational morphosyntactic analysis for the applicative -*i* in Indonesian. In Miriam Butt & Tracy Holloway King (eds.), *Proceedings of the LFG 2009 conference*, 85–105. Stanford, CA: CSLI Publications. http://csli-publications.stanford.edu/LFG/14/.

Arnold, Doug & Andrew Spencer. 2015. A constructional analysis for the skeptical. In Stefan Müller (ed.), *Proceedings of the 22nd International Conference on Head-Driven Phrase Structure Grammar, Nanyang Technological University (NTU), Singapore*, 41–60. Stanford, CA: CSLI Publications. http://csli-publications.stanford.edu/HPSG/2015/arnold-spencer.pdf.

Arnold, Jennifer E., Michael K. Tanenhaus, Rebecca J. Altmann & Maria Fagnano. 2004. The old and thee, uh, new. *Psychological Science* 15(9). 578–582.

Askedal, John Ole. 1986. Zur vergleichenden Stellungsfeldanalyse von Verbalsätzen und nichtverbalen Satzgliedern. *Deutsch als Fremdsprache* 23. 269–273 and 342–348.

Asudeh, Ash. 2004. *Resumption as resource management*: Stanford University dissertation.

Asudeh, Ash, Mary Dalrymple & Ida Toivonen. 2008. Constructions with lexical integrity: Templates as the lexicon-syntax interface. In Miriam Butt & Tracy Holloway King (eds.), *Proceedings of the LFG 2008 conference*, Stanford, CA: CSLI Publications. http://csli-publications.stanford.edu/LFG/13/.

Asudeh, Ash, Mary Dalrymple & Ida Toivonen. 2013. Constructions with lexical integrity. *Journal of Language Modelling* 1(1). 1–54.

Asudeh, Ash, Gianluca Giorgolo & Ida Toivonen. 2014. Meaning and valency. In Miriam Butt & Tracy Holloway King (eds.), *Proceedings of the LFG 2014 conference*, 68–88. Stanford, CA: CSLI Publications.

Asudeh, Ash & Ida Toivonen. 2014. *With* lexical integrity. *Theoretical Linguistics* 40(1–2). 175–186.

Attardi, Giuseppe. 2006. Experiments with a multilanguage non-projective dependency parser. In *Proceedings of the 10th Conference on Computational Natural Language Learning (CoNLL-X)*, 166–170. Association for Computational Linguistics.

Attia, Mohammed A. 2008. *Handling Arabic morphological and syntactic ambiguity within the LFG framework with a view to machine translation*: School of Languages, Linguistics and Cultures, University of Manchester dissertation.

Avgustinova, Tania & Yi Zhang. 2009. Exploiting the Russian national corpus in the development of a Russian Resource Grammar. In Núria Bel, Erhard Hinrichs, Kiril Simov & Petya Osenova (eds.), *Adaptation of language resources and technology to new domains at the RANLP 2009 Conference, Borovets, Bulgaria*, 1–11. Shoumen, Bulgaria: INCOMA Ltd.

Bach, Emmon. 1962. The order of elements in a Transformational Grammar of German. *Language* 8(3). 263–269.

Bach, Emmon. 1976. An extension of classical Transformation Grammar. In *Problems in linguistic metatheory, Proceedings of the 1976 Conference at the Michigan State University*, 183–224.

Bahrani, Mohammad, Hossein Sameti & Mehdi Hafezi Manshadi. 2011. A computational grammar for Persian based on GPSG. *Language Resources and Evaluation* 45(4). 387–408.

Baker, Carl Lee. 1978. *Introduction to Generative-Transformational Syntax*. Englewood Cliffs, NJ: Prentice-Hall.

Baker, Mark C. 2003. Linguistic differences and language design. *Trends in Cognitive Sciences* 7(8). 349–353.

Baker, Mark C. 2009. Language universals: Abstract but not mythological. *The Behavioral and Brain Sciences* 32(5). 448–449.

Baldridge, Jason. 2002. *Lexically specified derivational control in Combinatory Categorial Grammar*: University of Edinburgh dissertation.

Baldridge, Jason, Sudipta Chatterjee, Alexis Palmer & Ben Wing. 2007. DotCCG and VisCCG: Wiki and programming paradigms for improved grammar engineering with OpenCCG. In Tracy Holloway King & Emily M. Bender (eds.), *Grammar Engineering across Frameworks 2007* (Studies in Computational Linguistics ONLINE), 5–25. Stanford, CA: CSLI Publications. http://csli-publications.stanford.edu/GEAF/2007/.

Baldridge, Jason & Geert-Jan M. Kruijff. 2002. Coupling CCG and Hybrid Logic Dependency Semantics. In Pierre Isabelle (ed.), *40th Annual Meeting of the Association for Computational Linguistics: Proceedings of the conference*, 319–326. University of Pennsylvania, Philadelphia: Association for Computational Linguistics. http://aclanthology.info/events/acl-2002.

Ballweg, Joachim. 1997. Stellungsregularitäten in der Nominalphrase. In Hans-Werner Eroms, Gerhard Stickel & Gisela Zifonun (eds.), *Grammatik der deutschen Sprache*, vol. 7.3 (Schriften des Instituts für deutsche Sprache), 2062–2072. Berlin: Walter de Gruyter.

Baltin, Mark. 1981. Strict bounding. In Carl Lee Baker & John J. McCarthy (eds.), *The logical problem of language acquisition*, 257–295. Cambridge, MA/London, England: MIT Press.

Baltin, Mark. 2004. Remarks on the relation between language typology and Universal Grammar: Commentary on Newmeyer. *Studies in Language* 28(3). 549–553.

Baltin, Mark. 2006. Extraposition. In Martin Everaert, Henk van Riemsdijk, Rob Goedemans & Bart Hollebrandse (eds.), *The Blackwell companion to syntax* (Blackwell Handbooks in Linguistics), 237–271. Oxford: Blackwell Publishing Ltd.

Bangalore, Srinivas, Aravind K. Joshi & Owen Rambow. 2003. Dependency and valency in other theories: Tree Adjoining Grammar. In Vilmos Ágel, Ludwig M. Eichinger, Hans Werner Eroms, Peter Hellwig, Hans Jürgen Heringer & Henning Lobin (eds.), *Dependenz und Valenz / Dependency and valency: Ein internationales Handbuch der zeitgenössischen Forschung / An international handbook of contemporary research*, vol. 25.1 (Handbücher zur Sprach- und Kommunikationswissenschaft), 669–678. Berlin: Walter de Gruyter.

Bannard, Colin, Elena Lieven & Michael Tomasello. 2009. Modeling children's early grammatical knowledge. *Proceedings of the National Academy of Sciences* 106(41). 17284–17289.

Bar-Hillel, Yehoshua, Micha A. Perles & Eliahu Shamir. 1961. On formal properties of simple phrase-structure grammars. *Zeitschrift für Phonetik, Sprachwissenschaft und Kommunikationsforschung* 14(2). 143–172.

Bartsch, Renate & Theo Vennemann. 1972. *Semantic structures: A study in the relation between semantics and syntax* (Athenäum-Skripten Linguistik 9). Frankfurt/Main: Athenäum.

Barwise, Jon & John Perry. 1983. *Situations and attitudes*. Cambridge, MA/London, England: MIT Press.

Barwise, Jon & John Perry. 1987. *Situationen und Einstellungen – Grundlagen der Situationssemantik*. Berlin, New York: de Gruyter.

Baschung, K., G. G. Bes, A. Corluy & T. Guillotin. 1987. Auxiliaries and clitics in French UCG grammar. In Bente Maegaard (ed.), *Proceedings of the Third Conference of the European Chapter of the Association for Computational Linguistics*, 173–178. Copenhagen, Denmark: Association for Computational Linguistics.

Bates, Elizabeth A. 1984. Bioprograms and the innateness hypothesis. *The Behavioral and Brain Sciences* 7(2). 188–190.

Baumgärtner, Klaus. 1965. Spracherklärung mit den Mitteln der Abhängigkeitsstruktur. *Beiträge zur Sprachkunde und Informationsverarbeitung* 5. 31–53.

Baumgärtner, Klaus. 1970. Konstituenz und Dependenz: Zur Integration beider grammatischer Prinzipien. In Hugo Steger (ed.), *Vorschläge für eine strukturelle Grammatik des Deutschen* (Wege der Forschung 144), 52–77. Darmstadt: Wissenschaftliche Buchgesellschaft.

Bausewein, Karin. 1990. Haben kopflose Relativsätze tatsächlich keine Köpfe? In Gisbert Fanselow & Sascha W. Felix (eds.), *Strukturen und Merkmale syntaktischer Kategorien* (Studien zur deutschen Grammatik 39), 144–158. Tübingen: originally Gunter Narr Verlag now Stauffenburg Verlag.

Bayer, Josef & Jaklin Kornfilt. 1989. Restructuring effects in German. DYANA Report University of Edinburgh.

Beavers, John. 2003. A CCG implementation for the LKB. LinGO Working Paper 2002-08 CSLI Stanford Stanford, CA. http://lingo.stanford.edu/pubs/WP-2002-08.ps.gz.

Beavers, John. 2004. Type-inheritance Combinatory Categorial Grammar. In *Proceedings of COLING 2004*, 57–63. Geneva, Switzerland: Association for Computational Linguistics.

Beavers, John, Elias Ponvert & Stephen Mark Wechsler. 2008. Possession of a controlled substantive. In T. Friedman & S. Ito (eds.), *Proceedings of Semantics and Linguistic Theory (SALT) XVIII*, 108–125. Ithaca, NY: Cornell University.

Beavers, John & Ivan A. Sag. 2004. Coordinate ellipsis and apparent non-constituent coordination. In Stefan Müller (ed.), *Proceedings of the 11th International Conference on Head-Driven Phrase Structure Grammar, Center for Computational Linguistics, Katholieke Universiteit Leuven*, 48–69. Stanford, CA: CSLI Publications. http://csli-publications.stanford.edu/HPSG/2004/.

Bech, Gunnar. 1955. *Studien über das deutsche Verbum infinitum* (Linguistische Arbeiten 139). Tübingen: Max Niemeyer Verlag. 2nd unchanged edition 1983.

Becker, Tilman, Aravind K. Joshi & Owen Rambow. 1991. Long-distance scrambling and Tree Adjoining Grammars. In *Fifth Conference of the European Chapter of the Association for Computational Linguistics. Proceedings of the conference*, 21–26. Berlin: Association for Computational Linguistics. http://www.aclweb.org/anthology/E91-1005.pdf.

Beermann, Dorothee & Lars Hellan. 2004. A treatment of directionals in two implemented HPSG grammars. In Stefan Müller (ed.), *Proceedings of the 11th International Conference on Head-Driven Phrase Structure Grammar, Center for Computational Linguistics, Katholieke Universiteit Leuven*, 357–377. Stanford, CA: CSLI Publications. http://csli-publications.stanford.edu/HPSG/2004/.

Beghelli, Filippo & Timothy Stowell. 1997. Distributivity and negation: The syntax of *each* and *every*. In Anna Szabolcsi (ed.), *Ways of scope taking*, 71–107. Dordrecht: Kluwer Academic Publishers.

Behaghel, Otto. 1909. Beziehung zwischen Umfang und Reihenfolge von Satzgliedern. *Indogermanische Forschungen* 25. 110–142.

Behaghel, Otto. 1930. Von deutscher Wortstellung. *Zeitschrift für Deutschkunde* 44. 81–89.

Behrens, Heike. 2009. Konstruktionen im Spracherwerb. *Zeitschrift für Germanistische Linguistik* 37(3). 427–444.

Bellugi, Ursula, Liz Lichtenberger, Wendy Jones, Zona Lai & Marie St. George. 2000. The neurocognitive profile of Williams Syndrome: A complex pattern of strengths and weaknesses. *Journal of Cognitive Neuroscience* 12. 7–29.

Bender, Emily & Daniel P. Flickinger. 1999. Peripheral constructions and core phenomena: Agreement in tag questions. In Gert Webelhuth, Jean-Pierre Koenig & Andreas Kathol (eds.), *Lexical and Constructional aspects of linguistic explanation* (Studies in Constraint-Based Lexicalism 1), 199–214. Stanford, CA: CSLI Publications.

Bender, Emily M. 2000. *Syntactic variation and linguistic competence: The case of AAVE copula absence*: Stanford University dissertation. http://faculty.washington.edu/ebender/dissertation/.

Bender, Emily M. 2008a. Evaluating a crosslinguistic grammar resource: A case study of Wambaya. In Johanna D. Moore, Simone Teufel, James Allan & Sadaoki Furui (eds.), *Proceedings of the 46th Annual Meeting of the Association for Computational Linguistics: Human Language Technologies*, 977–985. Columbus, Ohio: Association for Computational Linguistics. http://aclweb.org/anthology-new/P/P08/P08-1111.pdf.

Bender, Emily M. 2008b. Grammar engineering for linguistic hypothesis testing. In Nicholas Gaylord, Alexis Palmer & Elias Ponvert (eds.), *Proceedings of the Texas Linguistics Society X Conference: Computational linguistics for less-studied languages*, 16–36. Stanford CA: CSLI Publications ONLINE.

Bender, Emily M. 2008c. Radical non-configurationality without shuffle operators: An analysis of Wambaya. In Stefan Müller (ed.), *Proceedings of the 15th International Conference on Head-Driven Phrase Structure Grammar*, 6–24. Stanford, CA: CSLI Publications. http://csli-publications.stanford.edu/HPSG/2008/.

Bender, Emily M. 2010. Reweaving a grammar for Wambaya: A case study in grammar engineering for linguistic hypothesis testing. *Linguistic Issues in Language Technology – LiLT* 3(3). 1–34. http://journals.linguisticsociety.org/elanguage/lilt/article/view/662/523.html.

Bender, Emily M., Daniel P. Flickinger & Stephan Oepen. 2002. The Grammar Matrix: An open-source starter-kit for the rapid development of cross-linguistically consistent broad-coverage precision grammars. In John Carroll, Nelleke Oostdijk & Richard Sutcliffe (eds.), *Proceedings of the Workshop on Grammar Engineering and Evaluation at the 19th International Conference on Computational Linguistics*, 8–14. Taipei, Taiwan.

Bender, Emily M. & Melanie Siegel. 2005. Implementing the syntax of Japanese numeral classifiers. In Keh-Yih Su, Oi Yee Kwong, Jn'ichi Tsujii & Jong-Hyeok Lee (eds.), *Natural language processing IJCNLP 2004* (Lecture Notes in Artificial Intelligence 3248), 626–635. Berlin: Springer Verlag.

Bergen, Benjamin K. & Nancy Chang. 2005. Embodied Construction Grammar in simulation-based language understanding. In Jan-Ola Östman & Mirjam Fried (eds.),

Construction Grammars: Cognitive grounding and theoretical extensions, 147–190. Amsterdam: John Benjamins Publishing Co.

Berman, Judith. 1996. Eine LFG-Grammatik des Deutschen. In *Deutsche und französische Syntax im Formalismus der LFG* (Linguistische Arbeiten 344), 11–96. Tübingen: Max Niemeyer Verlag.

Berman, Judith. 1999. Does German satisfy the Subject Condition? In Miriam Butt & Tracy Holloway King (eds.), *Proceedings of the LFG '99 conference, University of Manchester*, Stanford, CA: CSLI Publications. http://csli-publications.stanford.edu/LFG/4/.

Berman, Judith. 2003a. *Clausal syntax of German* (Studies in Constraint-Based Lexicalism). Stanford, CA: CSLI Publications.

Berman, Judith. 2003b. Zum Einfluss der strukturellen Position auf die syntaktische Funktion der Komplementsätze. *Deutsche Sprache* 3. 263–286.

Berman, Judith. 2007. Functional identification of complement clauses in German and the specification of COMP. In Annie Zaenen, Jane Simpson, Tracy Holloway King, Jane Grimshaw, Joan Maling & Chris Manning (eds.), *Architectures, rules, and preferences: Variations on themes by Joan W. Bresnan*, 69–83. Stanford, CA: CSLI Publications.

Berwick, Robert C. 1982. Computational complexity and Lexical-Functional Grammar. *American Journal of Computational Linguistics* 8(3–4). 97–109.

Berwick, Robert C. & Samuel David Epstein. 1995. On the convergence of the 'Minimalist' Syntax and Categorial Grammar. In Anton Nijholt, Giuseppe Scollo & Rene Steetskamp (eds.), *Algebraic methods in language processing*, 143–148. Enschede: University of Twente. http://eprints.eemcs.utwente.nl/9555/01/twlt10.pdf.

Berwick, Robert C. & Partha Niyogi. 1996. Learning from triggers. *Linguistic Inquiry* 27. 605–622.

Berwick, Robert C., Paul Pietroski, Beracah Yankama & Noam Chomsky. 2011. Poverty of the Stimulus revisited. *Cognitive Science* 35(7). 1207–1242.

Bick, Eckhard. 2001. En Constraint Grammar parser for dansk. In Peter Widell & Mette Kunøe (eds.), *8. Møde om Udforskningen af Dansk Sprog, 12.–13. October 2000*, vol. 8, 40–50. Århus: Århus University.

Bick, Eckhard. 2003. A Constraint Grammar-based question answering system for Portuguese. In Fernando Moura Pires & Salvador Abreu (eds.), *Progress in artificial intelligence: 11th Protuguese Conference on Artificial Intelligence, EPIA 2003, Beja, Portugal, December 4–7, 2003, proceedings* (Lecture Notes in Computer Science 2902), 414–418. Berlin: Springer Verlag.

Bick, Eckhard. 2006. A Constraint Grammar parser for Spanish. In *Proceedings of TIL 2006 – 4th Workshop on Information and Human Language Technology (Ribeirão Preto, October 27–28, 2006)*, 3–10. http://www.nilc.icmc.usp.br/til/til2006/.

Bick, Eckhard. 2009. A Dependency Constraint Grammar for Esperanto. In Eckhard Bick, Kristin Hagen, Kaili Müürisep & Trond Trosterud (eds.), *Constraint Grammar and robust parsing: Proceedings of the NODALIDA 2009 workshop* (NEALT Proceedings Series 8), 8–12. Northern European Association for Language Technologie Tartu: Tartu University Library.

Bick, Eckhard. 2010. FrAG: A hybrid Constraint Grammar parser for French. In Nicoletta Calzolari, Khalid Choukri, Bente Maegaard, Joseph Mariani, Jan Odijk, Stelios Piperidis, Mike Rosner & Daniel Tapias (eds.), *Proceedings of the Seventh International Conference on Language Resources and Evaluation (LREC'10)*, 794–798. Valletta, Malta: European Language Resources Association (ELRA).

Bick, Eckhard & Lars Nygaard. 2007. Using Danish as a CG interlingua: A wide-coverage Norwegian-English machine translation system. In Joakim Nivre, Heiki-Jaan Kaalep, Kadri Muischnek & Mare Koit (eds.), *Proceedings of the 16th Nordic Conference of Computational Linguistics*, 21–28. Forlag uden navn.

Bickerton, Derek. 1984a. Creol is still king. *The Behavioral and Brain Sciences* 7(2). 212–218.

Bickerton, Derek. 1984b. The Language Bioprogram Hypothesis. *The Behavioral and Brain Sciences* 7(2). 173–188.

Bickerton, Derek. 1997. How to acquire language without positive evidence: What acquisitionists can learn from Creoles. In Michel DeGraff (ed.), *Language creation and language change: Creolization, diachrony, and development* (Learning, Development, and Conceptual Change), 49–74. Cambridge, MA: MIT Press.

Bierwisch, Manfred. 1963. *Grammatik des deutschen Verbs* (studia grammatica 2). Berlin: Akademie Verlag.

Bierwisch, Manfred. 1966. Strukturalismus: Geschichte, Probleme und Methoden. *Kursbuch* 5. 77–152.

Bierwisch, Manfred. 1992. Grammatikforschung in der DDR: Auch ein Rückblick. *Linguistische Berichte* 139. 169–181.

Bildhauer, Felix. 2008. *Representing information structure in an HPSG grammar of Spanish*: Universität Bremen Dissertation.

Bildhauer, Felix. 2011. Mehrfache Vorfeldbesetzung und Informationsstruktur: Eine Bestandsaufnahme. *Deutsche Sprache* 39(4). 362–379.

Bildhauer, Felix. 2014. Head-Driven Phrase Structure Grammar. In Andrew Carnie, Yosuke Sato & Dan Siddiqi (eds.), *The Routledge handbook of syntax*, 526–555. Oxford: Routledge.

Bildhauer, Felix & Philippa Helen Cook. 2010. German multiple fronting and expected topic-hood. In Stefan Müller (ed.), *Proceedings of the 17th International Conference on Head-Driven Phrase Structure Grammar, Université Paris Diderot*, 68–79. Stanford, CA: CSLI Publications.

Bird, Steven & Ewan Klein. 1994. Phonological analysis in typed feature systems. *Computational Linguistics* 20(3). 455–491.

Bishop, Dorothy V. M. 2002. Putting language genes in perspective. *TRENDS in Genetics* 18(2). 57–59.

Bjerre, Tavs. 2006. Object positions in a topological sentence model for Danish: A linearization-based HPSG approach. Presentation at Ph.D.-Course at Sandbjerg, Denmark. http://www.hum.au.dk/engelsk/engsv/objectpositions/workshop/Bjerre.pdf.

Blackburn, Patrick & Johan Bos. 2005. *Representation and inference for natural language: A first course in computational semantics*. Stanford, CA: CSLI Publications.

Blackburn, Patrick, Claire Gardent & Wilfried Meyer-Viol. 1993. Talking about trees. In Steven Krauwer, Michael Moortgat & Louis des Tombe (eds.), *Sixth Conference of the European Chapter of the Association for Computational Linguistics. Proceedings of the conference*, 21–29. Uetrecht: Association for Computational Linguistics.

Błaszczak, Joanna & Hans-Martin Gärtner. 2005. Intonational phrasing, discontinuity, and the scope of negation. *Syntax* 8(1). 1–22.

Blevins, James P. 2003. Passives and impersonals. *Journal of Linguistics* 39(3). 473–520.

Block, Hans-Ulrich & Rudolf Hunze. 1986. Incremental construction of c- and f-structure in a LFG-parser. In Makoto Nagao (ed.), *Proceedings of COLING 86*, 490–493. University of Bonn: Association for Computational Linguistics.

Blom, Corrien. 2005. *Complex predicates in Dutch: Synchrony and diachrony* (LOT Dissertation Series 111). Utrecht: Utrecht University.

Bloom, Paul. 1993. Grammatical continuity in language development: The case of subjectless sentences. *Linguistic Inquiry* 24(4). 721–734.

Boas, Hans C. 2003. *A Constructional approach to resultatives* (Stanford Monographs in Linguistics). Stanford, CA: CSLI Publications.

Boas, Hans C. 2014. Lexical approaches to argument structure: Two sides of the same coin. *Theoretical Linguistics* 40(1–2). 89–112.

Bobaljik, Jonathan. 1999. Adverbs: The hierarchy paradox. *Glot International* 4(9/10). 27–28.

Bod, Rens. 2009a. Constructions at work or at rest? *Cognitive Linguistics* 20(1). 129–134.

Bod, Rens. 2009b. From exemplar to grammar: Integrating analogy and probability in language learning. *Cognitive Science* 33(4). 752–793.

Bögel, Tina, Miriam Butt & Sebastian Sulger. 2008. Urdu ezafe and the morphology-syntax interface. In Miriam Butt & Tracy Holloway King (eds.), *Proceedings of the LFG 2008 conference*, 129–149. Stanford, CA: CSLI Publications. http://csli-publications. stanford.edu/LFG/13/.

Bohnet, Bernd. 2010. Very high accuracy and fast Dependency Parsing is not a contradiction. In Chu-Ren Huang & Dan Jurafsky (eds.), *Proceedings of the 23rd International Conference on Computational Linguistics*, 89–97. Stroudsburg, PA, USA: Association for Computational Linguistics.

Bolc, Leonard, Krzysztof Czuba, Anna Kupść, Małgorzata Marciniak, Agnieszka Mykowiecka & Adam Przepiórkowski. 1996. A survey of systems for implementing HPSG grammars. Tech. Rep. 814 Institute of Computer Science, Polish Academy of Sciences Warsaw, Poland. http://www.cs.cmu.edu/~kczuba/systems-wide.ps.gz.

Booij, Geert E. 2002. Separable complex verbs in Dutch: A case of periphrastic word formation. In Nicole Dehé, Ray S. Jackendoff, Andrew McIntyre & Silke Urban (eds.), *Verb-particle explorations* (Interface Explorations 1), 21–41. Berlin: Mouton de Gruyter.

Booij, Geert E. 2005. Construction-Dependent Morphology. *Lingue e linguaggio* 4. 31–46.

Booij, Geert E. 2009. Lexical integrity as a formal universal: A Constructionist view. In Sergio Scalise, Elisabetta Magni & Antonietta Bisetto (eds.), *Universals of language today* (Studies in Natural Language and Linguistic Theory 76), 83–100. Berlin: Springer Verlag.

Booij, Geert E. 2010. Construction morphology. *Language and Linguistics Compass* 4(7). 543–555. DOI:10.1111/j.1749-818X.2010.00213.x.

Booij, Geert E. 2012. Construction morphology. Ms. Leiden University.

Borer, Hagit. 1994. The projection of arguments. In E. Benedicto & J. Runner (eds.), *Functional projections* (UMass Occasional Papers in Linguistics (UMOP) 17), 19–47. Massachusetts: University of Massachusetts Graduate Linguistic Student Association.

Borer, Hagit. 2003. Exo-skeletal vs. endo-skeletal explanations: Syntactic projections and the lexicon. In John Moore & Maria Polinsky (eds.), *The nature of explanation in linguistic theory*, 31–67. Stanford, CA: CSLI Publications.

Borer, Hagit. 2005. *Structuring sense: In name only*, vol. 1. Oxford: Oxford University Press.

Borsley, Robert D. 1987. Subjects and complements in HPSG. Report No. CSLI-87-107 Center for the Study of Language and Information Stanford, CA.

Borsley, Robert D. 1989. Phrase-Structure Grammar and the Barriers conception of clause structure. *Linguistics* 27(5). 843–863.

Borsley, Robert D. 1991. *Syntactic theory: A unified approach*. London: Edward Arnold.

Borsley, Robert D. 1999. *Syntactic theory: A unified approach*. London: Edward Arnold 2nd edn.

Borsley, Robert D. 2005. Against ConjP. *Lingua* 115(4). 461–482.

Borsley, Robert D. 2006. Syntactic and lexical approaches to unbounded dependencies. Essex Research Reports in Linguistics 49 University of Essex. http://core.ac.uk/download/pdf/4187949.pdf#page=35.

Borsley, Robert D. 2007. Hang on again! Are we 'on the right track'? In Andrew Radford (ed.), *Martin Atkinson – the Minimalist muse* (Essex Research Reports in Linguistics 53), 43–69. Essex: Department of Language and Linguistics, University of Essex.

Borsley, Robert D. 2012. Don't move! *Iberia: An International Journal of Theoretical Linguistics* 4(1). 110–139.

Bos, Johan. 1996. Predicate logic unplugged. In Paul J. E. Dekker & M. Stokhof (eds.), *Proceedings of the Tenth Amsterdam Colloquium*, 133–143. Amsterdam: ILLC/Department of Philosophy, University of Amsterdam.

Boukedi, Sirine & Kais Haddar. 2014. HPSG grammar treating of different forms of Arabic coordination. *Research in Computing Science* 86: Advances in Computational Linguistics and Intelligent Decision Making. 25–41.

Boullier, Pierre & Benoît Sagot. 2005a. Analyse syntaxique profonde à grande échelle: SxLFG. *Traitement Automatique des Langues (T.A.L.)* 46(2). 65–89.

Boullier, Pierre & Benoît Sagot. 2005b. Efficient and robust LFG parsing: SxLFG. In *Proceedings of IWPT 2005*, 1–10. Vancouver, Canada: Association for Computational Linguistics.

Boullier, Pierre, Benoît Sagot & Lionel Clément. 2005. Un analyseur LFG efficace pour le français: SxLfg. In *Actes de TALN 05*, 403–408. Dourdan, France.

Bouma, Gosse. 1996. Extraposition as a nonlocal dependency. In Geert-Jan Kruijff, Glynn V. Morrill & Dick Oehrle (eds.), *Proceedings of Formal Grammar 96*, 1–14. Prag. http://www.let.rug.nl/gosse/papers.html.

Bouma, Gosse, Robert Malouf & Ivan A. Sag. 2001a. Satisfying constraints on extraction and adjunction. *Natural Language and Linguistic Theory* 19(1). 1–65.

Bouma, Gosse & Gertjan van Noord. 1994. Constraint-based Categorial Grammar. In James Pustejovsky (ed.), *32th Annual Meeting of the Association for Computational Linguistics. Proceedings of the conference*, 147–154. Las Cruces: Association for Computational Linguistics.

Bouma, Gosse & Gertjan van Noord. 1998. Word order constraints on verb clusters in German and Dutch. In Erhard W. Hinrichs, Andreas Kathol & Tsuneko Nakazawa (eds.), *Complex predicates in nonderivational syntax* (Syntax and Semantics 30), 43–72. San Diego: Academic Press. http://www.let.rug.nl/~vannoord/papers/.

Bouma, Gosse, Gertjan van Noord & Robert Malouf. 2001b. Alpino: Wide-coverage computational analysis of Dutch. In Walter Daelemans, Khalil Sima'an, Jorn Veenstra & Jakub Zavrel (eds.), *Computational linguistics in the Netherlands 2000: Selected papers from the Eleventh CLIN Meeting* (Language and Computers 37), Amsterdam/New York, NY: Rodopi.

Bragmann, Sascha. 2015. Syntactically flexible VP-idioms and the N-after-N Construction. Poster presentation at the 5th General Meeting of PARSEME, Iasi, 23–24 September 2015.

Braine, Martin D. S. 1987. What is learned in acquiring word classes—A step toward an acquisition theory. In Brian MacWhinny (ed.), *Mechanisms of language acquisition*, 65–87. Hillsdale, NJ: Lawrence Erlbaum Associates, Publishers.

Branco, António & Francisco Costa. 2008a. A computational grammar for deep linguistic processing of Portuguese: LXGram, version A.4.1. Tech. Rep. TR-2008-17 Universidade de Lisboa, Faculdade de Ciências, Departamento de Informática.

Branco, António & Francisco Costa. 2008b. LXGram in the shared task 'comparing semantic representations' of STEP 2008. In Johan Bos & Rodolfo Delmonte (eds.), *Semantics in text processing: STEP 2008 conference proceedings*, vol. 1 (Research in Computational Semantics), 299–314. London: College Publications. http://www.aclweb.org/anthology/W08-2224.

Brants, Sabine, Stefanie Dipper, Peter Eisenberg, Silvia Hansen-Schirra, Esther König, Wolfgang Lezius, Christian Rohrer, George Smith & Hans Uszkoreit. 2004. TIGER: Linguistic interpretation of a German corpus. *Research on Language and Computation* 2(4). 597–620.

Bresnan, Joan. 1974. The position of certain clause-particles in phrase structure. *Linguistic Inquiry* 5(4). 614–619.

Bresnan, Joan. 1978. A realistic Transformational Grammar. In M. Halle, J. Bresnan & G. A. Miller (eds.), *Linguistic theory and psychological reality*, 1–59. Cambridge, MA: MIT Press.

Bresnan, Joan. 1982a. Control and complementation. *Linguistic Inquiry* 13(3). 343–434.

Bresnan, Joan. 1982b. The passive in lexical theory. In Joan Bresnan (ed.), *The mental representation of grammatical relations* (MIT Press Series on Cognitive Theory and Mental Representation), 3–86. Cambridge, MA/London: MIT Press.

Bresnan, Joan. 2001. *Lexical-Functional Syntax*. Oxford, UK/Cambridge, USA: Blackwell.

Bresnan, Joan & Jane Grimshaw. 1978. The syntax of free relatives in English. *Linguistic Inquiry* 9. 331–392.

Bresnan, Joan & Jonni M. Kanerva. 1989. Locative inversion in Chichewa: A case study of factorization in grammar. *Linguistic Inquiry* 20(1). 1–50.

Bresnan, Joan & Ronald M. Kaplan. 1982. Introduction: Grammars as mental representations of language. In Joan Bresnan (ed.), *The mental representation of grammatical relations* (MIT Press Series on Cognitive Theory and Mental Representation), xvii–lii. Cambridge, MA/London: MIT Press.

Bresnan, Joan & Sam A. Mchombo. 1995. The Lexical Integrity Principle: Evidence from Bantu. *Natural Language and Linguistic Theory* 13. 181–254.

Bresnan, Joan & Annie Zaenen. 1990. Deep unaccusativity in LFG. In Katarzyna Dziwirek, Patrick Farrell & Errapel Mejías-Bikandi (eds.), *Grammatical relations: A cross-theoretical perspective*, 45–57. Stanford, CA: CSLI Publications.

Brew, Chris. 1995. Stochastic HPSG. In Steven P. Abney & Erhard W. Hinrichs (eds.), *Proceedings of the Seventh Conference of the European Chapter of the Association for Computational Linguistics*, 83–89. Dublin: Association for Computational Linguistics.

Briscoe, Ted J. 1997. Review of Edward P. Stabler, Jr., The logical approach to syntax: Foundations, specifications, and implementations of theories of Government and Binding. *Journal of Linguistics* 33(1). 223–225.

Briscoe, Ted J. 2000. Grammatical acquisition: Inductive bias and coevolution of language and the language acquisition device. *Language* 76(2). 245–296.

Briscoe, Ted J. & Ann Copestake. 1999. Lexical rules in constraint-based grammar. *Computational Linguistics* 25(4). 487–526.

Bröker, Norbert. 2003. Formal foundations of Dependency Grammar. In Vilmos Ágel, Ludwig M. Eichinger, Hans Werner Eroms, Peter Hellwig, Hans Jürgen Heringer & Henning Lobin (eds.), *Dependenz und Valenz / Dependency and valency: Ein internationales Handbuch der zeitgenössischen Forschung / An international handbook of contemporary research*, vol. 25.1 (Handbücher zur Sprach- und Kommunikationswissenschaft), 294–310. Berlin: Walter de Gruyter.

Brosziewski, Ulf. 2003. *Syntactic derivations: A nontransformational view* (Linguistische Arbeiten 470). Tübingen: Max Niemeyer Verlag.

Brown, Roger & Camille Hanlon. 1970. Derivational complexity and order of acquisition in child speech. In John R. Hayes (ed.), *Cognition and the development of language*, 11–53. New York: John Wiley & Sons, Inc.

Bruening, Benjamin. 2009. Selectional asymmetries between CP and DP suggest that the DP hypothesis is wrong. In Laurel MacKenzie (ed.), *Proceedings of the 32th Annual Penn Linguistics Colloquium* (Penn Working Papers in Linguistics 15.1), 26–35. Philadelphia.

Bryant, John. 2003. *Constructional analysis*. University of Califorma at Berkeley MA thesis. http://www.icsi.berkeley.edu/~jbryant/old-analyzer.html.

Budde, Monika. 2010. Konstruktionen integrativ: Topik-Konstruktionen als rein-syntaktisches Pendant zu den lexikalisch verankerten Komplement-Konstruktionen. Vortrag auf der Tagung Konstruktionsgrammatik: Neue Perspektiven zur Untersuchung des Deutschen und Englischen. Internationale Fachtagung an der Christian-Albrechts-Universität zu Kiel vom 18. bis 20. Februar 2010.

Bungeroth, Jan. 2002. *A formal description of Sign Language using HPSG*. Karlsruhe Department of Computer Science, University of Stellenbosch, Lehrstuhl Informatik für Ingenieure und Naturwissenschaftler, Universität Karlsruhe (TH) Diploma thesis. http://www-i6.informatik.rwth-aachen.de/~bungeroth/diplarb.pdf.

Burzio, Luigi. 1981. *Intransitive verbs and Italian auxiliaries*: MIT dissertation.

Burzio, Luigi. 1986. *Italian syntax: A Government-Binding approach* (Studies in Natural Language and Linguistic Theory 1). Dordrecht: D. Reidel Publishing Company.

Busemann, Stephan. 1992. *Generierung natürlicher Sprache mit generalisierten Phrasenstrukturgrammatiken*, vol. 313 (Informatik-Fachberichte). Berlin: Springer Verlag.

Bußmann, Hadumod (ed.). 1983. *Lexikon der Sprachwissenschaft* (Kröners Taschenausgabe 452). Stuttgart: Alfred Kröner Verlag.

Bußmann, Hadumod (ed.). 1990. *Lexikon der Sprachwissenschaft* (Kröners Taschenausgabe 452). Stuttgart: Alfred Kröner Verlag 2nd edn.

Butt, Miriam. 2003. The light verb jungle. In C. Quinn, C. Bowern & G. Aygen (eds.), *Papers from the Harvard/Dudley House light verb workshop* (Harvard Working Papers in Linguistics 9), 1–49. Harvard University, Department of Linguistics.

Butt, Miriam, Stefanie Dipper, Anette Frank & Tracy Holloway King. 1999a. Writing large-scale parallel grammars for English, French and German. In Miriam Butt & Tracy Holloway King (eds.), *Proceedings of the LFG '99 conference, University of Manchester*, Stanford, CA: CSLI Publications. http://csli-publications.stanford.edu/LFG/4/.

Butt, Miriam, Helge Dyvik, Tracy Holloway King, Hiroshi Masuichi & Christian Rohrer. 2002. The Parallel Grammar Project. In *Proceedings of COLING-2002 Workshop on Grammar Engineering and Evaluation*, 1–7.

Butt, Miriam, Tracy Holloway King, María-Eugenia Niño & Frédérique Segond. 1999b. *A grammar writer's cookbook* (CSLI Lecture Notes 95). Stanford, CA: CSLI Publications.

Butt, Miriam, Tracy Holloway King & Sebastian Roth. 2007. Urdu correlatives: Theoretical and implementational issues. In Miriam Butt & Tracy Holloway King (eds.), *Proceedings of the LFG 2007 conference*, 107–127. Stanford, CA: CSLI Publications. http://csli-publications.stanford.edu/LFG/12/.

Cahill, Aoife, Michael Burke, Martin Forst, Ruth O'Donovan, Christian Rohrer, Josef van Genabith & Andy Way. 2005. Treebank-based acquisition of multilingual unification grammar resources. *Research on Language and Computation* 3(2). 247–279.

Cahill, Aoife, Michael Burke, Ruth O'Donovan, Stefan Riezler, Josef van Genabith & Andy Way. 2008. Wide-coverage deep statistical parsing using automatic dependency structure annotation. *Computational Linguistics* 34(1). 81–124.

Calder, Jonathan, Ewan Klein & Henk Zeevat. 1988. Unification Categorial Grammar: A concise, extendable grammar for natural language processing. In Dénes Vargha (ed.), *Proceedings of COLING 88*, 83–86. University of Budapest: Association for Computational Linguistics.

Callmeier, Ulrich. 2000. PET—A platform for experimentation with efficient HPSG processing techniques. *Journal of Natural Language Engineering* 1(6). 99–108. (Special Issue on Efficient Processing with HPSG: Methods, Systems, Evaluation).

Candito, Marie-Hélène. 1996. A principle-based hierarchical representation of LTAGs. In Jun-ichi Tsuji (ed.), *Proceedings of COLING-96. 16th International Conference on Computational Linguistics COLING96). Copenhagen, Denmark, August 5–9, 1996*, 194–199. Copenhagen, Denmark: Association for Computational Linguistics.

Candito, Marie-Hélène. 1998. Building parallel LTAG for French and Italian. In *Proceedings of the 36th Annual Meeting of the Association for Computational Linguistics and 17th International Conference on Computational Linguistics*, 211–217. Montreal, Quebec, Canada: Association for Computational Linguistics.

Candito, Marie-Hélène. 1999. *Organisation modulaire et paramétrable de grammaires électroniques lexicalisées. Application au français et à l'italien*: Université Paris 7 dissertation.

Candito, Marie-Hélène & Sylvain Kahane. 1998. Can the TAG derivation tree represent a semantic graph? An answer in the light of Meaning-Text Theory. In *TAG+4*, 25–28.

Cappelle, Bert. 2006. Particle placement and the case for "allostructions". *Constructions online* 1(7). 1–28.

Cappelle, Bert, Yury Shtyrov & Friedemann Pulvermüller. 2010. *Heating up* or *cooling up* the brain? MEG evidence that phrasal verbs are lexical units. *Brain and Language* 115. 189–201.

Carlson, Gregory N. & Michael K. Tanenhaus. 1988. Thematic roles and language comprehension. In Wendy Wilkins (ed.), *Thematic relations* (Syntax and Semantics 21), 263–289. San Diego: Academic Press.

Carpenter, Bob. 1992. *The logic of typed feature structures* (Tracts in Theoretical Computer Science). Cambridge: Cambridge University Press.

Carpenter, Bob. 1994. A natural deduction theorem prover for type-theoretic Categorial Grammars. Tech. rep. Carnegie Mellon Laboratory for Computational Linguistics. http://www.essex.ac.uk/linguistics/external/clmt/papers/cg/carp_cgparser_doc.ps.

Carpenter, Bob. 1998. *Type-logical semantics*. Cambridge, MA/London, England: MIT Press.

Carpenter, Bob & Gerald Penn. 1996. Efficient parsing of compiled typed attribute value logic grammars. In Harry Bunt & Masaru Tomita (eds.), *Recent advances in parsing technology* (Text, Speech and Language Technology 1), 145–168. Dordrecht: Kluwer Academic Publishers.

Çetinoğlu, Özlem & Kemal Oflazer. 2006. Morphology-syntax interface for Turkish LFG. In Nicoletta Calzolari, Claire Cardie & Pierre Isabelle (eds.), *Proceedings of the 21st International Conference on Computational Linguistics and 44th Annual Meeting of the Association for Computational Linguistics*, 153–160. Sydney, Australia: Association for Computational Linguistics.

Chang, Nancy Chih-Lin. 2008. Constructing grammar: A computational model of the emergence of early constructions. Technical Report UCB/EECS-2009-24 Electrical Engineering and Computer Sciences, University of California at Berkeley.

Chaves, Rui P. 2009. Construction-based cumulation and adjunct extraction. In Stefan Müller (ed.), *Proceedings of the 16th International Conference on Head-Driven Phrase Structure Grammar, University of Göttingen, Germany*, 47–67. Stanford, CA: CSLI Publications.

Choi, Hye-Won. 1999. *Optimizing structure in scrambling: Scrambling and information structure* (Dissertations in Linguistics). Stanford, CA: CSLI Publications.

Chomsky, Noam. 1956. Three models for the description of language. *IRE Transactions on Information Theory* 2. 113–124.

Chomsky, Noam. 1957. *Syntactic structures* (Janua Linguarum / Series Minor 4). The Hague/Paris: Mouton.

Chomsky, Noam. 1959. On certain formal properties of grammars. *Information and Control* 2(2). 137–167.

Chomsky, Noam. 1964a. *Current issues in linguistic theory* (Janua Linguarum / Series Minor 38). The Hague/Paris: Mouton.

Chomsky, Noam. 1964b. Degrees of grammaticalness. In Jerry A. Fodor & Jerrold J. Katz (eds.), *The structure of language*, 384–389. Englewood Cliffs, NJ: Prentice-Hall.

Chomsky, Noam. 1965. *Aspects of the theory of syntax*. Cambridge, MA: MIT Press.

Chomsky, Noam. 1968. Language and the mind. *Psychology Today* 1(9). 48–68. Reprint as: Chomsky (1976a).

Chomsky, Noam. 1970. Remarks on nominalization. In Roderick A. Jacobs & Peter S. Rosenbaum (eds.), *Readings in English Transformational Grammar*, chap. 12, 184–221. Waltham, MA/Toronto/London: Ginn and Company.

Chomsky, Noam. 1971. *Problems of knowledge and freedom*. London: Fontana.

Chomsky, Noam. 1973. Conditions on transformations. In Stephen R. Anderson & Paul Kiparski (eds.), *A festschrift for Morris Halle*, 232–286. New York: Holt, Rinehart & Winston.

Chomsky, Noam. 1975. *The logical structure of linguistic theory*. New York: Plenum Press.

Chomsky, Noam. 1976a. Language and the mind. In Diane D. Borstein (ed.), *Readings in the theory of grammar: From the 17th to the 20th century*, 241–251. Cambridge, MA: Winthrop. Reprint from: Chomsky (1968).

Chomsky, Noam. 1976b. *Reflections on language*. New York: Pantheon Books.

Chomsky, Noam. 1977. *Essays on form and interpretation*. New York: North Holland.

Chomsky, Noam. 1980. *Rules and representations*. Oxford: Basil Blackwell.

Chomsky, Noam. 1981a. *Lectures on government and binding*. Dordrecht: Foris Publications.

Chomsky, Noam. 1981b. Reply to comments of Thompson. *Philosophical Transactions of the Royal Society of London. Series B, Biological Sciences* 295(1077). 277–281.

Chomsky, Noam. 1982. *Some concepts and consequences of the theory of Government and Binding* (Linguistic Inquiry Monographs 5). Cambridge, MA/London, England: MIT Press.

Chomsky, Noam. 1986a. *Barriers* (Linguistic Inquiry Monographs 13). Cambridge, MA/London, England: MIT Press.

Chomsky, Noam. 1986b. *Knowledge of language: Its nature, origin, and use* (Convergence). New York/Westport, Connecticut/London: Praeger.

Chomsky, Noam. 1988. *Language and problems of knowledge: The Managua lectures* (Current Studies in Linguistics 16). Cambridge, MA: MIT Press.

Chomsky, Noam. 1989. Some notes on economy of derivation and representation. In I. Laka & Anoop Mahajan (eds.), *Functional heads and clause structure* (MIT Working Papers in Linguistics 10), 43–74. Cambridge, MA: Department of Linguistics and Philosophy.

Chomsky, Noam. 1990. On formalization and formal linguistics. *Natural Language and Linguistic Theory* 8(1). 143–147.

Chomsky, Noam. 1991. Some notes on economy of derivation and representation. In Robert Freidin (ed.), *Principles and parameters in Generative Grammar*, 417–454. Cambridge, MA: MIT Press. Reprint as: Chomsky (1995b: 129–166).

Chomsky, Noam. 1993. A Minimalist Program for linguistic theory. In Kenneth Hale & Samuel Jay Keyser (eds.), *The view from building 20: Essays in linguistics in honor of Sylvain Bromberger* (Current Studies in Linguistics 24), 1–52. Cambridge, MA/London: MIT Press.

Chomsky, Noam. 1995a. Bare phrase structure. In Hector Campos & Paula Kempchinsky (eds.), *Evolution and revolution in linguistic theory: Essays in honor of Carlos Otero*, 51–109. Washington, DC: Georgetown U Press.

Chomsky, Noam. 1995b. *The Minimalist Program* (Current Studies in Linguistics 28). Cambridge, MA/London, England: MIT Press.

Chomsky, Noam. 1998. Noam Chomsky's Minimalist Program and the philosophy of mind: An interview [with] Camilo J. Cela-Conde and Gisde Marty. *Syntax* 1(1). 19–36.

Chomsky, Noam. 1999. Derivation by phase. MIT Occasional Papers in Linguistics 18 MIT. Reprint in: Michael Kenstowicz, ed. 2001. Ken Hale. A Life in Language. Cambridge, MA: MIT Press, 1–52.

Chomsky, Noam. 2000. *New horizons in the study of language and mind*. Cambridge, UK: Cambridge University Press.

Chomsky, Noam. 2001. Derivation by phase. In Michael Kenstowicz (ed.), *Ken Hale: A life in language*, 1–52. Cambridge, MA: MIT Press.

Chomsky, Noam. 2002. *On nature and language*. Cambridge, UK: Cambridge University Press.

Chomsky, Noam. 2005. Three factors in language design. *Linguistic Inquiry* 36(1). 1–22.

Chomsky, Noam. 2007. Approaching UG from below. In Uli Sauerland & Hans-Martin Gärtner (eds.), *Interfaces + recursion = language? Chomsky's Minimalism and the view from syntax-semantics* (Studies in Generative Grammar 89), 1–29. Berlin: Mouton de Gruyter.

Chomsky, Noam. 2008. On phases. In Robert Freidin, Carlos P. Otero & Maria Luisa Zubizarreta (eds.), *Foundational issues in linguistic theory: Essays in honor of Jean-Roger Vergnaud*, 133–166. Cambridge, MA: MIT Press.

Chomsky, Noam. 2010. Restricting stipulations: Consequences and challenges. Talk given in Stuttgart.

Chomsky, Noam. 2013. Problems of projection. *Lingua* 130. 33–49.

Chomsky, Noam & George A. Miller. 1963. Introduction to the formal analysis of natural languages. In R. Duncan Luce, Robert R. Bush & Eugene Galanter (eds.), *Handbook of mathematical psychology*, vol. 2, 269–321. New York: John Wiley & Sons, Inc.

Chouinard, Michelle M. & Eve V. Clark. 2003. Adult reformulations of child errors as negative evidence. *Journal of Child Language* 30. 637–669.

Chrupala, Grzegorz & Josef van Genabith. 2006. Using machine-learning to assign function labels to parser output for Spanish. In Nicoletta Calzolari, Claire Cardie & Pierre Isabelle (eds.), *Proceedings of the 21st International Conference on Computational Linguistics and 44th Annual Meeting of the Association for Computational Linguistics*, 136–143. Sydney, Australia: Association for Computational Linguistics.

Chung, Sandra & James McCloskey. 1983. On the interpretation of certain island facts in GPSG. *Linguistic Inquiry* 14. 704–713.

Church, Kenneth. 2011. A pendulum swung too far. *Linguistic Issues in Language Technology* 6(5). 1–27. http://journals.linguisticsociety.org/elanguage/lilt/article/view/2581.html. Special Issue on Interaction of Linguistics and Computational Linguistics.

Cinque, Guglielmo. 1994. On the evidence for partial N movement in the Romance DP. In Guglielmo Cinque, Jan Koster, Jean-Yves Pollock, Luigi Rizzi & Raffaella Zanuttini (eds.), *Paths towards Universal Grammar: Studies in honor of Richard S. Kayne*, 85–110. Washington, D.C.: Georgetown University Press.

Cinque, Guglielmo. 1999. *Adverbs and functional heads: A cross-linguistic perspective*. New York, Oxford: Oxford University Press.

Cinque, Guglielmo & Luigi Rizzi. 2010. The cartography of syntactic structures. In Bernd Heine & Heiko Narrog (eds.), *The Oxford handbook of linguistic analysis*, 51–65. Oxford: Oxford University Press.

Citko, Barbara. 2008. Missing labels. *Lingua* 118(7). 907–944.

Clark, Alexander. 2000. Inducing syntactic categories by context distribution clustering. In *Proceedings CoNLL 2000*, 91–94. Stroudsburg, PA: Association for Computational Linguistics.

Clark, Herbert H. & Jean E. Fox Tree. 2002. Using *uh* and *um* in spontaneous speaking. *Cognition* 84(1). 73–111.

Clark, Herbert H. & Thomas Wasow. 1998. Repeating words in spontaneous speech. *Cognitive Psychology* 37(3). 201–242.

Clark, Stephen & James Curran. 2007. Wide-coverage efficient statistical parsing with CCG and log-linear models. *Computational Linguistics* 33(4). 493–552.

Clark, Stephen, Julia Hockenmaier & Mark J. Steedman. 2002. Building deep dependency structures with a wide-coverage CCG parser. In Pierre Isabelle (ed.), *40th Annual Meeting of the Association for Computational Linguistics: Proceedings of the conference*, 327–334. University of Pennsylvania, Philadelphia: Association for Computational Linguistics. http://aclanthology.info/events/acl-2002.

Clément, Lionel. 2009. XLFG5 documentation. Translated from French by Olivier Bonami. http://www.xlfg.org/.

Clément, Lionel & Alexandra Kinyon. 2001. XLFG—An LFG parsing scheme for French. In Miriam Butt & Tracy Holloway King (eds.), *Proceedings of the LFG 2001 conference*, Stanford, CA: CSLI Publications. http://csli-publications.stanford.edu/LFG/6/.

Clément, Lionel & Alexandra Kinyon. 2003. Generating parallel multilingual LFG-TAG grammars from a MetaGrammar. In Erhard Hinrichs & Dan Roth (eds.), *Proceedings of the 41st Annual Meeting of the Association for Computational Linguistics*, 184–191. Sapporo, Japan: Association for Computational Linguistics.

Clifton, Charles Jr. & Penelope Odom. 1966. Similarity relations among certain English sentence constructions. *Psychological Monographs: General and Applied* 80(5). 1–35.

Coch, Jose. 1996. Overview of AlethGen. In *Demonstrations and posters of the Eighth International Natural Language Generation Workshop (INLG'96)*, 25–28.

Cook, Philippa Helen. 2001. *Coherence in German: An information structure approach*: Departments of Linguistics and German, University of Manchester dissertation.

Cook, Philippa Helen. 2006. The datives that aren't born equal: Beneficiaries and the dative passive. In Daniel Hole, André Meinunger & Werner Abraham (eds.), *Datives and similar cases: Between argument structure and event structure*, 141–184. Amsterdam: John Benjamins Publishing Co.

Cooper, Robin, Kuniaki Mukai & John Perry (eds.). 1990. *Situation Theory and its applications*, vol. 1 (CSLI Lecture Notes 22). Stanford, CA: CSLI Publications.

Coopmans, Peter. 1989. Where stylistic and syntactic processes meet: Locative inversion in English. *Language* 65(4). 728–751.

Copestake, Ann. 2002. *Implementing typed feature structure grammars* (CSLI Lecture Notes 110). Stanford, CA: CSLI Publications.

Copestake, Ann. 2007. Applying robust semantics. In *Proceedings of the 10th Conference of the Pacific Assocation for Computational Linguistics (PACLING)*, 1–12.

Copestake, Ann & Ted Briscoe. 1995. Semi-productive polysemy and sense extension. *Journal of Semantics* 12(1). 15–67.

Copestake, Ann & Ted J. Briscoe. 1992. Lexical operations in a unification based framework. In James Pustejovsky & Sabine Bergler (eds.), *Lexical semantics and knowledge representation* (Lecture Notes in Artificial Intelligence 627), 101–119. Berlin: Springer Verlag.

Copestake, Ann & Daniel P. Flickinger. 2000. An open-source grammar development environment and broad-coverage English grammar using HPSG. In *Proceedings of the second Linguistic Resources and Evaluation Conference*, 591–600. Athens, Greece.

Copestake, Ann, Daniel P. Flickinger, Carl J. Pollard & Ivan A. Sag. 2005. Minimal Recursion Semantics: An introduction. *Research on Language and Computation* 4(3). 281–332.

Correa, Nelson. 1987. An Attribute-Grammar implementation of Government-Binding Theory. In Candy Sidner (ed.), *25th Annual Meeting of the Association for Computational Linguistics*, 45–51. Stanford, CA: Association for Computational Linguistics.

Costa, Francisco & António Branco. 2010. LXGram: A deep linguistic processing grammar for Portuguese. In Thiago A.S. Pardo (ed.), *Computational processing of the Portuguese language: 9th International Conference, PROPOR 2010, Porto Alegre, RS, Brazil,*

April 27–30, 2010. Proceedings (Lecture Notes in Artificial Intelligence 6001), 86–89. Berlin: Springer Verlag.

Covington, Michael A. 1990. Parsing discontinuous constituents in Dependency Grammar. *Computational Linguistics* 16(4). 234–236.

Crabbé, Benoit. 2005. *Représentation informatique de grammaires d'arbres fortement lexicalisées: le cas de la grammaire d'arbres adjoints*: Université Nancy 2 dissertation.

Crain, Stephen, Drew Khlentzos & Rosalind Thornton. 2010. Universal Grammar versus language diversity. *Lingua* 120(12). 2668–2672.

Crain, Stephen & Mineharu Nakayama. 1987. Structure dependence in grammar formation. *Language* 63(3). 522–543.

Crain, Stephen & Mark J. Steedman. 1985. On not being led up the garden path: The use of context by the psychological syntax processor. In David R. Dowty, Lauri Karttunen & Arnold M. Zwicky (eds.), *Natural language processing*, 320–358. Cambridge, UK: Cambridge University Press.

Crain, Stephen, Rosalind Thornton & Drew Khlentzos. 2009. The case of the missing generalizations. *Cognitive Linguistics* 20(1). 145–155.

Cramer, Bart & Yi Zhang. 2009. Construction of a German HPSG grammar from a detailed treebank. In Tracy Holloway King & Marianne Santaholma (eds.), *Proceedings of the 2009 Workshop on Grammar Engineering Across Frameworks (GEAF 2009)*, 37–45. Suntec, Singapore: Association for Computational Linguistics. http://www.aclweb.org/anthology/W/W09/#2600.

Crocker, Matthew Walter & Ian Lewin. 1992. Parsing as deduction: Rules versus principles. In Bernd Neumann (ed.), *ECAI 92. 10th European Conference on Artificial Intelligence*, 508–512. John Wiley & Sons, Inc.

Croft, William. 2001. *Radical Construction Grammar: Syntactic theory in typological perspective*. Oxford: Oxford University Press.

Croft, William. 2003. Lexical rules vs. constructions: A false dichotomy. In Hubert Cuyckens, Thomas Berg, René Dirven & Klaus-Uwe Panther (eds.), *Motivation in language: Studies in honour of Günter Radden*, 49–68. Amsterdam: John Benjamins Publishing Co.

Croft, William. 2009. Syntax is more diverse, and evolutionary linguistics is already here. *The Behavioral and Brain Sciences* 32(5). 457–458.

Crysmann, Berthold. 2001. Clitics and coordination in linear structure. In Birgit Gerlach & Janet Grijzenhout (eds.), *Clitics in phonology, morphology and syntax* (Linguistik Aktuell/Linguistics Today 36), 121–159. Amsterdam: John Benjamins Publishing Co.

Crysmann, Berthold. 2002. *Constraint-based co-analysis: Portuguese cliticisation and morphology-syntax interaction in HPSG* (Saarbrücken Dissertations in Computational Linguistics and Language Technology 15). Saarbrücken: Deutsches Forschungszentrum für Künstliche Intelligenz und Universität des Saarlandes.

Crysmann, Berthold. 2003. On the efficient implementation of German verb placement in HPSG. In *Proceedings of RANLP 2003*, 112–116. Borovets, Bulgaria.

Crysmann, Berthold. 2004. Underspecification of intersective modifier attachment: Some arguments from German. In Stefan Müller (ed.), *Proceedings of the 11th Interna-*

tional Conference on Head-Driven Phrase Structure Grammar, Center for Computational Linguistics, Katholieke Universiteit Leuven, 378–392. Stanford, CA: CSLI Publications. http://csli-publications.stanford.edu/HPSG/2004/.

Crysmann, Berthold. 2005a. An inflectional approach to Hausa final vowel shortening. In Geert Booij & Jaap van Marle (eds.), *Yearbook of morphology 2004,* 73–112. Dordrecht: Kluwer Academic Publishers.

Crysmann, Berthold. 2005b. Relative clause extraposition in German: An efficient and portable implementation. *Research on Language and Computation* 1(3). 61–82.

Crysmann, Berthold. 2005c. Syncretism in German: A unified approach to underspecification, indeterminacy, and likeness of case. In Stefan Müller (ed.), *Proceedings of the 12th International Conference on Head-Driven Phrase Structure Grammar, Department of Informatics, University of Lisbon,* 91–107. Stanford, CA: CSLI Publications. http://csli-publications.stanford.edu/HPSG/2005/.

Crysmann, Berthold. 2008. An asymmetric theory of peripheral sharing in HPSG: Conjunction reduction and coordination of unlikes. In Gerhard Jäger, Paola Monachesi, Gerald Penn & Shuly Wintner (eds.), *Proceedings of Formal Grammar 2003, Vienna, Austria,* 47–62. Stanford, CA: CSLI Publications.

Crysmann, Berthold. 2009. Autosegmental representations in an HPSG of Hausa. In Tracy Holloway King & Marianne Santaholma (eds.), *Proceedings of the 2009 Workshop on Grammar Engineering Across Frameworks (GEAF 2009),* 28–36. Suntec, Singapore: Association for Computational Linguistics. http://www.aclweb.org/anthology/W/W09/#2600.

Crysmann, Berthold. 2011. A unified account of Hausa genitive constructions. In Philippe de Groote, Markus Egg & Laura Kallmeyer (eds.), *Formal Grammar: 14th International Conference, FG 2009, Bordeaux, France, July 25–26, 2009, revised selected papers* (Lecture Notes in Artificial Intelligence 5591), 102–117. Berlin: Springer Verlag.

Crysmann, Berthold. 2012. HaG: A computational grammar of Hausa. In Michael R. Marlo, Nikki B. Adams, Christopher R. Green, Michelle Morrison & Tristan M. Purvis (eds.), *Selected proceedings of the 42nd Annual Conference on African Linguistics (ACAL 42),* 321–337. Somerville, MA: Cascadilla Press. http://www.lingref.com/cpp/acal/42/paper2780.pdf.

Culicover, Peter W. 1999. *Syntactic nuts: Hard cases, syntactic theory, and language acquisition,* vol. 1 (Foundations of Syntax). Oxford: Oxford University Press.

Culicover, Peter W. & Ray S. Jackendoff. 2005. *Simpler Syntax.* Oxford: Oxford University Press.

Culy, Christopher. 1985. The complexity of the vocabulary of Bambara. *Linguistics and Philosophy* 8. 345–351.

Curtiss, Susan. 1977. *Genie: A psycholinguistic study of a modern-day "wild child".* New York: Academic Press.

Dąbrowska, Ewa. 2001. From formula to schema: The acquisition of English questions. *Cognitive Linguistics* 11(1–2). 83–102.

Dąbrowska, Ewa. 2004. *Language, mind and brain: Some psychological and neurological constraints on theories of grammar.* Washington, D.C.: Georgetown University Press.

Dahl, Östen & Viveka Velupillai. 2013a. The past tense. In Matthew S. Dryer & Martin Haspelmath (eds.), *The world atlas of language structures online*, Leipzig: Max Planck Institute for Evolutionary Anthropology. http://wals.info/chapter/66.

Dahl, Östen & Viveka Velupillai. 2013b. Perfective/imperfective aspect. In Matthew S. Dryer & Martin Haspelmath (eds.), *The world atlas of language structures online*, Leipzig: Max Planck Institute for Evolutionary Anthropology. http://wals.info/chapter/65.

Dahllöf, Mats. 2002. Token dependency semantics and the paratactic analysis of intensional constructions. *Journal of Semantics* 19(4). 333–368.

Dahllöf, Mats. 2003. Two reports on computational syntax and semantics. Reports from Uppsala University (RUUL) 36 Department of Linguistics. http://stp.ling.uu.se/~matsd/pub/ruul36.pdf.

Dalrymple, Mary. 1993. *The syntax of anaphoric binding* (CSLI Lecture Notes 36). Stanford, CA: CSLI Publications.

Dalrymple, Mary (ed.). 1999. *Semantics and syntax in Lexical Functional Grammar: The Resource Logic approach*. Cambridge, MA: MIT Press.

Dalrymple, Mary. 2001. *Lexical Functional Grammar* (Syntax and Semantics 34). New York: Academic Press.

Dalrymple, Mary. 2006. Lexical Functional Grammar. In Keith Brown (ed.), *The encyclopedia of language and linguistics*, 82–94. Oxford: Elsevier Science Publisher B.V. (North-Holland) 2nd edn.

Dalrymple, Mary, Ronald M. Kaplan & Tracy Holloway King. 2004. Linguistic generalizations over descriptions. In Miriam Butt & Tracy Holloway King (eds.), *Proceedings of the LFG 2004 conference*, 199–208. Stanford, CA: CSLI Publications. http://csli-publications.stanford.edu/LFG/9/.

Dalrymple, Mary, Ronald M. Kaplan, John T. Maxwell III & Annie Zaenen (eds.). 1995. *Formal issues in Lexical-Functional Grammar* (CSLI Lecture Notes 47). Stanford, CA: CSLI Publications.

Dalrymple, Mary, John Lamping & Vijay Saraswat. 1993. LFG semantics via constraints. In Steven Krauwer, Michael Moortgat & Louis des Tombe (eds.), *Sixth Conference of the European Chapter of the Association for Computational Linguistics. Proceedings of the conference*, 97–105. Uetrecht: Association for Computational Linguistics. DOI:10.3115/976744.976757.

Dalrymple, Mary, Maria Liakata & Lisa Mackie. 2006. Tokenization and morphological analysis for Malagasy. *Computational Linguistics and Chinese Language Processing* 11(4). 315–332.

Dalrymple, Mary & Helge Lødrup. 2000. The grammatical functions of complement clauses. In Miriam Butt & Tracy Holloway King (eds.), *Proceedings of the LFG 2000 conference*, Stanford, CA: CSLI Publications. http://csli-publications.stanford.edu/LFG/5/lfg00dalrympl-lodrup.pdf.

Davidson, Donald. 1967. The logical form of action sentences. In Nicholas Rescher (ed.), *The logic of decision and action*, 81–95. Pittsburg: Pittsburg University Press.

Davis, Anthony R. 1996. *Lexical semantics and linking in the hierarchical lexicon*: Stanford University dissertation.

Davis, Anthony R. & Jean-Pierre Koenig. 2000. Linking as constraints on word classes in a hierarchical lexicon. *Language* 76(1). 56–91.

De Kuthy, Kordula. 2000. *Discontinuous NPs in German — A case study of the interaction of syntax, semantics and pragmatics*. Saarbrücken: Universität des Saarlandes dissertation.

De Kuthy, Kordula. 2001. Splitting PPs from NPs. In Walt Detmar Meurers & Tibor Kiss (eds.), *Constraint-based approaches to Germanic syntax* (Studies in Constraint-Based Lexicalism 7), 31–76. Stanford, CA: CSLI Publications.

De Kuthy, Kordula. 2002. *Discontinuous NPs in German* (Studies in Constraint-Based Lexicalism 14). Stanford, CA: CSLI Publications.

De Kuthy, Kordula, Vanessa Metcalf & Walt Detmar Meurers. 2004. Documentation of the implementation of the Milca English Resource Grammar in the Trale system. Ohio State University, ms.

De Kuthy, Kordula & Walt Detmar Meurers. 2001. On partial constituent fronting in German. *Journal of Comparative Germanic Linguistics* 3(3). 143–205.

De Kuthy, Kordula & Walt Detmar Meurers. 2003a. Dealing with optional complements in HPSG-based grammar implementations. In Stefan Müller (ed.), *Proceedings of the 10th International Conference on Head-Driven Phrase Structure Grammar, Michigan State University, East Lansing*, 88–96. Stanford, CA: CSLI Publications. http://csli-publications.stanford.edu/HPSG/2003/.

De Kuthy, Kordula & Walt Detmar Meurers. 2003b. The secret life of focus exponents, and what it tells us about fronted verbal projections. In Stefan Müller (ed.), *Proceedings of the 10th International Conference on Head-Driven Phrase Structure Grammar, Michigan State University, East Lansing*, 97–110. Stanford, CA: CSLI Publications. http://csli-publications.stanford.edu/HPSG/2003/.

de Saussure, Ferdinand. 1916a. *Cours de linguistique générale* (Bibliothèque Scientifique Payot). Paris: Payot. Edited by Charles Bally and Albert Sechehaye.

de Saussure, Ferdinand. 1916b. *Grundfragen der allgemeinen Sprachwissenschaft*. Berlin: Walter de Gruyter & Co. 2nd edition 1967.

Delmonte, Rodolfo. 1990. Semantic parsing with an LFG-based lexicon and conceptual representations. *Computers and the Humanities* 24(5–6). 461–488.

Demberg, Vera & Frank Keller. 2008. A psycholinguistically motivated version of TAG. In *Proceedings of the 9th International Workshop on Tree Adjoining Grammars and Related Formalisms TAG+9*, 25–32. Tübingen.

Demske, Ulrike. 2001. *Merkmale und Relationen: Diachrone Studien zur Nominalphrase des Deutschen* (Studia Linguistica Germanica 56). Berlin: Walter de Gruyter Verlag.

den Besten, Hans. 1983. On the interaction of root transformations and lexical deletive rules. In Werner Abraham (ed.), *On the formal syntax of the Westgermania: Papers from the 3rd Groningen Grammar Talks, Groningen, January 1981* (Linguistik Aktuell/Linguistics Today 3), 47–131. Amsterdam: John Benjamins Publishing Co.

den Besten, Hans. 1985. Some remarks on the Ergative Hypothesis. In Werner Abraham (ed.), *Erklärende Syntax des Deutschen* (Studien zur deutschen Grammatik 25), 53–74. Tübingen: originally Gunter Narr Verlag now Stauffenburg Verlag.

Deppermann, Arnulf. 2006. Construction Grammar – eine Grammatik für die Interaktion? In Arnulf Deppermann, Reinhard Fiehler & Thomas Spranz-Fogasy (eds.), *Grammatik und Interaktion*, 43–65. Radolfzell: Verlag für Gesprächsforschung.

Derbyshire, Desmond C. 1979. *Hixkaryana* (Lingua Descriptive Series 1). Amsterdam: North Holland.

Devlin, Keith. 1992. *Logic and information.* Cambridge: Cambridge University Press.

Dhonnchadha, E. Uí & Josef van Genabith. 2006. A part-of-speech tagger for Irish using finite-state morphology and Constraint Grammar disambiguation. In *Proceedings of lrec'06*, 2241–2244.

Diesing, Molly. 1992. *Indefinites.* Cambridge, MA/London, England: MIT Press.

Dione, Cheikh Mouhamadou Bamba. 2013. Handling Wolof Clitics in LFG. In Christine Meklenborg Salvesen & Hans Petter Helland (eds.), *Challenging clitics* (Linguistik Aktuell/Linguistics Today 206), 87–118. Amsterdam: John Benjamins Publishing Co.

Dione, Cheikh Mouhamadou Bamba. 2014. An LFG approach to Wolof cleft constructions. In Miriam Butt & Tracy Holloway King (eds.), *Proceedings of the LFG 2014 conference*, 157–176. Stanford, CA: CSLI Publications.

Dipper, Stefanie. 2003. *Implementing and documenting large-scale grammars – German LFG*: IMS, University of Stuttgart dissertation. Arbeitspapiere des Instituts für Maschinelle Sprachverarbeitung (AIMS), Volume 9, Number 1.

Donati, C. 2006. On *wh*-head-movement. In Lisa Lai-Shen Cheng & Norbert Corver (eds.), Wh-*movement: Moving on* (Current Studies in Linguistics 42), 21–46. Cambridge, MA: MIT Press.

Donohue, Cathryn & Ivan A. Sag. 1999. Domains in Warlpiri. In *Sixth International Conference on HPSG–Abstracts. 04–06 August 1999*, 101–106. Edinburgh.

Doran, Christine, Beth Ann Hockey, Anoop Sarkar, Bangalore Srinivas & Fei Xia. 2000. Evolution of the XTAG system. In Anne Abeillé & Owen Rambow (eds.), *Tree Adjoining Grammars: Formalisms, linguistic analysis and processing* (CSLI Lecture Notes 156), 371–403. Stanford, CA: CSLI Publications.

Dörre, Jochen & Michael Dorna. 1993. CUF: A formalism for linguistic knowledge representation. DYANA 2 deliverable R.1.2A IMS Stuttgart, Germany.

Dörre, Jochen & Roland Seiffert. 1991. A formalism for natural language — STUF. In Otthein Herzog & Claus-Rainer Rollinger (eds.), *Text understanding in LILOG* (Lecture Notes in Artificial Intelligence 546), 29–38. Berlin: Springer Verlag.

Dowty, David. 1997. Non-constituent coordination, wrapping, and Multimodal Categorial Grammars: Syntactic form as logical form. In Maria Luisa Dalla Chiara, Kees Doets, Daniele Mundici & Johan Van Benthem (eds.), *Structures and norms in science* (Synthese Library 260), 347–368. Springer.

Dowty, David R. 1978. Governed transformations as lexical rules in a Montague Grammar. *Linguistic Inquiry* 9(3). 393–426.

Dowty, David R. 1979. *Word meaning and Montague Grammar* (Synthese Language Library 7). Dordrecht: D. Reidel Publishing Company.

Dowty, David R. 1988. Type raising, functional composition, and nonconstituent coordination. In Richard Oehrle, Emmon Bach & Deirdre Wheeler (eds.), *Categorial Grammars and natural language structures*, 153–198. Dordrecht: D. Reidel Publishing Company.

Dowty, David R. 1989. On the semantic content of the notion 'thematic role'. In Gennaro Chierchia, Barbara H. Partee & Raymond Turner (eds.), *Properties, types and meaning*, vol. 2 (Studies in Linguistics and Philosophy), 69–130. Dordrecht: Kluwer Academic Publishers.

Dowty, David R. 1991. Thematic proto-roles and argument selection. *Language* 67(3). 547–619.

Dowty, David R. 2003. The dual analysis of adjuncts and complements in Categorial Grammar. In Ewald Lang, Claudia Maienborn & Cathrine Fabricius-Hansen (eds.), *Modifying adjuncts* (Interface Explorations 4), 33–66. Berlin: Mouton de Gruyter.

Dras, Mark, François Lareau, Benjamin Börschinger, Robert Dale, Yasaman Motazedi, Owen Rambow, Myfany Turpin & Morgan Ulinski. 2012. Complex predicates in Arrernte. In Miriam Butt & Tracy Holloway King (eds.), *Proceedings of the LFG 2012 conference*, 177–197. Stanford, CA: CSLI Publications.

Drellishak, Scott. 2009. *Widespread but not universal: Improving the typological coverage of the Grammar Matrix*: University of Washington Doctoral dissertation.

Drosdowski, Günther. 1984. *Duden: Grammatik der deutschen Gegenwartssprache*, vol. 4. Mannheim, Wien, Zürich: Dudenverlag 4th edn.

Drosdowski, Günther. 1995. *Duden: Die Grammatik*, vol. 4. Mannheim, Leipzig, Wien, Zürich: Dudenverlag 5th edn.

Dryer, Matthew S. 1992. The Greenbergian word order correlations. *Language* 68(1). 81–138.

Dryer, Matthew S. 1997. Are grammatical relations universal? In Joan Bybee, John Haiman & Sandra Thompson (eds.), *Essays on language function and language type: Dedicated to T. Givon*, 115–143. Amsterdam: John Benjamins Publishing Co.

Dryer, Matthew S. 2013a. Order of adposition and noun phrase. In Matthew S. Dryer & Martin Haspelmath (eds.), *The world atlas of language structures online*, Leipzig: Max Planck Institute for Evolutionary Anthropology. http://wals.info/chapter/85.

Dryer, Matthew S. 2013b. Order of object and verb. In Matthew S. Dryer & Martin Haspelmath (eds.), *The world atlas of language structures online*, Leipzig: Max Planck Institute for Evolutionary Anthropology. http://wals.info/chapter/83.

Dryer, Matthew S. 2013c. Order of subject, object and verb. In Matthew S. Dryer & Martin Haspelmath (eds.), *The world atlas of language structures online*, Leipzig: Max Planck Institute for Evolutionary Anthropology. http://wals.info/chapter/81.

Dürscheid, Christa. 1989. *Zur Vorfeldbesetzung in deutschen Verbzweit-Strukturen* (FOKUS 1). Trier: Wissenschaftlicher Verlag.

Dyvik, Helge, Paul Meurer & Victoria Rosén. 2005. LFG, Minimal Recursion Semantics and translation. Paper presented at the LFG conference 2005.

Egg, Markus. 1999. Derivation and resolution of ambiguities in *wieder*-sentences. In Paul
J. E. Dekker (ed.), *Proceedings of the 12th Amsterdam Colloquium*, 109–114.

Eisele, Andreas & Jochen Dorre. 1986. A Lexical Functional Grammar system in Prolog. In Makoto Nagao (ed.), *Proceedings of COLING 86*, 551–553. University of Bonn:
Association for Computational Linguistics.

Eisenberg, Peter. 1992. Platos Problem und die Lernbarkeit der Syntax. In Peter Suchsland
(ed.), *Biologische und soziale Grundlagen der Sprache* (Linguistische Arbeiten 280), 371–
378. Tübingen: Max Niemeyer Verlag.

Eisenberg, Peter. 1994a. German. In Ekkehard König & Johan van der Auwera (eds.),
The Germanic languages (Routledge Language Family Descriptions), 349–387. London
/ New York: Routledge.

Eisenberg, Peter. 1994b. *Grundriß der deutschen Grammatik*. Stuttgart, Weimar: Verlag
J. B. Metzler 3rd edn.

Eisenberg, Peter. 2004. *Grundriß der deutschen Grammatik*, vol. 2. Der Satz. Stuttgart,
Weimar: Verlag J. B. Metzler 2nd edn.

Eisenberg, Peter, Jörg Peters, Peter Gallmann, Cathrine Fabricius-Hansen, Damaris
Nübling, Irmhild Barz, Thomas A. Fritz & Reinhard Fiehler. 2005. *Duden: Die Grammatik*, vol. 4. Mannheim, Leipzig, Wien, Zürich: Dudenverlag 7th edn.

Ellefson, Michelle R. & Morten Christiansen. 2000. Subjacency constraints without Universal Grammar: Evidence from artificial language learning and connectionist modeling. In *Proceedings of the 22nd Annual Conference of the Cognitive Science Society*,
645–650. Mahwah, NJ: Lawrence Erlbaum Associates.

Elman, Jeffrey L. 1993. Learning and development in neural networks: The importance
of starting small. *Cognition* 48(1). 71–99.

Elman, Jeffrey L., Elizabeth A. Bates, Mark H. Johnson, Annette Karmiloff-Smith,
Domenico Parisi & Kim Plunkett. 1996. *Rethinking innateness: A connectionist perspective on development*. Cambridge, MA: Bradford Books/MIT Press.

Embick, David. 2004. On the structure of resultative participles in English. *Linguistic
Inquiry* 35(3). 355–392.

Emirkanian, Louisette, Lyne Da Sylva & Lorne H. Bouchard. 1996. The implementation of
a computational grammar of French using the Grammar Development Environment.
In Jun-ichi Tsuji (ed.), *Proceedings of COLING-96. 16th International Conference on Computational Linguistics COLING96). Copenhagen, Denmark, August 5–9, 1996*, 1024–1027.
Copenhagen, Denmark: Association for Computational Linguistics.

Engdahl, Elisabet & Enric Vallduví. 1996. Information packaging in HPSG. In Claire
Grover & Enric Vallduví (eds.), *Edinburgh Working Papers in Cognitive Science, vol. 12:
Studies in HPSG*, chap. 1, 1–32. Scotland: Centre for Cognitive Science, University of
Edinburgh. ftp://ftp.cogsci.ed.ac.uk/pub/CCS-WPs/wp-12.ps.gz.

Engel, Ulrich. 1970. Regeln zur Wortstellung. Forschungsberichte des Instituts für deutsche Sprache 5 Institut für deutsche Sprache Mannheim.

Engel, Ulrich. 1977. *Syntax der deutschen Gegenwartssprache*, vol. 22 (Grundlagen der
Germanistik). Berlin: Erich Schmidt Verlag.

Engel, Ulrich. 1996. Tesnière mißverstanden. In Gertrud Gréciano & Helmut Schumacher (eds.), *Lucien Tesnière – Syntaxe Structurale et Opèrations Mentales. Akten des deutsch-französischen Kolloquiums anläßlich der 100. Wiederkehr seines Geburtstages. Strasbourg 1993* (Linguistische Arbeiten 348), 53–61. Tübingen: Max Niemeyer Verlag.

Engel, Ulrich. 2014. Die dependenzielle Verbgrammatik (DVG). In Jörg Hagemann & Sven Staffeldt (eds.), *Syntaxtheorien: Analysen im Vergleich* (Stauffenburg Einführungen 28), 43–62. Tübingen: Stauffenburg Verlag.

Erbach, Gregor. 1995. ProFIT: Prolog with features, inheritance and templates. In Steven P. Abney & Erhard W. Hinrichs (eds.), *Proceedings of the Seventh Conference of the European Chapter of the Association for Computational Linguistics*, 180–187. Dublin: Association for Computational Linguistics.

Ernst, Thomas. 1992. The phrase structure of English negation. *The Linguistic Review* 9(2). 109–144.

Eroms, Hans-Werner. 1985. Eine reine Dependenzgrammatik für das Deutsche. *Deutsche Sprache* 13. 306–326.

Eroms, Hans-Werner. 1987. Passiv und Passivfunktionen im Rahmen einer Dependenzgrammatik. In Centre de Recherche en Linguistique Germanique (Nice) (ed.), *Das Passiv im Deutschen* (Linguistische Arbeiten 183), 73–95. Tübingen: Max Niemeyer Verlag.

Eroms, Hans-Werner. 2000. *Syntax der deutschen Sprache* (de Gruyter Studienbuch). Berlin: Walter de Gruyter Verlag.

Eroms, Hans-Werner & Hans Jürgen Heringer. 2003. Dependenz und lineare Ordnung. In Vilmos Ágel, Ludwig M. Eichinger, Hans Werner Eroms, Peter Hellwig, Hans Jürgen Heringer & Henning Lobin (eds.), *Dependenz und Valenz / Dependency and valency: Ein internationales Handbuch der zeitgenössischen Forschung / An international handbook of contemporary research*, vol. 25.1 (Handbücher zur Sprach- und Kommunikationswissenschaft), 247–263. Berlin: Walter de Gruyter.

Eroms, Hans-Werner, Gerhard Stickel & Gisela Zifonun (eds.). 1997. *Grammatik der deutschen Sprache*, vol. 7 (Schriften des Instituts für deutsche Sprache). Berlin: Walter de Gruyter.

Erteschik-Shir, Nomi. 1973. *On the nature of island constraints*. Cambridge, MA: MIT dissertation.

Erteschik-Shir, Nomi. 1981. More on extractability from quasi-NPs. *Linguistic Inquiry* 12(4). 665–670.

Erteschik-Shir, Nomi & Shalom Lappin. 1979. Dominance and the functional explanation of island phenomena. *Theoretical Linguistics* 6(1–3). 41–86.

Estigarribia, Bruno. 2009. Facilitation by variation: Right-to-left learning of English yes/no questions. *Cognitive Science* 34(1). 68–93.

Evans, Nicholas & Stephen C. Levinson. 2009a. The myth of language universals: Language diversity and its importance for cognitive science. *The Behavioral and Brain Sciences* 32(5). 429–448.

Evans, Nicholas & Stephen C. Levinson. 2009b. With diversity in mind: Freeing the language sciences from Universal Grammar. *The Behavioral and Brain Sciences* 32(5). 472–492.

Evans, Roger. 1985. ProGram: A development tool for GPSG grammars. *Linguistics* 23(2). 213–244.

Everett, Daniel L. 2005. Cultural constraints on grammar and cognition in Pirahã. *Current Anthropology* 46(4). 621–646.

Everett, Daniel L. 2009. Pirahã culture and grammar: A response to some criticisms. *Language* 85(2). 405–442.

Evers, Arnold. 1975. *The transformational cycle in Dutch and German*: University of Utrecht dissertation.

Faaß, Gertrud. 2010. *A morphosyntactic description of Northern Sotho as a basis for an automated translation from Northern Sotho into English*. Pretoria, South Africa: University of Pretoria dissertation. http://hdl.handle.net/2263/28569.

Fabregas, Antonio, Tom Stroik & Michael Putnam. 2016. Is simplest merge too simple? Ms. Penn State University.

Falk, Yehuda N. 1984. The English auxiliary system: A Lexical-Functional analysis. *Language* 60(3). 483–509.

Fan, Zhenzhen, Sanghoun Song & Francis Bond. 2015. An HPSG-based shared-grammar for the Chinese languages: ZHONG [|]. In Emily M. Bender, Lori Levin, Stefan Müller, Yannick Parmentier & Aarne Ranta (eds.), *Proceedings of the Grammar Engineering Across Frameworks (GEAF) Workshop*, 17–24. The Association for Computational Linguistics.

Fang, Ji & Tracy Holloway King. 2007. An LFG Chinese grammar for machine use. In Tracy Holloway King & Emily M. Bender (eds.), *Grammar Engineering across Frameworks 2007* (Studies in Computational Linguistics ONLINE), 144–160. Stanford, CA: CSLI Publications. http://csli-publications.stanford.edu/GEAF/2007/.

Fanselow, Gisbert. 1981. *Zur Syntax und Semantik der Nominalkomposition* (Linguistische Arbeiten 107). Tübingen: Max Niemeyer Verlag.

Fanselow, Gisbert. 1987. *Konfigurationalität* (Studien zur deutschen Grammatik 29). Tübingen: originally Gunter Narr Verlag now Stauffenburg Verlag.

Fanselow, Gisbert. 1988. Aufspaltung von NPn und das Problem der ‚freien‘ Wortstellung. *Linguistische Berichte* 114. 91–113.

Fanselow, Gisbert. 1990. Scrambling as NP-movement. In Günther Grewendorf & Wolfgang Sternefeld (eds.), *Scrambling and Barriers* (Linguistik Aktuell/Linguistics Today 5), 113–140. Amsterdam: John Benjamins Publishing Co.

Fanselow, Gisbert. 1992a. „Ergative“ Verben und die Struktur des deutschen Mittelfelds. In Ludger Hoffmann (ed.), *Deutsche Syntax: Ansichten und Aussichten* (Institut für deutsche Sprache, Jahrbuch 1991), 276–303. Berlin: de Gruyter.

Fanselow, Gisbert. 1992b. Zur biologischen Autonomie der Grammatik. In Peter Suchsland (ed.), *Biologische und soziale Grundlagen der Sprache* (Linguistische Arbeiten 280), 335–356. Tübingen: Max Niemeyer Verlag.

Fanselow, Gisbert. 1993. Die Rückkehr der Basisgenerierer. *Groninger Arbeiten zur Germanistischen Linguistik* 36. 1–74.

Fanselow, Gisbert. 2000a. Does constituent length predict German word order in the Middle Field? In Josef Bayer & Christine Römer (eds.), *Von der Philologie zur Grammatiktheorie: Peter Suchsland zum 65. Geburtstag*, 63–77. Tübingen: Max Niemeyer Verlag.

Fanselow, Gisbert. 2000b. Optimal exceptions. In Barbara Stiebels & Dieter Wunderlich (eds.), *The lexicon in focus* (studia grammatica 45), 173–209. Berlin: Akademie Verlag.

Fanselow, Gisbert. 2001. Features, θ-roles, and free constituent order. *Linguistic Inquiry* 32(3). 405–437.

Fanselow, Gisbert. 2002. Against remnant VP-movement. In Artemis Alexiadou, Elena Anagnostopoulou, Sjef Barbiers & Hans-Martin Gärtner (eds.), *Dimensions of movement: From features to remnants* (Linguistik Aktuell/Linguistics Today 48), 91–127. Amsterdam: John Benjamins Publishing Co.

Fanselow, Gisbert. 2003a. Free constituent order: A Minimalist interface account. *Folia Linguistica* 37(1–2). 191–231.

Fanselow, Gisbert. 2003b. Münchhausen-style head movement and the analysis of verb second. In Anoop Mahajan (ed.), *Proceedings of the workshop on head movement* (UCLA Working Papers in Linguistics 10), Los Angeles: UCLA, Linguistics Department.

Fanselow, Gisbert. 2003c. Zur Generierung der Abfolge der Satzglieder im Deutschen. *Neue Beiträge zur Germanistik* 112. 3–47.

Fanselow, Gisbert. 2004a. Cyclic phonology-syntax-interaction: PPT Movement in German (and other languages). In Shinichiro Ishihara, Michaela Schmitz & Anne Schwarz (eds.), *Interdisciplinary studies on information structure* (Working Papers of the SFB 632 1), 1–42. Potsdam: Universitätsverlag.

Fanselow, Gisbert. 2004b. Fakten, Fakten, Fakten! *Linguistische Berichte* 200. 481–493.

Fanselow, Gisbert. 2004c. Münchhausen-style head movement and the analysis of verb second. In Ralf Vogel (ed.), *Three papers on German verb movement* (Linguistics in Potsdam 22), 9–49. Universität Potsdam.

Fanselow, Gisbert. 2006. On pure syntax (uncontaminated by information structure). In Patrick Brandt & Eric Fuss (eds.), *Form, structure and grammar: A festschrift presented to Günther Grewendorf on occasion of his 60th birthday* (Studia grammatica 63), 137–157. Berlin: Akademie Verlag.

Fanselow, Gisbert. 2009. Die (generative) Syntax in den Zeiten der Empiriediskussion. *Zeitschrift für Sprachwissenschaft* 28(1). 133–139.

Fanselow, Gisbert & Sascha W. Felix. 1987. *Sprachtheorie 2. Die Rektions- und Bindungstheorie* (UTB für Wissenschaft: Uni-Taschenbücher 1442). Tübingen: A. Francke Verlag GmbH.

Fanselow, Gisbert, Matthias Schlesewsky, Damir Cavar & Reinhold Kliegl. 1999. Optimal parsing, syntactic parsing preferences, and Optimality Theory. Rutgers Optimality Archive (ROA) 367 Universität Potsdam. http://roa.rutgers.edu/view.php3?roa=367.

Feldhaus, Anke. 1997. Eine HPSG-Analyse ausgewählter Phänomene des deutschen *w*-Fragesatzes. Working Papers of the Institute for Logic and Linguistics 27 Institute for Logic and Linguistics IBM Scientific Center Heidelberg.

Feldman, Jerome. 1972. Some decidability results on grammatical inference and complexity. *Information and Control* 20(3). 244–262.

Fillmore, Charles J. 1968. The case for case. In Emmon Bach & Robert T. Harms (eds.), *Universals of linguistic theory*, 1–88. New York: Holt, Rinehart, and Winston.

Fillmore, Charles J. 1971. Plädoyer für Kasus. In Werner Abraham (ed.), *Kasustheorie* (Schwerpunkte Linguistik und Kommunikationswissenschaft 2), 1–118. Frankfurt/Main: Athenäum.

Fillmore, Charles J. 1988. The mechanisms of "Construction Grammar". In Shelley Axmaker, Annie Jaisser & Helen Singmaster (eds.), *Proceedings of the 14th Annual Meeting of the Berkeley Linguistics Society*, 35–55. Berkeley, CA: Berkeley Linguistics Society.

Fillmore, Charles J. 1999. Inversion and Constructional inheritance. In Gert Webelhuth, Jean-Pierre Koenig & Andreas Kathol (eds.), *Lexical and Constructional aspects of linguistic explanation* (Studies in Constraint-Based Lexicalism 1), 113–128. Stanford, CA: CSLI Publications.

Fillmore, Charles J., Paul Kay & Mary Catherine O'Connor. 1988. Regularity and idiomaticity in grammatical constructions: The case of *let alone*. *Language* 64(3). 501–538.

Fillmore, Charles J., Russell R. Lee-Goldmann & Russell Rhomieux. 2012. The FrameNet constructicon. In Hans C. Boas & Ivan A. Sag (eds.), *Sign-based Construction Grammar* (CSLI Lecture Notes 193), 309–372. Stanford, CA: CSLI Publications.

Fischer, Ingrid & Martina Keil. 1996. Parsing decomposable idioms. In Jun-ichi Tsuji (ed.), *Proceedings of COLING-96. 16th International Conference on Computational Linguistics COLING96). Copenhagen, Denmark, August 5–9, 1996*, 388–393. Copenhagen, Denmark: Association for Computational Linguistics.

Fischer, Kerstin & Anatol Stefanowitsch (eds.). 2006. *Konstruktionsgrammatik: Von der Anwendung zur Theorie* (Stauffenburg Linguistik 40). Tübingen: Stauffenburg Verlag.

Fisher, Simon E. & Gary F. Marcus. 2005. The eloquent ape: Genes, brains and the evolution of language. *Nature Reviews Genetics* 7(1). 9–20.

Fisher, Simon E., Faraneh Vargha-Khadem, Kate E. Watkins, Anthony P. Monaco & Marcus E. Pembrey. 1998. Localisation of a gene implicated in a severe speech and language disorder. *Nature Genetics* 18(2). 168–170.

Fitch, W. Tecumseh. 2010. Three meanings of "recursion": Key distinctions for biolinguistics. In Richard K. Larson, Viviane Déprez & Hiroko Yamakido (eds.), *The evolution of human language: Biolinguistic perspectives* (Approaches to the Evolution of Language 2), 73–90. Cambridge, UK: Cambridge University Press.

Fitch, W. Tecumseh, Marc D. Hauser & Noam Chomsky. 2005. The evolution of the language faculty: Clarifications and implications. *Cognition* 97(2). 179–210.

Flickinger, Daniel P. 1983. Lexical heads and phrasal gaps. In *Proceedings of the West Coast Conference on Formal Linguistics*, vol. 2, Stanford University Linguistics Dept.

Flickinger, Daniel P. 1987. *Lexical rules in the hierarchical lexicon*: Stanford University dissertation.

Flickinger, Daniel P. 2000. On building a more efficient grammar by exploiting types. *Natural Language Engineering* 6(1). 15–28.

Flickinger, Daniel P. 2008. Transparent heads. In Stefan Müller (ed.), *Proceedings of the 15th International Conference on Head-Driven Phrase Structure Grammar*, 87–94. Stanford, CA: CSLI Publications. http://csli-publications.stanford.edu/HPSG/2008/abstr-flickinger.shtml.

Flickinger, Daniel P. & Emily M. Bender. 2003. Compositional semantics in a multilingual grammar resource. In Emily M. Bender, Daniel P. Flickinger, Frederik Fouvry & Melanie Siegel (eds.), *Proceedings of the ESSLLI 2003 Workshop "Ideas and Strategies for Multilingual Grammar Development"*, 33–42. Vienna, Austria.

Flickinger, Daniel P., Ann Copestake & Ivan A. Sag. 2000. HPSG analysis of English. In Wolfgang Wahlster (ed.), *Verbmobil: Foundations of speech-to-speech translation* (Artificial Intelligence), 254–263. Berlin: Springer Verlag.

Flickinger, Daniel P., Carl J. Pollard & Thomas Wasow. 1985. Structure-sharing in lexical representation. In William C. Mann (ed.), *Proceedings of the Twenty-Third Annual Meeting of the Association for Computational Linguistics*, 262–267. Chicago, IL: Association for Computational Linguistics.

Fodor, Janet Dean. 1998a. Parsing to learn. *Journal of Psycholinguistic Research* 27(3). 339–374.

Fodor, Janet Dean. 1998b. Unambiguous triggers. *Linguistic Inquiry* 29(1). 1–36.

Fodor, Janet Dean. 2001. Parameters and the periphery: Reflections on *syntactic nuts*. *Journal of Linguistics* 37. 367–392.

Fodor, Jerry A., Thomas G. Bever & Merrill F. Garrett. 1974. *The psychology of language: An introduction to psycholinguistics and Generative Grammar*. New York: McGraw-Hill Book Co.

Fokkens, Antske. 2011. Metagrammar engineering: Towards systematic exploration of implemented grammars. In *Proceedings of the 49th Annual Meeting of the Association for Computational Linguistics: Human Language Technologies*, 1066–1076. Portland, Oregon, USA: Association for Computational Linguistics. http://www.aclweb.org/anthology/P11-1107.

Fokkens, Antske, Laurie Poulson & Emily M. Bender. 2009. Inflectional morphology in Turkish VP coordination. In Stefan Müller (ed.), *Proceedings of the 16th International Conference on Head-Driven Phrase Structure Grammar, University of Göttingen, Germany*, 110–130. Stanford, CA: CSLI Publications.

Fong, Sandiway. 1991. *Computational properties of principle-based grammatical theories*: MIT Artificial Intelligence Lab dissertation.

Fong, Sandiway. 2014. Unification and efficient computation in the Minimalist Program. In L. Francis & L. Laurent (eds.), *Language and recursion*, 129–138. Berlin: Springer Verlag.

Fong, Sandiway & Jason Ginsburg. 2012. Computation with doubling constituents: Pronouns and antecedents in Phase Theory. In Anna Maria Di Sciullo (ed.), *To-*

wards a Biolinguistic understanding of grammar: Essays on interfaces (Linguistik Aktuell/Linguistics Today 194), 303–338. Amsterdam: John Benjamins Publishing Co.

Fordham, Andrew & Matthew Walter Crocker. 1994. Parsing with principles and probabilities. In Judith L. Klavans Philip Resnik (ed.), *The balancing act: Combining symbolic and statistical approaches to language*, Las Cruces, New Mexico, USA: Association for Computational Linguistics.

Forst, Martin. 2006. COMP in (parallel) grammar writing. In Miriam Butt & Tracy Holloway King (eds.), *Proceedings of the LFG 2006 conference*, Stanford, CA: CSLI Publications. http://csli-publications.stanford.edu/LFG/11/lfg06forst.pdf.

Forst, Martin & Christian Rohrer. 2009. Problems of German VP coordination. In Miriam Butt & Tracy Holloway King (eds.), *Proceedings of the LFG 2009 conference*, 297–316. Stanford, CA: CSLI Publications. http://csli-publications.stanford.edu/LFG/14/.

Fortmann, Christian. 1996. *Konstituentenbewegung in der DP-Struktur: Zur funktionalen Analyse der Nominalphrase im Deutschen* (Linguistische Arbeiten 347). Tübingen: Max Niemeyer Verlag.

Fourquet, Jean. 1957. Review of: Heinz Anstock: Deutsche Syntax – Lehr- und Übungsbuch. *Wirkendes Wort* 8. 120–122.

Fourquet, Jean. 1970. *Prolegomena zu einer deutschen Grammatik* (Sprache der Gegenwart – Schriften des Instituts für deutsche Sprache in Mannheim 7). Düsseldorf: Pädagogischer Verlag Schwann.

Fouvry, Frederik. 2003. Lexicon acquisition with a large-coverage unification-based grammar. In *Proceedings of EACL 03, 10th Conference of the European Chapter of the Association for Computational Linguistics, research notes and demos, April 12–17, 2003, Budapest, Hungary*, 87–90.

Fraj, Fériel Ben, Chiraz Zribi & Mohamed Ben Ahmed. 2008. ArabTAG: A Tree Adjoining Grammar for Arabic syntactic structures. In *Proceedings of the International Arab Conference on Information Technology*, Sfax, Tunisia.

Frank, Anette. 1994. Verb second by lexical rule or by underspecification. Arbeitspapiere des SFB 340 No. 43 IBM Deutschland GmbH Heidelberg. ftp://ftp.ims.uni-stuttgart.de/pub/papers/anette/v2-usp.ps.gz.

Frank, Anette. 1996. Eine LFG-Grammatik des Französischen. In *Deutsche und französische Syntax im Formalismus der LFG* (Linguistische Arbeiten 344), 97–244. Tübingen: Max Niemeyer Verlag.

Frank, Anette. 2006. (Discourse-) functional analysis of asymmetric coordination. In Miriam Butt, Mary Dalrymple & Tracy Holloway King (eds.), *Intelligent linguistic architectures: Variations on themes by Ronald M. Kaplan*, 259–285. Stanford, CA: CSLI Publications.

Frank, Anette & Uwe Reyle. 1995. Principle based semantics for HPSG. In Steven P. Abney & Erhard W. Hinrichs (eds.), *Proceedings of the Seventh Conference of the European Chapter of the Association for Computational Linguistics*, 9–16. Dublin: Association for Computational Linguistics.

Frank, Anette & Annie Zaenen. 2002. Tense in LFG: Syntax and morphology. In Hans Kamp & Uwe Reyle (eds.), *How we say when it happens: Contributions to the theory of temporal reference in natural language*, 17–52. Tübingen: Max Niemeyer Verlag. Reprint as: Frank & Zaenen (2004).

Frank, Anette & Annie Zaenen. 2004. Tense in LFG: Syntax and morphology. In Louisa Sadler & Andrew Spencer (eds.), *Projecting morphology*, 23–66. Stanford, CA: CSLI Publications.

Frank, Robert. 2002. *Phrase structure composition and syntactic dependencies* (Current Studies in Linguistics 38). Cambridge, MA/London: MIT Press.

Franks, Steven. 1995. *Parameters in Slavic morphosyntax*. New York, Oxford: Oxford University Press.

Frazier, Lyn. 1985. Syntactic complexity. In David R. Dowty, Lauri Karttunen & Arnold M. Zwicky (eds.), *Natural language processing*, 129–189. Cambridge, UK: Cambridge University Press.

Frazier, Lyn & Charles Clifton. 1996. *Construal*. Cambridge, MA: MIT Press.

Freidin, Robert. 1975. The analysis of passives. *Language* 51(2). 384–405.

Freidin, Robert. 1997. Review article: The Minimalist Program. *Language* 73(3). 571–582.

Freidin, Robert. 2009. A note on methodology in linguistics. *The Behavioral and Brain Sciences* 32(5). 454–455.

Freudenthal, Daniel, Julian M. Pine, Javier Aguado-Orea & Fernand Gobet. 2007. Modeling the developmental patterning of finiteness marking in English, Dutch, German, and Spanish using MOSAIC. *Cognitive Science* 31(2). 311–341.

Freudenthal, Daniel, Julian M. Pine & Fernand Gobet. 2006. Modeling the development of children's use of optional infinitives in Dutch and English using MOSAIC. *Cognitive Science* 30(2). 277–310.

Freudenthal, Daniel, Julian M. Pine & Fernand Gobet. 2009. Simulating the referential properties of Dutch, German, and English root infinitives in MOSAIC. *Language Learning and Development* 5(1). 1–29.

Frey, Werner. 1993. *Syntaktische Bedingungen für die semantische Interpretation: Über Bindung, implizite Argumente und Skopus* (studia grammatica 35). Berlin: Akademie Verlag.

Frey, Werner. 2000. Über die syntaktische Position der Satztopiks im Deutschen. In Ewald Lang, Marzena Rochon, Kerstin Schwabe & Oliver Teuber (eds.), *Issues on topics* (ZAS Papers in Linguistics 20), 137–172. Berlin: ZAS, Humboldt-Universität zu Berlin.

Frey, Werner. 2001. About the whereabouts of indefinites. *Theoretical Linguistics* 27(2/3). 137–161. DOI:10.1515/thli.2001.27.2-3.137. Special Issue: NP Interpretation and Information Structure, Edited by Klaus von Heusinger and Kerstin Schwabe.

Frey, Werner. 2004a. The grammar-pragmatics interface and the German prefield. Forschungsprogramm Sprache und Pragmatik 52 Germanistisches Institut der Universität Lund.

Frey, Werner. 2004b. A medial topic position for German. *Linguistische Berichte* 198. 153–190.

Frey, Werner. 2005. Pragmatic properties of certain German and English left peripheral constructions. *Linguistics* 43(1). 89–129.

Frey, Werner & Hans-Martin Gärtner. 2002. On the treatment of scrambling and adjunction in Minimalist Grammars. In Gerhard Jäger, Paola Monachesi, Gerald Penn & Shuly Wintner (eds.), *Proceedings of Formal Grammar 2002*, 41–52. Trento.

Frey, Werner & Uwe Reyle. 1983a. Lexical Functional Grammar und Diskursrepräsentationstheorie als Grundlagen eines sprachverarbeitenden Systems. *Linguistische Berichte* 88. 79–100.

Frey, Werner & Uwe Reyle. 1983b. A Prolog implementation of Lexical Functional Grammar as a base for a natural language processing system. In Antonio Zampolli (ed.), *First Conference of the European Chapter of the Association for Computational Linguistics: Proceedings of the conference*, 52–57. Pisa, Italy: Association for Computational Linguistics. http://aclweb.org/anthology/E/E83/.

Fried, Mirjam. 2013. Principles of constructional change. In Thomas Hoffmann & Graeme Trousdale (eds.), *The Oxford handbook of Construction Grammar* (Oxford Handbooks), 419–437. Oxford: Oxford University Press.

Fried, Mirjam. 2015. Construction Grammar. In Tibor Kiss & Artemis Alexiadou (eds.), *Syntax – theory and analysis: An international handbook*, vol. 42 (Handbooks of Linguistics and Communication Science), 974–1003. Berlin: Mouton de Gruyter 2nd edn.

Friederici, Angela D. 2009. Pathways to language: Fiber tracts in the human brain. *Trends in Cognitive Sciences* 13(4). 175–181.

Friedman, Joyce. 1969. Applications of a computer system for Transformational Grammar. In Research Group for Quantitative Linguistics (ed.), *Proceedings of COLING 69*, 1–27.

Friedman, Joyce, Thomas H. Bredt, Robert W. Doran, Bary W. Pollack & Theodore S. Martner. 1971. *A computer model of Transformational Grammar* (Mathematical Linguistics and Automatic Language Processing 9). New York: Elsevier.

Fries, Norbert. 1988. Über das Null-Topik im Deutschen. Forschungsprogramm Sprache und Pragmatik 3 Germanistisches Institut der Universität Lund.

Fukui, Naoki & Margaret Speas. 1986. Specifiers and projection. In N. Fukui, T. R. Rapoport & E. Sagey (eds.), *Papers in theoretical linguistics* (MIT Working Papers 8), 128–172. Cambridge, MA: MIT.

Gaifman, Haim. 1965. Dependency systems and phrase-structure systems. *Information and Control* 8. 304–397.

Gallmann, Peter. 2003. Grundlagen der deutschen Grammatik. Lecture notes Friedrich-Schiller-Universität Jena. http://www.syntax-theorie.de.

Gardner, R. Allen. 1957. Probability-learning with two and three choices. *The American Journal of Psychology* 70(2). 174–185.

Gärtner, Hans-Martin & Jens Michaelis. 2007. Some remarks on locality conditions and Minimalist Grammars. In Uli Sauerland & Hans-Martin Gärtner (eds.), *Interfaces + recursion = language? Chomsky's Minimalism and the view from syntax-semantics* (Studies in Generative Grammar 89), 161–195. Berlin: Mouton de Gruyter.

Gärtner, Hans-Martin & Markus Steinbach. 1997. Anmerkungen zur Vorfeldphobie pronominaler Elemente. In Franz-Josef d'Avis & Uli Lutz (eds.), *Zur Satzstruktur im*

Deutschen (Arbeitspapiere des SFB 340 No. 90), 1–30. Tübingen: Eberhard-Karls-Universität Tübingen.

Gazdar, Gerald. 1981a. On syntactic categories. *Philosophical Transactions of the Royal Society of London. Series B, Biological Sciences* 295(1077). 267–283.

Gazdar, Gerald. 1981b. Unbounded dependencies and coordinate structure. *Linguistic Inquiry* 12. 155–184.

Gazdar, Gerald, Ewan Klein, Geoffrey K. Pullum & Ivan A. Sag. 1985. *Generalized Phrase Structure Grammar*. Cambridge, MA: Harvard University Press.

Gazdar, Gerald, Geoffrey K. Pullum, Bob Carpenter, Ewan Klein, Thomas E. Hukari & Robert D. Levine. 1988. Category structures. *Computational Linguistics* 14(1). 1–19.

Geach, Peter Thomas. 1970. A program for syntax. *Synthese* 22. 3–17.

Geißler, Stefan & Tibor Kiss. 1994. Erläuterungen zur Umsetzung einer HPSG im Basisformalismus STUF III. Tech. Rep. 19 IBM Informationssysteme GmbH – Institut für Logik und Linguistik (Verbundvorhaben Verbmobil) Heidelberg.

Gerdes, Kim. 2002a. DTAG? In *Proceedings of the Sixth International Workshop on Tree Adjoining Grammar and Related Frameworks (TAG+6)*, 242–251. Universitá di Venezia.

Gerdes, Kim. 2002b. *Topologie et grammaires formelles de l'allemand*: Ecole doctorale Science du langage, UFR de linguistique, Université Paris 7 dissertation.

Gerdes, Kim & Sylvain Kahane. 2001. Word order in German: A formal Dependency Grammar using a topological hierarchy. In *Proceedings of the 39th Annual Meeting on Association for Computational Linguistics*, 220–227. Stroudsburg, PA, USA: Association for Computational Linguistics. DOI:10.3115/1073012.1073041.

Gerken, LouAnn. 1991. The metrical basis for children's subjectless sentences. *Journal of Memory and Language* 30. 431–451.

Gibson, Edward. 1998. Linguistic complexity: Locality of syntactic dependencies. *Cognition* 68(1). 1–76.

Gibson, Edward & James Thomas. 1999. Memory limitations and structural forgetting: The perception of complex ungrammatical sentences as grammatical. *Language and Cognitive Processes* 14(3). 225–248.

Gibson, Edward & Kenneth Wexler. 1994. Triggers. *Linguistic Inquiry* 25(3). 407–454.

Ginzburg, Jonathan & Ivan A. Sag. 2000. *Interrogative investigations: The form, meaning, and use of English interrogatives* (CSLI Lecture Notes 123). Stanford, CA: CSLI Publications.

Gold, Mark E. 1967. Language identification in the limit. *Information and Control* 10(5). 447–474.

Goldberg, Adele E. 1995. *Constructions: A Construction Grammar approach to argument structure* (Cognitive Theory of Language and Culture). Chicago/London: The University of Chicago Press.

Goldberg, Adele E. 2003a. Constructions: A new theoretical approach to language. *Trends in Cognitive Sciences* 7(5). 219–224.

Goldberg, Adele E. 2003b. Words by default: The Persian Complex Predicate Construction. In Elaine J. Francis & Laura A. Michaelis (eds.), *Mismatch: Form-function incon-*

gruity and the architecture of grammar (CSLI Lecture Notes 163), 117–146. Stanford, CA: CSLI Publications.

Goldberg, Adele E. 2006. *Constructions at work: The nature of generalization in language* (Oxford Linguistics). Oxford, New York: Oxford University Press.

Goldberg, Adele E. 2009. Constructions work. [response]. *Cognitive Linguistics* 20(1). 201–224.

Goldberg, Adele E. 2013a. Argument structure Constructions vs. lexical rules or derivational verb templates. *Mind and Language* 28(4). 435–465.

Goldberg, Adele E. 2013b. Explanation and Constructions: Response to Adger. *Mind and Language* 28(4). 479–491.

Goldberg, Adele E. 2014. Fitting a slim dime between the verb template and argument structure construction approaches. *Theoretical Linguistics* 40(1–2). 113–135.

Goldberg, Adele E., Devin Casenhiser & Nitya Sethuraman. 2004. Learning argument structure generalizations. *Cognitive Linguistics* 15(3). 289–316.

Goldberg, Adele E. & Ray S. Jackendoff. 2004. The English resultative as a family of Constructions. *Language* 80(3). 532–568.

Gopnik, Myrna & Martha B. Cargo. 1991. Familial aggregation of a developmental language disorder. *Cognition* 39(1). 1–50.

Gordon, Peter. 1986. Level ordering in lexical development. *Cognition* 21(2). 73–93.

Gosch, Angela, Gabriele Städing & Rainer Pankau. 1994. Linguistic abilities in children with Williams-Beuren Syndrome. *American Journal of Medical Genetics* 52(3). 291–296.

Götz, Thilo, Walt Detmar Meurers & Dale Gerdemann. 1997. The ConTroll manual: (Con-Troll v.1.0 beta, XTroll v.5.0 beta). User's manual Seminar für Sprachwissenschaft Universität Tübingen. http://www.sfs.uni-tuebingen.de/controll/code.html.

Grebe, Paul & Helmut Gipper. 1966. *Duden: Grammatik der deutschen Gegenwartssprache*, vol. 4. Mannheim, Wien, Zürich: Dudenverlag 2nd edn.

Green, Georgia M. 2011. Modelling grammar growth: Universal Grammar without innate principles or parameters. In Robert D. Borsley & Kersti Börjars (eds.), *Non-transformational syntax: Formal and explicit models of grammar: A guide to current models*, 378–403. Oxford, UK/Cambridge, MA: Blackwell Publishing Ltd.

Grewendorf, Günther. 1983. Reflexivierungen in deutschen A.c.I.-Konstruktionen – kein transformationsgrammatisches Dilemma mehr. *Groninger Arbeiten zur Germanistischen Linguistik* 23. 120–196.

Grewendorf, Günther. 1985. Anaphern bei Objekt-Koreferenz im Deutschen: Ein Problem für die Rektions-Bindungs-Theorie. In Werner Abraham (ed.), *Erklärende Syntax des Deutschen* (Studien zur deutschen Grammatik 25), 137–171. Tübingen: originally Gunter Narr Verlag now Stauffenburg Verlag.

Grewendorf, Günther. 1987. Kohärenz und Restrukturierung: Zu verbalen Komplexen im Deutschen. In Brigitte Asbach-Schnitker & Johannes Roggenhofer (eds.), *Neuere Forschungen zur Wortbildung und Histographie: Festgabe für Herbert E. Brekle zum 50. Geburtstag* (Tübinger Beiträge zur Linguistik 284), 123–144. Tübingen: Gunter Narr Verlag.

Grewendorf, Günther. 1988. *Aspekte der deutschen Syntax: Eine Rektions-Bindungs-Analyse* (Studien zur deutschen Grammatik 33). Tübingen: originally Gunter Narr Verlag now Stauffenburg Verlag.

Grewendorf, Günther. 1989. *Ergativity in German* (Studies in Generative Grammar 35). Dordrecht: Foris Publications.

Grewendorf, Günther. 1993. German: A grammatical sketch. In Joachim Jacobs, Arnim von Stechow, Wolfgang Sternefeld & Theo Vennemann (eds.), *Syntax – Ein internationales Handbuch zeitgenössischer Forschung*, vol. 9.2 (Handbücher zur Sprach- und Kommunikationswissenschaft), 1288–1319. Berlin: Walter de Gruyter Verlag.

Grewendorf, Günther. 2002. *Minimalistische Syntax* (UTB für Wissenschaft: Uni-Taschenbücher 2313). Tübingen, Basel: A. Francke Verlag GmbH.

Grewendorf, Güther. 2009. The left clausal periphery: Clitic left dislocation in Italian and left dislocation in German. In Benjamin Shear, Philippa Helen Cook, Werner Frey & Claudia Maienborn (eds.), *Dislocated elements in discourse: Syntactic, semantic, and pragmatic perspectives* (Routledge Studies in Germanic Linguistics), 49–94. New York: Routledge.

Grimshaw, Jane. 1986. Subjacency and the S/S′ Parameter. *Linguistic Inquiry* 17(2). 364–369.

Grimshaw, Jane. 1997. Projections, heads, and optimality. *Linguistic Inquiry* 28. 373–422.

Grinberg, Dennis, John D. Lafferty & Daniel Dominic Sleator. 1995. A robust parsing algorithm for Link Grammars. In *Proceedings of the Fourth International Workshop on Parsing Technologies*, http://arxiv.org/abs/cmp-lg/9508003. Also as Carnegie Mellon University Computer Science Technical Report CMU-CS-95-125.

Groos, Anneke & Henk van Riemsdijk. 1981. Matching effects in free relatives: A parameter of core grammar. In A. Belletti, L. Brandi & L. Rizzi (eds.), *Theory of markedness in Generative Grammar*, 171–216. Pisa: Scuola Normale Superiore.

Groß, Thomas M. & Timothy Osborne. 2009. Toward a practical Dependency Grammar theory of discontinuities. *SKY Journal of Linguistics* 22. 43–90.

Groß, Thomas Michael. 2003. Dependency Grammar's limits – and ways of extending them. In Vilmos Ágel, Ludwig M. Eichinger, Hans Werner Eroms, Peter Hellwig, Hans Jürgen Heringer & Henning Lobin (eds.), *Dependenz und Valenz / Dependency and valency: Ein internationales Handbuch der zeitgenössischen Forschung / An international handbook of contemporary research*, vol. 25.1 (Handbücher zur Sprach- und Kommunikationswissenschaft), 331–351. Berlin: Walter de Gruyter.

Grosu, Alexander. 1973. On the status of the so-called Right Roof Constraint. *Language* 49(2). 294–311.

Grover, Claire, John Carroll & Ted J. Briscoe. 1993. The Alvey Natural Language Tools grammar (4th release). Technical Report 284 Computer Laboratory, Cambridge University, UK.

Grubačić, Emilija. 1965. *Untersuchungen zur Frage der Wortstellung in der deutschen Prosadichtung der letzten Jahrzehnte*. Zagreb: Philosophische Fakultät dissertation.

Gruber, Jeffrey. 1965. *Studies in lexical relations*: MIT dissertation.

Gunji, Takao. 1986. Subcategorization and word order. In William J. Poser (ed.), *Papers from the Second International Workshop on Japanese Syntax*, 1–21. Stanford, CA: CSLI Publications.

Günther, Carsten, Claudia Maienborn & Andrea Schopp. 1999. The processing of information structure. In Peter Bosch & Rob van der Sandt (eds.), *Focus: Linguistic, cognitive, and computational perspectives* (Studies in Natural Language Processing), 18–42. Cambridge, UK: Cambridge University Press. Rev. papers orig. presented at a conference held 1994, Schloss Wolfsbrunnen, Germany.

Guo, Yuqing, Haifeng Wang & Josef van Genabith. 2007. Recovering non-local dependencies for Chinese. In *Proceedings of the Joint Conference on Empirical Methods in Natural Language Processing and Natural Language Learning, (EMNLP-CoNLL 2007)*, 257–266. Prague, Czech Republic: Association for Computational Linguistics.

Guzmán Naranjo, Matías. 2015. Unifying everything: Integrating quantitative effects into formal models of grammar. In *Proceedings of the 6th Conference on Quantitative Investigations in Theoretical Linguistics*, DOI:10.15496/publikation-8636.

Haddar, Kais, Sirine Boukedi & Ines Zalila. 2010. Construction of an HPSG grammar for the Arabic language and its specification in TDL. *International Journal on Information and Communication Technologies* 3(3). 52–64.

Haegeman, Liliane. 1994. *Introduction to Government and Binding Theory* (Blackwell Textbooks in Linguistics 1). Oxford, UK/Cambridge, USA: Blackwell Publishing Ltd 2nd edn.

Haegeman, Liliane. 1995. *The syntax of negation*. Cambridge, UK: Cambridge University Press.

Haftka, Brigitta. 1995. Syntactic positions for topic and contrastive focus in the German middlefield. In Inga Kohlhof, Susanne Winkler & Hans-Bernhard Drubig (eds.), *Proceedings of the Göttingen Focus Workshop, 17 DGfS, March 1–3* (Arbeitspapiere des SFB 340 No. 69), 137–157. Eberhard-Karls-Universität Tübingen.

Haftka, Brigitta. 1996. Deutsch ist eine V/2-Sprache mit Verbendstellung und freier Wortfolge. In Ewald Lang & Gisela Zifonun (eds.), *Deutsch – typologisch* (Institut für deutsche Sprache, Jahrbuch 1995), 121–141. Berlin: Walter de Gruyter.

Hagen, Kristin, Janne Bondi Johannessen & Anders Nøklestad. 2000. A constraint-based tagger for Norwegian. In C.-E. Lindberg & S. N. Lund (eds.), *17th Scandinavian Conference of Linguistic, Odense*, vol. I (Odense Working Papers in Language and Communication 19), 1–15.

Hahn, Michael. 2011. Null conjuncts and bound pronouns in Arabic. In Stefan Müller (ed.), *Proceedings of the 18th International Conference on Head-Driven Phrase Structure Grammar, University of Washington*, 60–80. Stanford, CA: CSLI Publications. http://csli-publications.stanford.edu/HPSG/2011/.

Haider, Hubert. 1982. Dependenzen und Konfigurationen: Zur deutschen V-Projektion. *Groninger Arbeiten zur Germanistischen Linguistik* 21. 1–60.

Haider, Hubert. 1984. Was zu haben ist und was zu sein hat – Bemerkungen zum Infinitiv. *Papiere zur Linguistik* 30(1). 23–36.

Haider, Hubert. 1985a. The case of German. In Jindřich Toman (ed.), *Studies in German grammar* (Studies in Generative Grammar 21), 23–64. Dordrecht: Foris Publications.

Haider, Hubert. 1985b. Über *sein* oder nicht *sein*: Zur Grammatik des Pronomens *sich*. In Werner Abraham (ed.), *Erklärende Syntax des Deutschen* (Studien zur deutschen Grammatik 25), 223–254. Tübingen: originally Gunter Narr Verlag now Stauffenburg Verlag.

Haider, Hubert. 1986a. Fehlende Argumente: Vom Passiv zu kohärenten Infinitiven. *Linguistische Berichte* 101. 3–33.

Haider, Hubert. 1986b. Nicht-sententiale Infinitive. *Groninger Arbeiten zur Germanistischen Linguistik* 28. 73–114.

Haider, Hubert. 1990a. Pro-bleme? In Gisbert Fanselow & Sascha W. Felix (eds.), *Strukturen und Merkmale syntaktischer Kategorien* (Studien zur deutschen Grammatik 39), 121–143. Tübingen: originally Gunter Narr Verlag now Stauffenburg Verlag.

Haider, Hubert. 1990b. Topicalization and other puzzles of German syntax. In Günther Grewendorf & Wolfgang Sternefeld (eds.), *Scrambling and Barriers* (Linguistik Aktuell/ Linguistics Today 5), 93–112. Amsterdam: John Benjamins Publishing Co.

Haider, Hubert. 1991. Fakultativ kohärente Infinitivkonstruktionen im Deutschen. Arbeitspapiere des SFB 340 No. 17 IBM Deutschland GmbH Heidelberg.

Haider, Hubert. 1993. *Deutsche Syntax – generativ: Vorstudien zur Theorie einer projektiven Grammatik* (Tübinger Beiträge zur Linguistik 325). Tübingen: Gunter Narr Verlag.

Haider, Hubert. 1994. (Un-)heimliche Subjekte: Anmerkungen zur Pro-drop Causa, im Anschluß an die Lektüre von Osvaldo Jaeggli & Kenneth J. Safir, eds., The Null Subject Parameter. *Linguistische Berichte* 153. 372–385.

Haider, Hubert. 1995. Studies on phrase structure and economy. Arbeitspapiere des SFB 340 No. 70 Universität Stuttgart Stuttgart.

Haider, Hubert. 1997a. Projective economy: On the minimal functional structure of the German clause. In Werner Abraham & Elly van Gelderen (eds.), *German: Syntactic problems—Problematic syntax* (Linguistische Arbeiten 374), 83–103. Tübingen: Max Niemeyer Verlag.

Haider, Hubert. 1997b. Typological implications of a directionality constraint on projections. In Artemis Alexiadou & T. Alan Hall (eds.), *Studies on Universal Grammar and typological variation* (Linguistik Aktuell/Linguistics Today 13), 17–33. Amsterdam: John Benjamins Publishing Co.

Haider, Hubert. 1999. The license to license: Structural case plus economy yields Burzio's Generalization. In Eric Reuland (ed.), *Arguments and case: Explaining Burzio's Generalization* (Linguistik Aktuell/Linguistics Today 34), 31–55. Amsterdam: John Benjamins Publishing Co.

Haider, Hubert. 2000. OV is more basic than VO. In Peter Svenonius (ed.), *The derivation of VO and OV*, 45–67. Amsterdam: John Benjamins Publishing Co.

Haider, Hubert. 2001. Parametrisierung in der Generativen Grammatik. In Martin Haspelmath, Ekkehard König, Wulf Oesterreicher & Wolfgang Raible (eds.), *Sprachtypologie und sprachliche Universalien – Language typology and language universals: Ein internationales Handbuch – An international handbook*, 283–294. Berlin: Mouton de Gruyter.

Haider, Hubert. 2014. Scientific ideology in grammar theory. Ms. Universität Salzburg, Dept. of Linguistics and Centre for Cognitive Neuroscience.

Hajičová, Eva & Petr Sgall. 2003. Dependency Syntax in Functional Generative Description. In Vilmos Ágel, Ludwig M. Eichinger, Hans Werner Eroms, Peter Hellwig, Hans Jürgen Heringer & Henning Lobin (eds.), *Dependenz und Valenz / Dependency and valency: Ein internationales Handbuch der zeitgenössischen Forschung / An international handbook of contemporary research*, vol. 25.1 (Handbücher zur Sprach- und Kommunikationswissenschaft), 570–592. Berlin: Walter de Gruyter.

Hakuta, Kenji, Ellen Bialystok & Edward Wiley. 2003. Critical evidence: A test of the Critical-Period Hypothesis for second-language acquisition. *Psychological Science* 14(1). 31–38.

Hale, Kenneth. 1976. The adjoined relative clause in Australia. In R.M.W. Dixon (ed.), *Grammatical catgeories of Australian languages* (Linguistic Series 22), 78–105. New Jersey: Humanities Press.

Hale, Kenneth & Samuel Jay Keyser. 1993. On argument structure and the lexical expression of syntactic relations. In Kenneth Hale & Samuel Jay Keyser (eds.), *The view from building 20: Essays in linguistics in honor of Sylvain Bromberger* (Current Studies in Linguistics 24), 53–109. Cambridge, MA/London: MIT Press.

Hale, Kenneth & Samuel Jay Keyser. 1997. On the complex nature of simple predicators. In Alex Alsina, Joan Bresnan & Peter Sells (eds.), *Complex predicates* (CSLI Lecture Notes 64), 29–65. Stanford, CA: CSLI Publications.

Han, Chung-hye, Juntae Yoon, Nari Kim & Martha Palmer. 2000. A feature-based Lexicalized Tree Adjoining Grammar for Korean. Technical Report IRCS-00-04 University of Pennsylvania Institute for Research in Cognitive Science. http://repository.upenn. edu/ircs_reports/35/.

Harbour, Daniel. 2011. Mythomania? Methods and morals from 'The myth of language universals'. *Lingua* 121(12). 1820–1830.

Harley, Heidi & Rolf Noyer. 2000. Formal versus encyclopedic properties of vocabulary: Evidence from nominalizations. In Bert Peeters (ed.), *The lexicon–encyclopedia interface*, 349–374. Amsterdam: Elsevier.

Harman, Gilbert. 1963. Generative grammars without transformation rules: A defence of phrase structure. *Language* 39. 597–616.

Harris, Zellig S. 1957. Co-occurrence and transformation in linguistic structure. *Language* 33(3). 283–340.

Haspelmath, Martin. 2008. Parametric versus functional explanations of syntactic universals. In T. Biberauer (ed.), *The limits of syntactic variation*, 75–107. Amsterdam: John Benjamins Publishing Co.

Haspelmath, Martin. 2009. The best-supported language universals refer to scalar patterns deriving from processing costs. *The Behavioral and Brain Sciences* 32(5). 457–458.

Haspelmath, Martin. 2010a. Comparative concepts and descriptive categories in crosslinguistic studies. *Language* 86(3). 663–687.

Haspelmath, Martin. 2010b. Framework-free grammatical theory. In Bernd Heine & Heiko Narrog (eds.), *The Oxford handbook of grammatical analysis*, 341–365. Oxford: Oxford University Press.

Haspelmath, Martin. 2010c. The interplay between comparative concepts and descriptive categories (reply to Newmeyer). *Language* 86(3). 696–699.

Haugereid, Petter. 2007. Decomposed phrasal constructions. In Stefan Müller (ed.), *Proceedings of the 14th International Conference on Head-Driven Phrase Structure Grammar*, 120–129. Stanford, CA: CSLI Publications. http://csli-publications.stanford.edu/HPSG/2007/.

Haugereid, Petter. 2009. *Phrasal subconstructions: A Constructionalist grammar design, exemplified with Norwegian and English*: Norwegian University of Science and Technology dissertation.

Haugereid, Petter, Nurit Melnik & Shuly Wintner. 2013. Nonverbal predicates in Modern Hebrew. In Stefan Müller (ed.), *Proceedings of the 20th International Conference on Head-Driven Phrase Structure Grammar, Freie Universität Berlin*, 69–89. Stanford, CA: CSLI Publications. http://csli-publications.stanford.edu/HPSG/2013/hmw.pdf.

Hauser, Marc D., Noam Chomsky & W. Tecumseh Fitch. 2002. The faculty of language: What is it, who has it, and how did it evolve? *Science* 298. 1569–1579. DOI:10.1126/science.298.5598.1569.

Hausser, Roland. 1992. Complexity in left-associative grammar. *Theoretical Computer Science* 106(2). 283–308.

Hawkins, John A. 1999. Processing complexity and filler-gap dependencies across grammars. *Language* 75(2). 244–285.

Hawkins, John A. 2004. *Efficiency and complexity in grammars*. Oxford: Oxford University Press.

Hays, David G. 1964. Dependency Theory: A formalism and some observations. *Language* 40(4). 511–525.

Hays, David G. & T. W. Ziehe. 1960. Studies in machine translation: 10–Russian sentence-structure determination. Tech. rep. Rand Corporation.

Heinecke, Johannes, Jürgen Kunze, Wolfgang Menzel & Ingo Schröder. 1998. Eliminative parsing with graded constraints. In Pierre Isabelle (ed.), *Proceedings of the 36th Annual Meeting of the Association for Computational Linguistics and 17th International Conference on Computational Linguistics*, 526–530. Montreal, Quebec, Canada: Association for Computational Linguistics. DOI:10.3115/980845.980953.

Heinz, Wolfgang & Johannes Matiasek. 1994. Argument structure and case assignment in German. In John Nerbonne, Klaus Netter & Carl J. Pollard (eds.), *German in Head-Driven Phrase Structure Grammar* (CSLI Lecture Notes 46), 199–236. Stanford, CA: CSLI Publications.

Helbig, Gerhard & Joachim Buscha. 1969. *Deutsche Grammatik: Ein Handbuch für den Ausländerunterricht*. Leipzig: VEB Verlag Enzyklopädie.

Helbig, Gerhard & Joachim Buscha. 1998. *Deutsche Grammatik: Ein Handbuch für den Ausländerunterricht*. Leipzig Berlin München: Langenscheidt Verlag Enzyklopädie 18th edn.

Helbig, Gerhard & Wolfgang Schenkel. 1969. *Wörterbuch zur Valenz und Distribution deutscher Verben*. Leipzig: VEB Bibliographisches Institut Leipzig.

Hellan, Lars. 1986. The headedness of NPs in Norwegian. In Peter Muysken & Henk van Riemsdijk (eds.), *Features and projections*, 89–122. Dordrecht/Cinnaminson, U.S.A.: Foris Publications.

Hellan, Lars. 2007. On 'deep evaluation' for individual computational grammars and for cross-framework comparison. In Tracy Holloway King & Emily M. Bender (eds.), *Grammar Engineering across Frameworks 2007* (Studies in Computational Linguistics ONLINE), 161–181. Stanford, CA: CSLI Publications. http://csli-publications.stanford.edu/GEAF/2007/.

Hellan, Lars & Dorothee Beermann. 2006. The 'specifier' in an HPSG grammar implementation of Norwegian. In S. Werner (ed.), *Proceedings of the 15th NODALIDA Conference, Joensuu 2005* (Ling@JoY: University of Joensuu electronic publications in linguistics and language technology 1), 57–64. Joensuu: University of Joensuu.

Hellan, Lars & Petter Haugereid. 2003. Norsource – An excercise in the Matrix Grammar building design. In Emily M. Bender, Daniel P. Flickinger, Frederik Fouvry & Melanie Siegel (eds.), *Proceedings of the ESSLLI 2003 Workshop "Ideas and Strategies for Multilingual Grammar Development"*, Vienna, Austria.

Hellwig, Peter. 1978. PLAIN – Ein Programmsystem zur Sprachbeschreibung und maschinellen Sprachbearbeitung. *Sprache und Datenverarbeitung* 1(2). 16–31.

Hellwig, Peter. 1986. Dependency Unification Grammar. In Makoto Nagao (ed.), *Proceedings of COLING 86*, 195–198. University of Bonn: Association for Computational Linguistics.

Hellwig, Peter. 2003. Dependency Unification Grammar. In Vilmos Ágel, Ludwig M. Eichinger, Hans Werner Eroms, Peter Hellwig, Hans Jürgen Heringer & Henning Lobin (eds.), *Dependenz und Valenz / Dependency and valency: Ein internationales Handbuch der zeitgenössischen Forschung / An international handbook of contemporary research*, vol. 25.1 (Handbücher zur Sprach- und Kommunikationswissenschaft), 593–635. Berlin: Walter de Gruyter.

Hellwig, Peter. 2006. Parsing with Dependency Grammars. In Vilmos Ágel, Ludwig M. Eichinger, Hans Werner Eroms, Peter Hellwig, Hans Jürgen Heringer & Henning Lobin (eds.), *Dependenz und Valenz / Dependency and valency: Ein internationales Handbuch der zeitgenössischen Forschung / An international handbook of contemporary research*, vol. 25.2 (Handbücher zur Sprach- und Kommunikationswissenschaft), 1081–1109. Berlin: Walter de Gruyter.

Her, One-Soon, Dan Higinbotham & Joseph Pentheroudakis. 1991. An LFG-based machine translation system. *Computer Processing of Chinese and Oriental Languages* 5(3–4). 285–297.

Heringer, Hans-Jürgen. 1996. *Deutsche Syntax dependentiell* (Stauffenburg Linguistik). Tübingen: Stauffenburg Verlag.

Higginbotham, James. 1985. On semantics. *Linguistic Inquiry* 16(4). 547–593.

Hinrichs, Erhard W., Walt Detmar Meurers, Frank Richter, Manfred Sailer & Heike Win-hart (eds.). 1997. *Ein HPSG-Fragment des Deutschen. Teil 1: Theorie*, vol. No. 95 (Arbeits-papiere des SFB 340). Tübingen: Eberhard-Karls-Universität Tübingen.

Hinrichs, Erhard W. & Tsuneko Nakazawa. 1989a. Flipped out: AUX in German. In *Aspects of German VP structure* (SfS-Report-01-93), Tübingen: Eberhard-Karls-Univer-sität Tübingen.

Hinrichs, Erhard W. & Tsuneko Nakazawa. 1989b. Subcategorization and VP structure in German. In *Aspects of German VP structure* (SfS-Report-01-93), Tübingen: Eberhard-Karls-Universität Tübingen.

Hinrichs, Erhard W. & Tsuneko Nakazawa. 1994. Linearizing AUXs in German verbal complexes. In John Nerbonne, Klaus Netter & Carl J. Pollard (eds.), *German in Head-Driven Phrase Structure Grammar* (CSLI Lecture Notes 46), 11–38. Stanford, CA: CSLI Publications.

Hinterhölzel, Roland. 2004. Language change versus grammar change: What diachronic data reveal about the interaction between core grammar and periphery. In Carola Trips & Eric Fuß (eds.), *Diachronic clues to synchronic grammar*, 131–160. Amsterdam: John Benjamins Publishing Co.

Hoberg, Ursula. 1981. *Die Wortstellung in der geschriebenen deutschen Gegenwartssprache* (Heutiges Deutsch. Linguistische Grundlagen. Forschungen des Instituts für deutsche Sprache 10). München: Max Hueber Verlag.

Hockett, Charles F. 1960. The origin of speech. *Scientific American* 203. 88–96.

Hoeksema, Jack. 1991. Theoretische Aspekten van Partikelvooropplaatsing. *TABU Bul-letin voor Taalwetenschap* 21(1). 18–26.

Hoffman, Beryl Ann. 1995. *The computational analysis of the syntax and interpretation of "free" word order in Turkish*: University of Pennsylvania dissertation.

Höhle, Tilman N. 1978. *Lexikalische Syntax: Die Aktiv-Passiv-Relation und andere Infinit-konstruktionen im Deutschen* (Linguistische Arbeiten 67). Tübingen: Max Niemeyer Verlag.

Höhle, Tilman N. 1982. Explikationen für „normale Betonung" und „normale Wortstel-lung". In Werner Abraham (ed.), *Satzglieder im Deutschen – Vorschläge zur syntak-tischen, semantischen und pragmatischen Fundierung* (Studien zur deutschen Gramma-tik 15), 75–153. Tübingen: originally Gunter Narr Verlag now Stauffenburg Verlag. Republished as Höhle (2016c).

Höhle, Tilman N. 1983. Topologische Felder. Köln, ms, Published as Höhle (2016g).

Höhle, Tilman N. 1986. Der Begriff „Mittelfeld", Anmerkungen über die Theorie der topologischen Felder. In Walter Weiss, Herbert Ernst Wiegand & Marga Reis (eds.), *Ak-ten des VII. Kongresses der Internationalen Vereinigung für germanische Sprach-und Lit-eraturwissenschaft. Göttingen 1985. Band 3. Textlinguistik contra Stilistik? – Wortschatz und Wörterbuch – Grammatische oder pragmatische Organisation von Rede?* (Kontro-versen, alte und neue 4), 329–340. Tübingen: Max Niemeyer Verlag. Republished as Höhle (2016b).

Höhle, Tilman N. 1988. Verum-Fokus. Netzwerk Sprache und Pragmatik 5 Universität Lund, Germananistisches Institut Lund. Republished as Höhle (2016h).

Höhle, Tilman N. 1991a. On reconstruction and coordination. In Hubert Haider & Klaus Netter (eds.), *Representation and derivation in the theory of grammar* (Studies in Natural Language and Linguistic Theory 22), 139–197. Dordrecht: Kluwer Academic Publishers. Republished as Höhle (2016d).

Höhle, Tilman N. 1991b. Projektionsstufen bei V-Projektionen: Bemerkungen zu F/T. Ms. Published as Höhle (2016e).

Höhle, Tilman N. 1994. Spuren in HPSG. Vortrag auf der GGS-Tagung in Tübingen am 14. Mai 1994, published as Höhle (2016f).

Höhle, Tilman N. 1997. Vorangestellte Verben und Komplementierer sind eine natürliche Klasse. In Christa Dürscheid, Karl Heinz Ramers & Monika Schwarz (eds.), *Sprache im Fokus: Festschrift für Heinz Vater zum 65. Geburtstag*, 107–120. Tübingen: Max Niemeyer Verlag. Republished as Höhle (2016i).

Höhle, Tilman N. 1999. An architecture for phonology. In Robert D. Borsley & Adam Przepiórkowski (eds.), *Slavic in Head-Driven Phrase Structure Grammar*, 61–90. Stanford, CA: CSLI Publications. Republished as Höhle (2016a).

Höhle, Tilman N. 2016a. An architecture for phonology. In Stefan Müller, Marga Reis & Frank Richter (eds.), *Beiträge zur Grammatik des Deutschen* (Classics in Linguistics), Berlin: Language Science Press. Originally published as Höhle (1999).

Höhle, Tilman N. 2016b. Der Begriff „Mittelfeld", Anmerkungen über die Theorie der topologischen Felder. In Stefan Müller, Marga Reis & Frank Richter (eds.), *Beiträge zur Grammatik des Deutschen* (Classics in Linguistics), Berlin: Language Science Press. First published as Höhle (1986).

Höhle, Tilman N. 2016c. Explikationen für „normale Betonung" und „normale Wortstellung". In Stefan Müller, Marga Reis & Frank Richter (eds.), *Beiträge zur Grammatik des Deutschen* (Classics in Linguistics), Berlin: Language Science Press. In Preparation.

Höhle, Tilman N. 2016d. On reconstruction and coordination. In Stefan Müller, Marga Reis & Frank Richter (eds.), *Beiträge zur Grammatik des Deutschen* (Classics in Linguistics), Berlin: Language Science Press. In Preparation.

Höhle, Tilman N. 2016e. Projektionsstufen bei V-Projektionen: Bemerkungen zu F/T. In Stefan Müller, Marga Reis & Frank Richter (eds.), *Beiträge zur Grammatik des Deutschen* (Classics in Linguistics), Berlin: Language Science Press. First circulated in 1991.

Höhle, Tilman N. 2016f. Spuren in HPSG. In Stefan Müller, Marga Reis & Frank Richter (eds.), *Beiträge zur Grammatik des Deutschen* (Classics in Linguistics), Berlin: Language Science Press. Vortrag auf der GGS-Tagung in Tübingen am 14. Mai 1994.

Höhle, Tilman N. 2016g. Topologische Felder. In Stefan Müller, Marga Reis & Frank Richter (eds.), *Beiträge zur Grammatik des Deutschen* (Classics in Linguistics), Berlin: Language Science Press. First circulated as draft in 1983.

Höhle, Tilman N. 2016h. Verum-Fokus. In Stefan Müller, Marga Reis & Frank Richter (eds.), *Beiträge zur Grammatik des Deutschen* (Classics in Linguistics), Berlin: Language Science Press. Originally published as Höhle (1988).

Höhle, Tilman N. 2016i. Vorangestellte Verben und Komplementierer sind eine natürliche Klasse. In Stefan Müller, Marga Reis & Frank Richter (eds.), *Beiträge zur*

Grammatik des Deutschen (Classics in Linguistics), Berlin: Language Science Press. First published as Höhle (1997).

Holler, Anke. 2005. *Weiterführende Relativsätze: Empirische und theoretische Aspekte* (studia grammatica 60). Berlin: Akademie Verlag.

Hornstein, Norbert. 2013. Three grades of grammatical involvement: Syntax from a Minimalist perspective. *Mind and Language* 28(4). 392–420.

Hornstein, Norbert, Jairo Nunes & Kleantes K. Grohmann. 2005. *Understanding Minimalism* (Cambridge Textbooks in Linguistics). Cambridge, UK: Cambridge University Press.

Hudson, Carla L. & Elissa L. Newport. 1999. Creolization: Could adults really have done it all? In Annabel Greenhill, Heather Littlefield & Cheryl Tano (eds.), *Proceedings of the Boston University Conference on Language Development*, vol. 23, 265–276. Somerville, MA: Cascadilla Press.

Hudson, Richard. 1980. Constituency and dependency. *Linguistics* 18. 179–198.

Hudson, Richard. 1984. *Word grammar*. Oxford: Basil Blackwell.

Hudson, Richard. 1989. Towards a computer-testable Word Grammar of English. *UCL Working Papers in Linguistics* 1. 321–339.

Hudson, Richard. 1990. *English Word Grammar*. Oxford: Basil Blackwell.

Hudson, Richard. 1991. *English Word Grammar*. Oxford: Basil Blackwell.

Hudson, Richard. 2003. Mismatches in default inheritance. In Elaine J. Francis & Laura A. Michaelis (eds.), *Mismatch: Form-function incongruity and the architecture of grammar* (CSLI Lecture Notes 163), 355–402. Stanford, CA: CSLI Publications.

Hudson, Richard. 2004. Are determiners heads? *Functions of Language* 11(1). 7–42.

Hudson, Richard. 2010a. Reaction to: "The myth of language universals and cognitive science": On the choice between phrase structure and dependency structure. *Lingua* 120(12). 2676–2679.

Hudson, Richard. 2015. Pied piping in cognition. Ms. London. http://dickhudson.com/papers/.

Hudson, Richard A. 1988. Coordination and grammatical relations. *Journal of Linguistics* 24(2). 303–342.

Hudson, Richard A. 1997. German partial VP fronting. Ms. University College London. http://dickhudson.com/papers/.

Hudson, Richard A. 2000. Discontinuity. *Dependency Grammars, TAL* 41(1). 15–56.

Hudson, Richard A. 2007. *Language networks: The new Word Grammar*. Oxford: Oxford University Press.

Hudson, Richard A. 2010b. *An introduction to Word Grammar* (Cambridge Textbooks in Linguistics). Cambridge, UK: Cambridge University Press.

Hudson Kam, Carla L. & Elissa L. Newport. 2005. Regularizing unpredictable variation: The roles of adult and child learners in language formation and change. *Language Learning and Development* 1. 151–195.

Humboldt, Wilhelm von. 1988. *Gesammelte Werke*. Berlin, New York: Walter de Gruyter.

Hurford, James R. 2002. Expression/induction models of language evolution: Dimensions and issues. In Ted J. Briscoe (ed.), *Linguistic evolution through language acquisition*, 301–344. Cambridge, UK: Cambridge University Press.

Hurskainen, Arvi. 2006. Constraint Grammar in unconventional use: Handling complex Swahili idioms and proverbs. *Suominen, Mickael et.al.: A Man of Measure: Festschrift in Honour of Fred Karlsson on his 60th Birthday. Special Supplement to SKY Jounal of Linguistics* 19. 397–406.

Ingram, David & William Thompson. 1996. Early syntactic acquisition in German: Evidence for the modal hypothesis. *Language* 72(1). 97–120.

Iordanskaja, L., M. Kim, R. Kittredge, B. Lavoie & A. Polguère. 1992. Generation of extended bilingual statistical reports. In Antonio Zampolli (ed.), *14th International Conference on Computational Linguistics (COLING '92), August 23–28*, vol. 3, 1019–1023. Nantes, France: Association for Computational Linguistics.

Islam, Md. Asfaqul, K. M. Azharul Hasan & Md. Mizanur Rahman. 2012. Basic HPSG structure for Bangla grammar. In *15th International Conference on Computer and Information Technology (ICCIT)*, 185–189. Curran Associates. DOI:10.1109/ICCITechn.2012.6509749.

Jackendoff, Ray S. 1972. *Semantic interpretation in Generative Grammar*. Cambridge, MA/London, England: MIT Press.

Jackendoff, Ray S. 1975. Morphological and semantic regularities in the lexikon. *Language* 51(3). 639–671.

Jackendoff, Ray S. 1977. $\overline{X}$ *syntax: A study of phrase structure*. Cambridge, MA/London, England: MIT Press.

Jackendoff, Ray S. 1997. *The architecture of the language faculty* (Linguistic Inquiry Monographs 28). Cambridge, MA/London: MIT Press.

Jackendoff, Ray S. 2000. Fodorian modularity and representational modularity. In Yosef Grodzinsky, Lewis P. Shapiro & David Swinney (eds.), *Language and the brain: Representation and processing* (Foundations of Neuropsychology), 3–30. San Diego: Academic Press.

Jackendoff, Ray S. 2002. *Foundations of language*. Oxford: Oxford University Press.

Jackendoff, Ray S. 2007. A parallel architecture perspective on language processing. *Brain Research* 1146. 2–22.

Jackendoff, Ray S. 2008. Construction after Construction and its theoretical challenges. *Language* 84(1). 8–28.

Jackendoff, Ray S. 2011. What is the human language faculty? Two views. *Language* 87(3). 586–624.

Jackendoff, Ray S. & Steven Pinker. 2005. The nature of the language faculty and its implications for evolution of language (reply to Fitch, Hauser, and Chomsky). *Cognition* 97(2). 211–225.

Jackendoff, Ray S. & Steven Pinker. 2009. The reality of a universal language faculty. *The Behavioral and Brain Sciences* 32(5). 465–466.

Jacobs, Joachim. 1986. The syntax of focus and adverbials in German. In Werner Abraham & S. de Meij (eds.), *Topic, focus, and configurationality: Papers from the 6th Gronin-*

gen Grammar Talks, Groningen, 1984 (Linguistik Aktuell/Linguistics Today 4), 103–127. Amsterdam: John Benjamins Publishing Co.

Jacobs, Joachim. 1991. Bewegung als Valenztransfer. SFB 282: Theorie des Lexikons 1 Heinrich Heine Uni/BUGH Düsseldorf/Wuppertal.

Jacobs, Joachim. 2008. Wozu Konstruktionen? *Linguistische Berichte* 213. 3–44.

Jacobson, Pauline. 1987a. Phrase structure, grammatical relations, and discontinuous constituents. In Geoffrey J. Huck & Almerindo E. Ojeda (eds.), *Discontinuous constituency* (Syntax and Semantics 20), 27–69. New York: Academic Press.

Jacobson, Pauline. 1987b. Review of generalized phrase structure grammar. *Linguistics and Philosophy* 10(3). 389–426.

Jaeggli, Osvaldo A. 1986. Passive. *Linguistic Inquiry* 17(4). 587–622.

Jäger, Gerhard & Reinhard Blutner. 2003. Competition and interpretation: The German adverb *wieder* 'again'. In Ewald Lang, Claudia Maienborn & Cathrine Fabricius-Hansen (eds.), *Modifying adjuncts* (Interface Explorations 4), 393–416. Berlin: Mouton de Gruyter.

Jäppinen, H., A. Lehtola & K. Valkonen. 1986. Functional structures for parsing dependency constraints. In Makoto Nagao (ed.), *Proceedings of COLING 86*, 461–463. University of Bonn: Association for Computational Linguistics. DOI:10.3115/991365.991501.

Johnson, David E. & Shalom Lappin. 1997. A critique of the Minimalist Programm. *Linguistics and Philosophy* 20(3). 273–333.

Johnson, David E. & Shalom Lappin. 1999. *Local constraints vs. economy* (Stanford Monographs in Linguistics). Stanford, CA: CSLI Publications.

Johnson, David E. & Paul M. Postal. 1980. *Arc Pair Grammar.* Princeton, NJ: Princeton University Press.

Johnson, Jacqueline S. & Elissa L. Newport. 1989. Critical period effects in second language learning: The influence of maturational state on the acquisition of English as a second language. *Cognitive Psychology* 21(1). 60–99.

Johnson, Kent. 2004. Gold's theorem and cognitive science. *Philosophy of Science* 71(4). 571–592.

Johnson, Mark. 1986. A GPSG account of VP structure in German. *Linguistics* 24(5). 871–882.

Johnson, Mark. 1988. *Attribute-value logic and the theory of grammar* (CSLI Lecture Notes 14). Stanford, CA: CSLI Publications.

Johnson, Mark. 1989. Parsing as deduction: The use of knowledge of language. *Journal of Psycholinguistic Research* 18(1). 105–128.

Johnson, Mark, Stuart Geman, Stephen Canon, Zhiyi Chi & Stefan Riezler. 1999. Estimators for stochastic "unification-based" grammars. In Robert Dale & Ken Church (eds.), *Proceedings of the Thirty-Seventh Annual Meeting of the ACL*, 535–541. Association for Computational Linguistics.

Joshi, Aravind K. 1985. Tree Adjoining Grammars: How much context-sensitivity is required to provide reasonable structural descriptions? In David Dowty, Lauri Karttunen & Arnold Zwicky (eds.), *Natural language parsing*, 206–250. Cambridge University Press.

Joshi, Aravind K. 1987a. Introduction to Tree Adjoining Grammar. In Alexis Manaster-Ramer (ed.), *The mathematics of language*, 87–114. Amsterdam: John Benjamins Publishing Co.

Joshi, Aravind K. 1987b. Word-order variation in natural language generation. In *AAAI 87, Sixth National Conference on Artificial Intelligence*, 550–555. Seattle.

Joshi, Aravind K., Tilman Becker & Owen Rambow. 2000. Complexity of scrambling: A new twist to the competence-performance distinction. In Anne Abeillé & Owen Rambow (eds.), *Tree Adjoining Grammars: Formalisms, linguistic analysis and processing* (CSLI Lecture Notes 156), 167–181. Stanford, CA: CSLI Publications.

Joshi, Aravind K., Leon S. Levy & Masako Takahashi. 1975. Tree Adjunct Grammar. *Journal of Computer and System Science* 10(2). 136–163.

Joshi, Aravind K. & Yves Schabes. 1997. Tree-Adjoining Grammars. In G. Rozenberg & A. Salomaa (eds.), *Handbook of formal languages*, 69–123. Berlin: Springer Verlag.

Joshi, Aravind K., K. Vijay Shanker & David Weir. 1990. The convergence of mildly context-sensitive grammar formalisms. Tech. Rep. MS-CIS-90-01 Department of Computer and Information Science, University of Pennsylvania. http://repository.upenn.edu/cis_reports/539/.

Jungen, Oliver & Horst Lohnstein. 2006. *Einführung in die Grammatiktheorie* (UTB 2676). München: Wilhelm Fink Verlag.

Jurafsky, Daniel. 1996. A probabilistic model of lexical and syntactic access and disambiguation. *Cognitive Science* 20(2). 137–194.

Kahane, Sylvain. 1997. Bubble trees and syntactic representations. In Tilman Becker & Hans-Ulrich Krieger (eds.), *Proceedings of Mathematics of Language (MOL5) Meeting*, 70–76. Saarbrücken: DFKI.

Kahane, Sylvain. 2003. The Meaning-Text Theory. In Vilmos Ágel, Ludwig M. Eichinger, Hans Werner Eroms, Peter Hellwig, Hans Jürgen Heringer & Henning Lobin (eds.), *Dependenz und Valenz / Dependency and valency: Ein internationales Handbuch der zeitgenössischen Forschung / An international handbook of contemporary research*, vol. 25.1 (Handbücher zur Sprach- und Kommunikationswissenschaft), 546–570. Berlin: Walter de Gruyter.

Kahane, Sylvain. 2009. On the status of phrases in Head-Driven Phrase Structure Grammar: Illustration by a fully lexical treatment of extraction. In Alain Polguère & Igor A. Mel'čuk (eds.), *Dependency in linguistic description* (Studies in Language Companion Series 111), 111–150. Amsterdam: John Benjamins Publishing Co.

Kahane, Sylvain, Alexis Nasr & Owen Rambow. 1998. Pseudo-projectivity: A polynomially parsable non-projective Dependency Grammar. In Pierre Isabelle (ed.), *Proceedings of the 36th Annual Meeting of the Association for Computational Linguistics and 17th International Conference on Computational Linguistics*, 646–652. Montreal, Quebec, Canada: Association for Computational Linguistics. DOI:10.3115/980845.980953. http://www.aclweb.org/anthology/P98-1106.

Kallmeyer, Laura. 2005. Tree-local Multicomponent Tree Adjoining Grammars with shared nodes. *Computational Linguistics* 31(2). 187–225.

Kallmeyer, Laura & Aravind K. Joshi. 2003. Factoring predicate argument and scope semantics: Underspecified semantics with LTAG. *Research on Language and Computation* 1(1–2). 3–58. DOI:10.1023/A:1024564228892.

Kallmeyer, Laura, Timm Lichte, Wolfgang Maier, Yannick Parmentier, Johannes Dellert & Kilian Evang. 2008. TuLiPA: Towards a multi-formalism parsing environment for grammar engineering. In Stephen Clark & Tracy Holloway King (eds.), *Coling 2008: Proceedings of the Workshop on Grammar Engineering Across Frameworks*, 1–8. Manchester, England: Association for Computational Linguistics.

Kallmeyer, Laura & Rainer Osswald. 2012. A frame-based semantics of the dative alternation in Lexicalized Tree Adjoining Grammars. In Christopher Piñón (ed.), *Empirical issues in syntax and semantics*, vol. 9, 167–184. Paris: CNRS.

Kallmeyer, Laura & Maribel Romero. 2008. Scope and situation binding in LTAG using semantic unification. *Research on Language and Computation* 6(1). 3–52.

Kallmeyer, Laura & Sinwon Yoon. 2004. Tree-local MCTAG with shared nodes: An analysis of word order variation in German and Korean. *Traitement automatique des langues TAL* 45(3). 49–69.

Kamp, Hans & Uwe Reyle. 1993. *From discourse to logic: Introduction to modeltheoretic semantics of natural language, formal logic and Discourse Representation Theory* (Studies in Linguistics and Philosophy 42). Dordrecht: Kluwer Academic Publishers.

Kaplan, Ronald M. 1995. The formal architecture of Lexical-Functional Grammar. In Dalrymple et al. (1995) 7–27.

Kaplan, Ronald M. & Joan Bresnan. 1982. Lexical-Functional Grammar: A formal system for grammatical representation. In Joan Bresnan (ed.), *The mental representation of grammatical relations* (MIT Press Series on Cognitive Theory and Mental Representation), 173–281. Cambridge, MA/London: MIT Press. Reprint in: Dalrymple et al. (1995: 29–130).

Kaplan, Ronald M. & John T. Maxwell III. 1996. LFG grammar writer's workbench. Tech. rep. Xerox PARC.

Kaplan, Ronald M., Stefan Riezler, Tracy Holloway King, John T. Maxwell III, Alexander Vasserman & Richard Crouch. 2004. Speed and accuracy in shallow and deep stochastic parsing. In *Proceedings of the Human Language Technology Conference and the 4th Annual Meeting of the North American Chapter of the Association for Computational Linguistics (HLT-NAACL'04)*, Boston, MA: Association for Computational Linguistics.

Kaplan, Ronald M. & Annie Zaenen. 1989. Long-distance dependencies, constituent structure and functional uncertainty. In Mark R. Baltin & Anthony S. Kroch (eds.), *Alternative conceptions of phrase structure*, 17–42. Chicago/London: The University of Chicago Press.

Karimi, Simin. 2005. *A Minimalist approach to scrambling: Evidence from Persian* (Studies in Generative Grammar 76). Berlin, New York: Mouton de Gruyter.

Karimi-Doostan, Gholamhossein. 2005. Light verbs and structural case. *Lingua* 115(12). 1737–1756.

Karlsson, Fred. 1990. Constraint Grammar as a framework for parsing running text. In Hans Karlgren (ed.), *COLING-90: Papers presented to the 13th International Conference on Computational Linguistics*, 168–173. Helsinki: Association for Computational Linguistics.

Karmiloff-Smith, Annette. 1998. Development itself is the key to understanding developmental disorders. *Trends in Cognitive Sciences* 2(10). 389–398.

Karmiloff-Smith, Annette, Julia Grant, Ioanna Berthoud, Mark Davies, Patricia Howlin & Orlee Udwin. 1997. Language in Williams Syndrome: How intact is 'intact'? *Child Development* 68(2). 246–262.

Karttunen, Lauri. 1986. Radical lexicalism. Report No. CSLI-86-68 Center for the Study of Language and Information.

Karttunen, Lauri. 1989. Radical lexicalism. In Mark R. Baltin & Anthony S. Kroch (eds.), *Alternative conceptions of phrase structure*, 43–65. Chicago/London: The University of Chicago Press.

Kasper, Robert T. 1994. Adjuncts in the Mittelfeld. In John Nerbonne, Klaus Netter & Carl J. Pollard (eds.), *German in Head-Driven Phrase Structure Grammar* (CSLI Lecture Notes 46), 39–70. Stanford, CA: CSLI Publications.

Kasper, Robert T., Bernd Kiefer, Klaus Netter & Vijay K. Shanker. 1995. Compilation of HPSG to TAG. In Hans Uszkoreit (ed.), *33rd Annual Meeting of the Association for Computational Linguistics. Proceedings of the conference*, 92–99. Cambridge, MA: Association for Computational Linguistics.

Kathol, Andreas. 1995. *Linearization-based German syntax*: Ohio State University dissertation.

Kathol, Andreas. 2000. *Linear syntax*. New York, Oxford: Oxford University Press.

Kathol, Andreas. 2001. Positional effects in a monostratal grammar of German. *Journal of Linguistics* 37(1). 35–66.

Kathol, Andreas & Carl J. Pollard. 1995. Extraposition via complex domain formation. In Hans Uszkoreit (ed.), *33rd Annual Meeting of the Association for Computational Linguistics. Proceedings of the conference*, 174–180. Cambridge, MA: Association for Computational Linguistics.

Kaufmann, Ingrid & Dieter Wunderlich. 1998. Cross-linguistic patterns of resultatives. SFB 282: Theorie des Lexikons 109 Heinrich Heine Uni/BUGH Düsseldorf.

Kaufmann, Tobias. 2009. *A rule-based language model for speech recognition*: Computer Engineering and Networks Laboratory, ETH Zürich dissertation.

Kaufmann, Tobias & Beat Pfister. 2007. Applying licenser rules to a grammar with continuous constituents. In Stefan Müller (ed.), *Proceedings of the 14th International Conference on Head-Driven Phrase Structure Grammar*, 150–162. Stanford, CA: CSLI Publications. http://csli-publications.stanford.edu/HPSG/2007/.

Kaufmann, Tobias & Beat Pfister. 2008. Applying a grammar-based language model to a broadcast-news transcription task. In Johanna D. Moore, Simone Teufel, James Allan & Sadaoki Furui (eds.), *Proceedings of the 46th Annual Meeting of the Association for Computational Linguistics: Human Language Technologies*, 106–113. Columbus, Ohio: Association for Computational Linguistics. http://www.aclweb.org/anthology/P/P08/P08-1013.pdf.

Kay, Martin. 1967. Experiments with a powerful parser. In *Proceedings of Conference Internationale Sur Le Traitement Automatique Des Langues (COLING 1967)*, Grenoble. http://aclweb.org/anthology/C/C67/C67-1009.pdf.

Kay, Martin. 2000. David G. Hays. In William J. Hutchins (ed.), *Early years in machine translation* (Amsterdam Studies in the Theory and History of Linguistics Science Series 3), 165–170. Amsterdam: John Benjamins Publishing Co.

Kay, Martin. 2011. Zipf's law and *L'Arbitraire du Signe*. *Linguistic Issues in Language Technology* 6(8). 1–25. http://journals.linguisticsociety.org/elanguage/lilt/article/view/2584.html. Special Issue on Interaction of Linguistics and Computational Linguistics.

Kay, Paul. 2002. An informal sketch of a formal architecture for Construction Grammar. *Grammars* 5(1). 1–19.

Kay, Paul. 2005. Argument structure constructions and the argument-adjunct distinction. In Mirjam Fried & Hans C. Boas (eds.), *Grammatical constructions: Back to the roots* (Constructional Approaches to Language 4), 71–98. Amsterdam: John Benjamins Publishing Co.

Kay, Paul & Charles J. Fillmore. 1999. Grammatical Constructions and linguistic generalizations: The What's X Doing Y? Construction. *Language* 75(1). 1–33.

Kay, Paul, Ivan A. Sag & Daniel P. Flickinger. 2015. A lexical theory of phrasal idioms. Ms. CSLI Stanford.

Kayne, Richard S. 1994. *The antisymmetry of syntax* (Linguistic Inquiry Monographs 25). Cambridge, MA: MIT Press.

Kayne, Richard S. 2011. Why are there no directionality parameters? In Mary Byram Washburn, Katherine McKinney-Bock, Erika Varis, Ann Sawyer & Barbara Tomaszewicz (eds.), *Proceedings of the 28th West Coast Conference on Formal Linguistics*, 1–23. Somerville, MA: Cascadilla Press.

Keenan, Edward L. & Bernard Comrie. 1977. Noun phrase accessibility and Universal Grammar. *Linguistic Inquiry* 8(1). 63–99.

Keller, Frank. 1994. German functional HPSG – An experimental CUF encoding. Tech. rep. Institut für Maschinelle Sprachverarbeitung Stuttgart.

Keller, Frank. 1995. Towards an account of extraposition in HPSG. In Steven P. Abney & Erhard W. Hinrichs (eds.), *Proceedings of the Seventh Conference of the European Chapter of the Association for Computational Linguistics*, Dublin: Association for Computational Linguistics.

Kettunen, Kimmo. 1986. On modelling dependency-oriented parsing. In Fred Karlsson (ed.), *Papers from the Fifth Scandinavian Conference of Computational Linguistics*, 113–120. Helsinki.

Kiefer, Bernd, Hans-Ulrich Krieger & Mark-Jan Nederhof. 2000. Efficient and robust parsing of word hypotheses graphs. In Wolfgang Wahlster (ed.), *Verbmobil: Foundations of speech-to-speech translation* (Artificial Intelligence), 280–295. Berlin: Springer Verlag.

Kifle, Nazareth Amlesom. 2012. *Tigrinya applicatives in Lexical-Functional Grammar*: University of Bergen dissertation. http://hdl.handle.net/1956/5730.

Kim, Jong-Bok & Peter Sells. 2008. *English syntax: An introduction* (CSLI Lecture Notes 185). Stanford, CA: CSLI Publications.

Kim, Jong-Bok, Peter Sells & Jaehyung Yang. 2007. Parsing two types of multiple nominative constructions: A Constructional approach. *Language and Information* 11(1). 25–37.

Kim, Jong-Bok & Jaehyung Yang. 2003. Korean phrase structure grammar and its implementations into the LKB system. In Dong Hong Ji & Kim Teng Lua (eds.), *Proceedings of the 17th Pacific Asia Conference on Language, Information and Computation*, 88–97. National University of Singapore: COLIPS Publications.

Kim, Jong-Bok & Jaehyung Yang. 2004. Projections from morphology to syntax in the Korean Resource Grammar: Implementing typed feature structures. In Alexander Gelbukh (ed.), *Computational linguistics and intelligent text processing: 5th International Conference, CICLing 2004, Seoul, Korea, February 15-21, 2004, Proceedings* (Lecture Notes in Computer Science 2945), 13–24. Berlin: Springer Verlag.

Kim, Jong-Bok & Jaehyung Yang. 2006. Coordination structures in a typed feature structure grammar: Formalization and implementation. In Tapio Salakoski, Filip Ginter, Sampo Pyysalo & Tapio Pahikkala (eds.), *Advances in natural language processing: 5th International Conference, FinTAL 2006 Turku, Finland, August 23-25, 2006 proceedings* (Lecture Notes in Artificial Intelligence 4139), 194–205. Berlin: Springer Verlag.

Kim, Jong-Bok & Jaehyung Yang. 2009. Processing three types of Korean cleft constructions in a typed feature structure grammar. *Korean Journal of Cognitive Science* 20(1). 1–28.

Kim, Jong-Bok, Jaehyung Yang, Sanghoun Song & Francis Bond. 2011. Deep processing of Korean and the development of the Korean Resource Grammar. *Linguistic Research* 28(3). 635–672.

Kimball, John P. 1973. *The formal theory of grammar* (Foundations of Modern Linguistics). Englewood Cliffs, NJ: Prentice-Hall.

King, Paul. 1994. An expanded logical formalism for Head-Driven Phrase Structure Grammar. Arbeitspapiere des SFB 340 No. 59 Eberhard-Karls-Universität Tübingen. http://www.sfs.uni-tuebingen.de/sfb/reports/berichte/59/59abs.html.

King, Paul. 1999. Towards truth in Head-Driven Phrase Structure Grammar. In Valia Kordoni (ed.), *Tübingen studies in Head-Driven Phrase Structure Grammar* (Arbeitsberichte des SFB 340 No. 132), 301–352. Tübingen: Universität Tübingen. http://www.sfs.uni-tuebingen.de/sfb/reports/berichte/132/132abs.html.

King, Tracy Holloway & John T. Maxwell III. 2007. Overlay mechanisms for multi-level deep processing applications. In Tracy Holloway King & Emily M. Bender (eds.), *Grammar Engineering across Frameworks 2007* (Studies in Computational Linguistics ONLINE), 182–202. Stanford, CA: CSLI Publications. http://csli-publications.stanford.edu/GEAF/2007/.

Kinyon, Alexandra, Owen Rambow, Tatjana Scheffler, SinWon Yoon & Aravind K. Joshi. 2006. The Metagrammar goes multilingual: A cross-linguistic look at the V2-phenomenon. In Laura Kallmeyer & Tilman Becker (eds.), *TAG+8: The Eighth Inter-*

national *Workshop on Tree Adjoining Grammar and Related Formalisms: Proceedings of the workshop*, 17–24. Sydney, Australia: Association for Computational Linguistics.

Kiparsky, Paul. 1987. Morphology and grammatical relations. Unpublished paper, Stanford University, Stanford.

Kiparsky, Paul. 1988. Agreement and linking theory. Unpublished paper, Stanford University, Stanford.

Kiparsky, Paul & Carol Kiparsky. 1970. Fact. In Manfred Bierwisch & Karl Erich Heidolph (eds.), *Progress in linguistics*, 143–173. The Hague/Paris: Mouton.

Kiss, Katalin E. 2003. Argument scrambling, focus movement and topic movement in Hungarian. In Simin Karimi (ed.), *Word order and scrambling*, 22–43. London: Blackwell.

Kiss, Tibor. 1991. The grammars of LILOG. In Otthein Herzog & Claus-Rainer Rollinger (eds.), *Text understanding in LILOG* (Lecture Notes in Artificial Intelligence 546), 183–199. Berlin: Springer Verlag.

Kiss, Tibor. 1992. Variable Subkategorisierung: Eine Theorie unpersönlicher Einbettungen im Deutschen. *Linguistische Berichte* 140. 256–293.

Kiss, Tibor. 1993. Infinite Komplementation – Neue Studien zum deutschen Verbum infinitum. Arbeiten des SFB 282 No. 42 Bergische Universität Gesamthochschule Wuppertal.

Kiss, Tibor. 1995. *Infinite Komplementation: Neue Studien zum deutschen Verbum infinitum* (Linguistische Arbeiten 333). Tübingen: Max Niemeyer Verlag.

Kiss, Tibor. 2001. Configurational and relational scope determination in German. In Walt Detmar Meurers & Tibor Kiss (eds.), *Constraint-based approaches to Germanic syntax* (Studies in Constraint-Based Lexicalism 7), 141–175. Stanford, CA: CSLI Publications.

Kiss, Tibor. 2005. Semantic constraints on relative clause extraposition. *Natural Language and Linguistic Theory* 23(2). 281–334.

Kiss, Tibor & Birgit Wesche. 1991. Verb order and head movement. In Otthein Herzog & Claus-Rainer Rollinger (eds.), *Text understanding in LILOG* (Lecture Notes in Artificial Intelligence 546), 216–242. Berlin: Springer Verlag.

Klann-Delius, Gisela. 2008. *Spracherwerb*. Stuttgart: J.B. Metzler–Verlag 2nd edn.

Klein, Wolfgang. 1971. *Parsing: Studien zur maschinellen Satzanalyse mit Abhängigkeitsgrammatiken und Transformationsgrammatiken*, vol. 2. Frankfurt a. M.: Athenäum Verlag.

Klein, Wolfgang. 1985. Ellipse, Fokusgliederung und thematischer Stand. In Reinhard Meyer-Hermann & Hannes Rieser (eds.), *Ellipsen und fragmentarische Ausdrücke*, 1–24. Tübingen: Max Niemeyer Verlag.

Klein, Wolfgang. 1986. *Second language acquisition* (Cambridge Textbooks in Linguistics). Cambridge, UK: Cambridge University Press.

Klein, Wolfgang. 2009. Finiteness, Universal Grammar and the language faculty. In Jiansheng Guo, Elena Lieven, Nancy Budwig, Susan Ervin-Tripp, Keiko Nakamura & Seyda Ozcaliskan (eds.), *Cross-linguistic approaches to the study of language: Research in the tradition of Dan Isaac Slobin* (Psychology Press Festschrift Series), 333–344. New York: Psychology Press.

Klenk, Ursula. 2003. *Generative Syntax* (Narr Studienbücher). Tübingen: Gunter Narr Verlag.

Kluender, Robert. 1992. Deriving island constraints from principles of predication. In Helen Goodluck & Michael Rochemont (eds.), *Island constraints: Theory, acquisition, and processing*, 223–258. Dordrecht: Kluwer Academic Publishers.

Kluender, Robert & Marta Kutas. 1993. Subjacency as a processing phenomenon. *Language and Cognitive Processes* 8(4). 573–633.

Knecht, Laura. 1985. *Subject and object in Turkish*: M.I.T. dissertation.

Kobele, Gregory M. 2008. Across-the-board extraction in Minimalist Grammars. In *Proceedings of the Ninth International Workshop on Tree Adjoining Grammar and Related Formalisms (TAG+9)*, 113–128.

Koenig, Jean-Pierre. 1999. *Lexical relations* (Stanford Monographs in Linguistics). Stanford, CA: CSLI Publications.

Koenig, Jean-Pierre & Karin Michelson. 2010. Argument structure of Oneida kinship terms. *International Journal of American Linguistics* 76(2). 169–205.

Koenig, Jean-Pierre & Karin Michelson. 2012. The (non)universality of syntactic selection and functional application. In Christopher Piñón (ed.), *Empirical issues in syntax and semantics*, vol. 9, 185–205. Paris: CNRS.

Kohl, Dieter. 1992. Generation from under- and overspecified structures. In Antonio Zampolli (ed.), *14th International Conference on Computational Linguistics (COLING '92), August 23–28*, 686–692. Nantes, France: Association for Computational Linguistics.

Kohl, Dieter, Claire Gardent, Agnes Plainfossé, Mike Reape & Stefan Momma. 1992. Text generation from semantic representation. In Gabriel G. Bes & Thierry Guillotin (eds.), *The construction of a natural language and graphic interface: Results and perspectives from the ACORD project*, 94–161. Berlin: Springer Verlag.

Kohl, Karen T. 1999. *An analysis of finite parameter learning in linguistic spaces*. Massachusetts Institute of Technology MA thesis. http://karentkohl.org/papers/SM.pdf.

Kohl, Karen T. 2000. Language learning in large parameter spaces. In *Proceedings of the Seventeenth National Conference on Artificial Intelligence and Twelfth Conference on Innovative Applications of Artificial Intelligence*, 1080. AAAI Press / The MIT Press.

Kolb, Hans-Peter. 1997. GB blues: Two essays on procedures and structures in Generative Syntax. Arbeitspapiere des SFB 340 No. 110 Eberhard-Karls-Universität Tübingen.

Kolb, Hans-Peter & Craig L. Thiersch. 1991. Levels and empty categories in a Principles and Parameters based approach to parsing. In Hubert Haider & Klaus Netter (eds.), *Representation and derivation in the theory of grammar* (Studies in Natural Language and Linguistic Theory 22), 251–301. Dordrecht: Kluwer Academic Publishers.

Konieczny, Lars. 1996. *Human sentence processing: A semantics-oriented parsing approach*: Universität Freiburg Dissertation. IIG-Berichte 3/96.

König, Esther. 1999. LexGram: A practical Categorial Grammar formalism. *Journal of Language and Computation* 1(1). 33–52.

Koopman, Hilda & Dominique Sportiche. 1991. The position of subjects. *Lingua* 85(2–3). 211–258.

Kordoni, Valia (ed.). 1999. *Tübingen studies in Head-Driven Phrase Structure Grammar* (Arbeitspapiere des SFB 340, No. 132, Volume 1). Tübingen: Eberhard-Karls-Universität Tübingen.

Kordoni, Valia. 2001. Linking experiencer-subject psych verb constructions in Modern Greek. In Daniel P. Flickinger & Andreas Kathol (eds.), *Proceedings of the HPSG-2000 Conference, University of California, Berkeley*, 198–213. CSLI Publications. http://csli-publications.stanford.edu/HPSG/1/.

Kordoni, Valia & Julia Neu. 2005. Deep analysis of Modern Greek. In Keh-Yih Su, Oi Yee Kwong, Jn'ichi Tsujii & Jong-Hyeok Lee (eds.), *Natural language processing IJCNLP 2004* (Lecture Notes in Artificial Intelligence 3248), 674–683. Berlin: Springer Verlag.

Kornai, András & Geoffrey K. Pullum. 1990. The X-bar Theory of phrase structure. *Language* 66(1). 24–50.

Koster, Jan. 1975. Dutch as an SOV language. *Linguistic Analysis* 1(2). 111–136.

Koster, Jan. 1978. *Locality principles in syntax*. Dordrecht: Foris Publications.

Koster, Jan. 1986. The relation between pro-drop, scrambling, and verb movements. *Groningen Papers in Theoretical and Applied Linguistics* 1. 1–43.

Koster, Jan. 1987. *Domains and dynasties: The radical autonomy of syntax*. Dordrecht: Foris Publications.

Kratzer, Angelika. 1984. On deriving syntactic differences between German and English. TU Berlin, ms.

Kratzer, Angelika. 1996. Severing the external argument from its verb. In Johan Rooryck & Laurie Zaring (eds.), *Phrase structure and the lexicon*, 109–137. Dordrecht: Kluwer Academic Publishers.

Krieger, Hans-Ulrich & John Nerbonne. 1993. Feature-based inheritance networks for computational lexicons. In Ted Briscoe, Ann Copestake & Valeria de Paiva (eds.), *Inheritance, defaults, and the lexicon*, 90–136. Cambridge, UK: Cambridge University Press. A version of this paper is available as DFKI Research Report RR-91-31. Also published in: Proceedings of the ACQUILEX Workshop on Default Inheritance in the Lexicon, Technical Report No. 238, University of Cambridge, Computer Laboratory, October 1991.

Kroch, Anthony S. 1987. Unbounded dependencies and subjacency in a Tree Adjoining Grammar. In Alexis Manaster-Ramer (ed.), *Mathematics of language*, 143–172. Amsterdam: John Benjamins Publishing Co.

Kroch, Anthony S. & Aravind K. Joshi. 1985. The linguistic relevance of Tree Adjoining Grammar. Tech. Rep. MS-CIS-85-16 University of Pennsylvania. http://repository.upenn.edu/cgi/viewcontent.cgi?article=1706&context=cis_reports.

Kroch, Anthony S. & Aravind K. Joshi. 1987. Analyzing extraposition in a Tree Adjoining Grammar. In Geoffrey J. Huck & Almerindo E. Ojeda (eds.), *Discontinuous constituency* (Syntax and Semantics 20), 107–149. New York: Academic Press.

Kropp Dakubu, Mary Esther, Lars Hellan & Dorothee Beermann. 2007. Verb sequencing constraints in Ga: Serial verb constructions and the extended verb complex. In Stefan

Müller (ed.), *Proceedings of the 14th International Conference on Head-Driven Phrase Structure Grammar*, 99–119. Stanford, CA: CSLI Publications. http://csli-publications. stanford.edu/HPSG/2007/.

Kruijff-Korbayová, Ivana & Mark J. Steedman. 2003. Discourse and information structure. *Journal of Logic, Language and Information: Special Issue on Discourse and Information Structure* 12(3). 249–259.

Kübler, Sandra, Ryan McDonald & Joakim Nivre. 2009. *Dependency Parsing* (Synthesis Lectures on Human Language Technologies 2). San Rafael, U.S.A: Morgan & Claypool Publishers.

Kuhn, Jonas. 1995. Information packaging in German: Some motivation from HPSG-based translation. Universität Stuttgart, ms. ftp://ftp.ims.uni-stuttgart.de/pub/papers/kuhn/Info-Pack.pdf.

Kuhn, Jonas. 1996. An underspecified HPSG representation for information structure. In Jun-ichi Tsuji (ed.), *Proceedings of COLING-96. 16th International Conference on Computational Linguistics COLING96). Copenhagen, Denmark, August 5–9, 1996*, 670–675. Copenhagen, Denmark: Association for Computational Linguistics.

Kuhn, Jonas. 2007. Interfaces in constraint-based theories of grammar. In Gillian Ramchand & Charles Reiss (eds.), *The Oxford handbook of linguistic interfaces*, 613–650. Oxford: Oxford University Press.

Kuhn, Jonas & Christian Rohrer. 1997. Approaching ambiguity in real-life sentences: The application of an Optimality Theory-inspired constraint ranking in a large-scale LFG grammar. In *Proceedings of DGfS/CL 97*, Heidelberg.

Kuhns, Robert J. 1986. A PROLOG implementation of Government-Binding Theory. In Alan W. Biermann (ed.), *Proceedings of the Twenty-Fourth Annual Meeting of the Association for Computational Linguistics*, 546–550. Columbia University, New York: Association for Computational Linguistics.

Kunze, Jürgen. 1968. The treatment of non-projective structures in the syntactic analysis and synthesis of English and German. *Computational Linguistics* 7. 67–77.

Kunze, Jürgen. 1975. *Abhängigkeitsgrammatik* (studia grammatica 12). Berlin: Akademie Verlag.

Kunze, Jürgen. 1991. *Kasusrelationen und semantische Emphase* (studia grammatica XXXII). Berlin: Akademie Verlag.

Kunze, Jürgen. 1993. *Sememstrukturen und Feldstrukturen* (studia grammatica 36). Berlin: Akademie Verlag. Unter Mitarbeit von Beate Firzlaff.

Labelle, Marie. 2007. Biolinguistics, the Minimalist Program, and psycholinguistic reality. *Snippets* 14. 6–7. http://www.ledonline.it/snippets/.

Laczkó, Tibor, György Rákosi & Ágoston Tóth. 2010. HunGram vs. EngGram in ParGram: On the comparison of Hungarian and English in an international computational linguistics project. In Irén Hegedűs & Sándor Martsa (eds.), *Selected papers in linguistics from the 9th HUSSE Conference*, vol. 1, 81–95. Pécs: Institute of English Studies, Faculty of Humanities, University of Pécs.

Laenzlinger, Christoph. 2004. A feature-based theory of adverb syntax. In Jennifer R. Austin, Stefan Engelberg & Gisa Rauh (eds.), *Adverbials: The interplay between mean-*

ing, context, and syntactic structure (Linguistik Aktuell/Linguistics Today 70), 205–252. Amsterdam: John Benjamins Publishing Co.

Lai, Cecilia S. L., Simon E. Fisher, Jane A. Hurst, Faraneh Vargha-Khadem & Anthony P. Monaco. 2001. A forkhead-domain gene is mutated in a severe speech and language disorder. *Nature* 413(6855). 519–523. DOI:10.1038/35097076.

Lakoff, George. 1987. *Women, fire, and dangerous things: What categories reveal about the mind.* Chicago: The University of Chicago Press.

Langacker, Ronald W. 1987. *Foundations of Cognitive Grammar,* vol. 1. Stanford, CA: Stanford University Press.

Langacker, Ronald W. 2000. A dynamic usage-based model. In Michael Barlow & Suzanne Kemmer (eds.), *Usage-based models of language,* 1–63. Stanford, CA: CSLI Publications.

Langacker, Ronald W. 2008. *Cognitive Grammar: A basic introduction.* Oxford: Oxford University Press.

Langacker, Ronald W. 2009. Cognitive (Construction) Grammar. *Cognitive Linguistics* 20(1). 167–176.

Lappin, Shalom, Robert D. Levine & David E. Johnson. 2000a. The revolution confused: A response to our critics. *Natural Language and Linguistic Theory* 18(4). 873–890.

Lappin, Shalom, Robert D. Levine & David E. Johnson. 2000b. The structure of unscientific revolutions. *Natural Language and Linguistic Theory* 18(3). 665–671.

Lappin, Shalom, Robert D. Levine & David E. Johnson. 2001. The revolution maximally confused. *Natural Language and Linguistic Theory* 19(4). 901–919.

Larson, Richard K. 1988. On the double object construction. *Linguistic Inquiry* 19(3). 335–391.

Lascarides, Alex & Ann Copestake. 1999. Default representation in constraint-based frameworks. *Computational Linguistics* 25(1). 55–105.

Lasnik, Howard & Mamoru Saito. 1992. *Move α: Conditions on its application and output* (Current Studies in Linguistics 22). Cambridge, MA: MIT Press.

Lasnik, Howard & Juan Uriagereka. 2002. On the poverty of the challenge. *The Linguistic Review* 19(1–2). 147–150.

Lavoie, Benoit & Owen Rambow. 1997. RealPro–A fast, portable sentence realizer. In *Proceedings of the Conference on Applied Natural Language Processing (ANLP'97),* .

Le, Hong Phuong, Thi Minh Huyen Nguyen & Azim Roussanaly. 2008. Metagrammar for Vietnamese LTAG. In *Proceedings of the Ninth International Workshop on Tree Adjoining Grammars and Related Formalisms (TAG+9),* 129–132. Tübingen.

Legate, Julie & Charles D. Yang. 2002. Empirical re-assessment of stimulus poverty arguments. *The Linguistic Review* 19(1–2). 151–162.

Lehtola, Aarno. 1986. DPL: A computational method for describing grammars and modelling parsers. In Fred Karlsson (ed.), *Papers from the Fifth Scandinavian Conference of Computational Linguistics,* 151–159. Helsinki.

Leiss, Elisabeth. 2003. Empirische Argumente für Dependenz. In Vilmos Ágel, Ludwig M. Eichinger, Hans Werner Eroms, Peter Hellwig, Hans Jürgen Heringer & Henning Lobin (eds.), *Dependenz und Valenz / Dependency and valency: Ein internationales*

Handbuch der zeitgenössischen Forschung / An international handbook of contemporary research, vol. 25.1 (Handbücher zur Sprach- und Kommunikationswissenschaft), 311–324. Berlin: Walter de Gruyter.

Leiss, Elisabeth. 2009. *Sprachphilosophie* (de Gruyter Studienbuch). Berlin: Walter de Gruyter.

Lenerz, Jürgen. 1977. *Zur Abfolge nominaler Satzglieder im Deutschen* (Studien zur deutschen Grammatik 5). Tübingen: originally Gunter Narr Verlag now Stauffenburg Verlag.

Lenerz, Jürgen. 1994. Pronomenprobleme. In Brigitta Haftka (ed.), *Was determiniert Wortstellungsvariation? Studien zu einem Interaktionsfeld von Grammatik, Pragmatik und Sprachtypologie*, 161–174. Opladen: Westdeutscher Verlag.

Lenneberg, Eric H. 1964. The capacity for language acquisition. In Jerry A. Fodor & Jerrold J. Katz (eds.), *The structure of language*, 579–603. Englewood Cliffs, NJ: Prentice-Hall.

Lenneberg, Eric H. 1967. *Biological foundations of language*. New York: John Wiley & Sons, Inc.

Levelt, Willem J. M. 1989. *Speaking: From intonation to articulation* (ACL-MIT Press Series in Natural Language Processing). Cambridge, MA: MIT Press.

Levin, Beth. 1993. *English verb classes and alternations: A preliminary investigation*. Chicago, Illinois: University of Chicago Press.

Levin, Beth & Malka Rappaport Hovav. 2005. *Argument realization*. Cambridge University Press.

Levine, Robert D. 2003. Adjunct valents, cumulative scopings and impossible descriptions. In Jongbok Kim & Stephen Mark Wechsler (eds.), *The proceedings of the 9th International Conference on Head-Driven Phrase Structure Grammar*, 209–232. Stanford, CA: CSLI Publications. http://csli-publications.stanford.edu/HPSG/3/.

Levine, Robert D. & Thomas E. Hukari. 2006. *The unity of unbounded dependency constructions* (CSLI Lecture Notes 166). Stanford, CA: CSLI Publications.

Levine, Robert D. & Walt Detmar Meurers. 2006. Head-Driven Phrase Structure Grammar: Linguistic approach, formal foundations, and computational realization. In Keith Brown (ed.), *The encyclopedia of language and linguistics*, 237–252. Oxford: Elsevier Science Publisher B.V. (North-Holland) 2nd edn.

Lewis, Geoffrey L. 1967. *Turkish grammar*. Oxford: Clarendon Press.

Lewis, John D. & Jeffrey L. Elman. 2001. Learnability and the statistical structure of language: Poverty of Stimulus arguments revisited. In Barbora Skarabela, Sarah Fish & Anna H.-J. Do (eds.), *Proceedings of the 26th Annual Boston University Conference on Language Development*, 359–370. http://crl.ucsd.edu/~elman/Papers/BU2001.pdf.

Li, Charles N. & Sandra A. Thompson. 1981. *Mandarin Chinese: A functional reference grammar*. Berkeley and Los Angeles: University of California Press.

Li, Wei. 1996. Esperanto inflection and its interface in HPSG. Working papers of the linguistics circle University of Victoria.

Lichte, Timm. 2007. An MCTAG with tuples for coherent constructions in German. In Laura Kallmeyer, Paola Monachesi, Gerald Penn & Giorgio Satta (eds.), *Proceedings of the 12th Conference on Formal Grammar 2007*, Dublin, Ireland.

Lieb, Hans-Heinrich. 1983. *Integrational linguistics: Vol. I.: General outline* (Current Issues in Linguistic Theory 17). Amsterdam: John Benjamins Publishing Co.

Lightfoot, David W. 1997. Catastrophic change and learning theory. *Lingua* 100(1). 171–192.

Link, Godehard. 1984. Hydras: On the logic of relative constructions with multiple heads. In Fred Landmann & Frank Veltman (eds.), *Varieties of formal semantics*, 245–257. Dordrecht: Foris Publications.

Lipenkova, Janna. 2009. *Serienverbkonstruktionen im Chinesischen und ihre Analyse im Rahmen von HPSG*. Institut für Sinologie, Freie Universität Berlin MA thesis.

Liu, Gang. 1997. *Eine unifikations-basierte Grammatik für das moderne Chinesisch – dargestellt in der HPSG*: FG Sprachwissenschaft, Universität Konstanz dissertation. http://www.ub.uni-konstanz.de/kops/volltexte/1999/191/.

Liu, Haitao. 2009. *Dependency Grammar: From theory to practice*. Beijing: Science Press.

Liu, Haitao & Wei Huang. 2006. Chinese Dependency Syntax for treebanking. In *Proceedings of the Twentieth Pacific Asia Conference on Language, Information and Computation*, 126–133. Beijing: Tsinghua University Press.

Lloré, F. Xavier. 1995. *Un Método de 'Parsing' para Gramáticas Categoriales Multimodales*: I.C.E. de la Universidad Politécnica de Catalunya dissertation.

Lobin, Henning. 1993. *Koordinationssyntax als strukturales Phänomen* (Studien zur Grammatik 46). Tübingen: Gunter Narr Verlag.

Lobin, Henning. 2003. Dependenzgrammatik und Kategorialgrammatik. In Vilmos Ágel, Ludwig M. Eichinger, Hans Werner Eroms, Peter Hellwig, Hans Jürgen Heringer & Henning Lobin (eds.), *Dependenz und Valenz / Dependency and valency: Ein internationales Handbuch der zeitgenössischen Forschung / An international handbook of contemporary research*, vol. 25.1 (Handbücher zur Sprach- und Kommunikationswissenschaft), 325–330. Berlin: Walter de Gruyter.

Löbner, Sebastian. 1986. In Sachen Nullartikel. *Linguistische Berichte* 101. 64–65. http://user.phil-fak.uni-duesseldorf.de/~loebner/publ/Nullartikel.html.

Lohndal, Terje. 2012. Toward the end of argument structure. In María Cristina Cuervo & Yves Roberge (eds.), *The end of argument structure?*, vol. 38 (Syntax and Semantics), 155–184. Bingley, UK: Emerald Group Publishing.

Lohnstein, Horst. 1993. *Projektion und Linking: Ein prinzipienbasierter Parser fürs Deutsche* (Linguistische Arbeiten 287). Tübingen: Max Niemeyer Verlag.

Lohnstein, Horst. 2014. Artenvielfalt in freier Wildbahn: Generative Grammatik. In Jörg Hagemann & Sven Staffeldt (eds.), *Syntaxtheorien: Analysen im Vergleich* (Stauffenburg Einführungen 28), 165–185. Tübingen: Stauffenburg Verlag.

Longobardi, Giuseppe & Ian Roberts. 2010. Universals, diversity and change in the science of language: Reaction to "The myth of language universals and cognitive science". *Lingua* 120(12). 2699–2703.

Lorenz, Konrad. 1970. *Studies in human and animal behavior*, vol. I. Cambridge, MA: Harvard University Press.

Lötscher, Andreas. 1985. Syntaktische Bedingungen der Topikalisierung. *Deutsche Sprache* 13(3). 207–229.

Loukam, Mourad, Amar Balla & Mohamed Tayeb Laskri. 2015. Towards an open platform based on HPSG formalism for the Standard Arabic language. *International Journal of Speech Technology* DOI:10.1007/s10772-015-9314-4.

Lüdeling, Anke. 2001. *On particle verbs and similar constructions in German* (Dissertations in Linguistics). Stanford, CA: CSLI Publications.

Luuk, Erkki & Hendrik Luuk. 2011. The redundancy of recursion and infinity for natural language. *Cognitive Processing* 12(1). 1–11.

Maas, Heinz Dieter. 1977. The Saarbrücken Automatic Translation System (SUSY). In Eric James Coates (ed.), *Proceedings of the Third European Congress on Information Systems and Networks: Overcoming the Language Barrier*, vol. 1, 585–592. München: Verlag Dokumentation.

Maché, Jakob. 2010. Towards a compositional analysis of verbless directives in German. Paper presented at the HPSG 2010 Conference.

Machicao y Priemer, Antonio. 2015. SpaGram: An implemented grammar fragment of Spanish. Ms. Humboldt Universität zu Berlin. In Preparation.

MacWhinney, Brian. 1995. *The CHILDES project: Tools for analyzing talk*. Hillsdale, NJ: Erlbaum 2nd edn.

Maess, Burkhard, Stefan Koelsch, Thomas C. Gunter & Angela D. Friederici. 2001. Musical syntax is processed in Broca's area: An MEG study. *Nature Neuroscience* 4(5). 540–545.

Marantz, Alec. 1984. *On the nature of grammatical relations* (Linguistic Inquiry Monographs 10). Cambridge, MA: MIT Press.

Marantz, Alec. 1997. No escape from syntax: Don't try morphological analysis in the privacy of your own lexicon. *U. Penn Working Papers in Linguistics* 4(2). 201–225. http://www.ling.upenn.edu/papers/v4.2-contents.html.

Marantz, Alec. 2005. Generative linguistics within the cognitive neuroscience of language. *The Linguistic Review* 22(2–4). 429–445.

Marcus, Gary F. 1993. Negative evidence in language acquisition. *Cognition* 46(1). 53–85.

Marcus, Gary F. & Simon E. Fisher. 2003. FOXP2 in focus: What can genes tell us about speech and language? *TRENDS in Cognitive Sciences* 7(6). 257–262.

Marcus, Mitchell P. 1980. *A theory of syntactic recognition for natural language*. London, England/Cambridge, MA: MIT Press.

Marimon, Montserrat. 2013. The Spanish DELPH-IN grammar. *Language Resources and Evaluation* 47(2). 371–397. DOI:10.1007/s10579-012-9199-7.

Marshall, Ian & Éva Sáfár. 2004. Sign Language generation in an ALE HPSG. In Stefan Müller (ed.), *Proceedings of the 11th International Conference on Head-Driven Phrase Structure Grammar, Center for Computational Linguistics, Katholieke Universiteit Leuven*, 189–201. Stanford, CA: CSLI Publications. http://csli-publications.stanford.edu/HPSG/2004/.

Marslen-Wilson, William. 1975. Sentence perception as an interactive parallel process. *Science* 189(4198). 226–228.

Masuichi, Hiroshi & Tomoko Ohkuma. 2003. Constructing a practical Japanese parser based on Lexical-Functional Grammar. *Journal of Natural Language Processing* 10. 79–109. In Japanese.

Masum, Mahmudul Hasan, Muhammad Sadiqul Islam, M. Sohel Rahman & Reaz Ahmed. 2012. HPSG analysis of type-based Arabic nominal declension. In *The 13th International Arab Conference*, 272–279.

Mayo, Bruce. 1997. Die Konstanzer LFG-Umgebung. Arbeitspapier 82 des Fachbereichs Sprachwissenschaft der Universität Konstanz Universität Konstanz.

Mayo, Bruce. 1999. *A computational model of derivational morphology*: Universität Hamburg dissertation. http://www.sub.uni-hamburg.de/opus/volltexte/1999/386/.

Meinunger, André. 2000. *Syntactic aspects of topic and comment* (Linguistik Aktuell/ Linguistics Today 38). Amsterdam: John Benjamins Publishing Co.

Meisel, Jürgen. 1995. Parameters in acquisition. In Paul Fletcher & Brian MacWhinny (eds.), *The handbook of child language*, 10–35. Oxford: Blackwell Publishing Ltd.

Mel'čuk, Igor A. 1964. *Avtomatičeskij sintaksičeskij analiz*, vol. 1. Novosibirsk: Izdatel'stvo SO AN SSSR.

Mel'čuk, Igor A. 1981. Meaning-Text Models: A recent trend in Soviet linguistics. *Annual Review of Anthropology* 10. 27–62.

Mel'čuk, Igor A. 1988. *Dependency Syntax: Theory and practice* (SUNY Series in Linguistics). Albany, NY: SUNY Press.

Mel'čuk, Igor A. 2003. Levels of dependency description: Concepts and problems. In Vilmos Ágel, Ludwig M. Eichinger, Hans Werner Eroms, Peter Hellwig, Hans Jürgen Heringer & Henning Lobin (eds.), *Dependenz und Valenz / Dependency and valency: Ein internationales Handbuch der zeitgenössischen Forschung / An international handbook of contemporary research*, vol. 25.1 (Handbücher zur Sprach- und Kommunikationswissenschaft), 188–230. Berlin: Walter de Gruyter.

Melnik, Nurit. 2007. From "hand-written" to computationally implemented HPSG theories. *Research on Language and Computation* 5(2). 199–236.

Mensching, Guido & Eva-Maria Remberger. 2011. Syntactic variation and change in Romance: A Minimalist approach. In Peter Siemund (ed.), *Linguistic universals and language variation* (Trends in Linguistics. Studies and Monographs 231), 361–403. Berlin: Mouton de Gruyter.

Menzel, Wolfgang. 1998. Constraint satisfaction for robust parsing of spoken language. *Journal of Experimental & Theoretical Artificial Intelligence* 10(1). 77–89.

Menzel, Wolfgang & Ingo Schröder. 1998a. Constraint-based diagnosis for intelligent language tutoring systems. In *Proceedings of the ITF & KNOWS Conference at the 1FIP '98 Congress*, Wien/Budapest.

Menzel, Wolfgang & Ingo Schröder. 1998b. Decision procedures for Dependency Parsing using graded constraints. In Alain Polguère & Sylvain Kahane (eds.), *Processing of dependency-based grammars: Proceedings of the workshop at COLING-ACL'98*, 78–

87. Association for Computational Linguistics. http://www.aclweb.org/anthology/W/W98/#0500.

Meurer, Paul. 2009. A computational grammar for Georgian. In Peter Bosch, David Gabelaia & Jérôme Lang (eds.), *Logic, language, and computation: 7th International Tbilisi Symposium on Logic, Language, and Computation, TbiLLC 2007, Tbilisi, Georgia, October 2007, revised selected papers* (Lecture Notes in Artificial Intelligence 5422), 1–15. Berlin: Springer Verlag.

Meurers, Walt Detmar. 1994. On implementing an HPSG theory. In Erhard W. Hinrichs, Walt Detmar Meurers & Tsuneko Nakazawa (eds.), *Partial-VP and split-NP topicalization in German – An HPSG analysis and its implementation* (Arbeitspapiere des SFB 340 No. 58), 47–155. Tübingen: Eberhard-Karls-Universität. http://www.sfs.uni-tuebingen.de/~dm/papers/on-implementing.html.

Meurers, Walt Detmar. 1999a. German partial-VP fronting revisited. In Gert Webelhuth, Jean-Pierre Koenig & Andreas Kathol (eds.), *Lexical and Constructional aspects of linguistic explanation* (Studies in Constraint-Based Lexicalism 1), 129–144. Stanford, CA: CSLI Publications.

Meurers, Walt Detmar. 1999b. *Lexical generalizations in the syntax of German non-finite constructions.* Tübingen: Eberhard-Karls-Universität dissertation.

Meurers, Walt Detmar. 1999c. Raising spirits (and assigning them case). *Groninger Arbeiten zur Germanistischen Linguistik (GAGL)* 43. 173–226. http://www.sfs.uni-tuebingen.de/~dm/papers/gagl99.html.

Meurers, Walt Detmar. 2000. Lexical generalizations in the syntax of German non-finite constructions. Arbeitspapiere des SFB 340 No. 145 Eberhard-Karls-Universität Tübingen. http://www.sfs.uni-tuebingen.de/~dm/papers/diss.html.

Meurers, Walt Detmar. 2001. On expressing lexical generalizations in HPSG. *Nordic Journal of Linguistics* 24(2). 161–217.

Meurers, Walt Detmar, Kordula De Kuthy & Vanessa Metcalf. 2003. Modularity of grammatical constraints in HPSG-based grammar implementations. In Emily M. Bender, Daniel P. Flickinger, Frederik Fouvry & Melanie Siegel (eds.), *Proceedings of the ESSLLI 2003 Workshop "Ideas and Strategies for Multilingual Grammar Development"*, 83–90. Vienna, Austria. http://www.sfs.uni-tuebingen.de/~dm/papers/meurers-dekuthy-metcalf-03.html.

Meurers, Walt Detmar & Stefan Müller. 2009. Corpora and syntax. In Anke Lüdeling & Merja Kytö (eds.), *Corpus linguistics: An international handbook*, vol. 29 (Handbücher zur Sprach- und Kommunikationswissenschaft), chap. 42, 920–933. Berlin: Mouton de Gruyter.

Meurers, Walt Detmar, Gerald Penn & Frank Richter. 2002. A web-based instructional platform for constraint-based grammar formalisms and parsing. In Dragomir Radev & Chris Brew (eds.), *Effective tools and methodologies for teaching NLP and CL*, 18–25. Association for Computational Linguistics. Proceedings of the Workshop held at 40th Annual Meeting of the Association for Computational Linguistics. Philadelphia, PA.

Micelli, Vanessa. 2012. Field topology and information structure: A case study for German constituent order. In Luc Steels (ed.), *Computational issues in Fluid Construction Grammar* (Lecture Notes in Computer Science 7249), 178–211. Berlin: Springer Verlag.

Michaelis, Jens. 2001. *On formal properties of Minimalist Grammars*: Universität Potsdam dissertation.

Michaelis, Laura A. 2006. Construction Grammar. In Keith Brown (ed.), *The encyclopedia of language and linguistics*, 73–84. Oxford: Elsevier Science Publisher B.V. (North-Holland) 2nd edn.

Michaelis, Laura A. & Josef Ruppenhofer. 2001. *Beyond alternations: A Constructional model of the German applicative pattern* (Stanford Monographs in Linguistics). Stanford, CA: CSLI Publications.

Miller, George A. & Kathryn Ojemann McKean. 1964. A chronometric study of some relations between sentences. *Quarterly Journal of Experimental Psychology* 16(4). 297–308.

Mittendorf, Ingo & Louisa Sadler. 2005. Numerals, nouns and number in Welsh NPs. In Miriam Butt & Tracy Holloway King (eds.), *Proceedings of the LFG 2005 conference*, 294–312. Stanford, CA: CSLI Publications. http://csli-publications.stanford.edu/LFG/10/.

Miyao, Yusuke, Takashi Ninomiya & Jun'ichi Tsujii. 2005. Corpus-oriented grammar development for acquiring a Head-Driven Phrase Structure Grammar from the Penn Treebank. In Keh-Yih Su, Oi Yee Kwong, Jn'ichi Tsujii & Jong-Hyeok Lee (eds.), *Natural language processing IJCNLP 2004* (Lecture Notes in Artificial Intelligence 3248), 684–693. Berlin: Springer Verlag.

Miyao, Yusuke & Jun'ichi Tsujii. 2008. Feature forest models for probabilistic HPSG parsing. *Computational Linguistics* 34(1). 35–80.

Moens, Marc, Jo Calder, Ewan Klein, Mike Reape & Henk Zeevat. 1989. Expressing generalizations in unification-based grammar formalisms. In Harold Somers & Mary McGee Wood (eds.), *Proceedings of the Fourth Conference of the European Chapter of the Association for Computational Linguistics*, 174–181. Manchester, England: Association for Computational Linguistics.

Montague, Richard. 1974. *Formal philosophy*. New Haven: Yale University Press.

Moortgat, Michael. 1989. *Categorial investigations: Logical and linguistic aspects of the Lambek Calculus* (Groningen Amsterdam Studies in Semantics 9). Dordrecht/Cinnaminson, U.S.A.: Foris Publications.

Moortgat, Michael. 2011. Categorial type logics. In Johan F. A. K. van Benthem & G. B. Alice ter Meulen (eds.), *Handbook of logic and language*, 95–179. Amsterdam: Elsevier 2nd edn.

Moot, Richard. 2002. *Proof nets for linguistic analysis*: University of Utrecht dissertation.

Morgan, James L. 1989. Learnability considerations and the nature of trigger experiences in language acquisition. *Behavioral and Brain Sciences* 12(2). 352–353.

Morin, Yves Ch. 1973. A computer tested Transformational Grammar of French. *Linguistics* 116(11). 49–114.

Morrill, Glyn V. 1994. *Type Logical Grammars: Categorial logic of signs.* Dordrecht: Kluwer Academic Publishers.

Morrill, Glyn V. 1995. Discontinuity in Categorial Grammar. *Linguistics and Philosophy* 18(2). 175–219.

Morrill, Glyn V. 2012. CatLog: A Categorial parser/theorem-prover. In *Logical aspects of computational linguistics: System demonstrations*, 13–16. Nantes, France: University of Nantes.

Müller, Gereon. 1996a. A constraint on remnant movement. *Natural Language and Linguistic Theory* 14(2). 355–407.

Müller, Gereon. 1996b. On extraposition and successive cyclicity. In Uli Lutz & Jürgen Pafel (eds.), *On extraction and extraposition in German* (Linguistik Aktuell/Linguistics Today 11), 213–243. Amsterdam: John Benjamins Publishing Co.

Müller, Gereon. 1998. *Incomplete category fronting: A derivational approach to remnant movement in German* (Studies in Natural Language and Linguistic Theory 42). Dordrecht: Kluwer Academic Publishers.

Müller, Gereon. 2000. *Elemente der optimalitätstheoretischen Syntax* (Stauffenburg Linguistik 20). Tübingen: Stauffenburg Verlag.

Müller, Gereon. 2009a. There are no Constructions. Handout Ringvorlesung: *Algorithmen und Muster: Strukturen in der Sprache.* Freie Universität Berlin, 20. Mai.

Müller, Gereon. 2011. Regeln oder Konstruktionen? Von verblosen Direktiven zur sequentiellen Nominalreduplikation. In Stefan Engelberg, Anke Holler & Kristel Proost (eds.), *Sprachliches Wissen zwischen Lexikon und Grammatik* (Institut für Deutsche Sprache, Jahrbuch 2010), 211–249. Berlin: de Gruyter.

Müller, Gereon. 2014a. Syntactic buffers. Linguistische Arbeitsberichte 91 Institut für Linguistic Universität Leipzig. http://www.uni-leipzig.de/~muellerg/mu765.pdf.

Müller, Natascha & Beate Riemer. 1998. *Generative Syntax der romanischen Sprachen: Französisch, Italienisch, Portugiesisch, Spanisch* (Stauffenburg Einführungen 17). Tübingen: Stauffenburg Verlag.

Müller, Stefan. 1995. Scrambling in German – Extraction into the *Mittelfeld.* In Benjamin K. T'sou & Tom Bong Yeung Lai (eds.), *Proceedings of the Tenth Pacific Asia Conference on Language, Information and Computation*, 79–83. City University of Hong Kong.

Müller, Stefan. 1996c. The Babel-System—An HPSG fragment for German, a parser, and a dialogue component. In *Proceedings of the Fourth International Conference on the Practical Application of Prolog*, 263–277. London.

Müller, Stefan. 1996d. Yet another paper about partial verb phrase fronting in German. In Jun-ichi Tsuji (ed.), *Proceedings of COLING-96: 16th International Conference on Computational Linguistics (COLING96). Copenhagen, Denmark, August 5–9, 1996*, 800–805. Copenhagen, Denmark: Association for Computational Linguistics.

Müller, Stefan. 1999a. *Deutsche Syntax deklarativ: Head-Driven Phrase Structure Grammar für das Deutsche* (Linguistische Arbeiten 394). Tübingen: Max Niemeyer Verlag.

Müller, Stefan. 1999b. An HPSG-analysis for free relative clauses in German. *Grammars* 2(1). 53–105.

Müller, Stefan. 1999c. Restricting discontinuity. In *Proceedings of the 5th Natural Language Processing Pacific Rim Symposium 1999 (NLPRS'99)*, 85–90. Peking.

Müller, Stefan. 1999d. Restricting discontinuity. Verbmobil Report 237 Deutsches Forschungszentrum für Künstliche Intelligenz Saarbrücken. This report is also published in the Proceedings Proceedings of GLDV 99 (Frankfurt/Main). The initial part is contained in the proceedings of the 5th Natural Language Processing Pacific Rim Symposium 1999 (NLPRS'99).

Müller, Stefan. 2001. Case in German – towards an HPSG analysis. In Walt Detmar Meurers & Tibor Kiss (eds.), *Constraint-based approaches to Germanic syntax* (Studies in Constraint-Based Lexicalism 7), 217–255. Stanford, CA: CSLI Publications.

Müller, Stefan. 2002a. *Complex predicates: Verbal complexes, resultative constructions, and particle verbs in German* (Studies in Constraint-Based Lexicalism 13). Stanford, CA: CSLI Publications.

Müller, Stefan. 2002b. Multiple frontings in German. In Gerhard Jäger, Paola Monachesi, Gerald Penn & Shuly Wintner (eds.), *Proceedings of Formal Grammar 2002*, 113–124. Trento.

Müller, Stefan. 2002c. Syntax or morphology: German particle verbs revisited. In Nicole Dehé, Ray S. Jackendoff, Andrew McIntyre & Silke Urban (eds.), *Verb-particle explorations* (Interface Explorations 1), 119–139. Berlin: Mouton de Gruyter.

Müller, Stefan. 2003a. Mehrfache Vorfeldbesetzung. *Deutsche Sprache* 31(1). 29–62.

Müller, Stefan. 2003b. Object-to-subject-raising and lexical rule: An analysis of the German passive. In Stefan Müller (ed.), *Proceedings of the 10th International Conference on Head-Driven Phrase Structure Grammar, Michigan State University, East Lansing*, 278–297. Stanford, CA: CSLI Publications.

Müller, Stefan. 2003c. Solving the bracketing paradox: An analysis of the morphology of German particle verbs. *Journal of Linguistics* 39(2). 275–325.

Müller, Stefan. 2004a. An analysis of depictive secondary predicates in German without discontinuous constituents. In Stefan Müller (ed.), *Proceedings of the 11th International Conference on Head-Driven Phrase Structure Grammar, Center for Computational Linguistics, Katholieke Universiteit Leuven*, 202–222. Stanford, CA: CSLI Publications.

Müller, Stefan. 2004b. Complex NPs, subjacency, and extraposition. *Snippets* 8. 10–11.

Müller, Stefan. 2004c. Continuous or discontinuous constituents? A comparison between syntactic analyses for constituent order and their processing systems. *Research on Language and Computation, Special Issue on Linguistic Theory and Grammar Implementation* 2(2). 209–257.

Müller, Stefan. 2004d. An HPSG analysis of German depictive secondary predicates. In Lawrence S. Moss & Richard T. Oehrle (eds.), *Proceedings of the joint meeting of the 6th Conference on Formal Grammar and the 7th Conference on Mathematics of Language* (Electronic Notes in Theoretical Computer Science 53), 233–245. Helsinki: Elsevier Science Publisher B.V. (North-Holland). DOI:10.1016/S1571-0661(05)82585-X.

Müller, Stefan. 2005a. Resultative Constructions: Syntax, world knowledge, and collocational restrictions: Review of Hans C. Boas: A Constructional approach to resultatives. *Studies in Language* 29(3). 651–681.

Müller, Stefan. 2005b. Zur Analyse der deutschen Satzstruktur. *Linguistische Berichte* 201. 3–39.

Müller, Stefan. 2005c. Zur Analyse der scheinbar mehrfachen Vorfeldbesetzung. *Linguistische Berichte* 203. 297–330.

Müller, Stefan. 2006. Phrasal or lexical Constructions? *Language* 82(4). 850–883.

Müller, Stefan. 2007a. The Grammix CD Rom: A software collection for developing typed feature structure grammars. In Tracy Holloway King & Emily M. Bender (eds.), *Grammar Engineering across Frameworks 2007* (Studies in Computational Linguistics ONLINE), 259–266. Stanford, CA: CSLI Publications. http://csli-publications.stanford.edu/GEAF/2007/.

Müller, Stefan. 2007b. *Head-Driven Phrase Structure Grammar: Eine Einführung* (Stauffenburg Einführungen 17). Tübingen: Stauffenburg Verlag 1st edn.

Müller, Stefan. 2007c. Phrasal or lexical Constructions: Some comments on underspecification of constituent order, compositionality, and control. In Stefan Müller (ed.), *Proceedings of the 14th International Conference on Head-Driven Phrase Structure Grammar*, 373–393. Stanford, CA: CSLI Publications.

Müller, Stefan. 2007d. Qualitative Korpusanalyse für die Grammatiktheorie: Introspektion vs. Korpus. In Gisela Zifonun & Werner Kallmeyer (eds.), *Sprachkorpora – Datenmengen und Erkenntnisfortschritt* (Institut für Deutsche Sprache Jahrbuch 2006), 70–90. Berlin: Walter de Gruyter.

Müller, Stefan. 2008. Depictive secondary predicates in German and English. In Christoph Schroeder, Gerd Hentschel & Winfried Boeder (eds.), *Secondary predicates in Eastern European languages and beyond* (Studia Slavica Oldenburgensia 16), 255–273. Oldenburg: BIS-Verlag.

Müller, Stefan. 2009b. A Head-Driven Phrase Structure Grammar for Maltese. In Bernard Comrie, Ray Fabri, Beth Hume, Manwel Mifsud, Thomas Stolz & Martine Vanhove (eds.), *Introducing Maltese linguistics: Papers from the 1st International Conference on Maltese Linguistics (Bremen/Germany, 18–20 October, 2007)* (Studies in Language Companion Series 113), 83–112. Amsterdam: John Benjamins Publishing Co.

Müller, Stefan. 2009c. On predication. In Stefan Müller (ed.), *Proceedings of the 16th International Conference on Head-Driven Phrase Structure Grammar, University of Göttingen, Germany*, 213–233. Stanford, CA: CSLI Publications.

Müller, Stefan. 2010a. *Grammatiktheorie* (Stauffenburg Einführungen 20). Tübingen: Stauffenburg Verlag.

Müller, Stefan. 2010b. Persian complex predicates and the limits of inheritance-based analyses. *Journal of Linguistics* 46(3). 601–655.

Müller, Stefan. 2012a. On the copula, specificational constructions and type shifting. Ms. Freie Universität Berlin.

Müller, Stefan. 2012b. A personal note on open access in linguistics. *Journal of Language Modelling* 0(1). 9–39.

Müller, Stefan. 2013a. The CoreGram project: A brief overview and motivation. In Denys Duchier & Yannick Parmentier (eds.), *Proceedings of the workshop on high-level methodologies for grammar engineering (HMGE 2013), Düsseldorf*, 93–104.

Müller, Stefan. 2013b. *Grammatiktheorie* (Stauffenburg Einführungen 20). Tübingen: Stauffenburg Verlag 2nd edn.

Müller, Stefan. 2013c. Unifying everything: Some remarks on Simpler Syntax, Construction Grammar, Minimalism and HPSG. *Language* 89(4). 920–950.

Müller, Stefan. 2014b. Artenvielfalt und Head-Driven Phrase Structure Grammar. In Jörg Hagemann & Sven Staffeldt (eds.), *Syntaxtheorien: Analysen im Vergleich* (Stauffenburg Einführungen 28), 187–233. Tübingen: Stauffenburg Verlag.

Müller, Stefan. 2014c. Elliptical constructions, multiple frontings, and surface-based syntax. In Paola Monachesi, Gerhard Jäger, Gerald Penn & Shuly Wintner (eds.), *Proceedings of Formal Grammar 2004, Nancy*, 91–109. Stanford, CA: CSLI Publications.

Müller, Stefan. 2014d. Kernigkeit: Anmerkungen zur Kern-Peripherie-Unterscheidung. In Antonio Machicao y Priemer, Andreas Nolda & Athina Sioupi (eds.), *Zwischen Kern und Peripherie* (studia grammatica 76), 25–39. Berlin: de Gruyter.

Müller, Stefan. 2015a. The CoreGram project: Theoretical linguistics, theory development and verification. *Journal of Language Modelling* 3(1). 21–86. DOI:10.15398/jlm.v3i1.91.

Müller, Stefan. 2015b. *German sentence structure: An analysis with special consideration of so-called multiple fronting* (Empirically Oriented Theoretical Morphology and Syntax). Berlin: Language Science Press. Submitted.

Müller, Stefan. 2015c. HPSG – A synopsis. In Tibor Kiss & Artemis Alexiadou (eds.), *Syntax – Theory and analysis: An international handbook* (Handbooks of Linguistics and Communication Science 42.2), 937–973. Berlin: Walter de Gruyter 2nd edn.

Müller, Stefan. 2016a. *Germanic syntax* (Textbooks in Language Sciences). Berlin: Language Science Press. In Preparation.

Müller, Stefan. 2016b. Satztypen: Lexikalisch oder/und phrasal. In Rita Finkbeiner & Jörg Meibauer (eds.), *Satztypen und Konstruktionen im Deutschen* (Linguistik – Impulse und Tendenzen 65), 72–105. Berlin, Boston: de Gruyter.

Müller, Stefan & Masood Ghayoomi. 2010. PerGram: A TRALE implementation of an HPSG fragment of Persian. In *Proceedings of 2010 IEEE International Multiconference on Computer Science and Information Technology – Computational Linguistics Applications (CLA'10). Wisła, Poland, 18–20 October 2010*, vol. 5, 461–467. Polnish Information Processing Society.

Müller, Stefan & Martin Haspelmath. 2013. Language Science Press: A publication model for open-access books in linguistics. Grant Proposal to the DFG.

Müller, Stefan & Walter Kasper. 2000. HPSG analysis of German. In Wolfgang Wahlster (ed.), *Verbmobil: Foundations of speech-to-speech translation* (Artificial Intelligence), 238–253. Berlin: Springer Verlag.

Müller, Stefan & Janna Lipenkova. 2009. Serial verb constructions in Chinese: An HPSG account. In Stefan Müller (ed.), *Proceedings of the 16th International Conference on Head-Driven Phrase Structure Grammar, University of Göttingen, Germany*, 234–254. Stanford, CA: CSLI Publications.

Müller, Stefan & Janna Lipenkova. 2013. ChinGram: A TRALE implementation of an HPSG fragment of Mandarin Chinese. In Huei ling Lai & Kawai Chui (eds.), *Proceedings of the 27th Pacific Asia Conference on Language, Information, and Computation*

(PACLIC 27), 240–249. Taipei, Taiwan: Department of English, National Chengchi University.

Müller, Stefan & Janna Lipenkova. 2016. *Mandarin Chinese in Head-Driven Phrase Structure Grammar* (Empirically Oriented Theoretical Morphology and Syntax). Berlin: Language Science Press. In Preparation.

Müller, Stefan & Bjarne Ørsnes. 2011. Positional expletives in Danish, German, and Yiddish. In Stefan Müller (ed.), *Proceedings of the 18th International Conference on Head-Driven Phrase Structure Grammar, University of Washington, U.S.A.*, 167–187. Stanford, CA: CSLI Publications.

Müller, Stefan & Bjarne Ørsnes. 2013a. Passive in Danish, English, and German. In Stefan Müller (ed.), *Proceedings of the 20th International Conference on Head-Driven Phrase Structure Grammar, Freie Universität Berlin*, 140–160. Stanford, CA: CSLI Publications.

Müller, Stefan & Bjarne Ørsnes. 2013b. Towards an HPSG analysis of object shift in Danish. In Glyn Morrill & Mark-Jan Nederhof (eds.), *Formal Grammar: 17th and 18th International Conferences, FG 2012, Opole, Poland, August 2012, revised selected papers, FG 2013, Düsseldorf, Germany, August 2013: Proceedings* (Lecture Notes in Computer Science 8036), 69–89. Berlin: Springer Verlag.

Müller, Stefan & Bjarne Ørsnes. 2015. *Danish in Head-Driven Phrase Structure Grammar* (Empirically Oriented Theoretical Morphology and Syntax). Berlin: Language Science Press. In Preparation.

Müller, Stefan & Stephen Mark Wechsler. 2014a. Lexical approaches to argument structure. *Theoretical Linguistics* 40(1–2). 1–76.

Müller, Stefan & Stephen Mark Wechsler. 2014b. Two sides of the same slim Boojum: Further arguments for a lexical approach to argument structure. *Theoretical Linguistics* 40(1–2). 187–224.

Muraki, Kazunori, Shunji Ichiyama & Yasutomo Fukumochi. 1985. Augmented Dependency Grammar: A simple interface between the grammar rule and the knowledge. In Maghi King (ed.), *Proceedings of the 2nd European Meeting of the Association for Computational Linguistics*, 198–204. Geneva: Association for Computational Linguistics. http://aclweb.org/anthology/E/E85/.

Musso, Mariacristina, Andrea Moro, Volkmar Glauche, Michel Rijntjes, Jürgen Reichenbach, Christian Büchel & Cornelius Weiller. 2003. Broca's area and the language instinct. *Nature Neuroscience* 6(7). 774–781.

Müürisep, Kaili. 1999. Determination of syntactic functions in Estonian Constraint Grammar. In Henry S. Thompson & Alex Lascarides (eds.), *Ninth conference of the European Chapter of the Association for Computational Linguistics*, 291–292. Bergen, Norway.

Müürisep, Kaili, Tiina Puolakainen, Kadri Muischnek, Mare Koit, Tiit Roosmaa & Heli Uibo. 2003. A new language for Constraint Grammar: Estonian. In *International Conference Recent Advances in Natural Language Processing*, 304–310.

Muysken, Peter. 1982. Parameterizing the notion of "head". *Journal of Linguistic Research* 2. 57–75.

Mykowiecka, Agnieszka, Małgorzata Marciniak, Adam Przepiórkowski & Anna Kupść. 2003. An implementation of a Generative Grammar of Polish. In Peter Kosta, Joanna

Błaszczak, Jens Frasek, Ljudmila Geist & Marzena Żygis (eds.), *Investigations into formal Slavic linguistics: Contributions of the Fourth European Conference on Formal Description of Slavic Languages – FDSL IV held at Potsdam University, November 28–30, 2001*, 271–285. Frankfurt am Main: Peter Lang.

Naumann, Sven. 1987. Ein einfacher Parser für generalisierte Phrasenstrukturgrammatiken. *Zeitschrift für Sprachwissenschaft* 6(2). 206–226.

Naumann, Sven. 1988. *Generalisierte Phrasenstrukturgrammatik: Parsingstrategien, Regelorganisation und Unifikation* (Linguistische Arbeiten 212). Tübingen: Max Niemeyer Verlag.

Neeleman, Ad. 1994. *Complex predicates.* Utrecht: Onderzoeksinstituut voor Taal en Spraak (OTS) dissertation.

Nelimarkka, Esa, Harri Jäppinen & Aarno Lehtola. 1984. Two-way finite automata and Dependency Grammar: A parsing method for inflectional free word order languages. In Yorick Wilks (ed.), *Proceedings of the 10th International Conference on Computational Linguistics and 22nd Annual Meeting of the Association for Computational Linguistics,* 389–392. Stanford University, California: Association for Computational Linguistics.

Nerbonne, John. 1986a. 'Phantoms' and German fronting: Poltergeist constituents? *Linguistics* 24(5). 857–870.

Nerbonne, John. 1986b. A phrase-structure grammar for German passives. *Linguistics* 24(5). 907–938.

Nerbonne, John. 1993. A feature-based syntax/semantics interface. *Annals of Mathematics and Artificial Intelligence* 8(1–2). 107–132. Special issue on Mathematics of Language edited by Alexis Manaster-Ramer and Wlodek Zadrozsny, selected from the 2nd Conference on Mathematics of Language. Also published as DFKI Research Report RR-92-42.

Nerbonne, John, Klaus Netter & Carl J. Pollard (eds.). 1994. *German in Head-Driven Phrase Structure Grammar* (CSLI Lecture Notes 46). Stanford, CA: CSLI Publications.

Netter, Klaus. 1991. Clause union phenomena and complex predicates in German. DYANA Report, Deliverable R1.1.B University of Edinburgh.

Netter, Klaus. 1992. On non-head non-movement: An HPSG treatment of finite verb position in German. In Günther Görz (ed.), *Konvens 92. 1. Konferenz „Verarbeitung natürlicher Sprache". Nürnberg 7.–9. Oktober 1992* (Informatik aktuell), 218–227. Berlin: Springer Verlag.

Netter, Klaus. 1993. Architecture and coverage of the DISCO Grammar. In Stephan Busemann & Karin Harbusch (eds.), *DFKI Workshop on Natural Language Systems: Re-Usability and Modularity, October 23* (DFKI Document D-93-03), 1–10. Saarbrücken, Germany: DFKI.

Netter, Klaus. 1994. Towards a theory of functional heads: German nominal phrases. In John Nerbonne, Klaus Netter & Carl J. Pollard (eds.), *German in Head-Driven Phrase Structure Grammar* (CSLI Lecture Notes 46), 297–340. Stanford, CA: CSLI Publications.

Netter, Klaus. 1996. *Functional categories in an HPSG for German.* Saarbrücken: Universität des Saarlandes Dissertation.

Netter, Klaus. 1998. *Functional categories in an HPSG for German* (Saarbrücken Dissertations in Computational Linguistics and Language Technology 3). Saarbrücken: Deutsches Forschungszentrum für Künstliche Intelligenz Universität des Saarlandes.

Neville, Anne & Patrizia Paggio. 2004. Developing a Danish grammar in the GRASP project: A construction-based approach to topology and extraction in Danish. In Lawrence S. Moss & Richard T. Oehrle (eds.), *Proceedings of the joint meeting of the 6th Conference on Formal Grammar and the 7th Conference on Mathematics of Language* (Electronic Notes in Theoretical Computer Science 53), 246–259. Helsinki: Elsevier Science Publisher B.V. (North-Holland).

Nevins, Andrew Ira, David Pesetsky & Cilene Rodrigues. 2009. Pirahã exceptionality: A reassessment. *Language* 85(2). 355–404.

Newmeyer, Frederick J. 2004a. Against a parameter-setting approach to language variation. *Linguistic Variation Yearbook* 4. 181–234.

Newmeyer, Frederick J. 2004b. Typological evidence and Universal Grammar. *Studies in Language* 28(3). 527–548.

Newmeyer, Frederick J. 2005. *Possible and probable languages: A Generative perspective on linguistic typology.* Oxford: Oxford University Press.

Newmeyer, Frederick J. 2010. On comparative concepts and descriptive categories: A reply to Haspelmath. *Language* 86(3). 688–695.

Newport, Elissa L. 1990. Maturational constraints on language learning. *Cognitive Science* 14(1). 11–28.

Ng, Say Kiat. 1997. *A double-specifier account of Chinese NPs using Head-Driven Phrase Structure Grammar.* University of Edinburgh, Department of Linguistics MSc speech and language processing.

Nivre, Joakim. 2003. An efficient algorithm for projective dependency parsing. In Gertjan van Noord (ed.), *Proceedings of the 8th International Workshop on Parsing Technologies (IWPT 03)*, Nancy.

Nolda, Andreas. 2007. *Die Thema-Integration: Syntax und Semantik der gespaltenen Topikalisierung im Deutschen* (Studien zur deutschen Grammatik 72). Tübingen: Stauffenburg Verlag.

Noonan, Michael. 1994. A tale of two passives in Irish. In Barbara Fox & Paul J. Hopper (eds.), *Voice: Form and function* (Typological Studies in Language 27), 279–311. Amsterdam: John Benjamins Publishing Co.

van Noord, Gertjan & Gosse Bouma. 1994. The scope of adjuncts and the processing of lexical rules. In Makoto Nagao (ed.), *Proceedings of COLING 94*, 250–256. Kyoto, Japan: Association for Computational Linguistics.

Nordgård, Torbjørn. 1994. E-Parser: An implementation of a deterministic GB-related parsing system. *Computers and the Humanities* 28(4–5). 259–272.

Nordlinger, Rachel. 1998. *Constructive case: Evidence from Australia* (Dissertations in Linguistics). Stanford, CA: CSLI Publications.

Nowak, Martin A., Natalia L. Komarova & Partha Niyogi. 2001. Evolution of Universal Grammar. *Science* 291(5501). 114–118.

Nozohoor-Farshi, R. 1986. On formalizations of Marcus' parser. In Makoto Nagao (ed.), *Proceedings of COLING 86*, 533–535. University of Bonn: Association for Computational Linguistics.

Nozohoor-Farshi, R. 1987. Context-freeness of the language accepted by Marcus' parser. In Candy Sidner (ed.), *25th Annual Meeting of the Association for Computational Linguistics*, 117–122. Stanford, CA: Association for Computational Linguistics.

Nunberg, Geoffrey. 1995. Transfers of meaning. *Journal of Semantics* 12(2). 109–132.

Nunberg, Geoffrey, Ivan A. Sag & Thomas Wasow. 1994. Idioms. *Language* 70(3). 491–538.

Nunes, Jairo. 2004. *Linearization of chains and Sideward Movement* (Linguistic Inquiry Monographs 43). Cambridge, MA/London, England: MIT Press.

Ochs, Elinor. 1982. Talking to children in Western Samoa. *Language and Society* 11(1). 77–104.

Ochs, Elinor & Bambi B. Schieffelin. 1985. Language acquisition and socialization: Three developmental stories. In Richard A. Shweder & Robert A. LeVine (eds.), *Culture theory: Essays in mind, self and emotion*, 276–320. Cambridge, UK: Cambridge University Press.

O'Donovan, Ruth, Michael Burke, Aoife Cahill, Josef van Genabith & Andy Way. 2005. Large-scale induction and evaluation of lexical resources from the Penn-II and Penn-III Treebanks. *Computational Linguistics* 31(3). 328–365.

Oepen, Stephan & Daniel P. Flickinger. 1998. Towards systematic grammar profiling: Test suite technology ten years after. *Journal of Computer Speech and Language* 12(4). 411–436. http://www.delph-in.net/itsdb/publications/profiling.ps.gz. (Special Issue on Evaluation).

Özkaragöz, İnci. 1986. Monoclausal double passives in Turkish. In Dan I. Slobin & Karl Zimmer (eds.), *Studies in Turkish linguistics* (Typological Studies in Language 8), 77–91. Amsterdam: John Benjamins Publishing Co.

Oliva, Karel. 1992. Word order constraints in binary branching syntactic structures. CLAUS-Report 20 Universität des Saarlandes Saarbrücken.

Oliva, Karel. 2003. Dependency, valency and Head-Driven Phrase-Structure Grammar. In Vilmos Ágel, Ludwig M. Eichinger, Hans Werner Eroms, Peter Hellwig, Hans Jürgen Heringer & Henning Lobin (eds.), *Dependenz und Valenz / Dependency and valency: Ein internationales Handbuch der zeitgenössischen Forschung / An international handbook of contemporary research*, vol. 25.1 (Handbücher zur Sprach- und Kommunikationswissenschaft), 660–668. Berlin: Walter de Gruyter.

O'Neill, Michael & Randall Wood. 2012. The grammar of happiness. Essential Media & Entertainment / Smithsonian Networks. https://www.youtube.com/watch?v=er2VAk4uXUs#t=1519.

Oppenrieder, Wilhelm. 1991. *Von Subjekten, Sätzen und Subjektsätzen* (Linguisitische Arbeiten 241). Tübingen: Max Niemeyer Verlag.

Orgun, Cemil Orhan. 1996. *Sign-based morphology and phonology*: University of California, Berkeley dissertation.

Osborne, Miles & Ted J. Briscoe. 1997. Learning Stochastic Categorial Grammars. In T. Mark Ellison (ed.), *CoNLL97: Computational Natural Language Learning: Proceedings of the 1997 meeting of the ACL Special Interest Group in Natural Language Learning*, 80–87. Madrid: Association for Computational Linguistics. http://www.aclweb.org/anthology-new/signll.html#1997-0.

Osborne, Timothy. 2014. Dependency Grammar. In Andrew Carnie, Yosuke Sato & Dan Siddiqi (eds.), *The Routledge handbook of syntax*, 604–626. Oxford: Routledge.

Osborne, Timothy. 2016. Ellipsis in Dependency Grammar. In Jeroen van Craenenbrok (ed.), *Oxford handbook of ellipsis*, Oxford: Oxford University Press. To appear.

Osborne, Timothy & Thomas M. Groß. 2012. Constructions are catenae: Construction Grammar meets Dependency Grammar. *Cognitive Linguistics* 23(1). 165–216.

Osborne, Timothy & Sylvain Kahane. 2015. Translators' introduction. In *Elements of structural syntax*, xxix–lxxiii. Amsterdam: John Benjamins Publishing Co. Translated by Timothy Osborne and Sylvain Kahane.

Osborne, Timothy, Michael Putnam & Thomas M. Groß. 2011. Bare Phrase Structure, label-less trees, and specifier-less syntax: Is Minimalism becoming a Dependency Grammar? *The Linguistic Review* 28(3). 315–364.

Osenova, Petya. 2010a. Bulgarian Resource Grammar – efficient and realistic (BURGER). Tech. rep. LingoLab, CSLI Stanford. http://www.bultreebank.org/BURGER/BURGER3.pdf.

Osenova, Petya. 2010b. *Bulgarian Resource Grammar: Modeling Bulgarian in HPSG.* Saarbrücken: VDM Verlag Dr. Müller.

Osenova, Petya. 2011. Localizing a core HPSG-based grammar for Bulgarian. In Hanna Hedeland, Thomas Schmidt & Kai Wörner (eds.), *Multilingual resources and multilingual applications: Proceedings of the Conference of the German Society for Computational Linguistics and Language Technology (GSCL) 2011* (Arbeiten zur Mehrsprachigkeit/Working Papers in Multilingualism, Folge B/Series B 96), 175–182. Hamburg: Universitat Hamburg.

Ott, Dennis. 2011. A note on free relative clauses in the theory of Phases. *Linguistic Inquiry* 42(1). 183–192.

Ørsnes, Bjarne. 1995. *The derivation and compounding of complex event nominals in Modern Danish: An HPSG approach with an implementation in Prolog*: University of Copenhagen dissertation.

Ørsnes, Bjarne. 2002. Case marking and subject extraction in Danish. In Miriam Butt & Tracy Holloway King (eds.), *Proceedings of the LFG 2002 conference*, 333–353. Stanford, CA: CSLI Publications. http://csli-publications.stanford.edu/LFG/7/.

Ørsnes, Bjarne. 2009a. Das Verbalfeldmodell: Ein Stellungsfeldermodell für den kontrastiven DaF-Unterricht. *Deutsch als Fremdsprache* 46(3). 143–149.

Ørsnes, Bjarne. 2009b. Preposed negation in Danish. In Stefan Müller (ed.), *Proceedings of the 16th International Conference on Head-Driven Phrase Structure Grammar, University of Göttingen, Germany*, 255–275. Stanford, CA: CSLI Publications.

Ørsnes, Bjarne & Jürgen Wedekind. 2003. Paralelle datamatiske grammatikker for Norsk og Dansk [parallel computational grammars for Norwegian and Danish]. In Henrik Holmboe (ed.), *Årbog for nordisk sprogteknologisk forskningsprogram 2000–2004*, 113–130. Kopenhagen: Museum Tusculanums Forlag.

Ørsnes, Bjarne & Jürgen Wedekind. 2004. Paralelle datamatiske grammatikker for Norsk og Dansk: Analyse og disambiguering af modalverber [parallel computational grammars for Norwegian and Danish: Analysis and disambiguation of modal verbs]. In Henrik Holmboe (ed.), *Årbog for Nordisk Sprogteknologisk forskningsprogram 2000–2004*, 165–182. Kopenhagen: Museum Tusculanums Forlag.

Pafel, Jürgen. 1993. Ein Überblick über die Extraktion aus Nominalphrasen im Deutschen. In Franz-Josef d'Avis, Sigrid Beck, Uli Lutz, Jürgen Pafel & Susanne Trissler (eds.), *Extraktion im Deutschen I* (Arbeitspapiere des SFB 340 No. 34), 191–245. Tübingen: Eberhard-Karls-Universität Tübingen.

Paggio, Patrizia. 2005. Representing information structure in a formal grammar of Danish. In *Proceedings of the 2nd International Workshop on Logic and Engineering of Natural Language Semantics (LENLS2005). Kitakyushu, Japan. June 13–14,* .

Parmentier, Yannick, Laura Kallmeyer, Wolfgang Maier, Timm Lichte & Johannes Dellert. 2008. TuLiPA: A syntax-semantics parsing environment for mildly context-sensitive formalisms. In *Proceedings of the Ninth International Workshop on Tree Adjoining Grammars and Related Formalisms (TAG+9)*, 121–128. Tübingen. http://www.sfs.uni-tuebingen.de/~lk/papers/tag+9-parmentier-et-al.pdf.

Partee, Barbara H. 1987. Noun phrase interpretation and type-shifting principles. In Jeroen A. G. Groenendijk, Dick de Jongh & Martin J. B. Stokhof (eds.), *Studies in Discourse Representation Theory and the theory of generalized quantifiers*, 115–143. Dordrecht: Foris Publications.

Patejuk, Agnieszka & Adam Przepiórkowski. 2012. Towards an LFG parser for Polish: An exercise in parasitic grammar development. In *Proceedings of the Eighth International Conference on Language Resources and Evaluation, LREC 2012*, 3849–3852. Istanbul, Turkey: ELRA.

Paul, Hermann. 1919. *Deutsche Grammatik. Teil IV: Syntax*, vol. 3. Halle an der Saale: Max Niemeyer Verlag. 2nd unchanged edition 1968, Tübingen: Max Niemeyer Verlag.

Paul, Soma. 2004. *An HPSG account of Bangla compound verbs with LKB implementation*. Hyderabad, India: CALTS, University of Hyderabad, India dissertation.

Penn, Gerald. 2004. Balancing clarity and efficiency in typed feature logic through delaying. In Donia Scott (ed.), *Proceedings of the 42nd Meeting of the Association for Computational Linguistics (ACL'04), main volume*, 239–246. Barcelona, Spain.

Penn, Gerald & Bob Carpenter. 1999. ALE for speech: A translation prototype. In Géza Gordos (ed.), *Proceedings of the 6th Conference on Speech Communication and Technology (EUROSPEECH)*, Budapest, Hungary.

Perlmutter, David M. 1978. Impersonal passives and the Unaccusative Hypothesis. In *Proceedings of the 4th Annual Meeting of the Berkeley Linguistics Society*, 157–189. Berkeley Linguistic Society.

Perlmutter, David M. (ed.). 1983. *Studies in relational grammar*, vol. 1. Chicago: The University of Chicago Press.

Perlmutter, David M. (ed.). 1984. *Studies in relational grammar*, vol. 2. Chicago: The University of Chicago Press.

Perlmutter, David M. & John Robert Ross. 1970. Relative clauses with split antecedents. *Linguistic Inquiry* 1(3). 350.

Pesetsky, David. 1996. *Zero syntax: Experiencers and cascades*. Cambridge, MA: MIT Press.

Peters, Stanley & R. W. Ritchie. 1973. On the generative power of Transformational Grammar. *Information Sciences* 6(C). 49–83.

Petrick, Stanley Roy. 1965. *A recognition procedure for Transformational Grammars*: Massachusetts Institute of Technology. Dept. of Modern Languages dissertation. http://hdl.handle.net/1721.1/13013.

Phillips, Colin. 2003. Linear order and constituency. *Linguistic Inquiry* 34(1). 37–90.

Phillips, John D. 1992. A computational representation for Generalised Phrase Structure Grammars. *Linguistics and Philosophy* 15(3). 255–287.

Phillips, John D. & Henry S. Thompson. 1985. GPSGP – A parser for Generalized Phrase Structure Grammar. *Linguistics* 23(2). 245–261.

Piattelli-Palmarini, Massimo (ed.). 1980. *Language and learning: The debate between Jean Piaget and Noam Chomsky*. Cambridge: Harvard University Press.

Pickering, Martin & Guy Barry. 1993. Dependency Categorial Grammar and coordination. *Linguistics* 31(5). 855–902.

Pienemann, Manfred. 2005. An introduction to Processability Theory. In Manfred Pienemann (ed.), *Cross-linguistic aspects of processablity theory*, 1–60. Amsterdam: John Benjamins Publishing Co.

Piñango, Maria Mercedes, Jennifer Mack & Ray S. Jackendoff. 2006. Semantic combinatorial processes in argument structure: Evidence from light-verbs. In *Proceedings of the 32nd Annual Meeting of the Berkeley Linguistics Society: Theoretical approaches to argument structure*, vol. 32, Berkeley, CA: BLS.

Pineda, Luis Alberto & Iván V. Meza. 2005a. A computational model of the Spanish clitic system. In Alexander Gelbkuh (ed.), *Computational linguistics and intelligent language processing*, 73–82. Berlin: Springer Verlag.

Pineda, Luis Alberto & Iván V. Meza. 2005b. The Spanish pronominal clitic system. *Procesamiento del Lenguaje Natural* 34. 67–103.

Pinker, Steven. 1984. *Learnability and cognition: The acquisition of argument structure*. London/Cambridge, MA: MIT Press.

Pinker, Steven. 1994. *The language instinct: How the mind creates language*. New York: William Morrow.

Pinker, Steven & Ray S. Jackendoff. 2005. The faculty of language: What's special about it? *Cognition* 95(2). 201–236.

Pittner, Karin. 1995. Regeln für die Bildung von freien Relativsätzen: Eine Antwort an Oddleif Leirbukt. *Deutsch als Fremdsprache* 32(4). 195–200.

Plank, Frans & Elena Filimonova. 2000. The universals archive: A brief introduction for prospective users. *Sprachtypologie und Universalienforschung* 53(1). 109–123.

Poletto, Cecilia. 2000. *The higher functional field: Evidence from Northern Italian Dialects*. Oxford: Oxford University Press.

Pollard, Carl J. 1984. *Generalized Phrase Structure Grammars, Head Grammars, and natural language*: Stanford University dissertation.

Pollard, Carl J. 1988. Categorial Grammar and Phrase Structure Grammar: An excursion on the syntax-semantics frontier. In Richard Oehrle, Emmon Bach & Deirdre Wheeler (eds.), *Categorial Grammars and natural language structures*, 391–415. Dordrecht: D. Reidel Publishing Company.

Pollard, Carl J. 1994. Toward a unified account of passive in German. In John Nerbonne, Klaus Netter & Carl J. Pollard (eds.), *German in Head-Driven Phrase Structure Grammar* (CSLI Lecture Notes 46), 273–296. Stanford, CA: CSLI Publications.

Pollard, Carl J. 1996a. The nature of constraint-based grammar. Paper presented at the Pacific Asia Conference on Language, Information, and Computation, Kyung Hee University, Seoul, Korea. http://lingo.stanford.edu/sag/L221a/pollard-96.txt.

Pollard, Carl J. 1996b. On head non-movement. In Harry Bunt & Arthur van Horck (eds.), *Discontinuous constituency* (Natural Language Processing 6), 279–305. Berlin: Mouton de Gruyter. Published version of a Ms. dated January 1990.

Pollard, Carl J. 1999. Strong generative capacity in HPSG. In Gert Webelhuth, Jean-Pierre Koenig & Andreas Kathol (eds.), *Lexical and Constructional aspects of linguistic explanation* (Studies in Constraint-Based Lexicalism 1), 281–298. Stanford, CA: CSLI Publications.

Pollard, Carl J. & Andrew M. Moshier. 1990. Unifying partial descriptions of sets. In Philip P. Hanson (ed.), *Information, language and cognition* (Vancouver Studies in Cognitive Science 1), 285–322. Vancouver: University of British Columbia Press.

Pollard, Carl J. & Ivan A. Sag. 1987. *Information-based syntax and semantics* (CSLI Lecture Notes 13). Stanford, CA: CSLI Publications.

Pollard, Carl J. & Ivan A. Sag. 1992. Anaphors in English and the scope of Binding Theory. *Linguistic Inquiry* 23(2). 261–303.

Pollard, Carl J. & Ivan A. Sag. 1994. *Head-Driven Phrase Structure Grammar* (Studies in Contemporary Linguistics). Chicago: The University of Chicago Press.

Pollock, Jean-Yves. 1989. Verb movement, Universal Grammar and the structure of IP. *Linguistic Inquiry* 20(3). 365–424.

Popowich, Fred & Carl Vogel. 1991. A logic based implementation of Head-Driven Phrase Structure Grammar. In Charles Grant Brown & Gregers Koch (eds.), *Natural Language Understanding and Logic Programming, III. The 3rd International Workshop, Stockholm, Sweden, 23–25 Jan., 1991*, 227–246. Amsterdam: Elsevier, North-Holland.

Porzel, Robert, Vanessa Micelli, Hidir Aras & Hans-Peter Zorn. 2006. Tying the knot: Ground entities, descriptions and information objects for Construction-based information extraction. In *Proceedings of the OntoLex Workshop at LREC, May 2006. Genoa, Italy*, 35–40.

Postal, Paul M. 2004. *Skeptical linguistic essays*. Oxford: Oxford University Press.

Postal, Paul M. 2009. The incoherence of Chomsky's 'Biolinguistic' ontology. *Biolinguistics* 3(1). 104–123.

Postal, Paul M. & Geoffrey K. Pullum. 1986. Misgovernment. *Linguistic Inquiry* 17(1). 104–110.

Prince, Alan & Paul Smolensky. 1993. Optimality Theory: Constraint interaction in Generative Grammar. RuCCS Technical Report 2 Center for Cognitive Science, Rutgers University, Piscataway, N.J., and Computer Science Department, University of Colorado, Boulder. http://roa.rutgers.edu/files/537-0802/537-0802-PRINCE-0-0.PDF.

Przepiórkowski, Adam. 1999a. *Case assignment and the complement-adjunct dichotomy: A non-configurational constraint-based approach*: Eberhard-Karls-Universität Tübingen dissertation. https://publikationen.uni-tuebingen.de/xmlui/handle/10900/46147.

Przepiórkowski, Adam. 1999b. On case assignment and "adjuncts as complements". In Gert Webelhuth, Jean-Pierre Koenig & Andreas Kathol (eds.), *Lexical and Constructional aspects of linguistic explanation* (Studies in Constraint-Based Lexicalism 1), 231–245. Stanford, CA: CSLI Publications.

Przepiórkowski, Adam & Anna Kupść. 2006. HPSG for Slavicists. *Glossos* 8. 1–68.

Przepiórkowski, Adam, Anna Kupść, Małgorzata Marciniak & Agnieszka Mykowiecka. 2002. *Formalny opis języka polskiego: Teoria i implementacja*. Warsaw: Akademicka Oficyna Wydawnicza EXIT.

Pullum, Geoffrey K. 1977. Word order universals and grammatical relations. In Peter Cole & Jerrold M. Sadock (eds.), *Grammatical relations* (Syntax and Semantics 8), 249–277. New York, San Francisco, London: Academic Press.

Pullum, Geoffrey K. 1982. Free word order and phrase structure rules. In James Pustejovsky & Peter Sells (eds.), *Proceedings of the 12th Anual Meeting of the Northeast Linguistic Society*, 209–220. Amherst: Graduate Linguistics Student Association.

Pullum, Geoffrey K. 1983. How many possible human languages are there? *Linguistic Inquiry* 14(3). 447–467.

Pullum, Geoffrey K. 1984. Stalking the perfect journal. *Natural Language and Linguistic Theory* 2(2). 261–267.

Pullum, Geoffrey K. 1985. Assuming some version of X-bar Theory. In *Papers from the 21st Annual Meeting of the Chicago Linguistic Society*, 323–353.

Pullum, Geoffrey K. 1986. Footloose and context-free. *Natural Language and Linguistic Theory* 4(3). 409–414.

Pullum, Geoffrey K. 1988. Citation etiquette beyond thunderdome. *Natural Language and Linguistic Theory* 6(4). 579–588.

Pullum, Geoffrey K. 1989a. Formal linguistics meets the Boojum. *Natural Language and Linguistic Theory* 7(1). 137–143. DOI:10.1007/BF00141350.

Pullum, Geoffrey K. 1989b. The incident of the node vortex problem. *Natural Language and Linguistic Theory* 7(3). 473–479.

Pullum, Geoffrey K. 1991. *The great Eskimo vocabulary hoax and other irreverent essays on the study of language*. Chicago: The University of Chicago Press.

Pullum, Geoffrey K. 1996. Learnability, hyperlearning, and the Poverty of the Stimulus. In J. Johnson, M. L. Juge & J. L. Moxley (eds.), *Proceedings of the 22nd Annual Meeting of the Berkeley Linguistics Society: General session and parasession on the role of learnability in grammatical theory*, 498–513. Berkeley, CA: Berkeley Linguistic Society. http://users.ecs.soton.ac.uk/harnad/Papers/Py104/pullum.learn.html.

Pullum, Geoffrey K. 2003. Learnability: Mathematical aspects. In William J. Frawley (ed.), *Oxford international encyclopedia of linguistics*, 431–434. Oxford: Oxford University Press 2nd edn.

Pullum, Geoffrey K. 2007. The evolution of model-theoretic frameworks in linguistics. In James Rogers & Stephan Kepser (eds.), *Model-theoretic syntax at 10 – Proceedings of the ESSLLI 2007 MTS@10 Workshop, August 13–17*, 1–10. Dublin: Trinity College Dublin.

Pullum, Geoffrey K. 2009. Response to Anderson. *Language* 85(2). 245–247.

Pullum, Geoffrey K. 2013. The central question in comparative syntactic metatheory. *Mind and Language* 28(4). 492–521.

Pullum, Geoffrey K. & Barbara C. Scholz. 2001. On the distinction between Generative-Enumerative and Model-Theoretic syntactic frameworks. In Philippe de Groote, Glyn Morrill & Christian Retor (eds.), *Logical Aspects of Computational Linguistics: 4th International Conference* (Lecture Notes in Computer Science 2099), 17–43. Berlin: Springer Verlag.

Pullum, Geoffrey K. & Barbara C. Scholz. 2002. Empirical assessment of stimulus poverty arguments. *The Linguistic Review* 19(1–2). 9–50.

Pullum, Geoffrey K. & Barbara C. Scholz. 2010. Recursion and the infinitude claim. In Harry van der Hulst (ed.), *Recursion in human language* (Studies in Generative Grammar 104), 113–138. Berlin: Mouton de Gruyter.

Pulman, Stephen G. 1985. A parser that doesn't. In Maghi King (ed.), *Proceedings of the 2nd European Meeting of the Association for Computational Linguistics*, 128–135. Geneva: Association for Computational Linguistics. http://aclweb.org/anthology/E/E85/.

Pulvermüller, Friedemann. 2003. *The neuroscience of language: On brain circuits of words and serial order*. Cambridge, UK: Cambridge University Press.

Pulvermüller, Friedemann. 2010. Brain embodiment of syntax and grammar: Discrete combinatorial mechanisms spelt out in neuronal circuits. *Brain & Language* 112(3). 167–179.

Pulvermüller, Friedemann, Bert Cappelle & Yury Shtyrov. 2013. Brain basis of meaning, words, constructions, and grammar. In Thomas Hoffmann & Graeme Trousdale (eds.), *The Oxford handbook of Construction Grammar* (Oxford Handbooks), 397–416. Oxford: Oxford University Press.

Quaglia, Stefano. 2014. On the syntax of some apparent spatial particles in Italian. In Miriam Butt & Tracy Holloway King (eds.), *Proceedings of the LFG 2014 conference*, 503–523. Stanford, CA: CSLI Publications.

Radford, Andrew. 1990. *Syntactic theory and the acquisition of English syntax*. Cambridge, MA: Blackwell Publishing Ltd.

Radford, Andrew. 1997. *Syntactic theory and the structure of English: A Minimalist approach* (Cambridge Textbooks in Linguistics). Cambridge, UK: Cambridge University Press.

Rákosi, György, Tibor Laczkó & Gábor Csernyi. 2011. On English phrasal verbs and their Hungarian counterparts: From the perspective of a computational linguistic project. *Argumentum* 7. 80–89.

Rambow, Owen. 1994. *Formal and computational aspects of natural language syntax*: University of Pennsylvania dissertation.

Ramchand, Gillian. 2005. Post-Davidsonianism. *Theoretical Linguistics* 31(3). 359–373.

Randriamasimanana, Charles. 2006. Simple sentences in Malagasy. In Henry Y. Chang, Lillian M. Huang & Dah ah Ho (eds.), *Streams converging into an ocean: Festschrift in honor of Professor Paul Jen-kuei Li on his 70th birthday*, 71–96. Taipei, Taiwan: Institute of Linguistics, Academia Sinica.

Raposo, Eduardo & Juan Uriagereka. 1990. Long-distance case assignment. *Linguistic Inquiry* 21(4). 505–537.

Rappaport, Malka. 1983. On the nature of derived nominals. In Lori S. Levin, Malka Rappaport & Annie Zaenen (eds.), *Papers in Lexical Functional Grammar*, 113–42. Indiana: Indiana University Linguistics Club.

Rauh, Gisa. 2013. Linguistic categories and the syntax-semantics interface: Evaluating competing approaches. Ms. Universität Wuppertal.

Reape, Mike. 1991. Word order variation in Germanic and parsing. DYANA Report Deliverable R1.1.C University of Edinburgh.

Reape, Mike. 1992. *A formal theory of word order: A case study in West Germanic*: University of Edinburgh dissertation.

Reape, Mike. 1994. Domain union and word order variation in German. In John Nerbonne, Klaus Netter & Carl J. Pollard (eds.), *German in Head-Driven Phrase Structure Grammar* (CSLI Lecture Notes 46), 151–198. Stanford, CA: CSLI Publications.

Reape, Mike. 2000. Formalisation and abstraction in linguistic theory II: Toward a radical Linearisation Theory of German. unpublished paper.

Redington, Martin, Nick Chater & Steven Finch. 1998. Distributional information: A powerful cue for acquiring syntactic categories. *Cognitive Science* 22(4). 425–469.

Reis, Marga. 1974. Syntaktische Hauptsatzprivilegien und das Problem der deutschen Wortstellung. *Zeitschrift für Germanistische Linguistik* 2(3). 299–327.

Reis, Marga. 1980. On justifying topological frames: 'Positional field' and the order of nonverbal constituents in German. *Documentation et Recherche en Linguistique Allemande Contemporaine* 22/23. 59–85.

Reis, Marga. 1982. Zum Subjektbegriff im Deutschen. In Werner Abraham (ed.), *Satzglieder im Deutschen – Vorschläge zur syntaktischen, semantischen und pragmatischen Fundierung* (Studien zur deutschen Grammatik 15), 171–211. Tübingen: originally Gunter Narr Verlag now Stauffenburg Verlag.

Remberger, Eva-Maria. 2009. Null subjects, expletives and locatives in Sardinian. In Georg A. Kaiser & Eva-Maria Remberger (eds.), *Proceedings of the workshop* Null-Subjects, Expletives, and Locatives in Romance (Arbeitspapier 123), 231–261. Konstanz: Fachbereich Sprachwissenschaft, Universität Konstanz.

Resnik, Philip. 1992. Probabilistic Tree-Adjoining Grammar as a framework for statistical natural language processing. In Antonio Zampolli (ed.), *14th International Conference on Computational Linguistics (COLING '92), August 23–28*, 418–424. Nantes, France: Association for Computational Linguistics.

Reyle, Uwe. 1993. Dealing with ambiguities by underspecification: Construction, representation and deduction. *Jounal of Semantics* 10(2). 123–179.

Richards, Marc. 2015. Minimalism. In Tibor Kiss & Artemis Alexiadou (eds.), *Syntax – theory and analysis: An international handbook*, vol. 42 (Handbooks of Linguistics and Communication Science), 803–839. Berlin: Mouton de Gruyter 2nd edn.

Richter, Frank. 2004. *A mathematical formalism for linguistic theories with an application in Head-Driven Phrase Structure Grammar*: Eberhard-Karls-Universität Tübingen Phil. Dissertation (2000). https://publikationen.uni-tuebingen.de/xmlui/handle/10900/46230.

Richter, Frank. 2007. Closer to the truth: A new model theory for HPSG. In James Rogers & Stephan Kepser (eds.), *Model-theoretic syntax at 10 – Proceedings of the ESSLLI 2007 MTS@10 Workshop, August 13–17*, 101–110. Dublin: Trinity College Dublin.

Richter, Frank & Manfred Sailer. 1999a. A lexicalist collocation analysis of sentential negation in French. In Valia Kordoni (ed.), *Tübingen studies in Head-Driven Phrase Structure Grammar* (Arbeitspapiere des SFB 340, No. 132, Volume 1), 231–300. Tübingen: Eberhard-Karls-Universität Tübingen.

Richter, Frank & Manfred Sailer. 1999b. Lexicalizing the left periphery of German finite sentences. In Valia Kordoni (ed.), *Tübingen studies in Head-Driven Phrase Structure Grammar* (Arbeitspapiere des SFB 340, No. 132, Volume 1), 116–154. Tübingen: Eberhard-Karls-Universität Tübingen.

Richter, Frank & Manfred Sailer. 2004. Basic concepts of lexical resource semantics. In Arnold Beckmann & Norbert Preining (eds.), *ESSLLI 2003 – Course material I* (Collegium Logicum 5), 87–143. Wien: Kurt Gödel Society.

Richter, Frank & Manfred Sailer. 2009. Phraseological clauses as Constructions in HPSG. In Stefan Müller (ed.), *Proceedings of the 16th International Conference on Head-Driven Phrase Structure Grammar, University of Göttingen, Germany*, 297–317. Stanford, CA: CSLI Publications.

Riehemann, Susanne. 1993. *Word formation in lexical type hierarchies: A case study of bar-adjectives in German*. Eberhard-Karls-Universität Tübingen MA thesis. Also published as SfS-Report-02-93, Seminar für Sprachwissenschaft, University of Tübingen.

Riehemann, Susanne Z. 1998. Type-based derivational morphology. *Journal of Comparative Germanic Linguistics* 2(1). 49–77.

Riemsdijk, Henk van. 1978. *A case study in syntactic markedness: The binding nature of prepositional phrases*. Lisse: The Peter de Ridder Press.

Riezler, Stefan, Tracy Holloway King, Ronald M. Kaplan, Richard Crouch, John T. Maxwell III & Mark Johnson. 2002. Parsing the Wall Street Journal using a Lexical-Functional Grammar and discriminative estimation techniques. In Pierre Isabelle (ed.), *40th Annual Meeting of the Association for Computational Linguistics: Proceedings of the conference*, 271–278. University of Pennsylvania, Philadelphia: Association for Computational Linguistics. http://aclanthology.info/events/acl-2002.

Rizzi, Luigi. 1982. Violations of the *wh* island constraint and the Subjacency Condition. In Luigi Rizzi (ed.), *Issues in Italian syntax* (Studies in Generative Grammar 11), 49–76. Dordrecht: Foris Publications.

Rizzi, Luigi. 1986. Null objects in Italian and the theory of *pro*. *Linguistic Inquiry* 17(3). 501–577.

Rizzi, Luigi. 1997. The fine structure of the left periphery. In Liliane Haegeman (ed.), *Elements of grammar*, 281–337. Dordrecht: Kluwer Academic Publishers.

Rizzi, Luigi. 2009a. The discovery of language invariance and variation, and its relevance for the cognitive sciences. *The Behavioral and Brain Sciences* 32(5). 467–468.

Rizzi, Luigi. 2009b. Language variation and universals: Some notes on N. Evans and S. C. Levinson (2009) "The myth of language universals: Language diversity and its importance for cognitive science". In Paola Cotticelli-Kurras & Alessandra Tomaselli (eds.), *La Grammatica tra storia e teoria. Studi in onore di Giorgio Graffi*, 153–162. Alessandra: Edizioni dell'Orso.

Roberts, Ian F. & Anders Holmberg. 2005. On the role of parameters in Universal Grammar: A reply to Newmeyer. In Hans Broekhuis, N. Corver, Riny Huybregts, Ursula Kleinhenz & Jan Koster (eds.), *Organizing grammar: Linguistic studies in honor of Henk van Riemsdijk* (Studies in Generative Grammar 86), 538–553. Berlin: Mouton de Gruyter.

Robins, Robert Henry. 1997. *A short history of linguistics* (Longman Linguistics Library). London: Routledge 4th edn.

Rogers, James. 1994. Obtaining trees from their descriptions: An application to Tree-Adjoining Grammars. *Computational Intelligence* 10(4). 401–421.

Rogers, James. 1997. "Grammarless" Phrase Structure Grammar. *Linguistics and Philosophy* 20. 721–746.

Rogers, James. 1998. *A descriptive approach to language-theoretic complexity* (Studies in Logic, Language and Information). Stanford, CA: CSLI Publications.

Rohrer, Christian. 1996. Fakultativ kohärente Infinitkonstruktionen im Deutschen und deren Behandlung in der Lexikalisch Funktionalen Grammatik. In Gisela Harras & Manfred Bierwisch (eds.), *Wenn die Semantik arbeitet: Klaus Baumgärtner zum 65. Geburtstag*, 89–108. Tübingen: Max Niemeyer Verlag.

Rohrer, Christian & Martin Forst. 2006. Improving coverage and parsing quality of a large-scale LFG for German. In *Proceedings of the Language Resources and Evaluation Conference (LREC-2006)*, Genoa, Italy.

Ross, John Robert. 1967. *Constraints on variables in syntax*: MIT dissertation. http://files.eric.ed.gov/fulltext/ED016965.pdf. Reproduced by the Indiana University Linguistics Club and later published as Ross (1986).

Ross, John Robert. 1986. *Infinite syntax!* Norwood, New Jersey: Ablex Publishing Corporation.

Rothkegel, Annely. 1976. *Valenzgrammatik* (Linguistische Arbeiten 19). Saarbrücken, Germany: Sonderforschungsbereich Elektronische Sprachforschung, Universität des Saarlandes.

Sabel, Joachim. 1999. Das Passiv im Deutschen: Derivationale Ökonomie vs. optionale Bewegung. *Linguistische Berichte* 177. 87–112.

Sáfár, Éva & John Glauert. 2010. Sign Language HPSG. In *Proceedings of the 4th Workshop on the Representation and Processing of Sign Languages: Corpora and Sign Language Technologies, LREC 2010, 22–23 May 2010, Malta*, 204–207.

Sáfár, Éva & Ian Marshall. 2002. Sign language translation via DRT and HPSG. In Alexander Gelbukh (ed.), *Computational linguistics and intelligent text processing: Third International Conference, CICLing 2002 Mexico City, Mexico, February 17–23, 2002 Proceedings* (Lecture Notes in Computer Science 2276), 58–68. Berlin: Springer Verlag.

Sag, Ivan A. 1997. English relative clause constructions. *Journal of Linguistics* 33(2). 431–484.

Sag, Ivan A. 2000. Another argument against *Wh*-trace. Jorge Hankamer Webfest. http://ling.ucsc.edu/Jorge/sag.html.

Sag, Ivan A. 2007. Remarks on locality. In Stefan Müller (ed.), *Proceedings of the 14th International Conference on Head-Driven Phrase Structure Grammar*, 394–414. Stanford, CA: CSLI Publications. http://csli-publications.stanford.edu/HPSG/2007/.

Sag, Ivan A. 2010. English filler-gap constructions. *Language* 86(3). 486–545.

Sag, Ivan A. 2012. Sign-Based Construction Grammar: An informal synopsis. In Hans C. Boas & Ivan A. Sag (eds.), *Sign-based Construction Grammar* (CSLI Lecture Notes 193), 69–202. Stanford, CA: CSLI Publications.

Sag, Ivan A., Hans C. Boas & Paul Kay. 2012. Introducing Sign-Based Construction Grammar. In Hans C. Boas & Ivan A. Sag (eds.), *Sign-based Construction Grammar* (CSLI Lecture Notes 193), 1–29. Stanford, CA: CSLI Publications.

Sag, Ivan A., Philip Hofmeister & Neal Snider. 2007. Processing complexity in subjacency violations: The Complex Noun Phrase Constraint. In Malcolm Elliott, James Kirby, Osamu Sawada, Eleni Staraki & Suwon Yoon (eds.), *Proceedings of the 43rd Annual Meeting of the Chicago Linguistic Society*, 215–229. Chicago: Chicago Linguistic Society.

Sag, Ivan A. & Carl J. Pollard. 1991. An integrated theory of complement control. *Language* 67(1). 63–113.

Sag, Ivan A. & Thomas Wasow. 2011. Performance-compatible competence grammar. In Robert D. Borsley & Kersti Börjars (eds.), *Non-transformational syntax: Formal and explicit models of grammar: A guide to current models*, 359–377. Oxford, UK/Cambridge, MA: Blackwell Publishing Ltd.

Sag, Ivan A., Thomas Wasow & Emily M. Bender. 2003. *Syntactic theory: A formal introduction* (CSLI Lecture Notes 152). Stanford, CA: CSLI Publications 2nd edn.

Sag, Ivan A. & Tom Wasow. 2015. Flexible processing and the design of grammar. *Journal of Psycholinguistic Research* 44(1). 47–63.

Sailer, Manfred. 2000. *Combinatorial semantics and idiomatic expressions in Head-Driven Phrase Structure Grammar*: Eberhard-Karls-Universität Tübingen Dissertation. https://publikationen.uni-tuebingen.de/xmlui/handle/10900/46191.

Samarin, William J. 1984. Socioprogrammed linguistics. *The Behavioral and Brain Sciences* 7(2). 206–207.

Sampson, Geoffrey. 1989. Language acquisition: Growth or learning? *Philosophical Papers* 18(3). 203–240.

Samvelian, Pollet. 2007. A (phrasal) affix analysis of the Persian Ezafe. *Journal of Linguistics* 43. 605–645.

Sarkar, Anoop & Aravind K. Joshi. 1996. Coordination in Tree Adjoining Grammars: Formalization and implementation. In Jun-ichi Tsuji (ed.), *Proceedings of COLING-96. 16th International Conference on Computational Linguistics COLING96). Copenhagen, Denmark, August 5–9, 1996*, 610–615. Copenhagen, Denmark: Association for Computational Linguistics.

Sato, Yo. 2006. Constrained free word order parsing with Lexicalised Linearisation Grammar. In *Proceedings of 9th Annual CLUK Research Colloquium*, Open University, UK.

Sato, Yo. 2008. *Implementing Head-Driven Linearisation Grammar*: King's College London dissertation.

Sauerland, Uli & Paul Elbourne. 2002. Total reconstruction, PF movement, and derivational order. *Linguistic Inquiry* 33(2). 283–319.

Savin, Harris B. & Ellen Perchonock. 1965. Grammatical structure and the immediate recall of English sentences. *Journal of Verbal Learning and Verbal Behavior* 4(5). 348–353.

Schein, Barry. 1993. *Plurals and events* (Current Studies in Linguistics 23). Cambridge, MA: MIT Press.

Scherpenisse, Wim. 1986. *The connection between base structure and linearization restrictions in German and Dutch* (Europäische Hochschulschriften, Reihe XXI, Linguistik 47). Frankfurt/M.: Peter Lang.

Schluter, Natalie & Josef van Genabith. 2009. Dependency parsing resources for French: Converting acquired Lexical Functional Grammar f-structure annotations and parsing f-structures directly. In Kristiina Jokinen & Eckhard Bick (eds.), *Nodalida 2009 conference proceedings*, 166–173.

Schmidt, Paul, Sibylle Rieder & Axel Theofilidis. 1996a. Final documentation of the German LS-GRAM lingware. Deliverable DC-WP6e (German) IAI Saarbrücken.

Schmidt, Paul, Axel Theofilidis, Sibylle Rieder & Thierry Declerck. 1996b. Lean formalisms, linguistic theory, and applications: Grammar development in ALEP. In Jun-ichi Tsuji (ed.), *Proceedings of COLING-96. 16th International Conference on Computational Linguistics COLING96). Copenhagen, Denmark, August 5–9, 1996*, 286–291. Copenhagen, Denmark: Association for Computational Linguistics. DOI:10.3115/992628.992679.

Scholz, Barbara C. & Geoffrey K. Pullum. 2002. Searching for arguments to support linguistic nativism. *The Linguistic Review* 19(1–2). 185–223.

Schubert, K. 1987. *Metataxis: Contrastive Dependency Syntax for machine translation*. Dordrecht: Foris Publications.

Schumacher, Helmut, Jacqueline Kubczak, Renate Schmidt & Vera de Ruiter. 2004. *VALBU – Valenzwörterbuch deutscher Verben*. Tübingen: Gunter Narr Verlag.

Schütz, Jörg. 1996. The ALEP formalism in a nutshell. Tech. rep. IAI Saarbrücken. http://www.iai-sb.de/docs/alep-nutshell.pdf.

Schwarze, Christoph & Leonel de Alencar. 2016. *Lexikalisch-funktionale Grammatik: Eine Einführung am Beispiel des Französischen, mit computerlinguistischer Implementierung* (Stauffenburg Einführungen 30). Tübingen: Stauffenburg Verlag.

Seiss, Melanie & Rachel Nordlinger. 2012. An electronic dictionary and translation system for Murrinh-Patha. *The EUROCALL Review: Proceedings of the EUROCALL 2011 Conference* 20(1). 135–138.

Sengupta, Probal & B. B. Chaudhuri. 1997. A delayed syntactic-encoding-based LFG parsing strategy for an Indian language—Bangla. *Computational Linguistics* 23(2). 345–351.

Seuren, Pieter A. M. 1984. The Bioprogram Hypothesis: Facts and fancy. *The Behavioral and Brain Sciences* 7(2). 208–209.

Seuren, Pieter A. M. 2004. *Chomsky's Minimalism*. Oxford: Oxford University Press.

Shieber, Stuart M. 1985. Evidence against the context-freeness of natural language. *Linguistics and Philosophy* 8(3). 333–343.

Shieber, Stuart M. 1986. *An introduction to unification-based approaches to grammar* (CSLI Lecture Notes 4). Stanford, CA: CSLI Publications.

Shieber, Stuart M. & Mark Johnson. 1993. Variations on incremental interpretation. *Journal of Psycholinguistic Research* 22(2). 287–318.

Shieber, Stuart M., Hans Uszkoreit, Fernando Pereira, Jane Robinson & Mabry Tyson. 1983. The formalism and implementation of PATR-II. In *Research on interactive acquisition and use of knowledge*, 39–79. Menlo Park, CA: Artificial Intelligence Center, SRI International.

Shtyrov, Y., E. Pihko & F. Pulvermüller. 2005. Determinants of dominance: Is language laterality explained by physical or linguistic features of speech? *Neuroimage* 27(1). 37–47.

Siegel, Melanie. 2000. HPSG analysis of Japanese. In Wolfgang Wahlster (ed.), *Verbmobil: Foundations of speech-to-speech translation* (Artificial Intelligence), 264–279. Berlin: Springer Verlag.

Siegel, Melanie & Emily M. Bender. 2002. Efficient deep processing of Japanese. In *Proceedings of the 3rd Workshop on Asian Language Resources and International Standardization at the 19th International Conference on Computational Linguistics. Taipei, Taiwan*, http://www.aclweb.org/anthology-new/W/W02/W02-1210.pdf.

Simov, Kiril, Petya Osenova, Alexander Simov & Milen Kouylekov. 2004. Design and implementation of the Bulgarian HPSG-based treebank. *Research on Language and Computation* 2(4). 495–522.

Simpson, Jane. 1983. Resultatives. In Lori S. Levin, Malka Rappaport & Annie Zaenen (eds.), *Papers in Lexical Functional Grammar*, 143–157. Indiana: Indiana University Linguistics Club. Reprint: Simpson (2005b).

Simpson, Jane. 2005a. Depictives in English and Warlpiri. In Nikolaus P. Himmelmann & Eva Schultze-Berndt (eds.), *Secondary predication and adverbial modification: The typology of depictives*, 69–106. Oxford: Oxford University Press.

Simpson, Jane. 2005b. Resultatives. In Miriam Butt & Tracy Holloway King (eds.), *Lexical semantics in LFG*, 149–161. Stanford, CA: CSLI Publications.

Singleton, Jenny L. & Elissa L. Newport. 2004. When learners surpass their models: The acquisition of American Sign Language from inconsistent input. *Cognitive Psychology* 49(4). 370–407.

Sleator, Daniel D. K. & Davy Temperley. 1991. Parsing English with a Link Grammar. CMU-CS-TR-91-126 School of Computer Science, Carnegie Mellon University.

Smith, Carlota S. 1970. Jespersen's "move and change" class and causative verbs in English. In Bert Peeters (ed.), *The lexicon–encyclopedia interface*, 101–109. Amsterdam: Elsevier.

Smith, Carlota S. 1972. On causative verbs and derived nominals in English. *Linguistic Inquiry* 3(1). 136–138.

Snyder, William. 2001. On the nature of syntactic variation: Evidence from complex predicates and complex word-formation. *Language* 77(2). 324–342.

Soehn, Jan-Philipp & Manfred Sailer. 2008. At first blush on tenterhooks: About selectional restrictions imposed by nonheads. In Gerhard Jäger, Paola Monachesi, Gerald Penn & Shuly Wintner (eds.), *Proceedings of Formal Grammar 2003, Vienna, Austria*, 149–161. Stanford, CA: CSLI Publications. http://csli-publications.stanford.edu/FG/2003/soehn.pdf.

Son, Minjeong. 2007. Directionality and resultativity: The cross-linguistic correlation revisited. *Tromsø University Working Papers on Language & Linguistics* 34. 126–164. http://hdl.handle.net/10037/3191.

Son, Minjeong & Peter Svenonius. 2008. Microparameters of cross-linguistic variation: Directed motion and resultatives. In Natasha Abner & Jason Bishop (eds.), *Proceedings of the 27th West Coast Conference on Formal Linguistics*, 388–396. Somerville, MA: Cascadilla Proceedings Project.

Song, Sanghoun, Jong-Bok Kim, Francis Bond & Jaehyung Yang. 2010. Development of the Korean Resource Grammar: Towards grammar customization. In *Proceedings of the 8th Workshop on Asian Language Resources, Beijing, China, 21–22 August 2010*, 144–152. Asian Federation for Natural Language Processing.

Sorace, Antonella. 2003. Near-nativeness. In Catherine J. Doughty & Michael H. Long (eds.), *The handbook of second language acquisition* (Blackwell Handbooks in Linguistics), 130–151. Oxford, UK/Cambridge, USA: Blackwell Publishing Ltd.

Stabler, Edward P. 1987. Restricting logic grammars with Government-Binding Theory. *Computational Linguistics* 13(1–2). 1–10.

Stabler, Edward P. 1991. Avoid the pedestrian's paradox. In Robert C. Berwick, Steven P. Abney & Carol Tenny (eds.), *Principle-based parsing: Computation and psycholinguistics*, 199–237. Dordrecht: Kluwer Academic Publishers.

Stabler, Edward P. 1992. *The logical approach to syntax: Foundations, specifications, and implementations of theories of Government and Binding* (ACL-MIT Press Series in Natural Language Processing). Cambridge, MA: MIT Press.

Stabler, Edward P. 2001. Minimalist Grammars and recognition. In Christian Rohrer, Antje Rossdeutscher & Hans Kamp (eds.), *Linguistic form and its computation* (Studies in Computational Linguistics 1), 327–352. Stanford, CA: CSLI Publications.

Stabler, Edward P. 2011a. After Governement and Binding Theory. In Johan F. A. K. van Benthem & G. B. Alice ter Meulen (eds.), *Handbook of logic and language*, 395–414. Amsterdam: Elsevier 2nd edn.

Stabler, Edward P. 2011b. Computational perspectives on Minimalism. In Cedric Boeckx (ed.), *The Oxford handbook of linguistic Minimalism* (Oxford Handbooks in Linguistics), chap. 27, 616–641. Oxford: Oxford University Press.

Starosta, Stanley. 1988. *The case for Lexicase* (Open Linguistics Series). London: Pinter Publishers.

Starosta, Stanley & Hirosato Nomura. 1986. Lexicase parsing: A lexicon-driven approach to syntactic analysis. In Makoto Nagao (ed.), *Proceedings of COL-ING 86*, 127–132. University of Bonn: Association for Computational Linguistics. DOI:10.3115/991365.991400.

von Stechow, Arnim. 1979. Deutsche Wortstellung und Montague-Grammatik. In Jürgen M. Meisel & Martin D. Pam (eds.), *Linear order and Generative theory*, 317–490. Amsterdam: John Benjamins Publishing Co.

von Stechow, Arnim. 1989. Distinguo: Eine Antwort auf Dieter Wunderlich. *Linguistische Berichte* 122. 330–339.

von Stechow, Arnim. 1996. The different readings of *wieder* 'again': A structural account. *Journal of Semantics* 13(2). 87–138.

von Stechow, Arnim & Wolfgang Sternefeld. 1988. *Bausteine syntaktischen Wissens: Ein Lehrbuch der Generativen Grammatik*. Opladen/Wiesbaden: Westdeutscher Verlag.

Steedman, Mark J. 1985. Dependency and coordination in the grammar of Dutch and English. *Language* 61(3). 523–568.

Steedman, Mark J. 1989. Constituency and coordination in a Combinatory Grammar. In Mark R. Baltin & Anthony S. Kroch (eds.), *Alternative conceptions of phrase structure*, 201–231. Chicago/London: The University of Chicago Press.

Steedman, Mark J. 1991. Structure and intonation. *Language* 67(2). 260–296.

Steedman, Mark J. 1997. *Surface structure and interpretation* (Linguistic Inquiry Monographs 30). Cambridge, MA/London, England: MIT Press.

Steedman, Mark J. 2000. *The syntactic process* (Language, Speech, and Communication). Cambridge, MA/London, England: MIT Press.

Steedman, Mark J. 2011. Romantics and revolutionaries. *Linguistic Issues in Language Technology* 6(11). 1–20. http://journals.linguisticsociety.org/elanguage/lilt/article/view/2587.html. Special Issue on Interaction of Linguistics and Computational Linguistics.

Steedman, Mark J. & Jason Baldridge. 2006. Combinatory Categorial Grammar. In Keith Brown (ed.), *Encyclopedia of language and linguistics*, 610–621. Oxford: Elsevier 2nd edn.

Steels, Luc. 2003. Evolving grounded communication for robots. *Trends in Cognitive Science* 7(7). 308–312.

Steels, Luc (ed.). 2011. *Design patterns in Fluid Construction Grammar* (Constructional Approaches to Language 11). Amsterdam: John Benjamins Publishing Co.

Steels, Luc (ed.). 2012. *Computational issues in Fluid Construction Grammar* (Lecture Notes in Computer Science 7249). Berlin: Springer Verlag.

Steels, Luc. 2013. Fluid Construction Grammar. In Thomas Hoffmann & Graeme Trousdale (eds.), *The Oxford handbook of Construction Grammar* (Oxford Handbooks), 153–167. Oxford: Oxford University Press.

Steels, Luc. 2015. *The Talking Heads experiment: Origins of words and meanings* (Computational Models of Language Evolution 1). Berlin: Language Science Press.

Steels, Luc & Joachim De Beule. 2006. A (very) brief introduction to Fluid Construction Grammar. Paper presented at the Third International Workshop on Scalable Natural Language Understanding (ScaNaLU 2006) June 8, 2006, following HLT/NAACL, New York City.

Steels, Luc & Remi van Trijp. 2011. How to make Construction Grammars fluid and robust. In Luc Steels (ed.), *Design patterns in Fluid Construction Grammar* (Constructional Approaches to Language 11), 301–330. Amsterdam: John Benjamins Publishing Co.

Stefanowitsch, Anatol. 2008. Negative entrenchment: A usage-based approach to negative evidence. *Cognitive Linguistics* 19(3). 513–531.

Stefanowitsch, Anatol & Kerstin Fischer (eds.). 2008. *Konstruktionsgrammatik II: Von der Konstruktion zur Grammatik* (Stauffenburg Linguistik 47). Tübingen: Stauffenburg Verlag.

Stefanowitsch, Anatol & Stephan Th. Gries. 2009. Corpora and grammar. In Anke Lüdeling & Merja Kytö (eds.), *Corpus linguistics: An international handbook*, vol. 29 (Handbücher zur Sprach- und Kommunikationswissenschaft), chap. 43, 933–952. Berlin: Mouton de Gruyter.

Sternefeld, Wolfgang. 1985a. Deutsch ohne grammatische Funktionen: Ein Beitrag zur Rektions- und Bindungstheorie. *Linguistische Berichte* 99. 394–439.

Sternefeld, Wolfgang. 1985b. On case and binding theory. In Jindřich Toman (ed.), *Studies in German grammar* (Studies in Generative Grammar 21), 231–285. Dordrecht: Foris Publications.

Sternefeld, Wolfgang. 1995. Voice phrases and their specifiers. *FAS Papers in Linguistics* 3. 48–85.

Sternefeld, Wolfgang. 2006. *Syntax: Eine morphologisch motivierte generative Beschreibung des Deutschen* (Stauffenburg Linguistik 31). Tübingen: Stauffenburg Verlag.

Sternefeld, Wolfgang & Frank Richter. 2012. Wo stehen wir in der Grammatiktheorie? — Bemerkungen anläßlich eines Buchs von Stefan Müller. *Zeitschrift für Sprachwissenschaft* 31(2). 263–291.

Stiebels, Barbara. 1996. *Lexikalische Argumente und Adjunkte: Zum semantischen Beitrag verbaler Präfixe und Partikeln* (studia grammatica 39). Berlin: Akademie Verlag.

Stowell, Timothy. 1981. *Origins of phrase structure*: MIT dissertation. http://hdl.handle.net/1721.1/15626.

Strunk, Jan & Nil Snider. 2013. Subclausal locality constraints on relative clause extraposition. In Gert Webelhuth, Manfred Sailer & Heike Walker (eds.), *Rightward movement in a comparative perspective* (Linguistik Aktuell/Linguistics Today 200), 99–143. Amsterdam: John Benjamins Publishing Co.

Suchsland, Peter. 1997. *Syntax-Theorie: Ein zusammengefaßter Zugang* (Konzepte der Sprach- und Literaturwissenschaft 55). Tübingen: Max Niemeyer Verlag. Deutsche Bearbeitung von Borsley (1991) durch Peter Suchsland.

Sulger, Sebastian. 2009. Irish clefting and information-structure. In Miriam Butt & Tracy Holloway King (eds.), *Proceedings of the LFG 2009 conference*, 562–582. Stanford, CA: CSLI Publications. http://csli-publications.stanford.edu/LFG/14/.

Sulger, Sebastian. 2010. Analytic and synthetic verb forms in Irish – An agreement-based implementation in LFG. In Manfred Pinkal, Ines Rehbein, Sabine Schulte im Walde & Angelika Storrer (eds.), *Semantic approaches in natural language processing: Proceedings of the Conference on Natural Language Processing 2010*, 169–173. Saarbrücken: Saarland University Press (universaar).

Svenononius, Peter. 2004. Slavic prefixes inside and outside VP. *Nordlyd. Special Issue on Slavic Prefixes* 32(2). 205–253.

Takami, Ken-ichi. 1988. Preposition stranding: Arguments against syntactic analyses and an alternative functional explanation. *Lingua* 76(4). 299–335.

Tanenhaus, Michael K., Michael J. Spivey-Knowlton, Kathleen M. Eberhard & Julie C. Sedivy. 1995. Integration of visual and linguistic information in spoken language comprehension. *Science* 268(5217). 1632–1634.

Tanenhaus, Michael K., Michael J. Spivey-Knowlton, Kathleen M. Eberhard & Julie C. Sedivy. 1996. Using eye movements to study spoken language comprehension: Evidence for visually mediated incremental interpretation. In Toshio Inui & James L. McClelland (eds.), *Information integration in perception and communication* (Attention and Performance XVI), 457–478. Cambridge, MA: MIT Press.

ten Hacken, Pius. 2007. *Chomskyan linguistics and its competitors*. London: Equinox Publishing Ltd.

Tesnière, Lucien. 1959. *Eléments de syntaxe structurale*. Paris: Librairie C. Klincksieck.

Tesnière, Lucien. 1980. *Grundzüge der strukturalen Syntax*. Stuttgart: Klett-Cotta. Translated by Ulrich Engel.

Tesnière, Lucien. 2015. *Elements of structural syntax*. Amsterdam: John Benjamins Publishing Co. Translated by Timothy Osborne and Sylvain Kahane.

Thiersch, Craig L. 1978. *Topics in German syntax*: M.I.T. Dissertation.

Thompson, Henry S. 1982. Handling metarules in a parser for GPSG. D.A.I. Research 175 University of Edinburgh.

Timberlake, Alan. 1982. The impersonal passive in Lithuanian. In Monica Macaulay, Orin D. Gensler, Claudia Brugmann, Inese Čivkulis, Amy Dahlstrom, Katherine Krile & Rob Sturm (eds.), *Proceedings of the Eighth Annual Meeting of the Berkeley Linguistics Society*, 508–524. Berkeley: University of California.

Tomasello, Michael. 1995. Language is not an instinct. *Cognitive Development* 10(1). 131–156.

Tomasello, Michael. 2000. Do young children have adult syntactic competence? *Cognition* 74(3). 209–253.

Tomasello, Michael. 2003. *Constructing a language: A usage-based theory of language acquisition*. Cambridge, MA: Harvard University Press.

Tomasello, Michael. 2005. Beyond formalities: The case of language acquisition. *The Linguistic Review* 22(2–4). 183–197.

Tomasello, Michael. 2006a. Acquiring linguistic constructions. In Deanna Kuhn & Robert Siegler (eds.), *Handbook of child psychology*, vol. 2, New York: John Wiley & Sons, Inc. 6th edn.

Tomasello, Michael. 2006b. Construction Grammar for kids. *Constructions* Special Volume 1. http://www.constructions-journal.com/.

Tomasello, Michael. 2006c. Konstruktionsgrammatik und früher Erstspracherwerb. In Kerstin Fischer & Anatol Stefanowitsch (eds.), *Konstruktionsgrammatik: Von der Anwendung zur Theorie* (Stauffenburg Linguistik 40), 19–37. Tübingen: Stauffenburg Verlag.

Tomasello, Michael. 2009. Universal Grammar is dead. *The Behavioral and Brain Sciences* 32(5). 470–471.

Tomasello, Michael, Nameera Akhtar, Kelly Dodsen & Laura Rekau. 1997. Differential productivity in young children's use of nouns and verbs. *Journal of Child Language* 24(2). 373–387.

Tomasello, Michael, Malinda Carpenter, Josep Call, Tanya Behne & Henrike Moll. 2005. Understanding and sharing intentions: The origins of cultural cognition. *The Behavioral and Brain Sciences* 28(5). 675–735.

Travis, Lisa. 1984. *Parameters and effects of word order variation*. Cambridge, MA: M.I.T. Dissertation.

Trosterud, Trond. 2009. A Constraint Grammar for Faroese. In Eckhard Bick, Kristin Hagen, Kaili Müürisep & Trond Trosterud (eds.), *Constraint Grammar and robust parsing: Proceedings of the NODALIDA 2009 workshop*, vol. 8 (NEALT Proceedings Series 8), 1–7. Northern European Association for Language Technologie Tartu: Tartu University Library.

Tseng, Jesse (ed.). 2000. *Aspekte eines HPSG-Fragments des Deutschen* (Arbeitspapiere des SFB 340 No. 156). Tübingen: Eberhard-Karls-Universität Tübingen. http://www.sfs.uni-tuebingen.de/sfb/reports/berichte/156/156abs.html.

Tseng, Jesse L. 2003. LKB grammar implementation: French and beyond. In Emily M. Bender, Daniel P. Flickinger, Frederik Fouvry & Melanie Siegel (eds.), *Proceedings of the ESSLLI 2003 Workshop "Ideas and Strategies for Multilingual Grammar Development"*, 91–97. Vienna, Austria. http://w3.erss.univ-tlse2.fr/textes/pagespersos/tseng/Pubs/mgd03.pdf.

Tseng, Jesse L. 2007. English prepositional passive constructions. In Stefan Müller (ed.), *Proceedings of the 14th International Conference on Head-Driven Phrase Structure Grammar*, 271–286. Stanford, CA: CSLI Publications. http://csli-publications.stanford.edu/HPSG/2007/.

Umemoto, Hiroshi. 2006. Implementing a Japanese semantic parser based on glue approach. In *Proceedings of The 20th Pacific Asia Conference on Language, Information and Computation*, 418–425. http://dspace.wul.waseda.ac.jp/dspace/handle/2065/29076.

Uszkoreit, Hans. 1986a. Categorial Unification Grammars. In Makoto Nagao (ed.), *Proceedings of COLING 86*, 187–194. University of Bonn: Association for Computational Linguistics. http://aclweb.org/anthology-new/C/C86/C86-1045.pdf.

Uszkoreit, Hans. 1986b. Linear precedence in discontinuous constituents: Complex fronting in German. Report No. CSLI-86-47 Center for the Study of Language and Information Stanford, CA.

Uszkoreit, Hans. 1987. *Word order and constituent structure in German* (CSLI Lecture Notes 8). Stanford, CA: CSLI Publications.

Uszkoreit, Hans. 1990. Extraposition and adjunct attachment in Categorial Unification Grammar. In Werner Bahner, Joachim Schildt & Dieter Viehweger (eds.), *Proceedings of the Fourteenth International Congress of Linguists, Berlin/GDR, August 10–15, 1987*, vol. 3, 2331–2336. Berlin: Akademie Verlag.

Uszkoreit, Hans, Rolf Backofen, Stephan Busemann, Abdel Kader Diagne, Elizabeth A. Hinkelman, Walter Kasper, Bernd Kiefer, Hans-Ulrich Krieger, Klaus Netter, Günter Neumann, Stephan Oepen & Stephen P. Spackman. 1994. DISCO—An HPSG-based NLP system and its application for appointment scheduling. In Makoto Nagao (ed.), *Proceedings of COLING 94*, 436–440. Kyoto, Japan: Association for Computational Linguistics.

Uszkoreit, Hans, Rolf Backofen, Jo Calder, Joanne Capstick, Luca Dini, Jochen Dörre, Gregor Erbach, Dominique Estival, Suresh Manandhar, Anne-Marie Mineur & Stephan Oepen. 1996. The EAGLES formalisms working group: Final report Expert Advisory Group on Language Engineering Standards. Technical Report LRE 61–100. http://www.coli.uni-sb.de/publikationen/softcopies/Uszkoreit:1996:EFW.pdf.

Valian, Virginia. 1991. Syntactic subjects in the early speech of American and Italian children. *Cognition* 40(1–2). 21–81.

Van Eynde, Frank. 2015. Sign-Based Construction Grammar: A guided tour. *Journal of Linguistics* DOI:10.1017/S0022226715000341.

Van Langendonck, Willy. 1994. Determiners as heads? *Cognitive Linguistics* 5. 243–259.

van Trijp, Remi. 2011. A design pattern for argument structure constructions. In Luc Steels (ed.), *Design patterns in Fluid Construction Grammar* (Constructional Approaches to Language 11), 115–145. Amsterdam: John Benjamins Publishing Co.

van Trijp, Remi. 2013. A comparison between Fluid Construction Grammar and Sign-Based Construction Grammar. *Constructions and Frames* 5(1). 88–116.

van Trijp, Remi. 2014. Long-distance dependencies without filler–gaps: A cognitive-functional alternative in Fluid Construction Grammar. *Language and Cognition* 6(2). 242–270.

Van Valin, Robert D. Jr. (ed.). 1993. *Advances in Role and Reference Grammar*. Amsterdam: John Benjamins Publishing Co.

Van Valin, Robert D. Jr. 1998. The acquisition of *wh*-questions and the mechanisms of language acquisition. In Michael Tomasello (ed.), *The new psychology of language: Cognitive and functional approaches to language structure*, 221–249. Hillsdale, NJ: Lawrence Erlbaum.

Vancoppenolle, Jean, Eric Tabbert, Gerlof Bouma & Manfred Stede. 2011. A German grammar for generation in Open CCG. In Hanna Hedeland, Thomas Schmidt & Kai Wörner (eds.), *Multilingual resources and multilingual applications: Proceedings of the Conference of the German Society for Computational Linguistics and Language Technology (GSCL) 2011* (Arbeiten zur Mehrsprachigkeit/Working Papers in Multilingualism, Folge B/Series B 96), 145–150. Hamburg: Universität Hamburg.

Vargha-Khadem, Faraneh, Kate E. Watkins, Katie Alcock, Paul Fletcher & Richard Passingham. 1995. Praxic and nonverbal cognitive deficits in a large family with a genetically transmitted speech and language disorder. In *Proceedings of the National Academy of Sciences of the United States of America*, vol. 92, 930–933.

Vasishth, Shravan & Richard L. Lewis. 2006. Human language processing: Symbolic models. In Keith Brown (ed.), *The encyclopedia of language and linguistics*, vol. 5, 410–419. Oxford: Elsevier Science Publisher B.V. (North-Holland) 2nd edn.

Vasishth, Shravan, Katja Suckow, Richard L. Lewis & Sabine Kern. 2010. Short-term forgetting in sentence comprehension: Crosslinguistic evidence from verb-final structures. *Language and Cognitive Processes* 25(4). 533–567.

Vater, Heinz. 2010. Strukturalismus und generative Grammatik in Deutschland. In Hans-Harald Müller, Marcel Lepper & Andreas Gardt (eds.), *Strukturalismus in Deutschland: Literatur- und Sprachwissenschaft 1910–1975* (Marbacher Schriften. Neue Folge 5), 125–160. Göttingen: Wallstein Verlag.

Veenstra, Mettina Jolanda Arnoldina. 1998. *Formalizing the Minimalist Program*: Rijksuniversiteit Groningen Ph.d. thesis.

Vennemann, Theo & Ray Harlow. 1977. Categorial Grammar and consistent basic VX serialization. *Theoretical Linguistics* 4(1–3). 227–254.

Verhagen, Arie. 2010. What do you think is the proper place of recursion? Conceptual and empirical issues. In Harry van der Hulst (ed.), *Recursion in human language* (Studies in Generative Grammar 104), 93–110. Berlin: Mouton de Gruyter.

Verspoor, Cornelia Maria. 1997. *Contextually-dependent lexical semantics*: University of Edinburgh dissertation. ftp://ftp.cogsci.ed.ac.uk/pub/kversp/thesis.ps.gz.

Vierhuff, Tilman, Bernd Hildebrandt & Hans-Jürgen Eikmeyer. 2003. Effiziente Verarbeitung deutscher Konstituentenstellung mit der Combinatorial Categorial Grammar. *Linguistische Berichte* 194. 213–237.

Vijay-Shanker, K. & Aravind K. Joshi. 1988. Feature structures based Tree Adjoining Grammars. In Dénes Vargha (ed.), *Proceedings of COLING 88*, vol. 1, 714–719. University of Budapest: Association for Computational Linguistics. http://www.aclweb.org/anthology-new/C/C88/C88-2147.pdf.

Villavicencio, Aline. 2002. The acquisition of a unification-based Generalised Categorial Grammar. UCAM-CL-TR-533 University of Cambridge Computer Laboratory.

Vogel, Ralf. 2001. Case conflict in German free relative constructions: An Optimality Theoretic treatment. In Gereon Müller & Wolfgang Sternefeld (eds.), *Competition in syntax*, 341–375. Berlin: Mouton de Gruyter.

Vogel, Ralf & Markus Steinbach. 1998. The dative – An oblique case. *Linguistische Berichte* 173. 65–91.

Volk, Martin. 1988. *Parsing German with GPSG: The problem of separable-prefix verbs.* University of Georgia MA thesis.

Voutilainen, Atro, Juha Heikkilä & Arto Anttila. 1992. *Constraint Grammar of English: A performance-oriented introduction* (Publications of the Department of General Linguistics 21). Helsinki: University of Helsinki.

Wada, Hajime & Nicholas Asher. 1986. BUILDRS: An implementation of DR Theory and LFG. In Makoto Nagao (ed.), *Proceedings of COLING 86*, 540–545. University of Bonn: Association for Computational Linguistics.

Wahlster, Wolfgang (ed.). 2000. *Verbmobil: Foundations of speech-to-speech translation* (Artificial Intelligence). Berlin: Springer Verlag.

Walther, Markus. 1999. *Deklarative prosodische Morphologie: Constraint-basierte Analysen und Computermodelle zum Finnischen und Tigrinya* (Linguistische Arbeiten 399). Tübingen: Max Niemeyer Verlag.

Webelhuth, Gert. 1985. German is configurational. *The Linguistic Review* 4(3). 203–246.

Webelhuth, Gert. 1990. Diagnostics for structure. In Günther Grewendorf & Wolfgang Sternefeld (eds.), *Scrambling and Barriers* (Linguistik Aktuell/Linguistics Today 5), 41–75. Amsterdam: John Benjamins Publishing Co.

Webelhuth, Gert. 1995. X-bar Theory and Case Theory. In Gert Webelhuth (ed.), *Government and Binding Theory and the Minimalist Program: Principles and Parameters in syntactic theory* (Generative Syntax), 15–95. Oxford, UK & Cambrigde, USA: Blackwell Publishing Ltd.

Webelhuth, Gert. 2011. Paradigmenwechsel rückwärts: Die Renaissance der grammatischen Konstruktion. In Stefan Engelberg, Anke Holler & Kristel Proost (eds.), *Sprachliches Wissen zwischen Lexikon und Grammatik* (Institut für Deutsche Sprache, Jahrbuch 2010), 149–180. Berlin: de Gruyter.

Weber, Heinz J. 1997. *Dependenzgrammatik: Ein interaktives Arbeitsbuch* (Narr Studienbücher). Tübingen: Gunter Narr Verlag 2nd edn.

Wechsler, Stephen Mark. 1991. *Argument structure and linking*: Stanford University dissertation.

Wechsler, Stephen Mark. 1995. *The semantic basis of argument structure* (Dissertations in Linguistics). Stanford, CA: CSLI Publications.

Wechsler, Stephen Mark. 1997. Resultative predicates and control. In Ralph C. Blight & Michelle J. Moosally (eds.), *Texas Linguistic Forum 38: The syntax and semantics of predication: Proceedings of the 1997 Texas Linguistics Society Conference*, 307–321. Austin, Texas: University of Texas, Department of Linguistics.

Wechsler, Stephen Mark. 2005. What is right and wrong about little v. In *Grammar and beyond—Essays in honour of Lars Hellan*, 179–195. Oslo, Norway: Novus Press.

Wechsler, Stephen Mark. 2008a. A diachronic account of English deverbal nominals. In Charles B. Chang & Hannah J. Haynie (eds.), *Proceedings of the 26th West Coast Conference on Formal Linguistics*, 498–506. Somerville, MA: Cascadilla Proceedings Project.

Wechsler, Stephen Mark. 2008b. Dualist syntax. In Stefan Müller (ed.), *Proceedings of the 15th International Conference on Head-Driven Phrase Structure Grammar*, 294–304. Stanford, CA: CSLI Publications. http://csli-publications.stanford.edu/HPSG/2008/.

Wechsler, Stephen Mark & Bokyung Noh. 2001. On resultative predicates and clauses: Parallels between Korean and English. *Language Sciences* 23(4). 391–423.

Wegener, Heide. 1985. *Der Dativ im heutigen Deutsch* (Studien zur deutschen Grammatik 28). Tübingen: originally Gunter Narr Verlag now Stauffenburg Verlag.

Weir, Morton W. 1964. Developmental changes in problem-solving strategies. *Psychological Review* 71(6). 473–490.

Weissgerber, Monika. 1983. *Valenz und Kongruenzbeziehungen: Ein Modell zur Vereindeutigung von Verben in der maschinellen Analyse und Übersetzung*. Frankfurt a. M.: Peter Lang.

Weisweber, Wilhelm. 1987. Ein Dominanz-Chart-Parser für generalisierte Phrasenstrukturgrammatiken. KIT-Report 45 Technische Universität Berlin Berlin.

Weisweber, Wilhelm & Susanne Preuss. 1992. Direct parsing with metarules. In Antonio Zampolli (ed.), *14th International Conference on Computational Linguistics (COLING '92), August 23–28*, 1111–1115. Nantes, France: Association for Computational Linguistics.

Welke, Klaus. 1988. *Einführung in die Valenz- und Kasustheorie*. Leipzig: Bibliographisches Institut.

Welke, Klaus. 2009. Konstruktionsvererbung, Valenzvererbung und die Reichweite von Konstruktionen. *Zeitschrift für Germanistische Linguistik* 37(3). 514–543.

Welke, Klaus. 2011. *Valenzgrammatik des Deutschen: Eine Einführung* (De Gruyter Studium). Berlin: de Gruyter.

Wells, Rulon S. 1947. Immediate constituents. *Language* 23(2). 81–117.

Werner, Edeltraud. 1993. *Translationstheorie und Dependenzmodell: Kritik und Reinterpretation des Ansatzes von Lucien Tesnière* (Kultur und Erkenntnis: Schriften der Philosophischen Fakultät der Heinrich-Heine-Universität Düsseldorf 10). Tübingen: Francke Verlag.

Wetta, Andrew C. 2011. A Construction-based cross-linguistic analysis of V2 word order. In Stefan Müller (ed.), *Proceedings of the 18th International Conference on Head-Driven Phrase Structure Grammar, University of Washington*, 248–268. Stanford, CA: CSLI Publications. http://csli-publications.stanford.edu/HPSG/2011/.

Wexler, Kenneth. 1998. Very early parameter setting and the unique checking constraint: A new explanation of the optional infinitive stage. *Lingua* 106(1–4). 23–79.

Wexler, Kenneth & Peter W. Culicover. 1980. *Formal principles of language acquisition*. Cambridge, MA/London: MIT Press.

Weydt, Harald. 1972. „Unendlicher Gebrauch von endlichen Mitteln": Mißverständnisse um ein linguistisches Theorem. *Poetica* 5(3/4). 249–267.

Wharton, R. M. 1974. Approximate language identification. *Information and Control* 26(3). 236–255.

White, Mike & Jason Baldridge. 2003. Adapting chart realization to CCG. In Ehud Reiter, Helmut Horacek & Kees van Deemter (eds.), *Proceedings of the 9th European Workshop on Natural Language Generation (ENLG-2003) at EACL 2003*, 119–126.

Wijnen, Frank, Masja Kempen & Steven Gillis. 2001. Root infinitives in Dutch early child language: An effect of input? *Journal of Child Language* 28(3). 629–660.

Wiklund, Anna-Lena, Gunnar Hrafn Hrafnbjargarson, Kristine Bentzen & Þorbjörg Hróarsdóttir. 2007. Rethinking Scandinavian verb movement. *Journal of Comparative Germanic Linguistics* 10(3). 203–233.

Wilcock, Graham. 2001. Towards a discourse-oriented representation of information structure in HPSG. In *13th Nordic Conference on Computational Linguistics, Uppsala, Sweden*, http://www.ling.helsinki.fi/~gwilcock/Pubs/2001/Nodalida-01.pdf.

Wilder, Chris. 1991. Small clauses and related objects. *Groninger Arbeiten zur Germanistischen Linguistik* 34. 215–236.

Williams, Edwin. 1984. Grammatical relations. *Linguistic Inquiry* 15(4). 639–673.

Winkler, Susanne. 1997. *Focus and secondary predication* (Studies in Generative Grammar 43). Berlin, New York: Mouton de Gruyter.

Wittenberg, Eva, Ray S. Jackendoff, Gina Kuperberg, Martin Paczynski, Jesse Snedeker & Heike Wiese. 2014. The processing and representation of light verb constructions. In Asaf Bachrach, Isabelle Roy & Linnaea Stockall (eds.), *Structuring the argument* (Language Faculty and Beyond 10), 61–80. Amsterdam: John Benjamins Publishing Co.

Wittenberg, Eva & Maria Mercedes Piñango. 2011. Processing light verb constructions. *The Mental Lexicon* 6(3). 393–413.

Wöllstein, Angelika. 2010. *Topologisches Satzmodell* (Kurze Einführungen in die Germanistische Linguistik 8). Heidelberg: Universitätsverlag Winter.

Wunderlich, Dieter. 1987. Vermeide Pronomen – Vermeide leere Kategorien. *Studium Linguistik* 21. 36–44.

Wunderlich, Dieter. 1989. Arnim von Stechow, das Nichts und die Lexikalisten. *Linguistische Berichte* 122. 321–333.

Wunderlich, Dieter. 1992. CAUSE and the structure of verbs. Arbeiten des SFB 282 No. 36 Heinrich Heine Uni/BUGH Düsseldorf/Wuppertal.

Wunderlich, Dieter. 1997. Argument extension by lexical adjunction. *Journal of Semantics* 14(2). 95–142.

Wunderlich, Dieter. 2004. Why assume UG? *Studies in Language* 28(3). 615–641.

Wunderlich, Dieter. 2008. Spekulationen zum Anfang von Sprache. *Zeitschrift für Sprachwissenschaft* 27(2). 229–265.

Wurmbrand, Susanne. 2003a. *Infinitives: Restructuring and clause structure* (Studies in Generative Grammar 55). Berlin: Mouton de Gruyter.

Wurmbrand, Susanne. 2003b. Long passive (corpus search results).

XTAG Research Group. 2001. A lexicalized Tree Adjoining Grammar for English. Tech. rep. Institute for Research in Cognitive Science Philadelphia. ftp://ftp.cis.upenn.edu/pub/xtag/release-2.24.2001/tech-report.pdf.

Yamada, Hiroyasu & Yuji Matsumoto. 2003. Statistical dependency analysis with support vector machines. In Gertjan van Noord (ed.), *Proceedings of the 8th International Workshop on Parsing Technologies (IWPT 03)*, Nancy.

Yamada, Jeni. 1981. Evidence for the independence of language and cognition: Case study of a "hyperlinguistic" adolescent. UCLA Working Papers in Cognitive Linguistics 3 University of California, Los Angeles.

Yampol, Todd & Lauri Karttunen. 1990. An efficient implementation of PATR for Categorial Unification Grammar. In Hans Karlgren (ed.), *COLING-90: Papers presented to the 13th International Conference on Computational Linguistics*, 419–424. Helsinki: Association for Computational Linguistics.

Yang, Charles D. 2004. Universal Grammar, statistics or both? *Trends in Cognitive Sciences* 8(10). 451–456. DOI:10.1016/j.tics.2004.08.006.

Yasukawa, Hidekl. 1984. LFG System in Prolog. In Yorick Wilks (ed.), *Proceedings of the 10th International Conference on Computational Linguistics and 22nd Annual Meeting of the Association for Computational Linguistics*, 358–361. Stanford University, California: Association for Computational Linguistics.

Yip, Moira, Joan Maling & Ray S. Jackendoff. 1987. Case in tiers. *Language* 63(2). 217–250.

Yoshinaga, Naoki, Yusuke Miyao, Kentaro Torisawa & Jun'ichi Tsujii. 2001. Resource sharing amongst HPSG and LTAG communities by a method of grammar conversion between FB-LTAG and HPSG. In *Proceedings of ACL/EACL workshop on Sharing Tools and Resources for Research and Education*, 39–46. Toulouse, France.

Zaenen, Annie & Ronald M. Kaplan. 1995. Formal devices for linguistic generalizations: West Germanic word order in LFG. In Dalrymple et al. (1995) 215–239.

Zaenen, Annie, Joan Maling & Höskuldur Thráinsson. 1985. Case and grammatical functions: The Icelandic passive. *Natural Language and Linguistic Theory* 3(4). 441–483.

Zappa, Frank. 1986. Does humor belong in music? EMI Music Germany GmbH & Co.KG.

Zucchi, Alessandro. 1993. *The language of propositions and events: Issues in the syntax and the semantics of nominalization* (Studies in Linguistics and Philosophy 51). Berlin: Springer Verlag.

Zwart, C. Jan-Wouter. 1994. Dutch is head-initial. *The Linguistic Review* 11(3–4). 377–406.

Zweigenbaum, Pierre. 1991. Un analyseur pour grammaires lexicales-fonctionnelles. *TA Informations* 32(2). 19–34.

Zwicky, Arnold M., Joyce Friedman, Barbara C. Hall & Donald E. Walker. 1965. The MITRE syntactic analysis procedure for Transformational Grammars. In *Proceedings – FALL Joint Computer Conference*, 317–326. DOI:10.1109/AFIPS.1965.108.

Name index

Name index

Newport, Elissa L., 458, 459, 461
Ng, Say Kiat, 256
Nguyen, Thi Minh Huyen, 404
Niño, María-Eugenia, 214
Ninomiya, Takashi, 257
Nivre, Joakim, 356
Niyogi, Partha, 4, 452, 512–514
Noh, Bokyung, 565, 592, 610
Nøklestad, Anders, 357
Nolda, Andreas, xvi
Nomura, Hirosato, 356, 357
Noonan, Michael, 311, 614
Nordgård, Torbjørn, 117
Nordhoff, Sebastian, xvi
Nordlinger, Rachel, 214, 300, 544
Nowak, Martin A., 4, 452, 512
Noyer, Rolf, 601–603
Nozohoor-Farshi, R., 117
Nübling, Damaris, 13, 23–25, 42, 48, 71
Nunberg, Geoffrey, 520, 583, 600, 601, 616, 632
Nunes, Jairo, 145, 166, 172, 453, 454
Nygaard, Lars, 357

Ochs, Elinor, 475, 485
O'Connor, Mary Catherine, 303, 585
Odom, Penelope, 501
O'Donovan, Ruth, 214
Oepen, Stephan, 116, 255, 257
Özkaragöz, İnci, 311, 614
Oflazer, Kemal, 214
Ohkuma, Tomoko, 214
Oliva, Karel, 99, 283, 387, 396, 402
O'Neill, Michael, 4, 452
Oppenrieder, Wilhelm, 113, 574
Orgun, Cemil Orhan, 258
Ørsnes, Bjarne, xvi
Osborne, Miles, 238
Osborne, Timothy, xvi, 153, 191, 364, 366, 368–370, 378–380, 384, 385, 397, 400, 402, 550, 575, 576, 633
Osenova, Petya, 255
Osswald, Rainer, 308, 613, 615
Ott, Dennis, 153

Paczynski, Martin, 630
Pafel, Jürgen, 530
Paggio, Patrizia, 255, 339

Palmer, Alexis, 237, 238
Palmer, Martha, 404
Pankau, Andreas, xvi, xviii
Pankau, Rainer, 462
Parisi, Domenico, 458, 461, 487
Parmentier, Yannick, 403
Partee, Barbara H., 566
Passingham, Richard, 463
Patejuk, Agnieszka, 214
Paul, Hermann, 46
Paul, Soma, 255
Pembrey, Marcus E., 463
Penn, Gerald, 255, 347
Pentheroudakis, Joseph, 213, 214
Perchonock, Ellen, 501
Pereira, Fernando, 330
Perles, Micha A., 549, 551
Perlmutter, David M., 91, 115, 135, 275, 437
Perry, John, 270
Pesetsky, David, 454, 601, 603, 663
Peters, Jörg, 13, 23–25, 42, 48, 71
Peters, Stanley, 84
Petrick, Stanley Roy, 117
Pfister, Beat, 256, 669
Phillips, Colin, 501, 507
Phillips, John D., 175
Pickering, Martin, 253
Pienemann, Manfred, 235
Pietroski, Paul, 171, 471
Pietsch, Christian, xvi
Pihko, E., 634
Piñango, Maria Mercedes, 630, 631
Pine, Julian M., 471, 476, 477, 483, 521–523
Pineda, Luis Alberto, 257
Pinker, Steven, 84, 139, 235, 433–435, 438, 449, 450, 453, 456, 461, 487, 640
Pittner, Karin, 276
Plainfossé, Agnes, 213
Plank, Frans, 433
Plunkett, Kim, 458, 461, 487
Poletto, Cecilia, 142, 148
Polguère, A., 357
Pollack, Bary W., 117
Pollard, Carl J., 29, 35, 151, 158, 164–166, 196, 197, 202, 248, 249, 251, 255, 257, 262, 264, 270–272, 274, 276, 279, 287, 290, 293–295, 297, 298, 300,

Language index

Subject index

www.ingramcontent.com/pod-product-compliance
Lightning Source LLC
Chambersburg PA
CBHW080918100426
42812CB00007B/2317